Tenth Edition

EVOLUTION AND PREHISTORY

THE HUMAN CHALLENGE

WILLIAM A. HAVILAND
Professor Emeritus, University of Vermont

DANA WALRATH
University of Vermont

HARALD E. L. PRINS
Kansas State University

BUNNY MCBRIDE
Kansas State University

 **WADSWORTH**
CENGAGE Learning

Australia • Brazil • Japan • Korea • Mexico • Singapore • Spain • United Kingdom • United States

Evolution and Prehistory: The Human Challenge, Tenth Edition
William A. Haviland, Dana Walrath, Harald E. L. Prins, Bunny McBride

Publisher: Yolanda Cossio

Senior Acquisitions Editor: Aileen Berg

Senior Developmental Editor: Lin Gaylord

Assistant Editor: Margaux Cameron

Editorial Assistant: Victor Luu

Media Editor: John Chell

Senior Brand Manager: Liz Rhoden

Senior Market Development Manager: Michelle Williams

Senior Content Project Manager: Cheri Palmer

Senior Art Director: Caryl Gorska

Manufacturing Planner: Judy Inouye

Rights Acquisitions Specialist: Don Schlotman

Production Service: Joan Keyes, Dovetail Publishing Services

Photo Researcher: Sarah Evertson

Text Researcher: Sarah D'Stair

Copy Editor: Jennifer Gordon

Text Designer: Lisa Buckley

Cover Designer: Larry Didona

Cover Image: Cave with eleven sitting Buddhas, Po Win Taung, Myanmar (Burma): Hemis.fr / SuperStock. / Archaeologists brush skeletons discovered in Tyre, southern Lebanon: Hassan Bahsoun. / Murals at Bonampak / Mayan ruins, Chiapas state, Mexico: Christian Kober. / Globe image: Ocean. / Scientist examines fir seedling to research pollution damage: Maximilian Stock Ltd. / DNA (deoxyribonucleic acid) autoradiogram: Tek Image. / Lion Tamarin: Frans Lanting. / Cave painting petroglyph, Utah: ImageState. / Jeweled gold rings still encircle a skeleton's finger at Herculaneum (Ercolano), Italy: Jonathan Blair.

Compositor: PreMediaGlobal

For product information and technology assistance, contact us at
Cengage Learning Customer & Sales Support, 1-800-354-9706.

For permission to use material from this text or product,
submit all requests online at **www.cengage.com/permissions.**
Further permissions questions can be e-mailed to
permissionrequest@cengage.com.

Library of Congress Control Number: 2012949868

Student Edition:
ISBN-13: 978-1-285-06141-2
ISBN-10: 1-285-06141-1

Loose-leaf Edition:
ISBN-13: 978-1-285-06145-0
ISBN-10: 1-285-06145-4

Wadsworth
20 Davis Drive
Belmont, CA 94002-3098
USA

Cengage Learning is a leading provider of customized learning solutions with office locations around the globe, including Singapore, the United Kingdom, Australia, Mexico, Brazil, and Japan. Locate your local office at **www.cengage.com/global.**

Cengage Learning products are represented in Canada by Nelson Education, Ltd.

To learn more about Wadsworth, visit **www.cengage.com/wadsworth**
Purchase any of our products at your local college store or at our preferred online store **www.cengagebrain.com.**

Printed in the United States of America
1 2 3 4 5 6 7 17 16 15 14 13

DEDICATION

To **Philip Tobias** (1925–2012), South African paleoanthropologist
and antiapartheid activist whose integration of scientific and political facts
profoundly shaped evolutionary discourse, the social fabric in his beloved
homeland, and countless scholars from across the globe and a diverse
range of disciplines who were fortunate to call him professor.

Putting the World in Perspective

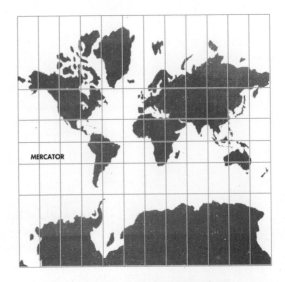

Although all humans we know about are capable of producing accurate sketches of localities and regions with which they are familiar, **cartography** (the craft of mapmaking as we know it today) had its beginnings in 16th-century Europe, and its subsequent development is related to the expansion of Europeans to all parts of the globe. From the beginning, there have been two problems with maps: the technical one of how to depict on a two-dimensional, flat surface a three-dimensional spherical object, and the cultural one of whose worldview they reflect. In fact, the two issues are inseparable, for the particular projection one uses inevitably makes a statement about how one views one's own people and their place in the world. Indeed, maps often shape our perception of reality as much as they reflect it.

In cartography, a **projection** refers to the system of intersecting lines (of longitude and latitude) by which part or all of the globe is represented on a flat surface. There are more than a hundred different projections in use today, ranging from polar perspectives to interrupted "butterflies" to rectangles to heart shapes. Each projection causes distortion in size, shape, or distance in some way or another. A map that correctly shows the shape of a landmass will of necessity misrepresent the size. A map that is accurate along the equator will be deceptive at the poles.

Perhaps no projection has had more influence on the way we see the world than that of Gerhardus Mercator, who devised his map in 1569 as a navigational aid for mariners. So well suited was Mercator's map for this purpose that it continues to be used for navigational charts today. At the same time, the Mercator projection became a standard for depicting landmasses, something for which it was never intended. Although an accurate navigational tool, the Mercator projection greatly exaggerates the size of landmasses in higher latitudes, giving about two-thirds of the map's surface to the northern hemisphere. Thus the lands occupied by Europeans and European descendants appear far larger than those of other people. For example, North America (19 million square kilometers) appears almost twice the size of Africa (30 million

square kilometers), whereas Europe is shown as equal in size to South America, which actually has nearly twice the landmass of Europe.

A map developed in 1805 by Karl B. Mollweide was one of the earlier *equal-area projections* of the world. Equal-area projections portray landmasses in correct relative size, but, as a result, distort the shape of continents more than other projections. They most often compress and warp lands in the higher latitudes and vertically stretch landmasses close to the equator. Other equal-area projections include the Lambert Cylindrical Equal-Area Projection (1772), the Hammer Equal-Area Projection (1892), and the Eckert Equal-Area Projection (1906).

The Van der Grinten Projection (1904) was a compromise aimed at minimizing both the distortions of size in the Mercator and the distortion of shape in equal-area maps such as the Mollweide. Although an improvement, the lands of the northern hemisphere are still emphasized at the expense of the southern. For example, in the Van der Grinten, the Commonwealth of Independent States (the former Soviet Union) and Canada are shown at more than twice their relative size.

The Robinson Projection, which was adopted by the National Geographic Society in 1988 to replace the Van der Grinten, is one of the best compromises to date between the distortions of size and shape. Although an improvement over the Van der Grinten, the Robinson Projection still depicts lands in the northern latitudes as proportionally larger at the same time that it depicts lands in the lower latitudes (representing most Third World nations) as proportionally smaller. Like European maps before it, the Robinson Projection places Europe at the center of the map with the Atlantic Ocean and the Americas to the left, emphasizing the cultural connection between Europe and North America, while neglecting the geographic closeness of northwestern North America to northeastern Asia.

The following pages show four maps that each convey quite different cultural messages. Included among them is the Peters Projection, an equal-area map that has been adopted as the official map of UNESCO (the United Nations Educational, Scientific, and Cultural Organization), and a map made in Japan, showing us how the world looks from the other side.

The Robinson Projection

The map below is based on the Robinson Projection, which is used today by the National Geographic Society and Rand McNally. Although the Robinson Projection distorts the relative size of landmasses, it does so much less than most other projections. Still, it places Europe at the center of the map. This particular view of the world has been used to identify the location of many of the cultures discussed in this text.

AMI

RUSSIANS

SLOVAKIANS

ERBS CHECHENS

OSNIANS

TURKS UZBEK TAJIK

KURDS KOHISTANI

BAKHTIARI

AWLAD ALI PASHTUN
BEDOUINS

BAHREIN

NUER TIGREANS

DINKA AFAR SOMALI

AZANDE

TURKANA

MBUTI NANDI

KIKUYU

HUTU GUSII

AND TUTSI MAASAI

TIRIKI

HADZA

SWAZI

ZULU

BASUTO

YUPIK
ESKIMO

MONGOLIANS

UYGHUR

JAPANESE

TIBETANS HAN CHINESE

MOSUO TAIWANESE

KAREN

SHAIVITE

TRUK

NAYAR

KOTA AND VEDDA
KURUMBA

MALDIVES TODA AND ACEH
BADAGA

MINANGKABAU

BALINESE

WAPE

KAPAUKU ENGA

TSEMBAGA

ARAPESH

DOBU

PINGELAP ISLANDERS

SOLOMON ISLANDERS

TROBRIANDERS

ABORIGINAL
AUSTRALIANS

MAORI

TASMANIANS

The Peters Projection

The map below is based on the Peters Projection, which has been adopted as the official map of UNESCO. Although it distorts the shape of continents (countries near the equator are vertically elongated by a ratio of 2 to 1), the Peters Projection does show all continents according to their correct relative size. Though Europe is still at the center, it is not shown as larger and more extensive than the Third World.

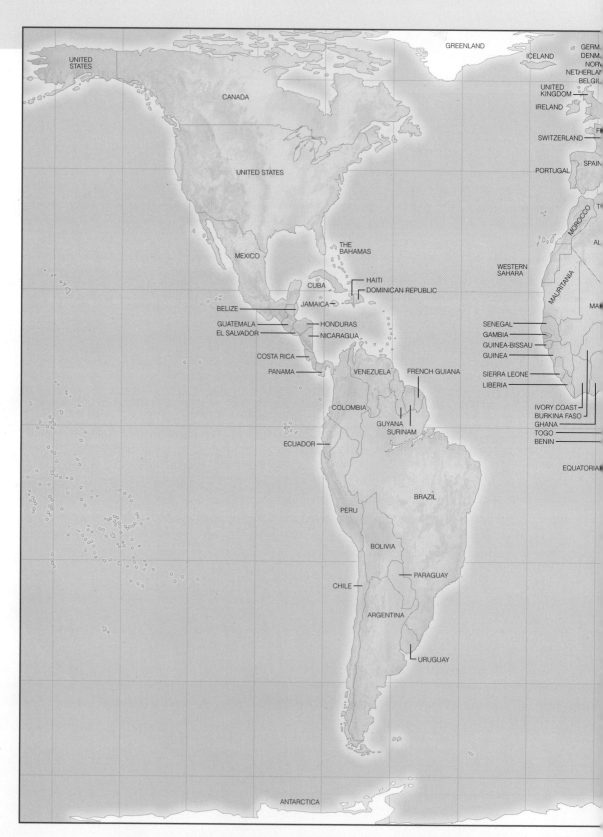

Japanese Map

Not all maps place Europe at the center of the world, as this Japanese map illustrates. Besides reflecting the importance the Japanese attach to themselves in the world, this map has the virtue of showing the geographic proximity of North America to Asia, a fact easily overlooked when maps place Europe at their center.

The Turnabout Map

The way maps may reflect (and influence) our thinking is exemplified by the Turnabout Map, which places the South Pole at the top and the North Pole at the bottom. Words and phrases such as "on top," "over," and "above" tend to be equated by some people with superiority. Turning things upside-down may cause us to rethink the way North Americans regard themselves in relation to the people of Central America.

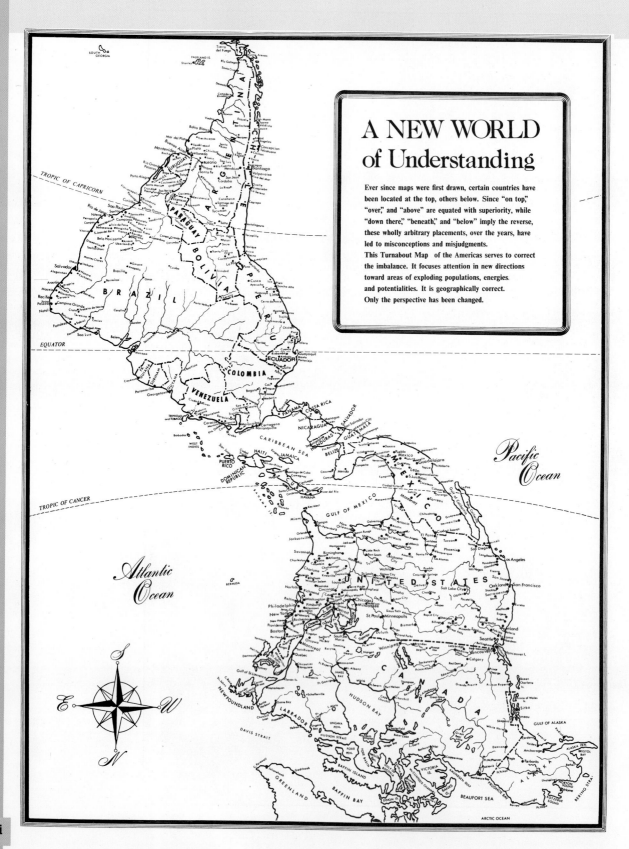

A NEW WORLD of Understanding

Ever since maps were first drawn, certain countries have been located at the top, others below. Since "on top," "over," and "above" are equated with superiority, while "down there," "beneath," and "below" imply the reverse, these wholly arbitrary placements, over the years, have led to misconceptions and misjudgments.

This Turnabout Map of the Americas serves to correct the imbalance. It focuses attention in new directions toward areas of exploding populations, energies and potentialities. It is geographically correct. Only the perspective has been changed.

Brief Contents

1 The Essence of Anthropology   2

2 Biology, Genetics, and Evolution   24

3 Living Primates   52

4 Primate Behavior   80

5 Field Methods in Archaeology and Paleoanthropology   102

6 From First Primates to First Bipeds   130

7 Origins of the Genus *Homo*   164

8 The Global Expansion of *Homo sapiens* and Their Technology   196

9 The Neolithic Revolution: The Domestication of Plants and Animals   224

10 The Emergence of Cities and States   248

11 Modern Human Diversity: Race and Racism   274

12 Human Adaptation to a Changing World   298

Features Contents

Anthropologists of Note

Franz Boas   13
Matilda Coxe Stevenson   13
Jane Goodall   85
Kinji Imanishi   85
Allan Wilson   127
Louis S. B. Leakey   140
Mary Leakey   140
Berhane Asfaw   201
Xinzhi Wu   201
Fatimah Jackson   278
Peter Ellison   304

Anthropology Applied

Forensic Anthropology: Voices for
    the Dead   14
The Congo Heartland Project   76
Stone Tools for Modern Surgeons   190
Pre-Columbian Fish Farming in the Amazon   260

Biocultural Connection

The Anthropology of Organ Transplantation   6
Bonds Beyond Blood: DNA Testing and Refugee
    Family Unification   36
Why Red Is Such a Potent Color   65
Chimpanzees in Biomedical Research: Time to End
    the Practice   98
Kennewick Man   120
Evolution and Human Birth   157
Sex, Gender, and Female Paleoanthropologists   168
Paleolithic Prescriptions for Diseases of Today   221
Dogs Get Right to the Point   232

Perilous Pigs: The Introduction of Swine-Borne
    Disease to the Americas   271
Beauty, Bigotry, and the Epicanthic Eyefold of the
    Beholder   289
Picturing Pesticides   322

Globalscape

A Global Body Shop?   20
Gorilla Hand Ashtrays?   75
Whose Lakes Are These?   217
Factory Farming Fiasco?   239
Iraqi Artifacts in New York City?   268
From Soap Opera to Clinic?   311

Original Study

Fighting HIV/AIDS in Africa: Traditional Healers on
    the Front Line   17
Ninety-Eight Percent Alike: What Our Similarity
    to Apes Tells Us about Our Understanding of
    Genetics   39
Gorilla Ecotourism: Ethical Considerations for
    Conservation   55
Disturbing Behaviors of the Orangutan   88
Whispers from the Ice   107
Ankles of the Australopithecines   147
Humans as Prey   170
Paleolithic Paint Job   212
The History of Mortality and Physiological Stress   243
Action Archaeology and the Community
    at El Pilar   256
Caveat Emptor: Genealogy for Sale   280
Dancing Skeletons: Life and Death in
    West Africa   312

Contents

Preface xx

Acknowledgments xxx

About the Authors xxxi

Chapter 1
The Essence of Anthropology 2

The Anthropological Perspective 3
Anthropology and Its Fields 5
    Cultural Anthropology 6
    Linguistic Anthropology 8
    Archaeology 9
    Physical Anthropology 11
Anthropology, Science, and the Humanities 16
Fieldwork 16
Questions of Ethics 19
Anthropology and Globalization 21

Biocultural Connection: The Anthropology of Organ Transplantation 6

Anthropologists of Note: Franz Boas, Matilda Coxe Stevenson 13

Anthropology Applied: Forensic Anthropology: Voices for the Dead 14

Original Study: Fighting HIV/AIDS in Africa: Traditional Healers on the Front Line 17

Chapter Checklist 22
Questions for Reflection 23
Online Study Resources 23

Chapter 2
Biology, Genetics, and Evolution 24

Evolution and Creation Stories 25
The Classification of Living Things 26
The Discovery of Evolution 28
Heredity 30
    The Transmission of Genes 31
    Genes and Alleles 32

    Cell Division 34
    Polygenetic Inheritance 39
Evolution, Individuals, and Populations 40
Evolutionary Forces 41
    Mutation 41
    Genetic Drift 42
    Gene Flow 43
    Natural Selection 43
The Case of Sickle-Cell Anemia 45
Adaptation and Physical Variation 47
Macroevolution and the Process of Speciation 47

Biocultural Connection: Bonds Beyond Blood: DNA Testing and Refugee Family Unification 36

Original Study: Ninety-Eight Percent Alike: What Our Similarity to Apes Tells Us about Our Understanding of Genetics 39

Chapter Checklist 49
Questions for Reflection 51
Online Study Resources 51

Chapter 3
Living Primates 52

Methods and Ethics in Primatology 54
Primates as Mammals 57
Primate Taxonomy 58
Primate Characteristics 62
    Primate Teeth 62
    Primate Sensory Organs 64
    The Primate Brain 66
    The Primate Skeleton 66
Living Primates 68
    Lemurs and Lorises 68
    Tarsiers 69
    New World Monkeys 69
    Old World Monkeys 70
    Small and Great Apes 71
Primate Conservation 74
    Threats to Primates 74
    Conservation Strategies 74

Original Study: Gorilla Ecotourism: Ethical Considerations for Conservation 55

Biocultural Connection: Why Red Is Such a Potent Color 65

Anthropology Applied: The Congo Heartland Project 76

Chapter Checklist 78
Questions for Reflection 79
Online Study Resources 79

Chapter 4
Primate Behavior 80

Primates as Models for Human Evolution 81
Primate Social Organization 83
    Home Range 84
    Social Hierarchy 84
    Individual Interaction and Bonding 87
    Sexual Behavior 87
    Reproduction and Care of Young 91
Communication and Learning 92
    Use of Objects as Tools 96
    Hunting 97
The Question of Culture 99

Anthropologists of Note: Jane Goodall, Kinji Imanishi 85

Original Study: Disturbing Behaviors of the Orangutan 88

Biocultural Connection: Chimpanzees in Biomedical Research: Time to End the Practice 98

Chapter Checklist 100
Questions for Reflection 101
Online Study Resources 101

Chapter 5
Field Methods in Archaeology and Paleoanthropology 102

Recovering Cultural and Biological Remains 104
    The Nature of Fossils 104
    Burial of the Dead 106
Searching for Artifacts and Fossils 109
    Site Identification 109
    Cultural Resource Management 111
    Excavation 111
    Excavation of Bones 113
    State of Preservation of Archaeological
        and Fossil Evidence 114
Sorting Out the Evidence 115
Dating the Past 121
    Relative Dating 121
    Chronometric Dating 123

Concepts and Methods for the Most
    Distant Past 125
        Continental Drift and Geologic Time 125
        The Molecular Clock 126
Sciences of Discovery 128

Original Study: Whispers from the Ice 107

Biocultural Connection: Kennewick Man 120

Anthropologist of Note: Allan Wilson 127

Chapter Checklist 128
Questions for Reflection 129
Online Study Resources 129

© Yves Herman/Reuters/Corbis

Chapter 6
From First Primates to First Bipeds 130

Primate Origins 131
    Oligocene Anthropoids 133
    New World Monkeys 134
Miocene Apes and Human Origins 134
The Anatomy of Bipedalism 137
Ardipithecus 140
Australopithecus 142
The Pliocene Environment and Hominin
    Diversity 144
        Diverse Australopithecine Species 144
        East Africa 145
        Central Africa 149
        South Africa 150
        Robust Australopithecines 151
        Australopithecines and the Genus *Homo* 152
Environment, Diet, and Origins of the Human
    Line 154

Humans Stand on Their Own Two Feet **155**
Early Representatives of the Genus *Homo* **159**
    Lumpers or Splitters? **160**
    Differences Between Early *Homo* and
    Australopithecus **161**

Anthropologists of Note: Louis S. B. Leakey,
Mary Leakey **140**

Original Study: Ankles of the Australopithecines **147**

Biocultural Connection: Evolution and Human Birth **157**

Chapter Checklist **161**
Questions for Reflection **163**
Online Study Resources **163**

Chapter 7
Origins of the Genus *Homo* 164

The Discovery of the First Stone Toolmaker **166**
Sex, Gender, and the Behavior of Early *Homo* **167**
    Hunters or Scavengers? **168**
    Brain Size and Diet **172**
Homo erectus **172**
    Fossils of *Homo erectus* **173**
    Physical Characteristics of *Homo erectus* **174**
Relationship among *Homo erectus, Homo habilis,*
    and Other Proposed Fossil Groups **175**
    Homo erectus from Africa **176**
    Homo erectus Entering Eurasia **176**
    Homo erectus from Indonesia **176**
    Homo erectus from China **177**
    Homo erectus from Western Europe **178**
The Culture of *Homo erectus* **178**
    Acheulean Tool Tradition **179**
    Use of Fire **179**
    Hunting **181**
    Other Evidence of Complex Thought **181**
The Question of Language **182**
Archaic *Homo sapiens* and the Appearance
    of Modern-Sized Brains **183**
    Levalloisian Technique **184**
    Other Cultural Innovations **184**
The Neandertals **185**
Javanese, African, and Chinese Archaic
    Homo sapiens **187**
Middle Paleolithic Culture **188**
    The Mousterian Tool Tradition **189**
    The Symbolic Life of Neandertals **191**
    Speech and Language in the Middle
        Paleolithic **192**

Culture, Skulls, and Modern Human Origins **193**

Biocultural Connection: Sex, Gender, and Female
Paleoanthropologists **168**

Original Study: Humans as Prey **170**

Anthropology Applied: Stone Tools for Modern
Surgeons **190**

Chapter Checklist **194**
Questions for Reflection **195**
Online Study Resources **195**

Chapter 8
The Global Expansion of *Homo sapiens* and Their Technology 196

Upper Paleolithic Peoples: The First Modern
    Humans **198**
The Human Origins Debate **199**
    The Multiregional Hypothesis **199**
    The Recent African Origins Hypothesis **200**
Reconciling the Evidence **202**
    The Genetic Evidence **202**
    The Anatomical Evidence **202**
    The Cultural Evidence **204**
    Coexistence and Cultural Continuity **204**
Race and Human Evolution **206**
Upper Paleolithic Technology **206**
Upper Paleolithic Art **209**
    Music **210**
    Cave or Rock Art **210**
    Ornamental Art **214**
    Gender and Art **214**
Other Aspects of Upper Paleolithic Culture **215**
The Spread of Upper Paleolithic Peoples **215**
    The Sahul **216**
    The Americas **219**
Major Paleolithic Trends **220**

Anthropologists of Note: Berhane Asfaw,
Xinzhi Wu **201**

Original Study: Paleolithic Paint Job **212**

Biocultural Connection: Paleolithic Prescriptions
for Diseases of Today **221**

Chapter Checklist **222**
Questions for Reflection **223**
Online Study Resources **223**

Chapter 9

The Neolithic Revolution: The Domestication of Plants and Animals   224

The Mesolithic Roots of Farming and
    Pastoralism   225
The Neolithic Revolution   227
    What Is Domestication?   227
    Evidence of Early Plant Domestication   228
    Evidence of Early Animal Domestication   228
Why Humans Became Food Producers   229
    The Fertile Crescent   220
    Other Centers of Domestication   232
Food Production and Population Size   236
The Spread of Food Production   237
The Culture of Neolithic Settlements   238
    Jericho: An Early Farming Community   238
    Neolithic Material Culture   240
    Social Structure   241
Neolithic Cultures in the Americas   242
The Neolithic and Human Biology   243
The Neolithic and the Idea of Progress   245

Biocultural Connection: Dogs Get Right
to the Point   232

Original Study: The History of Mortality
and Physiological Stress   243

Chapter Checklist   246
Questions for Reflection   247
Online Study Resources   247

Chapter 10

The Emergence of Cities and States   248

Defining Civilization   250
Tikal: A Case Study   253
    Surveying and Excavating the Site   254
    Evidence from the Excavation   254
Cities and Cultural Change   258
    Agricultural Innovation   258
    Diversification of Labor   259
    Central Government   262
    Social Stratification   266
The Making of States   267
    Ecological Theories   267
    Action Theory   269

Civilization and Its Discontents   270
    Social Stratification and Disease   270
    Colonialism and Disease   270
Anthropology and Cities of the Future   272

Original Study: Action Archaeology and the Community
at El Pilar   256

Anthropology Applied: Pre-Columbian Fish Farming
in the Amazon   260

Biocultural Connection: Perilous Pigs:
The Introduction of Swine-Borne Disease
to the Americas   271

Chapter Checklist   272
Questions for Reflection   273
Online Study Resources   273

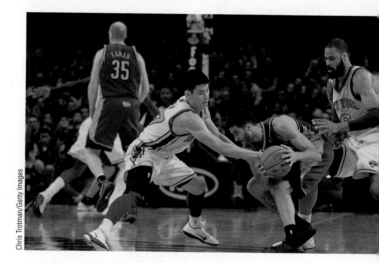

Chris Trotman/Getty Images

Chapter 11

Modern Human Diversity: Race and Racism   274

The History of Human Classification   276
Race as a Biological Concept   278
The Conflation of the Biological into the Cultural
    Category of Race   282
The Social Significance of Race: Racism   285
    Race and Behavior   285
    Race and Intelligence   285
Studying Human Biological Diversity   287
    Skin Color: A Case Study in Adaptation   290
    Culture and Biological Diversity   290
    Beans, Enzymes, and Adaptation to
        Malaria   293
Race and Human Evolution   294

Anthropologist of Note: Fatimah Jackson   278

Original Study: Caveat Emptor: Genealogy for Sale   **280**

Biocultural Connection: Beauty, Bigotry, and the Epicanthic Eyefold of the Beholder   **289**

Chapter Checklist   **296**
Questions for Reflection   **297**
Online Study Resources   **297**

Chapter 12
Human Adaptation to a Changing World   298

Human Adaptation to Natural Environmental
  Stressors   **300**
  Adaptation to High Altitude   **304**
  Adaptation to Cold   **306**
  Adaptation to Heat   **307**
Human-Made Stressors of a Changing World   **308**
The Development of Medical Anthropology   **308**
Science, Illness, and Disease   **310**
Evolutionary Medicine   **314**
  Symptoms as Defense Mechanisms   **314**
  Evolution and Infectious Disease   **315**

The Political Ecology of Disease   **317**
  Prion Diseases   **317**
  Medical Pluralism   **318**
Globalization, Health, and Structural Violence   **318**
  Population Size and Health   **318**
  Poverty and Health   **319**
  Environmental Impact and Health   **320**
The Future of *Homo sapiens*   **321**

Anthropologist of Note: Peter Ellison   **304**

Original Study: Dancing Skeletons: Life and Death in West Africa   **312**

Biocultural Connection: Picturing Pesticides   **322**

Chapter Checklist   **324**
Questions for Reflection   **325**
Online Study Resources   **325**

Glossary   **326**

References   **332**

Bibliography   **337**

Index   **349**

Preface

There comes a time when we need to clean out the basement—to sort through the piles clear down to the bottom, to determine what should be kept and what should be tossed, to make room for new things that warrant a place in a limited space. That's what has happened with this edition of *Evolution and Prehistory: The Human Challenge*—more thoroughly revised than any new edition since Bill Haviland took on coauthors a dozen years ago.

Evolution and Prehistory: The Human Challenge introduces students to biological anthropology and archaeology from an integrated, four-field anthropological perspective. By emphasizing the fundamental connection between biology and culture, the archaeology student learns more about the biological basis of human cultural capabilities and the many ways that culture has impacted human biology, past and present. Similarly, this combination provides more of the cultural context of human evolutionary history, the development of scientific thought, and present-day biological diversity than a student would get in a course restricted to biological anthropology. There has been much debate about the future of four-field anthropology. In our view, its future will be assured through collaboration among anthropologists with diverse backgrounds, as exemplified in this book.

Fueled by our own ongoing research, along with vital feedback from students and anthropology professors who have used and reviewed previous editions, we have scrutinized the archetypal examples of our discipline and weighed them against the latest innovative research methodologies, archaeological discoveries, genetic and other biological findings, linguistic insights, ethnographic descriptions, theoretical revelations, and significant examples of applied anthropology. We believe that these considerations, combined with paying attention to compelling issues in our global theater, have resulted in a lively and relevant textbook that presents both classical and fresh material in ways that stimulate student interest, stir critical reflection, and prompt "ah-ha" moments.

Our Mission

Most students enter an introductory anthropology class intrigued by the general subject but with little more than a vague sense of what it is all about. Thus, the first and most obvious task of our text is to provide a thorough introduction to the discipline—its foundations as a domain of knowledge and its major insights into the rich diversity of humans as a culture-making species. Recognizing the wide spectrum of students enrolled in entry-level anthropology courses, we cover the fundamentals of the discipline in an engaging, illustrative fashion—creating a textbook that establishes a broad platform on which teachers can expand the exploration of concepts and topics in ways that are particularly meaningful to them and their students.

In doing this, we draw from the research and ideas of a number of traditions of anthropological thought, exposing students to a mix of theoretical perspectives and methodologies. Such inclusiveness reflects our conviction that different approaches offer distinctly important insights about human biology, behavior, and beliefs.

If most students start out with only a vague sense of what anthropology is, they often have even less clearly defined—and potentially problematic—views concerning the position of their own species and cultures within the larger world. A second task for this text, then, is to encourage students to appreciate the richness and complexity of human diversity. Along with this goal is the aim of helping them to understand why there are so many differences and similarities in the human condition, past and present.

Debates regarding globalization and notions of progress; the "naturalness" of the mother, father, child(ren) nuclear family; new genetic technologies; and how gender roles relate to biological variation all benefit greatly from the distinct insights gained through anthropology's wide-ranging, holistic perspective. This aspect of the discipline is one of the most valuable gifts we can pass on to those who take our classes. If we as teachers (and textbook authors) do our jobs well, students will gain a wider and more open-minded outlook on the world and a critical but constructive perspective on human origins and on their own biology and culture today. To borrow a favorite line from the famous poet T. S. Eliot, we'll know we've reached the end of our journey when we "arrive where we started / And know the place for the first time" ("Little Gidding" from *The Four Quartets*).

We have written this text, in large part, to help students make sense of our increasingly complex world and to navigate through its interrelated biological and cultural networks with knowledge and skill, whatever professional path they take. We see the book as a guide for people entering the often-bewildering maze of global crossroads in the 21st century.

A Distinctive Approach

Two key factors distinguish *Evolution and Prehistory: The Human Challenge* from other introductory anthropology texts: our integrative presentation of the discipline's four fields and a trio of unifying themes that tie the book together.

Integration of the Four Fields

Unlike traditional texts that present anthropology's four fields—physical or biological anthropology, archaeology, linguistics, and cultural or social anthropology—as if they were separate or independent, our book takes an integrative approach. This reflects the holistic character of the discipline in which members of our species are studied in their totality—as social creatures biologically evolved with the inherent capacity for learning and sharing culture by means of symbolic communication. This approach also reflects our collective experience as practicing anthropologists who recognize that we cannot fully understand humanity in all its fascinating complexity unless we see the systemic interplay among environmental, physiological, material, social, ideological, psychological, and symbolic factors, both past and present.

For analytical purposes, however, we discuss physical anthropology as distinct from archaeology, linguistics, and sociocultural anthropology. Accordingly, there are separate chapters that focus primarily on each field, but the links among them are shown repeatedly. Among many examples of this integrative approach, Chapter 11, "Modern Human Diversity: Race and Racism," discusses the social context of race and recent cultural practices that have impacted the human genome. Similarly, material concerning linguistics appears not only in the chapter on living primates (Chapter 3), but also in the chapters on primate behavior (Chapter 4), on early *Homo* and the origins of culture (Chapters 7 and 8), and on the emergence of cities and states (Chapter 10). In addition, every chapter includes a Biocultural Connection feature to further illustrate the interplay of biological and cultural processes in shaping the human experience.

Unifying Themes

In our own teaching, we recognize the value of marking out unifying themes that help students see the big picture as they grapple with the vast array of material involved with the study of human beings. In *Evolution and Prehistory: The Human Challenge* we employ three such themes.

1. ***Systemic adaptation.*** We emphasize that every culture, past and present, like the human species itself, is an integrated and dynamic system of adaptation that responds to a combination of internal and external factors, including influences of the environment.
2. ***Biocultural connection.*** We highlight the integration of human culture and biology in the steps humans take to meet the challenges of survival. The biocultural connection theme is interwoven throughout the text—as a thread in the main narrative and in boxed features that highlight this connection with a topical example for nearly every chapter.
3. ***Globalization.*** We track the emergence of globalization and its disparate impact on various peoples and cultures around the world. European colonization was a global force for centuries, leaving a significant and often devastating footprint on the affected peoples in Asia, Africa, and the Americas. Decolonization began about 200 years ago and became a worldwide wave in the mid-1900s. However, since the 1960s, political and economic hegemony has taken a new and fast-paced form: globalization (in many ways a process that expands or builds on imperialism). Attention to both forms of global domination—colonialism and globalization—runs through *Evolution and Prehistory: The Human Challenge*, culminating in the final chapter where we apply the concept of structural power to globalization, discussing it in terms of hard and soft power and linking it to structural violence.

Pedagogy

Evolution and Prehistory: The Human Challenge features a range of learning aids, in addition to the three unifying themes described previously. Each pedagogical piece plays an important role in the learning process—from clarifying and enlivening the material to revealing relevancy and aiding recall.

Accessible Language and a Cross-Cultural Voice

In the writing of this text, we consciously cut through unnecessary jargon to speak directly to students. Manuscript reviewers have recognized this, noting that even the most difficult concepts are presented in straightforward and understandable prose for today's first- and second-year college students. Where technical terms are necessary, they appear in bold type with a clear definition in the narrative. The definition appears again in the running glossary at the bottom of our pages, and again in a summary glossary at the end of the book.

To make the narrative more accessible to students, we deliver it in chewable bites—short paragraphs. Numerous subheads provide visual cues to help students track what has been read and what is coming next.

Accessibility involves not only clear writing enhanced by visual cues, but also an engaging voice or style. The voice of *Evolution and Prehistory: The Human Challenge* is distinct among introductory texts in the discipline because it has been written from a cross-cultural perspective. We avoid the typical Western "we/they" voice in favor of a more inclusive one to make sure the narrative resonates with both Western and non-Western students and professors. Also, we highlight the theories and work of anthropologists from all over the world. Finally, we have drawn the text's cultural examples from industrial and postindustrial societies as well as nonindustrial ones.

Compelling Visuals

The Haviland et al. texts garner praise from students and faculty for having a rich array of visuals, including maps, photographs, and figures. This is important because humans—like all primates—are visually oriented, and a well-chosen image may serve to "fix" key information in a student's mind. Unlike some competing texts, all of our visuals are in color, enhancing their appeal and impact. Notably, all maps and figures are created with a colorblind-sensitive palette.

Photographs

Our pages feature a hard-sought collection of compelling, content-rich photographs. Large in size, many of them come with substantial captions composed to help students do a "deep read" of the image. Each chapter features more than a dozen pictures, including our popular Visual Counterpoints—side-by-side photos that effectively compare and contrast biological or cultural features.

Maps

Map features include our "Putting the World in Perspective" map series, locator maps, and distribution maps that provide overviews of key issues such as pollution and energy consumption. Of special note are the Globalscape maps and stories, described in the boxed features section a bit farther on.

Challenge Issues

Each chapter opens with a Challenge Issue and accompanying photograph, which together carry forward the book's theme of humankind's responses through time to the fundamental challenges of survival within the context of the particular chapter.

Student Learning Objectives, Knowledge Skills, and Chapter Checklist

New to this edition is the set of learning objectives presented at the start of every chapter just after the Challenge Issue and photograph. These objectives focus students on the main goals, identifying the knowledge skills they are expected to have mastered after studying each chapter. The main goals are incorporated in a closing Chapter Checklist, which is also new to this edition. The Chapter Checklist summarizes the chapter's content in an easy-to-follow format.

Thought-Provoking Questions

Each chapter closes with five Questions for Reflection, including one that relates back to the Challenge Issue introduced in the chapter's opening. Presented right after the Chapter Checklist, these questions ask students to apply the concepts they have learned by analyzing and evaluating situations. They are designed to stimulate and deepen thought, trigger class discussion, and link the material to the students' own lives.

In addition, the Biocultural Connection essay featured in every chapter ends with a probing question designed to help students grapple with and firmly grasp that connection.

Integrated Gender Coverage

In contrast to many introductory texts, *Evolution and Prehistory: The Human Challenge* integrates coverage of gender throughout the book. Thus, material on gender-related issues is included in *every* chapter. As a result of this approach, gender-related material in *Evolution and Prehistory: The Human Challenge* far exceeds the single chapter that most books devote to the subject.

We have chosen to integrate this material because concepts and issues surrounding gender are almost always too complicated to remove from their context. Spreading this material through all of the chapters has a pedagogical purpose because it emphasizes how considerations of gender enter into virtually everything people do. Gender-related material ranges from discussions of gender roles in evolutionary discourse and studies of nonhuman primates to intersexuality, homosexual identity, same-sex marriage, and female genital mutilation. Through a steady drumbeat of such coverage, this edition avoids ghettoizing gender to a single chapter that is preceded and followed by resounding silence.

Glossary as You Go

The running glossary is designed to catch the student's eye, reinforcing the meaning of each newly introduced term. It is also useful for chapter review, enabling students to readily isolate the new terms from those introduced in earlier chapters. A complete glossary is also included at the back of the book. In the glossaries, each term is defined in clear, understandable language. As a result, less class time is required for going over terms, leaving instructors free to pursue other matters of interest.

Special Boxed Features

Our text includes five types of special boxed features. Each chapter contains a Biocultural Connection, along with two of the following three features: an Original Study, Anthropology Applied, and Anthropologist of Note. In addition, about half of the chapters include a Globalscape. These features are carefully placed and introduced within the main narrative to alert students to their importance and relevance. A complete listing of features is presented just before the detailed table of contents.

Biocultural Connection

Appearing in every chapter, this signature feature of the Haviland et al. textbooks illustrates how cultural and biological processes interact to shape human biology, beliefs, and behavior. It reflects the integrated biocultural approach central to the field of anthropology today. All of the Biocultural Connections include a critical thinking question. For a quick peek at titles, see the listing of features on page xiv.

Original Study

Written expressly for this text, or adapted from ethnographies and other original works by anthropologists, these studies present concrete examples that bring specific concepts to life and convey the passion of the authors. Each study sheds additional light on an important anthropological concept or subject area for the chapter in which it appears. Notably, each Original Study is carefully integrated within the flow of the chapter narrative, signaling students that its content is not extraneous or supplemental. Appearing in twelve chapters, Original Studies cover a wide range of topics, evident from their titles (see page xiv).

Anthropology Applied

Featured in four chapters, these succinct and fascinating profiles illustrate anthropology's wide-ranging relevance in today's world and give students a glimpse into a variety of the careers anthropologists enjoy (see page xiv for a listing).

Anthropologists of Note

Profiling pioneering and contemporary anthropologists from many corners of the world, this feature puts the work of noted anthropologists in historical perspective and draws attention to the international nature of the discipline in terms of both subject matter and practitioners. This edition highlights eleven distinct anthropologists from all four fields of the discipline (see page xiv for a list of the profiles).

Globalscape

Appearing in about half of the chapters, this unique feature charts the global flow of people, goods, and services, as well as pollutants and pathogens. With a map, a story, and a photo highlighting a topic geared toward student interests, every Globalscape shows how the world is interconnected through human activity. Each one ends with a Global Twister—a question that prods students to think critically about globalization. Check out the titles of Globalscapes on page xiv.

Changes and Highlights in the Fourteenth Edition

We have extensively reworked and updated this edition. Definitions of key terms have been honed. Many new visuals and ethnographic examples have been added and others dropped. Every chapter features a new opening photograph and related Challenge Issue that is revised or new. The much-used Questions for Reflection include at least one new question per chapter, plus revisions of effective questions that have been included in previous editions.

As with earlier editions, we further chiseled the writing to make it all the more clear, lively, engaging, and streamlined. On average, chapter narratives have been trimmed by about 10 percent. Also, we have eliminated the chapter "Macroevolution and the Early Primates" by incorporating relevant macroevolutionary material into our chapter on biology, genetics, and evolution (Chapter 2); the primate material from that chapter is now in the chapter on living primates (Chapter 3) and in a new Chapter 6, "From First Primates to First Bipeds." Material on molecular clocks, geologic time, and continental drift is placed in the chapter on methods for studying the past (Chapter 5).

New to this edition is the list of student learning objectives at the start of every chapter, tied to the new Chapter Checklists at the end of every chapter. (Both are described in the pedagogy inventory mentioned earlier.)

In addition to numerous revisions of boxed features, many of these are completely new, including Biocultural Connections "Bonds Beyond Blood: DNA Testing and Refugee Family Unification," "Chimpanzees in Biomedical Research: Time to End the Practice," "Dogs Get Right to the Point," and "Beauty, Bigotry, and the Epicanthic Eyefold of the Beholder"; Original Studies "Disturbing Behaviors of the Orangutan" by Anne Nacey Maggioncalda and Robert M. Sapolsky and "Caveat Emptor: Genealogy for Sale" by Jonathan Marks; and an Anthropology Applied essay "Pre-Columbian Fish Farming in the Amazon" by Clark L. Erickson.

Finally, we have replaced footnotes with in-text parenthetical citations, making sources and dates more visible and freeing up space for larger visuals. The complete citations appear in the references section at the end of the book.

Beyond these across-the-board changes, significant changes have been made within each chapter.

Chapter 1: The Essence of Anthropology

This chapter gives students a broad-stroke introduction to the holistic discipline of anthropology, the distinct focus of each of its fields, and the common philosophical perspectives and methodological approaches they share. It opens with a new Challenge Issue centered on the mining of coltan—the key component of capacitors in small electronic devices—illustrating our globalized world by revealing the link between the miners and students who use the devices. The lead section on the development of anthropology has been dropped to avoid redundancy with the chapter on ethnographic research. The main narrative now begins with a reworked explanation of the anthropological perspective. As revised, this discussion more carefully contrasts anthropology to other disciplines.

The chapter also offers a brief overview of fieldwork and the comparative method, along with ethical issues and examples of applied anthropology in all four fields, providing a foundation for our two methods chapters—one that explores field methods in cultural anthropology and the other that examines the tools for studying the past shared by archaeology and paleoanthropology. Our presentation of the four fields has been reorganized, starting with cultural anthropology, followed by linguistics, archaeology, and physical or biological anthropology.

This chapter's overview of cultural anthropology has been substantially modified. Changes include a new discussion about how the concept of culture is integral to each of anthropology's four fields. To our narrative on the University of Arizona's modern-day Garbage Project, we added an introductory paragraph about anthropologists studying older garbage dumps, such as shell middens, describing how much these explorations can reveal about everyday life in societies past and present.

The chapter also introduces the concept of ethnocentrism and begins a discussion of globalization that is woven through the text. In addition, this first chapter rejects the characterization of a liberal bias in anthropology, identifying instead the discipline's critical evaluation of the status quo. The ideological diversity among anthropologists is explored while emphasizing their shared methodology that avoids ethnocentrism.

Finally, Chapter 1 introduces the five types of special boxed features that appear in the text, describing the purpose of each, along with an example: a Biocultural Connection on the anthropology of organ transplantation; a Globalscape about the global trafficking of human organs; an Original Study on traditional African healers dealing with HIV/AIDS; an Anthropology Applied about forensic anthropology's role in speaking for the dead; and an Anthropologists of Note profiling two of the discipline's pioneers: Franz Boas and Matilda Coxe Stevenson.

Chapter 2: Biology, Genetics, and Evolution

Covering all the basics of genetics and evolution, this revised chapter's content has been streamlined so that macroevolution, previously covered in a different chapter, can follow right on the heels of our detailed discussion of the microevolutionary process. From a pedagogical standpoint, this helps students make the connections between molecular processes and macroevolutionary change through time.

In order to make the content relevant to students' lives, we emphasize the relationship between culture and science beginning with the new Challenge Issue, featuring a large tattoo of DNA on a freckled upper arm, that illustrates how individuals increasingly turn to DNA to form their identity. A new Biocultural Connection, "Bonds Beyond Blood: DNA Testing and Refugee Family Unification" by Jason Silverstein, likewise shows that the use of genetic testing in isolation does not take into account alternate family structures present in other cultures, particularly those arrangements arising from war and genocide.

A variety of new photos, figures, and content-rich captions reinforce these connections, including a new image of the Great Chain of Being to show the transition from spiritual descriptions of nature toward those with a more scientific basis; a new figure showing Darwin's journey on the HMS *Beagle*; new figures illustrating cladogenesis and anagenesis; new and revised figures on the social consequences of prenatal genetic testing including the use of prenatal testing for sex selection, as well as transnational surrogacy as a social solution to the challenges of infertility for the privileged and wealthy; a new figure illustrating the relation between toxic exposure and mutation; and a revised figure on Darwin's finches that illustrates the connection between gradualism and punctuated equilibria.

Chapter 3: Living Primates

As we trace the basic biology of the living primates, this chapter emphasizes the place of humans within this group, instead of erecting barriers between "us" and "them." A new chapter introduction featuring the early fieldwork of Jane Goodall and a new Challenge Issue on primate conservation set the tone of the chapter.

Biological content is also strengthened through the incorporation of pertinent macroevolutionary concepts such as an expanded comparison of mammalian to reptilian biology that includes a discussion of homeotherms versus isotherms and k-selected versus r-selected species; ancestral and derived characteristics; convergent evolution; preadaptation, adaptive radiation, and ecological niche.

In addition, Michele Goldsmith has updated her exclusive Original Study on ecotourism and primate conservation to illustrate recent changes at her field sites. A new content-rich photo and caption on sexual dimorphism among gorillas expands the discussion of this concept. A new Question for Reflection, comparing mammals and reptiles, prompts students to apply the macroevolutionary concepts of ancestral and derived characteristics.

Chapter 4: Primate Behavior

The new Challenge Issue featuring bonobo sexuality asks students to think about nature versus nurture, a theme that builds throughout the chapter, concluding with our discussion of primate culture.

Frans de Waal's work on reconciliation is now featured in the body of the text to allow for Anne Maggioncalda and Robert Sapolsky's Original Study "Disturbing Behaviors of the Orangutan" on orangutan sexual behavior. Formerly a Biocultural Connection, this reorganization better integrates its content with the text and further develops the theme of how we project our cultural notions onto the study of primates.

A new figure illustrates the various forms of primate social organization, and the text provides more details on marmoset polyandry. We have also augmented our discussion of birth intervals and population size among primates. The chapter closes with an update on NIH policy regarding the use of chimps

in biomedical research and a new Biocultural Connection titled "Chimpanzees in Biomedical Research: Time to End the Practice."

Chapter 5: Field Methods in Archaeology and Paleoanthropology

This comprehensive chapter covering methods of investigation opens with the vital question of who owns the past. The Challenge Issue focuses on the current political upheaval in Timbuktu and the potential destruction of monuments, artifacts, and manuscripts in this ancient Muslim city.

Broad chapter changes include moving the material from our old macroevolution chapter on molecular clocks, geologic time, and continental drift into this chapter along with the Anthropologist of Note feature on Allan Wilson. Due to its importance, we moved the material on cultural resource management from a boxed feature into the text proper where students cannot miss it.

Chapter refinements comprise: a revision of the table on dating methods to include more information on process and use of techniques; more emphasis on the human skeleton figure and an insert of the sexually dimorphic pelvis; distinction between frozen remains such as the Ice Man Ötzi and fossil remains; a discussion of the possible deliberate burial at Sima de los Huesos; introduction of the term *archaeological profile*; and a clarified explanation of paleoanthropological and archaeological excavation techniques that avoids suggesting that one is more exacting than the other and that illustrates the laboratory techniques shared by paleoanthropologists, bioarchaeologists, and forensic anthropologists. Finally, a new content-rich photo highlights the difference between looting and real archaeological excavation.

Chapter 6: From First Primates to First Bipeds

Capturing the new inclusion of primate evolution into this chapter, we open with a tightrope-walking chimp from Fongoli to challenge students to think about bipedalism as the defining feature of the hominins. A streamlined introduction to primate evolution follows, including our cladogram illustrating the relationships among the primates, which has been revised to include the chimp–bonobo split.

We also moved the evidence for the earliest potential fossil hominins to this chapter, reorganizing the chapter to make room for this new material. Chapter updates based on recent discoveries include the South African species *Australopithecus sediba*; we both describe and integrate these findings into the discussion about which of these early bipeds led to the human line. We have added thought questions to several figure captions to urge students to participate in the process of paleoanthropological reconstruction. A new photo of reconstructed Laetoli footprints also encourages students to distinguish reenactment based on concrete data from imaginings of the past.

Chapter 7: Origins of the Genus *Homo*

Building on the theme of bringing students into the process of paleoanthropological reconstruction, we open the chapter with paleoartist Elisabeth Daynès bringing a fossil species to life, thus challenging students to think about how to avoid bias. This thread connects to our discussion of Neandertals including a new Visual Counterpoint featuring the varied reenactments that have surrounded their lifeways.

We have dropped "origins of culture" from the chapter title to reflect the current state of primatological research, which has established distinct cultural traditions among our closest relatives. Similarly, this chapter reengages with the notion of purported human uniqueness.

Our section on gender in paleoanthropological reconstructions now includes recent studies on strontium and female dispersal among early hominins. We have tied our discussion on precision grip and cranial capacity back to the previous chapter's discussion of the newly discovered species *Australopithecus sediba*.

Experimental archaeology, a new bolded key term, weaves into our discussion of Oldowan tools and other archaeological assemblages. A photo of the captive bonobo Kanzi making tools helps students visualize the process of reconstructing the past. We have added new material on the potential location of the lost "Peking Man" remains, as well as new evidence for paint fabrication in South Africa 100,000 years ago. Finally, our discussion of the Flores hominins has been placed in this chapter, separating it from the modern human origins controversy.

Chapter 8: The Global Expansion of *Homo sapiens* and Their Technology

To illustrate that paleoanthropology is a science of discovery, we open the chapter with the new, earlier dates for the cave paintings from Spain's El Castillo. This challenges students to consider whether art, once thought to be an accomplishment only of the Cro-Magnons, may have in fact been a part of the Neandertal repertoire. Similarly, our discussion of the recent discoveries related to the Denisovan hominins, and their genetic continuity with extant Asians, shows how paleoanthropologists reshape their understanding of the past as new evidence is discovered.

Our experimental archaeology thread continues in this chapter with a new photo illustrating Upper Paleolithic flint-knapping as well as the content-enriched caption on intricately constructed dwellings made from mammoth bones. We have updated the Biocultural Connection on paleolithic prescriptions for contemporary ailments and made it more relevant to college students by including substances abused today, such as alcohol and tobacco.

The chapter is also enhanced by various other new discoveries including a discussion of the Blombos Cave paint factories, cave flutings by Upper Paleolithic children, as well as new genetic data on peopling of Australia. We have updated our timeline of Upper Paleolithic innovations to include these recent discoveries.

Chapter 9: The Neolithic Revolution: The Domestication of Plants and Animals

This streamlined and updated chapter emphasizes the contemporary relevance of the Neolithic revolution. A new Challenge Issue shows the competition for resources set into motion during the Neolithic, playing out in the context of globalization today as Andean potato farmers battle with industrial asparagus farms that are lowering the aquifers to produce this water-intensive crop for global distribution. The theme of competition for resources threads throughout the chapter.

By incorporating relevant sections of the Biocultural Connection from previous editions on breastfeeding, fertility, and beliefs into the text, we made space for a new Biocultural Connection on the coevolution of humans and dogs featuring the work of evolutionary anthropologist Brian Hare titled "Dogs Get Right to the Point." We have reorganized the heads in the section on why humans became food producers to streamline the content, and we moved the definitions of horticulture and pastoralism to early in the chapter to improve the chapter's conceptual flow. A new Question for Reflection on today's genetically modified crops also drives home the point that today we are still facing challenges introduced during the Neolithic.

Chapter 10: The Emergence of Cities and States

The interrelation of war, power, and monumental structures thematically weaves through this updated chapter. This begins with the new Challenge Issue focusing on the temple at Angkor Wat in Cambodia and the way that the magnificent structure has been the site of violent struggles nearly since its dedication in the 12th century.

An updated introductory section on the interdependence of cities includes Hurricane Katrina, the 2011 Japanese earthquake and tsunami, as well as the role of social media in the Arab Spring of 2011. In a detailed caption, we incorporated key points from the Anthropology

Applied feature from previous editions on the U.S. military's employment of archaeologists to train personnel in war zones to preserve archaeological remains. This allowed us to include a new Anthropology Applied feature on rainforest fishing weirs by Clark Erickson titled "Pre-Columbian Fish Farming in the Amazon."

This chapter's rich new visuals include locator maps indicating Mesopotamian sites and the Inca empire; an intriguing photo of a Maya calendar, explaining how it connects to the current doomsday predictions; and a photo of Cairo's "City of the Dead" to illustrate the problems of social stratification today.

Chapter 11: Modern Human Diversity: Race and Racism

Enlivened writing throughout this chapter improves the pedagogy and makes the challenging concepts of race and racism more interesting and accessible for today's students. The new Challenge Issue features NBA star Jeremy Lin to illustrate the social meaning of biological difference.

The chapter now includes the seminal work of Audrey Smedley on the roots of racism in North America, focusing on the English treatment of the Irish along with reference to Bacon's Rebellion. As well, a photo and caption illustrate the Nazi expedition to Tibet in search of the origins of the pure Aryan race.

An updated section includes a discussion of the 2010 census categories of race, and a new footnote to the Tiger Woods story updates the history of African Americans in golf. We also use the families of two U.S. presidents—Thomas Jefferson and Barack Obama—to illustrate cultural beliefs about gene flow.

A new reference to structural violence and race details differences in prison sentences for crack versus powdered cocaine users, a disparity that preferentially privileges the predominantly white users of the more expensive powdered cocaine. Accordingly, we have added the term *structural violence* to the glossary along with the term *genocide*.

Links between Mendel's work on heredity from Chapter 2 strengthen this chapter's discussion of the faults inherent in theories of race and intelligence. The chapter's section on true biological adaptations across populations now includes the work of Gary Nabhan and Laurie Monti on "slow release" foods and activity, instead of the thrifty genotype, and also mentions the rising importance of epigenetics. We moved material on fava beans and G-6-PD to the body of the text to make space for a new Biocultural Connection on ethnic plastic surgery titled "Beauty, Bigotry, and the Epicanthic Eyefold of the Beholder." We are pleased to include as well a new Original Study by Jonathan Marks on the perils and pitfalls of commercial genetic testing titled "Caveat Emptor: Genealogy for Sale."

Chapter 12: Human Adaptation to a Changing World

This chapter provides a broad introduction to human biology and human adaptation, while also reinforcing the powerful influence of culture on all aspects of human biology. The Challenge Issue offers a stunning body map, a life-size depiction of the experience of being an HIV-positive woman in South Africa, to help students see themselves as fully biocultural beings.

A suite of new and revised figures illustrates a variety of biological concepts including a new figure on long bone growth, a new figure on sweat glands, a new figure showing the growth trajectory of different body systems, and a revised figure on human population growth. New figures also help students see the myriad connections between human biology and culture including an intriguing photo of the ship-breaking yards of Bangladesh and a figure on the use of military metaphors in immunology.

We have also expanded our discussion of body fat and fertility globally and added relevant key terms such as *menarche* and *menopause* to the running glossary. As well, our discussion of genetic, developmental, and physiological adaptation has been refined and clarified, again adding the relevant key terms such as *hypoxia* to the glossary.

We close the chapter with new examples of how an integrated anthropological perspective to questions of human health. Topics include the recent appointment of medical anthropologist Jim Yong Kim as the president of the World Bank and ongoing biological evolution in Kenyan sex workers who seem to be HIV-resistant despite constant exposure. Biological and cultural processes both contribute to human health.

Supplements

Evolution and Prehistory: The Human Challenge comes with a comprehensive supplements program to help instructors create an effective learning environment both inside and outside the classroom and to aid students in mastering the material.

Supplements for Instructors

Online Instructor's Manual and Test Bank

The Instructor's Manual offers detailed chapter outlines, lecture suggestions, key terms, and student activities such as video exercises and Internet exercises. In addition, there are over seventy-five chapter test questions including multiple choice, true/false, fill-in-the-blank, short answer, and essay.

PowerLecture™ with ExamView®

This one-stop class preparation tool contains ready-to-use Microsoft® PowerPoint® slides, enabling you to assemble, edit, publish, and present custom lectures with ease. PowerLecture helps you bring together text-specific lecture outlines and art from Haviland et al.'s text along with videos and your own materials—culminating in powerful, personalized, media-enhanced presentations. Featuring automatic grading, ExamView is also available within PowerLecture, allowing you to create, deliver, and customize tests and study guides (both print and online) in minutes. See assessments onscreen exactly as they will print or display online. Build tests of up to 250 questions using up to twelve question types, and enter an unlimited number of new questions or edit existing questions. PowerLecture also includes the text's Instructor's Resource Manual and Test Bank as Word documents.

WebTutor™ on Blackboard® and WebCT™

Jumpstart your course with customizable, rich, text-specific content within your course management system. Whether you want to web-enable your class or put an entire course online, WebTutor delivers. WebTutor offers a wide array of resources including access to the eBook, glossaries, flash cards, quizzes, videos, and more.

Anthropology Coursereader

Anthropology Coursereader allows you to create a fully customized online reader in minutes. Access a rich collection of thousands of primary and secondary sources, readings, and audio and video selections from multiple disciplines. Each selection includes a descriptive introduction that puts it into context, and the selection is further supported by both critical thinking and multiple-choice questions designed to reinforce key points. This easy-to-use solution allows you to select exactly the content you need for your courses and is loaded with convenient pedagogical features like highlighting, printing, note taking, and downloadable MP3 audio files for each reading. You have the freedom to assign and customize individualized content at an affordable price.

The Wadsworth Anthropology Video Library: Volumes I, II, and III

The Wadsworth Anthropology Video Library (featuring BBC Motion Gallery video clips) drives home the relevance of course topics through short, provocative clips of current and historical events. Perfect for enriching lectures and engaging students in discussion, many of the segments in these volumes have been gathered from the BBC Motion Gallery. Ask your Cengage Learning representative for a list of contents.

AIDS in Africa DVD

Southern Africa has been overcome by a pandemic of unparalleled proportions. This documentary series focuses on the democracy of Namibia and the nation's valiant actions to control HIV/AIDS.

Included in this series are four documentary films created by the Periclean Scholars at Elon University: (1) *Young Struggles, Eternal Faith*, which focuses on caregivers in the faith community; (2) *The Shining Lights of Opuwo*, which shows how young people share their messages of hope through song and dance; (3) *A Measure of Our Humanity*, which describes HIV/AIDS as an issue related to gender, poverty, stigma, education, and justice; and (4) *You Wake Me Up*, a story of two HIV-positive women and their acts of courage helping other women learn to survive.

Cengage/Wadsworth is excited to offer these award-winning films to instructors for use in class. When presenting topics such as gender, faith, culture, poverty, and so on, the films will be enlightening for students and will expand their global perspective of HIV/AIDS.

Online Resources for Instructors and Students

CourseMate

Cengage Learning's Anthropology CourseMate brings course concepts to life with interactive learning, study, and exam preparation tools that support the printed textbook. CourseMate includes an integrated eBook, glossaries, flash cards, quizzes, videos, and more—as well as EngagementTracker, an original tool that monitors student engagement in the course. The accompanying instructor website, available through login.cengage.com, offers access to password-protected resources such as an electronic version of the Instructor's Manual, Test Bank files, and Power-Point® slides. CourseMate can be bundled with the student text. Contact your Cengage sales representative for information on getting access to CourseMate.

Supplements for Students

Telecourse Study Guide

The distance learning course, **Anthropology: The Four Fields**, provides online and print companion study guide options that include study aids, interactive exercises, videos, and more.

Additional Student Resources

Basic Genetics for Anthropology CD-ROM: Principles and Applications (stand-alone version), by Robert Jurmain and Lynn Kilgore

This student CD-ROM expands on such concepts as biological inheritance (genes, DNA sequencing, and so on) and applications of that to modern human populations at the molecular level (human variation and adaptation—to disease, diet, growth, and development). Interactive animations and simulations bring these important concepts to life for students so they can fully understand the essential biological principles required for physical anthropology. Also available are quizzes and interactive flashcards for further study.

Hominid Fossils CD-ROM: An Interactive Atlas, by James Ahern

The interactive atlas CD-ROM includes over seventy-five key fossils important for a clear understanding of human evolution. The QuickTime Virtual Reality (QTVR) "object" movie format for each fossil enables students to have a near-authentic experience of working with these important finds, by allowing them to rotate the fossils 360 degrees.

Unlike some VR media, QTVR objects are made using actual photographs of the real objects and thus better preserve details of color and texture. The fossils used are high-quality research casts as well as actual fossils. Because the atlas is not organized linearly, student are able to access levels and multiple paths, allowing them to see how the fossil fits into the map of human evolution in terms of geography, time, and evolution. The CD-ROM offers students an inviting, authentic learning environment, one that also contains a dynamic quizzing feature that permits students to test their knowledge of fossil and species identification, as well as providing detailed information about the fossil record.

Readings and Case Studies

Classic and Contemporary Readings in Physical Anthropology, edited by M. K. Sandford with Eileen M. Jackson

This highly accessible reader emphasizes science—its principles and methods—as well as the historical development of physical anthropology and the applications of new technology to the discipline. The editors provide an introduction to the reader as well as a brief overview of the article so students know what to look for. Each article also includes discussion questions and Internet resources.

Classic Readings in Cultural Anthropology, 3rd edition, edited by Gary Ferraro

Now in its third edition, this reader includes historical and recent articles that have had a profound effect on the field of anthropology. Organized according to the major topic areas found in most cultural anthropology courses, this reader includes an introduction to the material as well as a brief overview of each article, discussion questions, and InfoTrac College Edition key search terms.

Globalization and Change in Fifteen Cultures: Born in One World, Living in Another, edited by George Spindler and Janice E. Stockard

In this volume, fifteen case study authors write about cultural change in today's diverse settings around the world. Each original article provides insight into the dynamics and meanings of change, as well as the effects of globalization at the local level.

Case Studies in Cultural Anthropology, edited by George Spindler and Janice E. Stockard

Select from more than sixty classic and contemporary ethnographies representing geographic and topical diversity. Newer case studies focus on cultural change and cultural continuity, reflecting the globalization of the world.

Case Studies on Contemporary Social Issues, edited by John A. Young

Framed around social issues, these new contemporary case studies are globally comparative and represent the cutting-edge work of anthropologists today.

Case Studies in Archaeology, edited by Jeffrey Quilter

These engaging accounts of new archaeological techniques, issues, and solutions—as well as studies discussing the collection of material remains—range from site-specific excavations to types of archaeology practiced.

Acknowledgments

In this day and age, no textbook comes to fruition without extensive collaboration. Beyond the shared endeavors of our author team, this book owes its completion to a wide range of individuals, from colleagues in the discipline to those involved in development and production processes. Sincere thanks to colleagues who brought their expertise to bear—as sounding boards and in responding to questions concerning their specializations: Marta P. Alfonso-Durruty, Robert Bailey, Frans B. M. de Waal, Jessica Falcone, Michele Goldsmith, John Hawks, Amber Campbell Hibbs, Heather Loyd, Gillian E. Newell, Martin Ottenheimer, Svante Pääbo, Yvette Pigeon, Herbert Prins, and Michael Wesch. We are particularly grateful for the manuscript reviewers listed below, who provided detailed and thoughtful feedback that helped us to hone and re-hone our narrative.

We carefully considered and made use of the wide range of comments provided by these individuals. Our decisions on how to utilize their suggestions were influenced by our own perspectives on anthropology and teaching, combined with the priorities and page limits of this text. Thus, neither our reviewers nor any of the other anthropologists mentioned here should be held responsible for any shortcomings in this book. They should, however, be credited as contributors to many of the book's strengths: Philip Carr, University of South Alabama; Douglas Crews, Ohio State University; William Price, North Country Community College; Frank Salamone, Iona College; David Schwimmer, Columbus State University; and Donna Marshaye White, Webster University.

Thanks, too, go to colleagues who provided material for some of the Original Study, Biocultural Connection, and Anthropology Applied boxes in this text: Katherine Dettwyler, Clark L. Erickson, Anabel Ford, Michele Goldsmith, Donna Hart, John Hawks, Suzanne Leclerc-Madlala, Roger Lewin, Anne Nacey Maggioncalda, Charles C. Mann, Jonathan Marks, Anna Roosevelt, Robert M. Sapolsky, Jason Silverstein, Sherry Simpson, and Meredith F. Small.

We have debts of gratitude to office workers in our departments for their cheerful help in clerical matters: Karen Rundquist, Patty Redmond, and Tina Griffiths, along with research librarian extraordinaire Nancy Bianchi. Also worthy of note here are the introductory anthropology teaching assistants at Kansas State University and the College of Medicine and Honors College students at the University of Vermont who, through the years, have shed light for us on effective ways to reach new generations of students. And, finally, we recognize the introductory students themselves, who are at the heart of this educational endeavor and who continually provide feedback in formal and informal ways.

Our thanksgiving inventory would be incomplete without mentioning individuals at Wadsworth/ Cengage Learning who helped conceive of this text and bring it to fruition. Of special note is our senior development editor Lin Marshall Gaylord, who has been a shaping force for many generations of the Haviland et al. textbooks. She continues to grace our efforts with vision, resilience, constancy, and anthropological knowledge. We cannot imagine this endeavor without her. Our thanks also go out to Wadsworth's skilled and enthusiastic editorial, marketing, design, and production team: Aileen Berg (senior acquisitions sponsoring editor), Liz Rhoden (senior brand manager), Michelle Williams (senior market development manager), John Chell (media editor), Margaux Cameron (assistant editor), Victor Luu (editorial assistant), as well as Cheri Palmer (content project manager) and Caryl Gorska (art director).

In addition to all of the above, we have had the invaluable aid of several most able freelancers, including veteran photo researcher Sarah Evertson and our alert and artful art team at Graphic World. We are beyond grateful to have once again had the opportunity to work with copy editor Jennifer Gordon and production coordinator Joan Keyes of Dovetail Publishing Services. Consummate professionals and generous souls, both of them keep track of countless details and bring calm efficiency and grace to the demands of meeting difficult deadlines. Their efforts and skills play a major role in making our work doable and pleasurable.

And finally, all of us are indebted to family members and close friends who have not only put up with our textbook preoccupation but cheered us on in the endeavor.

About the Authors

Authors Bunny McBride, Dana Walrath, Harald Prins, and William Haviland

All four members of this author team share overlapping research interests and a similar vision of what anthropology is (and should be) about. For example, all are true believers in the four-field approach to anthropology and all have some involvement in applied work.

WILLIAM A. HAVILAND is professor emeritus at the University of Vermont, where he founded the Department of Anthropology and taught for thirty-two years. He holds a PhD in anthropology from the University of Pennsylvania.

He has carried out original research in archaeology in Guatemala and Vermont; ethnography in Maine and Vermont; and physical anthropology in Guatemala. This work has been the basis of numerous publications in various national and international books and journals, as well as in media intended for the general public. His books include *The Original Vermonters*, coauthored with Marjorie Power, and a technical monograph on ancient Maya settlement. He also served as consultant for the award-winning telecourse *Faces of Culture*, and he is coeditor of the series *Tikal Reports*, published by the University of Pennsylvania Museum of Archaeology and Anthropology.

Besides his teaching and writing, Dr. Haviland has lectured to numerous professional as well as non-professional audiences in Canada, Mexico, Lesotho, South Africa, and Spain, as well as in the United States.

A staunch supporter of indigenous rights, he served as expert witness for the Missisquoi Abenaki of Vermont in an important court case over aboriginal fishing rights.

Awards received by Dr. Haviland include being named University Scholar by the Graduate School of the University of Vermont in 1990; a Certificate of Appreciation from the Sovereign Republic of the Abenaki Nation of Missisquoi, St. Francis/Sokoki Band in 1996; and a Lifetime Achievement Award from the Center for Research on Vermont in 2006. Now retired from teaching, he continues his research, writing, and lecturing from the coast of Maine. He serves as a trustee for the Abbe Museum in Bar Harbor, focused on Maine's Native American history, culture, art, and archaeology. His most recent books are *At the Place of the Lobsters and Crabs* (2009) and *Canoe Indians of Down East Maine* (2012).

DANA WALRATH is assistant professor of family medicine at the University of Vermont and an affiliated faculty member for women's and gender studies. After earning her PhD from the University of Pennsylvania, she taught there and at Temple University. Dr. Walrath broke new ground in medical and biological anthropology through her work on biocultural aspects of childbirth. She has also written on a wide range of topics related to gender in paleoanthropology, the social production of sickness and health, sex differences, genetics, and evolutionary medicine. Her work has appeared in edited volumes and in journals such as *Current Anthropology, American Anthropologist, American Journal of Physical Anthropology*, and *Anthropology Now*. She developed a novel curriculum in medical education at the University of Vermont's College of Medicine that brings humanism, anthropological theory and practice, narrative medicine, and professionalism skills to first-year medical students.

Dr. Walrath also has an MFA in creative writing from Vermont College of Fine Arts and has shown her artwork in galleries throughout the country. Her recent work on Alzheimer's disease combines anthropology with memoir and visual art. Spanning a variety of disciplines, her work has been supported by diverse sources such as the National Science Foundation for the Arts, the Centers for Disease Control, the Health Resources and Services Administration, the Vermont Studio Center, the Vermont Arts Council, and the National Endowment for the Arts. She is currently a Fulbright Scholar at the American University of

Armenia and the Institute of Ethnography and Archaeology of the National Academy of Sciences of Armenia, where she is completing a project titled "The Narrative Anthropology of Aging in Armenia."

HARALD E. L. PRINS is a University Distinguished Professor of cultural anthropology at Kansas State University. Academically trained at half a dozen Dutch and U.S. universities, he previously taught at Radboud University (Netherlands), Bowdoin College and Colby College in Maine, and was a visiting professor at the University of Lund, Sweden. Also named a Distinguished University Teaching Scholar, he received numerous honors for his outstanding academic teaching, including the Presidential Award in 1999, Carnegie Professor of the Year for Kansas in 2006, and the AAA/Oxford University Press Award for Excellence in Undergraduate Teaching of Anthropology in 2010.

His fieldwork focuses on indigenous peoples in the western hemisphere, and he has long served as an advocacy anthropologist on land claims and other Native rights. In that capacity, Dr. Prins has been a key expert witness in both the U.S. Senate and Canadian courts. His numerous academic publications appear in seven languages, and his book include *The Mi'kmaq: Resistance, Accommodation, and Cultural Survival.*

Also trained in filmmaking, he was president of the Society for Visual Anthropology, and coproduced award-winning documentaries. He has been the visual anthropology editor of *American Anthropologist*, coprincipal investigator for the U.S. National Park Service, international observer in Paraguay's presidential elections, and a research associate at the National Museum of Natural History, Smithsonian Institution.

BUNNY MCBRIDE is an award-winning author specializing in cultural anthropology, indigenous peoples, international tourism, and nature conservation issues. Published in dozens of national and international print media, she has reported from Africa, Europe, China, and the Indian Ocean. Holding an MA from Columbia University, she is highly rated as a teacher, and she has served as visiting anthropology faculty at Principia College and the Salt Institute for Documentary Field Studies. Since 1996 she has been an adjunct lecturer of anthropology at Kansas State University.

Among her many publications are books such as *Women of the Dawn; Molly Spotted Elk: A Penobscot in Paris; Indians in Eden* (with Harald Prins); and *The Audubon Field Guide to African Wildlife*, which she co-authored. McBride has also authored numerous book chapters. Honors include a special commendation from the state legislature of Maine for significant contributions to Native women's history. A community activist and researcher for the Aroostook Band of Micmacs (1981–1991), she assisted this Maine Indian community in its successful efforts to reclaim lands, gain tribal status, and revitalize cultural traditions.

In recent years, she has served as coprincipal investigator for a National Park Service ethnography project and curated several museum exhibits, including "Journeys West: The David & Peggy Rockefeller American Indian Art Collection" for the Abbe Museum in Bar Harbor, Maine. Her latest exhibit, "Indians & Rusticators," received a 2012 Leadership in History Award from the American Association for State and Local History. Currently, she serves as vice president of the Women's World Summit Foundation, based in Geneva, Switzerland, and is completing a collection of essays.

EVOLUTION AND PREHISTORY

© Mark Craemer

Challenge Issue

It is a challenge to make sense of the world and our place in the universe. Who am I and how am I connected to the person in this picture? Why do I look different from so many other people in the world and why are there so many different languages? Who harvested the cotton for my shirt or felled the tree used to build my house? Why are some people immune from a virus that kills others? How is it that many believe in an afterlife but others do not? When did our ancestors first begin to think? What distinguishes us from other animals? Anthropologists take a holistic, integrated approach to such questions, framing them in a broad context and examining interconnections. Our discipline considers human culture and biology, in all times and places, as inextricably intertwined, each affecting the other. This photograph shows the hands of a miner holding coltan, a tarlike mineral mined in eastern Congo. Refined, coltan turns into a heat-resistant powder capable of storing energy. As the key component of capacitors in small electronic devices, it is highly valued on the global market. Coltan mines, enriching the warring Congolese factions that control them, are hellholes for the thousands of people, including children, who work the mines. Bought, transported, and processed by foreign merchants and corporations, small bits of this mineral eventually end up in mobile phones and laptop computers worldwide. Although the link between you and globalization is complex, no more than "six degrees of separation" exist between your hands and those of the miner in the heart of Africa. Anthropology's holistic and integrative perspective will equip you to explore and negotiate today's interconnected and globalized world.

The Essence of Anthropology

The Anthropological Perspective

Anthropology is the study of humankind in all times and places. Of course, many other disciplines focus on humans in one way or another. For example, anatomy and physiology concentrate on our species as biological organisms. The social sciences examine human relationships, leaving artistic and philosophical aspects of human cultures to the humanities. Anthropology focuses on the interconnections and interdependence of all aspects of the human experience in all places, in the present and deep into the past, well before written history. This unique, broad **holistic perspective** equips anthropologists to address that elusive thing we call *human nature.*

Anthropologists welcome the contributions of researchers from other disciplines, and in return offer their own findings to these other disciplines. An anthropologist may not know as much about the structure of the human eye as an anatomist or as much about the perception of color as a psychologist. As a synthesizer, however, the anthropologist seeks to understand how anatomy and psychology relate to color-naming practices in different societies. Because they look for the broad basis of human ideas and practices without limiting themselves to any single social or biological aspect, anthropologists can acquire an especially expansive and inclusive overview of human biology and culture.

Keeping a holistic perspective allows anthropologists to prevent their own cultural ideas and values from distorting their research. As the old saying goes, people often see what they believe, rather than what appears before their eyes. By maintaining a critical awareness of their own assumptions about human nature—checking and rechecking the ways their beliefs and actions might be shaping their research—anthropologists strive to gain objective knowledge about human beings. With this

anthropology The study of humankind in all times and places.

holistic perspective A fundamental principle of anthropology: The various parts of human culture and biology must be viewed in the broadest possible context in order to understand their interconnections and interdependence.

IN THIS CHAPTER YOU WILL LEARN TO

Describe the discipline of anthropology and make connections among its four fields.

Compare anthropology to the sciences and the humanities.

Identify the characteristics of anthropological field methods and the ethics of anthropological research.

Explain the usefulness of anthropology in light of globalization.

in mind, anthropologists aim to avoid the pitfalls of **ethnocentrism**, a belief that the ways of one's own culture are the only proper ones.

To some, an inclusive, holistic perspective that emphasizes the diversity within and among human cultures can be mistaken as shorthand for liberal politics among anthropologists. This is not the case. Anthropologists come from many different backgrounds, and individuals practicing the discipline vary in their personal, political, and religious beliefs (**Figure 1.1**). At the same time, they apply a rigorous methodology for researching cultural practices from the perspective of the culture being studied—a methodology that requires them to check for the influences of their own biases. This is as true for an anthropologist analyzing the culture of the global banking industry as it is for one investigating trance dancing among contemporary hunter-gatherers. We might say that anthropology is a discipline concerned with unbiased evaluation of diverse human systems, including one's own. At times this requires challenging the status quo that is maintained and defended by the power elites of the system under study.

While other social sciences have predominantly concentrated on contemporary peoples living in North American and European (Western) societies, anthropologists have traditionally focused on non-Western peoples and cultures. Anthropologists work with the understanding that to fully access the complexities of human ideas, behavior, and biology, *all* humans, wherever and whenever, must be studied. A cross-cultural and long-term evolutionary perspective distinguishes anthropology from other social sciences. This approach guards against theories about the world and reality that are **culture-bound**—based on the assumptions and values that come from the researcher's own culture.

As a case in point, consider the fact that infants in the United States typically sleep apart from their parents. To people accustomed to multibedroom houses, cribs, and car seats, this may seem normal, but cross-cultural research shows that *co-sleeping,* of mother and baby in particular, is the norm (**Figure 1.2**). Further, the practice of sleeping apart favored in the United States dates back only about 200 years.

Recent studies have shown that separation of mother and infant has important biological and cultural consequences. For one thing, it increases the length of the infant's crying bouts. Some mothers incorrectly interpret crying as an indication that the baby is not receiving sufficient breast milk and consequently switch to using bottled formula, which has been shown to be less healthy. In extreme cases, a baby's cries may provoke physical

Figure 1.1 Anthropologist Jayasinhji Jhala Anthropologists come from many corners of the world and carry out research in a huge variety of cultures all around the globe. Dr. Jayasinhji Jhala, pictured here, hails from the old city of Dhrangadhra in Gujarat, northwestern India. A member of the Jhala clan of Rajputs, an aristocratic caste of warriors, he grew up in the royal palace of his father, the maharaja. After earning a bachelor of arts degree in India, he came to the United States and earned a master's in visual studies from MIT, followed by a doctorate in anthropology from Harvard. Currently a professor and director of the programs of Visual Anthropology and the Visual Anthropology Media Laboratory at Temple University, he returns regularly to India with students to film cultural traditions in his own caste-stratified society.

abuse. But the benefits of co-sleeping go beyond significant reductions in crying: Infants who are breastfed receive more stimulation important for brain development, and they are apparently less susceptible to sudden infant death syndrome (SIDS or "crib death"), which occurs at a higher rate in the United States than in any other country. There are benefits to the mother as well: Frequent nursing prevents early ovulation after childbirth, promotes weight

ethnocentrism The belief that the ways of one's own culture are the only proper ones.

culture-bound A perspective that produces theories about the world and reality that are based on the assumptions and values from the researcher's own culture.

VISUAL COUNTERPOINT

Figure 1.2 Sleeping Habits across Cultures Although infants in the United States typically sleep apart from their parents, cross-cultural research shows that co-sleeping, particularly of mother and baby, is the rule. Without the breathing cues provided by someone sleeping nearby, an infant is more susceptible to sudden infant death syndrome (SIDS), a phenomenon in which a 4- to 6-month-old baby stops breathing and dies while asleep. The highest rates of SIDS are found among infants in the United States. The photo on the right shows a Nenet family sleeping together in their *chum* (reindeer-skin tent). Nenet people are Arctic reindeer pastoralists living in Siberia.

loss to shed pregnancy pounds, and allows nursing mothers at least as much sleep as mothers who sleep apart from their infants (McKenna & McDade, 2005).

Why do so many mothers continue to sleep separately from their infants? In the United States, the cultural values of independence and consumerism come into play. To begin building individual identities, babies are provided with rooms (or at least space) of their own. This room also gives parents a place to stow the toys, furniture, and other paraphernalia associated with good and caring childrearing in the United States.

Although the findings of anthropologists have often challenged the conclusions of sociologists, psychologists, and economists, anthropology is absolutely indispensable to those in other disciplines because it is the only consistent check against culture-bound assertions. In a sense, anthropology is to these disciplines what the laboratory is to physics and chemistry: an essential testing ground for their theories.

Anthropology and Its Fields

Individual anthropologists tend to specialize in one of four fields or subdisciplines: cultural anthropology, linguistic anthropology, archaeology, and physical (biological) anthropology (**Figure 1.3**). Some anthropologists consider

archaeology and linguistics to be part of the broader study of human cultures, but archaeology and linguistics also have close ties to physical anthropology. For example, while linguistic anthropology focuses on the social and cultural aspects of language, it has deep connections to the evolution of human language and to the biological basis of speech and language studied within physical anthropology.

Researchers in each of anthropology's fields gather and analyze data to explore similarities and differences among humans, across time and space. Moreover, individuals within

Figure 1.3 The Four Fields of Anthropology Note that the divisions among the fields are not sharp, indicating that their boundaries overlap. Note also that all four include the practice of applied anthropology.

BIOCULTURAL CONNECTION

The Anthropology of Organ Transplantation

In 1954, the first organ transplant occurred in Boston when surgeons removed a kidney from one identical twin to place it inside his sick brother. Today, transplants between unrelated individuals are common, so much so that organs are trafficked in the black market, often across continents from the poor to the wealthy. Though some transplants rely upon living donors, routine organ transplantation depends largely upon the availability of organs obtained from individuals who have died. To reduce illegal traffic, several European countries have enacted policies that assume that any individual who is "brain dead" is automatically an organ donor unless the person has "opted out" ahead of time.

A practice like organ transplantation can exist only if it fits with cultural beliefs about death and the human body. The North American and European view—that the body is a machine that can be repaired much like a car—makes a practice like organ transplantation acceptable. But this is not the view shared by all societies. Anthropologist Margaret Lock has explored differences between Japanese and North American acceptance of the biological state of brain death and how it affects the practice of organ transplantation.

The diagnosis of brain death relies upon the absence of measurable electrical currents in the brain and the inability to breathe without technological assistance. The brain-dead individual, though attached to machines, still seems alive with a beating heart and normal skin coloring. Part of the reason most North Americans find organ transplantation tolerable with the determination of brain death is that personhood and individuality are culturally ascribed to the mind, and thus located in the brain. North Americans' acceptance of brain death has allowed for the "gift of life" through sometimes anonymous organ donation and subsequent transplantation.

By contrast, in Japan, the concept of brain death is hotly contested, and organ transplants are rarely performed. The Japanese idea of personhood does not incorporate a mind–body split; instead, a person's identity is tied to the entire body rather than solely to the brain. Consequently, the Japanese reject that a warm body is a corpse from which organs can be harvested. Further, organs cannot be transformed into "gifts" because anonymous donation is incompatible with Japanese social patterns of reciprocal exchange.

Organ transplantation involves far greater social meaning than the purely biological movement of an organ from one individual to another. Cultural and biological processes are tightly woven into every aspect of this new social practice.

BIOCULTURAL QUESTION

What criteria do you use for death, and is it compatible with the idea of organ donation? Do you think that donated organs are fairly distributed in your society or throughout the globe?

For more on this subject, see Lock, M. (2001). Twice dead: Organ transplants and the reinvention of death. Berkeley: University of California Press.

---

each of the four fields practice **applied anthropology**, which entails the use of anthropological knowledge and methods to solve practical problems. Most applied anthropologists actively collaborate with the communities in which they work—setting goals, solving problems, and conducting research together. In this book, the Anthropology Applied features spotlight how anthropology contributes to solving a wide range of challenges.

applied anthropology The use of anthropological knowledge and methods to solve practical problems, often for a specific client.

medical anthropology A specialization in anthropology that brings theoretical and applied approaches from cultural and biological anthropology to the study of human health and disease.

cultural anthropology The study of patterns in human behavior, thought, and emotions, focusing on humans as culture-producing and culture-reproducing creatures. Also known as *social* or *sociocultural anthropology.*

An early example of the application of anthropological knowledge to a practical problem was the international public health movement that began in the 1920s. This marked the beginning of **medical anthropology**—a specialization that brings theoretical and applied approaches from cultural and biological anthropology to the study of human health and disease. The work of medical anthropologists sheds light on the connections between human health and political and economic forces, both locally and globally. Examples of this specialization appear in some of the Biocultural Connections featured in this text, including the one presented on this page, "The Anthropology of Organ Transplantation."

Cultural Anthropology

Cultural anthropology (also called *social* or *sociocultural anthropology*) is the study of patterns in human behavior, thought, and emotions. It focuses on humans as culture-producing and culture-reproducing creatures. To understand the work of the cultural anthropologist, we must clarify the meaning of **culture**—a society's shared and socially transmitted ideas, values, emotions, and perceptions, which are used to make sense of experience and which generate behavior and are reflected in that behavior. These are the (often unconscious) standards by which societies—structured groups of people—operate. These standards are socially learned, rather than acquired through biological inheritance. The manifestations of culture may vary considerably from place to place, but no individual is "more cultured" in the anthropological sense than any other.

Integral to all the anthropological fields, the concept of culture might be considered anthropology's distinguishing feature. After all, a biological anthropologist is distinct from a biologist *primarily* because he or she takes culture into account. Cultural anthropologists may study the legal, medical, economic, political, or religious system of a given society, knowing that all aspects of the culture interrelate as part of a unified whole. They may focus on divisions in a society—such as by gender, age, or class—factors we will explore in depth later in this text. But it is also worth noting the significance of these same categories to the archaeologist who studies a society through its material remains, to the linguistic anthropologist who examines ancient and modern languages, and to the biological anthropologist who investigates the physical human body.

Cultural anthropology has two main components: ethnography and ethnology. An **ethnography** is a detailed description of a particular culture primarily based on **fieldwork**, which is the term all anthropologists use for on-location research. Because the hallmark of ethnographic fieldwork is a combination of social participation and personal observation within the community being studied and interviews and discussions with individual members of a group, the ethnographic method is commonly referred to as **participant observation** (Figure 1.4). Ethnographies provide the information used to make systematic comparisons among cultures all across the world. Known as **ethnology**, such cross-cultural research allows anthropologists to develop theories that help explain why certain important differences or similarities occur among groups.

Ethnography

Through participant observation—eating a people's food, sleeping under their roof, learning how to speak and behave acceptably, and personally experiencing their habits and customs—the ethnographer seeks to gain the best possible understanding of a particular way of life. Being a participant observer does not mean that the anthropologist must join in battles to study a culture in which warfare is prominent; but by living among a warring people, the ethnographer should be able to understand how warfare fits into the overall cultural framework.

The ethnographer must observe carefully to gain an overview without placing too much emphasis on one

Matt Dyas/Courtesy of Florian Stammler

Figure 1.4 Fieldwork in the Arctic British anthropologist Florian Stammler engages in participant observation among Sami reindeer nomads in Siberia. Specializing in Arctic anthropology, particularly in the Russian far north, Stammler coordinates the anthropology research team at the University of Lapland's Arctic Centre. His interests include Arctic economy, human–animal relations, and the anthropology of place and belonging.

cultural feature at the expense of another. Only by discovering how *all* parts of a culture—its social, political, economic, and religious practices and institutions—relate to one another can the ethnographer begin to understand the cultural system. This is the holistic perspective so basic to the discipline.

The popular image of ethnographic fieldwork is that it occurs among hunters, herders, fishers, or farmers who live in far-off, isolated places. To be sure, much ethnographic work has been done in the remote villages of Asia, Africa, or Latin America, islands of the Pacific Ocean, deserts of Australia, and so on. However, as the discipline developed after the mid-1900s with the demise of colonialism, industrialized societies

culture A society's shared and socially transmitted ideas, values, and perceptions, which are used to make sense of experience and which generate behavior and are reflected in that behavior.

ethnography A detailed description of a particular culture primarily based on fieldwork.

fieldwork The term anthropologists use for on-location research.

participant observation In ethnography, the technique of learning a people's culture through social participation and personal observation within the community being studied, as well as interviews and discussion with individual members of the group over an extended period of time.

ethnology The study and analysis of different cultures from a comparative or historical point of view, utilizing ethnographic accounts and developing anthropological theories that help explain why certain important differences or similarities occur among groups.

and neighborhoods in modern cities have also become a significant focus of anthropological study.

Ethnographic fieldwork has transformed from expert Western anthropologists studying people in "other" places to a collaborative approach among anthropologists from all parts of the world and the varied communities in which they work. Today, anthropologists from around the globe employ the same research techniques that were used in the study of non-Western peoples to explore diverse subjects such as religious movements, street gangs, refugee settlements, land rights, conflict resolution, corporate bureaucracies, and health-care systems in Western cultures.

Ethnology

Largely descriptive in nature, *ethnography* provides the raw data needed for *ethnology*—the branch of cultural anthropology that involves cross-cultural comparisons and theories that explain differences or similarities among groups. Intriguing insights into one's own beliefs and practices may come from cross-cultural comparisons. Consider, for example, the amount of time spent on domestic chores by industrialized peoples and traditional food foragers—people who rely on wild plant and animal resources for subsistence.

Anthropological research has shown that food foragers work far less time at domestic tasks and other subsistence pursuits compared to people in industrialized societies. Despite access to "labor-saving" appliances such as dishwashers, washing machines, clothes dryers, vacuum cleaners, food processors, and microwave ovens, urban women in the United States who are not working for wages outside their homes put 55 hours a week into their housework. In contrast, aboriginal women in Australia devoted 20 hours a week to their chores (Bodley, 2008, p. 67). Nevertheless, consumer appliances have become important indicators of a high standard of living in the United States due to the widespread belief that household appliances reduce housework and increase leisure time.

By making systematic comparisons, ethnologists seek to arrive at scientific explanations of cultural features and social practices in all times and places. (The Biocultural Connection you read on page 6 is one of countless examples of anthropological insights gained through comparative research.)

Applied Cultural Anthropology

Today, cultural anthropologists contribute to applied anthropology in a variety of contexts ranging from business to education to health care to governmental interventions to humanitarian aid. For example, anthropologist Nancy Scheper-Hughes has taken her investigative work on the global problem of illegal trafficking of organs and used it to help found Organs Watch, an organization dedicated to solving this human rights issue (see the Globalscape later in this chapter).

Linguistic Anthropology

Perhaps the most distinctive feature of the human species is language. Although the sounds and gestures made by some other animals—especially by apes—may serve functions comparable to those of human language, no other animal has developed a system of symbolic communication as complex as that of humans. Language allows people to create, preserve, and transmit countless details of their culture from generation to generation.

Linguistic anthropology is the branch of anthropology that studies human languages; it investigates their structure, history, and relation to social and cultural contexts. Although it shares data, theories, and methods with the more general discipline of linguistics, it differs in that it includes distinctly anthropological questions, such as, how does language influence or reflect culture? And how does language use differ among distinct members of a society?

In its early years, linguistic anthropology emphasized the documentation of languages of cultures under ethnographic study—particularly those whose future seemed precarious due to colonization, forced assimilation, population decimation, capitalist expansion, or other destructive forces. When the first Europeans began to colonize the world five centuries ago, an estimated 12,000 distinct languages existed. By the early 1900s—when anthropological research began to take off—many languages and peoples had already disappeared or were on the brink of extinction. Sadly this trend continues, with predictions that nearly half of the world's remaining 6,000 languages will become extinct over the next hundred years (Crystal, 2002; Knight, Studdert-Kennedy, & Hurford, 2000).

Linguistic anthropology has three main branches: descriptive linguistics, historical linguistics, and language in relation to social and cultural settings. All three yield valuable information about how people communicate and how they understand the world around them.

Descriptive Linguistics

This branch of linguistic anthropology involves the painstaking work of dissecting a language by recording, delineating, and analyzing all of its features. It leads to a deeper understanding of a language—its structure (including grammar and syntax), its unique linguistic repertoire (figures of speech, word plays, and so on), and its relationship to other languages.

Historical Linguistics

While descriptive linguistics focuses on all features of a particular language at any one moment in time, historical

---

linguistic anthropology The study of human languages—looking at their structure, history, and relation to social and cultural contexts.

Figure 1.5 Preserving Endangered Languages Linguistic anthropologist David Anderson (right) has devoted his career to documenting and saving indigenous languages. He founded and heads the Living Tongues Institute for Endangered Languages and works throughout the globe to preserve languages that are dying out at a shocking rate of about one every two weeks. Here he is recording for the first time the language of Koro, spoken by some 1,000 people in India's remote northeastern state, Arunachal Pradesh. Situated near India's contested border with China, this region is considered a black hole in the study of languages.

Photo by Chris Rainier/Enduring Voices Project

linguistics deals with the fact that languages change. In addition to deciphering "dead" languages that are no longer spoken, specialists in this field examine interrelationships among different languages and investigate earlier and later forms of the same language. Their findings make significant contributions to our understanding of the human past. By working out relationships among languages and examining their spatial distributions, they may estimate how long the speakers of those languages have lived where they do. By identifying those words in related languages that have survived from an ancient ancestral tongue, they can also suggest not only where, but how, the speakers of the inherited language lived. Such work shows linguistic ties between geographically distant groups such as the Navajo in Arizona's desert and the Gwich'in above the Arctic Circle in Alaska, or between the Magyars in Hungary and the people of Finland.

Language in Its Social and Cultural Settings

Some linguistic anthropologists study the social and cultural contexts of a language. For example, they may research how factors such as age, gender, ethnicity, class, religion, occupation, or financial status affect speech. Because members of any culture may use a variety of different registers and inflections, the ones they choose (often unconsciously) to use at a specific instance convey particular meanings.

Scientists in this branch of linguistics also look into the dynamic relationship between language and culture—investigating to what degree they mutually influence and inform each other. In this vein, they may investigate how a language reflects culturally significant aspects of a people's environment or values.

Linguistic anthropologists may also focus on the socialization process through which an individual becomes part of a culture, moves up in social status, or takes on a new professional identity. First-year medical students, for example, amass 6,000 new terms and a series of linguistic conventions as they begin to take on the role of a physician. Individuals training for any specialized career, from lawyer to chef, face similar challenges in quickly expanding their vocabularies.

Applied Linguistic Anthropology

Linguistic anthropologists put their research to use in a number of settings. Some, for example, have collaborated with recently contacted cultural groups, small nations (or tribes), and ethnic minorities in the preservation or revival of languages suppressed or lost during periods of oppression by dominant societies. Their work has included helping to create written forms of languages that previously existed only orally. This sort of applied linguistic anthropology represents a trend in mutually useful collaboration that is characteristic of much anthropological research today (**Figure 1.5**).

Archaeology

Archaeology is the branch of anthropology that studies human cultures through the recovery and analysis of material remains and environmental data. Such material products include tools, pottery, hearths, and enclosures that remain as traces of cultural practices in the past, as well as human, plant, and marine remains, some of which date back 2.5 million years. The arrangement of these traces, as much as the traces themselves, reflects specific human ideas and behavior. For example, shallow, restricted concentrations of charcoal that include oxidized earth, bone fragments, and charred plant

---

archaeology The study of cultures through the recovery and analysis of material remains and environmental data.

Figure 1.6 Analyzing Human Remains in a Bioarchaeology Laboratory Bioarchaeology graduate students J. Marla Toyne and Mellisa Lund Valle are conducting a skeletal inventory and checking for pathological conditions in human remains from a 14th-century mass execution and sacrifice site at Punta Lobos in the Huarmey River Valley in northern Peru. Their work is part of a research project directed by Dr. John Verano of Tulane University, New Orleans.

Courtesy of John Verano

remains, located near pieces of fire-cracked rock, pottery, and tools suitable for food preparation, indicate cooking and food processing. Such remains can reveal much about a people's diet and subsistence practices.

In addition to specific questions about a single group of people at a particular place and time, archaeologists use material remains to investigate broad questions, including settlement or migration patterns across vast areas, such as the spread of the earliest humans from Africa or the first peopling of the Americas. Together with skeletal remains, material remains help archaeologists reconstruct the biocultural context of past human lifeways and patterns. Archaeologists organize this material and use it to explain cultural variability and change through time.

Because archaeological research is explicitly tied to unearthing material remains in particular environmental contexts, a variety of innovations in the geographic and geologic sciences have been readily incorporated into archaeological research. Innovations such as geographic information systems (GIS), remote sensing, and ground-penetrating radar (GPR) complement traditional explorations of the past through archaeological digs.

Although archaeologists tend to specialize in particular culture zones or time periods that are connected with particular regions of the world, a number of topical subspecializations also exist. We turn now to these.

historical archaeology The archaeological study of places for which written records exist.

bioarchaeology The archaeological study of human remains—bones, skulls, teeth, and sometimes hair, dried skin, or other tissue—to determine the influences of culture and environment on human biological variation.

Historical Archaeology

Archaeologists can reach back for clues to human behavior far beyond the maximal 5,000 years to which historians are confined by their reliance on written records. Calling this time period "prehistoric" does not mean that these societies were less interested in their history or that they did not have ways of recording and transmitting history. It simply means that written records do not exist.

That said, archaeologists are not limited to the study of societies without written records; they may study those for which historic documents are available to supplement the material remains. **Historical archaeology**, the archaeological study of places for which written records exist, often provides data that differ considerably from the historical record. In most literate societies, written records are associated with governing elites rather than with farmers, fishers, laborers, or slaves, and therefore they include the biases of the ruling classes. In fact, according to James Deetz, a pioneer in historical archaeology of the Americas, in many historical contexts, "material culture may be the most objective source of information we have" (Deetz, 1977, p. 160).

Bioarchaeology

Bioarchaeology is the study of human remains—bones, skulls, teeth, and sometimes hair, dried skin, or other tissue— to determine the influences of culture and environment on human biological variation. Whether mummified (as in the dry deserts of northwestern China, Egypt, or Peru) or not, human remains excavated at archaeological sites provide valuable clues about the lifestyle and health of prehistoric peoples, including information about activity, physiological stress, nutrition, disease, and social rank (**Figure 1.6**).

For example, mummified skeletal remains from the Andean highlands in South America not only reveal this burial practice but also provide evidence of some of the earliest brain surgery ever documented. In addition, these bioarchaeological remains exhibit skull deformation techniques that distinguish nobility from other members of society.

Some archaeologists specialize in *ethnobotany*, studying how people of a given culture made use of indigenous plants. Others specialize in *zooarchaeology*, tracking the animal remains recovered in archaeological excavations. Still others, maritime archaeologists, may research submerged sites or old sailing vessels sunk to the bottom of a sea, lake, or river hundreds or even thousands of years ago.

Contemporary Archaeology

Although most archaeologists concentrate on the past, some study material objects in contemporary settings, and that includes garbage dumps. Just as a 3,000-year-old shell mound (*midden*) on the seacoast of Denmark, New England, or Tiera del Fuego offers significant clues about prehistoric communities living on mussels, oysters, fish, and other natural resources, modern garbage dumps provide evidence of everyday life in contemporary societies. For large cities like New York, the accumulation of daily garbage is staggering. In just a few centuries, millions of inhabitants have dumped so much trash that this urban area has been physically raised 6 to 30 feet—primarily from discarded newspapers and rubble from demolition and building construction, but also from huge amounts of plastic and household and office supplies and equipment (Rathje & Murphy, 2001).

Among the first anthropologists to study modern garbage was William Rathje, who founded the Garbage Project at the University of Arizona in 1973. The project began with a study of household waste of Tucson residents and later expanded to other cities. When surveyed by questionnaires, only 15 percent of households reported consuming beer, and none reported an intake of more than eight cans a week. Analysis of garbage from the same area showed that 80 percent of the households consumed some beer, and 50 percent discarded more than eight cans per week (Rathje & Murphy, 2001).

Beyond providing data on beer consumption, the Garbage Project has tested the validity of research survey techniques, upon which sociologists, economists, other social scientists, and policymakers rely heavily. The tests show a significant difference between what people *say* they do and what the garbage analysis shows they *actually* do.

Applied Archaeology

The Garbage Project also gives us a fine example of applied archaeology producing useful, thought-provoking information about contemporary social issues. Its program of excavating landfills in different parts of North America, initiated in 1987, produced the first reliable data on what materials actually go into landfills and what happens to them there. Again, common beliefs turned out to be at odds with the actual situation. For example, when buried in deep compost

landfills, biodegradable materials such as newspapers take far longer to decay than anyone had expected. This kind of information is a vital step toward solving waste disposal problems. The data gathered from the Garbage Project's landfill studies on hazardous wastes and rates of decay of various materials play a major role in landfill regulation and management today (Rathje & Murphy, 2001).

Cultural Resource Management

While archaeology may conjure up images of ancient pyramids and the like, much archaeological fieldwork is carried out as **cultural resource management**. What distinguishes this work from traditional archaeological research is that it is a legally required part of any activity that might threaten important aspects of a country's prehistoric and historic heritage. Many countries, from Chile to China, use archaeological expertise to protect and manage their cultural heritage.

In the United States, for example, if a construction company plans to replace a highway bridge, it must first contract with archaeologists to identify and protect any significant prehistoric or historic resources that might be affected by this new construction. And when cultural resource management work or other archaeological investigation unearths Native American cultural items or human remains, federal laws come into the picture again. The Native American Graves Protection and Repatriation Act (NAGPRA), passed in 1990, provides a process for the return of these remains, especially human bones and burial gifts (such as copper jewelry, weapons, and ceramic bowls), to lineal descendants, culturally affiliated Indian tribes, and Native Hawaiian organizations.

In addition to working in all the capacities mentioned, archaeologists also consult for engineering firms to help them prepare environmental impact statements. Some of these archaeologists operate out of universities and colleges, while others are on the staff of independent consulting firms. When state legislation sponsors any kind of archaeological work, it is referred to as *contract archaeology*.

Physical Anthropology

Physical anthropology, also called *biological anthropology*, focuses on humans as biological organisms. Traditionally, physical anthropologists concentrated on human evolution, primatology, growth and development, human adaptation, and forensics. Today, **molecular anthropology**, or the anthropological study of genes

cultural resource management A branch of archaeology concerned with survey and/or excavation of archaeological and historical remains that might be threatened by construction or development; also involved with policy surrounding protection of cultural resources.
physical anthropology The systematic study of humans as biological organisms; also known as *biological anthropology*.
molecular anthropology The anthropological study of genes and genetic relationships, which contributes significantly to our understanding of human evolution, adaptation, and diversity.

and genetic relationships, contributes significantly to our understanding of human evolution, adaptation, and diversity. Comparisons among groups separated by time, geography, or the frequency of a particular gene can reveal how humans have adapted and where they have migrated. As experts in the anatomy of human bones and tissues, biological anthropologists lend their knowledge about the body to applied areas such as gross anatomy laboratories, public health, and criminal investigations.

Paleoanthropology

Dealing with much greater time spans than other branches of anthropology, **paleoanthropology** is the study of the origins, predecessors, and early representatives of the present human species. Focusing on long-time biological changes (evolution) paleo-anthropologists seek to understand how, when, and why we became the species we are today. In biological terms, we humans are *Homo sapiens,* a species in the larger order of primates, one of the many kinds of mammals. Because we share a common ancestry with other primates (monkeys and apes), paleoanthropologists look back to the earliest primates (about 65 million years ago, abbreviated mya) or even to the earliest mammals (225 mya) to reconstruct the intricate path of human evolution. At times, paleoanthropologists take a **biocultural** approach, focusing on the interaction of biology and culture.

Paleoanthropologists compare fossilized skeletons of our ancestors to other fossils and to the bones of living members of our species. Combining this knowledge with biochemical and genetic evidence, they strive to scientifically reconstruct the complex course of human evolutionary history. With each new fossil discovery, paleoanthropologists have another piece to add to the puzzle still far from fully solved. Further on in this text, we discuss how, genetic evidence establishes the close relationship between humans and ape species—chimpanzees, bonobos, and gorillas. Genetic analyses indicate that the distinctively human line split from the apes sometime between 5 and 8 million years ago.

Primatology

Studying the anatomy and behavior of the other primates helps us understand what we share with our closest living relatives and what makes humans unique. Therefore, **primatology**, or the study of living and fossil primates, is a vital part of physical anthropology. Primates include the

Penelope Breese/Liaison/Getty Images

Figure 1.7 Primatologist Jane Goodall Nearly forty-five years ago Jane Goodall began studying chimpanzees to shed light on the behavior of our distant ancestors. The knowledge she has amassed reveals striking similarities with our species. Goodall has devoted much of her career to championing the rights of our closest living relatives.

Asian and African apes, as well as monkeys, lemurs, lorises, and tarsiers.

Biologically, humans are members of the ape family—large-bodied, broad-shouldered primates with no tail. Detailed studies of ape behavior in the wild indicate that the sharing of learned behavior is a significant part of their social life. Increasingly, primatologists designate the shared, learned behavior of nonhuman apes as *culture*. For example, tool use and communication systems indicate the elementary basis of language in some ape societies.

Primate studies offer scientifically grounded perspectives on the behavior of our ancestors, as well as greater appreciation and respect for the abilities of our closest living relatives. As human activity encroaches on all parts of the world, many primate species are endangered. Primatologists, such as Jane Goodall (**Figure 1.7**), strongly advocate for the preservation of primate habitats so that these remarkable animals will be able to continue to inhabit the earth with us.

Human Growth, Adaptation, and Variation

Some physical anthropologists specialize in the study of human growth and development. They examine biological mechanisms of growth as well as the impact of the environment on the growth process. For example, Franz Boas, a pioneer of American anthropology of the early 20th century (see the Anthropologists of Note feature on the next page) compared the heights of immigrants who spent their

---

paleoanthropology The anthropological study of biological changes through time (evolution) to understand the origins and predecessors of the present human species.

biocultural An approach that focuses on the interaction of biology and culture.

primatology The study of living and fossil primates.

ANTHROPOLOGISTS OF NOTE

Franz Boas (1858–1942) • Matilda Coxe Stevenson (1849–1915)

Franz Boas on a sailing ship, about 1925.

Franz Boas was not the first to teach anthropology in the United States, but it was Boas and his students, with their insistence on scientific rigor, who made anthropology courses common in college and university curricula. Born and raised in Germany where he studied physics, mathematics, and geography, Boas did his first ethnographic research among the Inuit (Eskimos) in Arctic Canada in 1883 and 1884. After a brief academic career in Berlin, he came to the United States where he worked in museums interspersed with ethnographic research among the Kwakiutl (Kwakwaka'wakw) Indians in the Canadian Pacific. In 1896, he became a professor at Columbia University in New York City. He authored an incredible number of publications, founded professional organizations and journals, and taught two generations of great anthropologists, including numerous women and ethnic minorities.

As a Jewish immigrant, Boas recognized the dangers of ethnocentrism and especially racism. Through ethnographic fieldwork and comparative analysis, he demonstrated that white supremacy theories and other schemes ranking non-European peoples and cultures as inferior were biased, ill informed, and unscientific. Throughout his long and illustrious academic career, he promoted anthropology not only as a human science but also as an instrument to combat racism and prejudice in the world.

Among the founders of North American anthropology were a number of women, including **Matilda Coxe Stevenson**, who did fieldwork among the Zuni Indians of Arizona. In 1885, she founded the Women's Anthropological Society in Washington, DC, the first professional association for women scientists. Three years later, hired by the Smithsonian's Bureau of American Ethnology, she became one of the first women in the world to receive a full-time official position in science. Along with several other pioneering female anthropologists in North America, she was highly influential among women's rights advocates in the late 1800s. The tradition of women building careers in anthropology continues. In fact, since World War II more than half the presidents of the now 12,000-member American Anthropological Association have been women.

Matilda Coxe Stevenson in New Mexico, about 1900.

Recording observations on film as well as in notebooks, Stevenson and Boas were also pioneers in visual anthropology. Stevenson used an early box camera to document Pueblo Indian religious ceremonies and material culture, while Boas photographed Inuit and Kwakiutl Indians from the early 1890s for cultural as well as physical anthropological documentation. Today, their early photographs are greatly valued not only by anthropologists and historians, but also by indigenous peoples themselves.

childhood in the "old country" (Europe) to the increased heights reached by their children who grew up in the United States. Today, physical anthropologists study the impact of poverty, pollution, and disease on growth. Comparisons between human and nonhuman primate growth patterns can provide clues to the evolutionary history of humans. Detailed anthropological studies of the hormonal, genetic, and physiological bases of healthy growth in living humans also contribute significantly to the health of children today.

Studies of human adaptation focus on the capacity of humans to adapt or adjust to their material environment—biologically and culturally. This branch of physical anthropology takes a comparative approach to humans living today in a variety of environments. Human beings are the only primates to inhabit the entire earth. Although biological adaptations make it possible for people to live in environmentally extreme regions, cultural adaptations also contribute to our survival in places that are dangerously cold, hot, or of high altitude.

ECUADOR

PERU

Altiplano

BOLIVIA

CHILE

Pacific
Ocean

ARGENTINA

© Cengage Learning

Some of these biological adaptations are built into the genetic makeup of populations. The long period of human growth and development provides ample opportunity for the environment to shape the human body. *Developmental adaptations* are responsible for some features of human variation, such as the enlargement of the right ventricle of the heart to help push blood to the lungs among the Aymara Indians of the Bolivian altiplano—an extensive area of high plateau at the widest part of the Andes. *Physiological adaptations* are short-term changes in response to a particular environmental stimulus. For example, if a woman who normally lives at sea level flies to La Paz, a large Bolivian city in the altiplano at an altitude of 3,660 meters (nearly 12,000 feet), her body will undergo a series of physiological responses, such as increased production of the red blood cells that carry oxygen. These kinds of biological adaptation contribute to present-day human variation.

Genetically based human differences include visible traits such as height, body build, and skin color, as well as biochemical factors such as blood type and susceptibility to certain diseases. Still, we remain members of a single

ANTHROPOLOGY APPLIED

Forensic Anthropology: Voices for the Dead

The work of Clyde C. Snow, Michael Blakey, and Amy Zelson Mundorff

Forensic anthropology is the analysis of skeletal remains for legal purposes. Law enforcement authorities call upon forensic anthropologists to use skeletal remains to identify murder victims, missing persons, or people who have died in disasters, such as plane crashes. Forensic anthropologists have also contributed substantially to the investigation of human rights abuses in all parts of the world by identifying victims and documenting the cause of their death.

Among the best-known forensic anthropologists is Clyde C. Snow. He has been practicing in this field for over forty years, first for the Federal Aviation Administration and more recently as a freelance consultant. In addition to the usual police work, Snow has studied the remains of General George Armstrong Custer and his men from the 1876 battle at Little Big Horn, and in 1985 he went to Brazil, where he identified the remains of the notorious Nazi war criminal Josef Mengele.

Snow was also instrumental in establishing the first forensic team devoted to documenting cases of human rights abuses around the world. This began in 1984 when he went to Argentina at the request of a newly elected civilian government to help with the identification of remains of the *desaparecidos*, or "disappeared ones," the 9,000 or more people who were eliminated by death squads during seven years of military rule. A year later, he returned to give expert testimony at the trial of nine junta members and to teach Argentineans how to recover, clean, repair, preserve, photograph, x-ray, and analyze bones. Besides providing factual accounts of the fate of victims to their surviving kin and refuting the assertions of revisionists that the massacres never happened, the work of Snow and his Argentinean associates was crucial in convicting several military officers of kidnapping, torture, and murder.

Since Snow's pioneering work, forensic anthropologists have become increasingly involved in the investigation of human rights abuses in all parts of the world, from Chile to Guatemala, Haiti, the Philippines, Rwanda, Iraq, Bosnia, and Kosovo. Meanwhile, they continue to do important work for more typical clients. In the United States these clients include the Federal Bureau of Investigation and city, state, and county medical examiners' offices.

Forensic anthropologists specializing in skeletal remains commonly work closely with forensic archaeologists. The relation between them is rather like that between a forensic pathologist, who examines a corpse to establish time and manner of death, and a crime scene investigator, who searches the site for clues. While the forensic anthropologist deals with the human remains—often only bones and teeth—the forensic archaeologist controls the site, recording the position of relevant finds and recovering any clues associated with the remains.

In Rwanda, for example, a team assembled in 1995 to investigate mass murder (genocide) for the United Nations, which included archaeologists from the U.S. National Park Service's Midwest Archaeological Center. They performed the standard archaeological procedures of mapping the site, determining its boundaries, photographing and recording all surface finds, and excavating, photographing, and recording buried skeletons and associated materials in mass graves.[a]

In 1991, in another part of the world, construction workers in New York City discovered an African burial ground from the 17th and 18th centuries.

species. Physical anthropology applies all the techniques of modern biology to achieve fuller understanding of human variation and its relationship to the different environments in which people have lived. Physical anthropologists' research on human variation has debunked false notions of biologically defined races, a belief based on widespread misinterpretation of human variation.

Forensic Anthropology

One of the many practical applications of physical anthropology is **forensic anthropology**—the identification of human skeletal remains for legal purposes. In addition to helping law enforcement authorities identify murder victims, forensic anthropologists investigate human rights abuses such as systematic genocide, terrorism, and war crimes. These specialists use details of skeletal anatomy to establish the age, sex, population affiliation, and stature of the deceased. Forensic anthropologists can also determine whether the person was right- or left-handed, exhibited any physical abnormalities, or had experienced trauma.

While forensics relies upon differing frequencies of certain skeletal characteristics to establish population affiliation, it is nevertheless false to say that all people from a given population have a particular type of skeleton. (See the Anthropology Applied feature to read about the work of several forensic anthropologists and forensic archaeologists.)

forensic anthropology The identification of human skeletal remains for legal purposes.

The excavation of mass graves by the Guatemalan Foundation for Forensic Anthropology (Fernando Moscoso Moller, director) documents the human rights abuses committed during Guatemala's bloody civil war, a conflict that left 200,000 people dead and another 40,000 missing. In 2009, in a mass grave in the Quiche region, Diego Lux Tzunux uses his cell phone to photograph the skeletal remains believed to belong to his brother Manuel who disappeared in 1980. Genetic analyses allow forensic anthropologists to confirm the identity of individuals so that family members can know the fate of their loved ones. The analysis of skeletal remains provides evidence of the torture and massacre sustained by these individuals.

Ground Project provided incontrovertible evidence of the horror of slavery in North America, in the busy northern port of New York City. The more than 400 individuals, many of them children, were worked so far beyond their ability to endure that their spines were fractured.

A decade after construction workers happened upon the African Burial Ground, terrorists attacked the World Trade Center in lower Manhattan. Amy Zelson Mundorff, a forensic anthropologist for New York City's Office of the Chief Medical Examiner, was injured in the September 11 attack. But two days later she returned to work where she supervised and coordinated the management, treatment, and cataloguing of people who lost their lives in the tragedy.

Thus, several kinds of anthropologists analyze human remains for a variety of purposes. Their work contributes to the documentation and correction of violence committed by humans of the past and present.

Researchers used a bioarchaeological rather than a strictly forensic approach to examine the complete cultural and historical context and lifeways of the entire population buried there. Directed by Michael Blakey, the African Burial

[a]Haglund, W. D., Conner, M., & Scott, D. D. (2001). The archaeology of contemporary mass graves. *Historical Archaeology* 35 (1), 57–69.

Anthropology, Science, and the Humanities

Anthropology has sometimes been called the most humane of the sciences and the most scientific of the humanities—a designation that most anthropologists accept with pride. Given their intense involvement with people of all times and places, anthropologists have amassed considerable information about human failure and success, weakness and greatness—the real stuff of the humanities.

Anthropologists remain committed to the proposition that one cannot fully understand another culture by simply observing it; as the term *participant observation* implies, one must *experience* it as well. This same commitment to fieldwork and to the systematic collection of data, whether qualitative or quantitative, is also evidence of the scientific side of anthropology. Anthropology is an **empirical** social science based on observations or information taken in through the senses and verified by others rather than on intuition or faith. But anthropology is distinguished from other sciences by the diverse ways in which scientific research is conducted within the discipline.

Science, a carefully honed way of producing knowledge, aims to reveal and explain the underlying logic, the structural processes that make the world tick. The creative scientific endeavor seeks testable explanations for observed phenomena, ideally in terms of the workings of hidden but unchanging principles or laws. Two basic ingredients are essential for this: imagination and skepticism. Imagination, though having the potential to lead us astray, helps us recognize unexpected ways phenomena might be ordered and to think of old things in new ways. Without it, there can be no science. Skepticism allows us to distinguish fact (an observation verified by others) from fancy, to test our speculations, and to prevent our imaginations from running away with us.

In their search for explanations, scientists do not assume that things are always as they appear on the surface. After all, what could be more obvious to the scientifically uninformed observer than the earth staying still while the sun travels around it every day?

Like other scientists, anthropologists often begin their research with a **hypothesis** (a tentative explanation or hunch) about the possible relationships between certain observed facts or events. By gathering various kinds of data that seem to ground such suggested explanations on evidence, anthropologists come up with a **theory**, a coherent statement that provides an explanatory framework for understanding; an explanation or interpretation supported by a reliable body of data. In their effort to demonstrate links between *known* facts or events, anthropologists may discover *unexpected* facts, events, or relationships. An important function of theory is that it guides us in our explorations and may result in new knowledge. Equally important, the newly discovered facts may provide evidence that certain explanations, however popular or firmly believed, are unfounded. When the evidence is lacking or fails to support the suggested explanations, promising hypotheses or attractive hunches must be dropped. In other words, anthropology relies on empirical evidence. Moreover, no scientific theory—no matter how widely accepted by the international community of scholars—is beyond challenge. That includes the findings of some of anthropology's earliest and most respected scholars.

It is important to distinguish between scientific theories—which are always open to challenges born of new evidence or insights—and doctrine. A **doctrine**, or dogma, is an assertion of opinion or belief formally handed down by an authority as true and indisputable. For instance, those who accept a creationist doctrine on the origin of the human species as recounted in sacred texts or myths do so on the basis of religious authority, conceding that such views may be contrary to genetic, geological, biological, or other explanations. Such doctrines cannot be tested or proved one way or another: They are accepted as matters of faith.

Straightforward as the scientific approach may seem, its application is not always easy. For instance, once a hypothesis has been proposed, the person who suggested it is strongly motivated to verify it, and this can cause one to unwittingly overlook negative evidence and unanticipated findings. This is a familiar problem in all science as noted by paleontologist Stephen Jay Gould: "The greatest impediment to scientific innovation is usually a conceptual lock, not a factual lock" (Gould, 1989, p. 226). Because culture provides humans with concepts and shapes our very thoughts, it can be challenging to frame hypotheses or to develop interpretations that are not culture-bound. However, by encompassing both humanism and science, the discipline of anthropology can draw on its internal diversity to overcome conceptual locks.

empirical An approach based on observations of the world rather than on intuition or faith.

hypothesis A tentative explanation of the relationships among certain phenomena.

theory A coherent statement that provides an explanatory framework for understanding; an explanation or interpretation supported by a reliable body of data.

doctrine An assertion of opinion or belief formally handed down by an authority as true and indisputable.

culture shock In fieldwork, the anthropologist's personal disorientation and anxiety that may result in depression.

Fieldwork

Anthropologists are keenly aware that their personal identity and cultural background may shape their research questions, bear upon their factual observations, and even influence their interpretations and explanations. To avoid inadvertent bias or distortion, they immerse themselves in the data to the fullest extent possible through on-location research traditionally known as *fieldwork*.

Fieldwork, introduced earlier in this chapter in connection with cultural anthropology, is characteristic of *all* the anthropological subdisciplines. Archaeologists and paleoanthropologists excavate sites in the field, and, as already noted, cultural anthropologists observe human behavior while living and interacting with a group of people wherever the group may reside, work, or travel. Just as an ethnographer will study the culture of a human community by living in it, a primatologist might live among a group of chimpanzees or gorillas in the forest. Likewise, linguistic anthropologists interested in analyzing or comparing words and grammar from undocumented languages must first learn the languages, and they typically do so by living in communities where these are actually spoken. The same is true for colleagues studying how speech is actually "performed" in various social settings. Also, a physical anthropologist interested in the effects of globalization on nutrition and growth may reside in a particular community to research this issue.

Fieldwork requires researchers to step out of their cultural comfort zone into a world that is unfamiliar and sometimes unsettling. Anthropologists in the field are likely to face a host of challenges—physical, social, mental, political, and ethical. They often must deal with the physical challenges of unfamiliar food, climate, and hygiene conditions.

Typically, anthropologists in the field struggle with emotional challenges such as loneliness, feeling like a perpetual outsider, being socially awkward in their new cultural setting, and having to be alert around the clock because anything that is happening or being said may be significant to their research. Political challenges include the possibility of unwittingly letting oneself be used by factions within the community, or being regarded with suspicion by government authorities who may view the anthropologist as a spy. And there are ethical dilemmas: What does the anthropologist do if faced with a troubling cultural practice such as female circumcision? How does the anthropologist deal with demands for food supplies or medicine? Is it acceptable to use deception to gain vital information? Collectively, these multiple challenges may gradually amount to **culture shock**—personal disorientation and anxiety that may result in depression, forcing some anthropologists to abandon their fieldwork and return home for recovery.

More often, however, fieldwork leads to tangible and meaningful personal, professional, and social rewards, ranging from lasting friendships to significant knowledge and insights concerning the human condition. Something of the meaning of anthropological fieldwork—its usefulness and its impact on researcher and subject—is conveyed in the following Original Study by Suzanne Leclerc-Madlala, an anthropologist who left her familiar New England surroundings nearly thirty years ago to do AIDS research among Zulu-speaking people in South Africa. Her research interest has changed the course of her own life, not to mention the lives of many individuals who are dealing with AIDS/HIV.

ORIGINAL STUDY

Fighting HIV/AIDS in Africa: Traditional Healers on the Front Line BY SUZANNE LECLERC-MADLALA

In the 1980s, as an anthropology graduate student at George Washington University, I met and married a Zulu-speaking student from South Africa. It was the height of apartheid (racial segregation), and upon moving to that country I was classified as "honorary black" and forced to live in a segregated township with my husband. The AIDS epidemic was in its infancy, but it was clear from the start that an anthropological understanding of how people perceive and engage with this disease would be crucial for developing interventions. I wanted to learn all that I could to make a difference, and this culminated in earning a doctorate from the University of Natal on the cultural construction of AIDS among the Zulu. The HIV/AIDS pandemic in Africa became my professional passion.

Faced with overwhelming global health-care needs, the World Health Organization passed a series of resolutions in the 1970s promoting collaboration between traditional and modern medicine. Such moves held a special relevance for Africa where traditional healers typically outnumber practitioners of modern medicine by a ratio of 100 to 1 or more. Given Africa's disproportionate burden of disease, supporting partnership efforts with traditional healers makes sense. But what sounds sensible today was once considered absurd, even heretical. For centuries Westerners generally viewed traditional healing as a whole lot of primitive mumbo jumbo practiced by witchdoctors with demonic powers who perpetuated superstition. Yet, its practice survived. Today, as the African continent grapples with an HIV/AIDS epidemic of crisis proportion, millions of sick people who are either too poor or too distant to access modern health care are proving that traditional healers are an invaluable resource in the fight against AIDS.

Of the world's estimated 35 million people currently infected by HIV, nearly 70 percent live in sub-Saharan Africa, and the vast majority of children left orphaned by AIDS are African. From the 1980s onward, as Africa became synonymous with the rapid spread of HIV/AIDS, a number of prevention programs involved traditional healers. My initial research in South Africa's KwaZulu-Natal province—where almost 40 percent of the population is HIV infected—revealed that traditional Zulu healers were regularly consulted for the treatment of sexually transmitted disease (STD). I found that such diseases, along with HIV/AIDS, were usually attributed to transgressions of taboos related to birth, pregnancy, marriage, and death. Moreover, these diseases were often understood within a framework of pollution and contagion, and like most serious illnesses, ultimately believed to have their causal roots in witchcraft.

I investigated a pioneer program in STD and HIV education for traditional healers in the province. It aimed to provide basic biomedical knowledge about the various modes of disease transmission, the means available for prevention, the diagnosing of symptoms, the keeping of records, and the making of patient referrals to local clinics and hospitals.

Interviews with the healers showed that many were deeply suspicious of modern medicine. They perceived AIDS education as a one-way street intended to press them into formal health structures and convince them of the superiority of modern medicine. Yet, today, few of the 6,000-plus KwaZulu-Natal healers who have been trained in AIDS education say they would opt for less collaboration; most want to have more.

Treatments by Zulu healers for HIV/AIDS often take the form of infusions of bitter herbs to "cleanse" the body, strengthen the blood, and remove misfortune and "pollution." Some treatments provide effective relief from common ailments associated with AIDS such as itchy skin rashes, oral thrush, persistent diarrhea, and general debility. Indigenous plants such as *unwele (Sutherlandia frutescens)* and African potato *(Hypoxis hemerocallidea)* are well-known traditional medicines that have proven immuno-boosting properties. Both have recently become available in modern pharmacies packaged in tablet form. With modern anti-retroviral treatments still well beyond the reach of most South Africans, indigenous medicines that can delay or alleviate some of the suffering caused by AIDS are proving to be valuable and popular treatments.

Knowledge about potentially infectious bodily fluids has led healers to change some of their practices. Where porcupine quills were once used to give a type of indigenous injection, patients are now advised to bring their own

sewing needles to consultations. Patients provide their own individual razor blades for making incisions on their skin, where previously healers reused the same razor on many clients. Some healers claim they have given up the practice of biting clients' skin to remove foreign objects from the body. Today, especially in urban centers like Durban, it is not uncommon for healers to proudly display AIDS training certificates in their inner-city "surgeries" where they don white jackets and wear protective latex gloves.

Medical anthropologist Suzanne Leclerc-Madlala visits with "Doctor" Koloko in KwaZulu-Natal, South Africa. This Zulu traditional healer proudly displays her official AIDS training certificate.

Politics and controversy have dogged South Africa's official response to HIV/AIDS. But back home in the waddle-and-daub, animal-skin-draped herbariums and diving huts of traditional healers, the politics of AIDS holds little relevance. Here the sick and dying are coming in droves to be treated by healers who have been part and parcel of community life (and death) since time immemorial. In many cases traditional healers have transformed their homes into hospices for AIDS patients. Because of the strong negative stigma that still plagues the disease, those with AIDS symptoms are often abandoned or sometimes chased away from their homes by family members. They seek refuge with healers who provide them with comfort in their final days. Healers' homes are also becoming orphanages as healers respond to what has been called the "third wave" of AIDS destruction: the growing legions of orphaned children.

Those who are suffering go to traditional healers not only in search of relief for physical symptoms. They go to learn about the ultimate cause of their disease—something other than the immediate cause of a sexually transmitted "germ" or "virus." They go to find answers to the "why me and not him" questions, the "why now" and "why this." As with most traditional healing systems worldwide, healing among the Zulu and most all African ethnic groups cannot be separated from the spiritual concerns of the individual and the cosmological beliefs of the community at large. Traditional healers help to restore a sense of balance between the individual and the community, on one hand, and between the individual and the cosmos, or ancestors, on the other hand. They provide health care that is personalized, culturally appropriate, holistic, and tailored to meet the needs and expectations of the patient. In many ways it is a far more satisfactory form of healing than that offered by modern medicine.

Traditional healing in Africa is flourishing in the era of AIDS, and understanding why this is so requires a shift in the conceptual framework by which we understand, explain, and interpret health. Anthropological methods and its comparative and holistic perspective can facilitate, like no other discipline, the type of understanding that is urgently needed to address the AIDS crisis.

For more details, see Leclerc-Madlala, S. (2002). Bodies and politics: Healing rituals in the democratic South Africa. *In V. Faure (Ed.),* Les cahiers de 'l'IFAS, *no. 2. Johannesburg: The French Institute. Leclerc-Madlala now works for USAID.*

Questions of Ethics

Anthropologists deal with matters that are private and sensitive, including information that individuals would prefer not to have generally known about them. In the early years of the discipline, many anthropologists documented traditional cultures they assumed would disappear due to disease, warfare, or changes imposed by colonialism, growing state power, or international market expansion. Some worked as government administrators or consultants gathering data used to formulate policies concerning indigenous peoples. Others helped predict the behavior of enemies during wartime.

How does one write about important but delicate issues and at the same time protect the privacy of the individuals who have shared their stories? The kinds of research carried out by anthropologists, and the settings within which they work, raise important moral questions about the potential uses and abuses of our knowledge. Who will utilize our findings and for what purposes? Who decides what research questions are asked? Who, if anyone, will benefit from the research? For example, in the case of research on an ethnic or religious minority whose values may be at odds with the dominant society, will government bureaucracies or industrial corporations use anthropological data to suppress that group? And what of traditional communities around the world? Who is to decide what changes should, or should not, be introduced for community development? And who defines "development"—the community, a national government, or an international agency like the World Bank?

After the colonial era ended in the 1960s, and in reaction to controversial research practices by some anthropologists in or near violent conflict areas, anthropologists formulated a code of ethics to ensure that their research would not harm the groups being studied. Formalized in 1971 and revised in 1998 and again in 2009, the American Anthropological Association's (AAA) ethics code outlines a range of moral responsibilities and obligations. It includes this core principle: Anthropological researchers must do everything in their power to ensure that their research does not harm the safety, dignity, or privacy of the people with whom they work, conduct research, or perform other professional activities.

In recent years, some of the debates regarding this code have focused on the potential ethical breaches if anthropologists work for corporations or undertake classified contract work for the military. Although the AAA has no legal authority, it does issue policy statements on research ethics questions as they come up. For example, recently the AAA recommended that research notes from medical settings should be protected and not subject to subpoena in court. This honors the ethical imperative to protect the privacy of individuals who have shared with anthropologists their stories about personal health issues.

Emerging technologies have ethical implications that impact anthropological inquiry. For example, the ability to sequence and patent particular genes has led to debates about who has the right to hold a patent—the individuals from whom the particular genes were obtained or the researcher who studies the genes? Similarly, do ancient remains belong to the scientist, to the people living in the region under scientific investigation, or to whoever happens to have possession of them? Global market forces have converted these remains into expensive collectibles, resulting in a systematic looting of archaeological and fossil sites.

While seeking answers to these questions, anthropologists recognize that they have special obligations to three sets of people: those whom they study, those who fund the research, and those in the profession who rely on published findings to increase our collective knowledge. Because fieldwork requires a relationship of trust between researchers and the community in which they work, the anthropologist's first responsibility clearly is to the people who have shared their stories and their community. Everything possible must be done to protect their physical, social, and psychological welfare and to honor their dignity and privacy. This task is frequently complex. For example, telling the story of a people gives information both to relief agencies who might help them and to others who might take advantage of them.

Maintaining one's own culture is an internationally recognized basic human right, and any connection with

Globalscape

AP Images

© K. Bhagya Prakash in *Frontline*, Vol. 19,
Issue 7, March 30–April 12, 2002

A Global Body Shop?

Lakshmamma, pictured here with her daughter in southern India's rural village of Holalu, near Mandya, has sold one of her kidneys for about 30,000 rupees ($650). This is far below the average going rate of $6,000 per kidney in the global organ transplant business. But the broker took his commission, and corrupt officials needed to be paid as well. Although India passed a law in 1994 prohibiting the buying and selling of human organs, the business is booming. In Europe and North America, kidney transplants can cost over $200,000, plus the waiting list for donor kidneys is long, and dialysis is expensive. Thus "transplant tourism," in India and several other countries, caters to affluent patients in search of "fresh" kidneys to be harvested from poor people like Lakshmamma.[a]

The well-publicized arrest of Brooklyn-based organ broker Levy Izhak Rosenbaum in July 2009—part of an FBI sting operation that also led to the arrest of forty-five other individuals, including several public officials in New Jersey—represents some progress in combatting illegal trafficking of body parts. Charged with brokering illegal kidney transplants—purchasing the organs for $10,000–$25,000 and selling them for as much as $160,000—the Israeli immigrant pleaded guilty to three trafficking counts and agreed to forfeit $420,000 in broker fees. In July 2012, he was sentenced to 2½ years in prison and possible deportation.[b]

Medical anthropologist and activist Nancy Scheper-Hughes has researched the criminal and medical aspects of global organ trafficking for some two decades. Cofounder of Organs Watch in Berkeley, California, an organization working to stop the illegal traffic in organs, she notified the FBI about Rosenbaum in 2002.[c] International crackdowns and changes in local laws are now curbing illegal global networks in human organ trafficking.

Global Twister

Considering that $650 is a fortune in a poor village like Holalu, does medical globalization benefit or exploit people like Lakshmamma, who are looked upon as human commodities? What accounts for the gap between the $650 she received for her kidney and the fees Rosenbaum received for the organ sales he brokered?

---

[a]Vidya, R. (2002). Karnataka's unabating kidney trade. *Frontline*. www.frontlineonnet.com/fl1907/19070610.htm (retrieved June 10, 2012)

[b]Henry, S., & Porter, D. (2011, October 27). Levy Izhak Rosenbaum pleads guilty to selling black market kidneys. *Huffingtonpost.com*. www.huffingtonpost.com/2011/10/27/levy-izhak-rosenbaum-plea_n_1035624.html (retrieved June 10, 2012)

[c]Glovin, D., & Voreacos, D. (2012, July 12). Kidney broker sentenced to prison. *Bloomberg News*. Retrieved from http://www.businessweek.com/news/2012-07-11/n-dot-y-dot-man-gets-30-month-term-in-first-u-dot-s-dot-organ-case

outsiders can expose and therefore endanger the cultural integrity of the community being studied. To overcome some of these ethical challenges, anthropologists frequently collaborate with and contribute to the communities in which they are working, inviting the people being studied to have some say about if and how their stories are told. In research involving ancient human remains, collaboration with local people not only preserves the remains from market forces but also honors the connections of indigenous people to the places and remains under study.

Anthropology and Globalization

A holistic perspective and a long-term commitment to understanding the human species in all its variety equip anthropologists to grapple with a challenge that has overriding importance for each of us today: **globalization**. This concept refers to worldwide interconnectedness, evidenced in rapid global movement of natural resources, trade goods, human labor, finance capital, information, and infectious diseases. Although worldwide travel, trade relations, and information flow have existed for several centuries, the pace and magnitude of these long-distance exchanges have picked up enormously in recent decades; the Internet, in particular, has greatly expanded information exchange capacities.

The powerful forces driving globalization are technological innovations, cost differences among countries, faster knowledge transfers, and increased trade and financial integration among countries. Touching almost everybody's life on the planet, globalization is about economics as much as politics, and it changes human relations and ideas as well as our natural environments. Even geographically remote communities are quickly becoming interdependent—and often vulnerable—through globalization (see the Globalscape on the opposite page for an example).

Researching in all corners of the world, anthropologists witness the impact of globalization on human communities wherever they are located. They describe and try to explain how individuals and organizations respond to the massive changes confronting them. Dramatically increasing every year, globalization can be a two-edged sword. It may generate economic growth and prosperity, but it also undermines long-established institutions. Generally, globalization has brought significant gains to more-educated groups in wealthier countries, while at the same time contributing to the erosion of traditional cultures. Upheavals due to globalization are key causes for rising levels of ethnic and religious conflict throughout the world.

Because all of us now live in a global village, we can no longer afford the luxury of ignoring our neighbors, no matter how distant they may seem. In this age of globalization, anthropology may not only provide humanity with useful

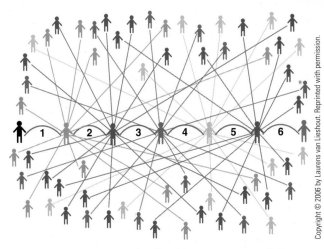

Figure 1.8 Six Degrees of Separation The phrase "six degrees of separation," diagrammed here, refers to the idea that everyone is on average approximately six steps away, by way of introduction, from any other person on earth. Thus, a chain of "a friend of a friend" statements can be made to connect any two people in six steps or fewer. Originally coined by Hungarian writer Frigyes Karinthy in his 1929 short story, "Chains," it was popularized by American playwright John Guare's 1993 film, *Six Degrees of Separation*. It became all the more popular after four college students invented the trivia game Six Degrees of Kevin Bacon, in which the goal is to link any actor to film star Kevin Bacon through no more than six performance connections.

insights concerning diversity, but it may also assist us in avoiding or overcoming significant problems born of that diversity. In countless social arenas, from schools to businesses to hospitals to emergency centers, anthropologists have done cross-cultural research that makes it possible for educators, businesspeople, doctors, and humanitarians to do their work more effectively.

As illustrated by many examples in this textbook, ignorance or ethnocentric (mis)information about other societies and their cultural beliefs and practices can cause or fuel serious problems throughout the world. This is especially true in an age when human interactions and interdependence have been transformed by global information exchange and transportation advances. As noted in the Challenge Issue at the start of this chapter, there are only six degrees of separation between each of us and any other person on earth (**Figure 1.8**). Anthropology offers a way of looking at and understanding the world's peoples—insights that are nothing less than basic skills for survival in this age of globalization.

globalization Worldwide interconnectedness, evidenced in rapid global movement of natural resources, trade goods, human labor, finance capital, information, and infectious diseases.

CHAPTER CHECKLIST

What is anthropology?

● Anthropology is the objective and systematic study of humankind in all times and places.

● Anthropology contains four major fields or subdisciplines: cultural anthropology, linguistic anthropology, archaeology, and physical or biological anthropology.

● In each of anthropology's fields some individuals practice applied anthropology, which uses anthropological knowledge to solve practical problems.

What do anthropologists do in each of its four fields?

● Cultural anthropologists study humans in terms of their cultures, the often-unconscious standards by which social groups operate.

● Linguistic anthropologists study human languages and may deal with the description of a language, with the history of languages, or with how languages are used in particular social settings.

● Archaeologists study human cultures through the recovery and analysis of material remains and environmental data.

● Physical anthropologists focus on humans as biological organisms; they particularly emphasize tracing the evolutionary development of the human animal and studying biological variation within the species today.

How is anthropology different from other disciplines?

● Unique among the sciences and humanities, anthropology has long emphasized the study of non-Western societies and a holistic approach, which aims to formulate theoretically valid explanations and interpretations of human diversity based on detailed studies of all aspects of human biology, behavior, and beliefs in all known societies, past and present.

● In anthropology, the humanities, social sciences, and natural sciences come together into a genuinely humanistic science. Anthropology's link with the humanities can be seen in its concern with people's beliefs, values, languages, arts, and literature—oral as well as written— but above all in its attempt to convey the experience of living in different cultures.

How do anthropologists conduct research?

● Fieldwork, characteristic of all the anthropological subdisciplines, includes complete immersion in

research settings ranging from archaeological and paleoanthropological survey and excavation, to living with a group of primates in their natural habitat, to biological data gathered while living with a group. Ethnographic participant observation with a particular culture or subculture is the classic field method of cultural anthropology.

● After the fieldwork of archaeologists and physical anthropologists, researchers conduct laboratory analyses of excavated remains or biological samples collected in the field.

● The comparative method is key to all branches of anthropology. Anthropologists make broad comparisons among peoples and cultures—past and present. They also compare related species and fossil groups. Ethnology, the comparative branch of cultural anthropologists, uses a range of ethnographic accounts to construct theories about cultures from a comparative or historical point of view. Ethnologists often focus on a particular aspect of culture, such as religious or economic practices.

How do anthropologists face the ethical challenges that emerge through conducting anthropological research?

● Anthropologists must stay aware of the potential uses and abuses of anthropological knowledge and the ways that it is obtained.

● The anthropological code of ethics, first formalized in 1971 and continually revised, outlines the moral and ethical responsibilities of anthropologists to the people whom they study, to those who fund the research, and to the profession as a whole.

What can anthropology contribute to the understanding of globalization?

● A long tradition of studying the connections among diverse peoples over time gives anthropology a theoretical framework to study globalization in a world increasingly linked through recent technological advancements.

● Anthropology equips global citizens to challenge ethnocentrism and to understand human diversity.

● Anthropology has essential insights to offer the modern world, particularly today, when understanding our neighbors in the global village has become a matter of survival for all.

QUESTIONS FOR REFLECTION

1. As noted in this chapter's opening Challenge Issue, there are only six degrees of separation between you and the pictured coltan miner working in the heart of Africa. Many miners are poor or orphaned children forced into hard labor and living in squalor, with short life expectancies. When you buy a new electronic device that uses coltan, do you think you contribute to the miserable exploitation of fellow humans?

2. Anthropology embraces a holistic approach to explain all aspects of human beliefs, behavior, and biology. How might anthropology challenge your personal perspective on the question, who am I?

3. From the holistic anthropological perspective, humans have one leg in culture and the other in nature. Are there examples from your life that illustrate the interconnectedness of human biology and culture?

4. Globalization can be described as a two-edged sword. How does it foster growth and destruction simultaneously?

5. The Biocultural Connection in this chapter contrasts different cultural perspectives on brain death, while the Original Study features a discussion about traditional Zulu healers and their role in dealing with AIDS victims. What do these two accounts suggest about the role of applied anthropology in dealing with cross-cultural health issues around the world?

ONLINE STUDY RESOURCES

CourseMate

Access chapter-specific learning tools, including learning objectives, practice quizzes, videos, flash cards, glossaries, and more in your Anthropology CourseMate.

Log into **www.cengagebrain.com** to access the resources your instructor has assigned and to purchase materials.

Challenge Issue

In the 21st century, a biomedical doctor in Brazil might urge his or her patient to undergo testing for a specific disease gene as part of predicting the patient's future health. A pregnant woman in Canada might choose to terminate her pregnancy if prenatal testing reveals the presence of genes for a specific disease in a developing fetus. A pregnant woman in India, a society that considers female children a liability, could opt for prenatal genetic testing to ensure she will have a boy. Genetic analyses have become routine in biomedicine. Genetics plays a role in law as well. Throughout the globe, police identify criminals through DNA fingerprinting. They also maintain DNA databases of convicts and suspects for solving crimes in the future. In the United States, individuals wrongfully imprisoned for many years have been freed after genetic testing. No wonder, then, that many individuals have come to see genes and DNA as integral to individual identity. This correspondence between self and genetics has even prompted some people to tattoo an image of the genetic code into their very skin. But is the human condition this simple? Are we merely our DNA? Do our genes determine our actions? And what will be the social consequences of depicting people as creatures programmed by their DNA, or by any other aspect of biology? Individuals and societies can answer these challenging questions using an anthropological perspective, which emphasizes the connections between human biology and culture.

Biology, Genetics, and Evolution

2

Evolution and Creation Stories

The mythology of most peoples includes a story explaining the appearance of humans on earth. The accounts of creation recorded in the Bible's Book of Genesis, for example, explain human origins. The Nez Perce, American Indians native to eastern Oregon and Idaho, provide us with a vastly different example that serves the same function. For the Nez Perce, human beings are the creation of Coyote, a trickster-transformer. Coyote chased the giant beaver monster Wishpoosh over the earth, leaving a trail to form the Columbia River. When Coyote caught Wishpoosh, he killed him, dragged his body to the riverbank, and cut it into pieces, each body part transforming into one of the various peoples of this region. The Nez Perce were made from Wishpoosh's head, thus conferring on them great intelligence and horsemanship (Clark, 1966).

Creation stories depict the relationship between humans and the rest of the natural world, sometimes reflecting a deep connection among people, other animals, and the earth. In the traditional Nez Perce creation story, groups of people derive from specific body parts—each possessing a special talent and relationship with a particular animal. By contrast, the story of creation in Genesis emphasizes human uniqueness and the concept of time. Creation takes place as a series of actions over the course of six days. God's final act of creation is to fashion the first human in his own image before the seventh day of rest.

This linear creation story from Genesis—shared by Jews, Christians, and Muslims—differs from the cyclical creation stories characteristic of Hinduism, which emphasize reincarnation and the cycle of life, including creation and destruction. For Hindus, the diversity of life on earth comes from three gods—Lord Brahma, the creator; Lord Vishnu, the preserver; and Lord Shiva, the destroyer and recreator—all of whom are part of the Supreme One. Lord Brahma destroys the world as he sleeps, then he recreates it again when he awakes. Similarly, intelligent design (ID)—championed by Seattle Washington's Discovery Institute to avoid the creation–evolution controversy and circumvent U.S. Supreme Court rulings—considers creation to be the result of an intelligent cause.

IN THIS CHAPTER YOU WILL LEARN TO

- Compare evolution to creation stories.

- Identify the place of humans in the classification of all living things.

- Explain the molecular basis of evolution and the four evolutionary processes: mutation, gene flow, genetic drift, and adaptation.

- Describe how evolutionary processes account for the diversity of life on earth.

- Contrast how evolutionary processes work at the individual and population level.

- Explain how humans have adapted to their environments.

- Identify how new species come into being.

Like creation stories, evolution, the major organizing principle of the biological sciences, accounts for the diversity of life on earth. Theories of evolution provide mechanisms for change and explanations for how the variety of organisms, both in the past and today, came into being. However, evolution differs from creation stories in that it explains the diversity of life in a consistent scientific language, using testable ideas (hypotheses). Contemporary scientists make comparisons among living organisms to test hypotheses drawn from evolutionary theory. Through their research, scientists have deciphered the molecular basis of evolution and the mechanisms through which evolutionary forces work on populations of organisms. At the same time, scientific thought does not come out of a vacuum. As you will see, historical and cultural processes contribute to scientific thought.

The Classification of Living Things

As European explorers exploited foreign lands, their approach to the natural world changed. The discovery of new life forms challenged the previously held notion of fixed, unchanging life on earth. As well, the invention of instruments, such as the microscope to study the previously invisible interior of cells, led to a new appreciation of life's diversity.

Before this time, Europeans organized living things and inanimate objects alike into a ladder or hierarchy known as the Great Chain of Being—an approach to nature first developed by the philosopher Aristotle in ancient Greece more than 2,000 years ago (**Figure 2.1**). The categories were based upon visible similarities, and one member of each category was considered its "primate" (from the Latin *primus*), meaning "the first" or "best" of the group. For example, the primate of rocks was the diamond, the primate of birds was the eagle, and so forth. Humans stood at the very top of the ladder, just below the angels.

This classificatory system was in place until Carolus Linnaeus (also known as Carl von Linné) developed the *Systema Naturae*, or system of nature, in the 18th century to classify the diversity of living things collected and brought

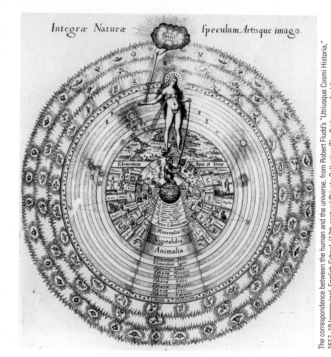

Figure 2.1 The Great Chain of Being This 17th-century drawing of the Great Chain of Being by Robert Flood shows that this system of classification was as much a spiritual system as a framework for organizing the natural world. Unlike Linnaeus's later classification scheme, the *Systema Naturae*, the Great Chain included minerals and astral bodies, which, though they can be studied scientifically, are not alive.

to Europe by ship from throughout the globe. Linnaeus's system reflected a new understanding of life on earth and of the place of humanity among the animals.

Linnaeus noted the similarity among humans, monkeys, and apes, classifying them together as **primates**. Not the first or the best of the animals on earth, primates are just one of several kinds of **mammal**, animals having body hair or fur who suckle or nurse their young. In other words, Linnaeus classified living things into a series of categories that are progressively more inclusive on the basis of internal and external visual similarities. **Species**, the smallest working units in biological classificatory systems, are reproductively isolated populations or groups of populations capable of interbreeding to produce fertile offspring. Species are subdivisions of larger, more inclusive groups, called **genera** (singular, **genus**). Humans, for example, are classified in the genus *Homo* and the species *sapiens*.

Linnaeus based his classificatory system on the following criteria:

1. *Body structure:* A Guernsey cow and a Holstein cow are the same species because they have identical body structure. A cow and a horse do not.
2. *Body function:* Cows and horses give birth to live young. Although they are different species, they are closer than either cows or horses are to chickens, which lay eggs and have no mammary glands.

primates The group of mammals that includes lemurs, lorisers, monkeys, apes, and humans.

mammals The class of vertebrate animals distinguished by bodies covered with hair or fur, self-regulating temperature, and in females, milk-producing mammary glands.

species The smallest working units in biological classificatory systems; reproductively isolated populations or groups of populations capable of interbreeding to produce fertile offspring.

genus (genera) In the system of plant and animal classification, a group of like species.

TABLE 2.1

The Classification of Humans

Taxonomic Category	Category to Which Humans Belong	Biological Features Used to Define and Place Humans in This Category
Kingdom	Animalia	Humans are animals. We do not make our own food (as plants do) but depend upon intake of living food.
Phylum	Chordata	Humans are chordates. We have a **notochord** (a rodlike structure of cartilage) and nerve chord running along the back of the body as well as gill slits in the embryonic stage of our life cycle.
Subphylum*	Vertebrata	Humans are vertebrates, possessing an internal backbone with a segmented spinal column.
Class	Mammalia	Humans are mammals: warm-blooded animals covered with fur and possessing mammary glands for nourishing their young after birth.
Order	Primates	Humans are primates: a kind of mammal with a generalized anatomy, a relatively large brain, and grasping hands and feet.
Suborder	Anthropoidea	Humans are anthropoids: social, daylight-active primates.
Superfamily	Hominoid	Humans are hominoids with broad, flexible shoulders and no tail. Chimps, bonobos, gorillas, orangutans, gibbons, and siamangs are also hominoids.
Family Subfamily	Hominid Hominin	Humans are hominids. We are hominoids from Africa, genetically more closely related to chimps, bonobos, and gorillas than to hominoids from Asia. Some scientists use "hominid" to refer only to humans and their ancestors. Others include chimps and gorillas in this category, using the subfamily "hominin" to distinguish humans and their ancestors from chimps and gorillas and their ancestors. The two taxonomies differ according to emphasis on genetic versus morphological similarities. Those who use "hominin" do so to emphasize the genetic relationship among humans, chimps, and gorillas. Those who refer to humans and their ancestor as "hominids" give preference to the similarities in body shape among chimpanzees, gorillas, and orangutans.
Genus Species	*Homo sapiens*	Humans have large brains and rely on cultural adaptations to survive. Ancestral fossils are placed in this genus and species depending upon details of the skull shape and interpretations of their cultural capabilities. Genus and species names are always italicized.

© Cengage Learning

*Most categories can be expanded or narrowed by adding the prefix "sub" or "super." A family could thus be part of a superfamily and in turn contain two or more subfamilies.

3. *Sequence of bodily growth:* At the time of birth—or hatching out of the egg—young cows and chickens possess body plans basically like that of their parents. They are therefore more closely related to each other than either one is to the frog, whose tadpoles undergo a series of changes before attaining the basic adult form.

Modern **taxonomy**, or the science of classification (from the Greek for "naming divisions"), while retaining the structure of the Linnaean system, takes more than body structure, function, and growth into account. Today's scientists also compare protein structure and genetic material to construct the relationships among living things. Such molecular comparisons can even be aimed at parasites, bacteria, and viruses, allowing scientists to classify or trace the origins of particular diseases, such as swine flu or HIV (human immunodeficiency virus). An emphasis on genetics rather than morphology has led to a reworking of

taxonomic designation in the human family, among other families, as is described in **Table 2.1**. Alternative taxonomies based on genetics compared to body form in the primate order will be discussed in detail in the next chapter.

Cross-species comparisons identify anatomical features of similar function as **analogies**, while anatomical features that have evolved from a common ancestral feature are called **homologies**. For example, the arm and

---

notochord A rodlike structure of cartilage that, in vertebrates, is replaced by the vertebral column.

taxonomy The science of classification.

analogies In biology, structures possessed by different organisms that are superficially similar due to similar function but that do not share a common developmental pathway or structure.

homologies In biology, structures possessed by two different organisms that arise in similar fashion and pass through similar stages during embryonic development, although they may have different functions.

VISUAL COUNTERPOINT

Figure 2.2 An Example of Homology The bat wing is homologous to the human hand. Look closely at the bones supporting the wing, and you can see that they are the same bones found in the human arm and hand. Homologous structures have the same embryonic origins but ultimately take on different functions. For humans, our grasping hands function in a variety of ways, including even language. Here two deaf children communicate through American Sign Language on their school playground.

hand of a human and the wing of a bat evolved from the front leg of a common ancestor, although they have acquired different functions: The human hand and bat wing are homologous structures (**Figure 2.2**). During their early embryonic development, homologous structures arise in a similar fashion and pass through similar stages before differentiating. The wings of birds and butterflies (**Figure 2.3**) look similar and have a similar function (flying): These are analogous, but not homologous, structures because they do not follow the same developmental sequence. When constructing evolutionary relationships, only homologies matter.

Through careful comparison and analysis of organisms, Linnaeus and his successors have grouped species into genera and into even larger groups such as families, orders, classes, phyla, and kingdoms. Characteristics shared by all the organisms in the group define each taxonomic level.

The Discovery of Evolution

Just as European seafaring and exploitation brought about an awareness of the diversity of life across the globe, industrialization in Europe brought about an awareness of change in life forms through time. As workers cut away the earth to lay railway tracks and excavated limestone for

Figure 2.3 Analogous Wings Butterflies, like bats and birds, use their wings to fly. But any resemblance of the insect wing to the analogous structures in a bird or mammal derives solely from their similar function. The course of insect wing development, as well as its structure, differs from that of a bat or bird.

buildings, fossils—preserved remains of past life forms—were brought into the light.

At first, the fossilized remains of elephants and giant saber-toothed tigers in Europe were interpreted according to religious doctrine. For example, the early 19th-century theory of *catastrophism,* championed by French paleontologist and anatomist George Cuvier, invoked natural events like the Great Flood described in Genesis to account for the disappearance of these species on European lands.

Another French scientist, Jean-Baptiste Lamarck, was among the first to suggest a mechanism to account for diversity among living creatures that did not rely upon scriptures. His theory of the *inheritance of acquired characteristics* proposed that behavior brought about changes in organisms' forms. The famed example was that the first giraffe gained its long neck by stretching to reach the leaves on the highest treetop branches and in turn passed this acquired long neck onto its offspring. While Lamarck's theory has long since been disproved as a mechanism to account for biological change, he was the first to make the connection between organisms and the environments they inhabit. As well, the mechanism he proposed for change over time works for qualities inherited via culture.

At about the same time, British geologist Sir Charles Lyell proposed a nonreligious theory to account for variations in the earth's surface. His theory, *uniformitarianism,* maintained that just as changes in the earth's surface that are immediately observable are caused by erosion and other natural processes, other changes are caused by gradual processes over extremely long periods of time. Lyell's theory was incompatible with religious accounts of creation because the length of time required for uniformitarianism far exceeded the biblical version that the earth is a mere 6,000 years old.

With industrialization, Europeans became more comfortable with the ideas of change and progress. In hindsight, it seems inevitable that someone would hit upon the idea of evolution. By the start of the 19th century, many naturalists had come to accept the idea that life had evolved, even though they were not clear about how it happened. It remained for Charles Darwin (1809–1882) to formulate a theory that has withstood the test of time.

Charles Darwin began the study of medicine at the University of Edinburgh in Scotland. Finding himself unfit for this profession, he went to Christ's College, Cambridge, to study theology. He then left Cambridge to take the position of companion to Captain Robert FitzRoy aboard the HMS *Beagle*, embarking on an expedition to various poorly mapped parts of the world. The voyage lasted almost five years, taking Darwin along the coasts of South America, to the Galapagos Islands, across the Pacific to Australia, and then across the Indian and Atlantic oceans to South America before returning to England in 1836 (**Figure 2.4**).

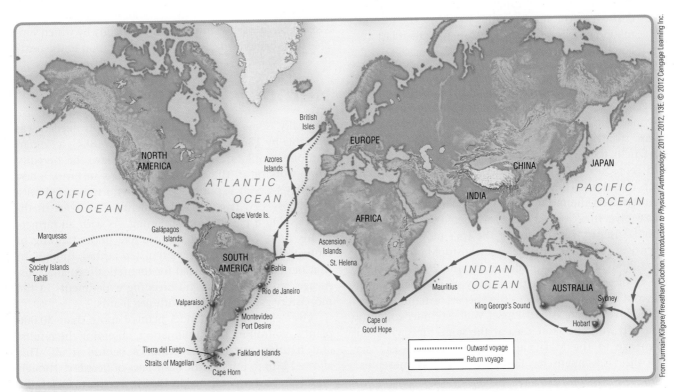

Figure 2.4 The Voyage of the HMS *Beagle* During his journey of almost five years, Darwin worked studiously on a manuscript about barnacles. At the same time, Darwin's exposure to the diversity of plant and animal life, as well as to the varied environments across the globe, planted the seeds of his evolutionary theory.

From Jurmain/Kilgore/Trevathan/Ciochon. *Introduction to Physical Anthropology,* 2011–2012, 13E. © 2012 Cengage Learning Inc.

Observing the tremendous diversity of living creatures as well as the astounding fossils of extinct animals, Darwin began to note that species varied according to the environments they inhabited. The observations he made on this voyage, his readings of Lyell's *Principles of Geology* (1830), and the arguments he had with the orthodox and dogmatic FitzRoy all contributed to the ideas culminating in Darwin's most famous book, *On the Origin of Species*. This book, published in 1859, twenty years after he returned from his voyage, describes a theory of evolution accounting for change within species and for the emergence of new species in purely naturalistic terms.

Darwin added observations from English farm life and intellectual thought to the ideas he began to develop on the *Beagle*. He paid particular attention to domesticated animals and farmers' "artificial selection," a practice of breeding their stock to select for specific traits. Darwin's theoretical breakthrough derived from an essay by economist Thomas Malthus (1766–1834), which warned of the potential consequences of increased human population, particularly of the poor. Malthus observed that animal populations, unlike human populations, remained stable, due to an overproduction of young followed by a large proportion of animal offspring not surviving to maturity. Darwin wrote in his autobiography,

> It at once struck me that under these circumstances favourable variations would tend to be preserved, and unfavourable ones to be destroyed. The results of this would be the formation of a new species. Here, then I had at last got a theory by which to work. (Darwin, 1887)

Darwin combined his observations into the theory of **natural selection** as follows: All species display a range of variation, and all have the ability to expand beyond their means of subsistence. It follows that, in their "struggle for existence," organisms with variations that help them to survive in a particular environment will reproduce with greater success than those without such variations. Thus, as generation succeeds generation, nature selects the most advantageous variations and species evolve. In retrospect, the idea seemed so obvious that Thomas Henry Huxley, one of the era's most prominent scientists, remarked, "How extremely stupid of me not to have thought of that" (quoted in Durant, 2000, p. 11).

As often happens in the history of science, Darwin was not alone in authoring the theory of natural selection. A Welshman, Alfred Russel Wallace, independently came up with the same idea at the same time while on a voyage to the Malay archipelago in Southeast Asia to collect specimens for European zoos and museums.

According to his autobiography, a theory came to Wallace while he was in a feverish delirium from malaria. He shared excitedly his idea with other scientists in England, including Darwin, whose own theory was yet unpublished. The two scientists jointly presented their findings.

However straightforward the idea of evolution by natural selection may appear, the theory was (and has continued to be) a source of considerable controversy. Darwin avoided the most contentious question of human origins, limiting his commentary in the original work to a single sentence near the end: "much light will be thrown on the origin of man and his history." However, the feisty Thomas Henry Huxley, in his book *On Man's Place in Nature* (1863), took up the subject of human origins explicitly through comparative anatomy of apes and humans and an examination of the fossils.

Two problems plagued Darwin's theory throughout his career: First, how did variation arise in the first place? Second, what was the mechanism of heredity by which variable traits could be passed from one generation to the next?

Heredity

Ironically, some of the information Darwin needed was available by 1866. Gregor Mendel (1822–1884), a Roman Catholic monk, developed the basic laws of heredity while working in the monastery gardens in Brno, a city in today's Czech Republic. Mendel, who was raised on a farm, possessed two particular talents: a flair for mathematics and a passion for gardening. As with all farmers of his time, Mendel had an intuitive understanding of biological inheritance. He went a step farther, though, in that he recognized the need for theoretical explanations. At age 34, he began careful breeding experiments in the monastery garden, starting with pea plants.

Over eight years, Mendel planted more than 30,000 plants, controlling their pollination, observing the results, and figuring out the mathematics behind it all. This allowed him to unravel the basic laws of heredity. Though his findings were published in 1866 in a respected scientific journal, no one recognized the importance of Mendel's work during his lifetime. Interestingly, a copy of this journal was found in Darwin's own library with the pages still uncut (journals were printed on long continuous sheets of

---

natural selection The evolutionary process through which factors in the environment exert pressure, favoring some individuals over others to produce the next generation.

paper and then folded into pages to be cut by the reader), an indication that the journal had never been read.

In 1900, cell biology had advanced to the point where rediscovery of Mendel's laws was inevitable, and in that year three European botanists, working independently of one another, rediscovered not only the laws but also Mendel's original paper. With this rediscovery, the science of genetics began. Still, it would be another fifty-three years before the molecular mechanisms of heredity and the discrete units of inheritance would be discovered. Today, a comprehensive understanding of heredity, molecular genetics, and population genetics supports Darwinian evolutionary theory.

The Transmission of Genes

Today, we define **genes** as portions of the DNA molecule containing a sequence of base pairs that encodes a particular protein. When biologists coined the term from the Greek word for "birth" at the turn of the 20th century, however, the molecular basis of the gene was still fifty years away from discovery. Mendel had deduced the presence and activity of genes by experimenting with garden peas to determine how various traits are passed from one generation to the next. Specifically, he discovered that inheritance was *particulate*, rather than *blending*, as Darwin and many others thought. That is, the units controlling the expression of visible traits come in pairs, one from each parent, and retain their separate identities over the generations rather than blending into a combination of parental traits in offspring. This was the basis of Mendel's first **law of segregation**, which states that pairs of genes separate, keep their individuality, and are passed on to the next generation unaltered. Another finding—Mendel's **law of independent assortment**—states that different traits (under the control of distinct genes) are inherited independently of one another.

Mendel based his laws on statistical frequencies of observed characteristics, such as color and texture in generations of plants. When **chromosomes**, the cellular structures containing the genetic information, were discovered at the start of the 20th century, they provided a visible vehicle for transmission of traits proposed in Mendel's laws.

Then in 1953 James Watson and Francis Crick found that genes are actually portions of molecules of **DNA (deoxyribonucleic acid)**—long strands of which form chromosomes. (Rosalind Franklin, shown in **Figure 2.5,**

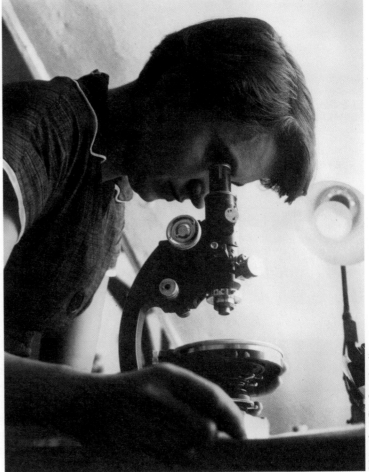

Figure 2.5 Rosalind Franklin and the Structure of DNA British scientist Rosalind Franklin's pioneering work in x-ray crystal photography played a vital role in unlocking the secret of the genetic code in 1953. Without her permission, Franklin's colleague Maurice Wilkins showed one of her images to James Watson. In his book *The Double Helix*, Watson wrote, "The instant I saw the picture my mouth fell open and my pulse began to race." While her research was published simultaneously in the prestigious journal *Nature* in 1953—alongside that of James Watson, Francis Crick, and Maurice Wilkins—her untimely death from cancer meant that only the gentlemen received the Nobel Prize for the double-helix model of DNA in 1962.

genes The portions of DNA molecules that direct the synthesis of specific proteins.

law of segregation The Mendelian principle that variants of genes for a particular trait retain their separate identities through the generations.

law of independent assortment The Mendelian principle that genes controlling different traits are inherited independently of one another.

chromosomes In the cell nucleus, the structures visible during cellular division containing long strands of DNA combined with a protein.

DNA (deoxyribonucleic acid) The genetic material consisting of a complex molecule whose base structure directs the synthesis of proteins.

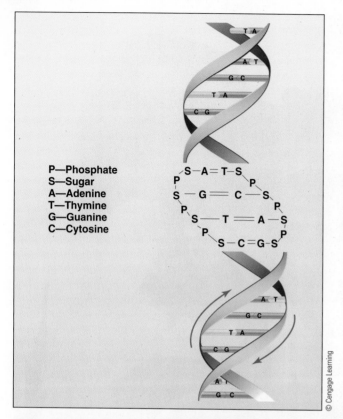

P—Phosphate
S—Sugar
A—Adenine
T—Thymine
G—Guanine
C—Cytosine

© Cengage Learning

Figure 2.6 The Structure of DNA This diagrammatic representation of a portion of DNA (deoxyribonucleic acid) illustrates its twisted ladderlike structure. Alternating sugar and phosphate groups form the structural sides of the ladder. The connecting "rungs" are formed by pairings between complementary bases—adenine with thymine and cytosine with guanine.

was a largely unknown contributor to this amazing breakthrough.) DNA is a complex molecule with an unusual shape, rather like two strands of a rope twisted around each other with ladderlike steps between the two strands (Figure 2.6). Alternating sugar and phosphate molecules form the backbone of these strands connected to each other by four base pairs: adenine, thymine, guanine, and cytosine (usually written as A, T, G, and C). Connections between the strands occur between so-called complementary pairs of bases (A to T, G to C).

chromatid One half of the X shape of chromosomes visible once replication is complete. Sister chromatids are exact copies of each other.

alleles Alternate forms of a single gene.

enzymes Proteins that initiate and direct chemical reactions.

karyotype The array of chromosomes found inside a single cell.

genome The complete structure sequence of DNA for a species.

codon Three-base sequence of a gene that specifies a particular amino acid for inclusion in a protein.

Sequences of three complementary bases specify the sequence of amino acids in protein synthesis. This arrangement also confers upon genes the unique property of replication—being able to make exact copies of themselves. The term **chromatid** refers to one half of the X shape of chromosomes visible once replication is complete. Sister chromatids are exact copies of each other.

Genes and Alleles

A sequence of chemical bases on a molecule of DNA (a gene) constitutes a recipe for making proteins. As science writer Matt Ridley puts it, "Proteins . . . do almost every chemical, structural, and regulatory thing that is done in the body: they generate energy, fight infection, digest food, form hair, carry oxygen, and so on and on" (Ridley, 1999, p. 40). Almost everything in the body is made of or by proteins.

There are alternate forms of genes, known as **alleles**. For example, the gene for a human blood type in the A-B-O system refers to a specific portion of a DNA molecule on chromosome 9 that in this case is 1,062 letters long (a medium-sized gene). This gene specifies the production of an **enzyme**, a kind of protein that initiates and directs a chemical reaction. This particular enzyme causes molecules involved in immune responses to attach to the surface of red blood cells. Alleles correspond to the specific blood type (the A allele and B allele). Genes, then, are not really separate structures, as had once been imagined, but locations, like dots on a map. (Figure 2.7 displays a **karyotype**, the array of chromosomes found inside a single cell.) These genes provide the recipe for the many proteins that keep us alive and healthy.

The human **genome**—the complete sequence of human DNA—contains 3 billion chemical bases, with 20,000 to 25,000 genes, a number similar to that found in most mammals. Of the 3 billion bases, humans and mice are about 90 percent identical. Both species have three times as many genes as does the fruit fly, but surprisingly humans and mice have half the number of genes found in the rice plant! In other words, the number of genes or base pairs does not explain every difference among organisms. At the same time, those 20,000 to 25,000 human genes account for only 1 to 1.5 percent of the entire genome, indicating that scientists still have far more to learn about how genes work. Frequently, genes themselves are split by long stretches of DNA that are not part of the known protein code; for example, the 1,062 bases of the A-B-O blood-group gene are interrupted by five such stretches. In the course of protein production, these stretches of DNA are metaphorically snipped out and left on the cutting room floor.

How is the DNA recipe converted into a protein? Through a series of intervening steps, each three-base sequence of a gene, called a **codon**, specifies production of a particular

Karyotype with a Few Genetic Loci

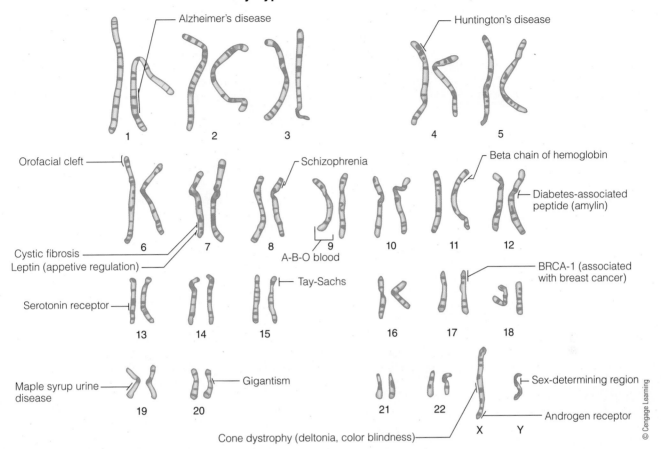

Figure 2.7 A Human Karyotype An array of chromosomes from inside the nucleus of one cell of one individual is called a karyotype. The twenty-three pairs of chromosomes humans possess include twenty-two pairs of somatic or body chromosomes, plus one pair of sex chromosomes, for a total of forty-six chromosomes. Here you can see the characteristic shape and relative size of each of the chromosomes. The locations of certain genes associated with various diseases and conditions identified by the Human Genome Project are labeled. Although we would need to sequence the DNA to see what alleles this individual had for various genes, a glance at the overall karyotype indicates a normal number of chromosomes and that this individual is genetically male. The female phenotype is determined by the presence of two X chromosomes. Offspring inherit an X chromosome from their mothers but either an X or a Y from their fathers, resulting in approximately equal numbers of male and female offspring in subsequent generations. Although the Y chromosome is critical for differentiation into a male phenotype, compared to other chromosomes the Y is tiny and carries little genetic information.

amino acid, strings of which build proteins. Because DNA cannot leave the cell's nucleus (**Figure 2.8**), the directions for a specific protein are first converted into **RNA (ribonucleic acid)** in a process called **transcription**. RNA differs from DNA in the structure of its sugar phosphate backbone and in the presence of the base uracil rather than thymine. Next, the RNA (called *messenger RNA* or *mRNA*) travels to the **ribosomes**, the cellular structure (**Figure 2.9**) where **translation** of the directions found in the codons occurs, producing proteins. Anticodons of *transfer RNA (tRNA)* transport the individual amino acids to the corresponding mRNA codons, and the amino acids are joined together by

peptide bonds to form polypeptide chains. For example, the sequence of AUG specifies the amino acid methionine, CCC proline, GAU aspartic acid, and so on.

RNA (ribonucleic acid) Similar to DNA but with uracil substituted for the base thymine. Transcribes and carries instructions from DNA from the nucleus to the ribosomes, where it directs protein synthesis. Some simple life forms contain RNA only.

transcription The process of conversion of instructions from DNA into RNA.

ribosomes Structures in the cell where translation occurs.

translation The process of conversion of RNA instructions into proteins.

Figure 2.8 A Eukaryotic Cell The figure shows the three-dimensional structure of a generalized eukaryotic, or nucleated, cell. DNA is located in the nucleus. Because DNA cannot leave the nucleus, genes must first be transcribed into RNA, which carries genetic information to the ribosomes, where protein synthesis occurs. Note also the mitochondria, which contain their own circular chromosomes and mitochondrial DNA.

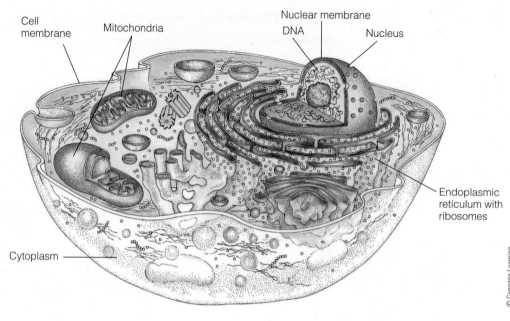

Figure 2.9 Transcription and Translation of DNA into Proteins Codons of DNA (a sequence of three bases) are transcribed into the complementary codons of a kind of RNA called messenger RNA (mRNA) in order to leave the nucleus. In the ribosomes, these codons are translated into proteins by transfer RNA (tRNA), which strings the amino acids together into particular chains. Can you think of the bases that would have been found in the DNA that correspond to the section of mRNA pictured here?

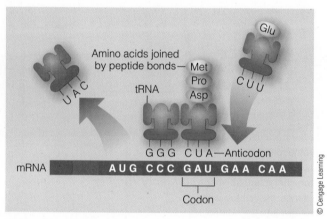

There are twenty amino acids, which are strung together in different amounts and sequences to produce an almost infinite number of different proteins. This is the so-called **genetic code**, and it is the same for every living thing, whether a worm or a human being. In addition to the genetic information stored in the chromosomes of the nucleus, complex organisms also possess cellular structures

called *mitochondria,* each of which has a single circular chromosome. The genetic material known as *mitochondrial DNA* or *mtDNA* has figured prominently in human evolutionary studies. On the other end of the spectrum, simple living things without nucleated cells, such as the retrovirus that causes AIDS, contain their genetic information only as RNA.

Much of this seemingly useless, noncoding DNA (often called *junk DNA*) has been inserted by retroviruses. *Retroviruses* are some of the most diverse and widespread infectious entities of vertebrates—responsible for AIDS, hepatitis, anemias, and some neurological disorders (Amábile-Cuevas & Chicurel, 1993). Other junk DNA consists of decaying hulks of once useful but now functionless genes: damaged genes that have been "turned off." As cells divide and reproduce, junk DNA, like known genes, also replicates. Mistakes can occur in the replication process, adding or subtracting repeats of the four bases: A, C, G, and T. This happens with some frequency and differently in every individual. As these "mistakes" accumulate over time, each person develops his or her unique DNA fingerprint.

Cell Division

In order to grow and maintain good health, the body cells of an organism must divide and produce new cells. Cell division begins when the chromosomes replicate, forming a second pair that duplicates the original pair of chromosomes in the nucleus. To do this, the DNA "unzips" between the base pairs—adenine from thymine and guanine from cytosine—and then each base on each now-single strand attracts its complementary base, reconstituting the second half of the double helix. After they separate, a new cell membrane surrounds each new chromosome pair and becomes the

genetic code The sequence of three bases (a codon) that specifies the sequence of amino acids in protein synthesis.

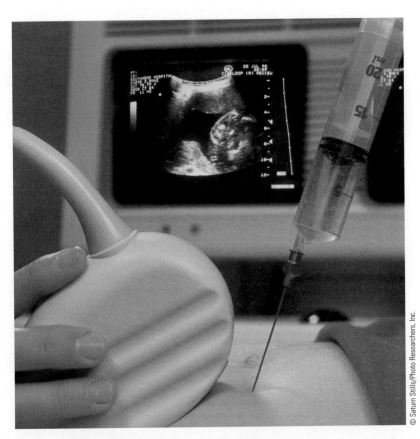

© Saturn Stills/Photo Researchers, Inc.

Figure 2.10 Prenatal Genetic Testing by Amniocentesis Prenatal genetic testing is conducted most frequently by amniocentesis, a technique that began in the 1960s through which a medical practitioner draws fluid, containing cells from the developing embryo, from the womb of a pregnant woman. Lab technicians then analyze the chromosomes and specific genes for abnormalities. Cultural anthropologists have shown that a biological fact (such as an extra 21st chromosome or Down syndrome) is open to diverse interpretations and reproductive choices by "potential parents" (Rapp, 1999). New reproductive technologies have far-reaching social consequences. Genetic testing may lead to the labeling of certain people as undesirable, pitting women's reproductive rights against the rights of the disabled.

Among wealthier parents-to-be, prenatal genetic testing has become increasingly common. As mentioned in this chapter's opening Challenge Issue, such testing aims to eliminate conditions not favored within a society. Generally, during the first two trimesters, women in the United States have a constitutionally protected right to decide whether to terminate or continue a pregnancy for any reason at all, including the diagnosis of a genetic anomaly. Following this window of time, federal law protects the rights of disabled individuals with these same anomalies. In other societies, the undesirable trait discovered through prenatal genetic testing can be as basic as the biological sex of the child (Figure 2.10). In India, where female children are undervalued, prenatal genetic testing has led to selective abortion of female fetuses (Arnold, Kishor, & Roy, 2002).

No aspect of human reproduction or genetics is simply biological. Social and political processes impact the interpretation and use of genetic technology. The technology, in turn, shapes social definitions of family, identity, and the types of citizens preferred by a given society. See this chapter's Biocultural Connection to read how DNA testing has made its way into the lives of African refugees seeking reunification with their families in the United States.

Sexual reproduction increases genetic diversity, which in turn has contributed to a multitude of adaptations among sexually reproducing species such as humans. Sexual reproduction involves the merging of two cells, one from each parent, to make a new individual. If two regular body cells, each containing twenty-three pairs of chromosomes, were to merge, the lethal result would be a new individual with forty-six pairs of chromosomes. Instead, sexual reproduction involves joining specialized sex cells (eggs and sperm) produced by a different kind of cell division, called **meiosis**.

Although meiosis begins like mitosis, with the replication and doubling of the original genes in chromosomes through the formation of sister chromatids, it proceeds to divide that number into four new cells rather than two

nucleus that directs the activities of a new cell. This kind of cell division is called **mitosis**. Barring errors in this replication process, cells divide mitotically to form daughter cells that are exact genetic copies of the parent cell.

Like most animals, humans reproduce sexually. The "popularity" of sex from an evolutionary perspective derives from the genetic variation that it provides. All animals contain two copies of each chromosome, having inherited one from each parent. In humans this involves twenty-three pairs of chromosomes. Sexual reproduction can bring favorable alleles together, purge the genome of harmful ones, and allow beneficial alleles to spread without being held back by the baggage of disadvantageous variants of other genes.

While human societies have always regulated sexual reproduction in some ways, the science of genetics has had a tremendous impact on social aspects of reproduction.

mitosis A kind of cell division that produces new cells having exactly the same number of chromosome pairs, and hence copies of genes, as the parent cell.

meiosis A kind of cell division that produces the sex cells, each of which has half the number of chromosomes found in other cells of the organism.

BIOCULTURAL CONNECTION

Bonds Beyond Blood: DNA Testing and Refugee Family Unification

By Jason Silverstein

In February of 2008, the U.S. government began to assess the use of DNA testing as documentary proof of familial relationship among asylum seekers from Africa attempting reunification with family members already in the United States. The pilot study began with

500 residents of the Dadaab refugee camp in Nairobi, Kenya, where an estimated 465,000 refugees currently live in a space designed for 90,000. DNA testing was later expanded to include 3,000 refugees in Ethiopia, Uganda, Ghana, Guinea, and Côte d'Ivoire.

The pilot program operated on the assumption of "guilty until proven family." Anything other than DNA proof of relationship was recorded as fraud. Refusal to test was recorded as fraud. On a petition with multiple family members, if one person refused, did not

Covering 50 square kilometers in northeastern Kenya, the Dadaab Refugee Camp is the largest such camp in the world. Originally designed in 1991 for 90,00, today over 400,000 people crowd into the camp. Each day, over 1,300 new refugees arrive seeking sanctuary from political persecution and starvation brought about by civil war and drought. Here Somali refugees pray during Eid al-Fitr, marking the end of the Muslim holy month of Ramadan.

(**Figure 2.11**). Thus, each new cell has only half the number of chromosomes compared to the parent cell. Human eggs and sperm have only twenty-three single chromosomes (half of a pair), whereas body cells have twenty-three pairs, or forty-six chromosomes.

The process of meiotic division has important implications for genetics. Because paired chromosomes are separated,

the daughter cells will not be identical. Two of the four new cells will have half of each pair of chromosomes, and the other two will have the second half of the original chromosome pair. In addition, corresponding portions of one chromosome may "cross over" to the other one, somewhat scrambling the genetic material compared to the original chromosomes.

Sometimes, the original pair is **homozygous**, possessing identical alleles for a specific gene. For example, if in both chromosomes of the original pair the gene for A-B-O blood type is represented by the allele for type A blood,

homozygous Refers to a chromosome pair that bears identical alleles for a single gene.

show up for, or failed the test, then the entire petition was recorded as fraud. Shockingly, the "anchor" (the person with whom the applicants desired to reunite) was never tested. Only the relationships between individuals on the application were tested. By the time the pilot phase ended, these policies resulted in the classification of 80 percent of family reunification claims as fraudulent, and the U.S. government suspended the reunification program. As DNA testing increasingly becomes the standard by which border security officials investigate kinship claims, what makes a family legitimate will be determined by the social prescriptions of the receiving community.

The definition of *family* is not necessarily portable across borders. Refugees are forced to conform their qualifications of family and, thus, their very life stories to the social norms of the receiving community. We should not confuse the neutrality of DNA as a hereditary material with the neutrality of those who collect, process, and interpret it. Far from value-neutral technology, DNA testing for family reunification reveals an allegiance to a particular social universe and often conceals the reality of the refugees' lived experience.

One especially lucid example of this claim is provided by a refugee case manager who remarked that polygamous families (those with more than one spouse) are never resettled (in other words, would never pass the family-relatedness test). Given the testing protocol of the pilot project (testing the genetic relationship between applicants and not between the applicant and the anchor), one readily can imagine that a mother as a primary applicant may not share DNA with her child. In such a case the entire application, and their relationship, would be officially recorded as fraudulent.

Family is not simply genetic or socially prescribed; it is also existentially evolved, especially for refugees, who have spent years if not decades in camps. An interviewer with the United Nations High Commissioner on Refugees related stories about parents who did not want to distinguish between their biological and adopted, often war-orphaned, children. Given that the verification interview takes place in front of the children, avoiding this distinction may have little to do with what security officials cruelly call fraud or abuse. As one case manager starkly put it, the DNA testing methodology overlooks that those who survive often do not survive unscathed.

For security officials, the DNA test is an attractive method of quantifying and eliminating fraud and abuse (and obeying the proposed refugee quota for the fiscal year). For caseworkers and interviewers, the DNA test alleviates officials' feelings of overwhelming responsibility and guilt stemming from their inability to resettle each of the worthy. But for the refugees themselves, the effect is a further widening of the divide between the world in which they are forced to live and a world of their own making. Indeed, if the refugee signifies that he or she is a person threatened by persecution, as defined by the 1951 United Nations Convention Relating to the Status of Refugees, then we must ask ourselves if our resettlement efforts return power to refugees or subject them to new narratives of domination and disregard.

BIOCULTURAL QUESTION

When DNA testing is used by the state for identification purposes, what rifts open between the truth of one's life and what can be extracted from one's blood? What should we be searching for when we want to know who a person truly is?

Adapted from Silverstein, J. (2012). Bonds beyond blood: DNA testing and refugee family resettlement. Anthropology News 53 *(4), 11. Reprinted by permission of the American Anthropological Association.*

then all new cells will have the A allele. But if the original pair is **heterozygous**, with the A allele on one chromosome and the allele for type B blood on the other, then half of the new cells will contain only the B allele; the offspring have a 50–50 chance of getting either one. It is impossible to predict any single individual's **genotype**, or genetic composition, but, as Mendel originally discovered, statistical probabilities can be established.

What happens when a child inherits the allele for type O blood from one parent and that for type A from the other? Will the child have blood of type A, O, or some mixture of the two? **Figure 2.12** illustrates some of the possible outcomes. Many of these questions were answered by Mendel's original experiments.

Mendel discovered that certain alleles are able to mask the presence of others; one allele is **dominant**, whereas the

---

heterozygous Refers to a chromosome pair that bears different alleles for a single gene.

genotype The alleles possessed for a particular trait.

dominant In genetics, a term to describe the ability of an allele for a trait to mask the presence of another allele.

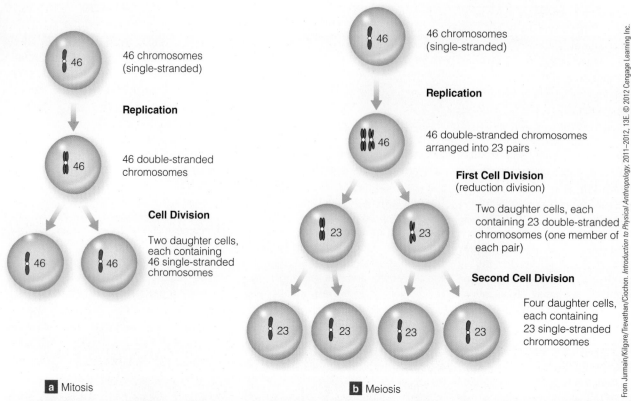

From Jurmain/Kilgore/Trevathan/Ciochon. *Introduction to Physical Anthropology, 2011–2012*, 13E. © 2012 Cengage Learning Inc.

Figure 2.11 Cell Division: Mitosis and Meiosis in Humans Each chromosome consists of two sister chromatids, which are exact copies of each other. During mitosis, these sister chromatids separate into two identical daughter cells. In meiosis, the cell division responsible for the formation of gametes, the first division halves the chromosome number. The second meiotic division is essentially like mitosis and involves the separation of sister chromatids. Chromosomes in red came from one parent; those in blue came from the other. Meiosis results in four daughter cells that are not identical.

Figure 2.12 Punnett Squares, Phenotype, and Genotype These four Punnett squares (named for British geneticist Reginald Punnett) illustrate some of the possible phenotypes and genotypes of offspring within the A-B-O system. Each individual possesses two alleles within this system, and together these two alleles constitute the individual's genotype. Phenotype refers to an individual's observed physical characteristics or traits. The alleles of one parent are listed on the left-hand side of the square, while the other parent's alleles are listed across the top. The potential genotypes of offspring are listed in the colored squares by letter. Offspring phenotypes are indicated by color: blue indicates the type A phenotype; orange indicates the B phenotype. Individuals with one A and one B allele have the AB phenotype and make both blood antigens. Individuals with the O phenotype (red) have two O alleles.

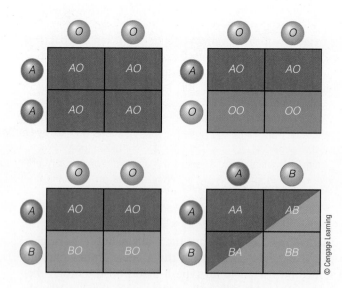

© Cengage Learning

recessive In genetics, a term to describe an allele for a trait whose expression is masked by the presence of a dominant allele.

phenotype The observable characteristic of an organism that may or may not reflect a particular genotype due to the variable expression of dominant and recessive alleles.

hemoglobin The protein that carries oxygen in red blood cells.

polygenetic inheritance Two or more genes contributing to the phenotypic expression of a single characteristic.

other is **recessive**. Actually, it is the traits that are dominant or recessive rather than the alleles themselves; geneticists merely refer to dominant and recessive alleles for the sake of convenience. Thus, one might speak of the allele for type A blood as being dominant to the one for type O. An individual whose blood type genes are heterozygous, with one A and one O allele, will have type A blood. In other words, the heterozygous condition (AO) will show exactly the same observed physical characteristic, or **phenotype**, as the homozygous (AA), even though the two have a somewhat different genetic composition, or genotype. Only the homozygous recessive genotype (OO) will show the phenotype of type O blood.

The dominance of one allele does not mean that the recessive one is lost or in some way blended. A type A heterozygous parent (AO) will produce sex cells containing both A and O alleles. (This is an example of Mendel's law of segregation, that alleles retain their separate identities.) Recessive alleles can be handed down for generations before they are matched with another recessive allele in the process of sexual reproduction and show up in the phenotype. The presence of the dominant allele simply masks the expression of the recessive allele.

All of the traits Mendel studied in garden peas showed this dominant–recessive relationship, and so for some years it was believed that this was the only relationship possible. Later studies, however, have indicated that patterns of inheritance are not always so simple. In some cases neither allele is dominant; they are both *co-dominant*. An example of co-dominance in human heredity can be seen also in the inheritance of blood types. Type A is produced by one allele; type B by another. A heterozygous individual will have a phenotype of AB because neither allele can dominate the other.

The inheritance of blood types points out another complexity of heredity. Although we each have at most two alleles for any given gene, the number of possible alleles for that gene found in a population is by no means limited to two. Certain traits have three or more allelic forms. For example, over 100 alleles exist for **hemoglobin**, the blood protein that carries oxygen. Only one allele can appear on each of the two homologous chromosomes, so each individual is limited to two genetic alleles.

Polygenetic Inheritance

So far, we have described the traits of organisms as if they are determined by just one gene. However, multiple genes control most physical traits, such as body build, skin color, or susceptibility to disease. In such cases, we speak of **polygenetic inheritance**, in which the respective alleles of two or more genes influence phenotype. For example, several individuals may have the exact same height, but because there is no single height gene that determines an individual's size, it is impossible to neatly unravel the genetic underpinnings of 5 foot 3 inches or 160 centimeters. Characteristics subject to polygenetic inheritance exhibit a continuous range of variation in their phenotypic expression that does not correspond to simple Mendelian rules. As biological anthropologist Jonathan Marks demonstrates in the following Original Study, the relationship between genetics and continuous traits remains a mystery.

ORIGINAL STUDY

Ninety-Eight Percent Alike: What Our Similarity to Apes Tells Us about Our Understanding of Genetics *BY JONATHAN MARKS*

It's not too hard to tell Jane Goodall from a chimpanzee. Goodall is the one with long legs and short arms, a prominent forehead, and whites in her eyes. She's the one with a significant amount of hair only on her head, not all over her body. She's the one who walks, talks, and wears clothing.

A few decades ago, however, the nascent field of molecular genetics recognized an apparent paradox: However easy it may be to tell Jane Goodall from a chimpanzee on the basis of physical characteristics, it is considerably harder to tell them apart according to their genes.

More recently, geneticists have been able to determine with

By Jonathan Marks (2000) "98% Alike: What Our Similarity to Apes Tells Us about Our Understanding Genetics." The Chronicle of Higher Education May 12, 1987

A true four-fielder, biological anthropologist Jonathan Marks is at the grave of Emile Durkheim, the French sociologist who profoundly influenced the founding of cultural anthropology.

precision that humans and chimpanzees are over 98 percent identical genetically, and that figure has become one of the most well-known factoids in the popular scientific literature. It has been invoked to argue that we are simply a third kind of chimpanzee, together with the common chimp and the rarer bonobo; to claim human rights for nonhuman apes; and to explain the roots of male aggression.

Using the figure in those ways, however, ignores the context necessary to make sense of it. Actually, our amazing genetic similarity to chimpanzees is a scientific fact constructed from two rather more mundane facts: our familiarity with the apes and our unfamiliarity with genetic comparisons.

To begin with, it is unfair to juxtapose the differences between the bodies of people and apes with the similarities in their genes. After all, we have been comparing the bodies of humans and chimpanzees for 300 years, and we have been comparing DNA sequences for less than 20 years.

Now that we are familiar with chimpanzees, we quickly see how different they look from us. But when the chimpanzee was a novelty, in the 18th century, scholars were struck by the overwhelming similarity of human and ape bodies. And why not? Bone for bone, muscle for muscle, organ for organ, the bodies of humans and apes differ only in subtle ways. And yet, it is impossible to say just how physically similar they are. Forty percent? Sixty percent? Ninety-eight percent? Three-dimensional beings that develop over their lifetimes don't lend themselves to a simple scale of similarity.

Genetics brings something different to the comparison. A DNA sequence is a one-dimensional entity, a long series of A, G, C, and T subunits. Align two sequences from different species and you can simply tabulate their similarities; if they match 98 out of 100 times, then the species are 98 percent genetically identical.

But is that more or less than their bodies match? We have no easy way to tell, for making sense of the question "How similar are a human and a chimp?" requires a frame of reference. In other words, we should be asking: "How similar are a human and a chimp, compared to what?" Let's try and answer the question. How similar are a human and a chimp, compared to, say, a sea urchin? The human and chimpanzee have limbs, skeletons, bilateral symmetry, a central nervous system; each bone, muscle, and organ matches. For all intents and purposes, the human and chimpanzee aren't 98 percent identical, they're 100 percent identical.

On the other hand, when we compare the DNA of humans and chimps, what does the percentage of similarity mean? We conceptualize it on a linear scale, on which 100 percent is perfectly identical, and 0 percent is totally different. But the structure of DNA gives the scale a statistical idiosyncrasy.

Because DNA is a linear array of those four bases—A, G, C, and T—only four possibilities exist at any specific point in a DNA sequence. The laws of chance tell us that two random sequences from species that have no ancestry in common will match at about one in every four sites.

Thus, even two unrelated DNA sequences will be 25 percent identical, not 0 percent identical. (You can, of course, generate sequences more different than that, but greater differences would not occur randomly.) The most different two DNA sequences can be, then, is 75 percent different.

Now consider that all multicellular life on earth is related. A human, a chimpanzee, and the banana the chimpanzee is eating share a remote common ancestry, but a common ancestry nevertheless. Therefore, if we compare any particular DNA sequence in a human and a banana, the sequence would have to be more than 25 percent identical. For the sake of argument, let's say 35 percent. In other words, your DNA is over one-third the same as a banana's. Yet, of course, there are few ways other than genetically in which a human could be shown to be one-third identical to a banana.

That context may help us to assess the 98 percent DNA similarity of humans and chimpanzees. The fact that our DNA is 98 percent identical to that of a chimp is not a transcendent statement about our natures, but merely a decontextualized and culturally interpreted datum.

Moreover, the genetic comparison is misleading because it ignores qualitative differences among genomes. Genetic evolution involves much more than simply replacing one base with another. Thus, even among such close relatives as human and chimpanzee, we find that the chimp's genome is estimated to be about 10 percent larger than the human's; that one human chromosome contains a fusion of two small chimpanzee chromosomes; and that the tips of each chimpanzee chromosome contain a DNA sequence that is not present in humans.

In other words, the pattern we encounter genetically is actually quite close to the pattern we encounter anatomically. In spite of the shock the figure of 98 percent may give us, humans are obviously identifiably different from, as well as very similar to, chimpanzees. The apparent paradox is simply a result of how mundane the apes have become and how exotic DNA still is.

Adapted from Marks, J. (2000, May 12). 98% alike (What our similarity to apes tells us about our understanding of genetics). The Chronicle of Higher Education, B7. Copyright © 2000 by Chronicle of Higher Education. Reprinted with permission of the author.

Evolution, Individuals, and Populations

At the level of the individual, the study of genetics shows how traits are transmitted from parent to offspring, enabling a prediction about the chances that any given individual will display some phenotypic characteristic.

At the level of the group, the study of genetics takes on additional significance, revealing how evolutionary processes account for the diversity of life on earth.

A key concept in genetics is that of the **population**, or a group of individuals within which breeding takes place. **Gene pool** refers to all the genetic variants possessed by members of a population. Natural selection takes place within populations as some members contribute a disproportionate share of the next generation. Over generations, the relative proportions of alleles in a population change (biological evolution) according to the varying reproductive success of individuals within that population. In other words, at the level of population genetics, **evolution** can be defined as changes in allele frequencies in populations. This is also known as *microevolution*. Evolution could not occur without variation. Four evolutionary forces—mutation, genetic drift, gene flow, and natural selection—create and pattern biological diversity.

In theory, the characteristics of any given population should remain stable. For example, generation after generation, the bullfrogs in a farm pond look much alike, have the same calls, and exhibit the same behavior when breeding. The gene pool of the population—the genetic variation available to that population—appears to remain stable over time.

Although some alleles may be dominant over others, recessive alleles are not just lost or destroyed. Statistically, an individual who is heterozygous for a particular gene with one dominant (A) and one recessive (a) allele has a 50 percent chance of passing on the dominant allele and a 50 percent chance of passing on the recessive allele. Even if another dominant allele masks the presence of the recessive allele in the next generation, the recessive allele nonetheless will continue to be a part of the gene pool.

Because alleles are not lost in the process of reproduction, the frequency of the different alleles within a population should remain exactly the same from one generation to the next in the absence of evolution. In 1908, the English mathematician Godfrey H. Hardy (1877–1947) and the German obstetrician Wilhelm Weinberg (1862–1937) worked this idea into a mathematical formula called the **Hardy-Weinberg principle**. The principle algebraically demonstrates that the percentages of individuals homozygous for the dominant allele, homozygous for the recessive allele, and heterozygous will remain the same from one generation to the next provided that the following conditions are met: mating is entirely random; the population is sufficiently large for a statistical average to express itself; no new variants will be introduced into the population's gene pool; and all individuals are equally successful at surviving and reproducing. As you will see in the following sections of this chapter, each of these conditions relates to one of the four forces responsible for microevolution or changes in allele frequency.

Evolutionary Forces

Mutation

Mutation, the ultimate source of evolutionary change, constantly introduces new genetic variation. Mutation occurs randomly. Although some mutations may be harmful or beneficial to individuals, most mutations are neutral. But in an evolutionary sense, random mutation is inherently positive: It provides the variation upon which the other evolutionary forces work. New body plans—such as walking on two legs compared to knuckle-walking like our closest relatives, chimpanzees and gorillas—ultimately depended on a series of genetic mutations. A random mutation might create a new allele that modifies protein, making possible a novel biological task. Without the variation brought in through random mutations, populations could not change over time in response to changing environments.

Mutations may arise whenever copying mistakes are made during cell division. This may involve a change in a single base of a DNA sequence or, at the other extreme, relocation of large segments of DNA, including entire chromosomes. As you read this page, the DNA in each cell of your body is being damaged (Culotta & Koshland, 1994). Fortunately, DNA repair enzymes constantly scan DNA for mistakes, slicing out damaged segments and patching up gaps. Moreover, for sexually reproducing species like humans, the only mutations of any evolutionary consequence are those occurring in sex cells because these cells form future generations.

New mutations arise continuously because no species has perfect DNA repair; thus all species continue to evolve. Geneticists have calculated the rate at which various types of mutant genes appear. In human populations, they run from a low of about five mutations per million sex cells formed, in the case of a gene abnormality that leads to the absence of an iris in the eye, to a high of about a hundred per million, in the case of a gene involved in a form of muscular dystrophy. The average is about thirty mutants per million. Environmental factors may increase the rate at which mutations occur. These factors include certain dyes, antibiotics, and chemicals used in the preservation of food. Radiation, whether of industrial or solar origin, represents another important cause of mutations (**Figure 2.13**). Even stress can increase mutation rates, augmenting the diversity necessary for selection if successful adaptation is to occur (Chicurel, 2001).

In humans, as in all multicellular animals, the very nature of genetic material ensures that mutations will occur. For instance, the fact that a gene can be split by stretches of DNA that are not part of that gene increases the chances that a mistake in the process of copying DNA will cause mutations. To cite one example, no fewer than fifty such segments of DNA fragment the gene for collagen—the main

population In biology, a group of similar individuals that can and do interbreed.

gene pool All the genetic variants possessed by members of a population.

evolution The changes in allele frequencies in populations; also known as *microevolution*.

Hardy-Weinberg principle The concept that demonstrates algebraically that the percentages of individuals that are homozygous for the dominant allele, homozygous for the recessive allele, and heterozygous should remain constant from one generation to the next, provided that certain specified conditions are met.

mutation The chance alteration of genetic material that produces new variation.

© Gerg Ludwig/INSTITUTE

Figure 2.13 From Toxic Dumps to Missing Hands These eight children, each missing a hand, were among 90 children born with missing terminal limbs over a twenty-year period in Moscow, Russia. Their family homes were all clustered in polluted industrialized sections of the city, and the missing limbs are the result of prenatal exposure to toxins. These children and their families certainly face many obstacles as a result of this birth defect. Yet from an evolutionary perspective, the mutations leading to limb loss will have no consequences unless they appear in the reproductive cells and are transmitted to future generations.

structural protein of the skin, bones, and cartilage. One possible benefit of this seemingly inefficient situation is that it allows the gene segments themselves to be shuffled like a deck of cards, sometimes creating new proteins with new functions. So although individuals may suffer as a result, mutations also confer versatility at the population level, making it possible for an evolving species to adapt more quickly to environmental changes. Remember, however, that mutations occur randomly and thus do not arise out of need for some new adaptation.

Genetic Drift

Genetic drift refers to chance fluctuations of allele frequencies in the gene pool of a population. This evolutionary force produces changes at the population level caused by random events at the individual level. Over the course of a lifetime, a number of random events affect each individual's survival. For example, an individual squirrel in good health and possessed of a number of advanta-

geous traits may be killed in a chance forest fire; a genetically well-adapted baby cougar may not live longer than a day if its mother gets caught in an avalanche, whereas the weaker offspring of another cougar mother may survive.

In a large population, such accidents of nature are unimportant; the accidents that preserve individuals with certain alleles will be balanced out by the accidents that destroy them. However, in small populations such averaging out may not be possible. Because today human populations are large, we might suppose that human beings are unaffected by genetic drift. But a chance event, like a rockslide that kills five people from a small town, say a population of 1,000, could significantly alter the frequencies of alleles in the local gene pool.

A specific kind of genetic drift known as **founder effects** may occur when an existing population splits up into two or more new ones, especially if a particularly small number of individuals founds one of the new populations. In such cases, the gene frequencies of the smaller population tend not to contain the full range of variation present in the larger one.

Isolated island populations may have limited variability due to founder effects. An interesting example can be seen on the Pacific Ocean island of Pingelap in Micronesia, where 5 percent of the population is completely colorblind, a condition known as *achromatopsia*. This is not the "normal"

genetic drift The chance fluctuations of allele frequencies in the gene pool of a population.
founder effects A particular form of genetic drift deriving from a small founding population not possessing all the alleles present in the original population.

red–green colorblindness that affects 8 to 20 percent of males in most populations but rather a complete inability to see color. The high frequency of achromatopsia occurred sometime around 1775 after a typhoon swept through the island, reducing its total population to only twenty individuals. Among the survivors was a single individual who was heterozygous for this condition. After a few genera-

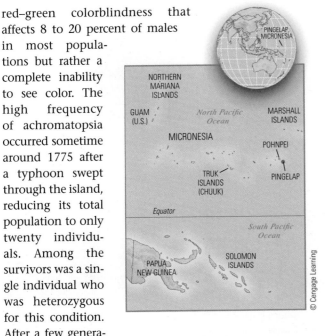

tions, this gene became fully embedded in the expanding population. Today a full 30 percent of the island's inhabitants are carriers of the colorblind gene, compared to a mere .003 percent seen in the United States (Sacks, 1998).

Genetic drift is likely to have been an important factor in human evolution because until 10,000 years ago all humans were food foragers generally living in relatively small communities. Whenever biological variation is observed, whether it is the distant past or the present, it is always possible that chance events of genetic drift are responsible for it.

Gene Flow

Gene flow, or the introduction of new alleles from nearby populations, brings new genetic variation into a population: Interbreeding allows "road-tested" genes to flow into and out of populations. Migration of individuals or groups into the territory occupied by others may lead to gene flow. Geographic factors also affect gene flow. For example, if a river separates two populations of small mammals, preventing interbreeding, these populations will begin to accrue random genetic differences due to their isolation (genetic drift). If the river changes course and the two populations can again interbreed freely, new alleles that may have been present in only one population will now be present in both populations due to gene flow.

Among humans, social factors—such as mating rules, intergroup conflict, and our ability to travel great distances—affect gene flow. For example, the last 500 years have seen the introduction of alleles into Central and South American populations from both the Spanish colonists and the Africans whom Europeans imported as slaves. More recent migrations of people from East Asia have added to this mix. Throughout the history of human life on earth, gene flow has prevented populations from developing into separate species.

Natural Selection

Although gene flow and genetic drift may produce changes in the allele frequency of a population, that change would not necessarily make the population better adapted to its biological and social environment. Natural selection, the evolutionary force described by Darwin, accounts for adaptive change. **Adaptation**—a series of beneficial adjustments to a particular environment—is the outcome of natural selection. As we will explore throughout this text, humans can adapt to their environment through culture as well as biology. When biological adaptation occurs at a genetic level, natural selection is at work.

Natural selection shapes genetic variation at the population level to fit local environmental conditions. In other words, instead of random individuals passing their traits on to the next generation, selection by the forces of nature favors some individuals over others. In the process, the frequency of genetic variants for harmful or nonadaptive traits within the population reduces while the frequency of genetic variants for adaptive traits increases. Over time, changes in the genetic structure of the population can result in the formation of new species.

Popular writing often reduces natural selection to the notion of the "survival of the fittest," a phrase coined by British philosopher Herbert Spencer (1820–1903). The phrase implies that disease, predation, and starvation eliminate the physically weak from the population. Obviously, the survival of the fittest has some bearing on natural selection. But at times "less fit" individuals survive, and even do quite well, but do not reproduce. They may be incapable of attracting mates, or they may be sterile, or they may produce offspring that do not survive after birth. For example, among the Uganda kob, a kind of antelope native to East Africa, males that are unable to attract females form bachelor herds in which they live out their lives. As members of a herd, they are reasonably well protected against predators, and so they may survive to relatively old ages. They do not, however, pass on their genes to succeeding generations.

Ultimately, all natural selection is measured in terms of **reproductive success**—mating and production of viable offspring who will in turn carry on one's genes. In some human societies, a woman's social worth is assessed in terms of reproductive success or her ability to bear children. In these contexts infertility becomes a human rights issue (Figure 2.13)

In human populations, changes in allele frequencies take place slowly. For example, if an environment changed such that a recessive allele that had been present in humans

---

gene flow The introduction of alleles from the gene pool of one population into that of another.

adaptation A series of beneficial adjustments to a particular environment.

reproductive success The relative production of fertile offspring by a genotype. In practical terms, the number of offspring produced by individual members of a population is tallied and compared to that of others.

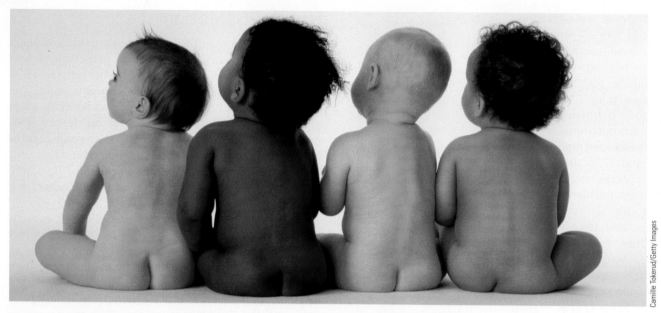

Camille Tokerud/Getty Images

Figure 2.14 Birth Weight and Stabilizing Selection Across the globe, newborn babies weigh on average between 5 and 8 pounds. Stabilizing selection seems to be operating here to keep infant size well matched to the size of the human birth canal for successful childbirth. Natural selection can promote stability as well as change.

at a modest frequency suddenly became lethal, this allele's frequency would still decrease only gradually. Even with complete selection against those homozygous for this allele, the allele would persist in the offspring of heterozygotes. In the first several generations, the frequency of the allele would decrease at a relatively rapid rate. However, with time, as the frequency of the recessive allele drops, the probability of forming a recessive homozygote also drops, so that it would take many generations to realize even a small decrease in allele frequency. Moreover, the twenty-five-year duration of a human generation (forty generations would span over a thousand years) contributes to the slow pace of evolutionary change. Nevertheless, even such small and slow changes can have a significant cumulative impact on both the genotypes and phenotypes of any population.

Through the process of natural selection, populations generally become well adapted to their environments. For example, consider the plants and animals that survive in the deserts of the western United States. Members of the cactus family have extensive root networks close to the surface of the soil, enabling them to soak up the slightest bit of moisture; they are able to store large quantities of water whenever it is available; they are shaped so as to expose the smallest possible surface to the dry air and are generally leafless as mature plants, thereby preventing water loss through evaporation; and a covering of spines discourages animals from chewing into the juicy flesh of the plant. Desert animals are also adapted to their environment. The kangaroo rat can survive without drinking water; many reptiles live

in burrows where the temperature is lower; most animals are nocturnal or active only in the cool of the night. By extrapolation, biologists assume that the same adaptive mechanisms also work on behavioral traits.

Natural selection often promotes stability instead of change. **Stabilizing selection** occurs in populations that are already well adapted or where change would be disadvantageous (**Figure 2.14**). In cases where change is disadvantageous, natural selection will favor the retention of allele frequencies more or less as they are. Evolution tends not to proceed as a steady, stately progression over vast periods of time. Instead, the life history of most species consists of relative stability or gradual change punctuated by shorter periods of more rapid change (or extinction) when altered conditions require new adaptations or when a new mutation produces an opportunity to adapt to some other available environment. According to the fossil record, most species survive between 3 and 5 million years (Thomson, 1997).

Despite the importance of adaptation and natural selection in shaping living organisms, many traits have no adaptive function. All male mammals, for example, possess nipples, even though they serve no useful purpose. For female mammals, however, nipples are essential to reproductive success, which is why males have them. The two sexes are not separate entities, shaped independently by natural selection, but are variants upon a single body plan, elaborated in later embryology. All mammalian fetuses possess precursors of mammary glands, enlarging later in the development of females but remaining small and without function in males.

Further, traits that seem nonadaptive in the present may be coopted for later use, and traits that appear adaptive might have come about due to unrelated changes in the pattern of growth and development. For instance, the

stabilizing selection Natural selection acting to promote stability rather than change in a population's gene pool.

 Otorohanga Zoological Society

Figure 2.15 Disproportionate Eggs This x-ray showing the unusually large size of a kiwi egg illustrates that evolution does not continue by preplanned design but rather by a process of tinkering with preexisting body forms.

unusually large size of a kiwi's egg enhances the survivability of kiwi chicks, in that they are particularly large and capable when hatched (**Figure 2.15**). Nevertheless, large kiwi egg size probably did not evolve because the size is adaptive. Instead, kiwis evolved from an ancestor that was the size of an ostrich, and in birds, egg size reduces at a slower rate than does body size. Therefore, the outsized eggs of kiwi birds seem to be no more than a developmental byproduct of a reduction in body size (Gould, 1991a).

Similarly, an existing adaptation may come under strong selective pressure for some new purpose. For instance, insect wings arose as structures that were used to "row," and later skim, across the surface of the water (Kaiser, 1994). Later, the larger ones by chance proved useful for purposes of flight. In both the kiwi eggs and the insect wings, what we see is natural selection operating as "a creative scavenger, taking what is available and putting it to new use" (Dorit, 1997, p. 475).

Natural selection differs from the concept of design as it works only with the existing store of genetic variation; it cannot create something entirely new. Variation protects populations from dying out or species from going extinct in changing environments. Evolution is a process of tinkering. Often tinkering involves balancing beneficial and harmful effects of a specific allele in a specific environment, as the following case study of sickle-cell anemia illustrates.

The Case of Sickle-Cell Anemia

Among human beings, **sickle-cell anemia** is a particularly well-studied case of adaptation. This painful disease, in which the oxygen-carrying red blood cells change shape (sickle) and clog the finest parts of the

circulatory system, first came to the attention of geneticists in Chicago who observed that the disease disproportionately impacted African Americans. Further investigation found that populations that live in a clearly defined belt across Central Africa had the sickle-cell allele at surprisingly high frequencies. Geneticists were curious to know why such a harmful hereditary disability persisted in these populations. **Figure 2.16** demonstrates the sickling shape of these abnormal red blood cells.

According to the theory of natural selection, any alleles that are harmful will tend to disappear from the group because the individuals who are homozygous for the abnormality generally die—are "selected out"—before they reproduce. Why, then, has this seemingly harmful condition persisted in populations from Central Africa?

The answer to this mystery began to emerge when researchers noticed that a particularly deadly form of malaria (falciparum malaria) was prevalent in the same areas that had high rates of sickle-cell anemia (**Figure 2.17**). This severe form of malaria causes many deaths or, in those who survive, high fever that significantly interferes with individuals' reproductive abilities. Moreover, researchers discovered hemoglobin abnormalities among people living in parts of the Arabian peninsula, Greece, Algeria, Syria, and India, all regions where malaria is (or was) common. Thus, selection favored heterozygous individuals with normal and sickling hemoglobin. The loss of alleles for abnormal hemoglobin caused by the death of those homozygous for it (from sickle-cell anemia) was balanced out by the loss of alleles for normal hemoglobin, as those homozygous for normal hemoglobin were more likely to die from malaria.

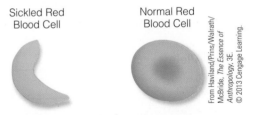

Sickled Red Blood Cell   Normal Red Blood Cell

From Haviland/Prins/Walrath/ McBride, *The Essence of Anthropology*, 3E. © 2013 Cengage Learning.

Figure 2.16 Sickle and Normal Red Blood Cells Sickle-cell anemia is caused by a genetic mutation in a single base of the hemoglobin gene, resulting in abnormal hemoglobin, called hemoglobin S or Hb^S. (The normal hemoglobin allele is called Hb^A not to be confused with blood type A.) Those afflicted by the disease are homozygous for the Hb^S allele, and all their red blood cells "sickle." Co-dominance is observable with the sickle and normal alleles. Heterozygotes (genotype $Hb^A Hb^S$) make 50 percent normal hemoglobin and 50 percent sickle hemoglobin. Shown here is a sickled red blood cell compared to a normal red blood cell.

sickle-cell anemia An inherited form of anemia produced by a mutation in the hemoglobin protein that causes the red blood cells to assume a sickle shape.

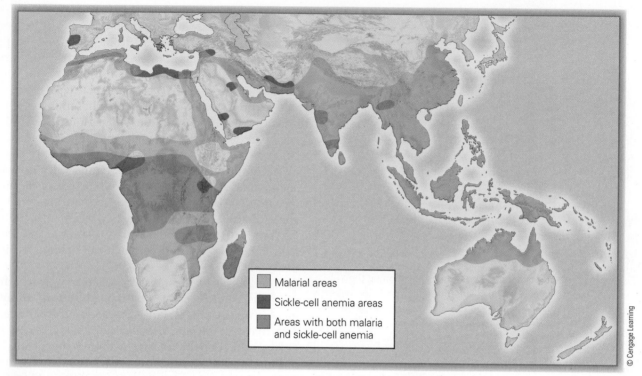

Figure 2.17 **The Distribution of Malaria and the Sickle-Cell Allele** In regions with a high incidence of falciparum malaria, people native to these areas have a higher than normal rate of the allele that causes sickle-cell anemia. Researchers have surmised that natural selection preserved the allele for the sickle-cell trait to protect individuals from the devastating effects of malaria.

The mutation that causes hemoglobin to sickle consists of a change in a single base of DNA, so it can arise readily by chance (**Figure 2.18**). The resulting mutant allele codes for an amino acid substitution in the beta chain of the hemoglobin protein that leads red blood cells to take on a characteristic sickle shape. In homozygous individuals with two sickle-hemoglobin alleles, collapse and clumping of the abnormal red blood cells block the capillaries and create tissue damage—causing the symptoms of sickle-cell disease.

Afflicted individuals commonly die before reaching adulthood. Except under low oxygen or other stressful conditions, heterozygous individuals suffer no ill effects. In regions with malaria, the heterozygous condition actually improves individuals' resilience to malaria and their reproductive success relative to the "normal" homozygous condition.

This example also points out how adaptations tend to be specific; the abnormal hemoglobin was adaptive only in environments in which the malarial parasite flourished.

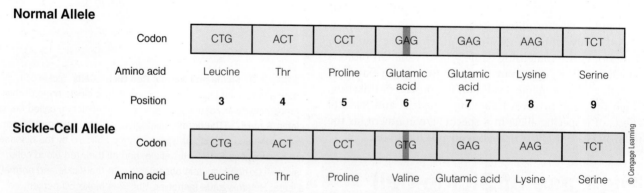

Figure 2.18 **Simple Mutation, Dramatic Consequences** Mutation of a single base of DNA can result in a dramatically different protein. Pictured here are codons 3 through 9 for the beta chain of hemoglobin, the protein that carries oxygen in red blood cells and the amino acids these codons specify. The top row depicts the normal allele, and the bottom row shows the single substitution that makes the red blood cells bend into a sickle shape (clogging the capillary beds and causing great pain, which is what occurs with sickle-cell anemia). Sickling occurs because the amino acid valine, compared to glutamic acid in the normal allele, gives the hemoglobin molecule different properties. The beta chain is 146 amino acids long. A simple mutation (the substitution of thymine for adenine in position 6 as indicated in red) has dramatic and tragic consequences.

When individuals adapted to malarial regions came to regions relatively free of malaria, the abnormal hemoglobin became comparatively disadvantageous. Although the rates of sickle-cell trait remain relatively high among African Americans—about 9 percent have the sickling trait—this has significantly declined from the 22 percent estimated among the first African captives who were shipped across the Atlantic and sold as slaves. A similar decline in the sickle-cell allele would occur over the course of several generations in malarial zones if this deadly disease were brought under control.

This example also illustrates the important role culture plays in biological adaptation. In Africa, the severe form of malaria was not a significant problem until humans abandoned food foraging for farming a few thousand years ago. In order to farm, people had to clear areas of the natural forest cover. In the forest, decaying vegetation on the forest floor gave the ground an absorbent quality so that the heavy rainfall rapidly soaked into the soil. But once stripped of its natural vegetation, the soil lost this quality. In addition, without the forest canopy to break the force of the rainfall, the heavy rains compacted the soil further. The stagnant puddles that formed after rains provided the perfect breeding environment for the type of mosquito that hosts the malarial parasite. These mosquitoes then began to flourish and transmit the malarial parasite to humans.

Thus, humans unwittingly created the kind of environment that made a disadvantageous trait, the abnormal hemoglobin associated with sickle-cell anemia, advantageous. While the biological process of evolution accounts for the frequency of the sickle-cell allele, cultural processes shape the environment to which humans adapt.

Adaptation and Physical Variation

Anthropologists study biological diversity in terms of **clines**, or the continuous gradation over space in the form or frequency of a trait. The spatial distribution or cline for the sickle-cell allele allowed anthropologists to identify the adaptive function of this gene in a malarial environment. Clinal analysis of a continuous trait such as body shape, which is controlled by a series of genes, allows anthropologists to interpret human global variation in body build as an adaptation to climate.

Generally, people long native to regions with cold climates tend to have greater body bulk (not to be equated with fat) relative to their extremities (arms and legs) than do people native to regions with hot climates, who tend to be relatively tall and slender. Interestingly, tall, slender bodies show up in human evolution perhaps as early as 1.5 million years ago. A person with larger body bulk and relatively short extremities may suffer more from summer heat than someone with a slender body and relatively long extremities. But this person will conserve needed body heat under cold conditions because a bulky body has less surface area relative to volume. In hot, open country, by contrast, people benefit from a long, slender body that can get rid of excess heat quickly. A small slender body can also promote heat loss due to a high surface area to volume ratio.

In addition to these sorts of very long-term effects that climate may have imposed on human variation, climate can also contribute to human variation through its impact on the process of growth and development (developmental adaptation). For example, some of the biological mechanisms for withstanding cold or dissipating heat have been shown to vary depending upon the climate an individual experiences as a child. People spending their youth in very cold climates develop circulatory system modifications that allow them to remain comfortable at temperatures that those from warmer climates cannot tolerate. Similarly, hot climate promotes the development of a higher density of sweat glands, creating a more efficient system for sweating to keep the body cool.

Cultural processes complicate studies of biological adaptation to climate. For example, a poor diet during childhood affects the growth process and ultimately impacts adult body shape and size. Clothing also complicates these studies. In fact, culture rather than biology accounts for much of the way people adapt to cold. For instance, to cope with bitter Arctic climates, the Iñuit peoples of northern Canada long ago developed efficient clothing to keep the body warm. The Iñuit (and other Eskimos) created artificial tropical environments for themselves inside their clothing. Such cultural adaptations allow humans to inhabit the entire globe.

Some anthropologists have suggested that variation in features such as face and eye shape relate to climate. For example, biological anthropologists once proposed that the flat facial profile and round head—common in populations native to East and Central Asia, as well as Arctic North America—derive from adaptation to very cold environments. Though these features are common in Asian and Native American populations, considerable physical variation exists within each population. Some individuals who spread to North America from Asia have a head shape that is more common among Europeans. Furthermore, genetic drift could also account for regional variation of traits. Because specific examples of adaptation, particularly of continuous traits, can be difficult to prove, scientists sometimes suggest that their colleagues' scenarios about adaptation are "Just So" stories.

Macroevolution and the Process of Speciation

While *microevolution* refers to changes in the allele frequencies of populations, **macroevolution** focuses on **speciation**—the formation of new species—and on

---

clines The gradual changes in the frequency of an allele or trait over space.
macroevolution Evolution above the species level or leading to the formation of new species.
speciation The process of forming new species.

the evolutionary relationships among groups of species. The microevolutionary forces of mutation, genetic drift, gene flow, and natural selection can lead to macroevolutionary change as species diverge.

As defined earlier in the chapter, *species*—a population or group of populations capable of interbreeding and producing viable, fertile offspring—are reproductively isolated. The bullfrogs in one farmer's pond are the same species as those in a neighboring pond, even though the two populations may never actually interbreed; in theory, they could interbreed if brought together. But isolated populations may be in the process of evolving into different species, and it is hard to tell exactly when they become biologically distinct.

Certain factors, known as *isolating mechanisms*, can separate breeding populations and lead to the appearance of new species. Because isolation prevents gene flow, changes that affect the gene pool of one population cannot be introduced into the gene pool of the other. Random mutation may introduce new alleles in one of the isolated populations but not in the other. Genetic drift and natural selection may affect the two populations in different ways. Over time, as the two populations continue to differ from each other, speciation occurs in a branching fashion known as **cladogenesis**. Speciation can also happen without branching, as a single population accumulates sufficient new mutations over time to be considered a separate species. This process is known as **anagenesis** (Figure 2.19). Speciation is inferred in the fossil record when a group of organisms takes on a different appearance over time.

Because speciation is a process, it can occur at various rates. Scholars generally consider speciation through the process of natural selection as proposed by Darwin to occur at a slow rate. In this model, speciation happens as organisms become better adapted to their environments. Sometimes, however, speciation can occur quite rapidly. For example, a genetic mutation such as one involving a key *regulatory gene*, a gene that turns other genes off and on, can lead to the formation of a new body plan. Such genetic accidents may involve material that is broken off, transposed, or transferred from one chromosome to another.

Genes that regulate the growth and development of an organism may have a major effect on its adult form. Scientists have discovered certain key genes called *homeobox genes* that are responsible for large-scale effects on the growth and development of the organism (Figure 2.20). If a new body plan happens to be adaptive, natural selection will maintain this new form during long periods of time rather than promoting change.

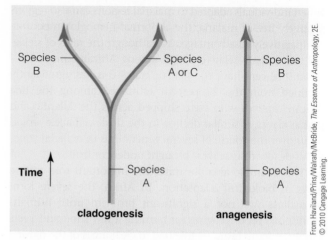

From Haviland/Prins/Walrath/McBride, *The Essence of Anthropology*, 2E. © 2010 Cengage Learning.

Figure 2.19 Mechanisms of Speciation Cladogenesis occurs as different populations of an ancestral species become reproductively isolated. Through genetic drift and differential selection, the number of descendant species increases. By contrast, anagenesis can occur through a process of variational change that takes place as small differences in traits that (by chance) are advantageous in a particular environment accumulate in a species' gene pool. Over time, this may produce sufficient change to transform an old species into a new one. Genetic drift may also account for anagenesis.

© David Scharf/Photo Researchers, Inc.

Figure 2.20 Homeobox Genes and New Body Plans Sometimes mutation in a single gene can cause reorganization of an organism's body plan. Here the "bithorax" homeobox gene has caused this fruit fly to have two thoraxes and two sets of wings. Another homeobox gene, "antennepedia," causes legs to develop in the place of antennae on the heads of fruit flies.

---

cladogenesis Speciation through a branching mechanism whereby an ancestral population gives rise to two or more descendant populations.

anagenesis A sustained directional shift in a population's average characteristics.

punctuated equilibria A model of macroevolutionary change that suggests evolution occurs via long periods of stability or stasis punctuated by periods of rapid change.

(a) Ground finch
Main food: seeds
Beak: heavy

(b) Tree finch
Main food: leaves, buds,
blossoms, fruits
Beak: thick, short

(c) Tree finch (called
woodpecker finch)
Main food: insects
Beak: stout, straight

(d) Ground finch (known
as warbler finch)
Main food: insects
Beak: slender

From Jurmain/Kilgore/Trevathan/Ciochon. *Introduction to Physical Anthropology*, 2009–2010, 12E. © 2010 Cengage Learning Inc.

Figure 2.21 Adaptation and Darwin's Finches Scientists have begun to unravel the genetic mechanisms controlling the shape and size of beaks of the finches studied by Darwin on the Galapagos Islands. Darwin noted how beak shape and size were related to each species' diet and used the birds to illustrate adaptation to a particular ecological niche. Finches with blunt crushing beaks are seedeaters while others with long probing beaks pick between cactus thorns for food or use the beaks to reach insects.

Paleontologists Stephen Jay Gould and Niles Eldredge have proposed that speciation occurs in a pattern of **punctuated equilibria**, or the alternation between periods of rapid speciation and times of stability. Often this model of evolutionary change is contrasted with speciation through adaptation, sometimes referred to as *Darwinian gradualism*. A close look at the genetics and the fossil record indicates that evolutionary change occurs via both mechanisms.

Genetic mechanisms underlie both rapid and gradual changes because mutations can have small or large effects. It is particularly interesting to see how molecular genetics supports Darwinian evolutionary change. For example, the tailoring of beak shape and size to diet among finches on the Galapagos Islands, in the Pacific Ocean west of Ecuador, constituted Darwin's classic example of natural selection

(Figure 2.21). Recently, scientists identified two proteins along with the underlying genes that control beak shape and size in birds. It is all the more impressive that Darwin was able to make his inferences about natural selection without the benefit of molecular genetics.

In biological terms, evolution accounts for all that humans share as well as the broad array of human diversity. Evolution is also responsible for the creation of new species over time. Primatologist Frans de Waal has said, "Evolution is a magnificent idea that has won over essentially everyone in the world willing to listen to scientific arguments" (de Waal, 2001, p. 77). We will return to the topic of human evolution in chapters that follow, but first we will look at the other living primates in order to understand the kinds of animals they are, what they have in common with humans, and what distinguishes the various forms.

CHAPTER CHECKLIST

How does evolutionary theory differ from creation stories?

● Scientific theories are based on testable hypotheses.

● Unlike existential or faith-based explanations, scientific theories of evolution propose mechanisms to account for the diversity of life on earth.

How are living things classified, and how did this system come about?

● The science of taxonomy classifies living organisms into a series of progressively more inclusive categories on the basis of internal and external visual similarities.

● In the 18th century, Carolus Linnaeus devised his *System Naturae*, the first system to classify living things then known on the basis of similarities in body structure, body function, and sequence of bodily growth.

● Modern taxonomy still uses the basic Linnaean system but now looks at such characteristics as chemical reactions of blood, protein structure, and the makeup of the genetic material itself. These new kinds of data have led to the revision of some existing taxonomies.

● Species, the smallest working units in biological classificatory systems, are reproductively isolated populations or groups of populations capable of interbreeding to produce fertile offspring.

What is evolution, and when was this central biological theory formulated?

● Charles Darwin formulated a theory of evolution in 1859. His conception of evolution was based on differential reproductive success among members of a population (a group of interbreeding individuals) that becomes adapted to its environment through natural selection.

● Today, evolution is understood in terms of the four evolutionary forces—mutation, genetic drift, gene flow, and natural selection—that affect the genetic structures of populations. Evolution at the level of population genetics is change in allele frequencies, which is also known as microevolution.

● Different versions or alternate forms of a gene for a given trait are called alleles. The total number of different alleles of genes available to a population is called its gene pool.

● Macroevolution focuses on the formation of new species (speciation) and on the evolutionary relationships among groups of species.

What is the molecular basis of evolution?

● Genes, the units of heredity, are segments of molecules of DNA (deoxyribonucleic acid), and the entire sequence of DNA is known as the genome.

● DNA is a complex molecule resembling two strands of rope twisted around each other with ladderlike rungs connecting the two strands.

● The sequence of bases along the DNA molecule directs the production of proteins. Proteins, in turn, constitute specific identifiable traits such as blood type. Just about everything in the human body is made of or by proteins, and human DNA provides the instructions for the thousands of proteins that keep us alive and healthy.

How do cells and organisms reproduce?

● DNA molecules have the unique property of being able to produce exact copies of themselves. As long as no errors are made in the process of replication, new daughter cells will be exact genetic copies of the parent cell.

● DNA molecules are located on chromosomes, structures found in the nucleus of each cell. Chromosomes consist of two sister chromatids, which are exact copies of each other.

● Each kind of organism has a characteristic number of chromosomes, which are usually found in pairs in sexually reproducing organisms. Humans have twenty-three pairs of chromosomes.

● Mitosis, one kind of cell division that results in new cells, begins when the chromosomes (hence, the genes) replicate, forming a duplicate of the original pair of chromosomes in the nucleus. Sister chromatids separate during mitosis and form identical daughter cells.

● Meiosis is related to sexual reproduction; it begins with the replication of original chromosomes, but these are divided into four cells, in humans each containing twenty-three single chromosomes. Fertilization, the union of an egg and a sperm cell, reestablishes the normal human number of twenty-three pairs of chromosomes.

How do different traits get inherited across generations?

● In the late 19th century Gregor Mendel discovered the particulate nature of heredity: Individuals inherit traits independently from each parent.

● Dominant alleles are able to mask the presence of recessive alleles. The allele for type A blood in humans, for example, is dominant to the allele for type O blood. Alleles that are both expressed when present are termed *co-dominant*. For example, an individual with the alleles for type A and type B blood has the AB blood type.

● *Phenotype* refers to the physical characteristics of an organism, whereas *genotype* refers to its genetic composition. Two organisms may have different genotypes but the same phenotype. An individual with the type A blood phenotype may possess either the AO or the AA genotype, having inherited one allele from each parent.

How do the four evolutionary forces contribute to the diversity of life on earth?

● Mutation provides the ultimate source of genetic variation. These changes in DNA may be helpful or harmful to the individual organism, though most mutations are simply neutral. Although mutations are inevitable given the nature of cellular chemistry, environmental factors—such as heat, chemicals, or radiation—can increase the mutation rate.

● *Genetic drift* refers to the effects of random events on the gene pool of a small population. Genetic drift may have been an important factor in human evolution because until 10,000 years ago humans lived in small isolated populations.

● Gene flow, the introduction of new variants of genes from nearby populations, distributes new variation to all populations and serves to prevent speciation.

● Natural selection, the evolutionary force involved in adaptive change, reduces the frequency of alleles for harmful or maladaptive traits within a population and increases the frequency of alleles for adaptive traits.

What are some examples of human adaptation through natural selection?

● A well-studied example of adaptation through natural selection in humans is inheritance of the trait for sickling red blood cells. The sickle-cell trait, caused by the inheritance of an abnormal form of hemoglobin, is an adaptation to life in regions in which malaria is common.

● Physical anthropologists have determined that some human physical variation appears related to climatic adaptation. People native to cold climates tend to have greater body bulk relative to their extremities than individuals from hot climates; the latter tend to be relatively tall and slender.

● Studies involving body build and climate are complicated by other factors such as the effects on physique of diet and clothing.

How are new species formed?

● Speciation can occur in a branching fashion (clado-genesis) or without branching (anagenesis) as a single population accumulates sufficient new mutations over time to be considered a separate species.

● Microevolutionary forces of mutation, genetic drift, gene flow, and natural selection can lead to macroevolutionary change, but the tempo of evolutionary change varies.

● A mutation in a regulatory gene can bring about rapid change. The punctuated equilibrium model proposes that macroevolution is characterized by long spans of relative stability interspersed with periods of rapid change.

QUESTIONS FOR REFLECTION

1. Have genetics and DNA become a part of your everyday experience? If so, how? How has the popularization of the human genetic code challenged your conception of what it means to be human? How much of your life, or of the lives of the people around you, is dictated by the structure of DNA?

2. Scientific fact and theory can challenge other belief systems. Is it possible for scientific models of human evolution and religious stories of creation to coexist? How do you personally reconcile science and religion?

3. The four evolutionary forces—mutation, genetic drift, gene flow, and natural selection—all affect biological variation. Some are at work in individuals while others function at the population level. Compare and contrast these evolutionary forces, outlining their contributions to biological variation.

4. The frequency of the sickle-cell allele in populations provides a classic example of adaptation on a genetic level. Describe the benefits of this deadly allele. Are mutations good or bad?

5. Are you likely to witness the appearance of a new species in your lifetime? If so, how might this come about? How would you recognize that this is truly a new species?

ONLINE STUDY RESOURCES

CourseMate

Access chapter-specific learning tools, including learning objectives, practice quizzes, videos, flash cards, glossaries, and more in your Anthropology CourseMate.

Log into **www.cengagebrain.com** to access the resources your instructor has assigned and to purchase materials.

Challenge Issue

One quick glance at this female gorilla and two children at play attests to all that we share with our closest living relatives. We are equipped to read their body language, their facial expressions. Our bodies possess the same basic form. In them we can discern the joy of play and the ease across generations, perhaps recalling our own experiences just from looking at them. It is no small wonder, then, that the other primates have long fascinated humans. But despite our biological and emotional closeness, humans threaten the survival of our primate cousins. Today, largely due to human action, all of the other great ape species—chimps, bonobos, gorillas, and orangutans—are endangered. The same holds true for many other primate species. We humans have brought war, a hunger for natural resources, and infectious disease into their habitats, with devastating results. If the difference between our primate relatives and us is our greater intelligence and complex language, it is time to use both these gifts to protect them. We humans face the challenge of speaking out and engaging in actions that ensure that other primates do not become extinct.

Living Primates

3

In October 1960, the young Jane Goodall sent word back to her mentor, paleoanthropologist Louis Leakey, that she had observed two chimps turning sticks into tools for fishing termites out of their nesting mounds. Leakey replied, "Now we must redefine 'tool,' redefine 'man,' or accept chimpanzees as humans" (Jane Goodall Institute, 2012).

Field studies of primates by Western scientists have always contained a degree of anthropocentrism and a focus on what nonhuman primates can tell us about ourselves. Indeed, that is the purpose of this chapter. By looking at the biology and behavior of the primates, we gain a firmer understanding of those characteristics we share with other primates, as well as those that distinguish us from them and make us distinctively human. Studying communication and tool use among our primate cousins today, for example, can help anthropologists reconstruct how and why humans developed as they did. Studies of primate behavior might unravel an old nature–nurture question: How much of human behavior is biologically determined and how much of it derives from culture?

Today, we are the only primate to inhabit the entire globe. As human population size rises to unsustainable levels, many primate groups are hovering on the brink of extinction. **Figure 3.1** shows the natural global distribution of living and fossil primates. It also indicates where the twenty-five most endangered species are struggling to survive. In this light, the purpose of this chapter is not just to learn more about ourselves, but to learn how to protect our primate cousins and the planet we share.

IN THIS CHAPTER YOU WILL LEARN TO

- Identify the key methods of primatologists and the ethics they uphold.

- Situate primates in the animal kingdom and compare them to other mammals and reptiles.

- Construct evolutionary relationships among the primates.

- Recognize the basic features of primate anatomy and behavior.

- Distinguish the characteristics of the five natural groups of primates.

- Identify critical issues and methods in primate conservation.

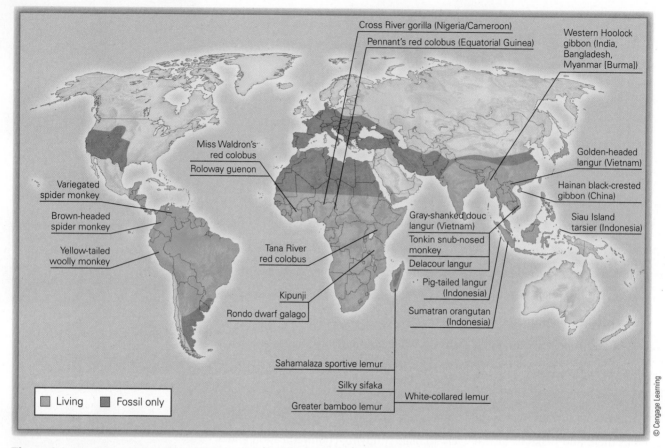

Figure 3.1 The Global Distribution of Living and Fossil Nonhuman Primates In the past, when more of the world was covered by tropical forests, the range of primates was far greater than it is now. Today, human activity threatens our primate cousins throughout the globe. The figure also shows the location of the twenty-five most endangered primate species today.

Methods and Ethics in Primatology

Just as anthropologists employ diverse methods to study humans, primatologists use a variety of methods to study the biology, behavior, and evolutionary history of our closest living relatives. Some primatologists concentrate on the comparative anatomy of ancient skeletons, whereas others trace evolutionary relationships by studying the comparative physiology and genetics of living species. Primatologists study the biology and behavior of living primates both in their natural habitats and in captivity in zoos, primate research colonies, and learning laboratories.

The primatologist most people recognize is Jane Goodall, a world-renowned British researcher who has devoted her career to in-depth observation of chimpanzees in their natural habitat. While documenting the range and nuance of chimpanzee behavior, she has also championed conservation of primate habitats and humane treatment of primates in captivity. The philosophy of conservation and preservation has led to further innovations in research methods. For example, primatologists have developed a number of noninvasive methods that allow them to study primate biology and behavior in the field while minimizing physical disruption. Primatologists gather hair, feces, and other body secretions left by the primates in the environment for later analysis in the laboratory. These analyses provide invaluable information about characteristics such as dietary habits or genetic relatedness among a group of individuals.

Work with captive animals provides more than knowledge about the basic biology of primates. It has also allowed primatologists to document the humanity of our primate cousins. Many of the amazing linguistic and conceptual abilities of primates became known through studies of captive animals. Individual primatologists have devoted their careers to working with primates in captivity, teaching them to communicate through pictures on a computer screen or American Sign Language. Of course, even compassionate captivity imposes stress on primates. Still, the knowledge gained through these studies ultimately will contribute to primate conservation and survival.

At first glance it might seem inherently more humane to work with animals in the field compared to captivity. But even field studies raise important ethical issues for primatologists to consider. Primatologists must maintain an awareness of how their presence affects the behavior of the group. For example, does becoming tolerant of human observers make the primates more vulnerable? Primates habituated to humans commonly range beyond established wilderness preserves and come in close contact with other humans who may be more interested in hunting than observing. Contact between primates and humans can also expose endangered primates to infectious diseases carried by humans.

Whether working with primates in captivity or in the field, primatologists seriously consider the well-being of the primates they study. Primatologist Michele Goldsmith explores these issues in depth in this chapter's Original Study.

ORIGINAL STUDY

Gorilla Ecotourism: Ethical Considerations for Conservation *BY MICHELE GOLDSMITH*

For the past 13 years, I have been studying and writing about the impact of ecotourism on mountain gorillas living in Bwindi Impenetrable National Park, Uganda. As a biological anthropologist and conservationist, my main focus has been on habituation, which is a necessary prerequisite for tourism, and how it influences gorilla behavior and well-being. *Habituation* refers to the acceptance by wild animals of a human observer as a neutral element in their environment. Although information from habituated primates has been instrumental in providing a wealth of information for research and conservation, little attention has been given to the costs these animals bear when their fear of humans is removed.

Primatologist Michele Goldsmith making observations of gorillas in the field.

The first impacts of habituation occur during the process of acclimation. Habituators follow the animals from a distance and, over time, slowly get closer and closer. Many factors contribute to the speed and success of the process, such as the terrain (open areas versus thick forest), prior exposure to humans, hunting pressure, and so on. The process can be stressful for the gorillas and even dangerous for the habituators. During the habituation process, a group of western lowland gorillas exhibited fear in their vocalizations, increased their aggressive behavior, and changed their daily ranging pattern.[a] Such fear and stress can lead to loss of reproductive function and to a weakened immune system. Aggressive behavior has resulted in habituators being charged by silverback males with some humans being hit and bitten.

Once fully habituated, gorillas may then experience unforeseen consequences. For example, gorillas that have lost their fear of humans are especially vulnerable to hunting. Five Bwindi gorillas habituated for research were found dead, having been killed by poachers so they could capture a young infant gorilla. In addition, humans have also brought great instability and warfare to areas where gorilla populations live. Sudden evacuation of research and tourist sites leaves behind habituated gorillas that become easy targets for the poacher's gun.

With regard to long-term changes in ecology and behavior, my research has shown that the diet, nesting, and ranging patterns of habituated gorilla groups are different from other "wild" gorillas in the same study area. The Nkuringo group, habituated in 1998 for tourism that started in 2004, lives near the edge of the protected Bwindi Impenetrable National Park. These gorillas spend close to 90 percent of their time outside the park, in and around human-inhabited areas and farms. These behavioral changes have many costs to the gorillas, such as increased contact with humans and human waste,

Michele L. Goldsmith/Photograph © Nate Boesch

Posho, a blackback gorilla from the Nkuringo tourist-habituated group, looks out over an area outside Bwindi Impenetrable National Park.

conflict with farmers that could result in injury, increased exposure to hunting given that these areas are mostly open fields, and increased risk of disease transmission.[b]

Another effect on behavior may be an artificial increase in group size. For example, a group of some forty-four animals now exists in the Virungas, where the average group size is usually ten individuals. Furthermore, it is thought that, due to their fear of humans, "wild" adult male gorillas that would normally challenge other dominant males are either deterred from presenting a challenge or are less successful in their challenge against habituated groups.

Perhaps the biggest threat to habituated great apes is disease.[c] There are over nineteen viruses and eighteen parasites that are known to infect both great apes and humans. These diseases have been responsible for between sixty-three and eighty-seven ape deaths in habituated groups (both research and tourist groups) in the Virungas, Bwindi, Mahale, Tai, and Gombe. As for the gorillas in Bwindi, it has been shown that parasites such as *Cryptosporidium* and *Giardia* are most prevalent in habituated groups living near humans along the border of the park.

Is gorilla tourism sustainable? Early gorilla tourism in the 1980s did appear to be a salvation because it helped to halt poaching and provide value to the living animal that was lacking. However, now the balance seems to have tipped. As of 2011, *61 percent* of the entire mountain gorilla population *is now habituated* for either research (17%) or tourism (44%). We know habituated gorillas are more susceptible to stress, experience changes in their behavior, and are more vulnerable to human disease. The fear remains that one deadly, highly infectious disease could travel quickly through the small isolated populations and leave few survivors. *What is most important is not habituating more groups but better managing of the already habituated groups.* Ethical considerations are crucial as we continue to put gorilla populations at risk.[d] Habituation, especially for tourism, may not be an ape's salvation.

Michele L. Goldsmith is a primatologist who has been studying the behavioral ecology of gorillas in Uganda and the Congo since 1991.

[a]Blom, A., et al. (2004). Behavioral responses of gorillas to habituation in the Dzanga-Ndoki National Park, Central African Republic. *International Journal of Primatology 25*, 179–196.

[b]Goldsmith, M. L., Glick, J., & Ngabirano, E. (2006). Gorillas living on the edge: Literally and figuratively. In N. E. Newton-Fisher, et al. (Eds.), *Primates of Western Uganda* (pp. 405–422). New York: Springer.

[c]Woodford, M. H., Butynski, T. M., & Karesh W. (2002). Habituating the great apes: The disease risks. *Oryx 36*, 153–160.

[d]Goldsmith, M. L. (2005). Habituating primates for field study: Ethical considerations for great apes. In T. Turner (Ed.), *Biological anthropology and ethics: From repatriation to genetic identity* (pp. 49–64). New York: SUNY Press.

Primates as Mammals

Biologists classify humans within the primate order, a subgroup of the class Mammalia. The other primates include lemurs, lorises, tarsiers, monkeys, and apes. Humans—together with chimpanzees, bonobos, gorillas, orangutans, gibbons, and siamangs—form the hominoids, colloquially known as apes, a superfamily within the primate order. Biologically speaking, as hominoids, humans are apes.

The primates are only one of several different kinds of mammals, such as rodents, carnivores, and ungulates (hoofed mammals). Primates, like other mammals, are intelligent animals, having more in the way of brains than reptiles or other kinds of vertebrates. Increased brainpower and the mammalian growth and development form the biological basis of the flexible behavior patterns typical of mammals. In most species, the young are born live, the egg being retained within the womb of the female until the embryo achieves an advanced state of growth.

Once born, the young receive milk from their mothers' mammary glands, the physical feature from which the class Mammalia gets its name (**Figure 3.2**). During this period of infant dependency, young mammals learn many of the things they will need for survival as adults. Primates in general, and apes in particular, have a long period of infant and childhood dependency in which the young learn the ways of their social group. Thus, primate behavioral patterns derive from mammalian primate biology.

In this regard, a comparison of mammals to reptiles clarifies much about the primate adaptation. The mammalian diversity with which we are familiar today is the product of an **adaptive radiation**: the rapid diversification of an evolving population following a change in the environment. Evidence from ancient skeletons indicates the first mammals appeared over 200 million years ago as small, often **nocturnal** (active at night) creatures. With the mass extinction of many reptiles including the dinosaurs some 65 million years ago, a number of existing **ecological niches**, or functional positions in their habitats, became available to mammals. A species' niche incorporates factors such as diet, activity, terrain, vegetation, predators, prey, and climate. New niches opened as the earth cooled during this time period, permitting mammals to fill them.

By chance, mammals were **preadapted**—possessing the biological equipment to take advantage of the new opportunities available to them through the mass extinction of the dinosaurs and other reptiles. As **homeotherms**, mammals have the ability to maintain a constant body temperature. Mammals can be active at a wide range of environmental temperatures, whereas reptiles, as **isotherms** that take their body temperature from the surrounding environment, become progressively sluggish as the surrounding temperature drops.

However, mammals require a diet high in calories in order to maintain a constant body temperature. To meet this need, mammals developed superior senses of smell and

Martin Harvey/Getty Images/Peter Arnold

Figure 3.2 Nursing Chimp Nursing their young is an important part of the general mammalian tendency to invest high amounts of energy into rearing relatively few young at a time. The reptilian pattern is to lay many eggs, with the young fending for themselves. Ape mothers tend to nurse their young for four or five years. The practice of bottle-feeding infants in North America and Europe is a massive departure from the ape pattern. Although the health benefits for mothers (such as lowered breast cancer rates) and children (strengthened immune systems) are clearly documented, cultural norms sometimes present obstacles to breastfeeding. In the United States, for example, only 44 percent of mothers were breastfeeding their 6-month-old infants. By contrast, across the globe women nurse their children on average for about three years.

adaptive radiation The rapid diversification of an evolving population as it adapts to a variety of available niches.

nocturnal Active at night and at rest during the day.

ecological niche A species' way of life considered in the full context of its environment including factors such as diet, activity, terrain, vegetation, predators, prey, and climate.

preadapted Possessing characteristics that, by chance, are advantageous in future environmental conditions.

homeotherm An animal that maintains a relatively constant body temperature despite environmental fluctuations.

isotherm An animal whose body temperature rises or falls according to the temperature of the surrounding environment.

hearing relative to reptiles. The mammalian pattern also differs from reptiles in terms of how they care for their young. Compared to reptiles, mammalian species are **k-selected**. This means that they produce relatively few offspring at a time, providing them with considerable parental care. Reptiles are **r-selected**, which means that they produce many young at a time and invest little effort caring for their young after they are born. Although among mammals some species are relatively more k- or r-selected, the higher energy requirements of mammals, entailed by parental investment and the maintenance of a constant body temperature, demand more nutrition than that required by reptiles.

Mammals tend to be more active than other members of the animal kingdom. Their high activity levels depend upon a relatively constant body temperature, an efficient respiratory system featuring a separation between the nasal (nose) and mouth cavities (allowing them to breathe while they eat), a diaphragm to assist in drawing in and letting out breath, and an efficient four-chambered heart that prevents mixing of oxygenated and deoxygenated blood.

Mammals possess a skeleton in which the limbs are positioned beneath the body, rather than out to the sides. This arrangement allows for direct support and easy, flexible movement. The bones of the limbs have joints constructed to permit growth in the young while simultaneously providing strong, hard joint surfaces that will stand up to the stresses of sustained activity. Mammals stop growing when they reach adulthood, whereas reptiles continue to grow throughout their lifespan.

Mammals and reptiles also differ in terms of their teeth. Reptilian teeth are pointed, peglike, and nearly identical in shape; mammalian teeth are specialized for particular purposes: incisors for nipping, gnawing, and cutting; canines for ripping, tearing, killing, and fighting; premolars for either slicing and tearing or crushing and grinding (depending on the kind of animal); and molars for crushing and grinding (**Figure 3.3**). This enables mammals to eat a wide variety of foods—an advantage given that they require more food than reptiles to sustain their high activity level.

But mammals pay a price for their dental specialization: Reptiles can repeatedly replace teeth throughout their lifespan, whereas mammals are limited to two sets. The first set serves the immature animal and is replaced by the "permanent" or adult teeth. The specializations of mammalian teeth allow species and evolutionary relationships to be identified through dental comparisons.

The earliest primatelike creatures emerged when a milder climate returned favoring the spread of dense tropical and

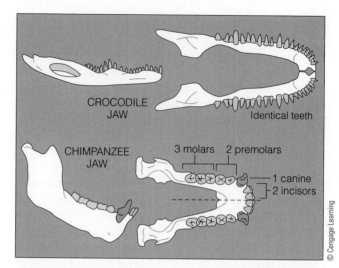

Figure 3.3 Comparison of Reptilian and Mammalian Teeth
The crocodile jaw, like the jaw of all reptiles, contains a series of nearly identical teeth. If a tooth breaks or falls out, a new tooth will emerge in its place. Mammals, by contrast, possess precise numbers of specialized teeth, each with a particular shape characteristic of the group, as indicated on the chimpanzee jaw: Incisors in front are shown in blue, canines behind in red, followed by two premolars and three molars in yellow (the last being the wisdom teeth in humans).

subtropical forests over much of the earth. The change in climate and habitat, combined with the earlier sudden extinction of dinosaurs, favored mammal diversification, including the evolutionary development of **arboreal** (tree-living) mammals from which primates evolved.

The ancestral primates possessed biological characteristics that allowed them to adapt to life in the forests. Their relatively small size enabled them to use tree branches not accessible to larger competitors and predators. Arboreal life opened up an abundant new food supply. The primates could gather leaves, flowers, fruits, insects, birds' eggs, and even nesting birds, rather than having to wait for them to fall to the ground. Natural selection favored those who judged depth correctly and gripped the branches tightly. Those individuals who survived life in the trees passed on their genes to succeeding generations.

Although the earliest primates were nocturnal, today most primate species are **diurnal**—active in the day. The transition to diurnal life in the trees involved important biological adjustments that helped shape the biology and behavior of humans today.

---

k-selected Reproduction involving the production of relatively few offspring with high parental investment in each.

r-selected Reproduction involving the production of large numbers of offspring with relatively low parental investment in each.

arboreal Living in the trees.

diurnal Active during the day and at rest at night.

Primate Taxonomy

Taxonomies reflect scientists' understanding of the natural world. Because scientific knowledge of evolutionary relationships among living things shifts over time, these classificatory systems are continually under construction. With new scientific discoveries, taxonomic categories have to be redrawn, and scientists often disagree about these categorical distinctions.

Taxonomies become contentious because classificatory systems make statements about evolutionary relationships. When creating a taxonomic grouping, scientists pay particular attention to features appearing more recently in evolutionary history that are unique to a group, calling these features **derived**. By contrast, **ancestral** characteristics occur not only in the present-day species but also in ancient forms. For example, bilateral symmetry, a body plan in which the right and left sides of the body are mirror images of each other, is an ancestral trait in humans. Because bilateral symmetry characterizes all vertebrates including fish, reptiles, birds, and mammals, it does not contribute to the reconstruction of evolutionary relationships among primates. Instead, scientists pay particular attention to recently evolved derived features in order to construct evolutionary relationships.

Convergent evolution—in which two more distant forms develop similarities to one another due to similar function rather than to shared ancestry—complicates taxonomic analyses. The classic examples of convergence involve analogies discussed in Chapter 2, such as the wings of birds and butterflies, which resemble each other because these structures serve similar functions. Convergent evolution occurs when an environment exerts similar pressures on distantly related organisms causing these species to resemble each other. Distinguishing the physical similarities produced by convergent evolution from those resulting from shared ancestry may be difficult.

Among more closely related groups, convergence of homologous structures can occur, such as when an identical structure present within several distinct species takes on a similar form in distantly related groups. Among the primates, an example is hind-leg dominance in both lemurs—a primate group found on Madagascar, an isolated but large island off the coast of Africa—and humans. Most primates possess hind limbs that are either shorter or of the same length as the forelimbs. Though their relationship is quite distant among the primates, lemurs and humans both have longer hind limbs because of their patterns of locomotion (**Figure 3.4**). Humans walk on two legs, while lemurs use their long legs to push off and propel them from tree to tree. Hind-leg dominance appeared separately in these two groups and is not indicative of a close evolutionary relationship. Only shared derived features can be used to establish relationships among groups of species.

Scientists have proposed alternate taxonomies to account for two hot spots in the classification of primates: one at the level of dividing the primate order into two suborders and the other at the level of the human family and subfamily. In both cases, the older classificatory systems, dating back to the time of Linnaeus, derive from shared visible physical characteristics. By contrast, the

Anup Shah/Getty Images/The Image Bank

Figure 3.4 Long-Legged Lemurs Lemurs, like humans, have longer hind limbs (legs) compared to their forelimbs (arms). Convergent evolution, rather than an especially close evolutionary relationship, accounts for this visible similarity. Long-legged lemurs move through the trees through vertical clinging and leaping, a mode of locomotion by which they cling to a tree trunk, push off with their powerful legs, do a "180," and grab another trunk. Human locomotion likewise benefits from long legs, but this characteristic evolved independently in these two primate groups.

newer taxonomic systems depend upon genetic analyses. Although molecular evidence has confirmed the close relationship between humans and other primates, these genetic comparisons have also challenged evolutionary relationships that had been inferred from physical characteristics. Laboratory methods involving genetic comparisons range from scanning species' entire genomes to comparing the precise sequences of base pairs in DNA, RNA, or amino acids in proteins.

Both genetic and morphological (body form and structure) data are useful. Biologists refer to the overall similarity

---

derived Characteristics that define a group of organisms and that did not exist in ancestral populations.

ancestral Characteristics that define a group of organisms that are due to shared ancestry.

convergent evolution In biological evolution, a process by which unrelated populations develop similarities to one another due to similar function rather than shared ancestry.

TABLE 3.1

Two Alternative Taxonomies for the Primate Order: Differing Placement of Tarsiers

Suborder	Infraorder	Superfamily (Family)	Location
I. Prosimii (lower primates)	Lemuriformes Lorisiformes	Lemuroidea (lemurs, indriids, and aye-ayes) Lorisoidea (lorises) Tarsioidea (tarsiers)	Madagascar Asia and Africa Asia
Anthropoidea (higher primates)	Platyrrhini (New World monkeys) Catarrhini	Ceboidea Cercopithecoidea (Old World monkeys) Hominoidea (apes and humans)	Tropical Americas Africa and Asia Africa and Asia (humans worldwide)
II. Strepsirhini	Lemuriformes Lorisiformes	Lemuroidea (lemurs, indriids, and aye-ayes) Lorisoidea (lorises)	Madagascar Asia and Africa
Haplorhini	Tarsiiformes Platyrrhini (New World monkeys) Catarrhini	Tarsioidea (tarsiers) Ceboidea Cercopithecoidea (Old World monkeys) Hominoidea (apes and humans)	Asia Tropical Americas Africa and Asia Africa and Asia (humans worldwide)

© Cengage Learning

of body plans within taxonomic groupings as a **grade**. The examination of shared sequences of DNA and RNA allows researchers to establish a **clade**, a taxonomic grouping that contains a single common ancestor and all of its descendants. Genetic analyses allow for precise quantification, but it is not always clear what the numbers mean (recall the Original Study from Chapter 2).

© Cengage Learning

The Linnaean system divides primates into two suborders: the **prosimians** (Prosimii, from the Latin for "before monkeys"), which includes lemurs, lorises, and tarsiers, and the **anthropoids** (Anthropoidea, from the Greek for "humanlike"), which includes monkeys, apes, and humans. Some call prosimians the "lower primates" because they resemble the earliest fossil primates. On the whole, most prosimians are cat-sized or smaller, although some larger forms existed in the past. The prosimians also retain certain ancestral features common among nonprimate mammals that the anthropoids have lost over time, such as claws and moist, naked skin on their noses.

In Asia and Africa, all prosimians are nocturnal and arboreal creatures—again, like the fossil primates. However, a variety of diurnal ground-dwelling prosimians inhabit the island of Madagascar. In the rest of the world, the diurnal primates are all anthropoids. This group is sometimes called the "higher primates" because they appeared later in evolutionary history and because of a lingering belief that the group including humans was more "evolved." From a contemporary biological perspective, no species is more evolved than any other.

Molecular evidence led to the proposal of a new primate taxonomy (**Table 3.1**). A close genetic relationship was discovered between the tarsiers—nocturnal treedwellers who resemble lemurs and lorises—and monkeys and apes (Goodman et al., 1994). The taxonomic scheme reflecting this genetic relationship places lemurs and lorises in the subdivision **strepsirhine** (Strepsirhini, from the Greek for "turned nose"). In turn, the subdivision **haplorhine** (Haplorhini, Greek for "simple nose") contains the tarsiers, monkeys, and apes. Tarsiers are separated from monkeys and apes at the infraorder level in this taxonomic scheme. Although this classificatory scheme accurately reflects genetic relationships, comparisons among grades, or general levels of organization, in the older prosimian and anthropoid classification make more sense when examining morphology and lifeways.

grade A general level of biological organization seen among a group of species; useful for constructing evolutionary relationships.

clade A taxonomic grouping that contains a single common ancestor and all of its descendants.

prosimians The suborder of primates that includes lemurs, lorises, and tarsiers.

anthropoids The suborder of primates that includes New World monkeys, Old World monkeys, and apes (including humans).

strepsirhines The subdivision within the primate order based on shared genetic characteristics; includes lemurs and lorises.

haplorhines The subdivision within the primate order based on shared genetic characteristics; includes tarsiers, New World monkeys, Old World monkeys, and apes (including humans).

The older taxonomic scheme divides the anthropoid suborder into two infraorders: the **platyrrhines** (*Platyrrhini*, Greek for "flat-nosed"), or New World monkeys, and the **catarrhines** (*Catarrhini*, Greek for "drooping nose"), consisting of the superfamilies Cercopithecoidea (Old World monkeys) and Hominoidea (apes). Although the terms *New World* and *Old World* reflect a Eurocentric vision of history (whereby the Americas were considered new only to European explorers and not to the indigenous people already living there), these terms have evolutionary and geologic relevance with respect to primates, as we will see in Chapters 5 and 6. Old World monkeys and apes, including humans, have a 40-million-year shared evolutionary history in Africa distinct from the course taken by anthropoid primates in the tropical Americas. "Old World" in this context represents the evolutionary origins of anthropoid primates rather than a political or historical focus on Europe.

In terms of human evolution, most of the taxonomic controversy derives from relationships established by the molecular evidence among the hominoids. Humans are placed in the **hominoid** or ape superfamily—with gibbons, siamangs, orangutans, gorillas, chimpanzees, and bonobos—due to physical similarities such as broad shoulders, absent tail, and long arms. Human characteristics such as bipedalism (walking on two legs) and culture led scientists to think that all the other apes were more closely related to one another than any of them were to humans. Thus, humans and their ancestors were classified in the **hominid** family to distinguish them from the other apes.

Advances in molecular analysis of blood proteins and DNA later demonstrated that humans are more closely related to African apes (chimps, bonobos, and gorillas) than we are to orangutans and the smaller apes (siamangs and gibbons). Some scientists then proposed that African apes should be included in the hominid family, with humans and their ancestors distinguished from the other African hominoids at the taxonomic level of subfamily, as **hominins** (Figure 3.5).

Although all scientists today agree about the close relationship among humans, chimpanzees, bonobos, and gorillas, they differ as to whether they use the term *hominid* or *hominin* to describe the taxonomic grouping of humans and their ancestors. Museum displays and much of the popular press tend to retain the old term *hominid*, emphasizing the visible differences between humans and the other African apes. Scientists and publications using *hominin* (such as *National Geographic*) emphasize the importance of genetics in establishing relationships among species. More than name games, these word choices reflect theoretical relationships among closely related species.

Though the DNA sequences of humans and African apes are 98 percent identical, the organization of DNA into chromosomes differs between humans and the other

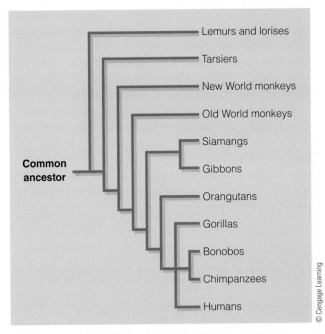

Figure 3.5 Relationships among the Primates Molecular evidence establishes these relationships among various primate groups. This evidence shows that tarsiers are more closely related to monkeys and apes than to the lemurs and lorises that they resemble physically. Present thinking is that the split between the human and African ape lines took place between 5 and 8 million years ago.

great apes. Bonobos and chimps, like gorillas and orangutans, possess an extra pair of chromosomes compared to humans, in which two medium-sized chromosomes have fused together to form chromosome 2. Chromosomes are numbered according to their size as they are viewed microscopically, so that chromosome 2 is the second largest of the human chromosomes (recall Figure 2.7). Of the other pairs, eighteen are virtually identical between humans and the African apes, whereas the remaining ones have been reshuffled.

platyrrhines The primate infraorder that includes New World monkeys.

catarrhines The primate infraorder that includes Old World monkeys, apes, and humans.

hominoid The taxonomic division superfamily within the Old World primates that includes gibbons, siamangs, orangutans, gorillas, chimpanzees, bonobos, and humans.

hominid African hominoid family that includes humans and their ancestors. Some scientists, recognizing the close relationship of humans, chimps, bonobos, and gorillas, use the term *hominid* to refer to all African hominoids. They then divide the hominid family into two subfamilies: the Paninae (chimps, bonobos, and gorillas) and the Homininae (humans and their ancestors).

hominin The taxonomic subfamily or tribe within the primates that includes humans and our ancestors.

Overall, there are fewer differences between humans and other African apes compared to those found between gibbons (with twenty-two pairs of chromosomes) and siamangs (twenty-five pairs of chromosomes). These two closely related species have, in captivity, produced live hybrid offspring. Most studies suggest a closer relationship between the two species in the genus *Pan* (chimps and bonobos) and humans than either has to gorillas. Other researchers disagree, suggesting that among *Pan*, humans, and gorillas there is an equal degree of relationship. Chimps and bonobos are, of course, more closely related to each other than either is to gorillas or humans (Rogers, 1994).

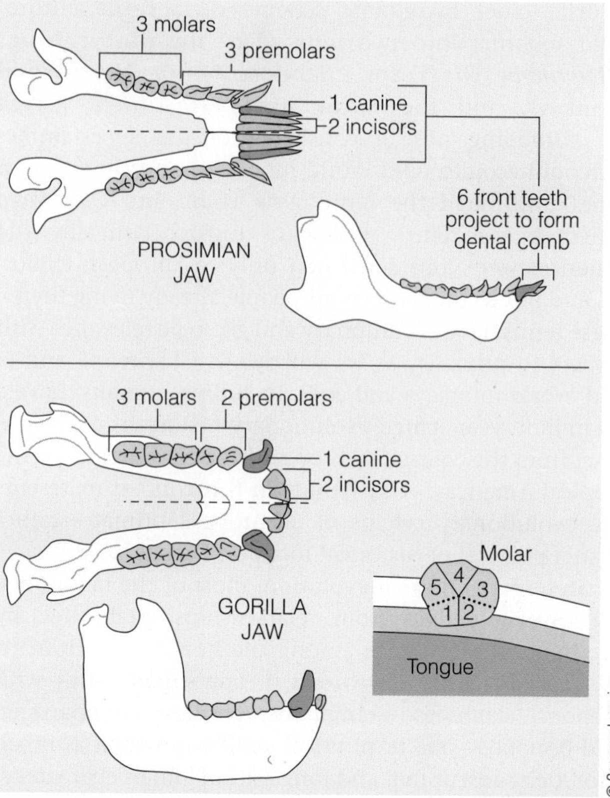

Primate Characteristics

The living primates, including humans, share a number of features. For instance, in baseball, a pitcher can strike out a batter due to the primate characteristics of grasping, throwing, and seeing in three dimensions. Compared to other mammals, primates possess a relatively unspecialized anatomy combined with diverse and flexible behavioral patterns.

Many primate characteristics developed from their arboreal niche. For animals preying upon the many insects living on the fruit and flowers of trees and shrubs, dexterous hands and keen vision would have been enormously adaptive. Life in the trees, along with the visual predation of insects, played a role in the evolution of primate biology.

Primate Teeth

The varied diet available to arboreal primates—shoots, leaves, insects, and fruits—did not require the specialization of teeth seen in other mammals. In most primates (humans included), on each side of each jaw, in front, are two straight-edged, chisel-like broad teeth called incisors (**Figure 3.6**). A large flaring and often fanglike canine tooth lies behind each incisor. The canines are used for defense as well as for tearing and shredding food.

Humans possess relatively small canine teeth with oversized roots, suggestive of larger canines some time back in our ancestry. Behind the canines, the premolars and molars (the "cheek teeth") grind and chew food. Molars erupt through the gums over the course of a young primate's growth and development (6-year molars,

Figure 3.6 Primate Dentition Because the exact number and shape of the teeth differ among primate groups, teeth are frequently used to identify evolutionary relationships and group membership. Prosimians (*top*), with a dental formula of 2-1-3-3, possess two incisors, one canine, three premolars, and three molars on each side of their upper and lower jaws. Also, lower canines and incisors project forward, forming a "dental comb," which is used for grooming. A dental formula of 2-1-2-3, typical of Old World monkeys and apes, can be seen in the gorilla jaw (*bottom*). Note the large projecting canines. On one of the molars, the cusps are numbered to illustrate the Y5 pattern found in hominoids.

12-year molars, and wisdom teeth in humans). Thus, the functions of grasping, cutting, and grinding were served by different kinds of teeth. The exact number of premolars and molars and the shape of individual teeth differ among primate groups (**Table 3.2**).

The course of primate evolution includes a trend toward a reduction in the number and size of the teeth. The ancestral **dental formula**, or pattern of tooth type and number in mammals, consists of three incisors, one canine, five premolars, and three molars (expressed as 3-1-5-3) on each side of the jaw, top and bottom, for a total of forty-eight teeth. In the early stages of primate evolution, one incisor and one premolar were lost on each side of each jaw, resulting in a dental pattern of 2-1-4-3 in the early fossil primates. This change differentiated primates from other mammals.

dental formula The number of each tooth type (incisors, canines, premolars, and molars) on one half of each jaw. Unlike other mammals, primates possess equal numbers on their upper and lower jaws so the dental formula for the species is a single series of numbers.

TABLE 3.2

Primate Anatomical Variation and Specialization

Primate Group	Skull and Face	Dental Formula and Specializations	Locomotor Pattern and Morphology	Tail and Other Skeletal Specializations
Earliest fossil primates	Eye not fully surrounded by bone	2-1-4-3		
Prosimians	Complete ring of bone surrounding eye Upper lip bound down to the gum Long snout	2-1-3-3 Dental comb for grooming	Hind-leg dominance for vertical clinging and leaping	Tail present
Anthropoids	Forward-facing eyes fully enclosed in bone Free upper lip Shorter snout			
New World monkeys		2-1-3-3	Quadrupedal	Prehensile (grasping) tail in some
Old World monkeys		2-1-2-3 Four-cusped molars	Quadrupedal	Tail present
Apes		2-1-2-3 Y5 molars on lower jaw	Suspensory hanging apparatus	No tail

© Cengage Learning

Over the millennia, as the first and second premolars became smaller and eventually disappeared altogether, the third and fourth premolars grew larger and added a second pointed projection, or cusp, thus becoming "bicuspid." In humans, all eight premolars are bicuspid, but in other Old World anthropoids, the lower first premolar is not bicuspid. Instead, it is a specialized, single-cusped tooth with a sharp edge to act with the upper canine as a shearing mechanism. The molars, meanwhile, evolved from a three-cusp pattern to one with four and even five cusps. The five-cusp pattern is characteristic of the lower molars of living and extinct hominoids (for instance, the mandrill in **Figure 3.7**). Because the grooves separating the five cusps of a hominoid lower molar looks like the letter Y, hominoid lower molars are said to have a Y5 pattern. Humans have departed somewhat from the Y5 pattern as tooth and jaw size reduced such that the second and third molars generally have only four cusps. Four- and five-cusp molars economically combined the functions of grasping, cutting, and grinding in one tooth.

The evolutionary trend for human dentition has generally been toward economy, with fewer, smaller, more efficient teeth doing more work. With thirty-two teeth (a 2-1-2-3 dental formula shared with the Old World monkeys and apes), we possess fewer teeth than some primates. However, this trend does not indicate that species with more teeth are less evolved; it only shows that their evolution followed a different path.

The canines of most primates develop into long daggerlike teeth that enable them to rip open tough husks of fruit and other foods (Figure 3.7). In many species, males possess larger canine teeth compared to females. This

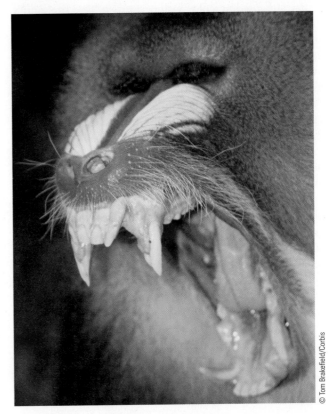

© Tom Brakefield/Corbis

Figure 3.7 Powerful Canines Though the massive canine teeth of some male primates are serious weapons, they are more often used to communicate rather than to draw blood. Raising his lip to flash his canines, this mandrill will get the young members of his group in line right away. Over the course of human evolution, overall canine size decreased as did differences in canine size between males and females.

sex difference is an example of **sexual dimorphism**—differences between the sexes in the shape or size of a feature. Adult males frequently use these large canines for social communication. If an adult male gorilla, baboon, or mandrill raises his upper lip to display his large, sharp canines, a youngster becomes submissive.

Primate Sensory Organs

The primates' adaptation to arboreal life involved changes in the form and function of their sensory organs. The sense of smell was vital for the earliest ground-dwelling, night-active mammals. It enabled them to operate in the dark, to sniff out their food, and to detect hidden predators. However, for active tree life during daylight, good vision is a better guide than smell in judging the location of the next branch or tasty morsel. Accordingly, the sense of smell declined in primates, while vision became highly developed.

Travel through the trees demands judgments concerning depth, direction, distance, and the relationships of objects hanging in space, such as vines or branches. Monkeys, apes, and humans achieved this through binocular stereoscopic color vision (**Figure 3.8**), the ability to see the world in the three dimensions of height, width, and depth. **Binocular vision** (in which two eyes sit next to each other on the same plane so that their visual fields overlap) and nerve connections that run from each eye to both sides of the brain confer complete depth perception characteristic of three-dimensional or **stereoscopic vision**. This arrangement allows nerve cells to integrate the images derived from each eye. Increased brain size in the visual area in primates, and a greater complexity at nerve connections, also contribute to stereoscopic color vision.

Visual acuity, however, varies throughout the primate order in terms of both color and spatial perception. Prosimians, most of whom are nocturnal, lack color vision. The eyes of lemurs and lorises (but not tarsiers) are capable of reflecting light off the retina, the surface where nerve fibers gather images in the back of the eye to intensify the limited light available in the forest at night. In

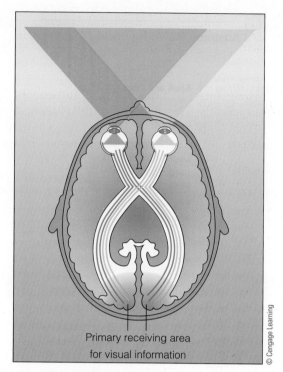

Primary receiving area
for visual information

© Cengage Learning

Figure 3.8 Primate Vision Monkeys, apes, and humans possess binocular stereoscopic vision. Binocular vision refers to overlapping visual fields due to forward-facing eyes. Three-dimensional or stereoscopic vision comes from binocular vision and the transmission of information from each eye to both sides of the brain.

addition, prosimian vision is binocular without the benefits of stereoscopy. Their eyes look out from either side of their muzzle or snout. Though there is some overlap of visual fields, their nerve fibers do not cross from each eye to both halves of the brain.

By contrast, monkeys, apes, and humans possess both color and stereoscopic vision. Color vision markedly improves the diet of these primates compared to most other mammals. The ability to distinguish colors allows anthropoid primates to choose ripe fruits or tender, immature leaves due to their red rather than green coloration. See this chapter's Biocultural Connection to see how our primate ancestry affects our response to color.

In addition to color vision, anthropoid primates possess a unique structure called the **fovea centralis**, or central pit, in the retina of each eye. Like a camera lens, this feature enables the animal to focus on a particular object for acutely clear perception without sacrificing visual contact with the object's surroundings.

The primates' emphasis on visual acuity came at the expense of their sense of smell. Smells are processed in the forebrain, and in animals that depend greatly on the sense of smell, the forebrain projects into the snout. A large protruding snout, however, interferes with stereoscopic vision. But as primates became diurnal tree-dwelling

sexual dimorphism Within a single species, differences between males and females in the shape or size of a feature not directly related to reproduction, such as body size or canine tooth shape and size.

binocular vision Vision with increased depth perception from two eyes set next to each other, allowing their visual fields to overlap.

stereoscopic vision Complete three-dimensional vision, or depth perception, from binocular vision and nerve connections that run from each eye to both sides of the brain, allowing nerve cells to integrate the images derived from each eye.

fovea centralis A shallow pit in the retina of the eye that enables an animal to focus on an object while maintaining visual contact with its surroundings.

BIOCULTURAL CONNECTION

Why Red Is Such a Potent Color

By Meredith F. Small

The Olympic athletes have been parading around like fashionistas in an array of colorful outfits, and we, their adoring public, can't resist commenting on the style and color of their high-end athletic wear. My favorite was the faux silk, faux embroidered, slinky red leotards of the Chinese women's gymnasts.

Apparently, as researchers have recently discovered, the choice of red for those leotards might also have given the Chinese gymnasts an advantage. But why is the color red so impressive?

The answer lies in our tree-living past.

The human response to the color red may well be rooted in our anthropoid heritage. Could this have given an edge to the Chinese gymnastic team? It is certain that our ape ancestry contributes to the human range of motion. Although we are all not able to move in the same ways that these talented gymnasts can, the human ability to grasp, swing, stretch, and throw things derives from characteristics of the hands and shoulders inherited from our ape ancestors.

In the back of the vertebrate eyeball are two kinds of cells called rods and cones that respond to light. Cones take in a wide range of light, which means they recognize colors, and they are stimulated best during daylight. Rods respond to a narrower range of light (meaning only white light) but notice that light from far away and at night.

Isaac Newton was the first person to hold up a prism and refract white light into a rainbow of colors and realize that there might be variation in what the eye can see. Color comes at us in electromagnetic waves. When the wavelength of light is short we perceive purple or blue. Medium wavelengths of lights tickle the cones in another way and we think green. Short light wavelengths make those cones stand up and dance as bright spots of yellow, orange, and red.

Various animals distinguish only parts of that rainbow because their cones respond in different ways. Butterflies, for example, see into the ultraviolet end of the rainbow, which allows them to see their own complex markings better than we can. Foxes and owls are basically colorblind, and it doesn't matter because they are awake at night when the light spectrum is limited anyway.

Humans are lucky enough to be primates, animals with decent color vision, and we can thank monkeys for this special ability.

Long ago, primitive primates that resemble today's lemurs and lorises saw only green and blue, the longer wavelengths of color. But when monkeys evolved, around 34 million years ago, their cones became sensitive to even shorter wavelengths of color and they saw red.

And what a difference. With red, the forest comes alive. Instead of a blanket of bluish-green leaves, the world is suddenly accented with ripe red, yellow, and orange fruits, and even the leaves look different.

For a monkey leaping through the forest canopy, color vision would be an essential advantage. Unripe fruit doesn't have enough carbs to sustain a hungry primate, and they taste really sour. Unripe leaves not only taste bad, they are toxic and indigestible.

For the first humans foraging about the forest and savannah around 5 million years ago, it would have been much more efficient to spot a ripe fruit or tuber than bite into a zillion just to get the right one. And so humans ended up with color vision even though we no longer live in trees.

But color is more than wavelengths, more than an indicator of ripeness, to us.

Color has become symbolic, meaning it has meaning, and that meaning is highly cultural.

Chinese athletes and Chinese brides wear red because red is considered lucky. The U.S. athletes also wear red because that bright color is in the U.S. flag, and because designers of athletic wear, as well as scientists, know that red gets you noticed.

BIOCULTURAL QUESTION

While the vast majority of humans see color as described here, 8 to 20 percent of human males have red-green color blindness. Do you know someone who is colorblind? What could a conversation with a colorblind person reveal about the anthropological perspective? What colors besides red have particular meanings? Do these meanings derive from biology or culture?

Adapted from Small, M. F. (2008, August 15). Why red is such a potent color. LiveScience. www.livescience.com/ 5043-red-potent-color.html (retrieved June 20, 2012). Reprinted by permission.

animals in search of insects, they no longer needed to live a "nose to the ground" existence, sniffing the earth in search of food. The anthropoids especially have the least-developed sense of smell of all land animals. Though our sense of smell allows humans to distinguish perfumes, and even to distinguish family members from strangers, our brains have come to emphasize vision rather than smell. Prosimians, by contrast, still rely more on smell than on vision, and they possess numerous scent glands for marking objects in their territories.

Arboreal primates also have an acute sense of touch. An effective feeling and grasping mechanism helps prevent them from falling and tumbling while speeding through the trees. The early mammals from which primates evolved possessed tiny touch-sensitive hairs at the tips of their hands and feet. In primates, sensitive pads backed up by nails on the tips of the animals' fingers and toes replaced these hairs.

The Primate Brain

These changes in sensory organs have corresponding changes in the primate brain. In addition, an increase in brain size, particularly in the cerebral hemispheres—the areas supporting conscious thought—occurred in the course of primate evolution. In monkeys, apes, and humans, the cerebral hemispheres completely cover the cerebellum, the part of the brain that coordinates the muscles and maintains body balance.

In turn, this development led to the flexibility seen in primate behavior. Rather than relying on reflexes controlled by the cerebellum, primates constantly react to a variety of features in the environment. Messages from the hands and feet, eyes and ears, and from the sensors of balance, movement, heat, touch, and pain are simultaneously relayed to the cerebral cortex. The cortex had to evolve considerably in order to receive, analyze, and coordinate these impressions and transmit the appropriate response back down to the motor nerves. This enlarged, responsive cerebral cortex provides the biological basis for flexible behavior patterns found in all primates, including humans.

The increased learning capacity of the primate brain likely started as the earliest primates, along with many other mammals, began to carry out their activities in the daylight hours. Prior to 65 million years ago, mammals seem to have been nocturnal in their habits. The extinction of the dinosaurs and climate change at that time opened new ecological niches. With the change to a diurnal life, the sense of vision took on greater importance, and so visual acuity was favored by natural selection. Unlike reptiles, who process visual information with neurons in the retina, mammals process visual information in the brain, permitting integration with information received through other senses such as sound, touch, taste, and smell.

If the evolution of visual acuity led to larger brains, it is likely that the primates' insect predation in an arboreal setting also played a role in enlargement of the brain. This would have required great agility and muscular coordination, favoring development of the brain centers. Interestingly, many higher mental faculties developed in an area alongside the motor centers of the brain (Romer, 1945).

Another hypothesis that may account for primate brain enlargement involves the use of hands as tactile instruments to replace the teeth and jaws or snout. The hands assumed some of the grasping, tearing, and dividing functions of the jaws, again requiring development of the brain centers for more complete coordination.

The Primate Skeleton

The skeleton gives animals with internal backbones, or **vertebrates**, their basic shape or silhouette, supports the soft tissues, and helps protect vital internal organs (Figure 3.9). In primates, for example, the skull protects the brain and the eyes. A number of factors are responsible for the shape of the primate skull as compared with those of most other mammals: changes in dentition, changes in the sensory organs of sight and smell, and increased brain size.

The primate braincase, or **cranium**, tends to be high and vaulted. Anthropoid primates have a solid partition between the eye and the temple, affording maximum protection to the eyes from the contraction of the chewing muscles, which are positioned directly next to the eyes.

The **foramen magnum** (the large opening at the base of the skull through which the spinal cord passes and connects to the brain) provides important clues about evolutionary relationships. In most mammals, as in dogs and horses, this opening faces directly backward, with the skull projecting forward from the vertebral column. In humans, by contrast, the vertebral column joins the skull toward the center of its base, thereby placing the skull in a balanced position as required for habitual upright posture. Other primates, though they frequently cling, sit, or hang with their body upright, are not as fully committed to upright posture as humans, and so their foramen magnum is not as far forward.

In anthropoid primates, the snout or muzzle portion of the skull reduced as the acuity of the sense of smell declined. The smaller snout offers less interference with stereoscopic vision; it also enables the eyes to take a frontal position. As a result, primates have flatter faces than some other mammals.

---

vertebrates Animals with a backbone, including fish, amphibians, reptiles, birds, and mammals.

cranium The braincase of the skull.

foramen magnum A large opening in the skull through which the spinal cord passes and connects to the brain.

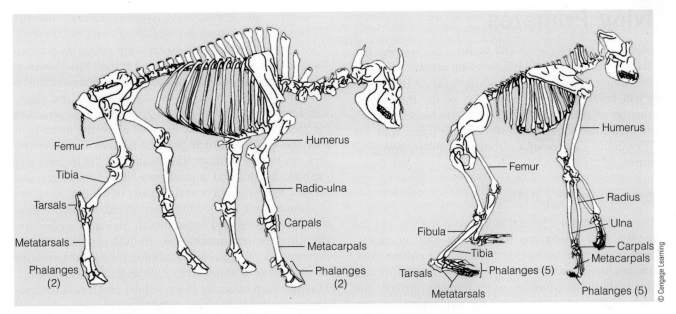

Figure 3.9 Skeletal Comparisons of Gorilla and Bison All primates possess the same ancestral vertebrate limb pattern seen in reptiles and amphibians, consisting of a single upper long bone, two lower long bones, and five radiating digits (fingers and toes), as seen in this gorilla skeleton (*right*). Other mammals such as bison (*left*) have a modified version of this pattern. In the course of evolution, bison have lost all but two of their digits, which form their hooves. The second long bone in the lower part of the limb is reduced. Note also the joining of the skull and vertebral column in these skeletons. In bison (as in most mammals) the skull projects forward from the vertebral column, but in semi-erect gorillas, the vertebral column is further beneath the skull.

Below the primate skull and the neck is the **clavicle**, or collarbone, a bone found in ancestral mammals though lost in some mammals such as cats. The size of the clavicle varies across the primate order according to pattern of locomotion. Quadrupedal primates like monkeys with a narrow, sturdy body plan possess smaller clavicles. Apes, by contrast, have broad clavicles that orient the arms at the side rather than at the front of the body and form part of the **suspensory hanging apparatus** of this group (see Table 3.2). The clavicle also supports the **scapula** (shoulder blade) and muscles required for flexible yet powerful arm movement—permitting large-bodied apes to hang suspended below tree branches and to move through **brachiation**, or swinging from tree to tree.

The limbs of the primate skeleton follow the same basic ancestral plan seen in the earliest vertebrates. Other animals possess limbs specialized to optimize a particular behavior, such as speed. In each primate arm or leg, the upper portion of the limb has a single long bone, the lower portion two long bones, and then hands or feet with five radiating digits (phalanges). Their grasping feet and hands have sensitive pads at the tips of their digits, backed up (except in some prosimians) by flattened nails. This unique combination of pad and nail provides the animal with an excellent **prehensile** (grasping) device for use when moving from branch to branch. The structural characteristics of the primate foot and hand make grasping possible; the digits are extremely flexible, the big toe is fully **opposable** to the other digits in all but humans and

their immediate ancestors, and the thumb is opposable to the other digits to varying degrees.

The retention of the flexible vertebrate limb pattern in primates was a valuable asset to evolving humans. It was, in part, having hands capable of grasping that enabled our own ancestors to manufacture and use tools and to embark on the pathway that led to the revolutionary ability to adapt through culture.

To sum up, a comparison of humans to other primates reveals how many of the characteristics we consider distinctly human are not in fact unique to us; rather, they are variants of typical primate traits. We humans look the way we do because we are primates, and the differences between us and our primate cousins—especially the apes—are more differences of degree than differences of kind.

clavicle The collarbone connecting the sternum (breastbone) with the scapula (shoulder blade).

suspensory hanging apparatus The broad powerful shoulder joints and muscles found in all the hominoids, allowing these large-bodied primates to hang suspended below the tree branches.

scapula The shoulder blade.

brachiation Moving from branch to branch using the arms, with the body hanging suspended below.

prehensile Having the ability to grasp.

opposable Having the ability to bring the thumb or big toe in contact with the tips of the other digits on the same hand or foot in order to grasp objects.

Living Primates

Except for a few species of Old World monkeys who live in temperate climates and humans who inhabit the entire globe, living primates inhabit warm areas of the world. We will briefly explore the diversity of the five natural groupings of living primates: lemurs and lorises, tarsiers, New World monkeys, Old World monkeys, and apes. We will examine each group's distinctive habitat, biological features, and behavior.

Lemurs and Lorises

Although the natural habitat of lemurs is restricted to the large island of Madagascar (off the east coast of Africa), lorises range from Africa to southern and eastern Asia. Only on Madagascar, where there was no competition from anthropoid primates until humans arrived, are lemurs diurnal, or active during the day; lorises, by contrast, are all nocturnal and arboreal (**Figure 3.10**).

All these animals are small, with none larger than a good-sized dog. In general body outline, they resemble rodents and insectivores, with short pointed snouts, large pointed ears, and big eyes. In the anatomy of the upper lip and snout, lemurs and lorises resemble nonprimate mammals in that the upper lip is bound down to the gums, thus limiting their range of facial expression. The split, moist naked skin on the nose around the nostrils facilitates a keen sense of smell. Most also have long tails, with that of a ring-tailed lemur somewhat like that of a raccoon.

Lemurs and lorises have typical primate "hands," although they use them in pairs, rather than one at a time. Their fingers and toes are particularly strong with sensitive pads and flattened nails located at their tips. However, they retain a claw on their second toe, sometimes called a grooming claw, which they use for scratching and cleaning. Lemurs and lorises possess another unique structure for grooming: a dental comb made up of the lower incisors and canines, which projects forward from the jaw and can be run through the fur. Behind the incisors and canines, lemurs and lorises have three premolars and molars, resulting in a dental formula of 2-1-3-3.

Lemurs and lorises have scent glands at their wrists, under their arms, and sometimes in their anal region that they use for communication. Individuals leave smelly messages for one another by rubbing their scent glands on tree branches or some other fixture of the environment. Through such olfactory clues, lemurs and lorises can recognize distinct individuals within their own group as well as pinpoint their location and physical state. They also use scent to mark their territory, thus communicating to members of other groups.

With hind legs longer than their front legs, lemurs and lorises keep their forelimbs in a palms-down position when they move on all fours. As mentioned previously, some species can also move from tree to tree by vertical clinging and leaping. With their distinctive mix of characteristics, lemurs and lorises appear to occupy a place between the anthropoid primates and insectivores, the mammalian order that includes moles and shrews.

VISUAL COUNTERPOINT

Figure 3.10 **Lemurs and Lorises** Wherever there is competition from the anthropoid primates, prosimian species, such as this loris on the right, retain the arboreal nocturnal patterns of the earliest fossil primates. Notice its large eyes, long snout, and moist split nose—all useful in its relatively solitary search for food in the trees at night. In contrast, only on the large island of Madagascar off the eastern coast of Africa, where no anthropoids existed until humans arrived, have prosimians come to occupy the diurnal ground-dwelling niche as do these ring-tailed lemurs. While all prosimians still rely on scent, marking their territory and communicating through smelly messages, daytime activity allowed the prosimians on Madagascar to become far less solitary. Also notice the difference in the size of the eyes in these two groups. Just as it would be incorrect to think of prosimians as "less evolved" than anthropoid primates because they bear a closer resemblance to the ancestral primate condition, it is also incorrect to think of lorises as less evolved compared to lemurs.

Tarsiers

Outwardly, tarsiers resemble lemurs and lorises (**Figure 3.11**). Molecular evidence, however, indicates a closer relationship to monkeys, apes, and humans. The head, eyes, and ears of these kitten-sized arboreal creatures are huge in proportion to the body. They have the remarkable ability to turn their heads 180 degrees, so they can see where they have been as well as where they are going. Their digits end in platelike adhesive discs.

Tarsiers are named for the elongated tarsal, or foot bone, that provides leverage for jumps of 6 feet or more. Tarsiers are mainly nocturnal insect-eaters and so occupy a niche that is similar to that of the earliest ancestral primates. In the structure of the nose and lips and in the part of the brain governing vision, tarsiers resemble monkeys.

© Danita Delimont/Alamy

Figure 3.11 Tarsiers With their large eyes, tarsiers are well adapted for nocturnal life. If humans possessed eyes proportionally the same size as tarsiers relative to the size of our faces, our eyes would be approximately as big as oranges. In their nocturnal habit and outward appearance, tarsiers resemble lemurs and lorises. Genetically, however, they are more closed related to monkeys and apes, causing scientists to rework the suborder divisions in primate taxonomy to reflect this evolutionary relationship.

New World Monkeys

New World monkeys live in tropical forests of South and Central America. In outward body plan they closely resemble Old World monkeys, except that New World monkeys possess flat noses with widely separated, outward-flaring nostrils. Their infraorder name platyrrhine (from the Greek for "flat-nosed") comes from this characteristic. There are five different families of New World monkeys, and they range in size from less than a pound to over 30 pounds.

New World monkeys have not been studied as extensively as other primates for two reasons. First, because of primatology's emphasis on human origins, researchers have tended to favor Old World species. The second reason is that the arboreal habitat of New World species makes it more difficult for researchers to observe them. In recent decades, however, primatologists have conducted numerous long-range field studies on a variety of species.

For example, anthropologist Karen Strier has studied the woolly spider monkey, or muriqui, in the state of Minas Gerais, Brazil, for close to three decades. Her field studies progressed from examining muriqui diet, social structure, and **demographics** (population characteristics such as the number of individuals of each age and sex) to tracking the reproductive cycles and health of these large, peaceful forest-dwellers. She pioneered a noninvasive method to measure reproductive hormone levels and the presence of parasites through analysis of the feces of individual animals—catching feces (in a gloved hand) the moment it dropped from the trees or quickly retrieving it from the ground. Through analysis of these samples, Strier was able to document correlations between diet and fertility.

© Cengage Learning

Strier also documented a reduced parasite load in muriquis that consumed certain plants—apparently for their medicinal or therapeutic value. Amazonian peoples have been known to use some of these plants for the same reason. As these human populations have become increasingly removed from their traditional lifeways due to globalization and modernization, the muriqui remain a valuable source to reclaim knowledge of the forest.

demographics Population characteristics such as the number of individuals of each age and sex.

According to Strier, "While traditional peoples of the Amazon have survived long enough to impart some of their knowledge of forest plants, the indigenous human societies of the Atlantic forest are long gone. The muriqui and other monkeys may provide humans with their best guides to the forest's medicinal values" (Strier, 1993, p. 42). Field studies like Strier's not only have contributed to our understanding of the behavior and biology of New World monkeys but have also played a major role in bringing back a number of species from the brink of extinction.

New World monkeys—unlike Old World monkeys, apes, and humans—possess a 2-1-3-3 dental formula (three, rather than two, premolars on each side of each jaw). This is not as much a functional distinction as it is a difference in evolutionary path. The common ancestor of Old World anthropoids and New World anthropoids possessed this 2-1-3-3 dental pattern. In the New World this pattern remained, while in Old World species a molar was lost.

Like Old World monkeys, New World monkeys have long tails. All members of one group, the family Atelidae, possess prehensile or grasping tails that they use as a fifth limb (**Figure 3.12**). The naked skin on the underside of their tail resembles the sensitive skin found at the tips of our fingers and is even covered with whorls like fingerprints.

Platyrrhines walk on all fours with their palms down and scamper along tree branches in search of fruit, which they eat sitting upright. Although New World monkeys spend much of their time in the trees, they rarely hang suspended below the branches or swing from limb to limb by their arms and have not developed the extremely long forelimbs and broad shoulders characteristic of the apes.

Old World Monkeys

Divided from the apes at the superfamily taxonomic level, Old World or catarrhine (from the Greek for "sharp-nosed") primates resemble New World monkeys in their basic body plan, but their noses are distinctive, with closely spaced, downward-pointing nostrils. Two subfamilies, the Cercopithecinae and the Colobinae, contain eleven and

Ingo Arndt/Getty Images/Minden Pictures

Figure 3.12 New World Spider Monkey Grasping hands and three-dimensional vision enable primates like this South American spider monkey to lead an active life in the trees. In some New World monkey species, a grasping or prehensile tail makes tree life even easier. The naked skin on the underside of the tail resembles the sensitive skin found at the tips of our fingers and is even covered with whorls like fingerprints. This sensory skin allows New World monkeys to use their tails as a fifth limb.

ten genera, respectively. Old World monkeys occupy a broader range of habitats compared to New World monkey species, which occupy only tropical forests.

Some Old World monkeys such as mandrills (pictured in Figure 3.7) have brightly colored faces and genitals. Others, like proboscis monkeys (**Figure 3.13**), have long droopy noses. They all possess a 2-1-2-3 dental formula (two, rather than three, premolars on each side of each jaw) and tails that are never prehensile. They may be either arboreal or terrestrial, using a quadrupedal pattern of locomotion on the ground or in the trees in a palms-down position. Their body plan is narrow with hind limbs and forelimbs of equal length, a reduced clavicle (collarbone), and relatively fixed and sturdy shoulder, elbow, and wrist joints.

Arboreal species of Old World monkeys include the mantled guereza (*Colobus guereza*) monkey, a species known to have been hunted by chimpanzees. Other Old World monkeys are equally at home on the ground and in the trees. These include the macaques—some nineteen

Figure 3.13 **The Proboscis Monkey** Although all Old World monkeys share certain features like a narrow body plan, a non-prehensile tail, and a 2-1-2-3 dental formula, some unusual specializations are also seen. The proboscis monkey, found in the mangrove swamps of Borneo, is known for its unusual protruding nose, which provides a chamber for extra resonance for its vocalizations. When a monkey is alarmed, the nose fills with blood so that the resonating chamber becomes even more enlarged.

Other Old World species also have much to tell us. For example, over the past several decades primatologists have documented primate social learning and innovation in colonies of macaques in Japan. Similarly, field studies of vervet monkeys in eastern and southern Africa have revealed that these Old World monkeys possess sophisticated communication abilities. In short, wherever primatologists study primates they make fascinating discoveries. These discoveries contribute not only to the disciplines of primatology, evolutionary biology, and ecology but also to our deepening understanding of who we are as primates. Chapter 4 includes more on the behavior of baboons and a variety of other Old World species, particularly the apes.

Small and Great Apes

Like us, the apes, our closest cousins in the animal world, are large, wide-bodied primates with no tails. As members of the hominoid superfamily, apes and humans possess a shoulder anatomy specialized for hanging suspended below tree branches. All apes have this suspensory hanging apparatus, although among apes only small, lithe gibbons and talented gymnasts swing from branch to branch in the pattern known as *brachiation*. At the opposite extreme are gorillas, which generally climb trees, using their prehensile hands and feet to grip the trunk and branches. Although small gorillas may swing between branches,

species that range from tropical Africa and Asia to Gibraltar on the southern coast of Spain to Japan. At the northernmost portions of their range, these primates inhabit temperate rather than strictly tropical environments.

Baboons, a kind of Old World monkey, have been of particular interest to paleoanthropologists because they live in environments similar to those in which humans may have originated. Largely terrestrial, baboons have abandoned trees (except for sleeping and refuge) and live in the savannahs, deserts, and highlands of Africa. Somewhat dog-faced, they have long muzzles and a fierce look. They eat a diet of leaves, seeds, insects, lizards, and small mammals. Baboons live in large, well-organized troops composed of related females and adult males that have transferred out of other troops.

larger individuals limit their swinging to leaning outward while reaching for fruit and clasping a limb for support. Still, gorillas spend most of their time on the ground. All apes except humans and their immediate ancestors possess arms that are longer than their legs.

In moving on the ground, African apes "knuckle-walk" on the backs of their hands, resting their weight on the middle joints of the fingers. They stand erect when reaching for fruit, looking over tall grass, or doing any activity where they find an erect position advantageous. The semi-erect posture is natural in apes when on the ground because the curvature of their vertebral column places their center of gravity, which is high in their body, in front of their hip joint. Thus, they are both top heavy and front heavy. Though apes can walk on two legs, or bipedally, for short distances, the structure of the ape pelvis is not well suited to support the weight of the torso and limbs for more than several minutes.

Gibbons and siamangs, the small apes that are native to Southeast Asia and Malaysia, have compact, slim bodies and stand about 3 feet high. They have extraordinarily long arms compared to their short legs. In addition to moving through treetops by brachiation (**Figure 3.14**), they can run erect, holding their arms out for balance.

Figure 3.14 Gibbons Swinging from Branch to Branch All apes or hominoids possess a suspensory hanging apparatus that allows them to hang from the branches of the forest canopy. But only the gibbon is a master of brachiation— swinging from branch to branch. These hominoids can also walk bipedally for brief periods of time when they need their arms free for carrying, but they cannot sustain bipedal locomotion for more than 50 to 100 yards. Hominoid anatomy, the human line excepted, is better adapted to knuckle-walking and hanging in the trees.

Gibbon and siamang males and females are similar in size, living in family groups of two parents and offspring.

Orangutans, found in Borneo and Sumatra, are divided into two distinct species. Considerably taller and much heavier than gibbons and siamangs, orangutans possess the bulk characteristic of the great apes. With close-set eyes and facial prominence, orangutans appear to be quite human. The people of Sumatra gave orangutans their name "person of the forest," using the Malay term *oran*, which means "person." On the ground, orangutans walk with their forelimbs in a fists-sideways or a palms-down position. They are, however, more arboreal than the African apes (**Figure 3.15**).

Although sociable by nature, the orangutans of Borneo spend most of their time alone (except in the case of females with young) because they have to forage over a wide area to obtain sufficient food. By contrast, in the swamps of Sumatra an abundance of fruits and insects sustains groups of adults and permits coordinated group travel. Thus, gregariousness is a function of habitat productivity (Normile, 1998).

Gorillas, found in equatorial Africa, are the largest of the apes; an adult male can weigh over 450 pounds, with females about half that size (**Figure 3.16**). Scientists distinguish between two gorilla species: the lowland and mountain varieties. A thick coat of glossy black hair covers gorilla bodies, and mature males have a silvery gray upper back. With a strikingly human look about the face, gorillas, like humans, focus on things in their field of vision by directing the eyes rather than moving the head.

Gorillas are mostly ground-dwellers, but the lighter females and young may sleep in trees in carefully constructed nests. Because of their weight, adult males spend less time in the trees but raise and lower themselves among the tree branches when searching for fruit. Gorillas knuckle-walk, using all four limbs with the fingers of the hand flexed, placing the knuckles instead of the palm of the hand on the ground. They stand erect to reach for fruit, to see something more easily, or to threaten perceived sources of danger with their famous chest-beating displays. Although known for these displays (which protect the members of their troop), adult male silverback gorillas are the gentle giants of the forest. As vegetarians, gorillas devote a major portion of each day to eating volumes of plant matter to sustain their massive size.

Figure 3.15 **Go Fish** This male orangutan was photographed off Kaja Island in the middle of the Gohong River in Borneo. A resident of a preserve where captive animals are rehabituated into the wild, the young male copied this hunting behavior by watching humans spear fishing along the same river. Although so far the orangutan has been unable to nab a fish with his spear tip, his intent is clear. This rare photograph, along with the first photograph of a swimming orangutan, appears in the beautiful book titled *Thinkers of the Jungle*, by Gerd Schuster, Willie Smits, and photographer Jay Ullal.

Figure 3.16 **Gorillas and Sexual Dimorphism** Compare this female gorilla to the adult male gorilla in this chapter's Globalscape. Not only are male gorillas nearly twice the size of females, but their faces also have a different shape. From the earliest embryological stage to adolescence, male and female sex hormones control the process of growth and development so that the male and female adult phenotypes differ in a variety of ways. Scientists have proposed that high levels of sexual dimorphism characterize primate groups in which male–male competition is high.

Although gorillas are gentle and tolerant, their behavioral repertoire includes bluffing aggression.

In the past, chimpanzees and bonobos (**Figure 3.17**), two closely related species of the genus (*Pan*), were thought to be the same species. Bonobos are restricted in their distribution to the rainforests of the Democratic Republic of Congo. The common chimpanzee, by contrast, widely inhabits the forested portions of sub-Saharan Africa. Probably the best known of the apes, chimpanzees and bonobos have long been favorites in zoos and circuses. When bonobos were recognized as a distinct species in 1929, they were commonly called "pygmy chimpanzees." *Bonobo* replaced this term because not only does their size range overlap with that of chimpanzees, but as we will explore in the next chapter, behavior rather than size constitutes the most striking difference between the two groups.

Although thought of as particularly quick and clever, all four great apes are of equal intelligence, despite some

© Steve Bloom Images/Alamy

Figure 3.17 **A Bonobo** Over a decade of civil war in the Democratic Republic of Congo, the natural habitat of bonobos, and the aftermath of the genocide in neighboring Rwanda have drastically threatened the survival of bonobos, a species known for harmonious social life. These violent times have prompted the hunting of bonobos to feed starving people and the illegal capture of baby bonobos as pets. Primatologists and local conservationists have turned from observational fieldwork to economic development projects aimed at restoring the stability in the region required for the continued survival of bonobos and mountain gorillas.

Threats to Primates

In Asia, the statistics are alarming, with more than 70 percent of species threatened and at least 80 percent at risk in Indonesia and Vietnam. Included among them are all of the great apes, as well as such formerly widespread and adaptable species as rhesus macaques. In the wild these animals are endangered by habitat destruction caused by economic development (farming, lumbering, cattle ranching, rubber tapping), as well as by hunters and trappers who pursue them for food, trophies, research, or as exotic pets. Primatologists have long known the devastating effects of habitat destruction through the traditional practice of slash-and-burn agriculture.

However, primate habitats are at far greater risk from contemporary hazards. War impacts primate habitats significantly, and the effects linger long after the battles. Hunters may use the automatic weapons left over from human conflicts in their pursuit of bushmeat. Also, because monkeys and apes are so closely related to humans, some scientists regard them as essential for biomedical research. Although captive breeding provides most of the primates used in laboratories, an active trade in live primates still threatens their native extinction. Globalization also exerts a profound impact on local conditions. This chapter's Globalscape illustrates how cell phones are impacting gorilla habitats and the survival of this species.

Primate Conservation

The aforementioned survey of living primates illustrates the diversity of our closest living relatives. To ensure that they will continue to share the planet with us, primate conservation has become an issue of vital importance. Nearly 50 percent of the known primate species and subspecies face extinction in the next decade (Kaplan, 2008).

differences in cognitive styles. More arboreal than gorillas but less so than orangutans, chimpanzees and bonobos forage on the ground much of the day, knuckle-walking like gorillas. At sunset, they return to the trees where they build their nests.

Conservation Strategies

Because of their vulnerability, the conservation of primates is an urgent matter. Traditional conservation efforts have emphasized habitat preservation above all else, but primatologists have expanded their efforts to include educating local communities and discouraging the hunting of primates for food and medical purposes. Some primatologists even help implement alternative economic strategies for local peoples so that human and primate populations can return to the successful coexistence that prevailed before colonialism and globalization contributed to the destabilization of tradition homelands. This chapter's Anthropology Applied looks at these economic development efforts in the Democratic Republic of Congo.

In direct conservation efforts, primatologists work to maintain some populations in the wild, either by

Globalscape

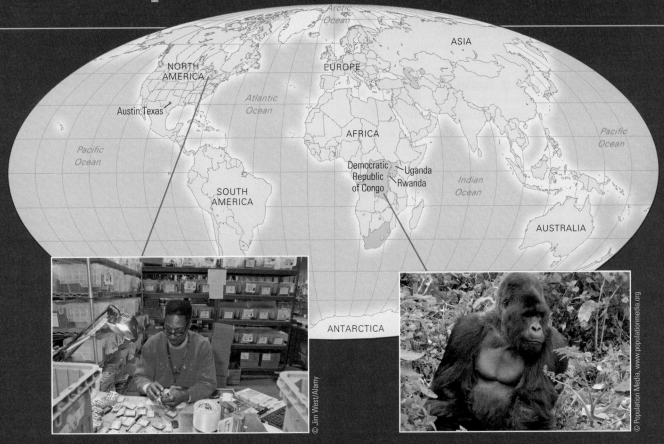

Gorilla Hand Ashtrays?

Tricia, a 20-year-old from Austin, Texas, once blogged: "At that party did you meet the guy from South Africa that looked like an exact replica of Dave Matthews (only skinnier) who was talking about gorilla hand ashtrays?"[a] The unnamed guy was talking about one of the many real threats to gorillas in the wild. With no natural enemies, human actions alone are responsible for the shrinking population of gorillas in their natural habitats in Rwanda, Uganda, and the Democratic Republic of Congo. Despite conservation work begun by the late primatologist Dian Fossey, who pioneered field studies of the gorillas in the 1970s, ashtrays made from gorilla hands and gorilla heads remain coveted souvenirs for unsavory tourists. A poacher can sell these body parts and the remaining bushmeat for a handsome profit.

Today, not only do logging and mining in gorilla habitats destroy these forests, but new roads make it easier for poach- ers to access the gorillas. Local governments of Rwanda and Uganda, in partnership with the Fossey Fund and the Bush Meat Project, have organized poaching patrols and community partnerships to protect the endangered gorillas. Thousands of miles away, Tricia and her friends can also help by recycling their cell phones. The mineral coltan (shown in Chapter 1's opening Challenge Issue) that is found in cell phones is mined primarily from gorilla habitats in the Democratic Republic of Congo. Recycling, as pictured here in a Michigan cell phone recycling plant, will reduce the amount of new coltan needed.

Global Twister

Encouraging recycling of cell phones and discouraging poaching both will impact gorilla survival. How would you go about convincing average cell phone users or poachers to change their habits or livelihood to protect endangered gorillas?

---

[a]http://profile.myspace.com/index.cfm?fuseaction=user. viewprofile&friendid=40312227 (accessed July 3, 2006)

ANTHROPOLOGY APPLIED

The Congo Heartland Project

Under the leadership of Belgian primatologist Jef Dupain, the African Wildlife Foundation has embarked on a number of projects to support the continued survival of bonobos and mountain gorillas in the Democratic Republic of Congo (DRC). Called the Congo Heartland Project, this work is designed to support the local human populations devastated by a decade of civil war in the Congo itself as well as the impact of the massive influx of refugees from war and genocide in neighboring Rwanda.

The rich rainforests along the tributaries of the mighty Congo River in the

As part of the African Wildlife Foundation's Congo Heartland Project, primatologist Jef Dupain (*second from left*) trains workers in the forest near the Lomako Conservation Science Center. In addition to classic research activities, the Congo Heartland Project provides jobs for local families and serves as an anchor for research, conservation, and microenterprise activities in the largely undisturbed Lomako Forest, which is the habitat of the bonobo, a rare great ape.

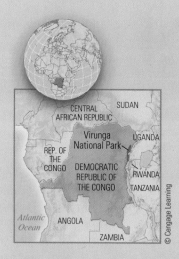

DRC are the only natural habitats for bonobos in the world. Mountain gorillas can be found in the DRC and in neighboring Uganda and Rwanda. Primatological fieldwork thrived in sites established during the 1970s until the mid-1990s when war and genocide led to the forced removal of primatologists. Although many left the region, Dupain stayed and monitored the kinds of bushmeat brought into the markets in Kinshasa. With the human population

establishing preserves in areas the animals already occupy or by moving populations to suitable habitats. These approaches require constant monitoring and management to ensure that sufficient space and resources remain available. As humans encroach on primate habitats, translocation of primates to protected areas is a viable strategy for primate conservation, and primatologists provide invaluable field studies to guide these relocations.

For example, when the troop of free-ranging baboons that primatologist Shirley Strum had been studying for

fifteen years in Kenya began raiding crops and garbage on newly established farms, she was instrumental in successfully moving this troop and two other local troops—130 animals in all—to more sparsely inhabited country 150 miles away. Knowing their habits, Strum was able to trap, tranquilize, and transport the animals to their new home while preserving the baboons' vital social relationships. Strum's careful work allowed for a smooth transition. With social relations intact, the baboons did not abandon their new homes nor did they block the transfer of desperate and starving and the poachers armed with automatic weapons, the park rangers charged with protecting the great apes were outnumbered, and many primates perished. Since a fragile peace was achieved in the region in 2003, initiatives of the Congo Heartland Project have been reestablished, including involving local communities in agricultural practices to protect the Congo River and its tributaries and to preserve their precious animal populations.

Congo Heartland Project initiatives typically empower local communities in development efforts using a participative, interactive, and transparent approach. For example, a range of different ethnic groups, including marginalized people such as Pygmies and women, met with local authorities to reestablish the management policies of Dupain's field site (the Lomako-Yokokala Faunal Reserve) as it reopened for researchers and ecotourists. Forty percent of the income generated in park revenues is to return to the local communities. According to Dupain, success for these projects is defined as follows:

Local communities take part in decision making on how the protected area will be managed, on how revenue will be shared, and as a result, local communities take up the defense of their protected area. In time, densities of bonobo, bongo, forest elephant, Congo peacock, leopard, Allen's swamp monkey, black and white colobus, and many others will increase, more tourists and researchers will come and will be willing to pay for this environmental service, local communities will have increased access to education, medical treatment, electricity, clean water . . . the list goes on. Mange Bofaso put it best: "In Katanga they have diamonds. Here in Lomako, we have bonobos."[a]

The Congo Heartland Project also includes encouraging a variety of alternative economic practices in communities bordering existing wildlife preserves. For example, around the Virunga National Park, home to the endangered mountain gorilla, Congolese Enterprise Officer Wellard Makambo encourages and monitors beekeeping and a mushroom farm collective, run by Congolese women. He also advises members of a conflict resolution team dealing with gorillas that have left the wildlife preserve to raid human crops. Local communities require reassurance and restitution, while gorillas need to be returned safely to the park. When Makambo made his first trip back to the Bukima Ranger Station after the war, he wrote,

While I was standing on the hill surveying the amazing Bukima view I felt like a mighty silverback gorilla looking at his bountiful bamboo kingdom—one whose life would be hopeless if this kingdom is destroyed. I tried to measure the effects of the war on people and on our activities and projects. It was tough getting my head around it: how to re-start things when you realise effort alone is not sufficient. You need stability as well, which is slowly coming back to this area.[b]

These economic development projects are playing a crucial role in restoring the stability in the region required for the continued survival of bonobos and mountain gorillas.

---

[a]African Wildlife Foundation, Facebook blog. www.facebook.com/AfricanWildlife Foundation
[b] Ibid.

new males, with their all-important knowledge of local resources, into the troop. The success of her effort, which had never been tried with baboons, proves that translocation is a realistic technique for saving endangered primate species. However, this conservation effort depends first on available land, where preserves can be established to provide habitats for endangered primates.

A second strategy has been developed to help primates that have been illegally trapped—either for market as pets or for biomedical research. This approach involves returning these recovered animals to their natural habitats. Researchers have established orphanages in which specially trained human substitute mothers support the young primates so that they can gain enough social skills to return to living with their own species.

A third strategy to preventing primate extinction is to maintain breeding colonies in captivity. These colonies encourage psychological and physical well-being, as well as reproductive success. Primates in zoos and laboratories do not successfully reproduce when deprived of amenities such as opportunities for climbing, materials for nest building, others with whom to socialize, and places for privacy. Although such features contribute to the success of breeding colonies in captivity, ensuring the survival of our primate cousins in suitable natural habitats is a far greater challenge that humans must meet in the years to come.

Intense primate conservation efforts are beginning to pay off. For example, in recent years, the population size of the mountain gorilla (*Gorilla beringei beringei*) has increased despite the political chaos of the Democratic Republic of Congo. Western lowland gorilla populations (*Gorilla gorilla*) are also on the rise. Similarly, tamarin monkey populations in Brazil (**Figure 3.18**) have stabilized despite being on the brink of extinction thirty-five years ago, demonstrating the effectiveness of the conservation initiatives put into place. According to primatologist Sylvia Atsalis, "The presence alone of scientists has been shown to protect primates, acting as a deterrent to habitat destruction and hunting. . . . The more people we can send, the more we can help to protect endangered primates" (quoted in Kaplan, 2008).

Figure 3.18 The Golden Lion Tamarin Because of their exceptional beauty, golden lion tamarin monkeys (or golden marmosets) have been kept as pets since colonial times. More recently, they have also been threatened by development given that they reside in the tropical forest habitats around the popular tourist destination of Rio de Janeiro, Brazil. A major conservation effort, initiated in the 1980s to save these monkeys, included planting wildlife corridors to connect the remaining forest patches and releasing animals bred in captivity into these newly created environments. Today, live wild births have increased steadily, and the golden lion tamarin population is recovering from the threat of extinction.

CHAPTER CHECKLIST

How do primatologists conduct field research?

● Researchers rely on observation and collection of feces and hair samples left behind in order to minimize contact that could endanger primate populations.

● Conservation efforts are combined with research to ensure the future study of wild populations.

● Animals in captivity have provided opportunities to interact with and discover the communicative capabilities of many primates.

How does mammalian biology compare to reptilian biology?

● As homeotherms, mammals can survive in a wider variety of climates than isothermic reptiles, but mammals require more calories to survive.

● Mammals are k-selected, rather than r-selected, meaning that parents spend much time rearing few offspring.

● Mammals possess various types of specialized teeth that are replaced only once over a lifetime. Reptile teeth are all nearly identical with unlimited replacement.

How does taxonomy apply to primates, and what issues does it pose?

● Taxonomists use shared derived characteristics to establish evolutionary relationships.

● The Linnaean system focuses on the measure of anatomical similarity known as a grade. By this system, primates consist of two subfamilies called *Prosimii* and *Anthropoidea*. Anthropoids are divided into the infraorders Platyrrhini and Catarrhini.

● A new taxonomic scheme based on quantifying genetic similarities proposes a regrouping of primates into two suborders: Strepsirhini and Haplorhini. It also distinguishes the hominin subfamily of hominids (humans and their ancestors) from the other African apes.

What features distinguish primates from other mammals?

● Primates have a long period of childhood dependency and are large-brained, which enables both learned and adaptive behavior.

● Primates developed binocular stereoscopic color vision as they became both diurnal and arboreal. Primate teeth reflect the diversity of food sources available among the trees.

● The fovea centralis is unique to primates and allows focusing the eye without sacrificing peripheral vision. Enhanced visual acuity has come at the expense of sense of smell.

● The primate foramen magnum is closer to the base of the skull, allowing an upright posture.

● Primate digits have sensitive pads, usually accompanied by flattened nails. Most species have opposable thumbs and big toes.

What features characterize the five natural groups of primates?

● Lemurs and lorises have large ears, big eyes, pointed snouts that limit facial expression, a claw on their second toe used for grooming, and several scent glands for communication. As a group, they retain more ancestral primate characteristics.

● Tarsiers are tiny arboreal creatures with oversized eyes and heads and elongated foot bones that allow for far jumps. They are genetically closer to monkeys and apes, though as nocturnal insect-eaters, they resemble early ancestral primates.

● New World monkeys are flat-nosed tree-dwellers that walk on all fours and rarely hang from trees by their arms. One subgroup possesses long prehensile tails that are used as an extra limb.

● Old World monkeys are alternately terrestrial and arboreal and have downward-pointing nostrils and non-prehensile tails. They walk on all fours with palms down, and many species exhibit sophisticated social organization, communication, and learning abilities.

● Having no tails, apes are all adapted to hanging by their arms and in some species to brachiate. Their clavicles position their arms at the sides of the body. They are able to stand erect due to the curvature of their vertebrae. African apes knuckle-walk when on the ground, and all apes but humans have forelimbs that are longer than their legs.

What pressures do primate populations currently face?

● Habitat destruction caused by economic development and globalization has led to the endangered status of many primate species, especially the great apes.

● Primates in war-torn regions are particularly threatened by the presence of automatic weapons and disruption to conservation efforts.

● Relocation, reintroduction, and captive colony strategies have met with success in recent years, and some populations are rebounding due to such conservation efforts.

QUESTIONS FOR REFLECTION

1. Has learning more about the numerous similarities between our primate cousins and us motivated you personally to meet the challenge of preventing their extinction? What human factors are causing endangerment of primates, and how can we prevent their extinction?

2. What are the main differences between mammals and reptiles? Do we share any ancestral features with reptiles? What are some of the derived features characteristic of mammals including humans?

3. Considering some of the trends seen among the primates, such as increased brain size or fewer teeth, why is it incorrect to say that some primates are more evolved than others? What is wrong with the statement that humans are more evolved than chimpanzees?

4. Two systems exist for dividing the primate order into suborders because of difficulties with classifying tarsiers. Should classification systems be based on genetic relationships or based on the biological concept of grade? Is the continued use of the older terminology an instance of unwillingness to change or a difference in philosophy? How do the issues brought up by the tarsier problem translate to the hominoids?

5. What aspects of mammalian primate biology do you see reflected in yourself or in people you know?

ONLINE STUDY RESOURCES

CourseMate

Access chapter-specific learning tools, including learning objectives, practice quizzes, videos, flash cards, glossaries, and more in your Anthropology CourseMate.

Log into **www.cengagebrain.com** to access the resources your instructor has assigned and to purchase materials.

Challenge Issue

Each new observation of primate behavior challenges us to rethink the old nature–nurture question: How much of human behavior is biologically determined and how much of it derives from culture? Early on, primate behavior was considered wholly natural or "acultural": Any behavior that humans shared with other primates was considered to have a biological basis. But repeated demonstration of the range of behaviors among our primate cousins has complicated such theories of human biological determinism. Consider, for example, the diverse sexual behaviors of bonobos, the species of the genus *Pan* that inhabits the war-torn rainforests of the Congo. The genital-genital or G-G rubbing between two females pictured here is one among the many sexual practices bonobos use to reduce tension and resolve social conflicts. Among bonobos, primatologists have observed every possible combination of ages and sexes engaging in a remarkable array of sexual activities that goes far beyond male–female mating for purposes of biological reproduction. Interestingly, female bonobos, like female humans, have no visible biological display of ovulation, or the moment when a fertile egg is released from the womb. Does this biological factor alone determine bonobos' diverse sexuality? And by extension, does concealed ovulation in human females indicate that our sexuality as a species is also untethered from the biological task of reproduction? What does it mean when individuals argue for a biological basis for human homosexuality or its opposite, that among humans, only heterosexuality is natural? Biology and culture clearly interact not only in generating behavioral variation, but also with the theories we humans generate about our behaviors.

Primate Behavior

Research into primate behavior has shown again and again the behavioral sophistication of our closest living relatives. Primates use tools, learn, and can be dishonest, just as humans can. Although the young Jane Goodall was criticized for naming the chimpanzees she studied, social interactions, particularly among the apes, demonstrate that they recognize one another as individuals and adjust their behavior accordingly. (Many other long-lived social mammals, such as elephants and dolphins, do the same.) Certainly, biology plays a role in such primate behaviors, but often, as with humans, the social traditions of the group also determine behavior. Nevertheless, some broad biological factors underlie the social traditions of the primates.

Compared to many other mammals, primates require more time to reach adulthood. During their lengthy growth and development, young primates learn the behaviors of their social group. Observations of primates in their natural habitats over the past decades have shown that social interaction, organization, learning, reproduction, care of the young, and communication among our primate relatives resemble human behavior. As we study primate behavior to learn about ourselves, who we are as a species today, and how we got here, it becomes clear that many of our differences reflect only the degree of expression of shared characteristics.

Primates as Models for Human Evolution

As we will explore in the human evolution chapters to come, the human line split from a common ancestor that we share with the African apes. Although this split occurred millions of years ago, paleoanthropologists in the mid-20th century were hopeful that observations made among the living apes might shed light on the lifeways of the fossil species they were discovering. Indeed, paleontologist Louis Leakey encouraged Jane Goodall to begin her research with chimpanzees in Gombe Stream Chimpanzee Reserve (now a national park) on the eastern shores

IN THIS CHAPTER YOU WILL LEARN TO

- Identify the range of variation of primate behavior and the theories that account for it.

- Distinguish different forms of primate social organization.

- Examine the biological basis of primate behavior, with particular emphasis on the primate life cycle, social learning, and the environment.

- Explore the cultural influences on theories of primate behavior.

- Distinguish the diverse behavioral patterns of our closest relatives—orangutans, gorillas, chimpanzees, and bonobos—with particular emphasis on sexual behavior, cooperation, hunting, and tool use.

- Describe the linguistic capacities of the great apes.

- Define *primate culture* in the context of human evolution.

- Explore the moral questions surrounding the use of chimpanzees in biomedical research.

of Lake Tanganyika in Tanzania for this reason. He also supported the fieldwork of two other primatologists: Dian Fossey, working with mountain gorillas in Rwanda, and Biruté Galdikas, working with orangutans in Borneo.

But as forest-dwellers, each of these ape species inhabited an environment that differed considerably from the grassy savannahs inhabited by the earliest human ancestors known at that time. Instead, paleoanthropologists turned to baboons: an Old World monkey native to the savannah environments of eastern Africa where the richest fossil evidence of our ancestors had also been found.

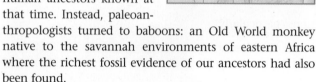

Although baboons differ considerably from our two-legged ancestors, their survival strategies provide some clues as to how early humans adapted to the savannah environment. Members of the genus *Papio*, baboons are among the largest of the Old World monkeys. Fully terrestrial, troops of baboons can be seen sitting together on the dry savannah earth to forage for corms (thick, nutritious underground reproductive parts of plants). They keep a watchful eye out for predators while feeding. At the first sight or sound of danger, alarm calls by members of the troop will signal for all the individuals to retreat to safety.

Baboons live in groups that vary dramatically in size, from less than ten individuals to hundreds. In some species the groups are multi-male multi-female while others are made up of a series of polygynous groups—one male with several females that he dominates (**Figure 4.1**). Sexual dimorphism—anatomical differences between males and females—is high in baboons, and therefore males can use their physical advantages to overpower females easily. But the degree to which males choose to do so varies from group to group.

Extrapolating from baboons to theories about our ancestors poses problems. To use the words of primatologists Shirley Strum and William Mitchell, these baboon "models" often became baboon "muddles" (Strum & Mitchell, 1987).

Figure 4.1 Baboon Social Learning The behavior of baboons, a type of Old World monkey, has been particularly well studied. There are several distinct species of baboon, each with its own social rules. Troops of hamadryas baboons, the sacred baboons of ancient Egypt pictured here, consist of a series of smaller groups made up of a single male and several females over which he dominates. Female hamadryas baboons, if transferred to a troop of olive baboons, where females are not as submissive, maintain the passive behaviors learned in their original troop. But a female olive baboon placed in the hamadryas troop quickly learns submissive behaviors in order to survive.

Paleoanthropologists did not expect our ancestors to possess tails or **ischial callosities**—the hardened, nerveless buttock pads that allow baboons to sit for long periods of time. Tails are strictly a monkey characteristic, not an ape one, and among the hominoids only gibbons and siamangs possess ischial callosities. Instead, paleoanthropologists were looking for examples of *convergence*—of behaviors that might appear in large-bodied, dimorphic primates living in large multimale multi-female groups in a savannah environment.

Paleoanthropology's "baboon hypothesis" led to many excellent long-term field studies of baboons that have yielded fascinating data on their social organization, omnivorous diet, mating patterns and other reproductive strategies, communication, and so forth. As with most primate field studies, the evolutionary questions remain in the background while the rich repertoire of primate behavior takes center stage.

While the savannah environment has certainly been important in human evolution, recent fossil discoveries and analyses have led paleoanthropologists back into the forest, where the earliest two-legged ancestors lived. Researchers now also focus on human origins and the transition from a forested environment to the savannah. Recent field studies of chimpanzees in more savannah-like environments, explored in this chapter, have yielded fascinating results.

Primate Social Organization

Primates are social animals, living and traveling in groups that vary in size and composition from species to species. Different environmental and biological factors have been linked to the group's size, and various primate species exhibit all the possible organizational forms (**Figure 4.2**).

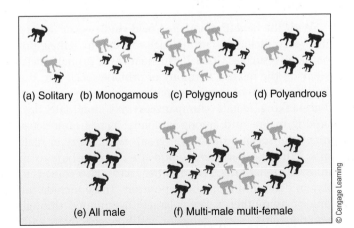

(a) Solitary (b) Monogamous (c) Polygynous (d) Polyandrous

(e) All male   (f) Multi-male multi-female

© Cengage Learning

Figure 4.2 Primate Social Organization Primate social organization ranges from (a) solitary to (b) monogamous to (c) polygynous (single male with many females and their young) to the rare (d) polyandrous (single female with multiple males and her young to (e) all male to (f) multi-male multi-female groups of various sizes and ages. In this figure, females are rust-colored, and males are dark brown.

For example, gibbons live in small nuclear family units consisting of a pair of bonded (*monogamous*) adults and their offspring, whereas orangutans tend to lead solitary existences, with males and females coming together only to mate. Young orangutans stay with their mothers until they reach adult status.

Some baboon species live in *polygynous* groups with one male and many females and their young. Only a very few New World species are *polyandrous* with a single female and more than one male and her young. Twins are common in these species, and the males all help with parenting.

Chimps and bonobos live in large multi-male multi-female groups. Among chimps and bonobos, the largest social organizational unit is the **community**, usually composed of fifty or more individuals who collectively inhabit a large geographic area. Rarely, however, do all of these animals congregate. Instead, they range singly or in small subgroups consisting of adult males, or females with their young, or males and females together with their young. In the course of their travels, subgroups may join forces and forage together, but sooner or later these will break up into smaller units. Typically, when some individuals split off, others join, so the composition of subunits shifts frequently.

The gorilla group is a "family" of five to thirty individuals led by a mature silver-backed male and including younger (black-backed) males, females, the young, and occasionally other silverbacks. The dominant male, however, usually prevents subordinate males from mating with the group's females. Thus, young, sexually mature males, who take on the characteristic silver color at the end of the sexual maturation process (about 11 to 13 years of age), are forced by the dominant silverback to leave their **natal group**—the community they have known since birth. After some time as a solitary male in the forest, a young silverback may find the opportunity to start his own social group by winning outside females. Occasionally, these solitary males will form an all-male group. In the natal group, if the dominant male is weakening with age, one of his sons may remain with the group to succeed to his father's position. Alternatively, an outside male may take over the group. With the dominant male controlling the group, gorillas rarely fight over food, territory, or sex, but they will fight fiercely to defend the group.

In many primate species, including humans, adolescence marks the time when individuals change the relationships they have had with the group they have known since birth. Among primates this change often takes the form of migration to new social groups. In many species, females constitute the core of the social system.

ischial callosities Hardened, nerveless pads on the buttocks that allow baboons and other primates to sit for long periods of time.

community In primatology, a unit of primate social organization composed of fifty or more individuals who collectively inhabit a large geographic area.

natal group The group or the community an animal has inhabited since birth.

For example, offspring tend to remain with the group to which their mother, rather than their father, belongs. Among gorillas, male adolescents leave their natal groups more frequently than females. However, adolescent female chimpanzees and bonobos are often the ones to migrate.

Among Tanzanian chimpanzee communities studied, about half the females leave the community they have known since birth to join another group (Moore, 1998). Other females may also temporarily leave their group to mate with males of another group. Among bonobos, adolescent females appear to always transfer to another group, where they promptly establish bonds with females of their new community. Although biological factors such as the hormonal influences on sexual maturity play a role in adolescent migration, the variation across species and within the chimpanzees in dispersal patterns indicates that differences may also derive from the learned social traditions of the group.

Home Range

Primates usually move about within a circumscribed area, or **home range**, which varies in size depending on the group and on ecological factors such as availability of food. Ranges often change seasonally, and the number of miles traveled daily by a group varies. Some areas, known as *core areas*, are used more often than others. Core areas typically contain water, food sources, resting places, and sleeping trees. The ranges of different groups may overlap, as among bonobos, where 65 percent of one community's range may overlap with that of another (Parish, 1998). By contrast, chimpanzee territories, at least in some regions, are exclusively occupied and will be defended from intrusion (**Figure 4.3**).

Gorillas do not defend their home range against incursions of others of their kind, although they will defend their group if it is in any way threatened. In the lowlands of Central Africa, it is not uncommon to find several families feeding in close proximity to one another (Parnell, 1999). In encounters with other communities, bonobos will defend their immediate space through vocalizations and displays but rarely through fighting. Usually, they settle down and feed side by side, not infrequently grooming, playing, and engaging in sexual activity between groups as well.

Chimpanzees, by contrast, have been observed patrolling their territories to ward off potential trespassers. Moreover, Jane Goodall (see Anthropologists of Note) has recorded the destruction of one chimpanzee community by another invading group. This sort of deadly intercommunity interaction has never been observed

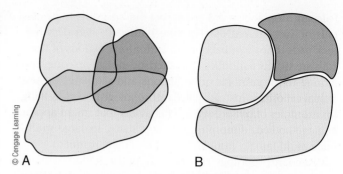

Figure 4.3 **Home Range and Territory** As illustrated in A, home ranges can overlap. When members of the same species meet one another in the shared parts of the range, there might be some tension, deference, or peaceful mingling. Some groups maintain clear territories (B) that are strictly defended from any intrusion by members of the same species.

among bonobos. Some have interpreted the apparent territorial behavior as an expression of the supposedly violent nature of chimpanzees. However, others have suggested that the violence Goodall witnessed was a response to overcrowding that resulted from human activity (Power, 1995).

Social Hierarchy

In the past, primatologists believed that male **dominance hierarchies**, in which some animals outrank and dominate others, formed the basis of primate social structures. They noted that physical strength and size play a role in determining an animal's rank. By this measure, males generally outrank females. However, the male-biased cultures of many early primatologists may have contributed to this theoretical perspective, with their emphasis on domination through superior size and strength. Male dominance hierarchies seemed "natural" to these initial researchers.

With the benefit of detailed field studies over the last fifty years, including cutting-edge research by female primatologists such as Goodall, the nuances of primate social behavior, the relative harmony of primate social life, and the importance of female primates are now documented. High-ranking female chimpanzees may dominate low-ranking males. And among bonobos, female rank determines the social order of the group far more than male rank. While greater strength and size do contribute to an animal's higher rank, several other factors also come into play in determining its social position. These include the rank of its mother, a factor largely determined through her cooperative social behavior and how effectively each individual animal creates alliances with others.

For males, drive or motivation to achieve high status also influences rank. For example, in the community studied by Goodall, one male chimp hit upon the idea of incorporating noisy kerosene cans into his charging displays, thereby intimidating all the other males (Goodall,

home range The geographic area within which a group of primates usually moves.

dominance hierarchies An observed ranking system in primate societies, ordering individuals from high (alpha) to low standing corresponding to predictable behavioral interactions including domination.

ANTHROPOLOGISTS OF NOTE

Jane Goodall (b. 1934) • Kinji Imanishi (1902–1992)

In July 1960, **Jane Goodall** arrived with her mother at the Gombe Chimpanzee Reserve on the shores of Lake Tanganyika in Tanzania. Goodall was the first of three women Kenyan anthropologist Louis Leakey sent to study great apes in the wild (the others were Dian Fossey and Biruté Galdikas, who studied gorillas and orangutans, respectively); her task was to begin a long-term study of chimpanzees. Little did she realize that, more than fifty years later, she would still be at it.

Jane Goodall in the field with chimpanzees at Gombe.

Born in London, Goodall grew up and was schooled in Bournemouth, England. As a child, she dreamed of going to live in Africa, so when an invitation arrived to visit a friend in Kenya, she jumped at the opportunity. While in Kenya, she met Leakey, who gave her a job as an assistant secretary. Before long, she was on her way to Gombe. Within a year, the outside world began to hear extraordinary things about this pioneering woman and her research: tales of tool-making apes, cooperative hunts by chimpanzees, and what seemed like exotic chimpanzee rain dances. By the mid-1960s, her work had earned her a doctorate from Cambridge University, and Gombe was on its way to becoming one of the most dynamic field stations for the study of animal behavior anywhere in the world.

Although Goodall is still very much involved with chimpanzees, she now spends a good deal of time lecturing, writing, and overseeing the work of other researchers. She is passionately committed to primate conservation and is dedicated to halting illegal trafficking in chimps as well as fighting for the humane treatment of captive chimps.

Long before Louis Leakey sent the first Western primatologists into the field, **Kinji Imanishi**—naturalist, explorer, and mountain climber—profoundly influenced primatology in Japan and throughout the world. Although fully aware of Western methods and theories, he developed a radically different approach to the scientific study of the natural world. Imanishi dates his transformation to a youthful encounter with a grasshopper:

> I was walking along a path in a valley, and there was a grasshopper on a leaf in a shrubbery. Until that moment I had happily caught insects, killed them with chloroform, impaled them on pins, and looked up their names, but I realized I knew nothing at all about how this grasshopper lived in the wild.[a]

Kinji Imanishi initiated the earliest field studies of bonobos in the 1940s.

In his most important work, *The World of Living Things*, first published in 1941, Imanishi developed a comprehensive theory about the natural world rooted in Japanese cultural beliefs and practices.

Imanishi's work challenged Western evolutionary theory in several ways. First, Imanishi's theory, like Japanese culture, does not emphasize differences between humans and other animals. Second, rather than focusing on the biology of individual organisms, Imanishi suggested that naturalists examine "specia" (a species society) to which individuals belong as the unit of analysis. Rather than focusing on time, Imanishi emphasized space in his approach to the natural world. He highlighted the harmony of all living things rather than conflict and competition among individual organisms.

Imanishi's research techniques, now standard worldwide, developed directly from his theories: long-term field study of primates in their natural societies using methods from ethnography. With his students, Imanishi conducted pioneering field studies of African apes and Japanese and Tibetan macaques. Japanese primatologists were the first to document the importance of kinship, the complexity of primate societies, patterns of social learning, and the unique character of each primate social group. Because of the work by Imanishi and his students, we now think about the distinct cultures of primate societies.

[a]Heita, K. (1999). Imanishi's world view. *Journal of Japanese Trade and Industry* 18 (2), 15.

1986). As a result, he rose from relatively low status to the number one (alpha) position.

On the whole, bonobo females form stronger bonds with one another than do chimpanzee females. Moreover, the strength of the bond between mother and son interferes with bonds among males. Bonobo males defer to females in feeding, and alpha (high-ranking) females have been observed chasing alpha males; such males may even yield to low-ranking females, particularly when groups of females form alliances. Further, allied females will band together to force an aggressive male out of the community. These bonobo females cooperate even though they are not genetically related to one another.

Alpha males even yield to low-ranking females, and groups of females form alliances in which they may cooperatively attack males, to the point of inflicting blood-drawing injuries (de Waal, Kano, & Parish, 1998). Thus, instead of the male dominance characteristic of chimps, female dominance prevails among bonobos.

Western primatologists' focus on social rank and attack behavior may be a legacy of the individualistic, competitive nature of the societies in which evolutionary theory originated. To a certain degree, natural selection relies upon struggle and competition among living creatures rather than peaceful coexistence within a fixed social order. By contrast, noted Japanese primatologist Kinji Imanishi (see Anthropologists of Note) developed a harmonious theory of evolution and initiated field studies of bonobos that have demonstrated the importance of social

cooperation rather than competition. According to Dutch primatologist Frans de Waal, in social species that cooperate and depend upon one another, **reconciliation**—a friendly reunion between former opponents not long after a conflict—has more evolutionary import than the fight that preceded it (Aureli & de Waal, 2000; de Waal, 2000).

As pictured in the chapter opener, female bonobos reconcile by rubbing their clitorises and swollen genitals. Chimpanzees reconcile with a hug and mouth-to-mouth kiss. The reconciliation techniques of a wide range of other primates and other mammalian species including dolphins and hyenas have been observed in the wild. Although some attribute reconciliation behavior to simple biology, de Waal carried out a series of experiments that demonstrate that primates *learn* these social skills. He took two species of Old World monkey, the aggressive rhesus macaque and the mellower stump-tailed macaque, and housed some of them together for five months. At the end of this period, rhesus macaques that had learned reconciliation from the stump-tailed macaques continued to practice these behaviors when living strictly with rhesus macaques.

Chimps, as de Waal observed, take reconciliation a step further: Some individuals, generally an older female, take on the role of mediator. Recognizing a dispute between two other individuals in the group who sit near one another but avoid eye contact, this mediator will groom one of the combatants for a bit (**Figure 4.4**). When she gets up to groom the other combatant, the first fighter follows and grooms her. She eventually leaves the two fighters grooming each other.

Figure 4.4 Primate Grooming Grooming is an important activity among all catarrhine primates, as shown here in a group of chimps grooming one another in a pattern known as the *domino effect*. Such activity is important for strengthening bonds among individual members of the group.

Gunter Ziesler/Getty Images/Peter Arnold

Individual Interaction and Bonding

As shown in Figure 4.4, **grooming**, the ritual cleaning of another animal to remove parasites and other matter from its skin or coat, has social as well as practical consequences. The grooming animal deftly parts the hair of the one being groomed and removes any foreign object, often eating it. Besides serving hygienic purposes, grooming can signify friendliness, closeness, appeasement, reconciliation, or even submission. Bonobos and chimpanzees have favorite grooming partners. Embracing, touching, and the joyous welcoming of other members of the ape community also demonstrate group sociability. These important behavioral traits undoubtedly existed among human ancestors.

Interestingly, different chimp communities have different styles of grooming. In one East African group, for example, the two chimps groom each other face-to-face, with one hand, while clasping their partner's free hand. In another group 90 miles distant, the handclasp does not occur. In East Africa, all communities incorporate leaves in their grooming, but in West Africa they do not.

Gorillas, though gentle and tolerant, tend toward aloofness and independence. Restraint characterizes individual interaction among adults, whereas friendship and closeness appear to typify only the relationships between adults and infants. Among bonobos, chimpanzees, gorillas, and orangutans, as among most other primates, the mother–infant bond is the strongest and longest lasting. It may endure for many years—commonly for the lifetime of the mother. Gorilla infants share their mothers' nests but have also been seen sharing nests with mature childless females. Bonobo, chimpanzee, and gorilla males pay attention to juveniles, thus contributing to their socialization. Bonobo males even carry infants on occasion. Their interest in a youngster does not elicit the nervous reaction from the mother that it does among chimps; chimp mothers may be reacting to the occasional infanticide on the part of chimpanzee males, a behavior never observed among bonobos.

Sexual Behavior

Most mammals mate only during specified breeding seasons occurring once or twice a year. While some primates have a fixed breeding season tied to a simultaneous increase in body fat, or to the consumption of specific plant foods, many primate species can breed throughout the course of the year. Among the African apes, as with humans, there is no fixed breeding season. In chimps, frequent sexual activity—initiated by either the male or the female—occurs during **estrus**, the period when the female is receptive to impregnation. Physically visible as a signal to potential mates (**Figure 4.5**), in chimpanzees the skin around the genitals swells during estrus. Bonobo females, by contrast, appear as if they are fertile at all

© Michel Gunther/Photo Researchers, Inc.

Figure 4.5 Gelada Estrus Because geladas, a kind of Old World monkey, spend far more time sitting than upright, signaling ovulation through genital swelling is not as practical as is signaling it through the reddening of a patch of furless skin on their chests. This way it is easy for other members of the group to see that they are fertile even while they are foraging.

times due to their constantly swollen genitals and interest in sex. Gorillas appear to show less interest in sex compared to either chimps or bonobos.

When in estrus, a chimpanzee female engages in lots of sexual activity, sometimes with as many as fifty copulations in one day with a dozen different partners. For the most part, females mate with males of their own group. Dominant males often try to monopolize females in full estrus, although this will not succeed without cooperation from the female. In addition, an individual female and a lower-ranking male sometimes form a temporary bond, leaving the group together for a few "private" days during the female's fertile period. Interestingly, the relationship between reproductive success and social rank differs for males and females. In the chimpanzee community

---

reconciliation In primatology, a friendly reunion between former opponents not long after a conflict.

grooming The ritual cleaning of another animal's coat to remove parasites and other matter.

estrus In some primate females, the time of sexual receptivity during which ovulation is visibly displayed.

studied by Goodall, low- or midlevel males sired about half the infants. Although for females high rank is linked with successful reproduction, social success for males—achieving alpha status—does not translate neatly into the evolutionary currency of reproductive success (Figure 4.6).

In contrast to chimpanzees, bonobos (like humans) do not limit their sexual behavior to times of female fertility. The constant genital swelling of bonobos, in effect, conceals the females' **ovulation**, or moment when an egg released into the womb is receptive for fertilization. Ovulation is also concealed in humans, by the absence of genital swelling at all times. Concealed ovulation in humans and bonobos may play a role in separating sexual activity for social and pleasurable reasons from the purely biological task of reproduction. In fact, among bonobos (as among humans) sexuality goes far beyond male–female mating for purposes of biological reproduction.

Primatologists have observed virtually every possible combination of ages and sexes engaging in a remarkable array of sexual activities, including oral sex, tongue-kissing, and massaging each other's genitals (de Waal, 2001). Male bonobos may mount each other, or one may rub his scrotum against that of the other. Researchers have also observed bonobos "penis fencing"—hanging face-to-face from a branch and rubbing their erect penises together as if crossing swords. Among females, genital rubbing is particularly common.

Most of this sex, both hetero- and homosexual, functions to reduce tensions and resolve social conflicts. Bonobo sexual activity is very frequent but also very brief, lasting only 8 to 10 seconds. Since the documentation of sexual activities among bonobos, field studies by primatologists have documented a variety of sexual behaviors

Figure 4.6 **Male Dominance Display and Reproductive Success** Although early primates studies focused on male dominance hierarchies, later research has shown that social dominance or alpha status does not automatically confer greater reproductive success for males as it does for females. As primates themselves, were the early primatologists impressed by male displays of power and bluster, such as seen here? Or did this emphasis on dominance hierarchies stem from the fact that Darwinian theory—itself in sync with its own cultural milieu—emphasized competition and a struggle for existence? With time, careful scientific study has confirmed that for primate survival, cooperation outranks aggression.

© Martin Harvey/Alamy

ovulation The moment when an egg released from an ovary into the womb is receptive for fertilization.

among other species as well. This chapter's Original Study by primatologists Anna Maggioncalda, and Robert Sapolsky offers a disturbing example of the diversity of sexual behavior of primates.

ORIGINAL STUDY

Disturbing Behaviors of the Orangutan

BY ANNE NACEY MAGGIONCALDA AND ROBERT M. SAPOLSKY

An adult male orangutan is an impressive sight. The animal has a pair of wide cheek pads, called flanges, and a well-developed throat sac used for emitting loud cries known as long calls. The mature male also has long, brightly colored hair on its body and face. These are secondary sexual characteristics, the flamboyant signals that male orangutans flaunt to proclaim their fertility and fitness to the opposite sex. The features emerge during orangutan adolescence: Males reach puberty at around 7 to 9 years of age, then spend a few years in a far-from-impressive "subadult" stage, during which they are

about the same size as mature females. The males reach their adult size and develop secondary sexual traits by ages 12 to 14. Or at least that's what primate researchers used to think.

As stable social groups of orangutans were established in zoos, however, it became clear that an adolescent male could remain a subadult, in a state of arrested development, until his late teens. In the 1970s, studies of orangutans in the rainforests of Southeast Asia by Biruté M. F. Galdikas . . . and others produced the same finding: Sometimes males were arrested adolescents for a decade or more, about half their potential reproductive lives. Variability of this magnitude is fascinating—it is like finding a species in which pregnancy could last anywhere from six months to five years.

Biologists are keenly interested in studying cases of arrested development because they often shed light on the processes of growth and maturation. . . . Environmental factors can . . . slow or halt an organism's development. For instance, food shortages delay maturation in humans and many other animals. This response is logical from an evolutionary standpoint—if it is unclear whether you will survive another week, it makes no sense to waste calories by adding bone mass or developing secondary sexual characteristics. Gymnasts and ballet dancers who exercise to extremes and anorexics who starve themselves sometimes experience delayed onset of puberty.

Among male orangutans, though, the cause of arrested development seems to lie in the animals' social environment. The presence of dominant adult males appears to delay the maturation of adolescent males in the same vicinity. Until recently, researchers believed that they were observing a stress-induced pathology—that is, the adolescent orangutans stopped developing because the adult males bullied and frightened them. Over the past few years, however, we have conducted studies (by measuring stress, growth, and reproductive hormone levels in urine) suggesting that arrested development among orangutans is not a pathology but an adaptive evolutionary strategy. The arrested adolescent males are capable of impregnating females, and by staying small and immature (in terms of secondary sexual features) they minimize the amount of food they need and lower the risk of serious conflict with adult males. But the strategy of these arrested adolescents has a disquieting aspect: They copulate forcibly with females. In other words, they rape.

These findings overturned some long-held assumptions about orangutans. Apparently, arrested adolescents are neither stressed nor reproductively suppressed. What is going on? It turns out that there is more than one way for a male orangutan to improve his chances of reproducing.

A cornerstone of modern evolutionary theory is that animal behavior has evolved not for the good of the species or the social group but to maximize the number of gene copies passed on by an individual and its close relatives. For a long time, the study of primates was dominated by simplistic models of how animals achieve this goal. According to these models, male behavior consists of virtually nothing but aggression and competition to gain access to females. If only one female is sexually receptive in a group with many males, this competition would result in the highest-ranking male mating with her; if two females are receptive, the males ranking first and second in the hierarchy would mate with them, and so on.

But this kind of behavior is rarely seen among social primates. Instead male primates can choose alternative strategies to maximize their reproductive success. Why should there be alternatives? Because the seemingly logical strategy—developing powerful muscles and dramatic secondary sexual characteristics to excel at male–male competition—has some serious drawbacks. In many species, maintaining those secondary characteristics requires elevated testosterone levels, which have a variety of adverse effects on health. The aggression that comes with such a strategy is not great for health either.

Furthermore, increased body mass means greater metabolic demands and more pressure for successful food acquisition. During famines, the bigger primates are less likely to survive. For an arboreal species such as the orangutan, the heavier body of the mature male also limits which trees and branches can be accessed for food. And the development of secondary sexual characteristics makes a male more conspicuous, both to predators and to other males that view those characteristics as a challenge.

In contrast, the key impression that a developmentally arrested male communicates to an adult male is a lack of threat or challenge because the immature male looks like a kid. Arrested male orangutans are apparently inconspicuous enough to be spared a certain amount of social stress. What is more, the "low profile" of these animals may actually give them a competitive advantage when it comes to reproduction. In many primate species, the low-ranking males are actually doing a fair share of the mating. Genetic paternity testing of these primates has shown that the subordinate males are quite successful in passing on their genes. . . .

The great majority of adult female orangutans are sexually receptive only to mature males. So how do the arrested males mate? Observations of orangutans both in the wild and in captive populations have indicated that the arrested males forcibly copulate with females. *Rape* is an apt term for these copulations: The adult females usually resist the arrested adolescents fiercely, biting the males whenever they can and emitting loud, guttural sounds (called rape grunts) that are heard only under these circumstances. Adult males sometimes rape, too, but not nearly as often as the arrested males.

Thus, two reproductive strategies appear to have evolved for adolescent male orangutans. If no fully mature males are nearby, the adolescent will most likely develop quickly in the hopes of attracting female attention. When adult males are present, however, a strategy of arrested development has its advantages. If the social environment changes—say, if the nearby adult males die off or migrate—the arrested males will rapidly develop secondary sexual features and change their behavior patterns. Researchers are now trying to determine exactly how the presence or absence of adult males triggers hormonal changes in the adolescents.

What are the lessons we can learn from the male orangutan? First, a situation that seems stressful from a

VISUAL COUNTERPOINT

The male orangutan on the right has retained his adolescent physique even though his primary sex characteristics are fully mature, allowing him to father offspring. The male on the left has developed the secondary sexual characteristics typical of the adult male orangutan. Though strikingly different in appearance, these two individuals might be very close to the same age.

human's perspective may not necessarily be so. Second, the existence of alternative reproductive strategies shows that the optimal approach can vary dramatically in different social and ecological settings. There is no single blueprint for understanding the evolution of behavior. Third, although the recognition of alternative strategies built around female choice has generally met with a receptive audience among scientists, the rape-oriented strategy of arrested male orangutans is not so pleasing. But the study of primates has demonstrated time and again that the behavior of these animals is far from Disney-esque.

One must be cautious, however, in trying to gain insights into human behavior by extrapolating from animal studies. There is a temptation to leap to a wrongheaded conclusion: Because forcible copulation occurs in orangutans and something similar occurs in humans, rape has a natural basis and is therefore unstoppable. This argument ignores the fact that the orangutan is the only nonhuman primate to engage in forcible copulation as a routine means of siring offspring. Furthermore, close observations of orangutan rape show that it is very different from human rape: For example, researchers have never seen a male orangutan injure a female during copulation in an apparently intentional manner. Most important, the orangutan's physiology, life history, and social structure are completely unlike those of any other primate. Orangutans have evolved a unique set of adaptations to survive in their environment, and hence it would be the height of absurdity to draw simpleminded parallels between their behaviors and those of humans.

Adapted from Maggioncalda, A. N., & Sapolsky, R. M. (2002, May 13). Disturbing behaviors of the orangutan. Scientific American 286 (6), 60–65. *Copyright © Scientific American, a division of Nature America, Inc. All rights reserved. Reprinted by permission.*

The behavior of the orangutans disturbs us in part because we see ourselves in their actions. Maggioncalda and Sapolsky call the forced copulations by arrested male orangutans "rape," but they also take pains to show how this differs from rape in humans. Likewise, individuals uncomfortable with human sexual diversity might see the sexual behavior of bonobos as deviant. As we study the sexual behavior of primates we must stay particularly aware of how we might impose our own cultural notions onto the behaviors of our closest living relatives.

Consider, for example, how previous editions of this text explained gorilla sexuality in terms of male control as follows: The dominant silverback was said to have exclusive breeding rights with the females; sometimes the silverback would tolerate the presence of a young adult male and allow him occasional access to a low-ranking female. Young males then enticed partners away from other established groups, in order to have reproductive success. Today we can look at this situation from the female gorilla's perspective and find an explanation for why males leave the home group by the time they become silverbacks. Could it be that females recognize the future potential in an incipient silverback and the possibility of forming a new group and thus will mate with these young adult males? Today's scientists studying animal behavior recognize the importance of female choice in reproduction.

Field studies have revealed variation in the typical gorilla pattern of a single dominant male. Gorilla groups in Uganda and Rwanda contain multiple silverback males. Still, in one of these multi-male groups studied in Rwanda, a single dominant male fathered all but one of ten juveniles (Gibbons, 2001a).

Although the vast majority of primate species are not **monogamous**—bonded exclusively to a single sexual partner—in their mating habits, many smaller species of New World monkeys, a few island-dwelling populations of leaf-eating Old World monkeys, and all of the smaller apes (gibbons and siamangs) appear to mate for life with a single individual of the opposite sex. These monogamous species have a lower degree of sexual dimorphism—anatomical differences between males and females—compared to our closest primate relatives (the great apes) or that was characteristic of our own ancient ancestors.

Evolutionary biologists, dating back to Charles Darwin himself, have proposed that sexual dimorphism (for example, larger male size in apes, beautiful feathers in peacocks) relates to competition among males for access to females. Females only evolved by what Canadian primatologist Linda Fedigan has called the "coat-tails theory" of evolution (Fedigan, 1992). She points out that evolutionary theories about sexual dimorphism and reproductive behaviors are particularly susceptible to becoming "gendered." That is, the gender norms of the scientists can easily creep their way (subconsciously, of course) into the theories they are creating. Darwin's era, despite the reign of Queen Victoria, was firmly patriarchal, and male–male competition prevailed in British society. Women of Darwin's time and class were denied basic rights, such as the right to vote. Inheritance laws favored first-born male heirs. Feminist analyses such as Fedigan's have contributed substantially to the developing discipline of primatology.

Primate field studies have revealed that male–male competition is just one of many factors playing a role in primate reproduction. Male–male competition can be reduced as it is in orangutans through arrested development. Further, a broad range of social processes contributes to reproductive success, with as much variation as the numerous biological factors that contribute to body size. For example, in baboons, a very sexually dimorphic species, the female chooses who her mate is just as often as the choice is determined through male–male competition. Females frequently choose to mate with lower-ranking males that show strong male–female **affiliative** actions (tending to promote social cohesion) and good parental behavior (Sapolsky, 2002).

Among baboons, paternal involvement has been shown to have distinct advantages for offspring, including more rapid growth in baboon infants if they receive attention from their fathers. In addition, adult males will also intercede on their offspring's behalf when the young ones are involved in fights. In short, choosing a good mate based on affiliative qualities can optimize the reproductive success of female baboons.

Reproduction and Care of Young

The average adult female monkey or ape spends most of her adult life either pregnant or nursing her young, times at which she is not sexually receptive. Apes generally nurse each of their young for about four to five years. After weaning her infant, she will come into estrus periodically, until she becomes pregnant again.

Among primates, as among some other mammals, females generally give birth to one infant at a time. Natural selection may have favored single births among primate tree-dwellers because the primate infant, having a highly developed grasping ability (human infants have this same grasping reflex), must be transported about by its mother. More than one clinging infant would interfere with movement in the trees. Only the smaller nocturnal prosimians, the primates closest to the ancestral condition, typically bear more than one infant at a time. Among the anthropoids, only the true marmoset, a kind of New World monkey, has a pattern of habitual twinning. Other species like humans will twin occasionally. In marmosets, both parents share infant care, with fathers doing most of the carrying. Polyandry also occurs

---

monogamous In primatology, mating for life with a single individual of the opposite sex.

affiliative Behaving in a manner that tends to promote social cohesion.

among marmosets, presumably as an adaptation to carrying multiple young.

Primates follow a pattern of bearing few young but devoting more time and effort to the care of each individual offspring. Compared to other mammals such as mice, which pass from birth to adulthood in a matter of weeks, primates spend a great deal of time growing up. As a general rule, the more closely related to humans the species is, the longer the period of infant and childhood dependency (**Figure 4.7**). For example, a lemur depends upon its mother for only a few months after birth, whereas an ape is dependent for four or five years. A chimpanzee infant cannot survive if its mother dies before it reaches the age of 4 at the very least. During the juvenile period, the larger social group, rather than just the mothers, sustain young primates. The young use this period to learn and refine a variety of behaviors. If the mother of a juvenile primate dies, an older male or female member of the social group may adopt the youngster. Among bonobos, a juvenile who has lost his or her mother has very little social standing in the group.

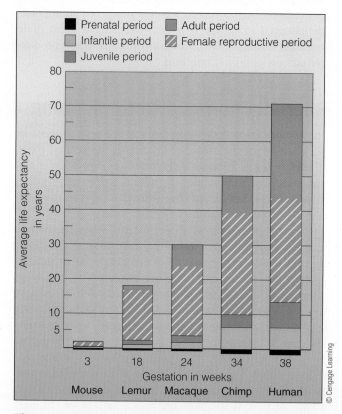

Figure 4.7 The Primate Life Cycle A long life cycle, including a long period of childhood dependency, is characteristic of the primates. In biological terms, infancy ends when young mammals are weaned, and adulthood is defined as *sexual maturation*. In many species, such as mice, animals become sexually mature as soon as they are weaned. Among primates, a juvenile period for social learning occurs between infancy and adulthood. For humans, the biological definitions of *infancy* and *adulthood* are modified according to cultural norms.

The long interval between births, particularly among the apes, results in small population size. A female chimpanzee, for example, does not reach sexual maturity until about the age of 10, and once she produces her first live offspring, five or six years passes before she will bear another. So, assuming that none of her offspring dies before adulthood, a female chimpanzee must survive for at least twenty or twenty-one years just to maintain the status quo in chimpanzee population. In fact, chimpanzee infants and juveniles do die from time to time, and not all females live full reproductive lives. This accounts for the lower population size of apes compared to monkeys. Likewise, the short intervals between births account for ever-increasing human population growth.

A long slow period of growth and development, particularly among the hominoids, also provides opportunities. Born without built-in responses dictating specific behavior in complex situations, the young monkey or ape, like the young human, learns how to strategically interact with others and even to manipulate them for his or her own benefit—by trial and error, observation, imitation, and practice. Young primates make mistakes along the way, learning to modify their behavior based on the reactions of other members of the group. Each member of the community has a unique physical appearance and personality. Youngsters learn to match their interactive behaviors according to each individual's social position and temperament. Anatomical features common to all monkeys and apes, such as a free upper lip (unlike lemurs and cats, for example), allow for varied facial expression, contributing to communication between individuals. Much of this learning takes place through play.

For primate infants and juveniles, play does more than pass the hours. Young primates play to learn about their environment, to learn social skills, and to test a variety of behaviors. Chimpanzee infants mimic the food-getting activities of adults, "attack" dozing adults, and "harass" adolescents. Observers have watched young gorillas do somersaults, wrestle, and play various organized games, such as jostling for position on the top of a hillside or following and mimicking a single youngster. One juvenile, becoming annoyed at repeated harassment by an infant, picked it up, climbed a tree, and deposited it on a branch from which it was unable to get down on its own; eventually, its mother came to retrieve it.

Communication and Learning

Primates, like many animals, vocalize. They have a great range of calls that are often used together with movements of the face or body to convey a message. Observers have not yet established the meaning of all the sounds, but a good number have been distinguished, such as warning calls, threat calls, defense calls, and gathering calls. Primatologists have studied the behavioral reactions of other animals hearing the call. Among bonobos, chimpanzees, and gorillas, most vocalizations communicate an emotional state rather than information. Much of the communication of these species takes place by using specific gestures and postures (Figure 4.8). Indeed, apes and humans share a number of these, such as kissing and embracing.

Primatologists have classified numerous chimpanzee vocalizations and visual communication signals. Facial expressions convey emotional states such as distress, fear, or excitement. Distinct vocalizations or calls have been associated with a variety of sensations. For example, chimps will smack their lips or clack their teeth to express pleasure with sociable body contact. Calls called "pant-hoots," which are used to announce the arrival of individuals or to inquire, can be differentiated into specific types. Together, these facilitate group protection, coordination of group efforts, and social interaction in general.

To what degree are various forms of communication universal and to what degree are they specific to a given group? On the group-specificity side, primatologists have recently documented within-species dialects of calls that emerge as groups are isolated in their habitats. Social factors, genetic drift, and habitat acoustics could all contribute to the appearance of these distinct dialects (de la Torre & Snowden, 2009).

Smiles and embraces have long been understood to be universal among humans and our closest relatives. But recently some additional universals have been documented. Athletes who are blind use the same gestures to express submission or victory that sighted athletes use at the end of a match, although they have never seen such gestures themselves (Figure 4.9) (Tracy & Matsumoto, 2008).

Figure 4.8 Universal Hominoid Expressions Many ape nonverbal communications are easily recognized by humans, as we share the same gestures. This capacity allows us to communicate across cultures and across species. Among humans, this capacity also makes miscommunication more likely when visual cues are missing or do not match the accompanying words.

This raises interesting questions about whether primate communications are biologically hardwired or learned.

Visual communication can also take place through objects. Bonobos do so with trail markers. When foraging, the community breaks up into smaller groups, rejoining

Figure 4.9 Gestures of the Blind Athletes who have been blind since birth use the same body gestures to express victory and defeat as sighted athletes. Because they do this without ever having seen an "end zone" celebration, this indicates that these body gestures are hardwired into humans and presumably derive from our primate heritage.

in the evening to nest together. To keep track of each party's whereabouts, those in the lead, at the intersections of trails or where downed trees obscure the path, will indicate their direction by deliberately stomping down the vegetation or by ripping off large leaves and placing them carefully. Thus, they all know where to come together at the end of the day (Recer, 1998).

Primatologists have also found that primates can communicate specific threats through their calls. Researchers have documented that the alarm calls of vervet monkeys communicate on several levels of meaning to elicit specific responses from others in the group (Seyfarth, Cheney, & Marler, 1980). The calls designated types of predators (birds of prey, big cats, snakes) and where the threat might arise. Further, they have documented how young vervets go about learning the appropriate use of the calls. If the young individual has uttered the correct call, adults will repeat the call, and the appropriate escape behavior will follow (heading into the trees to get away from a cat or into brush to be safe from an eagle). But if an infant utters the cry for an eagle in response to a leaf falling from the sky or for a nonthreatening bird, no adult calls will ensue.

From an evolutionary perspective, scientists have been puzzled about behaviors such as these vervet alarm calls. Biologists assume that the forces of natural selection work on behavioral traits just as they do on genetic traits. It seems reasonable that individuals in a group of vervet monkeys capable of warning one another of the presence of predators would have a significant survival advantage over those without this capability. However, these warning situations are enigmatic to evolutionary biologists because they would expect the animals to act in their own self-interest, with survival of self being paramount. By giving an alarm call, an individual calls attention to itself, thereby becoming an obvious target for the predator. How, then, could **altruism**, or concern for the welfare of others, evolve so that individuals place themselves at risk for the good of the group? One biologist's solution substitutes money for reproductive fitness to illustrate how such cooperative behavior may have come about:

> You are given a choice. Either you can receive $10 and keep it all or you can receive

The Great Ape Trust, photo courtesy of Sue Savage-Rumbaugh

Figure 4.10 **Bonobos and Pictorial Language** Kanzi, the 23-year-old bonobo at the Great Ape Trust of Iowa, communicates with primatologist Sue Savage-Rumbaugh by pointing to visual images called lexigrams. With hundreds of lexigrams, Kanzi can express his thoughts and feelings. He also understands spoken language and can reply in a conversation with the lexigrams. Kanzi began to learn this form of communication when he was a youngster, tagging along while his mother had language lessons. Though he showed no interest in the lessons, later he spontaneously began to use lexigrams himself.

> $10 million if you give $6 million to your next-door neighbor. Which would you do? Guessing that most selfish people would be happy with a net gain of $4 million, I consider the second option to be a form of selfish behavior in which a neighbor gains an incidental benefit. I have termed such selfish behavior benevolent. (Nunney, 1998, p. 1619)

Natural selection of beneficial social traits was probably an important influence on human evolution because in the primates some degree of cooperative social behavior became important for food-getting, defense, and mate attraction. Indeed, anthropologist Christopher Boehm argues, "If human nature were merely selfish, vigilant punishment of deviants would be expected, whereas the elaborate prosocial prescriptions that favor altruism would come as a surprise" (Boehm, 2000, p. 7).

With primate survival dependent on social cooperation, evolutionary forces have favored the development of strong communication skills. Experiments with captive apes, carried out over several decades, reveal remarkable communicative abilities. In some of these experiments, bonobos and chimpanzees have been taught to communicate using symbols, as in the case of Kanzi, a bonobo who uses a visual keyboard (**Figure 4.10**). Other chimpanzees, gorillas, and orangutans have been taught American Sign Language.

---

altruism Concern for the welfare of others expressed as increased risk undertaken by individuals for the good of the group.

Controversy surrounds this research in part because it challenges notions of human uniqueness. Nevertheless, it has become evident that apes are capable of understanding language quite well, even using rudimentary grammar. They generate original utterances, ask questions, distinguish naming something from asking for it, develop original ways to tell lies, coordinate their actions, and spontaneously teach language to others. Even though they cannot literally "speak," it is now clear that all of the great ape species can develop language skills to the level of a 2- to 3-year-old human child (Lestel, 1998; Miles, 1993). Interestingly, a Japanese research team recently demonstrated that chimps can outperform college students at a computer-based memory game (Inoue & Matsuzawa, 2007). The researchers propose that human brains have lost some of the spatial skill required to master this game to allow for more sophisticated human language.

Observations of monkeys and apes have shown learning abilities remarkably similar to those of humans. Numerous examples of inventive behavior have been observed among monkeys, as well as among apes. The snow monkeys or macaques of the research colony on Koshima Island, Japan, are particularly famous for demonstrating that individuals can invent new behaviors that then get passed on to the group through imitation.

In the 1950s and early 1960s, one particularly bright young female macaque named Imo (Japanese primatologists always considered it appropriate to name individual animals) started several innovative behaviors in her troop. She figured out that grain could be separated from sand if it was placed in water. The sand sank and the grain floated clean, making it much easier to eat. She also began the practice of washing the sweet potatoes that primatologists provided—first in fresh water but later in the ocean, presumably because of the pleasant taste the saltwater added. In each case, only the young animals imitated the innovations; Imo's mother was the lone older macaque to embrace them right away. Similarly, a female macaque named Mukbili at a field site in the Nagono Mountains initiated the

Figure 4.11 Macaque Social Learning In the same way that young Imo got her troop to begin washing sweet potatoes in saltwater, at Kyoto University's Koshima Island Primatology Research Preserve, another young female macaque recently taught other macaques to bathe in hot springs. In the Nagano Mountains of Japan, this macaque, named Mukbili, began bathing in the springs. Others followed her, and now this is an activity practiced by all members of the group.

practice of bathing in hot springs, a behavior that other members of the group adopted happily (**Figure 4.11**).

Another example of innovation in food manipulation was discovered among captive chimpanzees in the zoo of Madrid, Spain. It began when a 5-year-old female rubbed apples against a sharp corner of a concrete wall in order to lick the mashed pieces and juice left on the wall. From this youngster, the practice of "smearing" spread to her peers, and within five years most group members were performing the operation frequently and consistently. The innovation has become standardized and durable, having transcended two generations in the group (Fernandez-Carriba & Loeches, 2001).

Freely living chimpanzees in West Africa provide another dramatic example of learning in their method of cracking open hard-shelled oil-palm nuts. For this they use tools: an anvil stone with a level surface on which to place the nut and a good-sized hammer stone to crack it. Not just any stone will do; it must be of the right shape and weight, and the anvil may require leveling by placing smaller stones beneath one or more edges. Nor does random banging away do the job. The nut has to be hit at the right speed and the right trajectory, or else the nut simply flies off into the forest. Last but not least, the apes must avoid mashing their fingers, rather than the nut. According to fieldworkers, the expertise of the chimps far exceeds that of any human who tries cracking these hardest nuts in the world.

Youngsters learn this process by staying near to adults who are cracking nuts, where their mothers share some of the food. This teaches them about the edibility of the nuts but not how to get at what is edible. This they learn by observing and by "aping" (copying) the adults. At first they play with a nut or stone alone; later they begin to randomly combine objects. They soon learn, however, that placing nuts on anvils and hitting them with a hand or foot gets them nowhere.

Only after three years of futile effort do they begin to coordinate all of the multiple actions and objects, but even then only after a great deal of practice, by the age of 6 or 7 years, do they become proficient in this task. They practice this skill for over a thousand days. Evidently, social motivation accounts for their perseverance after at least three years of failure, with no reward to reinforce their effort. At first, a desire to act like the mother motivates them; only later does the desire to feed on the tasty nutmeat take over (de Waal, 2001).

Martin Harvey/Getty Images/Peter Arnold

Figure 4.12 Fishing for Termites Chimps use a variety of tools in the wild. Here a chimp uses a long stick stripped of its side branches to fish for termites—the first chimp tool use described by Jane Goodall in the 1960s. Chimps will select a stick when still quite far from the termite mound and modify its shape on the way to the snacking spot.

Use of Objects as Tools

A **tool** may be defined as an object used to facilitate some task or activity. The nut cracking just discussed is the most complex tool-use task observed by researchers in the wild, involving both hands, two tools, and exact coordination. Other examples of tool use among apes in the wild abound. Chimpanzees, bonobos, and orangutans all make and use tools.

Tool use and tool-making capacities remain distinct. Tool use, as in pounding something with a convenient

stone, requires far less acumen compared to tool making, which involves deliberate modification of some material for its intended use. Thus, otters that use unmodified stones to crack open clams may be tool users, but they are not toolmakers. Not only do chimpanzees modify objects to make them suitable for particular purposes, but chimps also modify these objects into regular and set patterns. They pick up and even prepare objects for future use at some other location, and they can use objects as tools to solve new problems.

Chimps have been observed using stalks of grass, twigs that they have stripped of leaves, and even sticks up to 3 feet long that they have smoothed down to "fish" for termites (**Figure 4.12**). They insert the modified stick into a termite nest, wait a few minutes, pull the stick out, and eat the insects clinging to it, all of which requires considerable dexterity. Chimpanzees are equally deliberate in their own nest

tool An object used to facilitate some task or activity. Although tool making involves intentional modification of the material of which it is made, tool use may involve objects either modified for some particular purpose or completely unmodified.

building. They test the vines and branches to make sure they are usable. If they are not, the animal moves to another site.

Other examples of chimpanzee use of tools involve leaves, used as wipes or as sponges, to get water out of a hollow to drink. Large sticks may serve as clubs or as missiles (as may stones) in aggressive or defensive displays. Chimps use twigs as toothpicks to clean teeth as well as to extract loose baby teeth. They use these dental tools not just on themselves but on other individuals as well (McGrew, 2000).

In the wild, bonobos have not been observed making and using tools to the extent seen in chimpanzees. However, their use of large leaves as trail markers may be considered a form of tool use. Further, a captive bonobo who has figured out how to make tools of stone that are remarkably like the earliest such tools made by our own ancestors provides further evidence of their tool-making capacities (Toth et al., 1993).

Chimpanzees also use plants for medicinal purposes, illustrating their selectivity with raw materials, a quality related to tool manufacture. Chimps that appear to observers to be ill have been seen seeking out specific plants of the genus *Aspilia*. They will eat the leaves singly without chewing them, letting the leaves soften in their mouths for a long time before swallowing. Primatologists have discovered that the leaves pass through the chimp's digestive system whole and relatively intact, having scraped parasites off the intestinal walls in the process.

Although gorillas (like bonobos and chimps) build nests, they have not been observed to make and use other tools in the wild. The lack of tools among gorillas likely stems from the fact that their easy diet of leaves and nettles makes tools of no particular use.

Hunting

Prior to the 1980s, most primates were thought to be vegetarian while humans alone were considered meat-eating hunters. Among the vegetarians, *folivores* were thought to eat only leaves while *frugivores* feasted on fruits. Though some primates do have specialized adaptations—such as a complex stomach and shearing teeth to aid in the digestion of leaves or an extra-long small intestine to slow the passage of juicy fruits so they can be readily absorbed—primate field studies have revealed that the diets of monkeys and apes are extremely varied.

Many primates are *omnivores* who eat a broad range of foods. Goodall's fieldwork among chimpanzees in their natural habitat at Gombe Stream demonstrates that these apes supplement their primary diet of fruits and other plant foods with insects and meat. Even more surprising, she found that in addition to killing small invertebrate animals for food, they also hunt and eat monkeys. Goodall observed chimpanzees grabbing adult red colobus monkeys and flailing them to death. Since her pioneering work, other primatologists have documented hunting behavior in baboons and capuchin monkeys, among others.

Chimpanzee females sometimes hunt, but males do so far more frequently. When on the hunt, they may spend hours watching, following, and chasing intended prey. Moreover, in contrast to the usual primate practice of each animal finding its own food, hunting frequently involves teamwork to trap and kill prey, particularly when hunting for baboons. Once a potential victim has been isolated from its troop, three or more adult chimps will carefully position themselves so as to block off escape routes while another pursues the prey. Following the kill, most who participated get a share of the meat, either by grabbing a piece as chance affords or by begging for it.

In addition to the nutritional value of meat, hunting appears to have social and reproductive value as well. Anthropologist Craig Stanford, who has been doing fieldwork among the chimpanzees of Gombe since the early 1990s, found that these sizable apes (100-pound males are common) frequently kill animals weighing up to 25 pounds and eat much more meat than previously believed. Their preferred prey is the red colobus monkey that shares their forested habitat. Annually, chimpanzee hunting parties at Gombe kill about 20 percent of these monkeys, many of them babies, often shaking them out of the tops of 30-foot trees. They may capture and kill as many as seven victims in a raid. These hunts usually take place during the dry season when plant foods are less available and when females display genital swelling, which signals that they are ready to mate. On average, each chimp at Gombe eats about a quarter-pound of meat per day during the dry season. For female chimps, a supply of protein-rich food helps support the increased nutritional requirements of pregnancy and lactation.

Somewhat different chimpanzee hunting practices have been observed in West Africa. At Tai National Park in Côte d'Ivoire, for instance, chimpanzees engage in highly coordinated team efforts to chase monkeys hiding in very tall trees in the dense tropical forest. Individuals who have especially distinguished themselves in a successful hunt see their contributions rewarded with more meat.

Recent research shows that bonobos in the Democratic Republic of Congo's rainforest also supplement their diet with meat obtained by means of hunting. Although their behavior resembles that of chimpanzees, crucial differences exist. Among bonobos, females predominantly hunt. Also, female hunters regularly share carcasses with

BIOCULTURAL CONNECTION

Chimpanzees in Biomedical Research: Time to End the Practice

Biological similarities among humans, apes, and Old World monkeys have led to the extensive use of nonhuman primate species in biomedical research aimed at preventing or curing disease in humans. Some biomedical research disturbs animals minimally. For example, DNA can be extracted from the hair naturally shed by living primates, allowing for cross-species comparisons of disease genes. To facilitate this process, cell repositories have been established for researchers to obtain samples of primate DNA. Other biomedical research is far more invasive to the individual primate. For example, to document the infectious nature of kuru, a disease closely related to mad cow disease, extract from the brains of sick humans was injected into the brains of living chimpanzees. A year and a half later, the chimpanzees began to sicken. They had the same classic features of kuru—uncontrollable spasticity, seizures, dementia, and ultimately death.

These research animals are subjected to procedures that would be considered morally questionable if done on humans. Mickey, pictured here, for example, was one of the hundreds of chimps who spent decades of her life alone in a concrete-and-steel windowless cage in a private research facility in New Mexico run by Frederick Coulston. After years of testing the effects of various infectious diseases, cosmetics, drugs, and pesticides on chimps like Mickey, the Coulston laboratory finally closed in 2002 when government research funding was withdrawn due to repeated violations of the Animal Welfare Act. But after years of abuse and neglect, research chimpanzees lack the skills to participate in chimpanzee social life. Furthermore, research animals have often been infected with deadly diseases such as HIV or hepatitis and cannot be released into the wild. Fortunately, Mickey and the other research chimps were given sanctuary through Save the Chimps, one of several organizations that rescue research animals.

The biological similarities of humans and other primates leading to such research practices derive from a long, shared evolutionary history. By comparison, the cultural rules that allow our closest relatives to be the subjects of biomedical research are relatively recent. Jane Goodall makes a convincing case for ending this practice:

> Surely it should be a matter of moral responsibility that we humans, differing from other animals mainly by virtue of our more highly developed intellect and, with it, our greater capacity for understanding and compassion, ensure that the medical progress slowly detaches its roots from the manure of nonhuman animal suffering and despair. Particularly when this involves the servitude of our closest relatives.[a]

BIOCULTURAL QUESTION

Those who fully support the use of nonhuman primates in biomedical research argue that using a limited number of chimpanzees or rhesus macaques to lessen human suffering and spare human lives is justified. Do you agree or disagree? What kinds of alternatives might be developed to replace nonhuman primates in biomedical research?

The toll of a life spent in the Coulston research facility is evident in Mickey who has since been rescued by Save the Chimp

Courtesy of Save the Chimps, the world's largest sanctuary for rescued chimpanzees; www.savethechimps.org

[a]Goodall, J. (1990). *Through a window: My thirty years with the chimpanzees of Gombe.* Boston: Houghton Mifflin.

other females but less often with males. Even when the most dominant male throws a tantrum nearby, he may still be denied a share of meat (Ingmanson, 1998). Female bonobos behave in much the same way when it comes to sharing other foods such as fruits.

While it had long been assumed that male chimpanzees were the primary hunters, primatologist Jill Pruetz and her colleagues researching in Fongoli, Senegal, documented habitual hunting by groups of young female and male chimpanzees using spears (Pruetz & Bertolani, 2007). The chimps took spears they had previously prepared and sharpened to a point and jabbed them repeatedly into the hollow parts of trees where small animals, including primates, might be hiding. The primatologists even observed the chimps extract bush babies from tree hollows with the spears.

The observation that young chimpanzees, one adolescent female in particular, are the most frequent spear hunters indicates that this innovation appeared in the group quite recently. Just as the young female Japanese macaques mentioned previously were the innovators in those groups, this young female chimp seems to be leading this behavior in Senegal. Further, the savannah conditions of the Fongoli Reserve make these observations particularly interesting in terms of human evolutionary studies: Paleoanthropologists have suggested that among our ancestors out on the savannah, males hunted while females gathered, a theory that seems to be undermined by the Fongoli observations.

The Question of Culture

The more we learn of the behavior of our nearest primate relatives, the more we become aware of the importance of learned, socially shared practices and knowledge in these creatures. Do chimpanzees, bonobos, and the other apes have culture? The answer appears to be yes. The detailed study of ape behavior has revealed varied use of tools and patterns of social engagement that seem to derive from the traditions of the specific group rather than from a biologically determined script. Humans share with the other apes an ability to learn the complex but flexible patterns of behavior particular to a social group during a long period of childhood dependency.

If we agree that these other primates possess culture, does this demand a reorientation in how humans behave toward

them, such as stopping the use of monkeys and apes in biomedical research? Jane Goodall argues vehemently for this change. She emphasizes that cultural processes determine the place of animals within biomedical research, and she advocates eliminating the cultural distinction between humans and our closest relatives for research purposes. Governments have begun responding to her calls as seen by the 2008 approval by the Spanish Parliament of the "Declaration on Great Apes," which extends some human rights to gorillas, chimpanzees, bonobos, and orangutans (O'Carroll, 2008).

In December 2010 the U.S. National Institutes of Health (NIH) commissioned the Institute of Medicine to study whether there was a need for chimps in biomedical and behavioral research. The answer was such an unequivocal no that the NIH will no longer fund any new projects involving research chimpanzees. The NIH also committed to reviewing all existing studies and dismantling any that do not meet the stringent criteria outlined in the Institute of Medicine's report. See this chapter's Biocultural Connection for more on the use of chimpanzees in medical research and the efforts to stop this practice.

Despite this progress, powerful social barriers still work against the well-being of our animal relatives. In Western societies there has been an unfortunate tendency to erect what paleontologist Stephen Jay Gould refers to as "golden barriers" that set us apart from the rest of the animal kingdom (quoted in de Waal, 2001). Sadly, this mindset blinds us to the fact that a continuum exists between us (humans) and them (animals). We have already seen that the physical differences between humans and apes are largely differences of degree, rather than kind. It now appears that the same is true with respect to behavior. As primatologist Richard Wrangham put it,

> Like humans, [chimpanzees] laugh, make up after a quarrel, support each other in times of trouble, medicate themselves with chemical and physical remedies, stop each other from eating poisonous foods, collaborate in the hunt, help each other over physical obstacles, raid neighboring groups, lose their tempers, get excited by dramatic weather, invent ways to show off, have family traditions and group traditions, make tools, devise plans, deceive, play tricks, grieve, are cruel and are kind. (quoted in Mydens, 2001, p. 5)

This is not to say that we are "just" another ape; obviously, degree does make a difference. Nevertheless, the continuities between our primate kin and us reflect a common evolutionary heritage, giving us the responsibility to help our cousins today. Because of our shared evolutionary heritage, the biology and behavior of the other living primates, like the contemporary study of genetics, provide valuable insight into our understanding of human origins. The methods scientists use to recover data directly from fossilized bones and preserved cultural remains in order to study the human past are the subject of the next chapter.

CHAPTER CHECKLIST

How does primate social organization differ among species?

● Chimps and bonobos compose communities of up to fifty members split among subgroups that change as individuals join and leave.

● Gorillas group into "families" led by a silver-backed male who tends to have exclusive mating rights. Upon maturity, younger males are forced to leave their natal group and may go on to form their own family or join an all-male group.

● Baboons live in troops of varying size that may comprise several smaller single male multi-female (polygynous) groups.

● Gibbons and a few other species are monogamous and live with only their nuclear families.

How does primate biology reflect behavior and environmental factors?

● Natural selection has favored single births among tree-dwelling primates whose young must cling to their mothers for transport. The long period until maturity provides opportunity for learning social behaviors, communication, and practical skills.

● Bonobo genitals maintain a constant state of swelling, which conceals ovulation and reflects their frequent and regular sexual activity. Sexual interactions are an important component of bonobo social organization and often mark reconciliation.

● A free upper lip allows apes a greater range of facial expression than that present in other primates, which contributes to their advanced communicative abilities.

● Baboons and some other species possess ischial callosities, permitting them to sit for long durations—an important feature for ground-dwellers. Primatologists have proposed that sexual dimorphism varies among primate species according to the degree of male–male competition.

● Rebalance columns as needed.

What are some possible cultural influences on primate behavior theories?

● Primatologists from male-biased cultures supposed that male-dominated hierarchies were the natural order of other primate social structures. However, female dominance is prevalent among some species, such as bonobos.

● A host of characteristics—including size, the rank of one's mother, motivation, and alliances—contribute to an individual's rank within primate groups.

● Western social norms may skew perceptions of the importance of social hierarchy and male–male competition in primatology. Cooperation and reconciliation are vitally important aspects of primate behavior.

● Female's choices in selection of mates based on affiliative and paternal behavioral qualities are important evolutionary forces among many primates.

How do the behavioral patterns and linguistic capabilities of the great apes compare?

● Apes combine vocalizations, gesturing, and facial expressions to communicate a variety of messages directly. Survival for many species depends on strong communication skills and effective social cooperation.

● Individuals in captivity have been taught to communicate using visual symbols and have learned American Sign Language. Innovation and adoption of new skills by whole groups is widespread.

● Chimps and bonobos are known for making tools whereas gorillas do not. Furthermore, chimps know to use certain plants for medicinal purposes and regularly hunt monkeys and other smaller animals, even using prepared spears.

What ethical concerns arise from the use of primates in biomedical research?

● The use of primates in medical research traditionally derived from a firm distinction between us and the other primates.

● The existence of primate culture runs counter to suppositions of human uniqueness. As our closest relatives, apes deserve the same rights we extend to fellow humans.

● Recent laws in several countries have begun to ban the use of apes in biomedical research.

QUESTIONS FOR REFLECTION

1. The range of sexual behavior among primates and the biological similarities that we share particularly with bonobos, our closest primate cousins, challenge us to apply the nature–nurture question to human sexuality. What does it mean when individuals argue for or against a biological basis for human homosexuality? Is there any evidence that homosexuality or heterosexuality is "natural"? Is it possible to consider human sexuality without taking culture into account?

2. What kinds of communication systems have been observed in primates? How do these differ from human language? How are they the same?

3. This chapter describes several instances of scientists revising their paradigms when it appeared that their work was overly influenced by their own cultural norms, such as prevailing gender roles. Can you think of ways that this might still be occurring? How do researchers prevent this from happening?

4. Given the variation seen in the specific behaviors of chimp, bonobo, and gorilla groups, is it fair to say that these primates possess culture?

5. Many primate species are endangered today due to human action. What features of ape biology also contribute to apes' limited population size? Do these biological limitations pertain to humans? Why or why not?

ONLINE STUDY RESOURCES

CourseMate

Access chapter-specific learning tools, including learning objectives, practice quizzes, videos, flash cards, glossaries, and more in your Anthropology CourseMate.

Log into **www.cengagebrain.com** to access the resources your instructor has assigned and to purchase materials.

Challenge Issue

The radical changes taking place in the world today make a scientific understanding of the past ever more important. Investigating and preserving ancient remains challenges us to collectively solve the complex questions of who owns the past and how can we protect its precious remains. These questions came into sharp focus in the spring of 2012 as ethnically Tuareg freedom fighters/separatist rebels (depending on one's perspective) occupied the ancient city of Timbuktu and declared it the capital of the new independent state Azawad. In the landlocked country of Mali on the southern edge of the Sahara Desert, Timbuktu, originally founded in the 4th century, has long been a crossroads, a trade center, a melting pot, and a hub of Islamic learning. In addition to unique ancient earthen mosques, Timbuktu also houses nearly 100,000 ancient manuscripts dating from its golden age, between the 12th and 15th centuries. Within days of the political shift, the world began hearing reports of looting and pillaging of the ancient libraries. Fearing that Islamic Sharia law was behind the destruction of early manuscripts relating to mathematics, medicine, astronomy, and music, people locally and across the world are struggling to preserve the unique treasure of Timbuktu. To whom do such remains belong—to the local government, to the global community, to researchers or scientific institutions, to people living in the region, to a rebel faction that has possession of them at that moment? The archaeological perspective holds that for the collective benefit of local peoples and the global community alike, these questions must be answered with an eye to long-term preservation, cooperation, and peace.

Field Methods in Archaeology and Paleoanthropology

5

IN THIS CHAPTER YOU WILL LEARN TO

- Define the site identification and excavation methods of archaeologists and paleoanthropologists.

- Describe the best excavation practices with particular emphasis on collaboration among diverse scientists and community members.

- Explain how archaeologists and paleoanthropologists employ a variety of laboratory techniques in their investigations once an excavation is complete.

- Distinguish among various absolute and relative dating methods.

- Describe geologic time, continental drift, and molecular clocks and their role in reconstructing the past.

Paleoanthropologists and archaeologists, anthropological specialists, reconstruct the biology and behavior of humans and their ancestors using a remarkable array of techniques. They share a focus on **prehistory**, a conventional term used to refer to the period of time before written records. For some people, the term *prehistoric* might conjure up images of "primitive" cavemen and cavewomen, but it does not imply a lack of history or any inferiority—merely a lack of *written* history. Archaeologists also focus on the cultural remains of peoples living since the invention of writing, such as the authors of the Timbuktu manuscripts as described in the chapter opener. The next several chapters of this book focus on the past; this chapter examines the methods archaeologists and paleoanthropologists use to study that past.

Most of us are familiar with some kind of archaeological material: a coin dug out of the earth, a fragment of an ancient pot, a spear point used by some ancient hunter. Archaeology consists of far more than finding and cataloguing such cultural treasures. Instead, archaeologists use material and ecological remains to reconstruct the culture and worldview of past human societies. Archaeologists examine every recoverable detail from past societies, including all kinds of structures (not just palaces and temples), hearths, garbage dumps, bones, and plant remains. Although it may appear that archaeologists are digging up *things*, they are really digging up human biology, behavior, and beliefs.

Similarly, paleoanthropologists who study the physical remains of our ancestors and other ancient primates do more than find and catalogue old bones. Paleoanthropologists recover, describe, and organize these remains to see what they can tell us about human biological evolution. True, paleoanthropologists find ancient bones, but more than that, they find out what these bones mean.

prehistory A conventional term used to refer to the period of time before the appearance of written records; does not deny the existence of history, merely of *written* history.

Recovering Cultural and Biological Remains

Archaeologists and paleoanthropologists face a dilemma. Their main investigative technique—excavation of sites containing biological and cultural remains—involves destruction of that site. Thus, competent and conscientious researchers precisely record the location and context of everything recovered, no matter how small, as they excavate. These records help scientists make sense of the data and enhance our knowledge of the past. Knowledge that can be derived from physical and cultural remains diminishes dramatically without such accurate and detailed records of the excavation. As anthropologist Brian Fagan has put it, "The fundamental premise of excavation is that all digging is destructive, even that done by experts. The archaeologist's primary responsibility, therefore, is to record a site for posterity as it is dug because there are no second chances" (Fagan, 1995, p. 19).

Archaeologists work with **artifacts**, any object fashioned or altered by humans—a flint scraper, a basket, an axe, the ruins of a house or its walls. An artifact expresses a facet of human culture. Artifacts, as products or representations of human behavior and beliefs, help archaeologists define durable aspects of culture such as tools, structures, and art as **material culture**.

Archaeologists do not consider artifacts in isolation; rather, they integrate them with biological and ecological remains. Such **ecofacts**, the natural remains of plants and animals found in the archaeological record, convey much about associated artifacts. Archaeologists also focus on **features**—nonportable elements such as hearths and architectural elements such as walls—that are preserved in the archaeological record. Archaeologists take into account how the artifacts and physical remains make their way into the ground. What people do with the things they have made, how they dispose of them, and how they lose them reflect important aspects of human culture. In other words, context allows archaeologists to understand the cultures of the past.

Similarly, context provides important information about biological remains, telling researchers which fossils are earlier or later in time compared to other fossils. Also, by noting the association of ancient human fossils with the remains of other species, the paleoanthropologist may make significant progress in reconstructing environmental settings of the past.

Cultural and physical remains represent distinct kinds of data, but the most comprehensive interpretation of the human past requires the integration of ancient human biology and culture. Often paleoanthropologists and archaeologists work together to systematically excavate and analyze fragmentary remains, placing scraps of bone, shattered pottery, and scattered campsites into broad interpretive contexts.

The Nature of Fossils

Broadly defined, a **fossil** is any mineralized trace or impression of an organism that has been preserved in the earth's crust from a past geologic time. Fossilization typically involves the hard parts of an organism. Bones, teeth, shells, horns, and the woody tissues of plants are the most successfully fossilized materials. Although the soft parts of an organism are rarely fossilized, casts or impressions of footprints, brains, and even whole bodies are sometimes found. Because dead animals quickly attract meat-eating scavengers and bacteria that cause decomposition, they rarely survive long enough to become fossilized. For an organism to become a fossil, it must be covered by some protective substance soon after death.

Preservation of an organism or part of an organism can take place in a number of ways that do not necessarily lead to fossilization. The whole animal may be frozen in ice (**Figure 5.1**), like the famous mammoths found in Siberia, safe from the forces of predators, weathering, and bacteria. Natural resins exuding from evergreen trees may enclose an organism allowing it to later become hardened and fossilized as amber. Specimens of spiders and insects dating back millions of years have been preserved in the Baltic Sea area in northeastern Europe, which is rich in resin-producing evergreens such as pine, spruce, and fir trees.

Lake bottoms and sea basins provide optimal conditions for preservation because sediment can quickly cover the organism. An entire organism may also be mummified or preserved in tar pits, peat, oil, or asphalt bogs, in which the chemical environment prevents the growth of decay-producing bacteria.

Entire organisms rarely fossilize, let alone an entire human. Fossils generally consist of scattered teeth and fragments of bones found embedded in rock deposits. Most have been altered in some way in the process of becoming fossilized. **Taphonomy** (from the Greek for "tomb"), the study of the biologic and geologic processes by which dead organisms become fossils, provides

---

artifact Any object fashioned or altered by humans.

material culture The durable aspects of culture, such as tools, structures, and art.

ecofact The natural remains of plants and animals found in the archaeological record.

feature A nonportable element such as a hearth or an architectural element such as a wall that is preserved in the archaeological record.

fossil The mineralized remains of past life forms.

taphonomy The study of how bones and other materials come to be preserved in the earth as fossils.

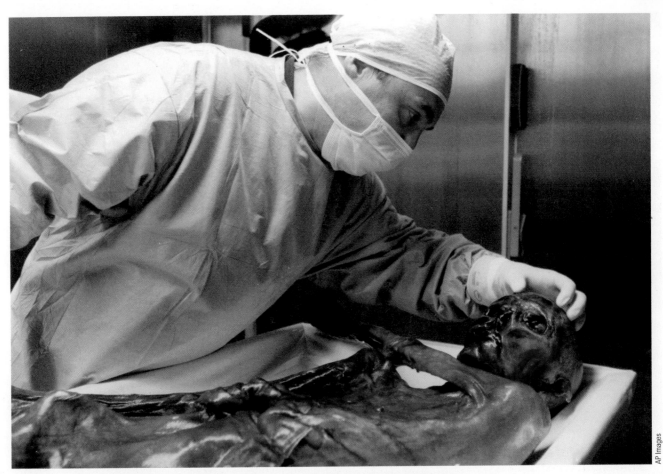

Figure 5.1 The Ice Man Ötzi In rare circumstances, human bodies are so well preserved that they could be mistaken for recent corpses. Such is the case of Ötzi, the 5,200-year-old Ice Man, exposed by the melting of an alpine glacier in the Tyrolean Alps in 1991. Both the Italian and the Austrian governments felt they had legitimate claims on this rare find, and they mounted legal, geographic, and taphonomic arguments for housing the body. These arguments continued as the specimen, just released from the ice, began to thaw.

systematic understanding of the fossilization process vital for the scientific interpretations of the fossils themselves.

Fossilization occurs most frequently among marine animals and other creatures living near water. Concentrations of shells and other parts of organisms are covered and completely enclosed by the soft waterborne sediments that eventually harden into shale and limestone in the following fashion: As the remains of organisms accumulate on the floor of shallow seas, rivers, or lakes, they become covered by sediment and silt, or sand. These materials gradually harden, forming a protective shell around the skeleton of the organism. The internal cavities of bones or teeth and other parts of the skeleton fill in with mineral deposits from the sediment immediately surrounding the specimen. Then the external walls of the bone decay and are replaced by calcium carbonate or silica.

Unless protected in some way, the bones of a land-dweller are generally scattered and exposed to the deteriorating influence of the elements, predators, and scavengers. Occasionally, terrestrial animals living near lakes or rivers become fossilized if they die next to or in the water. A land-dweller may also become fossilized if it happens to die in a cave (**Figure 5.2**), or if some other meat-eating animal drags its remains to a site protected from erosion and decay. In caves, conditions are often excellent for fossilization, as minerals contained in water dripping from the ceiling may harden over bones left on the cave floor. In northern China, for example, many fossils of *Homo erectus* (discussed in Chapter 7) and other animals were found in a cave near a village called Zhoukoudian, in deposits of consolidated clay and rock that had fallen from the cave's limestone ceiling. The cave had been frequented by both humans and predatory animals, which left the remains of many meals there.

Figure 5.2 Sima de los Huesos To excavate the ancient Stone Age site Sima de los Huesos or "Pit of Bones," Spanish paleoanthropologist Juan Luis Arsuaga and his team spend nearly an hour each day traveling underground through a narrow passage to a small enclosed space, rich with human remains. Here, the fossils are excavated with great care and transported back to the laboratory, where the long process of interpretation and analysis begins. Arsuaga's team has proposed that the high number of individuals recovered from this single cave site indicates some ritual surrounding death, a placement of the dead as in an ossuary rather than a burial. If true, this site, dated to sometime between 350,000 and 600,000 years ago, would provide the earliest evidence of ritualistic treatment of the dead.

Burial of the Dead

The cultural practice of burial that began (consistently) about 100,000 years ago has increased the preservation of complete fossil skeletons. The human fossil record from before this time consists primarily of fragmentary remains with an occasional complete skeleton. The fossil record for many other primates is even poorer because organic materials decay rapidly in the tropical forests where they lived. The records are more complete for primates (such as evolving humans) that lived on the grassy plains or in savannah environments, where conditions were more favorable to the formation of fossils. Places where ash deposited from volcanic eruptions or waterborne sediment along lakes and streams could quickly cover organisms

that died, favoring fossilization. Several localities in Ethiopia, Kenya, and Tanzania in East Africa, found near ancient lakes and streams and often sandwiched between layers of volcanic ash, yield numerous fossils important for our understanding of human evolution.

In more recent times, such complete remains are often quite spectacular and particularly informative. As an example, consider the recovery in 1994 of the remains of an Inupiat Eskimo girl in Barrow, Alaska, described in the Original Study. As seen in this case study, successful exploration of the past depends upon cooperation and respect between anthropologists and the living people with ancestral connections to the physical and cultural remains being studied.

Whispers from the Ice

BY SHERRY SIMPSON

People grew excited when a summer rainstorm softened the bluff known as Ukkuqsi, sloughing off huge chunks of earth containing remains of historic and prehistoric houses, part of the old village that predates the modern community of Barrow. Left protruding from the slope was a human head. Archaeologist Anne Jensen happened to be in Barrow buying strapping tape when the body appeared. Her firm, SJS Archaeological Services, Inc., was closing a field season at nearby Point Franklin, and Jensen offered the team's help in a kind of archaeological triage to remove the body before it eroded completely from the earth.

The North Slope Borough hired her and Glenn Sheehan, both associated with Pennsylvania's Bryn Mawr College, to conduct the work. The National Science Foundation, which supported the three-year Point Franklin Project, agreed to fund the autopsy and subsequent analysis of the body and artifacts. The Ukkuqsi excavation quickly became a community event. In remarkably sunny and calm weather, volunteers troweled and picked through the thawing soil, finding trade beads, animal bones, and other items. Teenage boys worked alongside grandmothers. The smell of sea mammal oil, sweet at first then corrupt, mingled with ancient organic odors of decomposed vegetation. One man searched the beach for artifacts that had eroded from the bluff, discovering such treasures as two feather parkas. Elder Silas Negovanna, originally of Wainwright, visited several times, "more or less out of curiosity to see what they have in mind," he said. George Leavitt, who lives in a house on the bluff, stopped by one day while carrying home groceries and suggested a way to spray water to thaw the soil without washing away valuable artifacts. Tour groups added the excavation to their rounds.

"This community has a great interest in archaeology up here just because it's so recent to their experience," says oral historian Karen Brewster, a tall young woman who interviews elders as part of her work with the North Slope Borough's division of Inupiat History, Language, and Culture. "The site's right in town, and everybody was really fascinated by it."

Slowly, as the workers scraped and shoveled, the earth surrendered its historical hoard: carved wooden bowls, ladles, and such clothing as a mitten made from polar bear hide, bird-skin parkas, and mukluks. The items spanned prehistoric times, dated in Barrow to before explorers first arrived in 1826.

The work prompted visiting elders to recall when they or their parents lived in traditional sod houses and relied wholly on the land and sea for sustenance. Some remembered sliding down the hill as children, before the sea gnawed away the slope. Others described the site's use as a lookout for whales or ships. For the archaeologists, having elders stand beside them and identify items and historical context is like hearing the past whispering in their ears. Elders often know from experience, or from stories, the answers to the scientists' questions about how items were used or made. "In this instance, usually the only puzzled people are the archaeologists," jokes archaeologist Sheehan.

A modern town of 4,000, Barrow exists in a cultural continuum, where history is not detached or remote but still pulses through contemporary life. People live, hunt, and fish where their ancestors did, but they can also buy fresh vegetables at the store and jet to other places. Elementary school classes include computer and Inupiaq language studies. Caribou skins, still ruddy with blood, and black brant carcasses hang near late-model cars outside homes equipped with television antennas. A man uses power tools to work on his whaling boat. And those who appear from the earth are not just bodies, but relatives. "We're not a people frozen in time," says Jana Harcharek, an Inupiat Eskimo who teaches Iñupiaq and nurtures her culture among young people. "There will always be that connection between us [and our ancestors]. They're not a separate entity."

The past drew still closer as the archaeologists neared the body. After several days of digging through thawed soil, they used water supplied by the local fire station's tanker truck to melt through permafrost until they reached the remains, about 3 feet below the surface. A shell of clear ice encased the body, which rested in what appeared to be a former meat cellar. With the low-pressure play of water from the tanker, the archaeologists teased the icy casket from the frozen earth, exposing a tiny foot. Only then did they realize they had uncovered a child. "That was kind of sad, because she was about my daughter's size," says archaeologist Jensen.

The girl was curled up beneath a baleen toboggan and part of a covering that Inupiat elder Bertha Leavitt identified as a kayak skin by its stitching. The child, who appeared to be 5 or 6, remained remarkably intact after her dark passage through time. Her face was cloaked by a covering that puzzled some onlookers. It didn't look like human hair, or even fur, but something with a feathery

In the long cool days of the Alaska summer, archaeologist Anne Jensen and her team excavate artifacts that will be exhibited at the Inupiat Heritage Center in Barrow, Alaska. In addition to traditional museum displays honoring the past, the center actively promotes the continuation of Inupiat Eskimo cultural traditions through innovations such as the elder-in-residence program.

residue. Finally, they concluded it was a hood from a feather parka made of bird skins. The rest of her body was delineated muscle that had freeze-dried into a dark brick-red color. Her hands rested on her knees, which were drawn up to her chin. Frost particles coated the bends of her arms and legs.

"We decided we needed to go talk to the elders and see what they wanted, to get some kind of feeling as to whether they wanted to bury her right away, or whether they were willing to allow some studies in a respectful manner—studies that would be of some use to residents of the North Slope," Jensen says. Working with community elders is not a radical idea to Jensen or Sheehan, whose previous work in the Arctic has earned them high regard from local officials who appreciate their sensitivity. The researchers feel obligated not only to follow community wishes, but to invite villagers to sites and to share all information through public presentations. In fact, Jensen is reluctant to discuss findings with the press before the townspeople themselves hear it.

"It seems like it's a matter of simple common courtesy," she says. Such consideration can only help researchers, she points out. "If people don't get along with you, they're not going to talk to you, and they're liable to throw you out on your ear." In the past, scientists were not terribly sensitive about such matters, generally regarding human remains—and sometimes living natives—as artifacts themselves. Once, the girl's body would have been hauled off to the catacombs of some university or museum, and relics would have disappeared into exhibit drawers in what Sheehan describes as "hit-and-run archaeology."

"Grave robbers" is how Inupiat Jana Harcharek refers to early Arctic researchers. "They took human remains and their burial goods. It's pretty gruesome. But, of course, at the time they thought they were doing science a big favor. Thank goodness attitudes have changed."

Today, not only scientists but municipal officials confer with the Barrow Elders Council when local people find skeletons from traditional platform burials out on the tundra, or when bodies appear in the house mounds. The elders appreciate such consultations, says Samuel Simmonds, a tall, dignified man known for his carving. A retired Presbyterian minister, he presided at burial ceremonies of the famous "frozen family," ancient Inupiats discovered in Barrow [about thirty years ago]. "They were part of us, we know that," he says simply, as if the connection between old bones and bodies and living relatives is self-evident. In the case of the newly discovered body, he says, "We were concerned that it was reburied in a respectful manner. They were nice enough to come over and ask us."

The elders also wanted to restrict media attention and prevent photographs of the body except for a few showing her position at the site. They approved a limited autopsy to help answer questions about the body's sex, age, and state of health. She was placed in an orange plastic body bag in a stainless steel morgue with the temperature turned down to below freezing.

With the help of staff at the Indian Health Service Hospital, Jensen sent the girl's still-frozen body to Anchorage's Providence Hospital. There she assisted with an autopsy performed by Dr. Michael Zimmerman of New York City's Mount Sinai Hospital. Zimmerman, an expert on prehistoric frozen bodies, had autopsied Barrow's frozen family in 1982 and was on his way to work on the prehistoric man recently discovered in the Alps.

The findings suggest the girl's life was very hard. She ultimately died of starvation, but also had emphysema caused by a rare congenital disease—the lack of an enzyme that protects the lungs. She probably was sickly and needed extra care all her brief life. The autopsy also found soot in her lungs from the family's sea mammal oil lamps, and she had osteoporosis, which was caused by a diet exclusively of meat from marine mammals. The girl's stomach was empty, but her intestinal tract contained dirt and animal fur. That remains a mystery and raises questions about the condition of the rest of the family. "It's not likely that she would be hungry and everyone else well fed," Jensen says.

That the girl appears to have been placed deliberately in the cellar provokes further questions about precontact burial practices, which the researchers hope Barrow elders can help answer. Historic accounts indicate the dead often were wrapped in skins and laid out on the tundra on wooden platforms, rather than buried in the frozen earth. But perhaps the entire family was starving and too weak to remove the dead girl from the house, Jensen speculates. "We probably won't ever be able to say, 'This is the way it was,'" she adds. "For that you need a time machine."

The scientific team reported to the elders that radio-carbon dating places the girl's death in about AD 1200. If correct—for dating is technically tricky in the Arctic—the date would set the girl's life about 100 years before her people formed settled whaling villages, Sheehan says.

Following the autopsy and the body's return to Barrow . . . , one last request by the elders was honored. The little girl, wrapped in her feather parka, was placed in a casket and buried in a small Christian ceremony next to the grave of the other prehistoric bodies. Hundreds of years after her death, an Inupiat daughter was welcomed back into the midst of her community.

The "rescue" of the little girl's body from the raw forces of time and nature means researchers and the Inupiat people will continue to learn still more about the region's culture. Sheehan and Jensen returned to Barrow in winter 1994 to explain their findings to townspeople. "We expect to learn just as much from them," Sheehan said before the trip. A North Slope Cultural Center . . . will store and display artifacts from the dig sites.

Laboratory tests and analyses also will contribute information. The archaeologists hope measurements of heavy metals in the girl's body will allow comparisons with modern-day pollution contaminating the sea mammals that Inupiats eat today. The soot damage in her lungs might offer health implications for Third World people who rely on oil lamps, dung fires, and charcoal for heat and light. Genetic tests could illuminate early population movements of Inupiats.

The project also serves as a model for good relations between archaeologists and Native people. "The larger overall message from this work is that scientists and communities don't have to be at odds," Sheehan says. "In fact, there are mutual interests that we all have. Scientists have obligations to communities. And when more scientists realize that, and when more communities hold scientists to those standards, then everybody will be happier."

Adapted from Simpson, S. (1995, April). Whispers from the ice. Alaska, 23–28.

Searching for Artifacts and Fossils

Where are artifacts and fossils found? Places containing archaeological remains of previous human activity are known as *sites*. Many kinds of sites exist, and sometimes it is difficult to define their boundaries, for remains may be strewn over large areas. Sites are even found under water. Some examples of sites identified by archaeologists and paleoanthropologists are hunting campsites, from which hunters went out to hunt game; kill sites, in which game was killed and butchered; village sites, in which domestic activities took place; and cemeteries, in which the dead, and sometimes their belongings, were buried.

Although skeletons of recent peoples are frequently associated with their cultural remains, archaeological sites may or may not contain any physical remains. As we go back in time, the association of physical and cultural remains becomes less likely. Physical remains dating from before 2.5 to 2.6 million years ago are found in isolation. This does not prove the absence of material culture; it simply indicates that the earliest forms of material culture were not preserved in the archaeological record. The earliest tools used by our ancestors were likely made of organic materials (such as the termite-fishing sticks used by chimpanzees) that were much less likely to be preserved. Although only geologic contexts with conditions favorable for fossilization yield physical remains, archaeological sites may be found just about anywhere. The more recent time depth of archaeological remains helps their preservation as well.

Site Identification

Archaeologists must first identify sites to investigate. Archaeological sites, particularly very old ones, frequently are buried underground, covered by layers of sediment deposited since the site was in use. The presence of artifacts indicates a potential site. Chance may play a crucial role in the site's discovery, as in the case discussed in Barrow, Alaska. Usually, however, the archaeologist will conduct surveys of a region in order to plot the sites available for excavation.

A survey can be made from the ground, but more territory can be covered from the air. Aerial photographs have been used by archaeologists since the 1920s and are widely used today. Among other purposes, such photographs were used for the discovery and interpretation of the huge geometric and zoomorphic (from Latin for "animal-shaped") markings on the coastal desert of Peru (**Figure 5.3**). More recently a variety of innovations in the geographic and geologic sciences have been incorporated into archaeological surveys and other aspects of research. Innovations such as geographic information systems (GIS), remote sensing, and ground-penetrating radar (GPR) complement traditional archaeological exploration methods.

High-resolution aerial photographs, including satellite imagery, resulted in the astonishing discovery of over 500 miles of prehistoric roadways connecting sites in the Four Corners region of the United States (where Arizona, New Mexico, Colorado, and Utah meet) with other sites in ways that archaeologists had never suspected. This discovery led to a new understanding of prehistoric Pueblo Indian economic, social, and political organization. Evidently, large centers in this region governed a number of smaller satellite communities, mobilized labor for large public works, and allowed for the distribution of goods over substantial distances.

In open country, archaeologists can easily identify more obvious sites, such as the human-made mounds or *tells* of the Middle East, that rise as swells from the ground. But a heavy forest cover poses extra challenges for site identification even when ruins rise above ground. Thus, local geography and climate impact the discovery of archaeological sites.

In the forests, a change in vegetation might indicate a potential site. For example, topsoil that is richer in organic matter than that of the surrounding areas often covers ancient storage and refuse pits and grows distinctive vegetation. At Tikal, an ancient Maya site in Guatemala, breadnut trees usually grow near the remains of ancient houses, so archaeologists can use these trees as guideposts.

Figure 5.3 Zoomorphs Some archaeological features are best seen from the air, such as this massive figure of a monkey made in prehistoric times on the Nazca Desert of Peru. Ancient people selectively removed the top layer of reddish stones thus exposing the light-colored earth below.

On the ground, **soil marks** or stains, showing up on the surface of recently plowed fields, can indicate a potential site. Soil marks led archaeologists to many of the Bronze Age burial mounds in Hertfordshire and Cambridgeshire, England. The mounds hardly rose out of the ground, yet each was circled at its core by chalky soil marks. Sometimes the very presence of a particular chalky rock is significant.

Archaeologists also use documents, maps, and folklore in the search for sites. For example, Homer's *Iliad* led Heinrich Schliemann, the famous and controversial 19th-century German archaeologist, to the discovery of Troy. (As was typical of that time, Schliemann's excavation methods destroyed much of the actual remains.) He assumed that the city described by Homer as Ilium was really Troy. Place names and local lore often indicate the presence of an archaeological site in an area. Archaeological surveys therefore often depend upon amateur collectors and local people who are usually familiar with the history of the land.

Sometimes natural processes, such as soil erosion or droughts, expose sites or fossils. For example, in eastern North America erosion along the coastlines and riverbanks has exposed prehistoric refuse mounds known as **middens** (the general term for a trash deposit), which in these regions are filled with the remains of mussels and/or oysters, indicating that shellfish consumption was common. Similarly, the gradual action of wind blowing away sand exposed a whole village of stone huts dug into the ground at Skara Brae in Scotland's Orkney Islands.

Sometimes natural forces expose fossils and sites, and sometimes human actions unrelated to anthropological

---

soil marks Stains that show up on the surface of recently plowed fields that reveal an archaeological site.

middens A refuse or garbage disposal area in an archaeological site.

investigations reveal physical and cultural remains. In Chapter 2 we noted how construction and quarrying work in Europe led to the discovery of fossils of extinct animals, which then played a role in the development of evolutionary theory. Similarly, limestone quarrying at a variety of sites in South Africa early in the 20th century led to the discovery of the earliest humanlike fossils from millions of years ago (see Chapter 6). Disturbances of the earth on a smaller scale, such as plowing, sometimes turn up bones, fragments of pots, and other archaeological objects.

Cultural Resource Management

Because construction projects frequently uncover archaeological remains, in many countries, including the United States, such projects require government approval in order to ensure the identification and protection of those finds. *Cultural resource management*, introduced in Chapter 1, is routinely included in the environmental review process for federally funded or licensed construction projects in the United States, as it is in Europe. For example, in the United States, if the transportation department of a state government plans to replace a highway bridge, the state must first contract with archaeologists to identify and protect any significant resources that might be affected by this new construction.

Since passage of the Historic Preservation Act of 1966, the National Environmental Policy Act of 1969, the Archaeological and Historical Preservation Act of 1974, and the Archaeological Resources Protection Act of 1979, cultural resource management has been required for any construction project that is partially funded or licensed by the U.S. government. As a result, the field of cultural resource management has flourished. Many archaeologists are employed by U.S. government agencies such as the Army Corps of Engineers, the National Park Service, the Forest Service, and the Natural Resource Conservation Service, assisting in the preservation, restoration, and salvage of archaeological resources. Canada and the United Kingdom have programs very similar to those of the United States. From Chile to China, various governments use archaeological expertise to manage their cultural heritage.

When cultural resource management work or other archaeological investigation unearths Native American cultural items or human remains, federal laws come into the picture again. The Native American Graves Protection and Repatriation Act (NAGPRA), passed in 1990, outlines a process for the return of these remains to lineal descendants, culturally affiliated Indian tribes, and Native Hawaiian organizations. NAGPRA has become central to the work of anthropologists who study Paleo-Indian and more recent Indian cultures in the United States. The Kennewick Man

controversy featured later in this chapter highlights some of the ethics debates surrounding NAGPRA.

In addition to working in all the capacities mentioned, archaeologists also consult for engineering firms to help them prepare environmental impact statements. Some of these archaeologists operate out of universities and colleges, whereas others are on the staff of independent consulting firms. When state legislation sponsors any kind of archaeological work, it is referred to as *contract archaeology*.

Excavation

Once a researcher identifies an appropriate site, the next step is to plan and carry out excavation. If not already a part of cultural resource management, the next step of excavation planning involves obtaining permission to excavate from a variety of local and national authorities. The excavation team begins by clearing the land and plotting the site as a **grid system** (Figure 5.4). The excavators divide the surface of the site into squares of equal size and number and mark each square with stakes. Each object found then may be located precisely in the square from which it came. (Remember, context is everything!) The starting point of a grid system, which is located precisely in three dimensions, may be a large rock, the edge of a stone wall, or an iron rod sunk into the ground. This point is also known as the reference or **datum point**.

At a large site covering several square miles, archaeologists may plot individual structures, numbered according to their location in a particular square of a giant grid. Archaeologists dig each square of the grid separately with great care. (In Figure 5.5, notice how archaeologists use the grid system even when under water.) They use trowels to scrape the soil and screens to sift all the loose soil so that they recover even the smallest artifacts, such as flint chips or beads.

Flotation, a technique employed when looking for very fine objects, such as fish scales or very small bones, consists of immersing soil in water, causing the particles to separate. Some will float, others will sink to the bottom, allowing for easy retrieval of the remains.

If the site is **stratified**—that is, if the remains lie in layers one upon the other—archaeologists will dig

---

grid system A system for recording data in three dimensions for an archaeological excavation.

datum point The starting point or reference for a grid system.

flotation An archaeological technique employed to recover very tiny objects by immersion of soil samples in water to separate heavy from light particles.

stratified Layered; term used to describe archaeological sites where the remains lie in layers, one upon another.

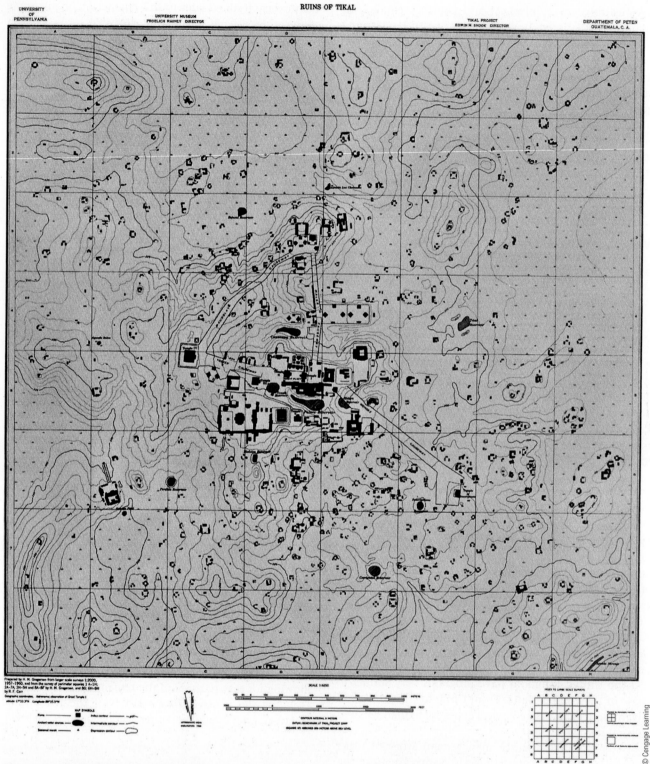

Figure 5.4 The Grid System At large sites covering several square miles, archaeologists construct a giant grid, as shown in this map of the center of the ancient Maya city of Tikal. Each square of the grid is one-quarter of a square kilometer; excavators number individual structures according to the square in which they are found.

each layer, or stratum, separately. Each layer represents a particular span of time and period of settlement. Thus, it will contain artifacts deposited at the same time and belonging to the same culture (**Figure 5.6**). Cultural change can be traced through the order in which artifacts were deposited—deeper layers reveal older artifacts.

Figure 5.5 Underwater Archaeology Here a diver recovers antique amphorae (the traditional containers for transporting wine, olives, olive oil, grain, and other commodities) from the site of a shipwreck in the Mediterranean Sea near the village of Kas, Turkey. The shipwreck dates back to the time of the Trojan War (over 3,000 years ago). Underwater archaeologists—led in this expedition by George Bass from the Institute of Nautical Archaeology of Texas A&M University collaborating with the Bodrum Museum of Underwater Archaeology in Istanbul, Turkey—reconstructs facets of the past, ranging from ancient trade routes and shipbuilding techniques, through the analysis of such remains.

However, archaeologists Frank Hole and Robert F. Heizer suggest care when analyzing stratified sites:

> because of difficulties in analyzing stratigraphy, archaeologists must use the greatest caution in drawing conclusions. Almost all interpretations of time, space, and culture contexts depend on stratigraphy. The refinements of laboratory techniques for analysis are wasted if archaeologists cannot specify the stratigraphic position of their artifacts. (Hole & Heizer, 1969, p. 113)

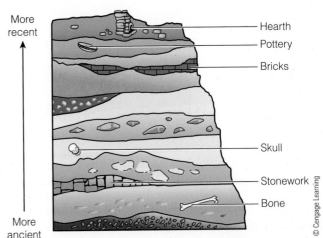

Figure 5.6 An Archaeological Profile Archaeologists create profiles or vertical representations of the sites they excavate. In stratified sites where archaeological remains lie in stacked layers, with older layers deeper or lower down and more recent layers above them, profiles are especially informative. Geologic processes will result in strata of different depths in different places. Interpretation of the site depends upon careful mapping of each stratum using the grid system.

If no stratification is present, then the archaeologist digs by arbitrary levels. Each square must be dug so that its edges and profiles are straight; walls between squares are often left standing to serve as visual correlates of the grid system.

Paleoanthropologists working on older sites, without the benefit of archaeological layers, must employ geological expertise because interpretation of a fossil depends utterly on its place in the sequence of rocks that contain it. The geological context provides the dates that place specimens in the human evolutionary sequence. More recent archaeological sites can be dated more reliably. Paleoanthropological expeditions today generally are made up of teams of specialists in various fields in addition to physical anthropology so that all the necessary expertise is available.

Excavation of Bones

Removing a fossil from its burial place without damage requires surgical skill and caution. Unusual tools and materials are found in the kit of the paleoanthropologist—pickaxes, dental instruments, enamel coating, burlap for bandages, and sculpting plaster.

To remove newly discovered bones, the paleoanthropologist and archaeologist begin uncovering the specimen, using pick and shovel for initial excavation, then small camel-hair brushes and dental picks to remove loose and easily detachable debris surrounding the bones. Once

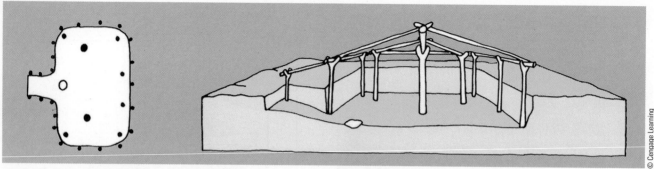

Figure 5.7 Reconstruction from Traces of Organic Remains Although the wooden posts of a house have long since decayed, their positions may still be marked by discoloration of the soil. The plan shown on the left—of an ancient post-hole pattern and depression at Snaketown, Arizona—permits the hypothetical house reconstruction on the right.

© Cengage Learning

the researchers uncover the entire specimen (a process that may take days of back-breaking patient labor), they cover the bones with shellac and tissue paper to prevent cracking and damage during further excavation and handling.

The excavation team prepares both the fossil and the earth immediately surrounding it, or the *matrix*, for removal as a single block. They cut the bones and matrix out of the earth but do not remove them. Next they add more shellac to the entire block to harden it. They cover the bones with burlap bandages dipped in plaster. Then they enclose the block in more plaster and burlap bandages, perhaps splinted with tree branches, and allow it to dry overnight. After it has hardened, they carefully remove the entire block from the earth, now ready for packing and transport to a laboratory. Before leaving the discovery area, the investigator makes a thorough sketch map of the terrain and pinpoints the find on geological maps to aid future investigators.

State of Preservation of Archaeological and Fossil Evidence

The results of an excavation depend greatly on the condition of the remains. Inorganic materials such as stone and metal are more resistant to decay than organic ones such as wood and bone. Sometimes the anthropologist discovers an *assemblage*—a collection of artifacts—made of durable inorganic materials, such as stone tools, and traces of organic ones long since decomposed, such as woodwork (**Figure 5.7**), textiles, or food.

Climate, local geological conditions, and cultural practices also play a role in the state of preservation. For example, our knowledge of ancient Egyptian culture stems not only from their burial practices but from the effects of climate and soil on preservation. The ancient Egyptians believed that eternal life could be achieved only if the dead were buried with their worldly possessions. Hence, these tombs are usually filled with a wealth of artifacts, including the skeletons of other humans owned by dynastic rulers.

Under favorable climatic conditions, even the most perishable objects may survive over vast periods of time. The earliest Egyptian burials, consisting of shallow pits in the sand with bodies buried long before mummification was practiced, often yield well-preserved corpses. Their preservation is the result of rapid desiccation, or complete drying out, in the warm desert climate (**Figure 5.8**). The elaborate tombs of the rulers of dynastic Egypt often contain wooden furniture, textiles, flowers, and written scrolls on paper made from papyrus reeds, barely touched by time, seemingly as fresh as they were when deposited in the tombs as long as 5,000 years ago—a consequence of the region's arid climatic conditions. Of course, the ancient Egyptian burial practices selectively preserved more information about the elite members of society than the average individual.

The dryness of certain caves also promotes the preservation of **coprolites**, the scientific term for fossilized human or animal feces. Coprolites provide information on prehistoric diet and health. From the analysis of elements preserved in coprolites such as seeds, insect skeletons, and tiny bones from fish or amphibians, archaeologists and paleoanthropologists can directly determine diets from the past. This information, in turn, can shed light on overall health. Because many sources of food are available only in certain seasons, researchers can even determine the time of year in which the food was eaten.

Certain climates can obliterate all evidence of organic remains. Maya ruins found in the tropical rainforests

coprolites Preserved fecal material providing evidence of the diet and health of past organisms.

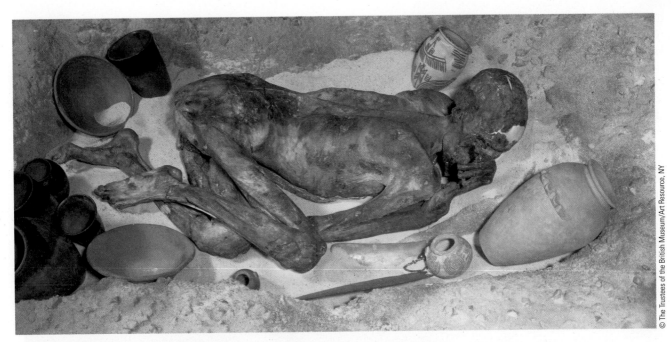

Figure 5.8 Preservation and Environment The preservation of archaeological remains is dependent upon the environment. Even before the invention of mummification technologies, buried bodies were very well preserved in Egypt because they dried so quickly in the extremely arid environment.

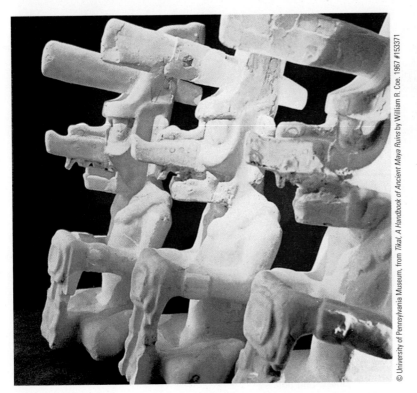

Figure 5.9 Reconstructing Decayed Wood Carvings At the Maya site of Tikal, these intricately carved figures, originally made of wood, were recovered from a king's tomb by pouring plaster into a cavity in the soil that was left when the original organic material decayed.

of Mesoamerica (the region encompassing central and southern Mexico and northern Central America) are often in a state of collapse—notwithstanding that many are massive structures of stone—as a result of the pressure exerted upon them by the heavy forest vegetation. The rain and humidity soon destroy almost all traces of woodwork, textiles, or basketry. Fortunately, impressions of these artifacts can sometimes be preserved in plaster (**Figure 5.9**). More easily preserved stone carvings and pottery figurines may depict some objects made of wood or plant fibers. Thus, even in the face of substantial decay of organic substances, archaeologists can still learn about these remains.

Sorting Out the Evidence

Excavation records include a scale map of all the features, the stratification of each excavated square, a description of the exact location and depth of every artifact or bone unearthed, and photographs and scale drawings of the objects. Such detailed records allow the researchers to piece together the archaeological and biological evidence so as to arrive at a plausible reconstruction of a culture. Although researchers conducting an excavation may focus only on certain kinds of remains, they must record every aspect of the site. Future researchers may need a piece of information to answer a question that no one thought of at the time of the initial investigation. In other words, archaeological sites are nonrenewable resources. Even the most meticulous excavation results in a permanent disturbance of the arrangement of artifacts.

Sometimes sites are illegally looted, which can result in loss not only of the artifacts themselves but of the site (**Figure 5.10**). Although looting has long been a threat to the archaeological record, today it is a high-tech endeavor. Avid collectors and fans of archaeological sites

unwittingly aid looting through sharing site and artifact location information on the Internet, which has also provided a market for artifacts.

Meticulous care does not end with excavation. Archaeologists and paleoanthropologists apply a variety of laboratory methods to studying the artifact or fossil, once freed from the surrounding matrix. Generally, archaeologists and paleoanthropologists plan on at least three hours of laboratory work for each hour of fieldwork (**Figure 5.11**).

In the lab, archaeologists first clean and catalogue—often a tedious and time-consuming job—all artifacts before beginning any analyses. From the shapes of the artifacts as well as from the traces of manufacture and wear, archaeologists can usually determine their function. For example, the Russian archaeologist S. A. Semenov devoted many years to the study of prehistoric technology. In the

© Arne Hodalic/Corbis

Figure 5.10 Looting When looters harvest artifacts for sale on the black market, they simply pull them from the ground. These looters steal far more than the artifacts themselves: They also steal all the information that could have been gleaned from a proper excavation of the site. Even if police ultimately recover the artifacts from the looters, or from the collectors who purchase such artifacts illegally, lack of context and precise location of the artifacts in relation to every other detail of the site severely limits the opportunity to reconstruct lifeways of past peoples. Further, looters often completely destroy the sites they loot, erasing evidence of their crime along with any details archaeologists might have salvaged.

AFP/Getty Images

Figure 5.11 Lucy's Child In September 2006, researchers announced the discovery of a spectacular new fossil—the skeleton of a young child dated to 3.3 million years ago. The fossil was actually discovered in the Dikika area of northern Ethiopia in 2000. Since then, researchers worked on careful recovery and analysis of the fossilized remains so that when the announcement was made, much was already known about the specimen. Their analyses have determined that this child, a little girl about 3 years old who likely died in a flash flood, was a member of *Australopithecus afarensis*, the same species as the famous Lucy specimen (see Chapter 6). Due to the importance of this find, some scientists have referred to this specimen as "Lucy's Baby" or "Lucy's Child," although the individual lived about 150,000 years before Lucy.

case of a flint tool used as a scraper, he was able to determine, by examining the wear patterns of the tool under a microscope, that the prehistoric individuals who used it began to scrape from right to left and then scraped from left to right, and in so doing avoided straining the muscles of the hand (Semenov, 1964). From the work of Semenov and others, we now know that right-handed individuals made most stone tools preserved in the archaeological record, a fact that has implications for brain structure. The relationships among populations can also be traced through material remains (**Figure 5.12**).

Paleoanthropologists, bioarchaeologists, and forensic anthropologists use a variety of investigative techniques to examine bones and teeth. For example, the examination of dental specimens under the microscope might reveal markings on teeth that provide clues about diet. Paleoanthropologists often make imprints or **endocasts** of the insides of skulls to determine the size and shape of ancient brains.

Just as DNA fingerprinting might be used in forensic investigations, paleoanthropologists apply advances in genetic technology to ancient human remains. By extracting genetic material from skeletal remains, they can make DNA comparisons among the specimen, other fossils, and living people. Small fragments of DNA are amplified or copied repeatedly using **polymerase chain reaction (PCR)** technology to provide a sufficient amount of material to perform these analyses. However, unless DNA is preserved in a stable material such as amber, it will decay over time. Therefore, analyses of DNA extracted from specimens older than about 50,000 years become increasingly unreliable due to the decay of DNA.

The bioarchaeologist combines the biological anthropologist's expertise in skeletal biology with the archaeological reconstruction of human cultures. Examination of human skeletal material provides important insights into ancient peoples' diets, gender roles, social status,

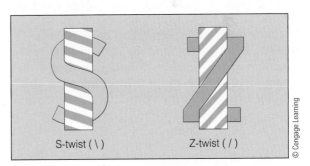

S-twist (\ )   Z-twist (/)

© Cengage Learning

Figure 5.12 Actions in Objects In northern New England, prehistoric pottery was often decorated by impressing the damp clay with a cord-wrapped stick. Examination of cord impressions reveals that coastal people made cordage by twisting fibers to the left (Z-twist), whereas those living inland did the opposite (S-twist). The nonfunctional differences reflect motor habits so deeply ingrained as to seem completely natural to the cordage makers. From this, we may infer two distinctively different populations.

endocast A cast of the inside of a skull; used to help determine the size and shape of the brain.

polymerase chain reaction (PCR) A technique for amplifying or creating multiple copies of fragments of DNA so that it can be studied in the laboratory.

and patterns of activity. For example, analysis of human skeletons shows that elite members of society had access to more nutritious foods, allowing them to reach their full growth potential.

Bioarchaeologists can assess the gender roles in a given society through skeletons as well. In fully preserved adult skeletons, the sex of the deceased individual can be determined with a high degree of accuracy, allowing for comparisons of male and female life expectancy, mortality, and health status (**Figure 5.13**). These analyses can help establish the social roles of men and women in past societies. Skeletal remains can also reveal aspects of an individual's social status (**Figure 5.14**).

Forensic anthropology, bioarchaeology's cousin discipline, also examines skeletal remains to determine characteristics of a deceased or injured individual. As does a bioarchaeologist, the forensic anthropologist integrates skeletal information with material remains. New biomedical technology also plays a role in the investigation of remains from both the past and the present. For example, CT (computed tomography) scans have added new information in forensic, bioarchaeological, and paleoanthropological investigations. Recent and ancient remains are now routinely scanned, yielding considerable information about the structural details of bones. Although a CT scan cannot substitute for an autopsy in forensic contexts, it facilitates identification in the context of mass disasters. In addition, it can provide evidence of past trauma that might otherwise remain hidden in an investigation aimed at determining the immediate cause of death (Leth, 2007).

In archaeological contexts, CT technology has been particularly useful for determining whether damage to remains took place during excavation or whether it preceded death. For example, after the remains of Egyptian King Tut were scanned, scientists uniformly agreed that the young king did not die of a head injury as previously thought; some suggested that a broken femur may have been the cause of his death (Handwerk, 2005). To minimize handling, scientists scan these rare specimens only once allowing future researchers to study the digital images instead of the remains.

Recently, it has become more complicated to carry out skeletal analyses, especially in the United States where the right of American Indian communities to request the return of archaeologically excavated skeletons for reburial is now supported by federal law. Anthropologists find themselves in a quandary over this requirement. As scientists, anthropologists know the importance of the information that can be gleaned from studies of human skeletons, but as scholars guided by ethical principles they are bound to respect the feelings of those for whom the skeletons possess cultural and spiritual significance.

New techniques, such as 3D digital images of Native American skeletons, help to resolve this conflict as they allow for both rapid repatriation and continued study

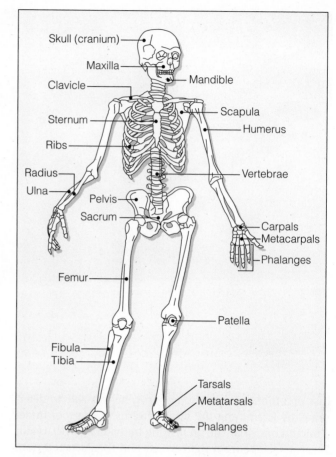

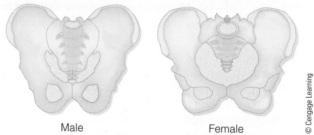

Male   Female

© Cengage Learning

Figure 5.13 **The Human Skeleton** Learning the basic skeleton will be useful in the chapters ahead as we trace the history of human evolution. In addition, bear in mind that the complete male and female skeletons differ on average in some consistent ways that allow skeletal biologists to identify the sex of the deceased individual. Some of these differences relate to the fact that generally males outsize females. But the successful adaptation of the human female pelvis to childbirth makes it the most dimorphic bone of the body and the best way for researchers to determine the sex of skeletal remains. Notice the typically more open space on the interior of the female pelvis corresponding to the birth canal. In males, bones project into this space.

of skeletal remains. But globally, many aboriginal groups question the practice of digitizing remains of their people without permission. For example, the University of Vienna in Austria has been challenged by representatives of the

Figure 5.14 **African Burial Ground** In 1991, federally mandated investigation of cultural remains, on the site of a proposed 34-story, $276-million federal office building in Lower Manhattan, led to the discovery of a massive African burial ground, covering nearly six acres. Though laws led to this discovery, ironically no laws automatically protected this site, one of the most important historical archaeological sites of colonial America. Activists, politicians, and anthropologists worked together to protect and ultimately excavate the site. The investigations documented the extreme physical hardships endured by these earliest American slaves, the vital contributions African men, women, and children made to economic and cultural development of colonial America, and the cultural continuity that these individuals maintained with their African homeland against great odds. After completing analyses of the skeletal remains of over 400 of the estimated 20,000 people buried there, the remains were respectfully reinterred in a commemorative ceremony, "Rites of Ancestral Return." Today, instead of an office building, a memorial and a historical exhibit mark the site.

Ju/'hoansi people of southern Africa because the remains that the Austrian ethnological museum holds were not donated; rather, they were taken early in the century by Rudolf Pöch, a Viennese anthropologist, as was common practice at that time. Roger Chennells, the South African legal advisor for the Ju/'hoansi, states their position as: "We have not been consulted, and we do not support any photographic archiving of our people's remains—we are opposed to it" (quoted in Scully, 2008, p. 1155).

By the standards of the 1990 Native American Graves Protection and Repatriation Act (NAGPRA), the Ju/'hoansi

would have legal decision-making authority over the fate of these remains; but the equivalent of NAGPRA has not yet been codified in international law. Even with NAGPRA in place, controversy still surrounds the handling of remains. Sometimes conflicting worldviews are at the heart of the controversy between scientists and American Indians, as seen with Kennewick Man, a 9,300-year-old skeleton that was dislodged by the Columbia River in Washington State in 1996. This chapter's Biocultural Connection focuses on how this controversy has been playing out in the federal courts.

BIOCULTURAL CONNECTION

Kennewick Man

The "Ancient One" and "Kennewick Man" both refer to the 9,300-year-old skeletal remains that were found in 1996 below the surface of Lake Wallula, part of the Columbia River, in Kennewick, Washington State. This discovery has been the center of continuing controversy since it was made. Who owns these human remains? Who can determine what shall be done with them? Do the biological characteristics preserved in these remains play a role in determining their fate?

This particular conflict involves three major parties. Because the skeleton was found on a location for which the U.S. Army Corps of Engineers is responsible, this federal agency first took possession of the remains. Appealing to NAGPRA, a nearby American Indian group—Confederated Tribes of the Umatilla Indian Reservation (representing the region's Umatilla, Cayuse, and Walla Walla nations)—claimed the remains. Because Kennewick Man was found within their ancestral homeland, they argue that they are "culturally affiliated" with the individual they refer to as the "Ancient One." Viewing these human bones as belonging to an ancestor, they wish to return them to the earth in a respectful ceremony.

This claim was challenged in federal court by a group of scientists, including archaeologists and biological anthropologists. They view these human remains, among the oldest ever discovered in the western hemisphere, as scientifically precious, with potential to shed light on the earliest population movements in the Americas. The scientists do not want to "own" the remains but want the opportunity to study them. By means of DNA analysis, for instance, these scientists expect to determine possible prehistoric linkages between this individual and ancient human remains found elsewhere, including Asia. Moreover, scientific analysis may determine whether there actually exists any biological connection between these remains and currently living Native peoples, including individuals residing on the Umatilla Indian Reservation.

Fearing the loss of a unique scientific specimen, the scientists filed a lawsuit in federal court to prevent reburial before the bones were researched and analyzed. Their legal challenge was based on the notion that "cultural affiliation" is a very difficult concept when it concerns such ancient human remains. The scientists focus on the fact that the region's Native peoples cannot prove they are

direct lineal descendants. Unless such ties have been objectively established, they argue, Kennewick Man should be released for scientific study.

In 2004 federal court rulings permitted initial scientific investigations. Just as these investigations were wrapping up in July 2005, the Senate Indian Affairs Committee heard testimony on a proposal by Arizona Senator John McCain to expand NAGPRA so that remains such as these would be once again prohibited from study. Congress adjourned without this bill becoming law, and the remains have been studied continually since then.

Doug Owsley, the forensic anthropologist from the Smithsonian Institution leading the research team, has said that scientific investigation is yielding even more information than expected. Because conflicting worldviews are at the center of this controversy, it is unlikely that it will be easily resolved.

BIOCULTURAL QUESTION

If the skeletons of your ancestors were the subject of scientific study, how would you react? Would you be comfortable donating your own body to biological research? What beliefs about life, death, and the body inform your responses to these questions?

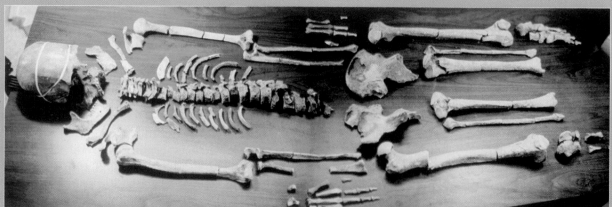

The names for this prehistoric skeleton, Ancient One and Kennewick Man, distill the debate between American Indians and scientists down to the level of two expressive words.

Dating the Past

With accurate and detailed records of their excavations in hand, archaeologists and paleoanthropologists can begin to investigate a crucial research issue: the question of age. As we have seen, analysis and interpretation of physical and cultural remains depends on accurate calculation of the age of the artifacts or specimens. How, then, do scientists reliably date the materials retrieved from excavations? Because archaeologists and paleoanthropologists often deal with peoples and events from long ago, the traditional calendar of historic times is of little use to them.

Scientists can date remains by noting their position in the earth, by measuring the amount of chemicals contained in fossil bones, or by association with other plant, animal, or cultural remains. These are known as **relative dating** techniques because they do not establish precise dates for specific remains but rather their relationship to a series of remains. Methods of **absolute dating** or **chronometric dating** (from the Latin for "measuring time") provide actual dates calculated in years "before the present" (BP). These methods rely on chemical and physical properties such as rates of decay of radioactive elements, which may be present in the remains themselves or in the surrounding soil. Absolute dating methods scientifically establish actual dates for the major events of geologic and evolutionary history. By comparing dates and remains across a variety of sites, anthropologists can reconstruct human origins, migrations, and technological developments.

Scientists use a wide range of relative and chronometric techniques. However, most of these methods work only for certain time spans and in certain environmental contexts. Bear in mind that each of the chronometric dating techniques also has a margin of error. Ideally, archaeologists and paleoanthropologists utilize as many methods as are appropriate, given the materials available and the funds at their disposal. By doing so, they significantly reduce the risk of error. Several of the most frequently employed dating techniques are presented in **Table 5.1**.

Relative Dating

Of the many relative dating techniques available, **stratigraphy** is probably the most reliable (recall Figure 5.6). Based on the simple principle that the oldest layer, or stratum, was deposited first (it is the deepest) whereas the newest layer was deposited last (in undisturbed situations, it lies at the top), stratigraphy establishes a reliable sequence of age at a given site. The archaeological evidence follows the same pattern with deposition in chronological order. The lowest stratum contains the oldest artifacts and possibly fossils whereas the uppermost stratum contains the most recent ones. Thus, even in the absence of precise dates, one knows the *relative* age of objects in one

stratum compared with the ages of those in other strata. However, defining the stratigraphy of a given site can be complicated by geologic activities such as earthquakes that shift the position of stratigraphic layers.

Archaeologists also use the relative dating technique of **fluorine dating**, based on the fact that the amount of fluorine deposited in bones is proportional to the amount of time they have been in the earth. The oldest bones contain the greatest amount of fluorine and vice versa. The fluorine test can help date bones that cannot be ascribed with certainty to any particular stratum. The variation in the amount of naturally occurring fluorine from region to region limits the validity of this method for cross-site comparisons of fluorine values. Fluorine dating was vital for exposing the infamous Piltdown hoax in England, in which a human skull and orangutan jaw were placed together in the earth as false evidence for an early human ancestor (see Chapter 6).

Relative dating can also be done by **seriation**, a method of establishing sequences of plant, animal, or even cultural remains. With seriation, the order of appearance of a succession (or series) of plants, animals, or artifacts provides relative dates for a site based on a series established in another area. An example of seriation based on cultural artifacts is the Stone–Bronze–Iron Age series used by prehistorians. Within a given region, sites containing artifacts made of iron are generally more recent than sites containing only stone tools. In well-investigated cultural areas, archaeologists have developed series for particular styles of pottery.

Scientists make similar inferences with animal or faunal series. For example, very early North American Indian sites have yielded the remains of mastodons and mammoths—animals now extinct. These remains allow scientists to date these sites to a time before these animals died out, roughly 10,000 years ago. For dating some of the earliest African fossils in human evolution, paleoanthropologists have developed faunal series in regions where accurate chronometric dates can be established. They then

relative dating In archaeology and paleoanthropology, designating an event, object, or fossil as being older or younger than another by noting the position in the earth, by measuring the amount of chemicals contained in fossil bones and artifacts, or by identifying its association with other plant, animal, or cultural remains.

absolute or chronometric dating In archaeology and paleoanthropology, dating archaeological or fossil materials in units of absolute time using scientific properties such as rates of decay of radioactive elements; also known as *chronometric dating*.

stratigraphy In archaeology and paleoanthropology, the most reliable method of relative dating by means of strata.

fluorine dating In archaeology or paleoanthropology, a technique for relative dating based on the fact that the amount of fluorine in bones is proportional to their age.

seriation In archaeology and paleoanthropology, a technique for relative dating based on putting groups of objects into a sequence in relation to one another.

TABLE 5.1

Absolute and Relative Dating Methods Used by Archaeologists and Paleoanthropologists

Dating Method	Time Period	Process and Use	Drawbacks
Stratigraphy	Relative only	Based on the law of superposition, which states that lower layers or strata are older than higher strata; establishing the age of biological and cultural remains based on the layer in which they are found	Site specific; natural forces, such as earthquakes, and human activity, such as burials, disturb stratigraphic relationships
Fluorine analysis	Relative only	Comparing the amount of fluorine from surrounding soil absorbed by specimens after deposition; older remains will have absorbed more fluorine	Site specific
Faunal and floral series	Relative only	Sequencing remains into relative chronological order based on an evolutionary order established in another region with reliable absolute dates; called *palynology* when done with pollen grains	Dependent upon known relationships established elsewhere
Seriation	Relative only	Sequencing cultural remains into relative chronological order based on stylistic features	Dependent on known relationships established elsewhere
Dendrochronology	About 3,000 years before present (BP) maximum	Comparing tree growth rings preserved in a site with a tree of known age	Requires ancient trees of known age
Radiocarbon	Accurate < 50,000 BP	Comparing the ratio of radioactive carbon 14 (^{14}C), with a half-life of 5,730 years, to stable carbon (^{12}C) in organic material; after organisms die, only the ^{14}C decays (half of it every 5,730 years), so the ratio between ^{14}C and ^{12}C determines an actual date since death	Increasingly inaccurate when assessing remains from more than 50,000 years ago
Potassium argon (K-Ar)	> 200,000 BP	Using volcanic ash, comparing the amount of radioactive potassium (^{40}K), with a half-life of 1.25 billion years, to stable argon (^{40}Ar)	Requires volcanic ash; requires cross checking due to contamination from atmospheric argon
Amino acid racemization	40,000–180,000 BP	Comparing the ratio of right- and left-sided proteins in a three-dimensional structure; decay after death causes these proteins to change	Amino acids leached out from soil variably cause error
Thermoluminescence	Possibly up to 200,000 BP	Measuring the amount of light given off due to radioactivity when the specimen is heated to high temperatures	Technique developed for recent materials such as Greek pottery; not clear how accurate the dates are for older remains
Electron spin resonance	Possibly up to about 200,000 BP	Measuring the resonance of trapped electrons in a magnetic field	Works with tooth enamel, not yet developed for bone; problems with accuracy
Fission track	Wide range of times	Measuring the tracks left in crystals by uranium as it decays; good cross check for K-Ar technique	Useful for dating crystals only
Paleomagnetic reversals	Wide range of times	Measuring the orientation of magnetic particles in stones and linking them to whether the earth's magnetic field pulled toward the north or south during their formation	Large periods of normal or reversed magnetic orientation require dating by some other method; some smaller events are known to interrupt the sequence
Uranium series	40,000–180,000	Measuring the amount of uranium decaying in cave sites	Large error range

use these series to establish relative sequences in other regions. Similar series have been established for plants, particularly using grains of pollen. With this approach, known as **palynology**, the kind of pollen found in any geologic stratum depends on the kind of vegetation that existed at the time that stratum was deposited. Identifying the type of pollen associated with a site or locality can establish its relative dates. In addition, palynology also helps to reconstruct the environments in which prehistoric peoples lived.

Chronometric Dating

Some archaeological sites yield written records that provide archaeologists with a fascinating account of dates and times (**Figure 5.15**). But generally precise dates derive

© University of Pennsylvania Museum CX 61–4–123

Figure 5.15 Maya Calendric Glyphs Some ancient societies devised precise ways of recording dates that archaeologists have been able to correlate with our own calendar. Here is the tomb of an important ruler, Siyaj Chan K'awil II, at the ancient Maya city of Tikal. The glyphs painted on the wall give the date of the burial in the Maya calendar, which is the same as March 18 of the year AD 457, in the Gregorian calendar.

from a variety of absolute or chronometric dating methods. These techniques apply chemistry and physics to calculate the ages of physical and cultural remains. Several methods use naturally occurring radioactive elements that are present either in the remains themselves or in the surrounding soil.

One of the most widely used methods of absolute dating is **radiocarbon dating**. This method uses the fact that while they are alive, all organisms absorb radioactive carbon (known as carbon 14 or ^{14}C) as well as ordinary carbon 12 (^{12}C) in proportions identical to those found in the atmosphere. Absorption of ^{14}C ceases at the time of death, and the ratio between the two forms of carbon begins to change as the unstable radioactive element ^{14}C begins to "decay." Each radioactive element decays, or transforms into a stable nonradioactive form, at a specific rate. The amount of time it takes for one-half of the material originally present to decay is expressed as the "half-life." In the case of ^{14}C, it takes 5,730 years for half of the amount of ^{14}C present to decay to stable nitrogen 14. In another 5,730 years (11,460 years total), half of the remaining amount will also decay to nitrogen 14 so that only one-quarter of the original amount of ^{14}C will be present. Thus, the age of an organic substance such as charcoal, wood, shell, or bone can be measured through determining the changing proportion of ^{14}C relative to the amount of stable ^{12}C.

Though scientists can measure the amount of radioactive carbon left in even a few milligrams of a given organic substance of a recent specimen, the miniscule amount of carbon 14 present in remains from the distant past limits accurate detection. The radiocarbon method can adequately date organic materials up to about 50,000 years old, but dating older material is far less reliable.

Of course, one has to be sure that the organic remains were truly contemporaneous with the archaeological materials. For example, charcoal found on a site may have gotten there from a recent forest fire rather than a more ancient activity, or wood found at a site may have been retrieved by the people who lived there from some older context.

Because there is always a certain amount of error involved, radiocarbon dates (like all chronometric dating methods) are not as absolute as is sometimes thought. This is why any stated date always has a plus-or-minus ($\pm$) factor attached to it corresponding to one standard deviation above and below the mean value. For example, a date of 5,200 $\pm$ 120 years ago means that there is about a 2 out of 3 chance (or a 67 percent chance) that the true date

palynology In archaeology and paleoanthropology, a technique of relative dating based on changes in fossil pollen over time.

radiocarbon dating In archaeology and paleoanthropology, a technique of chronometric dating based on measuring the amount of radioactive carbon (^{14}C) left in organic materials found in archaeological sites.

falls somewhere between 5,080 and 5,320 radiocarbon years ago. The qualification "radiocarbon years" is used because radiocarbon years are not precisely equivalent to calendar years.

That discovery—radiocarbon years are not precisely equivalent to calendar years—was made possible by another method of absolute dating: **dendrochronology** (derived from *dendron*, a Greek word meaning "tree"). Originally devised for dating Pueblo Indian sites in the North American Southwest, this method is based on the fact that in the right kind of climate, trees add one (and only one) new growth ring to their trunks every year. The rings vary in thickness, depending upon the amount of rainfall received in a year, so that tree ring growth registers climatic fluctuation. By taking a sample of wood, such as a beam from a Pueblo Indian house, and by comparing its pattern of rings with those in the trunk of a tree of known age, archaeologists can date the archaeological material.

Dendrochronology is applicable only to wooden objects. Furthermore, it works only in regions that contain trees of great age, such as giant sequoias and bristlecone pines. Radiocarbon dating of wood from bristlecone pines dated by dendrochronology allows scientists to correct the carbon 14 dates so as to bring them into agreement with calendar dates.

Potassium-argon dating, another commonly used method of absolute dating, is based on a technique similar to that of radiocarbon analysis. Following intense heating, as from a volcanic eruption, radioactive potassium decays at a known rate to form argon; any previously existing argon will have been released by the heating of the molten lava. The half-life of radioactive potassium is 1.3 billion years. Measuring the ratio of potassium to argon in a given rock accurately dates deposits dating back millions of years.

Potassium-argon analysis of volcanic debris at various fossil localities in East Africa indicates when the volcanic eruption occurred. Fossils or artifacts found sandwiched between layers of volcanic ash (as at Olduvai and other sites in East Africa) can be dated with some precision. As with radiocarbon dates, there are limits to that precision so potassium-argon dates are always stated with a plus-or-minus margin of error attached. Further, potassium-argon dating loses precision with materials younger than about 200,000 years.

Neither the radiocarbon nor the potassium-argon methods work well during the time period dating from about 50,000 years ago to about 200,000 years ago. Because this same time period happens to be very important in human evolutionary history, scientists have developed a number of other methods to obtain accurate dates for this critical period.

One such method, *amino acid racemization*, is based on the fact that amino acids trapped in organic materials gradually change, or racemize, after death, from left-handed forms to right-handed forms. Thus, the ratio of left- to right-handed forms should indicate the specimen's age. Unfortunately, in substances like bone, moisture and acids in the soil can leach out the amino acids, thereby introducing a serious source of error. However, ostrich eggshells have proved immune to this problem, the amino acids being so effectively locked up in a tight mineral matrix that they are preserved for thousands of years. Because ostrich eggs were widely used as food and the shells were used as containers in Africa and the Middle East, they provide a powerful means of dating sites of the later parts of the Old Stone Age (Paleolithic), between 40,000 and 180,000 years ago.

Electron spin resonance, which measures the number of trapped electrons in bone, and *thermoluminescence*, which measures the amount of light emitted from a specimen when heated to high temperatures, are two additional methods that have been developed to fill in prehistoric time gaps. Dates derived from these two methods changed the interpretation of key sites in present-day Israel vital for reconstructing human origins (see Chapters 7 and 8).

A few other chronometric techniques rely on the element uranium. *Fission track dating*, for example, counts radiation damage tracks on mineral crystals. Like amino acid racemization, all these methods have problems: They are complicated and tend to be expensive, many can be carried out only on specific kinds of materials, and some are so new that their reliability is not yet unequivocally established. It is for these reasons that they have not been as widely used as radiocarbon and potassium-argon dating techniques.

Paleomagnetic reversals contribute another interesting dimension to absolute dating methodologies by providing a method to crosscheck dates (**Figure 5.16**). This method is based on the shifting magnetic pole of the earth—the same force that controls the orientation of a compass needle. Today, a compass points to the north because we are in a period defined as the geomagnetic "normal." Over the past several million years, there have been extended periods of time during which the magnetic field of the earth pulled toward the south pole. Geologists call these periods *geomagnetic reversals*. Iron particles in stones will be oriented into positions determined by the dominant magnetic pole at the time of their formation, allowing scientists to derive broad ranges of dates for them. Human evolutionary history contains a geomagnetic reversal starting 5.2 million years ago that ended 3.4 million years ago, followed by a normal period until 2.6 million years ago; then a second reversal began, lasting until about 700,000 years ago when the present normal period began. This paleomagnetic sequence can be used to date sites to either normal or reversed periods and can be correlated with a variety of other dating methods to crosscheck their accuracy.

---

dendrochronology In archaeology and paleoanthropology, a technique of chronometric dating based on the number of rings of growth found in tree trunks.

potassium-argon dating In archaeology and paleoanthropology, a technique of chronometric dating that measures the ratio of radioactive potassium to argon in volcanic debris associated with human remains.

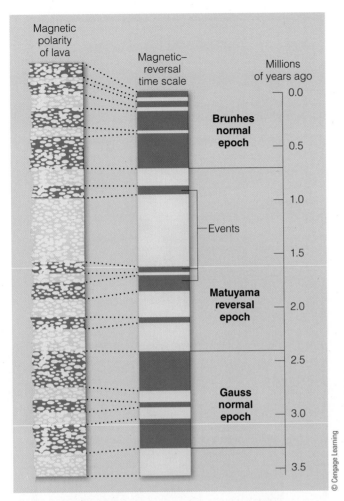

Figure 5.16 Paleomagnetic Reversals Scientists have documented a geomagnetic polarity time scale in which the changes in the earth's magnetic force—to north or south—have been calibrated. This geomagnetic time scale provides scientists with opportunities to cross check other dating methods.

Concepts and Methods for the Most Distant Past

As described previously, context and dating are vital for the interpretation of fossils and cultural remains. Because mammalian primate evolution extends so far back in time, paleoanthropologists reconstruct our evolutionary history in conjunction with information about the geologic history of the earth, which is 4.6 billion years old.

Continental Drift and Geologic Time

The geologic time scale is unfamiliar because few people deal with hundreds of millions of anything, let alone years, on a regular basis. To understand this type of scale, astronomer Carl Sagan correlated the geologic time scale for the history of the earth to a single calendar year. In this "cosmic calendar," the earth itself originates on January 1,

the first organisms appear approximately 9 months later around September 25, followed by the earliest vertebrates around December 20, mammals on December 25, primates on December 29, hominoids at 10:15 AM on New Year's Eve, bipeds at 9:30 PM, with our species appearing in the last minutes before midnight. Human evolutionary history begins with the December 25 appearance of the mammals in the Mesozoic era, roughly 245 million years ago (mya). **Figure 5.17** plots out the more recent events in

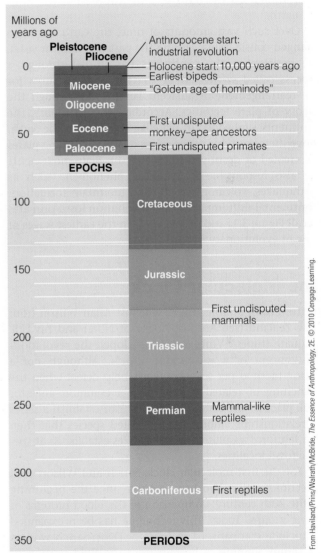

Figure 5.17 Milestones of Mammalian Primate Evolution This timeline highlights some major milestones in the course of mammalian primate evolution that ultimately led to humans and their ancestors. The Paleocene, Eocene, Oligocene, and Miocene epochs are subsets of the Tertiary period. The Quaternary period begins with the Pleistocene and continues today. It includes the Holocene epoch that began at the end of the last Ice Age around 12,000 years ago. In 2000, the Nobel Prize–winning chemist Paul Crutzen coined the term *Anthropocene* to describe the world since the industrial revolution because of the profound geologic changes human activity imposes on the earth. Geologic societies around the globe are currently debating the inclusion of Anthropocene as a formal geologic unit.

mammalian primate evolution that take place during the final week of Sagan's cosmic calendar.

By 190 million years ago—the end of what geologists call the Triassic period—true mammals were on the scene. Mammals from the Triassic, Jurassic (135–190 mya), and Cretaceous (65–135 mya) periods are largely known from hundreds of fossils, especially teeth and jaw parts. Because teeth are the hardest, most durable structures, they often outlast other parts of an animal's skeleton. Fortunately, investigators often are able to infer a good deal about the total animal on the basis of only a few teeth found in the earth.

Over such vast amounts of time, the earth itself has changed considerably. During the past 200 million years, the position of the continents has shifted through a process called **continental drift**, which accounts for the rearrangement of adjacent landmasses through the theory of plate tectonics. According to this theory, the continents, embedded in platelike segments of the earth, move their positions as the edges of the underlying plates are created or destroyed (**Figure 5.18**). Plate movements are also responsible for geologic phenomena such as earthquakes, volcanic activity, and mountain formation. Continental drift impacted the distribution fossil primates (recall Figure 3.1) and played a role in the earliest stages of human evolutionary history.

The Molecular Clock

In the 1960s, a molecular biochemist Allan Wilson from New Zealand (see Anthropologist of Note) and his U.S. graduate student Vince Sarich developed the revolutionary concept of a **molecular clock**. Although not a dating method per se, such clocks help detect when the branching of related species from a common ancestor took place in the distant past. They can establish a series of relationships among closely related species that then can reinforce absolute or relative dates established at specific fossil localities.

For the first molecular clock, Sarich and Wilson used a technique that had been around since the beginning of the 20th century: comparison of the blood proteins of living groups. Today, this technique has been expanded to include comparisons in bases of DNA. Sarich worked on serum albumin, a protein from the fluid portion of the blood (like the albumin that forms egg whites) that can be precipitated out of solution. *Precipitation* refers to

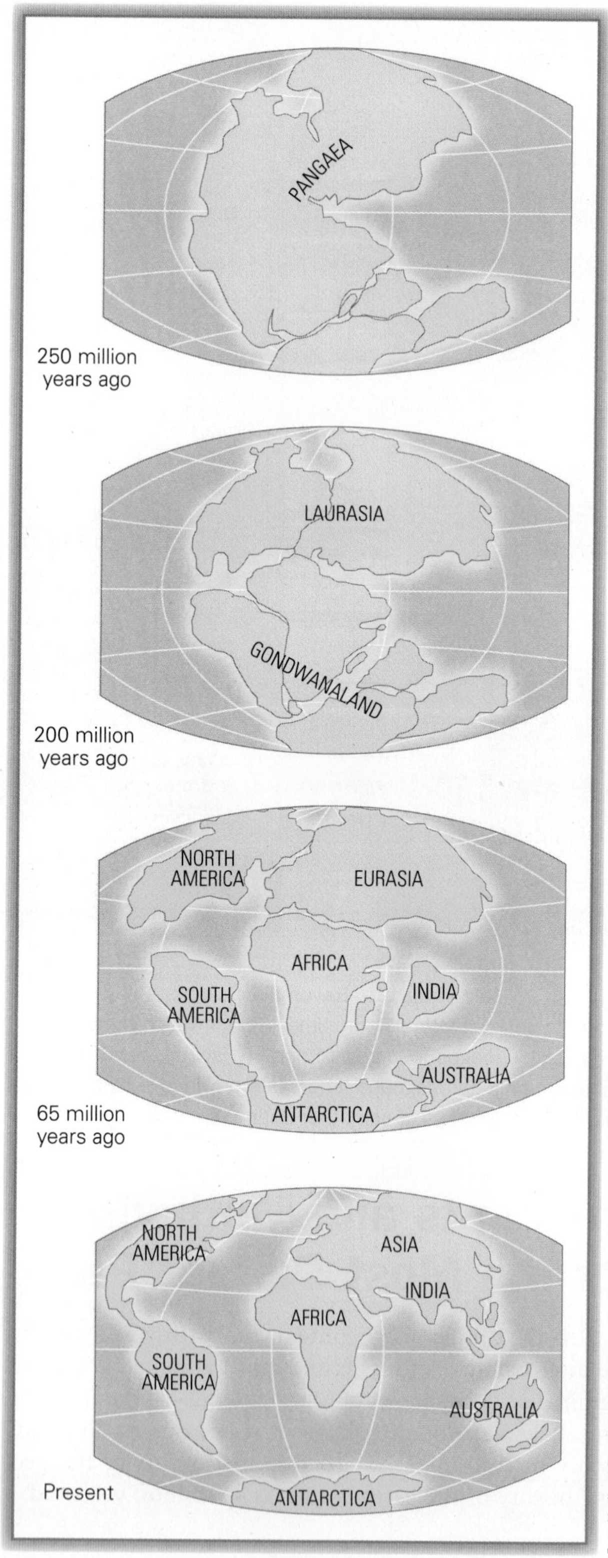

Figure 5.18 **Continental Drift** Continental drift is illustrated here during several geologic periods. At the time of the extinction of the dinosaurs 65 million years ago, the seas opened up by continental drift, creating isolating barriers between major landmasses. About 23 million years ago, at the start of the time period known as the Miocene epoch, African and Eurasian landmasses reconnected and the Indian subcontinent joined Asia.

From Haviland/Prins/Walrath/McBride, *The Essence of Anthropology*, 2E. © 2010 Cengage Learning.

continental drift According to the theory of plate tectonics, the movement of continents embedded in underlying plates on the earth's surface in relation to one another over the history of life on earth.

molecular clock The hypothesis that dates of divergences among related species can be calculated through an examination of the genetic mutations that have accrued since the divergence.

ANTHROPOLOGIST OF NOTE

Allan Wilson (1934–1991)

Though a biochemist by training, New Zealander **Allan Wilson** has made key contributions to anthropology through his pioneering work in applying the principles of biochemistry to human evolutionary questions. Wilson forged a new "hybrid science," combining fossil and molecular evidence with groundbreaking results. Because the molecular evidence required rethinking long-held theories about the relationships among fossil groups, Wilson's work has been surrounded by controversy. According to those close to Wilson, he enjoyed his role as an outsider—being on the edges of anthropology and shaking things up.

Wilson was born in Ngaruwahia, New Zealand, and grew up on a farm in Pukekohe. After attending school in New Zealand and Australia, he was invited to study biochemistry at the University of California, Berkeley, in 1955. His father was reluctant to have his son travel so far from home, but his mother saw this as an exciting opportunity and encouraged him to head to California.

Wilson stayed at Berkeley for the next thirty-five years, running one of the world's most creative biochemistry labs. In the 1960s, Berkeley was a center of academic liberalism and social protest. Wilson's highly original work was conducted with a similar revolutionary spirit, garnering him a MacArthur "Genius" grant, two Guggenheim fellowships, and a place on the short list for the Nobel Prize.

He developed the notion of a molecular clock with his graduate student Vince Sarich and published the groundbreaking paper "Immunological Time-Scale for Human Evolution" in the journal *Science* in 1967. The molecular clock proposes that evolutionary events such as the split between humans and apes can be dated through an examination of the number of genetic mutations that accumulated since two species diverged from a common ancestor. In the 1980s, his laboratory (including Rebecca Cann and Mark Stoneking) was also responsible for seminal work with the mitochondrial Eve hypothesis that continues to be widely debated today (see Chapters 8).

Wilson died from leukemia at the age of 56. Joseph Felsenstein, one of his biographers, stated in his obituary in the journal *Nature*, "While others concentrated on what evolution could tell them about molecules, Wilson always looked for ways that molecules could say something about evolution."

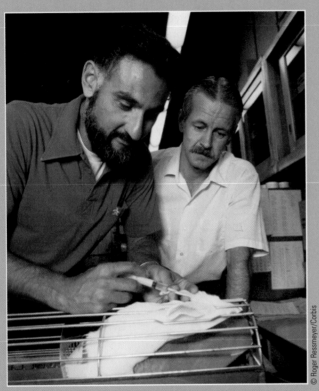

Allan Wilson (*right*) observes as Vince Sarich (*left*) injects a laboratory rabbit.

© Roger Ressmeyer/Corbis

the chemical transformation of a substance dissolved in a liquid back into its solid form. One of the forces that will cause such precipitation is contact of this protein with antibodies directed against it. Antibodies are proteins produced by organisms as part of an immune response to an infection. The technique relies on the notion that the stronger the biochemical reaction between the protein and the antibody (the more precipitate), the closer the evolutionary relationship. The antibodies and proteins of closely related species resemble one another more than the antibodies and proteins of distant species.

Sarich made immunological comparisons between a variety of species and suggested that he could establish dates for evolutionary events by calculating a molecular rate of change over time. By assuming a constant rate of change in the protein structure of each species, Sarich used these results to predict times of divergence between related groups. Each molecular clock needs to be set, or calibrated, by the dates associated with a known event, such as the divergence between prosimian and anthropoid primates or a major change in the continental plates, as established by absolute dating methods.

Using this technique, Sarich proposed a sequence of divergence for the living hominoids showing that human, chimp, and gorilla lines split roughly 5 million years ago (mya). He boldly stated that it was impossible to have a separate human line before 7 million years ago "no matter what it looked like." Before this work, anthropologists had thought that the great apes—chimpanzees and bonobos, gorillas, and orangutans—were more closely related to one another than any of them were to humans. This work was the first proof that human origins are firmly in Africa and that humans, chimps and bonobos, and gorillas are more closely related to one another than any of them are to the orangutans. A discovery in the laboratory, like the molecular clock, can drastically change the interpretation of the fossil evidence.

Sciences of Discovery

The previous discussion demonstrates that anthropologists participate in an unusual kind of science. Paleoanthropology and archaeology are sciences of discovery. As new fossil discoveries and artifacts come to light, interpretations inevitably change, making for better understanding of human evolutionary and cultural history. Today, discoveries can occur in the laboratory as easily as on the site of an excavation. Molecular studies since the 1970s provide a new line of evidence in much the same way that a fossil or pottery figurine or the remains of a preserved plant provides new data as it is unearthed. Just like detectives at an investigation, scientists use each new discovery to refine our collective understanding of the past.

The archaeological and fossil records are imperfect. Chance circumstances of preservation have determined what has and what has not survived the consequences of time. Thus, scientists reconstruct the biology and culture of our ancestors on the basis of fragmentary and at times unrepresentative samples of physical and cultural remains. Chance also impacts the discovery of prehistoric remains. Vestiges may come to light due to factors ranging from changing sea level, vegetation, or even a local government's decision to build a highway.

Ancient cultural processes have also shaped the archaeological and fossil record. We know more about the past due to the cultural practice of deliberate burial. We also know more about the elite segments of past societies because they have left more material culture behind. However, as archaeologists have shifted their focus from gathering treasures to the reconstruction of human behavior, they have gained a more complete picture of ancient societies. Similarly, paleoanthropologists no longer simply catalogue fossils; they interpret data about our ancestors in order to reconstruct the biological processes responsible for who we are today. The challenge of reconstructing our past will be met by a continual process of reexamination and modification as anthropologists discover evidence in the earth, among living people, and in the laboratory leading to new understandings of human origins.

CHAPTER CHECKLIST

How do archaeologists and paleoanthropologists identify sites for excavation?

- Aerial photographs and other surveying tools reveal environmental clues such as soil markings. Survey may be combined with documents, folklore, and found artifacts in order to locate important sites.

- Many excavations take place where natural forces such as erosion or drought leave sites exposed.

- Chance discoveries, like those from mining or construction, have led to the recovery of significant historical remains.

What excavation practices are preferred?

- Excavators map the land into a grid system in order to precisely record the location of found objects, and they choose a fixed landmark to use as the reference (datum point) of the grid. Photographs and scale drawings supplement the written excavation data.

- The destructive nature of excavation demands that researchers record information on all found objects including those irrelevant to their original purpose.

- Where stratification is present, layers corresponding to distinct time periods are dug carefully, one at a time. If searching for smaller objects, the excavation team may utilize the flotation technique to separate particles of varying density.

- For bone excavation, the earth matrix containing the specimen is cut out and hardened using shellac and plaster bandages. Then, the entire block is removed and shipped to a laboratory for the final stages of extraction.

How do scientists continue excavation analysis in the lab?

● Close examination of wear patterns on artifacts can lead to understanding of early human behaviors. Similarly, markings on teeth suggest dietary habits, and endocasts reveal brain size and shape.

● Bioarchaeologists use anatomical data to reconstruct cultures of the past.

● Technology such as CT scanning minimizes handling and potential damage to specimens; 3D digital images permit the continued scientific study of remains that must be repatriated.

● DNA samples can be extracted from more recent skeletal remains.

What are the important dating methods, and how do they differ?

● Relative dating techniques establish the age of remains by association with the surrounding earth or other nearby remains. Researchers may combine several techniques to create accurate timelines of the past. Relative dating methods include stratigraphy, the fluorine method, and seriation.

● Most absolute dating techniques rely on rates of decay of radioactive elements present in remains in order to estimate a numerical age. Absolute methods include techniques such as radiocarbon dating, potassium-argon dating, amino acid racemization, and, in the case of wooden remains, dendrochronology.

How do geologic phenomena contribute to our understanding of human history?

● Knowledge of geomagnetic reversals can be used to date ancient remains by examining the position of iron particles in stone artifacts.

● Continental drift has impacted the course of human evolution by separating populations that then diverged to become distinct species.

What is the molecular clock, and what does it reveal about human evolution?

● The evolutionary proximities of living species can be estimated by comparing their blood proteins. Assuming these proteins have changed at a constant rate over time, scientists estimate when two species' last common ancestor lived.

● Molecular clocks were used to determine that humans, chimps, bonobos, and gorillas split into different evolutionary branches between 5 and 7 million years ago in Africa. All African hominoids are more closely related to one another than any is to the orangutan.

QUESTIONS FOR REFLECTION

1. How would you decide who owns the past? Have there been any examples of contested ownership in your community?

2. The cultural practice of burial of the dead altered the fossil record and provided valuable insight into the beliefs and practices of past cultures. The same is true today. What beliefs are reflected in the traditions for treatment of the dead in your culture?

3. Controversy has surrounded Kennewick Man since this skeleton was discovered on the banks of the Columbia River in Washington in 1996. Scientists and American Indians both feel they have a right to these remains.

What kinds of evidence support these differing perspectives? How should this controversy be resolved?

4. Why is dating so important for paleoanthropologists and archaeologists? Would an interpretation of physical or cultural remains change depending upon the date assigned to the remains? Why are metaphors used in the context of geologic time?

5. The interpretation of fossil material changes with the discovery of new specimens and with findings in the laboratory. How has that happened? Why do we know more about some places and peoples than others?

ONLINE STUDY RESOURCES

CourseMate

Access chapter-specific learning tools, including learning objectives, practice quizzes, videos, flash cards, glossaries, and more in your Anthropology CourseMate.

Log into **www.cengagebrain.com** to access the resources your instructor has assigned and to purchase materials.

Challenge Issue

Who are we? How did we get here? Where and when did the unique human line first appear? What distinguishes us from the other animals in general, the other primates in particular? Paleoanthropologists seek answers to all these questions through scientific study of the fossil record, of our closest relatives, of molecules, and of geology, and they use this disparate fragmentary evidence to reconstruct a coherent trajectory of our evolutionary history. Each aspect of this narrative of human origins challenges us to think about what it means to be human. Although we might be tempted to say that our intellects distinguish us from the other primates, the hallmark of the hominin or human line is *bipedalism*—our ability to walk on two legs. Bone structure indicating that a fossil was fully bipedal makes it, by definition, a hominin. But as Nellie, a graceful tightrope-walking chimp from Fongoli, Senegal, demonstrates, our closest relatives can do this extremely well, if only for a few minutes at a time. The opposable big toe makes it far easier for a chimp than a human to grip a branch thirty feet above the forest floor, but the chimp has difficulty maintaining this posture for long periods of time, due to the position of the bones and muscles of the trunk and legs. Still, the discovery of rich fossil evidence for bipedal forest-dwelling primates who lived from 4.4 to 5.8 million years ago has made some scientists wonder if, like Nellie, our ancestors took their first bipedal steps in the trees instead of on the ground.

From First Primates to First Bipeds

**IN THIS CHAPTER
YOU WILL LEARN TO**

● Identify the course of
primate evolution and its
major geologic events.

● Recognize the anatomy
of bipedalism and how
paleoanthropologists
identify the hominin line
and distinct species in
the fossil record.

● Discuss how cultural
biases interfered with
scientific recognition of the
African origins of humans.

● Describe
paleoanthropology
in action: how
paleoanthropologists
construct the trajectory
of human origins from
fragmentary remains.

● Compare the earliest
bipeds to one another and
to chimps and humans.

● Identify two grades of
australopithecines: the
gracile and the robust.

● Describe the earliest
appearance of the genus
Homo in the fossil record.

In geologic terms, humans appeared in the world recently, though not as
recently as some new strains of bacteria. Our form—like that of any organism—
came about only as a consequence of a whole string of accidental happenings
in the past. The history of any species is an outcome of many such occurrences.
This chapter begins our focus on human origins, starting with our earliest primate ancestors. Much of who we are, as culture-bearing biological organisms,
derives from our mammalian primate heritage.

The successful adaptation of the primates largely reflects their intelligence, a
characteristic that provides for behavioral flexibility. Other physical traits, such
as stereoscopic vision and a grasping hand, have also been instrumental in the
success of the primates. In addition, the continued survival of our species and of
our world now depends on understanding evolutionary processes and the way
all organisms interact with their environment.

Primate Origins

Early primates began to emerge during a time of great global change at the start
of the Paleocene epoch 65 million years ago (mya). Evidence suggests that a
meteor or some other sort of extraterrestrial body slammed into the earth where
the Yucatan Peninsula of Mexico now exists, cooling global temperatures to
such an extent as to cause the extinction of the dinosaurs (and numerous other
species as well). For 100 million years, dinosaurs had dominated most terrestrial
environments suitable for vertebrate animals and would probably have continued to do so had the climate not changed. Although mammals appeared at
about the same time as reptiles, they existed as small, inconspicuous creatures.
But with the demise of the dinosaurs, new opportunities became available,
allowing mammals to begin their great adaptive radiation into a variety of species, including our own ancestors, the earliest primates (**Figure 6.1**).

Figure 6.1 Extinction of the Dinosaurs Though popular media depict the coexistence of humans and dinosaurs, in reality the extinction of the dinosaurs occurred 65 million years ago (mya), while the first bipeds ancestral to humans appeared between 5 and 8 million years ago. The climatic changes beginning 65 million years ago allowed for the adaptive radiation of the mammals and a diversification of plant life. The appearance of the true seed plants (the angiosperms) provided not only highly nutritious fruit seeds and flowers but also a host of habitats for numerous edible insects and worms—just the sorts of food required by mammals with their higher metabolism. For species like mammals to continue to survive, a wide diversity of plants, insects, and even single-celled organisms needs to be maintained. In ecosystems these organisms are dependent upon one another.

Newly evolved grasses, shrubs, and other flowering plants proliferated enormously during this same time period. This diversification, along with a milder climate, favored the spread of dense, lush tropical and subtropical forests over the earth. The spread of these huge belts of forest set the stage for the movement of some mammals into the trees. Forests provided our early ancestors with the ecological niches in which they would flourish. Fossil evidence of primatelike mammals from the Paleocene forests has been found in North America and Eurasia. See **Figure 6.2** for a full timeline of primate evolution.

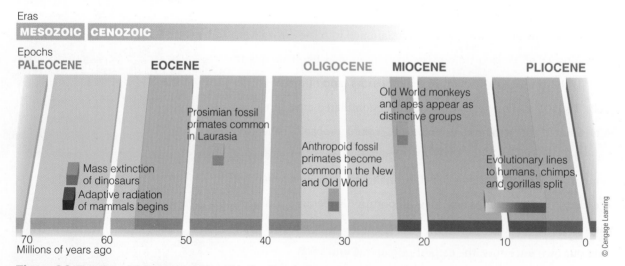

Figure 6.2 Timeline of Primate Evolution This timeline depicts some of the major events of primate evolution.

One theory for primate evolution, the **arboreal hypothesis**, proposes that life in the trees was responsible for enhanced visual acuity and manual dexterity in primates. Misjudgments and errors of coordination led to falls that injured or killed the individuals poorly adapted to arboreal life. Natural selection would favor those that judged depth correctly and gripped the branches strongly. Early primates that took to the trees were probably in some measure preadapted by virtue of behavioral flexibility, better vision, and more dexterous fingers than their contemporaries.

Primatologist Matt Cartmill's **visual predation hypothesis** suggests that primate visual and grasping abilities were also promoted through the activity of hunting for insects by sight. The relatively small size of the early primates allowed them to make use of the smaller branches of trees; larger, heavier competitors and most predators could not follow. The move to the smaller branches also gave them access to an abundant food supply; the primates were able to gather insects, leaves, flowers, and fruits directly rather than waiting for them to fall to the ground.

The strong selection in a new environment led to an acceleration in the rate of change of primate characteristics. Paradoxically, these changes eventually facilitated a return to the ground by some primates, including the ancestors of the genus *Homo*.

The first well-preserved "true" primates appeared by about 55 million years ago at the start of the Eocene epoch. During this time period, an abrupt warming trend caused the extinction of many older mammalian forms, which were replaced by recognizable forerunners of some of today's mammals, including the prosimians. Over fifty prosimian fossil genera have been found in Africa, North America, Europe, and Asia, where the warm, wet conditions of the Eocene sustained extensive rainforests. Relative to ancestral primatelike mammals, these early primate families had enlarged braincases, slightly reduced snouts, and a somewhat forward position of the eye orbits, which, though not completely walled in, were surrounded by a complete bony ring called a *postorbital bar* (**Figure 6.3**).

The fossil record indicates that Eocene primates, ancestors of today's prosimians and anthropoids, were abundant, diverse, and widespread. Among these, a spectacularly well-preserved 47-million-year-old specimen nicknamed "Ida" received a lot of media attention in 2009 when two sections of her remains were reunited (Dalton, 2009; Franzen et al., 2009; Gebo, Dagosto, Beard, & Tao, 2001; "Media frenzy," 2009; Seiffert et al., 2009; Simons et al., 2009). The remains of this potential anthropoid, originally discovered thirty years earlier during mining and drilling operations in Germany, were sold to two separate collections. Since being reunited, scientists are determining whether Ida is a true anthropoid, a distinction that places her on the line leading to humans.

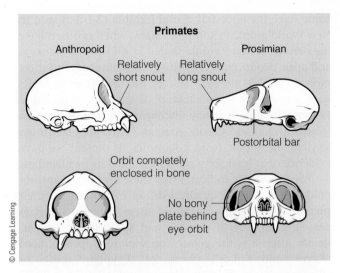

Figure 6.3 **Prosimian and Anthropoid Skulls** Ancestral features seen in Eocene and Oligocene primates are still seen in prosimians today. Like modern lemurs, these fossil prosimians have a postorbital bar, a bony ring around the eye socket that is open in the back. Anthropoid primates have orbits completely enclosed in bone. Note also the difference in the relative size of the snout in these two groups. Paleoanthropologists make these kinds of comparisons as they reconstruct our evolutionary history.

With the end of the Eocene, climates became somewhat cooler and drier, but then temperatures took a sudden dive, triggering the formation of an icecap over previously forested Antarctica. The result was a marked reduction in the range of suitable environments for primates. At the same time, cold climate led to lower sea levels through the formation of icecaps, perhaps changing opportunities for migration of primates. In North America, now well isolated from Eurasia, primates became extinct, and elsewhere their range seems to have been reduced considerably.

Oligocene Anthropoids

During the Oligocene epoch, from about 23 to 34 million years ago (mya), the anthropoid primates diversified and expanded their range, and prosimian fossil forms became far less prominent. Fossil evidence from Egypt's Fayum region has yielded sufficient fossils (more than 1,000) to reveal that by 33 million years ago, Old World anthropoid primates existed in considerable diversity.

arboreal hypothesis A theory for primate evolution that proposes that life in the trees was responsible for enhanced visual acuity and manual dexterity in primates.
visual predation hypothesis A theory for primate evolution that proposes that hunting behavior in tree-dwelling primates was responsible for their enhanced visual acuity and manual dexterity.

Some have the ancestral dental formula (2-1-3-3) seen in New World monkeys and prosimians, whereas others have the derived dental formula shared by Old World monkeys and apes: two incisors, a canine, two premolars, and three molars (2-1-2-3) on each side of the jaw. The eye orbits have a complete wall, a feature of anthropoid primates. Fayum, along with newly discovered localities in Algeria (North Africa) and Oman (Arabian Peninsula), continues to yield anthropoid fossil discoveries. At present, we have evidence of at least sixty genera included in two families.

Fossil evidence indicates that these Old World anthropoids were diurnal quadrupeds, as evidenced by their smaller orbits (eyes). Many of these Oligocene species possess a mixture of monkey and ape features. Of particular interest is the genus *Aegyptopithecus* (pronounced "Egypt-o-pith-ee-kus"; Greek for "Egyptian ape"), an Oligocene anthropoid that has sometimes been called a monkey with an ape's teeth. Its lower molars have the five cusps of an ape, and the upper canine and lower first premolar exhibit the sort of shearing surfaces found in monkeys and apes. Its skull has forward-facing eye sockets completely protected by a bony wall. The endocast of its skull indicates that it had a larger visual cortex than that found in prosimians. Relative to its body size, the brain of *Aegyptopithecus* was smaller than that of more recent anthropoids. Still, this primate seems to have had a larger brain than any prosimian, past or present. Possessed of a monkeylike skull and body, and fingers and toes capable of powerful grasping, it evidently moved about in a quadrupedal, monkeylike manner.

Although no bigger than a modern house cat, *Aegyptopithecus* was, nonetheless, one of the larger Oligocene primates. Primatologists consider the larger *Aegyptopithecus* fossils to be males, noting that these specimens also possess more formidable canine teeth and deeper mandibles (lower jaws) compared to the smaller females. In modern anthropoids, such sexual dimorphism correlates with social systems with high competition among males.

New World Monkeys

The earliest evidence of primates in Central and South America dates from the Oligocene epoch. Eyes fully encased in bone and limb bones for quadrupedal locomotion confirm these fossil primates' anthropoid status. Scientists hypothesize that these primates came to South America from Africa because the Old World contains the earliest fossil evidence of anthropoids.

Scientists surmise that some of the African anthropoids arrived in South America, which at the time was not attached to any other landmass, by means of giant floating clumps of vegetation of the sort that originate even today in the great rivers of West and Central Africa. In the Oligocene, the distance between the two continents, though still formidable, was far less than it is today. Favorable winds and currents could have carried New World monkey ancestors on these floating islands of vegetation to South America quickly enough for them to survive.

Miocene Apes and Human Origins

True apes first appeared in the fossil record during the Miocene epoch, 5 to 23 million years ago. It was also during this time period that the African and Eurasian landmasses made direct contact. For most of the preceding 100 million years, the Tethys Sea—a continuous body of water that joined what are now the Mediterranean Sea and the Black Sea to the Indian Ocean—created a barrier to migration between Africa and Eurasia. Once joined through the region of what is now the Middle East and Gibraltar, Old World primates, such as the apes, could extend their range from Africa into Eurasia. Miocene ape fossil remains have been found everywhere from the caves of China, to the forests of France, to East Africa, where scientists have recovered the oldest fossil remains of bipeds. So varied and ubiquitous were the fossil apes of this period that the Miocene has been called the "golden age of the hominoids." The word *hominoid* comes from the Latin roots *homo* and *homin* (meaning "human being") and the suffix *oïdes* ("resembling").

In addition to the Old World anthropoid dental formula of 2-1-2-3, hominoids can be characterized by the derived characteristics of Y5 molars, lack of a tail, and broad flexible shoulder joints. One of the Miocene apes is the direct ancestor of the human line; exactly which one remains a question. An examination of the history of the contenders for direct human ancestor among the Miocene apes demonstrates how reconstruction of evolutionary relationships draws on much more than simply bones. Scientists interpret fossil finds by drawing on existing beliefs and knowledge. With new discoveries, interpretations change.

The first Miocene ape fossil remains were found in Africa in the 1930s and 1940s by the British archaeologist A. T. Hopwood and the renowned Kenyan paleoanthropologist Louis Leakey. These fossils turned up on one of the many islands in Lake Victoria, the 27,000-square-mile lake where Kenya, Tanzania, and Uganda meet. Impressed with the chimplike appearance of these fossil remains, Hopwood suggested that the new species be named *Proconsul*, combining the Latin root for "before" (*pro*) with the stage name of a chimpanzee who was performing in London at the time.

Dated to the early Miocene (17 to 21 mya), *Proconsul* had some of the classic hominoid features, lacking a tail and having the characteristic pattern of Y5 grooves in the lower molar teeth. However, the adaptations of the upper body seen in later apes (including humans), such as a skeletal structure adapted for hanging suspended below tree branches, were absent. In other words, *Proconsul* had some apelike features as well as some features of four-footed Old World monkeys (**Figure 6.4**). This mixture of ape and monkey features makes *Proconsul* a contender for a missing link between monkeys and apes.

At least seven fossil hominoid groups besides *Proconsul* have been found in East Africa from the early to middle Miocene. Between 5 and 14 million years ago, however, this fossil record thins out because the tropical forests inhabited by ancestral chimps and gorillas were not optimal for the preservation of bones. The scarcity of African fossil evidence from this time period fit well with notions about human origins that prevailed in the past. European scientists in the early 20th century concentrated on the various species of European ape—all members of the genus *Dryopithecus* (pronounced "dry-o-pith-ee-kus"). They believed that humans evolved where "civilization" developed and that these apes could be the missing link to humans.

Moreover, investigators initially did not consider that humans were any more closely related to the African apes than they were to the other intelligent great ape—the Asian orangutan. Chimps, bonobos, gorillas, and orangutans were thought to be more closely related to one another than any of them were to humans. The construction of evolutionary relationships still relied upon visual similarities among species, much as it did in the mid-1700s

when Linnaeus developed the taxonomic scheme that grouped humans with other primates. Chimps, bonobos, gorillas, and orangutans all possess the same basic body plan, adapted to hanging by their arms from branches or knuckle-walking on the ground. Humans and their ancestors had an altogether different form of locomotion: walking upright on two legs. On an anatomical basis, the first Miocene ape to become bipedal could have come from any part of the vast Old World range of the Miocene apes.

Today, scientists agree that genetic evidence firmly establishes that the human line diverged from those leading to chimpanzees and gorillas between 5 and 8 million years ago. Although any fossil discoveries in Africa from this critical time period have the potential to be the missing link between humans and the other African ape species, the evidence from this period has been, until recently, particularly scrappy. Controversy surrounds the interpretation of many of these fossil finds, although scientists agree on the basic evolutionary relationships among the Old World anthropoid primates (**Figure 6.5**).

For example, in 2007 scientists announced a new 10-million-year-old ape species discovered in Ethiopia as ancestral to gorillas. Named *Chororapithecus abyssinicus,* after Chorora, the local area where the fossil was found, and Abyssinia, the ancient name of Ethiopia, the scientists who found the nine fossil teeth claim that this specimen indicates that the gorilla lineage had become distinct from the human and chimp lines 2 to 4 million years earlier than that. Other scientists require more fossil evidence before pushing back the timing of the split.

Some fossils have begun to fill in the critical period of 5 to 8 million years ago. In Chad in the summer of 2002, a team of international researchers led by Michael Brunet of France unearthed a well-preserved skull dated to between 6 and 7 million years ago (**Figure 6.6**). Calling their find *Sahelanthropus tchadensis* ("Sahel human of Chad," referring to the Sahel, a belt of semi-arid land bordering the southern edge of the Sahara Desert), the researchers suggested that this specimen represented the earliest known ancestor of humans (Brunet et al., 2002). Inclusion of any fossil specimen in the human evolutionary line depends upon evidence for **bipedalism** (also called *bipedality*), the shared derived characteristic distinguishing humans and their ancestors from the other African apes.

Some paleoanthropologists argue that this specimen, nicknamed "Toumai," from the region's Goran-language meaning "hope for life," cannot be established as a hominin from skull bones alone, especially considering the degree

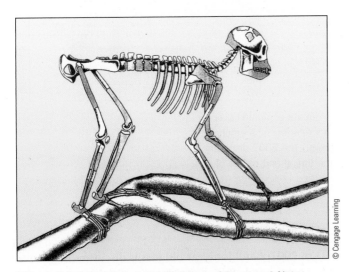

Figure 6.4 A Reconstructed Skeleton of *Proconsul* Note the apelike absence of a tail but monkeylike limb and body proportions. *Proconsul*, however, was capable of greater rotation of forelimbs than monkeys.

bipedalism A special form of locomotion, distinguishing humans and their ancestors from the African great apes, in which the organism walks upright on two feet; also called *bipedality*.

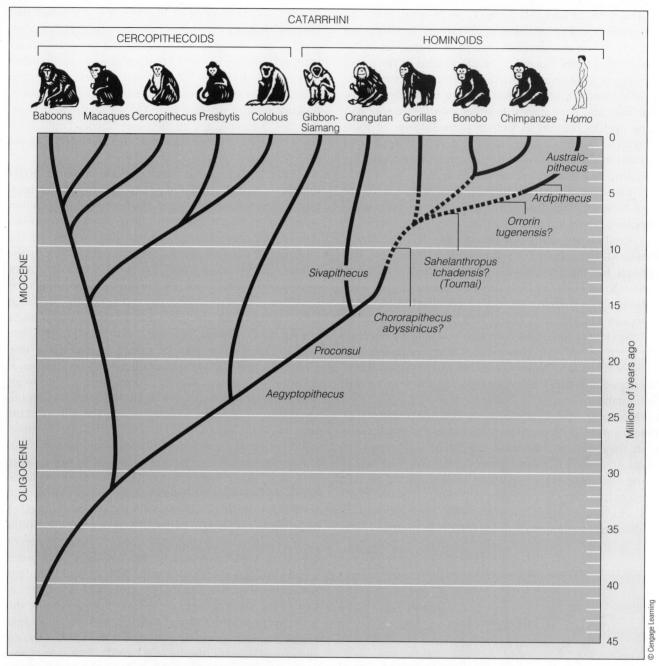

Figure 6.5 Relationships among the Old World Anthropoids Although debate continues over details, this chart represents a reasonable reconstruction of evolutionary relationships among the Old World anthropoid primates. (Extinct evolutionary lines are not shown.) The 2007 discovery of a fossil ancestor to gorillas has suggested a new interpretation of the timing and nature of the split between humans and the African apes.

of distortion present. The research team argues that derived features, such as a reduced canine tooth, indicate its status as a member of the human evolutionary line. Whether or not this specimen proves to be a direct human ancestor, as the only skull from this time period, it remains a very important find.

In 2001, 6-million-year-old fossils discovered in Kenya by French and British researchers Brigitte Senut and Martin Pickford were also reported as human ancestors (**Figure 6.7**). Officially given the species name *Orrorin tugenensis* (*Orrorin* meaning "original man" and *tugenensis* meaning "from the Tugen Hills") but nicknamed

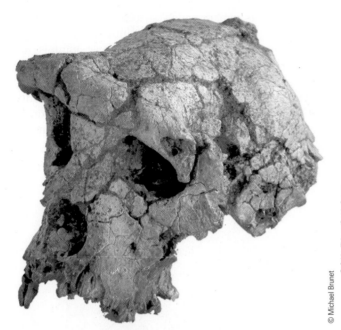

© Michael Brunet

Figure 6.6 *Sahelanthropus tchadensis* The spectacular skull from Chad nicknamed "Toumai" ("hope for life") has been proposed as the earliest direct human ancestor. Although the 6- to 7-million-year-old specimen is beautifully preserved and has some derived features, some paleoanthropologists feel that alone, it does not establish bipedalism, the derived trait characteristic of the human line.

© Orbin, Thierry/Corbis Sygma

Figure 6.7 *Orrorin tugenensis* These 6-million-year-old fossils, discovered in Kenya in 2001, represent a new species, *Orrorin tugenensis,* which has also been proposed as the earliest human ancestor. Like Toumai, these bones are surrounded by controversy. The thighbones (femora) strongly suggest bipedalism, and the upper arm bone (humerus) may be more like that of humans than it is like some of the later bipeds. More discoveries and scientific comparisons will solve controversies surrounding both *Orrorin* and Toumai.

"Millennium Man," controversy also surrounds these specimens (Senut et al., 2001).

The evidence for *Orrorin* consists of bone fragments from the arm and thigh, a finger bone, some jaw fragments, and teeth of at least five individuals. The thighbones demonstrate possible but not definite bipedalism. Unfortunately, the distal, or far ends, of the thighbone that would prove this are not fully preserved. The humerus (upper arm) appears to be more like that of humans, but arm bones cannot confirm bipedalism. Surprisingly, many other unexpected fragments can provide strong evidence of bipedalism, as we will explore following.

The Anatomy of Bipedalism

Anatomical changes accompany bipedalism literally from head to toe. Even an isolated skull can indicate bipedalism (**Figure 6.8**) because balancing the head in an upright posture requires a skull position relatively centered above the spinal column. The spinal cord leaves the skull at its base through an opening called the *foramen magnum* (Latin for "big opening"). In a knuckle-walker like a chimp, the foramen magnum sits toward the back of the skull whereas in a biped it is toward the front.

Extending down from the skull of a biped, the spinal column makes a series of convex and concave curves that together maintain the body in an upright posture by positioning the body's center of gravity above the legs rather than forward. The curves correspond to the neck (cervical), chest (thoracic), lower back (lumbar), and pelvic (sacral) regions of the spine, respectively. In a chimp, the shape of the spine

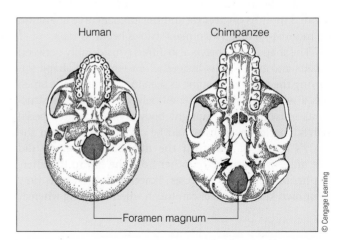

© Cengage Learning

Figure 6.8 **The Foramen Magnum** Bipedalism can be inferred from the position of the foramen magnum, the large opening at the base of the skull. Note its relatively forward position on the human skull (*left*) compared to the chimpanzee skull.

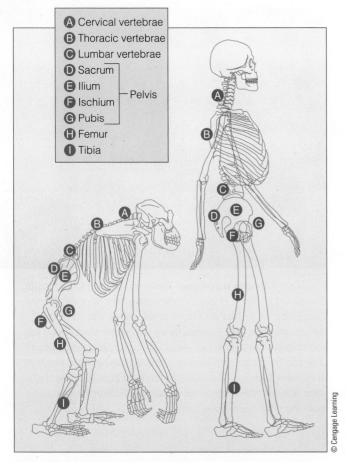

Figure 6.9 Chimp and Human Skeletons Differences between skeletons of chimps and humans reflect their habitual mode of locomotion. Notice the curves in the spinal column of the human as well as the basin-shaped pelvis.

© Cengage Learning

Legend (top left box):
- Ⓐ Cervical vertebrae
- Ⓑ Thoracic vertebrae
- Ⓒ Lumbar vertebrae
- Ⓓ Sacrum ⎫
- Ⓔ Ilium ⎪
- Ⓕ Ischium ⎬ Pelvis
- Ⓖ Pubis ⎪
- Ⓗ Femur
- Ⓘ Tibia

your hip joints remain widely spaced.) This angling does not continue past the knee to the shinbones (tibia), which are oriented vertically. The resulting knee joint is not symmetrical, allowing the thighbones and shinbones to meet despite their different orientations (**Figure 6.10**).

Other characteristics of bipeds are their stable arched feet and the absent opposable big toe. The position of the ape big toe is **abducted** (sticking out away from the midline) while the human big toe is **adducted** (pulled in

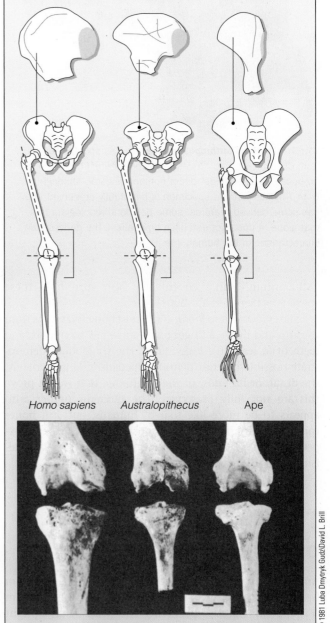

Homo sapiens   Australopithecus   Ape

© 1981 Luba Dmytryk Gudz/David L. Brill

Figure 6.10 Lower Limb Comparisons The upper hip bones and lower limbs of (*from left*) *Homo sapiens*, *Australopithecus* (an ancestral hominin species) and an ape can be used to determine means of locomotion. The striking similarities between the human and australopithecine bones are indicative of bipedal locomotion.

follows a single arching curve (**Figure 6.9**). Interestingly, at birth the spines of human babies have a single arching curve as seen in adult apes. As humans mature, the curves characteristic of bipedalism appear, the cervical curve at about 3 months on average and the lumbar curve at around 12 months—a time when many babies begin to walk.

The shape of the pelvis also differs considerably between bipeds and other apes. Instead of an elongated shape following the arch of the spine as seen in the chimp, the biped has a wider and foreshortened pelvis that provides structural support for the upright body. With a wide bipedal pelvis, the lower limbs would be oriented away from the body's center of gravity if the thighbones (femora) did not angle in toward each other from the hip to the knee, a phenomenon described as "kneeing-in." (Notice how your own knees and feet can touch when standing whereas

abduction Movement away from the midline of the body or from the center of the hand or foot.

adduction Movement toward the midline of the body or to the center of the hand or foot.

© Cengage Learning

Figure 6.11 Bipedal Gait The bipedal gait in some regards is really "serial monopedalism" or movement by means of one foot at a time through a series of controlled falls. Note how the body's weight shifts from one foot to the other as an individual moves through the swing phase to heel strike and toe off.

toward the midline). In general, humans and their ancestors possess shorter toes than the other apes.

These anatomical features allow paleoanthropologists to diagnose bipedal locomotion even in fragmentary remains such as the top of the shinbone or the base of a skull. Bipedal locomotion can also be established through fossilized footprints, which preserve the characteristic stride used by humans and their ancestors. In fact, bipedal locomotion is a process of shifting the body's weight from one foot to the other as the nonsupporting foot swings forward. While the body is supported in a one-legged stance, a biped takes a stride by swinging the other leg forward. The heel of the foot is the first part of the swinging leg to hit the ground. Then as the biped continues to move forward, the individual rolls from the heel toward the toe, pushing or "toeing off" into the next swing phase of the stride (**Figure 6.11**). While one leg is moving from

heel strike to toe off of the stance phase, the other leg is moving forward through the swing phase of walking.

The most dramatic confirmation of our ancestors' walking ability comes from Laetoli, Tanzania, where, 3.6 million years ago, two (perhaps three) individuals walked across newly fallen volcanic ash (**Figure 6.12**). Because it was damp, the ash took the impressions of their feet, and these were sealed beneath subsequent ash falls until discovered by chemist Paul Abell in 1978. Abell was part of a team led by British paleoanthropologist Mary Leakey in search of human origins at Laetoli (see Anthropologists of Note). The shape of the footprints and the linear distance between the heel strikes and toe offs are quite human.

Once bipedalism establishes a fossil specimen as a hominin, paleoanthropologists turn to other features, such as the skull or teeth, to reconstruct relationships among the various fossil hominin groups.

Photo by Denis Finnin and Craig Chesek. © American Museum of Natural History

Figure 6.12 Laetoli Footprints Paleoartists can reconstruct the soft tissues of individual fossil specimens using the data paleoanthropologists amass from their study of bones. They also reconstruct the setting based on data gathered by investigators. In this particular case, because the footprints were preserved in volcanic ash, paleoanthropologists can date when these steps were taken at the Laetoli site in Tanzania. The actual trail of footprints is 24 meters (80 feet) long. Does your sense of these ancient hominins change from looking at them fully fleshed out? What details are scientific? What details are imagined?

ANTHROPOLOGISTS OF NOTE

Louis S. B. Leakey (1903–1972) • Mary Leakey (1913–1996)

Few figures in the history of paleoanthropology discovered so many key fossils, received so much public acclaim, or stirred up as much controversy as **Louis Leakey** and his second wife, **Mary Leakey**.

Born in Kenya of missionary parents, Louis received his early education from an English governess and subsequently was sent to England for a university education. He returned to Kenya in the 1920s to begin his career there. It was in 1931 that Louis and his research assistant from England, Mary Nicol (whom he married in 1936), began working in their spare time at Olduvai Gorge in Tanzania, searching patiently and persistently for remains of early human ancestors. It seemed a good place to look, for there were numerous animal fossils as well as crude stone tools lying scattered on the ground and eroding out of the walls of the gorge.

Their patience and persistence were not rewarded until 1959, when Mary found the first fossil. A year later, another skull was found, and Olduvai was on its way to being recognized as one of the most important sources of fossils relevant to human evolution in all of Africa. While Louis reconstructed, described, and interpreted the fossil material, Mary made the definitive study of the Oldowan tools, a very early stone tool industry.

The Leakeys' important discoveries were not limited to those at Olduvai. In the early 1930s they found the first fossils of Miocene apes in Africa at Rusinga Island in Lake Victoria. Also in the 1930s, Louis found a number of skulls at Kanjera, Kenya, that show a mixture of derived and more ancestral features. In 1948, at Fort Ternan, Kenya, the Leakeys found the remains of a late Miocene ape with features that seemed appropriate for an ancestor of the bipeds. After Louis's death, Paul Abell, a member of an expedition led by Mary Leakey, found the first fossilized footprints of early bipeds at Laetoli, Tanzania.

In addition to their own work, Louis Leakey promoted a good deal of important work on the part of others. He made it possible for Jane Goodall to begin her landmark field studies of chimpanzees; later, he was instrumental in setting up similar studies among gorillas (by Dian Fossey) and orangutans (by Biruté Galdikas). He set into motion the fellowship program responsible for the training of numerous paleoanthropologists from Africa. The Leakey tradition has been continued by son Richard, his wife Meave, and their daughter Louise.

Louis Leakey had a flamboyant personality and a way of interpreting fossil materials that frequently did not stand up to careful scrutiny, but this did not stop him from publicly presenting his views as if they were the gospel truth. It was this aspect of the Leakeys' work that generated controversy. Nonetheless, the Leakeys produced a great deal of work that resulted in a much fuller understanding of human origins.

Mary and Louis Leakey at work at Olduvai Gorge. Not only did they contribute substantially to paleoanthropology through numerous fossil finds, but they also created a lineage of paleoanthropologists.

Ardipithecus

In the fall of 2009, a dramatic paleoanthropological find was announced: a remarkably complete skeleton of a putative human ancestor dated to 4.4 million years ago (Figure 6.13). Only half a dozen partially complete fossil skeletons on the human line older than 1 million years have ever been discovered, and this one is the oldest. Nicknamed "Ardi" for the new genus *Ardipithecus*, these fossil remains, first discovered between 1992 and

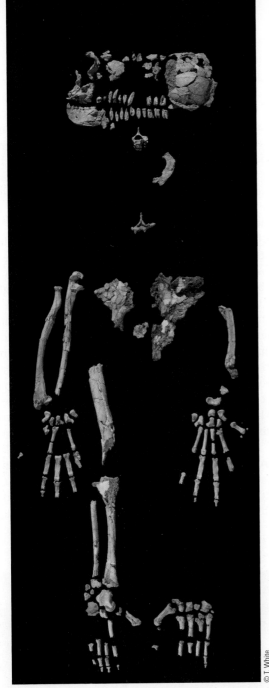

© T. White

Figure 6.13 *Ardipithecus ramidus* Early analyses of the Ardi remains in the early 1990s also established that there were forest- rather than savannah-dwellers on the human line. For the following fifteen-plus years, an international team of forty-seven scientists conducted painstaking excavation, reconstruction, and analysis to create a complete picture of the lifeways of this new species; through this process Ardi has become personified. A series of research papers in the prestigious journal *Science*, along with a Discovery Channel documentary about how the scientists went about their work, reveal not only the importance of the find but how Ardi has captured our collective imagination. Sophisticated computer graphics allow scientists to simulate how regulatory genes might have shaped the development of Ardi's bones that caused her to move in a more humanlike fashion. Gymnasts were asked to mimic her gait for scientific analysis, and advances in physics and chemistry were incorporated in the reconstruction of the ancient forested environment she inhabited.

1995, have dramatically changed what we know about the earliest bipeds (White et al., 2009). The genus actually contains two species, *Ardipithecus ramidus* and the older *Ardipithecus kadabba* dated to between 5.2 and 5.8 million years ago. The *Ardipithecus* remains show that some of the earliest bipeds inhabited a forested environment much like that of contemporary chimpanzees, bonobos, and gorillas; these remains were found in fossil-rich deposits along Ethiopia's Awash River accompanied by fossils of forest animals. The name *Ardipithecus ramidus* is fitting for an ultimate human ancestor as *Ardi* means "floor" and *ramid* means "root" in the local Afar language.

Now that the spectacular Ardi specimen has been sufficiently analyzed by the team who discovered her, paleoanthropologists debate her exact place on the human line. Because the other African apes share a body plan similar to one another, many paleoanthropologists expected the earliest bipeds to resemble something halfway between chimps and humans. Instead, Ardi shows that these forest creatures moved in a combination of ways: They traveled across the tops of branches with the palms of their hands and feet facing downward, and they walked between the trees on the ground in an upright position. The other African apes, as we saw in previous chapters, knuckle-walk on the forest floor and hang suspended below the branches. In other words, Ardi resembles some of the early Miocene apes more than she does the living African apes.

This calls into question what the last common ancestor of humans and the other African apes looked like. Does Ardi represent the more ancestral form, with the other apes evolving independently after they split from the human line but still converging to the typical African ape body plan? Or does Ardi represent a new body plan, characteristic of the earliest bipeds that evolved away from the African ape plan shared by chimps and gorillas? And what of Ardi's relationship to the later bipeds? Until fall 2009, *Ardipithecus* was generally considered a side branch on the human evolutionary tree. Now, the international team has proposed that Ardi may be a direct ancestor to the later bipeds, including humans.

In terms of size, at 120 centimeters tall and a weight of about 50 kilograms, Ardi resembles a female chimpanzee. The size and shape of this partial skeleton's brain and the enamel thickness of the specimen's teeth are similar to chimpanzees as well. Although possessing a grasping big toe like a chimp, scientists reconstruct Ardi's locomotion as bipedal when on the ground.

The *Ardipithecus* finds, along with the *Orrorin* and Toumai specimens, provide evidence for the time period

Ardipithecus One of the earliest genera of bipeds that lived in eastern Africa. *Ardipithecus* is actually divided into two species: the older, *Ardipithecus kadabba*, which dates to between 5.2 and 5.8 million years ago, and the younger, *Ardipithecus ramidus*, which dates to around 4.4 million years ago.

before the appearance of the ancient bipeds belonging to the genus *Australopithecus*. Paleoanthropologists discovered the first representatives of this group in the early 20th century, long before the majority of scientists were comfortable with the now-accepted notion that humans originated on the African continent.

Australopithecus

Most of the early bipeds from the Pliocene are members of the genus **Australopithecus**, a genus that includes species from southern and eastern Africa (**Figure 6.14**). The name for this group of fossils was coined back in 1924 when the first important fossil from Africa proposed to be a human ancestor came to light. This unusual fossil, consisting of a partial skull and natural brain cast of a young individual, was brought to the attention of anatomist Raymond Dart

of the University of Witwatersrand in Johannesburg, South Africa. The "Taung Child," named for the limestone quarry in the South African town of Taung (Tswana for "place of the lion") in which it was found, was unlike any creature Dart had seen before. Recognizing an intriguing mixture of ape and human characteristics in this unusual fossil, Dart proposed a new taxonomic category for his discovery—*Australopithecus africanus* or "southern ape of Africa"—suggesting that this specimen represented an extinct form that was ancestral to humans (**Figure 6.15**).

Although the anatomy of the base of the skull indicated that the Taung Child was probably a biped, the scientific community was not ready to accept the notion of a small-brained African ancestor to humans. Dart's original paper describing the Taung Child was published in the February 1925 edition of the prestigious journal *Nature*. The next month's issue was filled with venomous critiques rejecting Dart's proposal that this specimen represented a human ancestor. Criticisms of Dart ranged from biased to fussy to sound. Some scholars chastised Dart for incorrectly combining Latin and Greek in the genus and species name he coined. Other critics more justifiably questioned the wisdom of making inferences about the appearance of an adult of the species based only on the fossilized remains of a young individual. However, ethnocentric bias was the biggest obstacle to Dart's proposed human ancestor. Paleoanthropologists of the early 20th century expected that the ancestor to humans already had a large brain. Moreover, most European scientists expected to

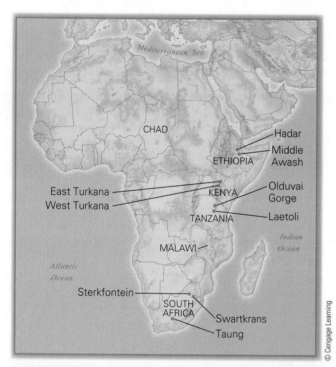

Figure 6.14 Map of Australopithecus Sites Australopithecine fossils have been found in South Africa, Malawi, Tanzania, Kenya, Ethiopia, and Chad. In the Miocene, the Eurasian and African continents made contact at the eastern and western ends of what now is the Mediterranean Sea. As these landmasses met, rifting also occurred, gradually raising the elevation of the eastern third of Africa. The drier climates that resulted may have played a role in human evolution in the distant past. This rifting also gives us excellent geologic conditions for finding fossils today.

Figure 6.15 The Taung Child Discovered in South Africa in 1924, the Taung Child was the first fossil specimen placed in the genus *Australopithecus*. Though Raymond Dart correctly diagnosed the Taung Child's bipedal mode of locomotion as well as its importance in human evolution, other scientists rejected Dart's claims that this small-brained biped with a humanlike face was a direct ancestor to humans. In the early 20th century, scientists expected ancestors to humans to possess a large brain and an apelike face and to originate from Europe or Asia rather than Africa.

Australopithecus The genus including several species of early bipeds from southern and eastern Africa living between about 1.1 and 4.3 million years ago, one of whom was directly ancestral to humans.

find evidence of this large-brained ancestor in Europe or, barring that, in Asia. No one at the time expected to find the ancestor to humans in Africa.

In fact, many scientists of the 1920s even believed that the ancestor to humans had already been found in the Piltdown gravels of Sussex, England, in 1910. The Piltdown specimens consisted of a humanlike skull and an apelike jaw that seemed to fit together, though the crucial joints connecting the two were missing (**Figure 6.16**). They were discovered along with the bones of some other animal species known to be extinct. Charles Dawson—the British amateur archaeologist, paleontologist, and practicing lawyer who found these remains—immodestly named them *Eoanthropus dawsoni* or "Dawson's Dawn Man." Until the 1950s the Piltdown remains were widely accepted as representing the missing link between apes and humans; today, they are known as one of the biggest hoaxes in the history of science.

There were several reasons for widespread acceptance of Dawson's Dawn Man. As Darwin's theory of evolution by natural selection began to gain acceptance in the early 20th century, intense interest developed in finding traces of prehistoric human ancestors. Accordingly, predictions were made as to what those ancestors looked like. Darwin himself, on the basis of his knowledge of embryology and the comparative anatomy of living apes and humans, suggested in his 1871 book *The Descent of Man* that early humans had, among other things, a large brain and an apelike face and jaw.

Although the tools made by prehistoric peoples were commonly found in Europe, their bones were not. A few fossilized skeletons had come to light in France and Germany, but they did not resemble the predicted missing link, nor had any human fossils been discovered in England ever before. Given this state of affairs, the Piltdown finds could not have come at a better time. Here at last was the long-awaited missing link, and it was almost exactly as predicted. Even better, so far as English-speaking scientists were concerned, it was found on English soil.

In the context of the evidence available in the early 1900s, the idea of an ancient human with a large brain

Discovery of the Piltdown Man in 1911, Cooke, Arthur Claude (1867–1951)/Geological Society, London, UK/The Bridgeman Art Library

Figure 6.16 The Piltdown Gang The Piltdown forgery was widely accepted as ancestral to humans, in large part because it fit with conventional expectations that the missing link would have a large brain and an apelike face. No one knows with certainty how many of the "Piltdown gang"—scientists supporting this specimen as the missing link—were actually involved in the forgery. It is likely that Charles Dawson had help from at least one scientist. Sir Arthur Conan Doyle, the author of the Sherlock Holmes detective stories, has also been implicated.

and an apelike face met expectations. Fortunately, the self-correcting nature of science has prevailed, exposing the Piltdown specimens as a forgery. First, discoveries—primarily in South Africa, China, and Java—of fossils of smaller-brained bipeds from the distant past caused scientists to question Piltdown's authenticity. Ultimately, the application of the newly developed fluorine dating method (described in Chapter 5) by British physical anthropologist Kenneth Oakley and colleagues in 1953 proved conclusively that Piltdown was a hoax. The forgery consisted of a human approximately 600 years old and a recent jaw from an orangutan. These findings fully vindicated Dart and the Taung Child.

The Pliocene Environment and Hominin Diversity

As mentioned previously, the Miocene epoch was a time of tremendous geologic change, and the effects of these changes continued into the Pliocene. The steady movement of geologic plates supporting the African and Eurasian continents resulted in a collision of the two landmasses at either end of what now is the Mediterranean Sea. This contact allowed for the spread of species between the continents.

A suite of geologic changes accompanied this collision. Among the changes was the creation of the Great Rift Valley system, a separation between geologic plates extending from the Middle East through the Red Sea and

eastern Africa into southern Africa. **Rifting** created the steady increase in the elevation of the eastern third of the African continent, which experienced a cooler and drier climate and a transformation of vegetation from forest to dry grassy **savannah**. The system also contributed to the volcanic activity in the region, which provides opportunities for accurate dating of fossil specimens.

Also in the Miocene, the Indian subcontinent, which had been a solitary landmass for many millions of years, came into its present position through a collision with Eurasia, contributing further to cooler, drier conditions globally. In addition to causing global climate change, these geologic events also provided excellent opportunities for the discovery of fossil specimens as layers of the earth became exposed through the rifting process.

Diverse Australopithecine Species

Since Dart's original find, hundreds of other fossil bipeds have been discovered, first in South Africa and later in Tanzania, Malawi, Kenya, Ethiopia, and Chad. As they were discovered, scientists defined a variety of different genera and species, but over time the single genus *Australopithecus* has come to include most of these species. Anthropologists recognize up to nine species of the genus (Table 6.1). In addition, some other groups of fossil bipeds from the Pliocene epoch (1.6 to around 5 mya) have been discovered, including the earliest representatives of the

TABLE 6.1

Species of *Australopithecus* and Other Pliocene Fossil Hominins*

Species	Location	Dates	Notable Features/Fossil Specimens
Ardipithecus ramidus	Ethiopia	4.4 mya†	Fossil remains of over thirty-five individuals including Ardi (another species, *Ardipithecus kadabba*, dates to 5.4–5.8 mya)
A. anamensis	Kenya	3.9–4.2 mya	Oldest australopithecine
Kenyanthropus platyops	Kenya	3.2–3.5 mya	Contemporary with australopithecines, believed by some to be a member of that genus
A. afarensis	East Africa	2.9–3.9 mya	Lucy, Lucy's Child, the Laetoli footprints
A. bahrelghazali	Chad	3–3.5 mya	Only australopithecine from Central Africa
A. africanus	South Africa	2.3–3 mya	First discovered, gracile, well represented in fossil record (Taung)
A. aethiopicus	Kenya	2.5 mya	Oldest robust australopithecine (Black Skull)
A. garhi	Ethiopia	2.5 mya	Later East African australopithecine with humanlike dentition
A. boisei	Kenya	1.2–2.3 mya	Later robust form coexisted with early *Homo* (Zinj)
A. robustus	South Africa	1–2 mya	Coexisted with early *Homo*
A. sediba	South Africa	1.97–1.98 mya	May be ancestral to early *Homo* and a descendant of *A. africanus*

*Paleoanthropologists differ in the number of species they recognize, some suggesting separate genera.
†Million years ago.

© Cengage Learning

genus *Homo*. Because the East African sites can be reliably dated we will look at these fossils first, followed by the South African australopithecines, and then we close the chapter with a late-appearing grade of australopithecine that coexisted with the genus *Homo*.

East Africa

The oldest australopithecine species known so far consists of some jaw and limb bones from Kenya that date to between 3.9 and 4.2 million years ago (see *Australopithecus anamensis* in Table 6.1). Meave and Louise Leakey, daughter-in-law and granddaughter of Louis and Mary Leakey, discovered these fossils in 1995 and decided to place them in a separate species from other known australopithecines. The name means "ape-man of the lake," and the jaw shows particularities in the teeth such as a true *sectorial*: a lower premolar tooth shaped to hone the upper canine as seen in apes. In humans and more recent ancestors, the premolar has a characteristic bicuspid shape and does not sharpen the canine each time the jaws come together. As in other australopithecines and humans, thick enamel coats the molar teeth. The limb bone fragments indicate bipedalism.

Moving closer to the present, the next species defined in the fossil record is *Australopithecus afarensis*. No longer considered the earliest australopithecine species, it still remains one of the best known due to the Laetoli footprints from Tanzania, the famous Lucy specimen (**Figure 6.17**), and the recent discovery of the 3.3-million-year-old remains of a young child called "Lucy's Baby," both from Ethiopia (recall Figure 5.11). Lucy consists of bones from almost all parts of a single 3.2-million-year-old skeleton discovered in 1974 in the Afar Triangle of Ethiopia (hence the name *afarensis*). Standing only 3½ feet tall, this adult female was named after the Beatles song "Lucy in the Sky with Diamonds," which the paleoanthropologists listened to as they celebrated her discovery. The Afar region also is the site of the "First Family"—a collection of bones from at least thirteen individuals, ranging in age from infancy to adulthood, who died together as a result of some single calamity.

Fossil localities in Ethiopia and Tanzania have yielded at least sixty individuals from *A. afarensis* (once the name of a genus has been established, it can be abbreviated with the first letter followed by the complete species name).

Figure 6.17 Lucy Here, Lucy, the 3.2-million-year-old fossil specimen, is on display in an exhibition space in New York City's Times Square as part of a traveling exhibit organized and curated by the Ethiopian government and the Houston Museum of Natural History. Though Lucy has done much to popularize paleoanthropology and evolutionary studies since her discovery in 1974, some paleoanthropologists have said that placing her fragile ancient skeleton on public display is far too risky. The Smithsonian Institution and the Cleveland Museum of Natural History declined to host the show for this reason. Others—like her discoverer Donald Johanson, pictured here with Lucy—feel that the benefits outweigh the risks. Benefits include the study of Lucy's remains via CT scans so that future generations of scientists can study them without actually handling the fragile bones. In addition, the revenues from the tour will be used to help modernize Ethiopia's museums. Finally, the exhibit will increase public awareness of human origins and the vital role of Africa and, in particular, Ethiopia in our evolutionary history. What's your opinion?

Potassium-argon techniques securely date the specimens from Ethiopia's Afar region to between 2.9 and 3.9 million years ago, and material from Laetoli, in Tanzania, to 3.6 million years ago. Altogether, *A. afarensis* appears to be a sexually

rifting In geology, the process by which a rift, or a long narrow zone of faulting, results when two geological plates come together.

savannah Semi-arid plains environment as in eastern Africa.

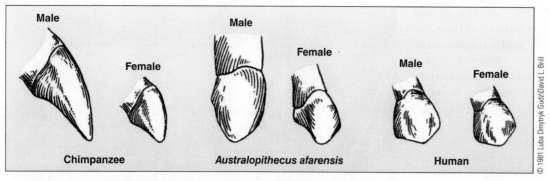

Figure 6.18 Sexual Dimorphism in Canine Teeth In addition to the difference in sexual dimorphism of canines seen in chimps, australopithecines, and humans, respectively, also note the more daggerlike shape of the chimp canines compared to the hominins.

dimorphic bipedal species with estimates of body size and weight ranging between 1.1 and 1.6 meters (3½–5 feet) and 29 and 45 kilograms (64–100 pounds), respectively.

Assuming that larger fossil specimens were males and smaller specimens females, males were about 1½ times the size of females. This resembles the sexual dimorphism of Miocene African apes but falls between the lesser degree of dimorphism present in a modern chimpanzee and the greater amount seen in gorillas and orangutans. Males possess canine teeth, significantly larger than those of females, though canine size is reduced compared to that of chimps (**Figure 6.18**).

Nearly 40 percent complete, the Lucy specimen has provided invaluable information about the shape of the pelvis and torso of early human ancestors. From the waist up, *A. afarensis* resembles an ape and from the waist down, a human (**Figure 6.19**). In addition, because her forearm bones are relatively shorter than those of apes, it is believed that Lucy's upper limbs were lighter and her center of gravity lower in the body than in apes. Still, Lucy and other early australopithecines possessed arms long in proportion to their legs when compared to the proportions seen in humans.

Though she lived about 150,000 years before her namesake, Lucy's Baby will add considerably to our knowledge about the biology and behavior of *A. afarensis* (Zeresenay et al., 2006). These well-preserved remains of a child, thought to have died in a flash flood, include a hyoid bone (located in the throat region) that will allow scientists to reconstruct australopithecine patterns of vocalization. Although the lower limbs clearly indicate bipedalism, the specimen's scapula and long curved finger bones are more apelike.

The curvature of the fingers and toes and the somewhat elevated position of the shoulder joint seen in adult specimens indicate that *A. afarensis* was better adapted to tree climbing compared to more recent human ancestors. In the following Original Study, paleoanthropologist John Hawks discusses the kinds of evidence used to reconstruct a behavior such as tree climbing in our ancestors.

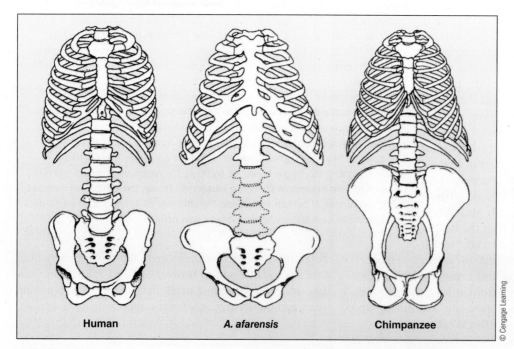

Figure 6.19 Comparisons of Trunk Skeletons of Modern Human, *A. afarensis*, and Chimp In its pelvis, the australopithecine resembles the modern human, but its rib cage shows the pyramidal configuration of the ape.

Ankles of the Australopithecines

BY JOHN HAWKS

Recent University of Michigan PhD Jeremy DeSilva gets some nice press about his work demonstrating that fossil hominins didn't climb like chimpanzees.

> "Frankly, I thought I was going to find that early humans would be quite capable, but their ankle morphology was decidedly maladaptive for the kind of climbing I was seeing in chimps," DeSilva told LiveScience. "It kind of reinvented in my mind what they were doing and how they could have survived in an African savannah without the ability to go up in the trees."[a]

This is a good example of the comparative method in paleoanthropology. We can't observe the behavior of extinct species; we can only observe the behavior of their living relatives. We can observe the anatomy of fossil specimens, but testing hypotheses about their behavior requires us to understand the relationship between anatomy and behavior in living species. We've known about the anatomy of fossil hominin ankles for a long time, but it's not so obvious how the anatomical differences between them and chimpanzee ankles relates to behavior.

DeSilva studied the tibiae and anklebones of early hominins and concludes "that if hominins included tree climbing as part of their locomotor repertoire, then they were performing this activity in a manner decidedly unlike modern chimpanzees."

DeSilva's conclusion is straightforward and easy to illustrate. Chimpanzees climb vertical tree trunks pretty much like a logger does. A logger slings a strap around the trunk and leans back on it. Friction from the strap holds him up as he moves his feet upward; spikes on his boots hold him while he moves the strap.

Of course, chimpanzees don't have spikes on their feet, and they don't use a strap. Instead, their arms are long enough to wrap around the trunk, and they can wedge a foot against the trunk by flexing their ankle upward—dorsiflexing it—or grip the trunk by bending the ankle sideways—inverting the foot—around it. . . .

You might wonder, yeah so what? Isn't it obvious that chimpanzees climb this way?

Well, it wasn't so obvious which features of the ankle might adapt chimpanzees to this style of climbing. By

The amount of dorsiflexion in a chimpanzee's foot allows it to climb trees with the feet in a position that is impossible for humans. Comparisons like this between living species allow paleoanthropologists to reconstruct the pattern of locomotion in fossil groups.

watching the chimpanzees (and other apes), DeSilva was able to determine the average amount (and range) of dorsiflexion and inversion of the feet while climbing, and could also assess the extent to which dorsiflexion is accomplished at the ankle joint (as opposed to the midfoot). In this case, the observations were pretty obvious—chimpanzees were habitually flexing their ankles in ways that would damage a human ankle. Then, by examining the bony limits on human ankle flexibility, DeSilva showed that fossil hominins shared the same constraints on ankle movement as recent people. They couldn't have climbed like chimpanzees.

Human Climbing

I would say that the ankle-joint observations match the rest of the skeleton. It seems pretty obvious that *Australopithecus afarensis* and later hominins couldn't possibly have climbed in the chimpanzee-like manner described in DeSilva's paper because the hominins' arms were too short. If a logger tried to climb with his arms instead of a strap, even spikes on his feet would be relatively ineffective holding him up. Dorsiflexion would be hopeless—the normal component of force against the tree trunk would be insufficient to prevent slipping.

Humans who *aren't* loggers use a different strategy to climb vertical tree trunks—they put a large fraction of the surface area of their legs directly in contact with the trunk. Wrapping legs around and pressing them together gives the necessary friction to hold the body up.

If you're like me, you'll remember this climbing strategy ruefully from gym class, where "rope climbing" is the lowest common denominator of fitness tests. The sad fact is that many otherwise-normal humans fall on the wrong side of the line between mass and muscle power. Straining my groin muscles to the max, I still could never pull my way up a rope.

There's nothing magical about getting a human to climb. Ladders, after all, are relatively easy for the large fraction of the population who can't climb a rope or tree trunk. The trick with a ladder is that friction is organized in a more effective way for our ankle mechanics and arm length. But you don't need to schlep a ladder, if you can manage a little extra arm strength and a low enough body mass.

Early Hominin Climbing

Australopithecines were light in mass, and from what we can tell, they had strong arms. So they had what it takes for humans today to climb trees effectively—not like chimpanzees, but like humans. Up to *A. afarensis*, every early hominin we know about lived in an environment that was at least partially wooded.

. . . DeSilva hypothesizes a trade-off between climbing ability and effective bipedality, so that early hominins could not have effectively adapted to both. I don't think a chimpanzee-like ankle would have been any use with arms as short as australopithecines'. So I don't see the necessity of a trade-off in ankle morphology. *A. afarensis*—long before any evidence of stone tool manufacture—had very non-apelike arms, hands and thumbs.

But there's one significant question that DeSilva omits discussing—the foot bones of a South African australopithecine: StW 573 (see Figure 6.22). Clarke and Tobias[b] describe the foot of StW 573 as having a big toe that is abducted (sticks out) from the foot, intermediate between the chimpanzee and human condition. They conclude:

> [W]e now have the best available evidence that the earliest South African australopithecine, while bipedal, was equipped to include arboreal, climbing activities in its locomotor repertoire. Its foot has departed to only a small degree from that of the chimpanzee. It is becoming clear that *Australopithecus* was not an obligate terrestrial biped, but rather a facultative biped and climber. (p. 524)

DeSilva studied the talus (an ankle bone), not the toe. StW 573 has a talus, and although it is not in DeSilva's sample, it probably would place very close to the other hominins in his comparison. Even Clarke and Tobias described its talus as humanlike—their argument for an intermediate form was based mostly on the toe.

But still, it's hard to believe that australopithecines would retain a chimpanzee-like big toe, if they couldn't use that big toe by inverting or dorsiflexing their foot in any significant way. By all other accounts, an abducted hallux (big toe) would only impede effective bipedality. It is of no use at all for a humanlike pattern of climbing. The only remaining utility would be for small-branch grasping, but small branches would seem unlikely as a support for hominin arboreality.

One possibility is that Clarke and Tobias were simply mistaken. That appears to be the explanation favored by Harcourt-Smith and Aiello[c] and McHenry and Jones,[d] who concluded that all known hominin feet appear to lack any "ape-like ability to oppose the big toe." They also point to the Laetoli footprint trails, most observers of which agree that the big toe was adducted, not abducted.

I tend to favor that explanation—australopithecines simply didn't have a grasping foot. But they may not have shared the medial longitudinal arch, at least not in the human configuration, and without it one might doubt that their gait featured as strong a toe-off as that of later humans. Who knows?

[a]DeSilva, J. M. (2009). Functional morphology of the ankle and the likelihood of climbing in early hominins. *Proceeding of the National Academy of Sciences, USA 106*, 6567–6572.

[b]Clarke, R. J., & Tobias, P. V. (1995). Sterkfontein Member 2 foot bones of the oldest South African hominid. *Science 269*, 521–524.

[c]Harcourt-Smith, W. E. H., & Aiello, L. C. (2004). Fossils, feet and the evolution of human bipedal locomotion. *Journal of Anatomy 204*, 412.

[d]McHenry, H. M., & Jones, A. L. (2006). Hallucial convergence in early hominids. *Journal of Human Evolution 50*, 534–539.

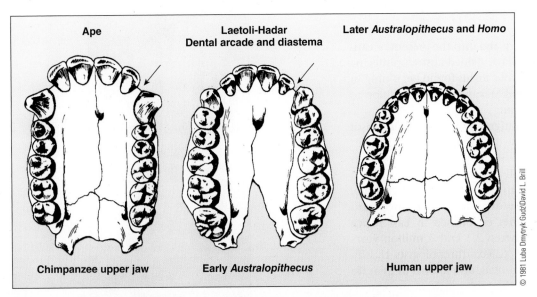

Figure 6.20 Upper Jaws of Chimps, Australopithecines, and Humans The upper jaws and teeth of these three groups differ in several ways. Note the difference in the shape of the dental arch and the spacing between the canines and the adjoining teeth. Only the earliest australopithecines possess a diastema (a large gap between the upper canine and incisor), which is found in chimpanzees.

At the other end of the body, skull bones are vital for the reconstruction of evolutionary relationships. They allow paleoanthropologists to learn about the cognitive capacities of ancestral species. For example, the brow of an *A. afarensis* skull slopes backward to a relatively low height and has the ridge that helps give apes such massive-looking foreheads. Other ape features include large jaws relative to the size of the skull, no chin, and a small brain. Even the semicircular canal, a part of the ear crucial to maintenance of balance, is apelike. Cranial capacity, commonly used as an index of brain size for *A. afarensis*, averages about 420 cubic centimeters (cc), roughly equivalent to the size of a chimpanzee and about one-third the size of living humans. In addition to absolute brain size, the ratio of brain to body size contributes to intelligence. Unfortunately, with such a wide range of adult weights, this ratio cannot be determined for australopithecines.

Australopithecine teeth constitute one of the primary means for distinguishing among closely related groups. In *A. afarensis*, unlike humans, the teeth are all quite large, particularly the molars. The premolar is no longer fully sectorial as in *A. anamensis*, but most other features of the teeth represent a more ancestral rather than derived condition. For example, instead of the dental arch seen in humans, australopithecines possess more parallel tooth rows (the ancestral ape condition). The canines project slightly, and a slight space or gap known as a **diastema** remains between the upper incisors and canines as found in the apes (**Figure 6.20**).

To further complicate the diversity seen in *A. afarensis*, in 2001 Meave and Louise Leakey announced the discovery of an almost complete cranium, parts of two upper jaws, and assorted teeth from a site in northern Kenya, dated to between 3.2 and 3.5 million years ago (Leakey et al., 2001). Contemporary with early East African *Australopithecus*, the Leakeys see this as a different genus and named it ***Kenyanthropus platyops*** ("flat-faced man of Kenya"). Unlike early australopithecines, *Kenyanthropus* has a small braincase and small molars set in a large, humanlike, flat face. The Leakeys regard the fossils as ancestral to the genus *Homo*. Other paleoanthropologists disagree suggesting that the Leakeys' interpretation rests on a questionable reconstruction of badly broken fossil specimens (White, 2003).

Central Africa

The first Central African australopithecine species, dated to the same time period as *Kenyanthropus platyops*, was discovered in Chad. Named *Australopithecus bahrelghazali* for a nearby riverbed, the specimen consists of a jaw and several teeth dated to between 3 and 3.5 million years ago. With time, perhaps more discoveries from this region (also home to the Toumai specimen discussed previously) will give a fuller understanding of the role of *A. bahrelghazali* in human evolution and its relationship to the possible bipeds from the Miocene.

diastema A space between the canines and other teeth allowing the large projecting canines to fit within the jaw.

Kenyanthropus platyops A proposed genus and species of biped contemporary with early australopithecines; may not be a separate genus.

South Africa

Throughout the 20th century and into the present, a variety of sites in South Africa have yielded australopithecine fossils. These include numerous fossils found beginning in the 1930s at Sterkfontein and Makapansgat, in addition to Dart's original find from Taung.

Absence of the clear stratigraphy and volcanic ash of East African sites makes these discoveries far more difficult to date and interpret (**Figure 6.21**). Paleomagnetism dates one unusually complete skull and skeleton and one partial foot skeleton (**Figure 6.22**) to about 3.3 million years ago. Until recently, dates for the other fossils remained hard to pin down. A faunal series established in East Africa places these specimens between 2.3 and 3 million years ago. Like the Taung Child, paleoanthropologists classify all these specimens as *A. africanus*, also known as **gracile australopithecines**.

Researchers debate the presence of human qualities in gracile australopithecines. Some see evidence for some

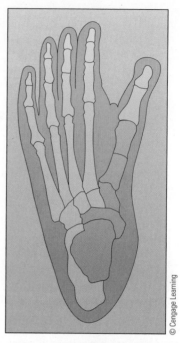

Figure 6.22 Gracile Australopithecine Foot Drawing of the foot bones of a 3- to 3.3-million-year-old *Australopithecus* from Sterkfontein, South Africa, as they would have been in the complete foot. Note the length and flexibility of the first toe (*at right*). This is a drawing of the StW 573 specimen referred to in this chapter's Original Study.

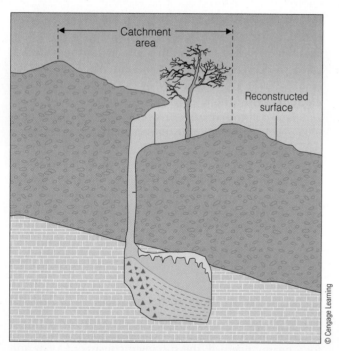

Figure 6.21 South African Limestone Cave Sites Many of the fossil sites in South Africa were limestone caverns connected to the surface by a shaft. Over time, dirt, bones, and other matter that fell down the shaft accumulated inside the cavern, becoming fossilized. In the Pliocene, trees that grew from earth next to the shaft's opening provided a sheltered location that may have been used by predators for eating without being bothered by scavengers.

expansion of the brain in *A. africanus*, whereas others vigorously disagree. The same is true for analyses of the outer surface of the brain, as revealed by casts of the insides of skulls. At the moment, the weight of the evidence favors mental capabilities for all gracile australopithecines as being comparable to those of modern great apes (chimps, bonobos, gorillas, orangutans).

Using patterns of tooth eruption in young australopithecines such as Taung, some paleoanthropologists suggest that the developmental pattern of australopithecines was more humanlike than apelike, though other paleoanthropologists do not agree. Evidence from the recent discovery of the young *A. afarensis* specimen (Lucy's Baby) will help scientists to resolve this debate. Our current understanding of genetics and the macroevolutionary process indicates that a developmental shift likely underlies a change in body plan such as the emergence of bipedalism among the African hominoids.

Other South African sites have yielded fossils whose skulls and teeth looked quite different from the gracile australopithecines described previously. Relative to the size of their braincases, these South African fossils, known as *Australopithecus robustus*, possess massive (robust) teeth, jaws, and chewing muscles. The slightly smaller gracile forms lack such robust chewing structures. Over the course of evolution, several distinct groups of

gracile australopithecines Members of the genus *Australopithecus* possessing a more lightly built chewing apparatus; likely had a diet that included more meat than that of the robust *australopithecines*; best represented by the South African species *A. africanus*.

robust australopithecines have appeared not only in South Africa but throughout East Africa as well.

Robust Australopithecines

The remains of robust australopithecines were first found at Kromdraai and Swartkrans in the 1930s in deposits that, unfortunately, cannot be securely dated. Current thinking puts them between 1 and 2 million years ago. Usually referred to as *A. robustus* (see Table 6.1), this species possessed a characteristic robust chewing apparatus including a **sagittal crest** running from front to back along the top of the skull (**Figure 6.23**). This feature provides sufficient area on a relatively small braincase for attachment of the huge temporal muscles required to operate powerful jaws. Present in robust australopithecines and gorillas today, the sagittal crest provides an example of convergent evolution.

The first East African robust australopithecine was discovered by Mary Leakey in the summer of 1959, the centennial year of the publication of Darwin's *On the Origin of Species*. She found it in Olduvai Gorge, a massive fossil-rich gash in the earth, near Ngorongoro Crater, on the Serengeti Plain of Tanzania. About 40 kilometers (25 miles) long and 91 meters (300 feet) deep, Olduvai Gorge cuts through Plio-Pleistocene and recent geologic strata revealing close to 2 million years of the earth's history.

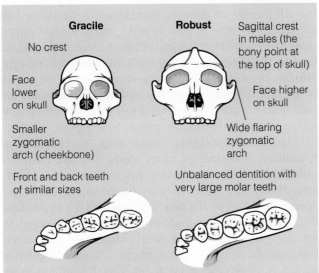

Figure 6.23 Gracile and Robust Australopithecines The differences between gracile and robust australopithecines relate primarily to their chewing apparatus. Robust species have extremely large cheek teeth, large chewing muscles, and a bony ridge on the top of their skulls for the attachment of large temporal muscles for chewing. The front and back teeth of gracile species are balanced in size, and their chewing muscles (reflected in a less massive skull) are more like those seen in the later genus *Homo*. If you place your hands on the sides of your skull above your ears while opening and closing your jaw, you can feel where your temporal muscles attach to your skull. Glide your hands toward the top of your skull while still moving your jaw to feel where these muscles end in humans.

Labels in Figure 6.23:
Gracile — No crest; Face lower on skull; Smaller zygomatic arch (cheekbone); Front and back teeth of similar sizes
Robust — Sagittal crest in males (the bony point at the top of skull); Face higher on skull; Wide flaring zygomatic arch; Unbalanced dentition with very large molar teeth
© Cengage Learning

© John Reader/Photo Researchers Inc.

Figure 6.24 Robust Australopithecines and the Genus *Homo* The robust australopithecines and the earliest members of genus *Homo* inhabited the earth at the same time. These particular skulls and leg bones were all found along the eastern shores of Lake Turkana in Kenya and are dated to between 1.7 and 1.9 million years ago. Many paleoanthropologists classify two specimens with the rounded skulls as members of the species *Homo habilis*. The robust australopithecine at the top of the photograph has the bony ridge (sagittal crest) along the top of its skull. Note that the dates for each of these species expands beyond the dates found at one particular site.

Louis Leakey reconstructed his wife Mary's discovery and gave it the name *Zinjanthropus boisei* (*Zinj*, an old Arabic name for East Africa that means literally "Land of the Blacks," *boisei* after the benefactor who funded their expedition). At first, the stone tools found in association with this specimen led Louis Leakey to suggest that this ancient fossil seemed more humanlike than *Australopithecus* and extremely close to modern humans in evolutionary development. Further study, however, revealed that *Zinjanthropus*, the remains of which consisted of a skull and a few limb bones, was an East African species of robust australopithecine, *Australopithecus boisei* (see Table 6.1). Potassium-argon dating places these fossils at about 1.75 million years old.

Since the time of Mary Leakey's original *A. boisei* find, numerous other fossils of this robust species have been found at Olduvai, as well as north and east of Lake Turkana in Kenya (**Figure 6.24**). These robust fossils date

robust australopithecines Several species within the genus *Australopithecus*, who lived from 1 to 2.5 million years ago in eastern and southern Africa; known for the rugged nature of their chewing apparatus (large back teeth, large chewing muscles, and a bony ridge on their skull tops to allow for these large muscles).

sagittal crest A crest running from front to back on the top of the skull along the midline to provide a surface of bone for the attachment of the large temporal muscles for chewing.

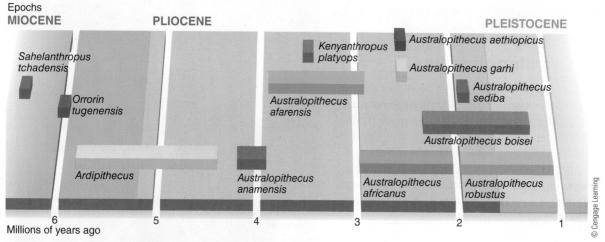

Figure 6.25 Timeline of Plio-Pleistocene Hominins This timeline shows the fossil bipeds who were not members of the genus *Homo* and the scientific names by which they have been known, arranged according to when they lived. The genus *Homo* first appears in the fossil record 2.5 million years ago and coexists with the gracile species *A. garhi* and *A. sediba*. There is also overlap between *Homo* and the robust australopithecines species *A. aethiopicus, A. boisei,* and *A. robustus.* Whether the different species names are warranted is a matter of debate.

from between 2.5 million years old and 1 mya. Like robust australopithecines from South Africa, East African robust forms possessed enormous molars and premolars. Despite a large mandible and palate, the anterior teeth (canines and incisors) were often crowded, owing to the room needed for the massive molars. The heavy skull, more massive even than seen in the robust forms from South Africa, has a sagittal crest and prominent brow ridges. Cranial capacity ranges from about 500 to 530 cubic centimeters. Body size, too, is somewhat larger; estimates for the weight of the South African robust forms range between 32 and 40 kilograms, while the East African robusts probably weighed from 34 to 49 kilograms.

Because the earliest robust skull from East Africa, the Black Skull from Kenya dated to 2.5 million years ago (see *A. aethiopicus* in Table 6.1), retains a number of ancestral features shared with earlier East African australopithecines, some suggest that it evolved from *A. afarensis*, giving rise to the later robust East African forms. Paleoanthropologists debate whether the South African robust australopithecines represent a southern offshoot of the East African line or convergent evolution from a South African ancestor. In either case, the later robust australopithecines developed molars and premolars that are both absolutely and relatively larger than those of earlier australopithecines, who possessed front and back teeth more in proportion to those seen in the genus *Homo*.

Larger teeth require more bone to support them, hence the prominent jaws of the robust australopithecines. Larger jaws and heavy chewing activity require more jaw musculature that attaches to the skull. The marked crests seen on skulls of the late australopithecines provide for the attachment of chewing muscles on a skull that has increased very little in size. In effect, robust australopithecines had evolved into highly efficient chewing machines. Clearly, their immense cheek teeth and powerful chewing muscles bespeak the heavy chewing required for a diet of uncooked plant foods. This general level of biological organization shared by separate fossil groups as seen in the robust australopithecines is referred to as a *grade*.

Many anthropologists believe that, by becoming a specialized consumer of plant foods, the late australopithecines avoided competing for the same niche with early *Homo*, with which they were contemporaries. In the course of evolution, the **law of competitive exclusion** dictates that when two closely related species compete for the same niche, one will outcompete the other, bringing about the loser's extinction. Their coexistence for 1.5 million years from about 1 to 2.5 million years ago suggests that early *Homo* and late *Australopithecus* did not compete for the same niche (**Figure 6.25**).

Australopithecines and the Genus *Homo*

A variety of bipeds inhabited Africa about 2.5 million years ago, around the time the first evidence for the genus *Homo* begins to appear. In 1999, discoveries in East Africa added another australopithecine to the mix. Found

law of competitive exclusion When two closely related species compete for the same niche, one will outcompete the other, bringing about the latter's extinction.

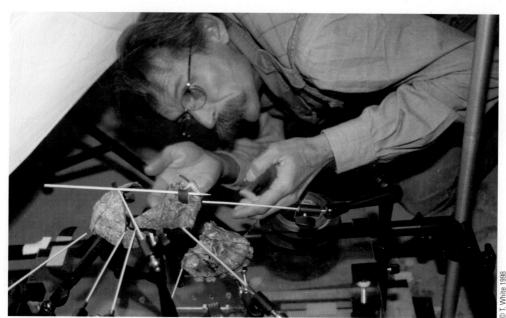

© T. White 1998

Figure 6.26

Reconstruction of Fossil Specimens Photographer David Brill, a specialist in images of fossils and paleoanthropologists, positions the upper jaw and the other skull fragments of *Australopithecus garhi* so that the fragments are aligned as they would be in a complete skull.

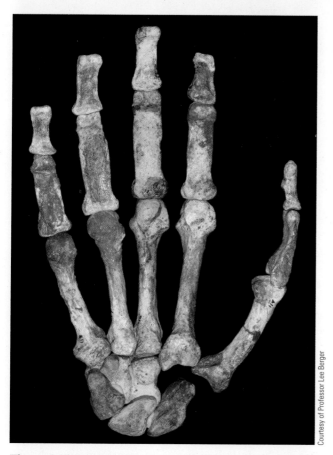

Courtesy of Professor Lee Berger

Figure 6.27 Exquisite Hands Derived features of the hand and forearm, which *Australopithecus sediba* shares with humans, have led some scientists to suggest that this is the ancestral hominin that gave rise to the human line. From the analysis of the well-preserved bones, it appears that these ancient hominins were anatomically capable of a "precision grip," a feature characteristic of humans. The *A. sediba* pelvis also has evidence of derived morphology that would contribute to a more efficient stride.

in the Afar region of Ethiopia, these fossils were named *Australopithecus garhi* from the word for "surprise" in the local Afar language (**Figure 6.26**). Though the teeth were large, this australopithecine possessed an arched dental arcade and a ratio between front and back teeth more like humans and South African gracile australopithecines than like robust groups. For this reason, some have proposed that *A. garhi* is ancestral to the genus *Homo*, though the question of which australopithecine was ancestral to humans remains particularly controversial.

The new discoveries continue. In 2010, a paleoanthropological team led by Lee Berger published a series of papers on a newly discovered South African gracile australopithecine they named ***Australopithecus sediba***. First discovered in 2008 by Berger's then 9-year-old son Matthew, who was exploring while his father excavated a formal site nearby, this new species consists of at least four partial skeletons, one of which is a well-preserved adolescent male. Best of all, *A. sediba* can be precisely dated to between 1.97 and 1.98 million years ago by paleomagnetism and uranium dating (Pickering et al., 2011). A variety of derived traits in the hand, forearm, and pelvis have led Berger's team to suggest that *A. sediba* is transitional between *A. africanus* and early *Homo* (**Figure 6.27**). Others argue that these specimens are part of the wide variation present in *A. africanus*. They also protest that *A. sediba* could not be ancestral to early *Homo* because the two groups seem to have coexisted.

A variety of scenarios have been proposed, each one giving a different australopithecine group the starring

Australopithecus sediba A newly identified species of South African gracile australopithecine dated precisely to between 1.97 and 1.98 million years ago, with derived *Homo*-like characteristics in the hands and pelvis.

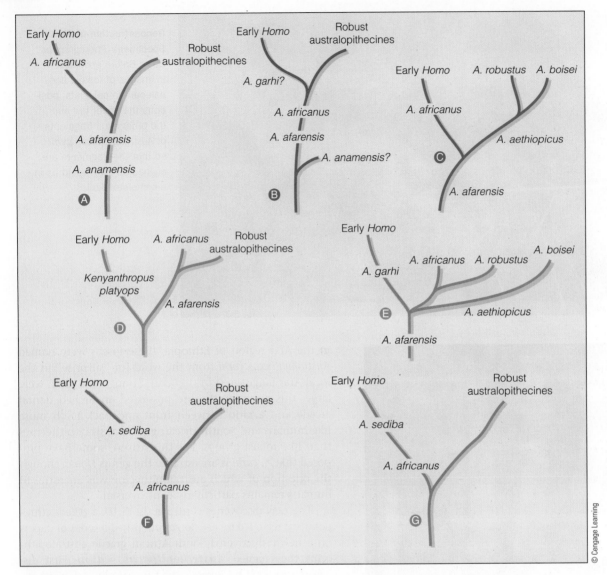

Figure 6.28 Scenarios for Human Origins Paleoanthropologists debate the relationship among the various australopithecine (and other) Pliocene groups and the question of which group is ancestral to the genus *Homo*. These diagrams present several alternative hypotheses. Most agree, however, that the robust australopithecines represent an evolutionary side branch and that *Ardipithecus ramidus* is ancestral to the australopithecines. The most recent point of contention is whether the newly discovered species, *Australopithecus sediba*, might be directly ancestral to the genus *Homo*.

role as the immediate human ancestor (**Figure 6.28**). Paleoanthropologists use the dates of the specimens as well as derived features to link the contending australopithecines to *Homo*. Pelvic shape and forearm anatomy make the case for *A. sediba*. An arched dental arcade is the evidence promoted for *A. garhi*. The flat face and perhaps larger cranial capacity of *Kenyanthropus platyops* is proposed as the link to *Homo*, but when cranial capacity becomes sufficiently large, the specimens are already classified as the genus *Homo*. Paleoanthropologists do agree, however, that the robust australopithecines, though successful in their time, ultimately represent an evolutionary side branch.

Environment, Diet, and Origins of the Human Line

How did evolutionary processes transform an early ape into a hominin? Hypotheses about hominin adaptation begin with the fossil evidence. For example, the fossil record indicates that once bipedalism appeared, over the next several million years the shape of the face and teeth shifted from an apelike to a humanlike condition. To refine their hypotheses, paleoanthropologists add scientific reconstructions of environmental conditions and

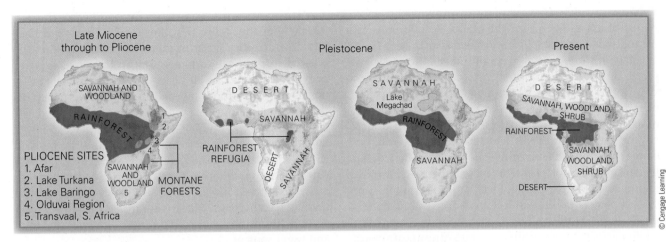

Figure 6.29 Climate Change and Vegetation Zones Since the late Miocene, the vegetation zones of Africa have changed considerably. Cooler, drier periods during the Pliocene reduced forested areas to far less than what exist today. The loss of forest likely created selective pressures that favored bipedalism.

inferences made from data gathered on living nonhuman primates and humans to the fossil evidence.

For many years, the emergence of the savannah environment in eastern Africa has dominated the human evolutionary narrative. Although the evidence from *Ardipithecus* shows that the earliest members of the human line were forest-dwellers, over time the size of tropical forests decreased or, more commonly, broke up into mosaics where patches of forest were interspersed with savannah or other types of open country. The forebears of the human line likely lived in places with access to both trees and open savannah.

With the breaking up of forests, these early ancestors found themselves spending more and more time on the ground and had to adapt to this new, more exposed environment. As the forest thinned or shrank, the traditional ape-type foods found in trees became less available, especially in seasons of reduced rainfall (**Figure 6.29**). Therefore, it became more and more necessary to forage on the ground for foods such as seeds, grasses, and roots. With reduced canine teeth, early bipeds were relatively defenseless when down on the ground and were easy targets for numerous carnivorous predators. The South African fossil evidence supports the notion that predators were a problem for early hominins. Most of the fossil specimens were dropped into rock fissures by predators such as leopards or, in the case of Dart's original find, by an eagle.

Many investigators have argued that the hands of early bipeds took over the weapon functions of reduced canine teeth. Hands enabled them to threaten predators by using wooden objects as clubs and throwing stones. Many of the other hominoids use their hands in this fashion. Recall the male chimpanzee (Chapter 4) clanging kerosene cans as part of his display to obtain alpha status. In australopithecines the use of clubs and throwing stones may have set the stage for the much later manufacture of more efficient weapons from bone, wood, and stone.

Although the hands of the later australopithecines were suitable for tool making, no evidence exists that any of them actually *made* stone tools. Still, using brain size as a measure, *Australopithecus* certainly had no less intelligence and dexterity than do modern great apes, all of whom make use of tools as described in Chapter 4. Most likely, the ability to make and use simple tools dates back to the last common ancestor of the Asian and African apes, before the appearance of the first bipeds.

Australopithecine tool use was likely similar to that of the other great apes. Unfortunately, these simple tools would not preserve well in the fossil record for a million and more years. Although we cannot be certain about this, in addition to clubs and objects thrown for defense, sturdy sticks may have been used to dig edible roots, and convenient stones may have been used (as some chimpanzees do) to crack open nuts. In fact, some animal bones from australopithecine sites in South Africa show microscopic wear patterns suggesting their use to dig edible roots from the ground. We may also allow the possibility that, like chimpanzees, females used tools more often to get and process food, while males more typically used tools as weapons. The female chimpanzees hunting with spears in Fongoli as described in Chapter 4 call into question these distinct roles for the sexes.

Humans Stand on Their Own Two Feet

From the broad-shouldered, long-armed, tailless ape body plan, the human line became fully bipedal. Our late Miocene forebears seem to have been primates that combined quadrupedal tree climbing with perhaps some swinging below the branches. On the ground, they were capable of assuming an upright stance, at least on occasion (optional, versus obligatory, bipedalism).

Paleoanthropologists generally take the negative aspects of bipedal locomotion into account when considering this pattern of locomotion. For example, paleoanthropologists have suggested that bipedalism makes an animal more visible to predators, exposes its soft underbelly or gut, and interferes with the ability to instantly change direction while running. They also emphasize that bipedalism does not result in particularly fast running; quadrupedal chimpanzees and baboons, for example, run 30 to 34 percent faster than we bipeds. For 100-meter distances, our best athletes today may attain speeds of 34 to 37 kilometers per hour, while the larger African carnivores from which bipeds might need to run can attain speeds up to 60 to 70 kilometers per hour. The consequences of a leg or foot injury are more serious for a biped whereas a quadruped can do amazingly well on three legs. Because each of these drawbacks would have placed our early ancestors at risk from predators, paleoanthropologists ask what made bipedal locomotion worth paying such a high price. What selective pressures favored bipedalism despite these disadvantages?

One older theory proposed that bipedal locomotion allowed males to obtain food on the savannah and transport it back to females, who were restricted from doing so by the dependence of their offspring. The fact that female apes, not to mention women among food-foraging peoples, routinely combine infant care with foraging for food negates this theory. Indeed, among most food foragers, it is the women who commonly supply the bulk of the food eaten by both sexes.

Moreover, this model presumed pair bonding (one male attached to one female), a form of social organization atypical of terrestrial primates displaying the degree of sexual dimorphism that was characteristic of *Australopithecus*. Nor is pair bonding really characteristic of *Homo sapiens*. In a substantial majority of recent human societies, including those in which people forage for their food, some form of polygamy—marriage to two or more individuals at the same time—is not only permitted but preferred. And even in the supposedly monogamous United States, many individuals marry (and hence mate with) two or more others (the only requirement is that the person not be married to more than one mate at the same time).

In the end, the idea of males provisioning stay-at-home moms appears to be more culture-bound than based on the fossil evidence. Paleoanthropologists, like all anthropologists, must exercise caution to avoid infusing theories about the fossil record with their own cultural beliefs. See the Biocultural Connection for another example of the influence of contemporary gender roles on paleoanthropological theories.

A fully erect biped on the ground—whether male or female—has the ability to gather food for transport back to a tree or other place of safety for consumption. The biped does not have to remain out in the open, exposed and vulnerable, to do all of its eating. Besides making it possible to carry food, bipedalism could have facilitated the food quest in other ways. With their hands free and body upright, the animals could reach otherwise unobtainable food on thorny trees too flimsy and too spiny to climb (Kaplan, 2007; Thorpe, Holder, & Crompton, 2007). Furthermore, with both hands free, they could gather other small foods more quickly using both hands. And in times of scarcity, being able to see farther, with the head in an upright position, would have helped them locate food and water sources.

Food may not have been the only thing transported by early bipeds. As we saw in Chapters 3 and 4, from birth primate infants must cling to their mothers, who use all their limbs in locomotion. Chimpanzee infants, for example, cling by themselves to their mother, and even up to 4 years of age they make long journeys on their mother's back. Injuries caused by falling from the mother account for a significant proportion of infant mortality among apes. Thus, the ability to carry infants would have made a significant contribution to the survival of offspring, and the ancestors of *Australopithecus* would have been capable of doing just this.

Although bipedalism appeared before our ancestors lived in the savannah, bipedalism likely served as a means to cope with heat stress out in the open as the forested environments disappeared. In addition to bipedalism, our relative nakedness constitutes one of the most obvious differences between humans and other living hominoids. Humans have only a fine sparse layer of body hair over most of the body with a very dense cover of hair limited primarily to the head. Peter Wheeler, a British physiologist, has suggested that bipedalism and the human pattern of body hair growth are both adaptations to the heat stress of the savannah environment. Building upon the earlier "radiator" theory of paleoanthropologist Dean Falk, Wheeler developed this hypothesis through comparative anatomy, experimental studies, and the observation that humans are the only apes to inhabit the savannah environment today.

Many other animals, however, inhabit the savannah, and each of them possesses some mechanism for coping with heat stress. Some animals, like many of the carnivores, limit their heavy activity to near dawn or dusk when the sun is low in the sky or to the cooler nights. Some, like antelope, have evolved to tolerate high body temperatures that would kill humans due to overheating of the brain tissue. They accomplish this through cooling their blood in their muzzles through evaporation before it enters the vessels leading to the delicate tissues of the brain.

BIOCULTURAL CONNECTION

Evolution and Human Birth

Because biology and culture have always shaped human experience, it can be a challenge to separate the influences of each of these factors on human practices. For example, in the 1950s, paleoanthropologists developed the theory that human childbirth is particularly difficult compared to birth in other mammals. This theory was based in part on the observation of a "tight fit" between the human mother's birth canal and the baby's head, though several other primates also possess similarly tight fits between the newborn's head or shoulders and the birth canal. Nevertheless, changes in the birth canal associated with bipedalism coupled with the evolution of large brains were held responsible for difficult birth in humans.

At the same historical moment, childbirth practices in the United States were changing. In one generation from the 1920s to the 1950s, birth shifted from the home to the hospital. In the process childbirth transformed from something a woman normally accomplished at home, perhaps with the help of a midwife or relatives, into the high-tech delivery of a neonate (the medical term for a newborn) with the assistance of medically trained personnel. Women in the 1950s were generally fully anesthetized during the birth process. Paleoanthropological theories mirrored the cultural norms, providing a scientific explanation for the change in U.S. childbirth practices.

As a scientific theory, the idea of difficult human birth stands on shaky ground. No fossil neonates have ever been recovered, and only a handful of complete pelves (the bones forming the birth canal) exist. Instead, scientists must examine the birth process in living humans and nonhuman primates to reconstruct the evolution of the human birth pattern.

Cultural beliefs and practices, however, shape every aspect of birth.

Tlazolteotl, the earth mother goddess of the Aztecs, is depicted here giving birth in a squatting position, which is favored by women throughout the world. For hospital births, women generally have to work against gravity to bring a child into the world because they tend to be placed on their backs with their legs in stirrups for the benefit of attending physicians.

© 2012 Man Ray Trust/Artists Rights Society (ARS), NY/ADAGP, Paris. Statuette of Ixcuina, Mexican Goddess of Maternity, 1890–1941. Gelatin silver print, 9-1/16 x 6-7/8". Gift of James Thrall Soby (204.1991). Digital Image © The Museum of Modern Art/Licensed by SCALA/Art Resource, NY.

Cultural factors determine where a birth occurs, the actions of the individuals present, and beliefs about the nature of the experience. When paleoanthropologists of the 1950s and 1960s asserted that human childbirth is more difficult than birth in other mammals, they were drawing upon their own cultural beliefs that childbirth is dangerous and belongs in a hospital.

A quick look at global neonatal mortality statistics indicates that in countries such as the Netherlands and Sweden, healthy well-nourished women give birth successfully outside of hospitals, as they did throughout human evolutionary history. In other countries, deaths related to childbirth reflect malnutrition, infectious disease, and the low social status of women, rather than an inherently faulty biology.

BIOCULTURAL QUESTION

Though well-nourished healthy women successfully birth their babies outside of hospital settings, caesarean section (C-section) rates have been rising in industrialized societies. In the United States one in three deliveries is by C-section, and in many Latin American countries more than half of all deliveries are by caesarean. What cultural factors have led to this practice? Would your personal approach to birth change with the knowledge that humans have successfully adapted to childbirth?

According to Wheeler, the interesting thing about humans and other primates is that

> We can't uncouple brain temperature from the rest of the body, the way an antelope does, so we've got to prevent any damaging elevations in body temperature. And of course the problem is even more acute for an ape, because in general, the larger and more complex the brain, the more easily it is damaged. So, there were incredible selective pressures on early hominids favoring adaptations that would reduce thermal stress—pressures that may have favored bipedalism. (quoted in *The Naked and the Bipedal* by Tim Folger, 1993, pp. 34–35)

Wheeler has studied this notion by taking measurements on the exposure of an early biped, like Lucy, to solar radiation in upright and quadrupedal stances. He found that the bipedal stance reduced exposure to solar radiation by 60 percent, indicating that a biped would require less water to stay cool in a savannah environment compared to a quadruped.

Wheeler further suggests that bipedalism made the human body hair pattern possible. Fur can keep out solar radiation as well as retain heat. A biped, with reduced exposure to the sun everywhere except the head, would benefit from hair loss on the body surface to increase the efficiency of sweating to cool down. On the head, hair serves as a shield, blocking solar radiation.

Some object to this scenario, citing that when bipedalism developed, savannah was not as extensive in Africa as it is today. In both East and South Africa, environments included closed and open bush and woodlands. Moreover, fossil flora and fauna found with *Ardipithecus* and the possible human ancestors from the Miocene are typical of a moist, closed, wooded habitat.

However, the presence of bipedalism in the fossil record without a savannah environment does not indicate that bipedalism was not adaptive to these conditions. It merely indicates that bipedalism appeared without any particular adaptive benefits at first, likely through a random macromutation. Bipedalism provided a body plan preadapted to the heat stress of the savannah environment.

Recall how in the early 20th century, larger brains were thought to have permitted the evolution of bipedalism. We now know not only that bipedalism preceded the evolution of larger brains by several million years, but we can also consider the possibility that bipedalism may have preadapted human ancestors for brain expansion. According to Wheeler,

> The brain is one of the most metabolically active tissues in the body. . . . In the case of humans it accounts for something like 20 percent of total energy consumption. So you've got an organ producing a lot of heat that you've got to dump. Once we'd become bipedal and naked and achieved this ability to dump heat, that may have allowed the expansion of the brain that took place later in human evolution. It didn't cause it, but you can't have a large brain unless you can cool it. (quoted in *The Naked and the Bipedal* by Tim Folger, 1993, pp. 34–35)

Consistent with Wheeler's hypothesis is the fact that the system for drainage of the blood from the cranium of the earlier australopithecines is significantly different from that of the genus *Homo* (**Figure 6.30**).

Though paleoanthropologists cannot resolve every detail of the course of human evolution from the available data, over time the narrative they have constructed has improved. Human evolution evidently took place in fits and starts, rather than at a steady pace. Today, we know that bipedalism preceded brain expansion by several million years. Bipedalism likely occurred as a sudden shift in body plan and after a viable bipedal adaptation was achieved; then stabilizing selection took over, and little change took place for at least a few million years.

Change again occurred about 2.5 million years ago, resulting in the branching out of new forms, including several robust species as well as the first appearance of the

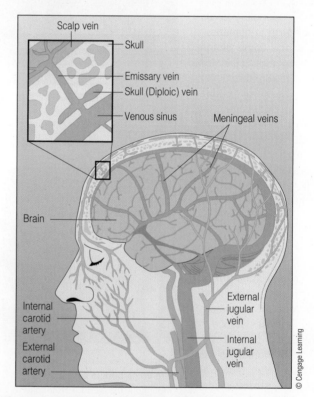

Figure 6.30 Cooling Hot-Headed Hominins In humans, blood from the face and scalp, instead of returning directly to the heart, may be directed instead into the braincase and then to the heart. Already cooled at the surface of the skin, blood is able to carry heat away from the brain.

genus *Homo*. From about 2.3 million years ago until robust australopithecines became extinct around 1 million years ago, however, the robust forms underwent relatively little alteration. By contrast, after its appearance 2.5 million years ago, *Homo* began a steady course of brain expansion that continued over the next 2.3 million years until brain size reached its current state. With the appearance of this new larger-brained hominin, the first stone tools appear in the archaeological record.

Early Representatives of the Genus *Homo*

Just as the Leakeys thought, Olduvai Gorge with its stone tool assemblages was a good place to search for human ancestors. Part of today's Olduvai Gorge was once a lake. Almost 2 million years ago, numerous wild animals including a variety of bipeds inhabited its shores. In 1959—when the Leakeys found the bones of the first specimen of robust *Australopithecus boisei* in association with some of these tools and the bones of birds, reptiles, antelopes, and pigs—they thought they had found the remains of one of the toolmakers. Fossils unearthed a few months later and a few feet below this first discovery led them to change their mind. These fossil remains consisted of more than one individual, including a few cranial bones, a lower jaw, a clavicle, some finger bones (**Figure 6.31**), and the nearly complete left foot of an adult (**Figure 6.32**). Skull and jaw fragments indicated that these specimens represented a larger-brained biped without the specialized chewing apparatus of the robust australopithecines.

The Leakeys and colleagues named that contemporary *Homo habilis* (Latin for "handy human") and suggested that tool-wielding *H. habilis* may have eaten the animals and possibly the *Australopithecus boisei*. Of course, we do not really know whether *A. boisei* from Olduvai Gorge met its end in this way, but we do know that cut marks from a stone tool are present on a jawbone from a 2.4-million-year-old australopithecine from South Africa (White & Toth, 2000). This was done, presumably, to remove the mandible, but for what purpose we do not know. In any event, it does lend credibility to the idea of *A. boisei* on occasion being dismembered by *H. habilis*.

Subsequent work at Olduvai has unearthed not only more skull fragments but other parts of the skeleton of *H. habilis* as well. Since the late 1960s, sites in South Africa, Ethiopia, and Kenya have yielded fossils of the genus *Homo* contemporaneous with those from Olduvai.

The eastern shores of Lake Turkana, on the border between Kenya and Ethiopia, have been particularly rich with fossils from earliest *Homo*. The Leakeys' son Richard discovered one well-known fossil, known as KNM ER 1470, at Koobi Fora. (The letters KNM stand for Kenya National

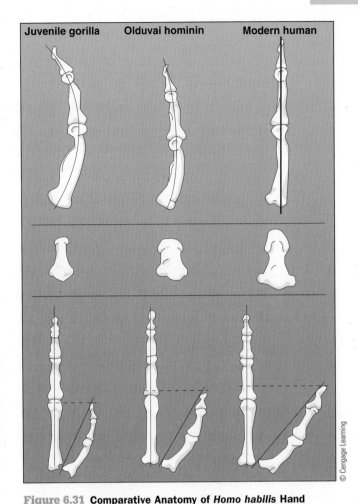

Figure 6.31 Comparative Anatomy of *Homo habilis* Hand Bones A comparison of hand bones of a juvenile gorilla, *Homo habilis* from Olduvai, and a modern human highlights important differences in the structure of fingers and thumbs. In the top row are fingers, and in the second row are terminal (end) thumb bones. Although terminal finger bones are more human, lower finger bones are more curved and powerful. The bottom row compares thumb length and angle relative to the index finger.

Museum; the ER, for East Rudolf, the name for Lake Turkana during the colonial era in Kenya.) The deposits in which it was found are about 1.9 million years old; these deposits, like those at Olduvai, also contain crude stone tools. The KNM ER 1470 skull is more modern in appearance than any *Australopithecus* skull and has a cranial capacity of 752 cubic centimeters (cc). However, the large

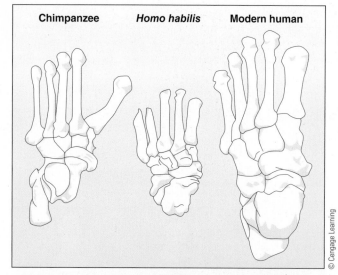

Figure 6.32 **Comparative Anatomy of *Homo habilis* Foot**
A partial foot skeleton of *Homo habilis* (*center*) is compared
with the same bones of a chimpanzee (*left*) and modern human
(*right*). Note how *H. habilis'* bone at the base of the great toe is
in line with the others, as it is in modern humans, making for
effective walking but poor grasping.

teeth and face of this specimen resemble the earlier australopithecines.

From this same site another well-preserved skull from
the same time period (KNM ER 1813) possesses a cranial
capacity of less than 600 cc but has the derived characteristics of a smaller, less projecting face and teeth (both
of these specimens are shown in Figure 6.24). Though
specimens attributed to *H. habilis* generally have cranial
capacities greater than 600 cc, the cranial capacity of any
individual is also in proportion to its body size. Therefore,
many paleoanthropologists interpret KNM ER 1813 and
ER 1470 as a female and male of a very sexually dimorphic
species, with the smaller cranial capacity of KNM ER 1813
a reflection of her smaller body size (**Figure 6.33**).

Lumpers or Splitters?

Other paleoanthropologists do not agree with placing
specimens as diverse as KNM ER 1813 and KNM ER 1470
in the single taxonomic group of *H. habilis*. Instead they
feel that the diversity represented in these specimens war-
rants separating the fossils like the larger-brained KNM
ER 1470 into a distinct coexisting group called *Homo
rudolphensis*. Whether one chooses to call these or any
other contemporary fossils *Homo rudolphensis* or *Homo
habilis* is more than a name game. Fossil names indicate
researchers' perspectives about evolutionary relationships among groups. Giving specimens separate species
names signifies that they form part of a reproductively
isolated group.

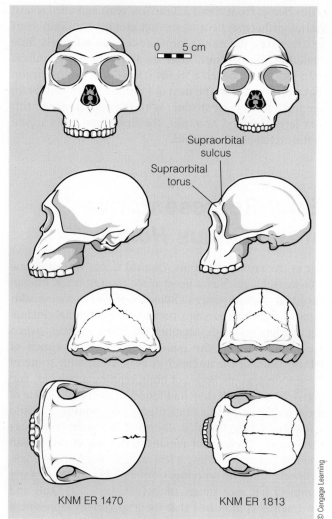

Figure 6.33 **One Diverse Species?** The KNM ER 1470 skull—
one of the most complete skulls of *Homo habilis*—is close to
2 million years old and is probably a male; it contrasts with the
considerably smaller KNM ER 1813 skull, probably a female.
Some paleoanthropologists feel this variation is too great to
place these specimens in the same species.

Some paleoanthropologists approach the fossil record
with the perspective that making such detailed biological determinations is arbitrary and that variability exists
within any group. Arguing that it is impossible to prove
whether a collection of ancient bones and teeth represents a distinct species, these paleoanthropologists tend
to be "lumpers," placing similar-looking fossil specimens
together in more inclusive groups. For example, gorillas
show a degree of sexual dimorphism that lumpers attribute to *H. habilis*.

"Splitters," by contrast, focus on the variation in the
fossil record, interpreting minor differences in the shape
of skeletons or skulls as evidence of distinct biological species with corresponding cultural capacities. The late great
South African paleoanthropologist Philip Tobias (to whose

memory this text is dedicated) once quipped about the variable shape of the bony ridge above ancient eyes: "Splitters will create a new species at the drop of a brow ridge."

Splitting has the advantage of specificity while lumping has the advantage of simplicity. We will use a lumping approach throughout our discussion of the genus *Homo*.

Differences Between Early *Homo* and *Australopithecus*

By 2.4 million years ago, the evolution of the genus *Homo* was proceeding in a different direction from that of *Australopithecus*. In terms of body size, early *Homo* differs little from *Australopithecus*. Although early *Homo* had teeth that are large by modern standards—or even by those of a half-million years ago—they are smaller in relation to the size of the skull than those of any australopithecine. Early *Homo* also had undergone enlargement of the brain indicating that early *Homo's* mental abilities probably exceeded those of *Australopithecus*. Early *Homo* likely possessed a marked increase in ability to learn and to process information compared with australopithecines.

The later robust australopithecines from East and South Africa that coexisted with early *Homo* evolved into more specialized "grinding machines" with massive jaws and back teeth for processing plant foods. Robust australopithecine brain size did not change, nor is there firm evidence that they made stone tools. Thus, in the period between 1 and 2.5 million years ago, two kinds of bipeds were headed in very different evolutionary directions: the robust australopithecines, specializing in plant foods and ultimately becoming extinct, and the genus *Homo*, with expanding cranial capacity, a varied diet that included meat, and the earliest evidence for stone tool making.

Without stone tools early *Homo* could eat few animals (only those that could be skinned by tooth or nail); therefore, their diet was limited in terms of animal protein. On the arid savannah, it is hard for a primate with a humanlike digestive system to satisfy its protein requirements from available plant resources. Moreover, failure to do so has serious consequences: stunted growth, malnutrition, starvation, and death. Leaves and legumes (nitrogen-fixing plants, familiar modern examples being beans and peas) provide the most readily accessible plant sources of protein. Unfortunately, substances in the leaves and legumes cause proteins to pass right through the gut without being absorbed unless cooked.

Chimpanzees have a similar problem when out on the savannah. Even with canine teeth far larger and sharper than ours or those of early *Homo*, chimpanzees frequently have trouble tearing through the skin of other animals. In savannah environments, chimps spend about a third of their time foraging for insects (ants and termites), eggs, and small vertebrate animals. Such animal foods not only are easily digestible, but they provide high-quality proteins that contain all the essential amino acids, the building blocks of protein. No single plant food can provide this nutritional balance. Only a combination of plants can supply the range of amino acids provided by meat alone.

Lacking long, sharp teeth for shearing meat, our earliest ancestors likely foraged for insects, but sharp tools for butchering made it possible to efficiently eat meat. The initial use of tools by early *Homo* may be related to adapting to an environment that we know was changing since the Miocene from forests to grasslands. The physical changes that adapted bipeds for spending increasing amounts of time on the new grassy terrain may have encouraged tool making.

Thus, with the appearance of the genus *Homo*, a feedback loop between biological characteristics and cultural innovations began to play a major role in our evolutionary history. This set the hominin line on a steady course of increasing brain size and a reliance on culture as the means of adaptation, as we explore in detail in the next chapter.

CHAPTER CHECKLIST

What was the course of primate evolution, and how was it affected by geologic events?

● Early primates began to emerge after the extinction of dinosaurs 65 million years ago, when a meteor hit the earth and dramatically cooled global temperatures. The new climate led to the growth of forests over the earth, creating an ideal environment for early arboreal primates.

● A warming trend 55 million years ago caused the extinction of many earlier mammals and led to the evolution of the first true primates, including the prosimians.

● Primates became extinct in North America at the end of the Eocene era, when the earth cooled and icecaps formed over Antarctica.

● By 33 million years ago, during the Oligocene epoch, a diverse array of Old World anthropoid primates existed, possessing a mixture of ape and monkey features. The earliest evidence of New World monkeys also dates from the Oligocene epoch.

What are the distinguishing features of bipedalism, and how do paleoanthropologists use fossil evidence to identify hominins?

● Bipedalism is the characteristic that separates humans and their ancestors from the other African apes.

● Distinguishing features of bipedalism include a skull centered above the spinal column; a series of convex and concave curves in the spine; a wide pelvis; femora that "knee in"; an asymmetrical knee joint; stable arched feet and an adducted big toe; and shorter toes than other apes. These anatomical features allow scientists to determine bipedalism in fossils, even from fragmentary remains.

● Bipedal locomotion is the process of shifting the body's weight from one foot to the other as the nonsupporting foot swings forward. Scientists can use fossilized footprints to determine bipedal locomotion.

● After bipedalism is determined in a fossil, scientists turn to other characteristics, such as skull and teeth, to reconstruct relationships among fossil groups.

How did cultural biases interfere with the recognition of Africa as the place of origin of the human species?

● During the Miocene epoch, 5 to 23 million years ago, the African and Eurasian landmasses made direct contact, and the first hominoids appeared.

● During the later Miocene 5 to 14 million years ago, the fossil record in Africa became scarce because the rainforest environment did not permit the preservation of fossils.

● Western scientists tended to focus on European apes as the possible missing link to humans, believing that humans had evolved where Western civilization had developed.

● Western scientists were eager to label the Piltdown remains, found in England, as evidence of a missing link in human ancestry due to its location on British soil and its large cranial capacity. The remains were later revealed to be a hoax.

● These biases impeded the acceptance of the small-brained bipedal Taung child from South Africa as one of our ancestors when it was first discovered. Ultimately, the self-correcting nature of science prevailed and today all agree that the human line originated in Africa as a small-brained biped.

How do the earliest bipeds compare to one another? How do they compare to chimps? To humans?

● The earliest bipeds belonged to the genus *Ardipithecus*, which contains the species *Ardipithecus ramidus* and the older *Ardipithecus kadabba*. Though bipedal, the remarkably complete specimen "Ardi" physically resembles a chimp and inhabited forested environments.

● Most bipeds from the Pliocene epoch belong to the genus *Australopithecus*, which includes eight known species.

● *Australopithecus afarensis* resembles an ape from the waist up and a human from the waist down and was better adapted to life in the trees than more recent human ancestors.

● Australopithecines probably used tools in ways similar to modern chimpanzees.

● Bipedalism would have allowed australopithecines, like humans, to carry their offspring in their arms, reducing the risk of infant mortality of chimps whose young must cling to the mother for safety.

What are the distinguishing characteristics of gracile and robust australopithecines?

● Gracile australopithecines had about the same mental capacity as modern great apes. Their teeth were smaller than those of robust australopithecines, and they likely ate meat.

● Robust australopithecines were larger and possessed massive teeth, jaws, and chewing muscles that were attached to a sagittal crest, making them adapted for plant consumption.

What is the earliest appearance of the genus *Homo* in the fossil record?

● The earliest specimen from the genus *Homo* is the stone toolmaking species *Homo habilis*, discovered by the Leakeys in Olduvai Gorge. Since then, similar fossils have been discovered throughout Kenya, Ethiopia, and South Africa.

● Early *Homo* had smaller teeth and a larger brain than early *Australopithecus*. Its body was about the same size.

QUESTIONS FOR REFLECTION

1. Although we often consider human intelligence as the quality that separates us from the other apes, bipedalism was the first feature to define the human evolutionary line. Does this surprise you? Does our early evolutionary history make us seem more like the other animals? Does this challenge your notions of what it means to be human?

2. Describe the anatomy of bipedalism, providing examples from head to toe of how bipedalism can be "diagnosed" from a single bone. Do you think evidence from a single bone is enough to determine whether an organism from the past was bipedal?

3. Who were the robust australopithecines? What evidence is used to demonstrate that they are an evolutionary dead end?

4. How do paleoanthropologists decide whether a fossil specimen from the distant past is male or female? Do our cultural ideas about males and females in the present affect the interpretation of behavior in human evolutionary history?

5. Do you think that members of the genera *Ardipithecus* and *Australopithecus* were tool users? What evidence would you use to support a case for tool use in these early bipeds?

ONLINE STUDY RESOURCES

CourseMate

Access chapter-specific learning tools, including learning objectives, practice quizzes, videos, flash cards, glossaries, and more in your Anthropology CourseMate.

Log into **www.cengagebrain.com** to access the resources your instructor has assigned and to purchase materials.

Challenge Issue

As we approach the later stages of human evolution, our ancestors become more familiar in every sense. This may be most apparent in the depictions of fossil specimens of this time period made by paleoartists using casts of fossilized skulls to accurately recreate the faces of our ancestors. Paleoartists like Elisabeth Daynès team with paleoanthropologists to produce striking yet faithful renderings of ancient individuals. In fact, by envisioning this era of human evolution, paleoartists document the essential human traits that make their craft possible: enlarged brains, sophisticated symbolic thought, and dexterous hands for wielding tools. These qualities, first appearing with the genus *Homo* 2.5 million years ago, allowed our ancestors to better meet the challenges of survival. In turn paleoartists are challenged to represent these ancient species accurately and without bias, drawing from all available information. For example, they assess brain expansion directly from fossil specimens and details of facial form and robusticity from muscle insertions on these ancient skeletons, but they imagine features such as facial expression, body language, body hair, and skin color. Paleoartists might also incorporate archaeological evidence starting with the earliest stone tools dating from 2.6 million years ago. We know that without the brain expansion that characterizes the genus *Homo*, reliance on culture could not have occurred, but the exact relationship between biological change and cultural capacity remains controversial. Does each cultural innovation mark the appearance of a new species? Does a 20 percent increase in brain tissue do the same? And what about all the cultural changes that have occurred after brain size reached modern proportions? Although the precise relationship between biology and cultural capacity remains unclear, paleoart provides a window into our past and serves as an important supplement to facts and figures in the effort to understand human origins.

Origins of the Genus *Homo*

7

In the quest for the origin of modern humans, paleoanthropologists confront mysteries by drawing from evidence that can be scant, misleading, and contradictory. Some of the mystery stems from the kind of evolutionary change that was set in motion with the appearance of the genus **Homo**. Beginning 2.5 million years ago (mya), several million years after the appearance of bipedalism separated the human evolutionary line from those of the other African apes, the brain size of our ancestors began to increase. Simultaneously, these early ancestors increased their cultural manipulation of the physical world through their use of stone tools. These new bipeds were the first members of the genus *Homo*. Over time, they increasingly relied on cultural adaptation as a rapid and effective way to adjust to the environment.

Although the evolution of culture became critical for human survival, it was intricately tied to underlying biological capacities, specifically the evolution of the human brain. Over the course of the next 2.2 million years, increasing brain size and specialization of function (evidence preserved in fossilized skulls) permitted the development of language, planning, new technologies, and artistic expression. With the evolution of a brain that made versatile behavior possible, members of the genus *Homo* became biocultural beings.

U.S. biological anthropologist Misia Landau has noted that the narrative of human evolutionary history takes the form of the heroic epic (Landau, 1991). The hero, or evolving human, faces a series of natural challenges that cannot be overcome from a strictly biological standpoint. Endowed with the gift of intelligence, the hero meets these challenges to become fully human. In this narrative, cultural capabilities increasingly separate humans from other evolving animals. As we saw in earlier chapters, recent advances in primatology keep undercutting this notion of human uniqueness.

Biological change and cultural change are very different phenomena. Cultural equipment and techniques can develop rapidly with innovations

Homo The genus of bipeds that appeared 2.5 million years ago, characterized by increased brain size compared to earlier bipeds. The genus is divided into various species based on features such as brain size, skull shape, and cultural capabilities.

IN THIS CHAPTER YOU WILL LEARN TO

Describe the cultural capacity of various members of the genus *Homo* and how these capacities relate to anatomy preserved in fossils.

Situate humans' place in the animal kingdom and recognize the cultural biases that have influenced the development of scientific theories about human evolution.

Describe the debates surrounding relationships among fossil groups of the genus *Homo*.

Identify the features that characterize the distinct eras of toolmaking.

Discuss the controversy surrounding Neandertals' place in human evolution.

occurring during the lifetime of individuals. By contrast, because it depends upon heritable traits, biological change requires many generations. Paleoanthropologists consider whether an evident cultural change, such as a new type of stone tool, corresponds to a major biological change, such as the appearance of a new species. Reconciling the relation between biological and cultural change is often a source of debate within paleoanthropology.

The Discovery of the First Stone Toolmaker

Paleoanthropologists Louis and Mary Leakey began their search for human origins at Olduvai Gorge, Tanzania, because of the presence of crude stone tools unearthed there. These tools found in deposits dating back to very early in the Pleistocene epoch (which began almost 2 mya), defined the **Oldowan tool tradition**.

These earliest identifiable tools consist of implements made using a system of manufacture called the **percussion method** (**Figure 7.1**). Sharp-edged flakes were obtained from a stone (often a large, water-worn cobble) either by using another stone as a hammer (a hammerstone) or by striking the cobble against a large rock (anvil) to remove the flakes. The finished flakes had sharp edges, effective for cutting and scraping. Microscopic wear patterns show that these flakes were used for cutting meat, reeds, sedges, and grasses and for cutting and scraping wood. Small indentations on their surfaces suggest that the leftover cores were transformed into choppers for breaking open bones, and they may also have been employed to defend the user. The appearance of these tools marks the beginning of the **Lower Paleolithic**, the first part of the Old Stone Age.

The tools from Olduvai Gorge are not the oldest stone tools known. Paleoanthropologists have dated the start of the Lower Paleolithic to between 2.5 and 2.6 million years ago from similar assemblages recently discovered in Gona, Ethiopia. (**Figure 7.2** shows the captive bonobo Kanzi who has made tools and used tools similar to those found in

Figure 7.1 **The Percussion Method** By 2.5 million years ago, early *Homo* in Africa had invented the percussion method of stone tool manufacture. This technological breakthrough, which is associated with a significant increase in brain size, made the butchering of meat from scavenged carcasses possible.

Gona.) Lower Paleolithic tools have also been found in the vicinity of Lake Turkana in northwestern Kenya, in southern Ethiopia, as well as in other sites near Gona in the Afar Triangle of Ethiopia. With these earliest stone tools, we have the beginning of the hominin archaeological record. Before this time, tool use among early bipeds probably consisted of heavy sticks to dig up roots or ward off animals, unshaped stones to throw for defense or to crack open nuts, and perhaps simple carrying devices made of knotted plant fibers. Perishable tools are not preserved in the archaeological record.

Paleoanthropologists have applied the methodology of **experimental archaeology**, the systematic recreation of ancient lifeways in order to test hypotheses, interpretations, and assumptions about the past. To understand the process of toolmaking, researchers work with raw materials to make stone tools themselves (Figure 7.2). The process of becoming skilled at fashioning

Oldowan tool tradition The first stone tool industry, beginning between 2.5 and 2.6 million years ago.

percussion method A technique of stone tool manufacture performed by striking the raw material with a hammerstone or by striking raw material against a stone anvil to remove flakes.

Lower Paleolithic The first part of the Old Stone Age beginning with the earliest Oldowan tools spanning from about 200,000 or 250,000 to 2.6 million years ago.

experimental archaeology The recreation of ancient lifeways by modern paleoanthropologists in order to test hypotheses, interpretations, and assumptions about the past.

Figure 7.2 Oldowan Toolmaking While we have no evidence of stone toolmaking by any hominoids in the wild, Kanzi, the captive bonobo, spontaneously began making stone tools thus providing us with some insight into the cognitive capacities that underlie this ancient task. The experimental archaeologist takes this many steps further. Through becoming skilled at ancient toolmaking techniques, an experimental archaeologist analyzes the exact processes involved. In essence, a form of participant observation across time, the experimental archaeologist takes on the lifeways of ancient hominins. He or she performs the same behaviors and creates the same artifacts, to discover which skills these lifeways required, knowledge that is indispensible for the interpretation of the material remains. Experimental archaeologists often master the entire range of ancient stone tool techniques described in this chapter in order to make comparisons among the various industries.

Sex, Gender, and the Behavior of Early *Homo*

When paleoanthropologists from the 1960s and 1970s depicted the lifeways of early *Homo*, they concentrated on "man the hunter," a tough guy with a killer instinct wielding tools on a savannah teeming with meat, while the female members of the species stayed at home tending their young. Similarly, until the 1960s, most cultural anthropologists doing fieldwork among foragers stressed the role of male hunters and underreported the significance of female gatherers in providing food for the community. Western notions of **gender**, the cultural elaborations and meanings assigned to the biological differentiation between the sexes, played a substantial role in creating these biases.

tools allows researchers to analyze what skills toolmaking requires. Through this work it is clear that the makers of these early tools were highly skilled, consistently and efficiently producing many well-formed sharp-edged flakes from raw materials with the least effort (Ambrose, 2001). To do this, the toolmaker had to have in mind an abstract idea of the tool to be made, as well as a specific set of steps to transform the raw material into the finished product. Furthermore, the toolmaker would have to know which kinds of stone have the flaking properties that would allow the transformation to take place, as well as where such stone could be found.

Sometimes tool fabrication required the transport of raw materials over great distances. Such planning for the future undoubtedly was associated with natural selection favoring changes in brain structure. These changes mark the beginning of the genus *Homo*. As described in the previous chapter, **Homo habilis** was the name given to the oldest members of the genus when first discovered in 1959. With larger brains and the stone tools preserved in the archaeological record, paleoanthropologists began to piece together a picture of the life of early *Homo*.

As anthropologists became aware of their own biases, they began to set the record straight, documenting the vital role of "woman the gatherer" in provisioning the social group in foraging cultures, past and present. (See this chapter's Biocultural Connection for the specific contributions of female paleoanthropologists.) The division of labor among contemporary food foragers, like all gender relations, does not conform to fixed boundaries defined through biologically based sex differences. Instead, it is influenced by cultural and environmental factors. It appears likely that the same principle applied to our human ancestors. Uncovering such biases is as important as any new discovery for interpreting the fossil record (**Figure 7.3**).

Studies of extant primates can allow paleoanthropologists to see when gender might appropriately be incorporated into their theories. For example, by finding sex

Homo habilis "Handy human." The first fossil members of the genus *Homo* appearing 2.5 million years ago, with larger brains and smaller faces than australopithecines.

gender The cultural elaborations and meanings assigned to the biological differentiation between the sexes.

BIOCULTURAL CONNECTION

Sex, Gender, and Female Paleoanthropologists

Until the 1970s, the study of human evolution was permeated by a deep-seated bias reflecting the privileged status enjoyed by men in Western society. Beyond the obvious labeling of fossils as particular types of "men," irrespective of the sex of the individual represented, males were portrayed as the active players in human evolution. Thus, males were seen as providers and innovators, using their wits to become ever-more effective suppliers of food and protection for passive females. Females were depicted as spending their time preparing food and caring for offspring, while the males were getting ahead by becoming ever smarter. Central to such thinking was the idea of "man the hunter," constantly honing his wits through the pursuit and killing of animals. Hunting by men was seen as the pivotal humanizing activity in evolution.

We now acknowledge that such ideas are culture-bound, reflecting the hopes and expectations of Western culture in the late 19th and early 20th centuries. This recognition came in the 1970s and was a direct consequence of the entry of a number of highly capable women into the profession of paleoanthropology.

Up until the 1960s, there were few women in any field of physical anthropology, but with the expansion of graduate programs and changing attitudes toward the role of women in society, increasing numbers of women went on to earn doctorates. One of these was Adrienne Zihlman, who earned her doctorate at the University of California at Berkeley in 1967. Subsequently, she authored a number of important papers critical of "man the hunter" scenarios. She was not the first to do so; as early as 1971, Sally Linton had published a preliminary paper on "woman the gatherer." But it was Zihlman who, from 1976 on, especially elaborated on the importance of female activities for human evolution. Others have joined in the effort, including Zihlman's graduate school companion and professional colleague Nancy Tanner, who has produced important works of her own.

The work of Zihlman and her coworkers was crucial in forcing a reexamination of existing "man the hunter" scenarios; this produced recognition of the importance of scavenging in early human evolution as well as the value of female gathering and other activities.

Although there is still plenty to learn about human evolution, thanks to these women we now know that it was not a case of females being "uplifted" as a consequence of their association with progressively evolving males. Rather, the two sexes evolved together, with each making its own important contribution to the process.

BIOCULTURAL QUESTION

Can you think of any examples of how gender norms are influencing theories about the biological basis of male and female behavior today?

---

differences in the levels of the mineral strontium in the teeth of 2-million-year-old fossil hominins, paleoanthropologists have deduced that these ancestors followed the same pattern of female dispersal at adolescence seen in chimps and bonobos (Copeland et al., 2011). However, female dispersal patterns cannot be extended to explain theories regarding the evolution of pair bonding or biologically encoded male aggression without introducing gender bias.

Similarly, evidence from chimpanzees and bonobos casts further doubt on the notion of a strict sex-based division of labor in human evolutionary history. As described in Chapter 4, female chimpanzees have been observed participating in hunting expeditions, even leading the hunt behavior with spears. Meat gained from the successful hunt of a smaller mammal is shared within the group whether provided by a male or a female chimpanzee. Among bonobos, females hunt regularly and share meat as well as plant foods with one another. In other words, patterns of food sharing and hunting behaviors in these apes are variable, supporting the notion that culture plays a role in establishing these behaviors. Similarly, in our evolutionary history it is likely that culture—the shared learned behaviors of each early *Homo* group—played a role in food-sharing behaviors rather than strict biological differences between the sexes.

No evidence exists to establish definitively how procured foods may have been shared among our ancestors. When the evidence is fragmentary, as it is in all paleoanthropological reconstructions of behavior, gaps are too easily filled in with behaviors that seem "natural" and familiar, such as the contemporary gender roles of the paleoanthropologist.

Hunters or Scavengers?

As biases in paleoanthropological interpretations were addressed, it became clear that early members of the genus *Homo* were not hunters of large game. Assemblages of Oldowan tools and broken animal bones tell us that both *H. habilis* and large carnivorous animals were active at these locations. In addition to marks on the bones made by slicing, scraping, and chopping with stone tools, there

© The Field Museum Neg A102513C, Ron Testa

Figure 7.3 Gender Bias In this artist's reconstruction, separate roles are portrayed for males and females. Do the roles depicted here derive from biological differences between the sexes or culturally established gender differences?

are marks made by gnawing teeth. Some of the gnawing marks overlie the butcher marks, indicating that enough flesh remained on the bones after *Homo* was done with them to attract other carnivores. In other cases, though, the butcher marks overlie the tooth marks of carnivores, indicating that the animals got there first. This is what we would expect if *H. habilis* was scavenging the kills of other animals, rather than doing its own killing.

Further, areas that appear to be ancient butchering sites lack whole carcasses; apparently, only parts were transported away from the original location where they were obtained—again, the pattern that we would expect if they were stolen from the kill of some other animal. The stone tools, too, were made of raw material procured at distances of up to 60 kilometers from where they were used to process pieces of carcasses. Finally, the incredible density of bones at some of the sites and patterns of weathering indicate that the sites were used repeatedly for perhaps five to fifteen years.

By contrast, historically known and contemporary hunters typically bring whole carcasses back to camp or form camp around a large animal in order to fully process it. After processing, nothing edible remains—neither meat nor **marrow** (the fatty nutritious tissue inside long bones where blood cells are produced). The bones themselves are broken up not just to get at the marrow (as at Oldowan sites) but to fabricate tools and other objects of bone (unlike at Oldowan sites).

It appears that our Oldowan forebears were scavengers, getting their meat from the Lower Paleolithic equivalent of modern-day roadkill, taking the spoils of their scavenging

to particular places where tools, and the raw materials for making them (often procured from faraway sources), had been stockpiled in advance for the purpose of butchering. At the least, this may have required fabrication of carrying devices such as net bags and trail signs of the sort (described in Chapter 4) used by modern bonobos. Quite likely, *H. habilis* continued to sleep in trees or rocky cliffs, as do modern small-bodied terrestrial or semiterrestrial primates, in order to be safe from predators.

Microscopic analysis of cut marks on bones has revealed that the earliest members of the genus *Homo* were actually **tertiary scavengers**—that is, third in line to get something from a carcass after a lion or leopard managed to kill the prey. After the initial kill, ferocious scavengers, such as hyenas and vultures, would swarm the rotting carcass. Next, our tool-wielding ancestors would scavenge for food, breaking open the shafts of long bones to get at the rich marrow inside. A small amount of marrow is a concentrated source of both protein and fat. Muscle alone, particularly from lean game animals, contains very little fat. Furthermore, as the following Original Study shows, perhaps evolving humans were prey themselves, and this selective pressure imposed by predators played a role in brain expansion (Hart & Sussman, 2005).

---

marrow The fatty nutritious tissue inside of long bones where blood cells are produced.

tertiary scavenger In a food chain, the third animal group (second to scavenge) to obtain meat from a kill made by a predator.

Humans as Prey BY DONNA HART

There's little doubt that humans, particularly those in Western cultures, think of themselves as the dominant form of life on earth. And we seldom question whether that view holds true for our species' distant past. . . . We swagger like the toughest kids on the block as we spread our technology over the landscape and irrevocably change it for other species.

. . . The vision of our utter superiority may even hold true for the last 500 years, but that's just the proverbial blink of an eye when compared to the 7 million years that our hominid ancestors wandered the planet.

"Where did we come from?" and "What were the first humans like?" are questions that have been asked since Darwin first proposed his theory of evolution. One commonly accepted answer is that our early ancestors were killers of other species and of their own kind, prone to violence and even cannibalism. In fact, a club-swinging "Man the Hunter" is the stereotype of early humans that permeates literature, film, and even much scientific writing. . . .

Even the great paleontologist Louis S. B. Leakey endorsed it when he emphatically declared that we were not "cat food." Another legendary figure in the annals of paleontology, Raymond A. Dart, launched the killer-ape-man scenario in the mid-20th century. . . .

Dart had interpreted the finds in South African caves of fossilized bones from savannah herbivores together with damaged hominid skulls as evidence that our ancestors had been hunters. The fact that the skulls were battered in a peculiar fashion led to Dart's firm conviction that violence and cannibalism on the part of killer ape-men formed the stem from which our own species eventually flowered. In his 1953 article "The Predatory Transition from Ape to Man," Dart wrote that early hominids were "carnivorous creatures, that seized living quarries by violence, battered them to death, tore apart their broken bodies, [and] dismembered them limb from limb, . . . greedily devouring livid writhing flesh."

But what is the evidence for Man the Hunter? Could smallish, upright creatures with relatively tiny canine teeth and flat nails instead of claws, and with no tools or weapons in the earliest millennia, really have been deadly predators? Is it possible that our ancestors lacked the spirit of cooperation and desire for social harmony? We have only two reliable sources to consult for clues: the fossilized remains of the human family tree and the behaviors and ecological relationships of our living primate relatives.

When we investigate those two sources, a different view of humankind emerges. First, consider the hominid fossils that have been discovered. Dart's first and most famous find, the cranium of an *Australopithecus* child who died over 2 million years ago (called the "Taung Child" after the quarry in which the fossil was unearthed), has been reassessed by Lee Berger and Ron Clarke of the University of the Witwatersrand, in light of recent research on eagle predation. The same marks that occur on the Taung cranium are found on the remains of similarly sized African monkeys eaten today by crowned hawk eagles, known to clutch the monkeys' heads with their sharp talons.

C. K. Brain, a South African paleontologist like Dart, started the process of relabeling Man the Hunter as Man the Hunted when he slid the lower fangs of a fossil leopard into perfectly matched punctures in the skull of another australopithecine who lived between 1 million and 2 million years ago. The paradigm change initiated by Brain continues to stimulate reassessment of hominid fossils.

The idea that our direct ancestor *Homo erectus* practiced cannibalism was based on the gruesome disfigurement of faces and brain-stem areas in a cache of skulls a half-million years old, found in the Zhoukoudian cave, in China. How else to explain these strange manipulations except as relics of Man the Hunter? But studies over the past few years by Noel T. Boaz and Russell L. Ciochon—of the Ross University School of Medicine and the University of Iowa, respectively—show that extinct giant hyenas could have left the marks as they crunched their way into the brains of their hominid prey.

The list of our ancestors' fossils showing evidence of predation continues to grow. A 1.75-million-year-old hominid skull unearthed in the Republic of Georgia shows punctures from the fangs of a saber-toothed cat. Another skull, about 900,000 years old, found in Kenya, exhibits carnivore bite marks on the brow ridge. . . . Those and other fossils provide rock-hard proof that a host of large, fierce animals preyed on human ancestors.

It is equally clear that, outside the West, no small amount of predation occurs today on modern humans. Although we are not likely to see these facts in American newspaper headlines, each year 3,000 people in sub-Saharan Africa are eaten by crocodiles, and 1,500 Tibetans are killed by bears about the size of grizzlies. In one Indian state between 1988 and 1998, over 200 people were attacked by leopards; 612 people were killed by tigers in the Sundarbans delta of India and Bangladesh between 1975 and 1985. The carnivore zoologist Hans Kruuk, of the University of Aberdeen, studied death records in eastern Europe and concluded that wolf predation on humans is still a fact of life in the region, as it was until the 19th century in western European countries like France and Holland.

The fact that humans and their ancestors are and were tasty meals for a wide range of predators is further supported by research on nonhuman primate species still in

Whether hunters or hunted, early *Homo* was in competition with formidable adversaries like hyenas. Communication and cooperation helped early *Homo* avoid carnivores that saw them as prey.

existence. My study of predation found that 178 species of predatory animals included primates in their diets. The predators ranged from tiny but fierce birds to 500-pound crocodiles, with a little of almost everything in between: tigers, lions, leopards, jaguars, jackals, hyenas, genets, civets, mongooses, Komodo dragons, pythons, eagles, hawks, owls, and even toucans.

Our closest genetic relatives, chimpanzees and gorillas, are prey to humans and other species. Who would have thought that gorillas, weighing as much as 400 pounds, would end up as cat food? Yet Michael Fay, a researcher with the Wildlife Conservation Society and the National Geographic Society, has found the remnants of a gorilla in leopard feces in the Central African Republic. Despite their obvious intelligence and strength, chimpanzees often fall victim to leopards and lions. In the Tai Forest in the Ivory Coast, Christophe Boesch, of the Max Planck Institute, found that over 5 percent of the chimp population in his study was consumed by leopards annually. Takahiro Tsukahara reported, in a 1993 article, that 6 percent of the chimpanzees in the Mahale Mountains National Park of Tanzania may fall victim to lions.

The theory of Man the Hunter as our archetypal ancestor isn't supported by archaeological evidence, either. Lewis R. Binford, one of the most influential figures in archaeology during the last half of the 20th century, dissented from the hunting theory on the ground that reconstructions of early humans as hunters were based on a priori positions and not on the archaeological record. Artifacts that would verify controlled fire and weapons, in particular, are lacking until relatively recent dates.

And, of course, there's also the problem of how a small hominid could subdue a large herbivore. . . . Large-scale, systematic hunting of big herbivores for meat may not have occurred any earlier than 60,000 years ago—over 6 million years after the first hominids evolved.

What I am suggesting, then, is a less powerful, more ignominious beginning for our species. Consider this alternate image: smallish beings (adult females maybe weighing 60 pounds, with males a bit heavier), not overly analytical because their brain-to-body ratio was rather small, possessing the ability to stand and move upright, who basically spent millions of years as meat walking around on two legs. Rather than Man the Hunter, we may need to visualize ourselves as more like Giant Hyena Chow, or Protein on the Go.

Our species began as just one of many that had to be careful, to depend on other group members, and to communicate danger. We were quite simply small beasts within a large and complex ecosystem.

Is Man the Hunter a cultural construction of the West? Belief in a sinful, violent ancestor does fit nicely with Christian views of original sin and the necessity to be saved from our own awful, yet natural, desires. Other religions don't necessarily emphasize the ancient savage in the human past; indeed, modern-day hunter-gatherers, who have to live as part of nature, hold animistic beliefs in which humans are a part of the web of life, not superior creatures who dominate or ravage nature and one another.

Think of Man the Hunted, and you put a different face on our past. . . . We needed to live in groups (like most other primates) and work together to avoid predators. Thus an urge to cooperate can clearly be seen as a functional tool rather than a Pollyannaish nicety, and deadly competition among individuals or nations may be highly aberrant behavior, not hardwired survival techniques. The same is true of our destructive domination of the earth by technological toys gone mad.

Raymond Dart declared that "the loathsome cruelty of mankind to man . . . is explicable only in terms of his carnivorous, and cannibalistic origin." But if our origin was not carnivorous and cannibalistic, we have no excuse for loathsome behavior. Our earliest evolutionary history is not pushing us to be awful bullies. Instead, our millions of years as prey suggest that we should be able to take our heritage of cooperation and interdependency to make a brighter future for ourselves and our planet.

Adapted from Hart, D. (2006, April 21). Humans as prey. Chronicle of Higher Education Review, April 21, 2006. Reprinted by permission of Donna Hart.

Whether as hunters or as the hunted, brain expansion and tool use played a significant role in the evolution of the genus *Homo*. The advanced preparation for meat processing implied by the storing of stone tools, and the raw materials for making them, attest to considerable foresight, an ability to plan ahead, and cooperation among our ancestors.

Brain Size and Diet

From its appearance 2.5 million years ago, the genus *Homo* began a course of brain expansion that continued until about 200,000 years ago. By this point, brain size had approximately tripled, reaching the proportion of contemporary people. The cranial capacity of the largely plant-eating robust australopithecines ranged from 310 to 530 cubic centimeters (cc). Likewise the cranial capacity of the contemporaneous *Australopithecus sediba* was also small though they possessed some more *Homo*-like skeletal features. The cranial capacity of the earliest known meat-eater, *Homo habilis* from East Africa, ranged from 580 to 752 cc; whereas *Homo erectus*, who eventually hunted as well as scavenged for meat, possessed a cranial capacity of 775 to 1,225 cc.

Larger brains, in turn, required parallel improvements in diet. The energy demands of nerve tissue, of which the brain is made, are high—higher, in fact, than the demands of other types of tissue in the human body. Although a mere 2 percent of body weight, the brain accounts for about 20 to 25 percent of energy consumed at resting metabolic rate in modern human adults. One can meet the brain's energy demands on a vegetarian diet, but generally a given amount of plant food contains less energy compared to the same amount of meat. Large animals that live on plant foods, such as gorillas, spend all day munching on plants to maintain their large bodies. Meat-eaters, by contrast, have no need to eat so much, or so often. Consequently, meat-eating bipeds of both sexes may have had more leisure time to explore and manipulate their environment.

The archaeological record provides us with a tangible account of our ancestors' cultural abilities that corresponds with the simultaneous biological expansion of the brain. Toolmaking itself puts a premium on manual dexterity, precision, and fine manipulation (**Figure 7.4**). Stone tools provide evidence of handedness that bespeaks specialization and lateralization of the brain associated with language.

Beginning with the appearance of the genus *Homo* in Africa 2.5 million years ago, increasing brain size and cultural development each presumably acted to promote the other. The behaviors made possible by larger brains conferred advantages to large-brained individuals, increasing their reproductive success. Over time, large-brained individuals contributed more to successive generations, so that the population evolved to a larger-brained form. Natural selection for increases in learning ability thus led to the evolution of larger and more complex brains over about 2 million years.

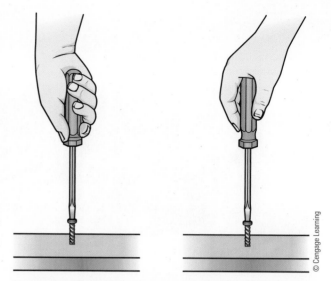

Figure 7.4 Power Versus Precision Grip A power grip (*left*) utilizes more of the hand whereas the precision grip (*right*) relies on the fingers for control, requiring corresponding organizational changes in the brain. Though *A. sediba* possessed a small brain, their hand anatomy indicates they could execute a precision grip.

Though it preceded increases in brain size by several million years, bipedalism set the stage for the evolution of large brains and human culture. It freed the hands for activities such as toolmaking and carrying of resources or infants. Thus, the bipedal body plan opened new opportunities for change.

Homo erectus

In 1887, long before the discovery of *Australopithecus* and early *Homo* in Africa, the Dutch physician Eugène Dubois set out to find the missing link between humans and apes. The presence of the humanlike orangutan in the Dutch East Indies (now Indonesia) led him to start his search there. He joined the colonial service as an army surgeon and set sail.

When Dubois found fossilized remains consisting of a skullcap, a few teeth, and a thighbone at Trinil on the island of Java, the features seemed to him part ape, part human. The flat skull with its low forehead and enormous brow ridges resembled that of an ape; but at about 775 cubic centimeters it possessed a much larger cranial capacity, even though small by modern human standards. The femur, or thighbone, was clearly human in shape, and its proportions indicated the creature was a biped. Believing that his specimens represented the missing link and that the thighbone indicated this creature was bipedal, Dubois named his find *Pithecanthropus erectus* (from the Greek *pithekos* meaning "ape," *anthropus* meaning "man") or "erect ape-man." Dubois used the genus name proposed

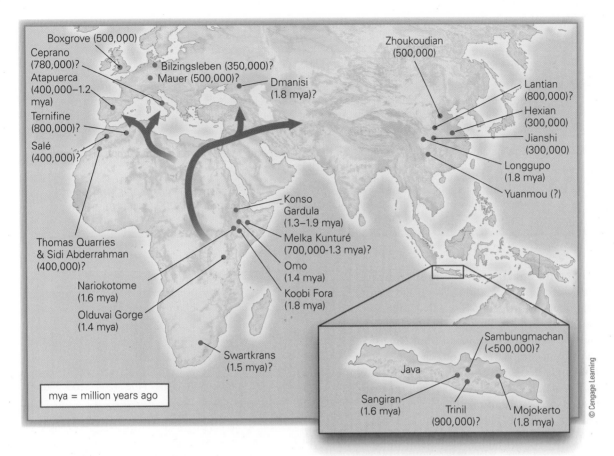

Figure 7.5 Map of *Homo erectus* Sites *Homo erectus* sites are shown here with their dates. The arrows indicated the proposed routes by which *Homo* spread from Africa to Eurasia. The question marks indicate the uncertain dating for particular sites. Splitters give some of these fossils different names.

in a paper by the German zoologist Ernst Haeckel, a strong supporter of Darwin's theory of evolution.

As with the Taung Child, the first australopithecine discovered in the 1920s, many in the scientific community ridiculed and criticized Dubois's claim, suggesting instead that the apelike skull and humanlike femur came from different individuals. Controversy surrounded these specimens throughout Dubois's lifetime. He eventually retreated from the controversy, keeping the fossil specimens stored safely under the floorboards of his dining room. Ultimately, the discovery of more fossils provided enough evidence to fully support his claim. In the 1950s, the Trinil skullcap and similar specimens from Indonesia and China were assigned to the species **Homo erectus** because they were more human than apelike.

Fossils of *Homo erectus*

Until about 1.8 million years ago, the bipedal primates inhabited only Africa. Both the first bipeds and the genus *Homo* originated there, and the first stone tools were also invented in Africa. But by the time of *H. erectus*, members

of the genus *Homo* had begun to spread far beyond their original homeland. Fossils of this species are now known from a number of localities not just in Africa, but in China, western Europe, Georgia (in the Caucasus Mountains), and India, as well as Java (**Figure 7.5**).

Although remains of *H. erectus* have been found in many different places in three continents, "lumpers," as discussed in the last chapter, emphasize that several shared characteristics unify them. However, because the fossil evidence also suggests some differences within and among populations of *H. erectus* inhabiting discrete regions of Africa, Asia, and Europe, "splitters" prefer to divide *H. erectus* into multiple distinct groups, limiting the species *H. erectus* only to the specimens from Asia. In this taxonomic scheme, *Homo ergaster* is used for African specimens from the early Pleistocene period that others describe as early *Homo erectus* (**Table 7.1**).

Homo erectus "Upright human." A species within the genus *Homo* first appearing just after 2 million years ago in Africa and ultimately spreading throughout the Old World.

TABLE 7.1

Alternate Species Designations for *Homo erectus* Fossils from Eurasia and Africa

Name	Explanation
Homo ergaster	Some paleoanthropologists feel that the large-brained successors to *H. habilis* from Africa and Asia are too different to be placed in the same species. Therefore, they use *H. ergaster* for the African specimens, saving *H. erectus* for the Asian fossils. Some paleoanthropologists place the recent discoveries from Dmanisi into this taxon.
Homo antecessor	This name was coined by "splitters" for the earliest *Homo* fossils from western Europe discovered in Spain; *antecessor* is Latin for "explorer" or "pioneer."
Homo heidelbergensis	Originally coined for the Mauer jaw (Mauer is not far from Heidelberg, Germany), this name is now used by some as a designation for all European fossils from about 500,000 years ago until the appearance of the Neandertals.

© Cengage Learning

Regardless of species designation, the fossil evidence indicates that beginning 1.8 million years ago these larger-brained members of the genus *Homo* lived not only in Africa but had also spread to Eurasia. Fossils dating to 1.8 million years old have been recovered from Dmanisi, Georgia, as well as from Mojokerto, Indonesia. A recently discovered and securely dated jaw from the Atapuerca site places the genus *Homo* in western Europe 1.2 million years ago (Carbonell et al., 2008). Many additional specimens have been found at a variety of sites in Europe and Asia.

Physical Characteristics of *Homo erectus*

Features of the skull best identify *H. erectus*. Cranial capacity ranges from 775 to 1,225 cc (average about 1,000 cc). Cranial capacity overlaps with both the nearly 2-million-year-old KNM ER 1470 skull from East Africa (752 cc) and the 1,000 to 2,000 cc range (average 1,300 cc) for modern human skulls (**Figure 7.6**).

The cranium itself has a low vault (height of the dome of the skull top), and the head is long and narrow. When viewed from behind, its width is greater than its height, with its greatest width at the base. The skulls of modern humans when similarly viewed are higher than they are wide, with the widest dimension in the region above the ears. The shape of the inside of *H. erectus'* braincase shows near-modern development of the brain, especially in the speech area. Although some anthropologists argue that the vocal apparatus was not adequate for speech, others claim that asymmetries of the brain suggest the same pattern of right-handedness with left cerebral dominance that, in modern peoples, is correlated with the capacity for language.

H. erectus possessed a massive brow ridge (**Figure 7.7**). When viewed from above, a marked constriction or "pinching in" of the skull can be seen just behind the brow ridge. *H. erectus* also possessed a sloping forehead and a

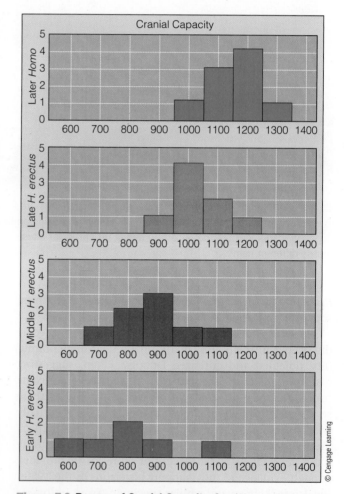

Figure 7.6 Ranges of Cranial Capacity Cranial capacity in *Homo erectus* increased over time, as illustrated by these bar graphs, shown in cubic centimeters. The cranial capacity of late *Homo erectus* overlaps with the range seen in contemporary humans.

receding chin. Powerful jaws with large teeth, a protruding mouth, and huge neck muscles added to *H. erectus'* generally rugged appearance. Nevertheless, the face, teeth, and jaws of this species are smaller than those of *H. habilis*.

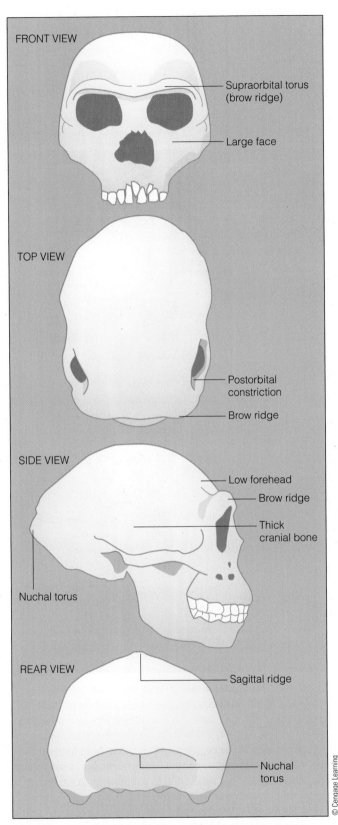

FRONT VIEW

— Supraorbital torus (brow ridge)

— Large face

TOP VIEW

— Postorbital constriction

— Brow ridge

SIDE VIEW

— Low forehead

— Brow ridge

— Thick cranial bone

Nuchal torus

REAR VIEW

— Sagittal ridge

— Nuchal torus

© Cengage Learning

Figure 7.7 The Skull of *Homo erectus* Note the enormous brow ridge of the *Homo erectus* skull, along with the sloping forehead and receding chin.

Apart from its skull, the skeleton of *H. erectus* differs only subtly from that of modern humans. Its bodily proportions resemble ours but with more robust muscles. Stature seems to have increased from the smaller size typical of the australopithecines and the earliest members of the genus *Homo*. The best evidence for this comes from a remarkably well-preserved skeleton of an adolescent male from Lake Turkana in Kenya. Sexual dimorphism in body size also appears to have decreased in *H. erectus* compared to earlier bipeds. A reduction in sexual dimorphism may be due to the increase in female size as an adaptation to childbirth. The recent discovery of a capacious female *Homo erectus* pelvis in Gona, Ethiopia, supports this notion (Simpson et al., 2008), although the large pelvis of *Australopithecus sediba* indicates that this trait might predate brain enlargement (Kibii et al., 2011).

Relationship among *Homo erectus*, *Homo habilis*, and Other Proposed Fossil Groups

The smaller teeth and larger brains of *Homo erectus* seem to mark the continuation of a trend first seen in *Homo habilis*. Newly derived characteristics for *H. erectus* include increased body size, reduced sexual dimorphism, and a more "human" body form. Nonetheless, some skeletal resemblance to *H. habilis* exists, for example, in the shape of the thighbone, the long low vault and marked constriction of the skull behind the eyes, and the smaller brain size in the earliest *H. erectus* fossils.

Presumably *H. erectus* evolved from *H. habilis* fairly abruptly, around 1.8 to 1.9 million years ago. Although Asian *H. erectus* possesses thicker bones and more pronounced brow ridges compared to *H. erectus* from Africa, detailed anatomical comparisons indicate levels of variation approximating those seen in *H. sapiens* (Rightmire, 1998). That the 1.8-million-year-old specimens from Dmanisi, in the Caucasus—a region that lies along the overland route between Africa and Eurasia—show a mix of characteristics seen in African and Asian *H. erectus* populations supports the notion of a single species. The recent discovery of the small-brained 1.9-million-year-old "gracile" *Australopithecus sediba*, coexisting with these early members of the genus *Homo*, complicates this picture. Its discoverers proposed that derived aspects of its skeleton, such as a precision grip and a large pelvis, place it too as a contender for our direct ancestor.

Despite this complexity, paleoanthropologists state that throughout the globe, the most recent fossils possess a more derived appearance, and the oldest fossils (up to 1.8 million years old) display features reminiscent of earlier *H. habilis.* Indeed, distinguishing early *H. erectus* from late *H. habilis* is problematic—precisely what one would expect if one evolved from the other. We will next explore the *H. erectus* finds by region.

Homo erectus from Africa

Although our samples of *H. erectus* fossils from Asia remain among the best, Africa has yielded several important specimens. Fossils now assigned to this species were discovered there as long ago as 1933, but the better-known finds have been made since 1960, at Olduvai Gorge and at Lake Turkana, Kenya. These include the most complete *H. erectus* skeleton ever found, the Nariokotome Boy, an adolescent who died 1.6 million years ago (Figure 7.8). Paleoanthropologists infer the age of this specimen from his teeth (the 12-year molars are fully erupted) and the stage of maturity of the bones. With a height of about 5 feet 3 inches at adolescence, the Nariokotome Boy was expected to attain a stature of about 6 feet by adulthood.

Recently, paleoanthropologists discovered a trail of *H. erectus* footprints, like those from Laetoli, along Lake Turkana. These footprints support the estimates of *H. erectus* body mass (weight) and stature made from more fragmentary remains.

Homo erectus Entering Eurasia

The site of Dmanisi in the Caucasus Mountains of Georgia preserves evidence of the spread of *H. erectus* from Africa into Eurasia. Dmanisi was first excavated as an archaeological site because of its importance as a crossroads for the caravan routes of ancient Armenia, Persia, and Byzantium. When Oldowan stone tools were found at this site in 1984, the hunt for fossil specimens began there as well.

Since then, paleoanthropologists have recovered some remarkable remains that can be accurately dated to 1.8 million years ago through past volcanic activity in the region. In 1999, two well-preserved skulls, one with a partial face, were discovered. Thus, the early habitation of this region by members of the genus *Homo* is supported at Dmanisi with archaeological, anatomical, and geological evidence.

Because rising sea levels since the Pleistocene make it impossible for paleoanthropologists to document coastal routes for the spread of *Homo* from Africa to Eurasia, the evidence from Georgia constitutes the only direct evidence of the spread of evolving humans from Africa to Europe and to Asia.

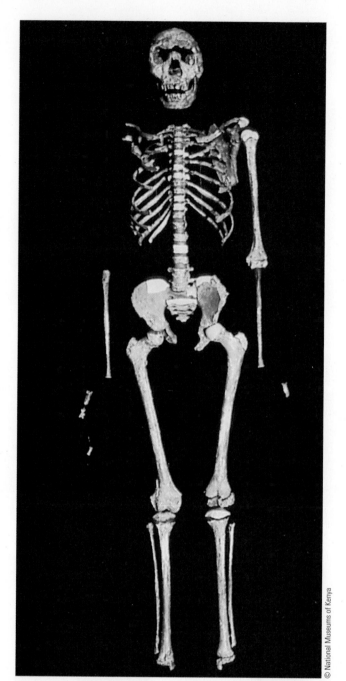

Figure 7.8 Nariokotome Boy One of the oldest and certainly one of the most complete *Homo erectus* fossils is the Nariokotome Boy from Lake Turkana, Kenya. How can scientists determine the age and sex of this specimen? Age comes from an examination of the degree to which bones have finished their growth and the emergence of the molar teeth; sex is determined from the shape of the pelvis, due to adaptations in the female pelvis that accommodate childbirth. Even though these remains come from a tall adolescent boy, this pelvis has been used to reconstruct theories about the evolution of human birth.

Homo erectus from Indonesia

Although it took many years for the skullcap and thighbone discovered by Dubois to be accepted as part of the human line, these specimens are now considered typical

Asian *H. erectus*. In the 1930s, a number of additional *H. erectus* fossils were discovered by German-Dutch paleoanthropologist G. H. R. von Königswald at Sangiran, Java (see Figure 7.5). Von Königswald found a small skull that fluorine analysis and (later) potassium-argon dating assigned to the early Pleistocene. This indicated that these fossils were older than the Trinil skullcap found by Dubois, dating to approximately 500,000 to 700,000 years ago.

Since 1960, additional fossils have been found in Java, and we now have remains of around forty individuals. A long continuity of *H. erectus* populations in Southeast Asia is indicated, from 500,000 to 1.8 million years ago. Interestingly, the teeth and jaws of some of the earliest Javanese fossils are in many ways quite similar to those of *H. habilis*. When considering the spread of *H. erectus* to Java, it is important to note that in the past, lower sea levels resulted in a continuous landmass between most of Indonesia and the Asian continent.

Homo erectus from China

In the mid-1920s a combination of serendipity and good anatomical knowledge led to the discovery of a site in China rich with fossils, now known as *H. erectus*. Davidson Black, a Canadian anatomist teaching at Peking Union Medical College, traveled to this site after purchasing a few ancient humanlike teeth offered for their medicinal properties from a Beijing drugstore. He set out for the nearby countryside to discover the "owner" of the teeth and perhaps a species of early human ancestor. At a place called Dragon Bone Hill in Zhoukoudian, 48 kilometers (30 miles) from Beijing (see Figure 7.5), on the day before closing camp at the end of his first year of excavation, he found one molar tooth. Subsequently, Chinese paleoanthropologist W. C. Pei, who worked closely with Black, found a skull encased in limestone.

Between 1929 and 1934, the year of his death from silicosis—a lung disease caused by exposure to silica particles in the cave—Black labored along with Pei and French Jesuit paleontologist Pierre Teilhard de Chardin in the fossil-rich deposits of Zhoukoudian, uncovering fragment after fragment of ancient remains. On the basis of the anatomy of that first molar tooth, Black

named these fossils *Sinanthropus pekinensis*, or "Chinese human of Peking" (Beijing), called "Peking Man" for short at the time. Today, paleoanthropologists consider these fossils an East Asian representative of *H. erectus*.

After Black's death, the Rockefeller Foundation sent Franz Weidenreich, a German anatomist and paleoanthropologist, to China to continue this work. As a Jew in Nazi Germany in the early 1930s, Weidenreich had sought refuge in the United States. By 1938, he and his colleagues recovered the remains of more than forty individuals, over half of them women and children, from the limestone deposits of Zhoukoudian. Fragmentary fossil remains included teeth, jawbones, and incomplete skulls. Weidenreich reconstructed a spectacular composite specimen from the most complete remains.

However, World War II (1939–1945) brought a halt to the digging, and the original Zhoukoudian specimens were lost during the Japanese occupation of China. The fossils had been carefully packed by Weidenreich and his team and placed with the U.S. Marines, but in the chaos of war, these precious fossils disappeared. Then, in 2012, an international team of paleoanthropologists followed the trail of the missing fossils, guided by information from a retired Marine, Richard Bowen Sr., who was stationed at the camp where the fossils were last seen. The potential location of the remains was pinpointed to a parking lot in the industrial city of Qinhuangdao (**Figure 7.9**).

Courtesy of Professor Lee Berger

Figure 7.9 Missing Peking Man Retired U.S. Marine Richard M. Bowen has led paleoanthropologists to think that the lost Peking Man fossils may be lying underneath this parking lot in Qinhuangdao, China. One of the last American soldiers to leave China at the end of World War II, Bowen vividly recalled finding a box of bones while digging a foxhole and reburying them when his small company was surrounded by the Communist 8th Route Army. After trying to pass this information on to Chinese authorities, Bowen's son Paul contacted paleoanthropologist Lee Berger, who has mobilized an investigation.

Paleoanthropologists are working with Chinese Cultural Heritage authorities to excavate the remains.

Fortunately, Weidenreich had made superb casts of most of the Zhoukoudian fossil specimens and sent them to the United States before leaving the site (Figure 7.10). After the war, other specimens of *H. erectus* were discovered in China, at Zhoukoudian and a number of other localities. The oldest skull is about 700,000 to 800,000 years old and comes from Lantian in central China. A fragment of a lower jaw from a cave in south-central China (Longgupo) is as old as the oldest Indonesian fossils. Like some of their Indonesian contemporaries, this Chinese fossil resembles African *H. habilis*. In contrast to these ancient remains, the original Zhoukoudian fossils appear to date between 300,000 and 600,000 years ago.

Although the two populations overlap in time, the majority of the Chinese fossils are, on the whole, slightly younger than those from Indonesia. Not surprisingly, Chinese *H. erectus* is less ancestral in appearance with an average cranial capacity of about 1,000 cc, compared to 900 cc for Indonesian *H. erectus*. The smaller teeth and short jaw of the Chinese fossil specimens provide further evidence of their more derived status.

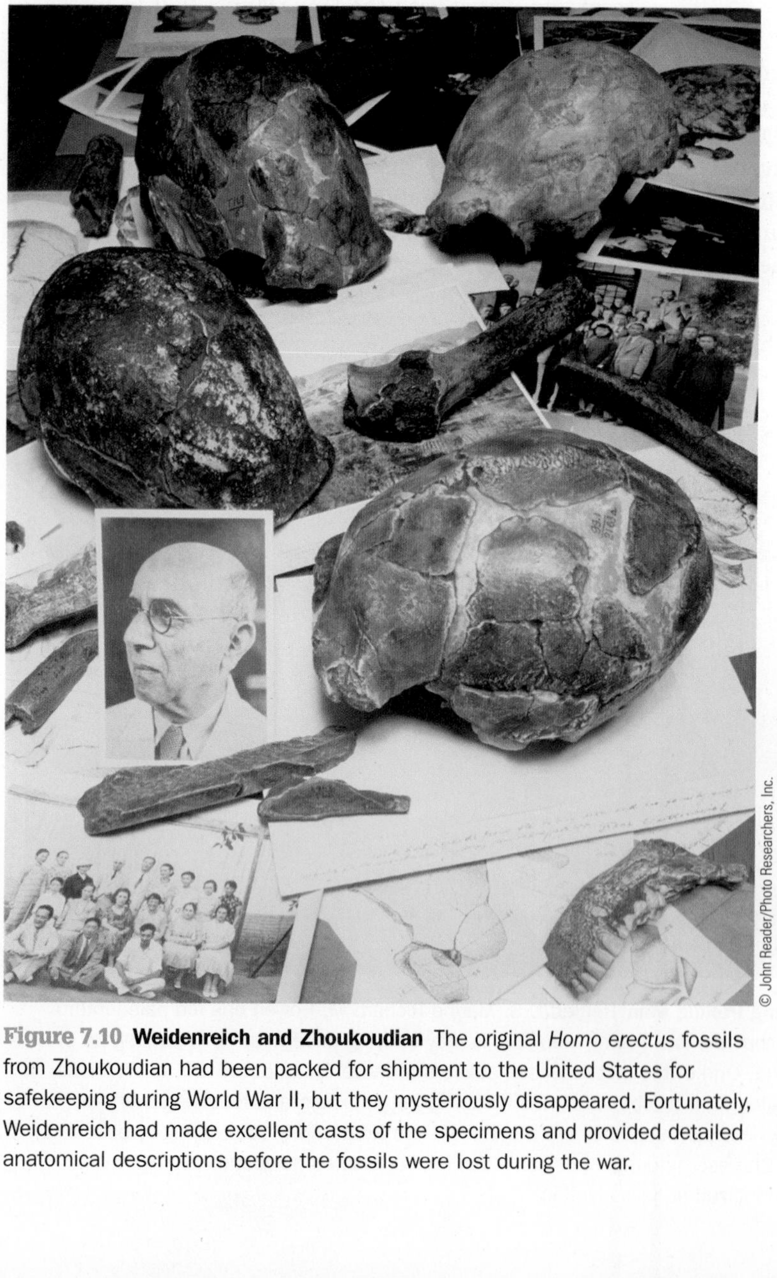

Homo erectus from Western Europe

Although the fossil evidence indicates the presence of the genus *Homo* on the Eurasian landmass 1.8 million years ago (at Dmanisi, Georgia), the fossil evidence from western Europe begins at about 1.2 million years ago with the new jawbone discovery at the Sima del Elefante ("Elephant's Pit") site in the Sierra de Atapuerca region of north-central Spain. The nearby Grand Dolina site has yielded fragments of four individuals dating to 1.2 million years ago. A skull from Ceprano in Italy is thought to be approximately the same age if not older. Again, whether one places these specimens into the inclusive but varied species *H. erectus* or into several separate species differs according to the approach taken by paleoanthropologists with regard to the fossil record (see Table 7.1).

Some other fossils attributable to *H. erectus*— such as a robust shinbone from Boxgrove, England, and a large lower jaw from Mauer, Germany—are close to half a million years old. The jaw came from a skull that was wide at the base, typical of *H. erectus*. These remains resemble *H. erectus* material from North Africa from the same time period. This observation and the fact that the earliest evidence of the genus *Homo* in western Europe comes from Spain and Italy suggest continued gene flow between this region and northern Africa (Balter, 2001). At the time, a mere 6 or 7 kilometers separated Gibraltar from Morocco (compared to 13 kilometers today), and islands dotted the straits from Tunisia to Sicily. The only direct land connection between Africa and Eurasia is through the Middle East and into Turkey and the Caucasus.

© John Reader/Photo Researchers, Inc.

Figure 7.10 Weidenreich and Zhoukoudian The original *Homo erectus* fossils from Zhoukoudian had been packed for shipment to the United States for safekeeping during World War II, but they mysteriously disappeared. Fortunately, Weidenreich had made excellent casts of the specimens and provided detailed anatomical descriptions before the fossils were lost during the war.

The Culture of *Homo erectus*

As one might expect given its larger brain, *Homo erectus* outstripped its predecessors in cultural ability. *H. erectus* refined the technology of stone toolmaking and at some point began to use fire for light, protection, warmth, and cooking, though precisely when is still a matter for debate. Indirect evidence indicates that the organizational and planning abilities of *H. erectus*, or at least the later ones, exceeded those of their predecessors.

Acheulean Tool Tradition

Implements of the **Acheulean tool tradition** accompany the remains of *H. erectus* in Africa, Europe, and southwestern Asia. Named for the stone tools first identified at St. Acheul, France, the signature piece of this tradition is the hand-axe: a teardrop-shaped tool pointed at one end with a sharp cutting edge all around (**Figure 7.11**).

The earliest hand-axes, from East Africa, date to about 1.6 million years ago. Those found in Europe are no older than about 500,000 years. At the same time that hand-axes appeared, archaeological sites in Europe became dramatically more common. This suggests an influx of individuals bringing Acheulean technology with them, implying continued gene flow into Europe. Because the spread of the genus *Homo* from Africa into Asia took place before the invention of the hand-axe, different forms of tools developed in East Asia.

Evidence from Olduvai Gorge indicates that the Acheulean grew out of the Oldowan tradition: In lower strata, chopper tools were found along with remains of *H. habilis*; above these, the first crude hand-axes intermingle with chopper tools; and higher strata contain more finished-looking Acheulean hand-axes along with *H. erectus* remains.

Early Acheulean tools represent a significant step beyond the generalized cutting, chopping, and scraping tools of the Oldowan tradition. The original form, size, and mechanical properties of raw materials largely controlled the shapes of Oldowan tools. The shapes of hand-axes and some other Acheulean tools, by contrast, were more standardized, apparently reflecting arbitrary preconceived designs imposed upon a diverse range of raw materials (Ambrose, 2001). Overall, Acheulean toolmakers could produce a sharper point and a more regular and larger cutting edge from the same amount of stone.

During this part of the Lower Paleolithic, toolkits began to diversify. Besides hand-axes, *H. erectus* used tools that functioned as cleavers (hand-axes with a straight, sharp edge where the point would otherwise be), picks and knives (variants of the hand-axe form), and flake tools (generally smaller tools made by hitting a flint core with a hammerstone, thus knocking off flakes with sharp edges). Many flake tools were byproducts of hand-axe and cleaver manufacture. Their sharp edges made them useful as is, but many were retouched (modified again by ancient flint-knappers) to make points, scrapers, borers, and other sorts of tools.

Toolkits diversified regionally during this period. In northern and eastern Europe, the archaeological record contains reduced numbers of hand-axes compared to Africa and southwestern Asia. People relied on simple flaked choppers, a wide variety of unstandardized flakes, and supplementary tools made of bone, antler, and wood. In eastern Asia, by contrast, people developed a variety of choppers, scrapers, points, and burins (chisel-like tools) different from those in southwestern Asia, Europe, and Africa.

Besides direct percussion, anvil (striking the raw material against a stationary stone) and bipolar percussion (holding the raw material against an anvil, but striking it at the same time with a hammerstone) other methods were used in tool manufacture. Although tens of thousands of stone tools have been found with *H. erectus* remains at Zhoukoudian, stone implements are not at all common in Southeast Asia. Here, favored materials likely were ones that do not preserve well, such as bamboo (**Figure 7.12**) and other local woods, from which excellent knives, scrapers, and so on can be made.

Use of Fire

With *H. erectus* came the first evidence of ancestral populations living outside the Old World tropics. Controlled use of fire allowed early humans to move successfully into regions where winter temperatures regularly dropped to temperate climate levels—as they must have in northern China, the mountain highlands of Central Asia, and most of Europe. Members of the genus *Homo* spread to these colder regions some 780,000 years ago.

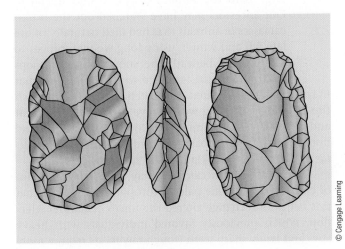

Figure 7.11 Acheulean Hand-Axe To fabricate this Acheulean hand-axe from flint, the toolmaker imposed a standardized arbitrary form on the naturally occurring raw material. The crafter made many separate strikes to create the sharp edge visible in profile.

Acheulean tool tradition The prevalent style of stone tools associated with *Homo erectus* remains and represented by the hand-axe.

Figure 7.12 **Bamboo Construction** In regions where bamboo is readily available for the fabrication of effective tools, the same stone tool industries might not have developed. Here, contemporary Chinese construction workers erecting a bamboo scaffolding demonstrate this material's strength and versatility.

rocks, more readily available in the shelter, cannot be used for hearths because, when burned, limestone produces quicklime, a caustic substance that causes itching and burning skin rashes. The hearth is associated with bones, showing clear evidence of cut marks from butchering as well as burning.

Evidence from Swartkrans in South Africa indicates that *H. erectus* may have been using fire even earlier. Here, deposits dated to between 1 and 1.3 million years ago contain bones that had been heated to temperatures far in excess of what one would expect as the result of natural fires. Furthermore, the burned bones at Swartkrans do not occur in older, deeper deposits. If these fires were natural, all archaeological layers would contain burned bones. Because the bones indicate heating to such high temperatures that any meat on them would have been inedible, paleoanthropologists suggest that the Swartkrans fires functioned as protection from predators.

H. erectus may have used fire not just for protection from animals out in the open but also to frighten away cave-dwelling predators allowing the fire users to live in the caves themselves. In addition, fire provided warmth and light in these otherwise cold and dark habitations. Although earlier bipeds likely used caves as part of their temperature regulation strategy as has been observed in nonhuman primates (Barrett et al., 2004), controlled use of fire expands the ability to regulate temperature considerably.

Fire may have assisted in the quest for food as well. In the long, cold winters of places like central Europe and China, food would have been hard to come by. Edible plants were unavailable, and the large herds of animals dispersed and migrated. Our ancestors may have searched out the frozen carcasses of animals that had died naturally in the late fall and winter, using long wooden probes to locate them beneath the snow, wooden scoops to dig them out, and fire to thaw them so that they could be butchered and eaten. Furthermore, such fire-assisted scavenging would have made available meat and hides of woolly mammoths, woolly rhinoceroses, and bison, which were probably beyond the ability of *H. erectus* to kill, at least until late in the species' career.

Using fire to thaw carcasses may have led to the idea of cooking food. Some paleoanthropologists suggest that this behavioral change altered the forces of natural selection, which previously favored individuals with heavy jaws and large, sharp teeth (tough raw foods require more chewing), favoring instead further reduction in tooth size along with supportive facial structure.

Alternatively, the reduction of tooth size and supporting structure may have occurred outside the context of adaptation. For example, the genetic changes responsible

The 700,000-year-old Kao Poh Nam rock shelter in Thailand provides compelling evidence for deliberate, controlled use of fire. Here, a roughly circular arrangement of fire-cracked basalt cobbles was discovered in association with artifacts and animal bones. Because basalt rocks are not native to the rock shelter and are quite heavy, they were likely carried in by *H. erectus*. Limestone

for increasing brain size may also have caused a reduction in tooth size as a secondary effect. The discovery of a genetic mutation, shared by all humans but absent in apes, that acts to prevent growth of powerful jaw muscles supports this hypothesis. Without heavy jaw muscles attached to the outside of the braincase, a significant constraint to brain growth was removed. In other words, humans may have developed large brains as an accidental byproduct of jaw-size reduction (Stedman et al., 2004).

Soft foods may have relaxed selection for massive jaws. But cooking does more than soften food. It detoxifies a number of otherwise poisonous plants; alters digestion-inhibiting substances so that important vitamins, minerals, and proteins can be absorbed while in the gut, rather than just passing through it unused; and makes high-energy complex carbohydrates like starch digestible. Cooking increased the nutritional resources available to humans and made them more secure.

The partial predigestion of food by cooking also may have allowed a reduction in the size of the digestive tract. Because paleoanthropologists do not have the benefit of fossilized digestive tracts to establish this biological change, they turn to comparative anatomy of the living hominoids. Despite its overall similarity of form to those of apes, contemporary humans possess substantially smaller digestive tracts. This reduced gut takes less energy to operate, thereby easing the competing energy demands of a larger brain.

Like tools, then, fire gave people more control over their environment. Fire modified the natural succession of day and night, perhaps encouraging *H. erectus* to stay up after dark to review the day's events and plan the next day's activities. Though we cannot know whether *H. erectus* enjoyed socializing and planning around campfires at night, we do have evidence at least of some planning behavior. The existence of populations in temperate climates implies planning because survival depended upon the ability to anticipate the needs of the winter season by advance preparation for the cold.

Although considerable variation exists, studies of modern humans indicate that most people can remain reasonably comfortable down to 50 degrees Fahrenheit (10 degrees Celsius) with minimal clothing as long as they keep active. Below that temperature, hands and feet cool to the point of pain. Clothing, like many other aspects of material culture, does not fossilize, so we have no direct evidence of the kind of clothing worn by *H. erectus*. We know only that colder climates required more sophisticated clothing. In short, when our human ancestors learned to use fire to warm and protect themselves and to cook their food, they dramatically increased their geographic range and nutritional options.

Hunting

Sites such as 400,000-year-old Ambrona and Torralba in Spain provide evidence that *Homo erectus* developed the ability to organize in order to hunt large animals.

The ancient swamp at Torralba contains dismembered scattered remains of several elephants, horses, red deer, wild oxen, and rhinoceroses. That no natural geologic process can account for this find indicates that these animals did not accidentally get mired in a swamp where they simply died and decayed. In fact, the bones are closely associated with a variety of stone tools—a few thousand of them. Furthermore, the site contains very little evidence of carnivorous animal activity and none at all for the really big carnivores. Clearly, the genus *Homo* was involved—not just in butchering the animals but evidently in killing them as well.

It appears that the animals were actually driven into the swamp so that they could be easily killed. The remains of charcoal and carbon, widely but thinly scattered in the vicinity, raise the possibility that grassfires were used to drive the animals into the swamp. This evidence indicates more than opportunistic scavenging. Not only was *H. erectus* able to hunt, but the evidence implies considerable organizational and communicative skills as well.

Other Evidence of Complex Thought

Other evidence of *H. erectus*' capabilities comes from the small island of Flores in Indonesia. Flores lies east of a deepwater strait that throughout the Pleistocene acted as a barrier to animals to and from Southeast Asia. Even at times of lowered sea levels, getting to Flores required crossing open water: at minimum 25 kilometers from Bali to Sumbawa, with an additional 19 kilometers to Flores. The presence of 800,000-year-old stone tools on Flores indicates that somehow our ancestors navigated across the deep, fast-moving water.

Flores is also the site where the "hobbit" species, *Homo floriensis* was discovered in 2003. Tiny in stature and possessing many ancestral characteristics, the Flores fossils date from 13,000 years ago to 73,000 years ago. Some paleoanthropologists have proposed that this dwarf species evolved directly from *H. erectus*, who arrived on the island with the aforementioned stone tools. In this model, the hominins then reduced in size, over generations, a phenomenon that can occur in isolated island populations.

Increased standardization and refinement of Acheulean hand-axes over time also provides evidence for a developing symbolic life. Moreover, deliberately marked objects of stone, bone, and ivory appear in Acheulean contexts at several sites in Europe. These include several objects from Bilzingsleben, Germany—among them a mastodon bone with a series of regular lines that appear to have been deliberately engraved. Similarly, the world's oldest known rock carvings are associated with Acheulean tools in a cave in India. Though a far cry from the later Upper Paleolithic cave art of France and Spain, these Paleolithic artifacts have no obvious utility or model in the natural world. Archaeologists have argued that the use of such symbolic images requires some sort of spoken language, not only to assign meaning to the images but to maintain the tradition they seem to represent.

The Question of Language

Though we have no definitive evidence of *Homo erectus'* linguistic abilities, indications of a developing symbolic life, as well as the need to plan for seasonal changes and to coordinate hunting activities (and cross stretches of open water), imply improving linguistic competence. In addition, the observation that right-handed individuals made the majority of stone tools supports the theory of the increased specialization and lateralization of the evolving brain. In other primates and most mammals, the right and left sides of the brain duplicate each other's function; these animals use the right and left sides of their bodies equally and interchangeably. In humans, the emergence of handedness seems closely linked both developmentally (at about the age of 1 year) and evolutionarily with the appearance of language. Thus, evidence of handedness in Lower Paleolithic tools indicates that the kind of brain specialization required for language was well under way (**Figure 7.13**).

The fossil record provides evidence for evolving humans' linguistic capability. The vocal tract and brain of *H. erectus* are intermediate between those of *H. sapiens* and earlier *Australopithecus*. The **hypoglossal canal**—the passageway through the skull that accommodates the nerve that controls tongue movement, which is so important for spoken language—has taken on the characteristic large size seen in contemporary humans in fossil skulls dated to 500,000 years ago (**Figure 7.14**).

Possibly, a changeover from reliance on gestural to spoken language was a driving force in these evolutionary changes. The reduction of tooth and jaw size, facilitating the ability to articulate speech sounds, may have also played a role. From an evolutionary standpoint, spoken language may provide some advantages over a gestural

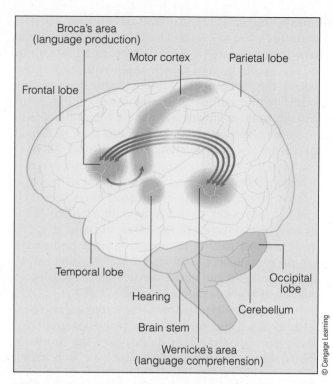

Figure 7.13 Language Areas of the Brain Language areas in the left side of the brain. The right side of the human brain has different specialized functions.

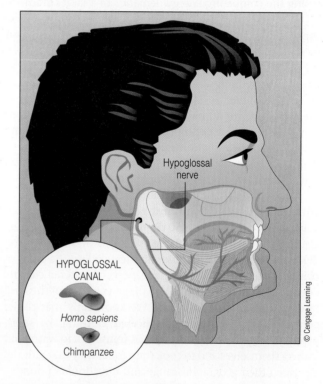

Figure 7.14 The Hypoglossal Canal The size of the hypoglossal canal is much larger in humans than in chimpanzees. The nerve that passes through this canal controls tongue movement, and complex tongue movements are involved in spoken language. All members of the genus *Homo* after about 500,000 years ago have an enlarged hypoglossal canal.

hypoglossal canal The opening in the skull that accommodates the tongue-controlling hypoglossal nerve.

one. Individuals do not have to stop whatever they are doing with their hands to "talk" (useful to a species increasingly dependent on tool use), and it is possible to communicate in the dark, past opaque objects, or among people whose gaze is concentrated on something else (potential prey, for example).

With *H. erectus*, then, we find a clearer manifestation of the interplay among cultural, physical, and environmental factors than ever before. However slowly, social organization, technology, and communication developed in tandem with an increase in brain size and complexity. In fact, the cranial capacity of late *H. erectus* is 31 percent greater than the mean for early *H. erectus*, a rate of increase more rapid than the average fossil vertebrate rate.

Archaic *Homo sapiens* and the Appearance of Modern-Sized Brains

Fossils from a number of sites in Africa, Asia, and Europe, dated to between 200,000 and 400,000 years ago, indicate that by this time cranial capacity reached modern proportions. Most fossil finds consist of parts of one or a very few individuals. The fossils from Sierra de Atapuerca in northern Spain provide the only evidence of a Paleolithic population (**Figure 7.15**). Dated to about 400,000 years ago (Parés et al., 2000), the remains of at least twenty-eight individuals of both sexes and of various ages were deliberately dumped (after defleshing their skulls) by their contemporaries into a deep cave shaft known today as Sima de los Huesos ("Pit of the Bones"). The presence of animal bones in the same pit with humans raises the possibility that early humans simply used the site as a dump. Alternatively, the treatment of the dead at Atapuerca may have involved ritual activity that presaged burial of the dead, a practice that became common after 100,000 years ago.

As with any population, this one displays a significant degree of variation. Cranial capacity, for example,

ranges from 1,125 to 1,390 cc, overlapping the upper end of the range for *H. erectus* and the average size of *H. sapiens* (1,300 cc). Overall, the bones display a mix of features, some typical of *H. erectus*, others of *H. sapiens*, including some incipient Neandertal characteristics. Despite this variation, the sample appears to show no more sexual dimorphism than displayed by modern humans.

Other remains from Africa and Europe dating from 200,000 to 400,000 years ago have shown a combination of *H. erectus* and *H. sapiens* features. Some—such as skulls from Ndutu in Tanzania, Swanscombe (England),

© Javier Trueba/Madrid Scientific Films

Figure 7.15 Sima de los Huesos These fossils from Sima de los Huesos ("Pit of the Bones"), Sierra de Atapuerca, Spain, are the best collection of *Homo* fossils from a single site. Although the remains possess cranial capacities overlapping with the average size of contemporary humans, the scientists who discovered them place them in the species *Homo antecessor*. These fossils fit into the complex period of our evolutionary history when brain size and cultural capability began to separate.

and Steinheim (Germany)—have been classified as *H. sapiens*, while others—from Arago (France), Bilzingsleben (Germany), Petralona (Greece), and several African sites—have been classified as *H. erectus*. Yet all have cranial capacities that fit within the range exhibited by the Sima de los Huesos skulls, which are classified as *H. antecessor* (see Table 7.1).

Comparisons of these skulls to those of living people or to *H. erectus* reflect their transitional nature. The Swanscombe and Steinheim skulls are large and robust, with their maximum breadth lower on the skull, more prominent brow ridges, larger faces, and bigger teeth. Similarly, the face of the Petralona skull from Greece resembles the later European Neandertals, whereas the back of the skull looks like *H. erectus*. Conversely, a skull from Salé in Morocco, which had a rather small brain for *H. sapiens* (930–960 cc), looks surprisingly modern from the back. Finally, various jaws from France and Morocco (in northern Africa) seem to combine features of *H. erectus* with those of the Neandertals. A similar situation exists in East Asia, where skulls from several sites in China exhibit the same mix of *H. erectus* and *H. sapiens* characteristics.

"Lumpers" suggest that calling some of these early humans "late *H. erectus*" or "early *H. sapiens*" (or any of the other proposed species names within the genus *Homo*) serves no useful purpose and merely obscures their transitional status. They tend to place these fossils in the **archaic *Homo sapiens*** category, a group that reflects both their large brain size and the ancestral features on the skull. "Splitters" use a series of discrete names for specimens from this period that take into account some of the geographic and morphologic variation exhibited by these fossils. Both approaches reflect their respective statements about evolutionary relationships among fossil groups.

Levalloisian Technique

With the appearance of large-brained members of the genus *Homo*, the pace of cultural change accelerated. These ancestors invented a new method of flake manufacture: the **Levalloisian technique**, so named for the French site where such tools were first excavated. Sites in Africa, Europe, southwestern Asia, and even China have yielded flake tools produced by this technique along with Acheulean tools. In China, the technique could represent a case of independent invention, or it could indicate the spread of ideas from one part of the inhabited world to another.

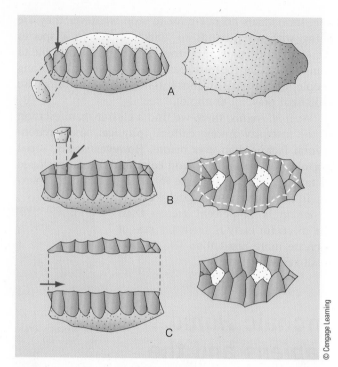

Figure 7.16 **The Levalloisian Technique** These drawings show side (*left*) and top (*right*) views of the steps in the Levalloisian technique. Arrows indicate where the toolmaker strikes the core with another stone in order to shape it. Drawing A shows the preparatory flaking of the stone core; B, the same on the top surface of that core (the dotted line indicates what will ultimately become a tool; and C, the final step of detaching a flake tool of a size and shape predetermined by the preceding steps.

© Cengage Learning

The Levalloisian technique initially involves preparing a core by removing small flakes over the stone's surface. Following this, the toolmaker sets up a platform by striking a crosswise blow at one end of the core of stone (Figure 7.16). Striking the platform removes three or four long flakes, whose size and shape have been predetermined by the preceding preparation, leaving behind a core nodule that looks like a tortoise shell and from which large preshaped flake tools can be removed. This method produces a longer edge for the same amount of flint than the previous ones used by evolving humans. It also produces sharper edges in less time.

Other Cultural Innovations

At about the same time the Levalloisian technique developed, our ancestors invented hafting—the fastening of small stone bifaces and flakes to handles of wood (Figure 7.17). Hafting led to the development of knives and more complex spears. Unlike the older handheld tools made simply by reduction (flaking of stone or working of wood), these new composite tools involved three components: a handle or shaft, a stone insert, and the materials to bind them. Manufacture involved planned sequences of actions that could be performed at different times and places.

archaic *Homo sapiens* A loosely defined group within the genus *Homo* that "lumpers" use for fossils with the combination of large brain size and ancestral features on the skull.

Levalloisian technique Toolmaking technique by which three or four long triangular flakes are detached from a specially prepared core; developed by members of the genus *Homo* transitional from *H. erectus* to *H. sapiens*.

© PhotoDisc/Getty Images

Figure 7.17 Hafting The practice of hafting, the fastening of small stone bifaces and flakes to handles of wood, was a major technological advance appearing in the archaeological record at about the same time as the invention of the Levalloisian technique.

With this new technology, regional stylistic and technological variants become more marked in the archaeological record, suggesting the emergence of distinct cultural traditions and culture areas. At the same time, the proportions of raw materials procured from faraway sources increased; whereas sources of stone for Acheulean tools were rarely more than 20 kilometers (12 miles) away, Levalloisian tools are found up to 320 kilometers (200 miles) from the sources of their stone (Ambrose, 2001).

The use of yellow and red pigments of iron oxide, called ochre, a development first identified in Africa, became especially common by 130,000 years ago. The use of ochre may signal a rise in ritual activity, similar to the deliberate placement of the human remains in the Sima de los Huesos, Atapuerca, already noted. The use of red ochre in ancient burials may relate to its similarity to the color of blood as a powerful symbol of life.

The Neandertals

To many outside the field of anthropology, **Neandertals** are the quintessential cavemen, portrayed by imaginative cartoonists as a slant-headed, stooped, dimwitted individuals clad in animal skins and carrying a big club as they plod across the prehistoric landscape, perhaps dragging an unwilling female or a dead saber-toothed tiger. The stereotype has been perpetuated in novels and film. The popular image of Neandertals as brutish and incapable of spoken language, much less abstract or innovative thinking, may, in turn, have influenced the interpretation of the fossil and archaeological evidence. One of the most contentious issues in paleoanthropology is the theory that the Neandertals represent an inferior side branch of human evolution that went extinct following the appearance of modern humans. The alternative view is that descendants of the Neandertals walk the earth today, and you may be one of them.

Neandertals were an extremely muscular people living from approximately 30,000 to 125,000 years ago in Europe, and southwestern and central Asia. Although having brains larger than the modern average size, Neandertals possessed faces distinctively different from those of modern humans. Their large noses and teeth projected forward. They had prominent bony brow ridges over their eyes. On the back of their skull, there was a bunlike bony mass for attachment of powerful neck muscles. These features, not in line with classic forms of Western beauty, may have contributed to the depiction of Neandertals as brutes. Their rude reputation may also derive from the timing of their discovery.

One of the first Neandertals was found in a cave in the Neander Valley (*tal* means "valley" in German, *thal* was the old German spelling) near Düsseldorf, Germany, in 1856. This was well before scientific theories to account for human evolution had gained acceptance. (Darwin published *On the Origins of Species* three years later in 1859.)

Initially, experts were at a loss as to what to make of this discovery. Examination of the fossil skull, a few ribs, and some limb bones revealed that the individual was a human being, but it did not look "normal." Some people believed the bones were those of a sickly and deformed contemporary. Others thought the skeleton belonged to a soldier who had succumbed to "water on the brain" during the Napoleonic Wars earlier that century. One prominent anatomist thought the remains were those of an idiot suffering from malnutrition, whose violent temper

Neandertals A distinct group within the genus *Homo* inhabiting Europe and southwestern Asia from approximately 30,000 to 125,000 years ago.

VISUAL COUNTERPOINT

Figure 7.18 Neandertal Depiction When Neandertals are portrayed as brutes as they were in this sketch from the early 20th century (*left*), based on the La Chapelle-aux-Saints skeleton, it is difficult to welcome them into our human ancestry. But when reconstructions portray them in a positive light, Neandertal ancestry seems more palatable. The image on the right depicts the reconstruction of Neandertal remains from the Shanidar site located in the Kurdistan region of today's Iraq. Excavated between 1957 and 1961, evidence from this site includes the deliberate burial of nine individuals. Ochre and pollen associated with the skeletons led to the nickname the "original flower people" for the Shanidar remains, as depicted here. Although some have claimed that the pollen is a modern contaminant, analysis of the bones reveals a rich cultural system. One of the buried individuals, an older male, had survived for many years after severe injuries that required amputating the lower half of one arm as well as a wound to his eye socket that would have left him partially blind. (The humerus or upper arm bone had withered—a gradual response to amputation of the lower arm.) Such survival demonstrates the caregiving capacities of his community to nurse him through these injuries.

had gotten him into many fights, flattening his forehead and making his brow ridges bumpy. Similarly, an analysis of a skeleton found in 1908 near La Chapelle-aux-Saints in France mistakenly concluded that the specimen's brain was apelike and that he walked like an ape (**Figure 7.18**).

The evidence indicates that Neandertals were nowhere near as brutish and apelike as originally portrayed, and some scholars now see them as the archaic *H. sapiens* of Europe and southwest and central Asia, ancestral to the more derived, anatomically modern populations of these regions of the last 30,000 years. For example, paleoanthropologist C. Loring Brace observed that "classic" Neandertal features (**Figure 7.19**) are commonly present in 10,000-year-old skulls from Denmark and Norway (Ferrie, 1997).

Nevertheless, Neandertals are somewhat distinctive when compared to more recent populations. Although they held modern-sized brains (average cranial capacity 1,400 cc versus 1,300 cc for modern *H. sapiens*), Neandertal skulls are notable for the protruding appearance of the midfacial region. The wear patterns on their large front teeth indicate that they may have been heavily used for tasks other than chewing. In many specimens,

front teeth were worn down to the root stub by 35 to 40 years of age. The large noses of Neandertals probably were necessary to warm, moisten, and clean the dry, dusty frigid air of the glacial climate, preventing damage to the lungs and brain as seen in cold-adapted people of recent times. At the back of the skull, the occipital bony bun allowed for attachment of the powerful neck muscles and counteracted the weight of a heavy face.

All Neandertal fossils indicate that both sexes were muscular, with extremely robust and dense limb bones. Relative to body mass, the limbs were short (as they are in modern humans native to especially cold climates). Their shoulder blades indicate the importance of over-arm and downward thrusting movements. Their arms were exceptionally powerful, and pronounced attachments on their hand bones attest to a remarkably strong grip. Science writer James Shreeve has suggested that a healthy Neandertal could lift an average North American football player over his head and throw him through the goalposts (Shreeve, 1995). Their massive, dense foot and leg bones suggest high levels of strength and endurance, comparable to robust individuals who live today (**Figure 7.20**).

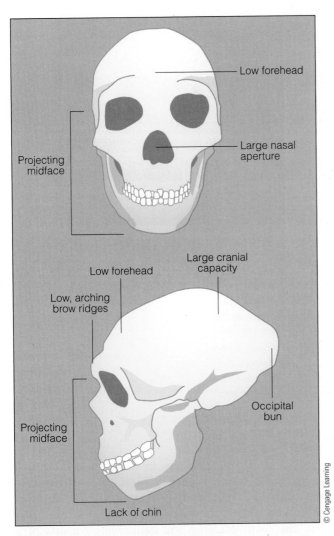

Figure 7.19 Neandertal Skulls Features of the skull seen in "classic" Neandertals.

Because brain size is related to overall body mass, heavy robust Neandertal bodies account for the large average size of the Neandertal brain. With *H. habilis* and *H. erectus*, increasing brain size has been linked to increasing cultural capabilities. Because Neandertal brain size falls at the high end of the human size range, paleoanthropologists have shifted to debating whether changes in the *shape*, rather than just the size, of the brain and skull is associated with changes in cultural capabilities.

Though the interpretation of Neandertal fossils has changed dramatically compared to when first discovered, they are still surrounded by controversy. Those who propose that the Neandertal line went extinct emphasize a notion of Neandertal biological difference and cultural inferiority. Those who include Neandertals in our direct ancestry emphasize the sophistication of Neandertal culture, attributing differences in skull shape and body form to regional adaptation to an extremely cold climate and the retention of ancestral traits in a somewhat isolated population.

Javanese, African, and Chinese Archaic *Homo sapiens*

While the large-brained Neandertals inhabited Europe and Southwest Asia, variants of archaic *H. sapiens* inhabited other parts of the world; these lacked the extreme midfacial projection and massive muscle attachments on the back of the skull characteristic of the Neandertals

Figure 7.20

Wolpoff Versus Neandertal As this face-off between paleoanthropologist Milford Wolpoff and his reconstruction of a Neandertal shows, the latter did not differ all that much from modern humans of European descent.

© The Natural History Museum, London

Figure 7.21 Comparing Crania The African archaic *Homo sapiens* from Kabwe, Zambia (*fourth from the left*) is pictured here with a variety of earlier hominins as well as Kabwe's contemporaries and later members of the genus *Homo*. The Kabwe specimen is likely to have died from a dental infection that spread to the brain of this individual. To the right of the Kabwe specimen is his contemporary, the original Neandertal cranium discovered in the Neander Valley, Germany, in 1856 (the only one without a face), followed by a cranium from a recent *Homo sapiens*. The other fossils, from the left, are a gracile australopithecine; *Homo habilis* (KNM ER 1470) discovered at Koobi Fora, Kenya; *Homo erectus* also from Koobi Fora. Increasing cranial capacity over time is evident from this series, as is the fact that Neandertal brains and that of Kabwe are in the modern human range. Even without the Neandertal face, some of the differences in the shape of the skull compared to *H. sapiens* are evident. The African archaic *H. sapiens* is also quite different from the contemporary skeleton.

(**Figure 7.21**). Skulls found in Java, Africa, and China date from roughly the same time period.

Eleven skulls found near the Solo River in Ngandong, Java, are a prime example. These skulls indicated modern-sized brains ranging from 1,013 to 1,252 cc, while retaining features of earlier Javanese *H. erectus*. When their dating was recently revised (to between 27,000 and 53,000 years ago), some researchers concluded that this proved a late survival of *H. erectus* in Asia, contemporary with *H. sapiens* elsewhere. But the Ngandong skulls remain what they always were: representatives of archaic *H. sapiens*, with modern-sized brains in otherwise ancient-looking skulls.

Fossils from various parts of Africa show a similar combination of ancient and modern traits. Equivalent remains have been found at several localities in China. Thus, the Neandertals could be said to represent an extreme form of archaic *H. sapiens*. Elsewhere, the archaics look like robust versions of the early modern populations that lived in the same regions or like somewhat more derived versions of the *H. erectus* populations that preceded them. All appear to have contained modern-sized brains, with their skulls retaining some ancestral features.

Exciting recent discoveries in southern Siberia bring a new group of archaic *Homo sapiens*, the **Denisovans**, into this mix. Dated to between 30,000 and 50,000 years ago and named for the cave in which they were discovered, the fossil evidence for Denisovans consists of a finger bone, a toe bone, and two molar teeth. Though scanty, these relatively recent remains were well enough preserved to allow for genetic analyses (Reich et al., 2010, 2012). They were also associated with blade tools and burins, more sophisticated stone tools characteristic of later peoples, as well as pendants made from the teeth of a variety of animals. Genetic analyses indicate that the Denisovans were local descendants of *Homo erectus*, who may have interbred with Neandertals, who also inhabited this region for a period of time, and with later waves of *Homo sapiens*. Features of both the Neandertal genome and the Denisovan genome live on in contemporary people today.

Middle Paleolithic Culture

Adaptations to the environment by *Homo* from the **Middle Paleolithic**, or middle part of the Old Stone Age, were both biological and cultural, but the capacity for cultural adaptation was predictably superior to what it had been in earlier members of the genus *Homo*. Possessing

Denisovans A newly discovered group of archaic *Homo sapiens* from southern Siberia dated to between 30,000 and 50,000 years ago.

Middle Paleolithic The middle part of the Old Stone Age characterized by the development of the Mousterian tool tradition and the earlier Levalloisian traditions.

brains of modern size, these members of the genus *Homo* had, as we would expect, greater cultural capabilities than their ancestors. Such a brain played a role in technological innovations, conceptual thought of considerable sophistication, and, almost surely, communication through spoken language. In addition to the Levalloisian technique already described, the Middle Paleolithic also included the development of the Mousterian tool tradition.

The Mousterian Tool Tradition

The **Mousterian tool tradition** and similar techniques of Europe, southwestern Asia, and northern Africa, dating between about 40,000 and 125,000 years ago, are the best known of these industries (**Figure 7.22**). Comparable traditions are found in China and Japan, where they likely arose independently from local toolmaking traditions.

All these traditions represent a technological advance over preceding industries. For example, the 40 centimeters (16 inches) of working edge that an Acheulean flint worker could get from a kilogram (2.2 pound) core compares with the nearly 200 centimeters (6 feet) of working edge the Mousterian could obtain from the same core. All people—Neandertals as well as other members of the genus *Homo* of this same time period who were said to possess more anatomically modern skulls, in Europe, northern Africa,

and southwestern Asia—used Mousterian tools. At around 35,000 years ago, the Mousterian traditions were replaced by the Upper Paleolithic traditions, which are the subject of Chapter 8. The following Anthropology Applied feature shows that stone tools continue to be important for humans today.

The Mousterian tradition is named after the Neandertal cave site of Le Moustier in southern France. The presence of Acheulean hand-axes at Mousterian sites is one indication that this culture was ultimately rooted in the older Acheulean tradition. Mousterian tools are generally lighter and smaller than those of earlier industries. Whereas previously only two or three flakes could be obtained from the entire core, Mousterian toolmakers obtained many smaller flakes, which they skillfully retouched and sharpened. Their toolkits also contained a greater variety of tool types: hand-axes, flakes, scrapers, borers, notched flakes for shaving wood, and many kinds of points that could be attached to wooden shafts to make spears. This variety of tools facilitated more effective use of food resources and enhanced the quality of clothing and shelter.

With the Mousterian cultural traditions, members of the genus *Homo* could cope with the frigid conditions that supervened in Eurasia as the glaciers expanded about 70,000 years ago. People likely came to live in cold climates as a result of a slow but steady population increase during the Pleistocene. Once there, they had little choice but to adapt as climates turned even colder.

Population expansion into previously uninhabited colder regions was made possible through a series of cultural adaptations. Under such cold conditions, vegetable foods are only rarely or seasonally available, and meat becomes a critical staple. In particular, animal fats, rather than carbohydrates, become the chief source of energy. Energy-rich animal fat in the diets of cold-climate meat-eaters provides them with the extra energy needed for hunting, as well as for keeping the body warm.

An abundance of associated animal bones, often clearly showing cut marks, indicates the importance of meat to Mousterian toolmakers. Frequently, the remains consist almost entirely of very large game—wild cattle (including the European bison known as the aurochs), wild horses, and even mammoths and woolly rhinoceroses. At several sites evidence indicates that particular species were singled out for the hunt. For example, at one site in the French Pyrenees, well over 90 percent of the faunal assemblage (representing at least 108 animals) consists of large members of the wild cattle family. These bones accumulated at the foot of a steep riverside escarpment, over which the animals were evidently stampeded. Evidence of similar cliff-fall hunting strategy is also found

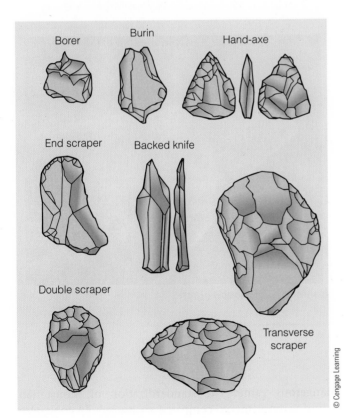

Borer   Burin   Hand-axe

End scraper   Backed knife

Double scraper

Transverse scraper

© Cengage Learning

Figure 7.22 The Mousterian Toolkit The Mousterian tool tradition includes a wide range of tool types with specific functions, which resulted in finer workmanship.

Mousterian tool tradition The tool industry of the Neandertals and their contemporaries of Europe, Southwest Asia, and North Africa from 40,000 to 125,000 years ago.

ANTHROPOLOGY APPLIED

Stone Tools for Modern Surgeons

When anthropologist Irven DeVore of Harvard University was to have some minor melanomas removed from his face, he did not leave it up to the surgeon to supply his own scalpels. Instead, he had graduate student John Shea create a scalpel. Making a blade of obsidian (a naturally occurring volcanic "glass") by the same techniques used by Upper Paleolithic people to create blades, he hafted this in a wooden handle, using melted pine resin as glue and then lashing it with sinew. After the procedure, the surgeon reported that the obsidian scalpel was superior to metal ones.[a]

DeVore was not the first to undergo surgery in which stone scalpels were used. In 1975, Don Crabtree, then at Idaho State University, prepared the scalpels that his surgeon would use in Crabtree's heart surgery. In 1980, Payson Sheets at the University of Colorado

created obsidian scalpels that were used successfully in eye surgery. And in 1986, David Pokotylo of the Museum of Anthropology at the University of British Columbia underwent reconstructive surgery on his hand with blades he himself had made (the hafting was done by his museum colleague, Len McFarlane).

The reason for the use of scalpels modeled on ancient stone tools is that the anthropologists realized that obsidian is superior in almost every way to materials normally used to make scalpels: It is 210 to 1,050 times sharper than surgical steel, 100 to 500 times sharper than a razor blade, and three times sharper than a diamond blade (which not only costs much more but cannot be made with more than 3 millimeters of cutting edge).

Obsidian blades are easier to cut with and do less damage in the process (under a microscope, incisions made

with the sharpest steel blades show torn, ragged edges and are littered with bits of displaced flesh).[b] As a consequence, the surgeon has better control over what she or he is doing, and the incisions heal faster with less scarring and pain. Because of the superiority of obsidian scalpels, Sheets went so far as to form a corporation in partnership with eye surgeon Dr. Firmon Hardenbergh. Together, they developed a means of producing cores of uniform size from molten glass, as well as a machine to detach blades from the cores.

---

[a]Shreeve, J. (1995). *The Neandertal enigma: Solving the mystery of modern human origins* (p. 134). New York: William Morrow.

[b]Sheets, P. D. (1993). Dawn of a New Stone Age in eye surgery. In R. J. Sharer & W. Ashmore (Eds.), *Archaeology: Discovering our past.* Palo Alto, CA: Mayfield.

 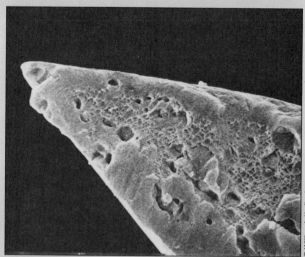

These electron micrographs of the tips of an obsidian blade (*left*) and a modern steel scalpel (*right*) illustrate the superiority of the obsidian.

at La Quina in southwestern France and at a site in the Channel Islands just off the northwest coast of France.

Clearly, the Neandertals were not merely casual or opportunistic hunters but engaged in carefully planned and organized hunting of very large and potentially

dangerous game. The standardization of Mousterian hunting implements compared to household tools also reflects the importance of hunting for these ancient peoples. At the same time, the complexity of the toolkit needed for survival in a cold climate may have decreased the users' mobility. Decreased mobility is suggested by the greater depth of deposits and thus longer habitation at Mousterian sites compared with those from the earlier Lower Paleolithic. Such sites contain evidence of long production sequences, resharpening and discarding of tools, and large-scale butchering and cooking of game. Pebble paving, construction of simple walls, and the digging of post holes and artificial pits show how the inhabitants worked to improve living conditions in some caves and rock shelters. This evidence suggests that Mousterian sites were not simply stopovers in a people's constant quest for food.

In addition, evidence suggests that Neandertal social organization had developed to the point of providing care for physically disabled members of the group. For the first time, the remains of old people are well represented in the fossil record. Furthermore, many elderly Neandertal skeletons show evidence of treatment for trauma, with extensive healing of wounds and little or no infection. The partially blind man with a withered upper arm from Shanidar in Iraq, described in Figure 7.18, provides one particularly dramatic example. Remains of another individual found at Krapina in Croatia suggest the possibility of surgical amputation of a hand. In La Chapelle, France, fossil remains indicate prolonged survival of a man badly crippled by arthritis. The earliest example comes from a 200,000-year-old site in France, where a toothless man was able to survive, probably because others in his group processed or prechewed his food so he could swallow it. Whether this evidence indicates true compassion on the part of these early people is not clear, but it is certain that cultural factors helped ensure survival, allowing individuals to provide care for others.

The Symbolic Life of Neandertals

There are indications of a rich symbolic life among the Neandertals. For example, several sites contain clear evidence for deliberate burial of the dead. This is one reason for the relative abundance of reasonably complete Neandertal skeletons. The difficulty of digging an adult-sized grave without access to metal shovels suggests how important a social activity this was. Moreover, intentional positioning of dead bodies, whatever the specific reason may have been, constitutes evidence of symbolism.

To date, at least seventeen sites in Europe, South Africa, and Southwest Asia include Middle Paleolithic burials. For example, at Kebara Cave in Israel, around 60,000 years ago, a Neandertal male between 25 and 35 years of age was placed in a pit on his back, with his arms folded over his chest and abdomen (**Figure 7.23**). Some time later, after complete decay of attaching ligaments, the grave was reopened and the skull removed (a practice that, interestingly, is sometimes seen in burials in the same region roughly 50,000 years later).

The rich Neandertal site of Krapina in Croatia contains the remains of at least 70 individuals. At first, cut marks on the bones were interpreted as evidence of cannibalism. Now scientists have come to recognize that these marks indicate deliberate defleshing of the skeletons of the dead that are consistent with later ceremonial practices.

Shanidar Cave provides evidence of a burial accompanied by what may have been a funeral ceremony. In the back of the cave a Neandertal was buried in a pit. Pollen analysis of the soil around the skeleton indicates that flowers had been placed below the body and in a wreath about the head. Because the key pollen types came from insect-pollinated flowers, few if any of the pollen grains could have found their way into the pit via air currents. The flowers in question consist solely of varieties valued in historic times for their medicinal properties.

Other evidence for symbolic behavior in Mousterian culture comes from the naturally occurring pigments: manganese dioxide and the red and yellow forms of ochre. Recovered chunks of these pigments reveal clear evidence of scraping to produce powder, as well as facets, like those that appear on a crayon, from use. A Mousterian artist also applied color to the carved and shaped section of a mammoth tooth about 50,000 years ago. This mammoth tooth may have been made for cultural symbolic purposes. Noteworthy is its similarity to ceremonial objects made

Figure 7.23 Kebara Burial The position of the body remains and the careful removal of the skull, without the lower jaw, indicate that the individual from Kebara Cave in Israel was deliberately buried there about 60,000 years ago.

© Cengage Learning

of bone and ivory dated to the later Upper Paleolithic and to the *churingas* made of wood by Australian Aborigines.

The mammoth tooth, which was once smeared with red ochre, has a highly polished face suggesting it was handled a lot. Microscopic examination reveals that it was never provided with a working edge for any utilitarian purpose. Such objects imply, as archaeologist Alexander Marshack has observed, "that the Neandertals did in fact have conceptual models and maps as well as problem-solving capacities comparable to, if not equal to, those found among anatomically modern humans" (Marshack, 1989, p. 22).

Recent discovery of a painting "toolkit" in a South African cave push this behavior back to 100,000 years ago and also to a region outside of the Neandertal range. Here we have evidence that the ancient artists made paint by mixing ground-stone pigments with bone marrow and charcoal (as binders) and a liquid, most likely water (Henshilwood et al., 2011). Whether a new kind of species is responsible for this or whether this paint manufacture was just a part of Mousterian culture will be taken up in detail in the next chapter.

Evidence for symbolic activity on the part of Neandertals raises the possibility of the presence and use of musical instruments, such as a proposed bone flute from a Mousterian site in Slovenia in southern Europe (**Figure 7.24**). This object, consisting of a hollow bone with perforations, has sparked controversy. Some see it as nothing more than a bone from a cave bear that was chewed on by carnivores—hence the perforations. Its discoverer, French archaeologist Marcel Otte, on the other hand, sees it as a flute.

Unfortunately, the object is fragmentary; surviving are five holes, four on one side and one on the opposite side. The regular spacing of the four holes, fitting perfectly to the fingers of a human hand, and the location of the fifth hole at the base of the opposite side, at the natural location of the thumb, all lend credence to the flute hypothesis. Although signs of gnawing by animals are present on this bone, they are superimposed on traces of human activity (Otte, 2000). Were it found in an Upper Paleolithic context as was the flute discovered in Hohle Fels Cave in southwestern Germany, it would probably be accepted as a flute without argument. However, because its early date indicates a Neandertal made it, the interpretation of this object is tied to the larger controversy about Neandertals' cultural abilities and their place in human evolutionary history.

Speech and Language in the Middle Paleolithic

Among modern humans, the sharing of thoughts and ideas, as well as the transmission of culture from one generation to the next, is dependent upon language. Because the Neandertals and other Middle Paleolithic *Homo* had modern-sized brains and a sophisticated Mousterian toolkit, or one that was even more sophisticated such as the Denisovan toolkit, it might be supposed that they had some form of language.

As pointed out by paleoanthropologist Stanley Ambrose, the Mousterian toolkit included composite tools involving the assembly of parts in different configurations to produce functionally different tools. He likens this ordered assembly of parts into tools to grammatical language "because hierarchical assemblies of sounds produce meaningful phrases and sentences, and changing word order changes meaning" . . . "a composite tool may be analogous to a sentence, but explaining how to make one is the equivalent of a recipe or a short story" (Ambrose, 2001, p. 1751). In addition, the evidence

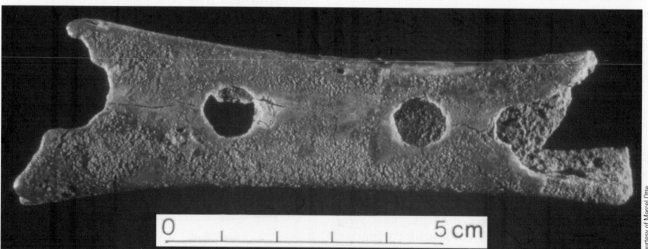

Courtesy of Marcel Otte

Figure 7.24 The First Musical Instrument? There is a strong possibility that this object, found in trash left by Neandertals, is the remains of a flute made of bone.

for the manufacture of objects of symbolic significance supports the presence of language in Middle Paleolithic *Homo*. Objects such as the colored section of mammoth tooth already described would seem to have required some form of explanation through language.

Although the archaeological evidence supports the symbolic thinking characteristic of language, specific anatomical features can be examined to determine whether this language was spoken or gestural. Some have argued that the Neandertals lacked the physical features necessary for speech. For example, an early 20th-century reconstruction of the angle at the base of the Neandertal skull was said to indicate that the larynx was higher in the throat than it is in modern humans, precluding humanlike speech. This reconstruction is now known to be faulty. Further, the hyoid bone associated with the muscles of speech in the larynx is preserved from the skeleton from the Kebara Cave burial in Israel. Its shape is identical to that of contemporary humans, indicating that the vocal tract was adequate for speech.

With respect to the brain, paleoneurologists, working from endocranial casts, agree that Neandertals had the neural development necessary for spoken language. Indeed, they argue that the changes associated with language began even before the appearance of archaic *Homo sapiens*, as described previously. Consistent, too, is an expanded thoracic vertebral canal (the thorax is the upper part of the body), a feature Neandertals share with modern humans but not with early *Homo erectus* (or any other primate). This feature suggests the increased breath control required for speech. This control enables production of long phrases or single expirations of breath, punctuated with quick inhalations at meaningful linguistic breaks.

Another argument—that a relatively flat base in Neandertal skulls would have prevented speech—has no merit, as some modern adults show as much flattening, yet have no trouble talking. Clearly, when the anatomical evidence is considered in its totality, there seems no compelling reason to deny Neandertals the ability to speak.

The discovery of a "language gene" by Swedish paleogeneticist Svante Pääbo and colleagues at the Max Planck Institute for Evolutionary Anthropology in Leipzig, Germany, adds an interesting new dimension to the study of the evolution of language (Lai et al., 2001). The gene, called FOXP2 found on chromosome 7, was identified through the analysis of a family in which members spanning several generations have severe language problems. Changes in the gene are hypothesized to control the ability to make fine movements of the mouth and larynx necessary for spoken language. The identification of this gene in humans allowed scientists to compare its structure to that found in other mammalian species.

The human FOXP2 gene differs from versions of the gene found in the chimpanzee, gorilla, orangutan, rhesus macaque, and mouse. Although these differences among living species can be known, applying this knowledge to the earlier members of the genus *Homo* is far more difficult. We do not know precisely when in human evolution the human form of the FOXP2 gene appeared or whether this gene was associated with the formation of a new species of *Homo*.

In light of these genetic discoveries it is also interesting to consider the work done on language capacity in the great apes. For example, in her work with the bonobo named Kanzi, Sue Savage-Rumbaugh documented his ability to understand hundreds of spoken words and associate them with lexigrams (pictures of words) on a computer display while unable to create the sounds himself (Savage-Rumbaugh & Lewin, 1994). Speech and language are not identical.

Culture, Skulls, and Modern Human Origins

For Middle Paleolithic *Homo*, cultural adaptive abilities relate to the fact that brain size was comparable to that of people living today. Archaeological evidence indicates sophisticated technology, as well as conceptual thought of considerable complexity, matching the increased cranial capacity. During this same time period, large-brained individuals with skulls with an anatomically modern shape began to appear. The earliest specimens with this skull shape—a more vertical forehead, diminished brow ridge, and a chin—appear first in Africa and later in Asia and Europe. Whether the derived features in the skull indicate the appearance of a new species with improved cultural capabilities is hotly debated.

The transition from the Middle Paleolithic to the tools of the Upper Paleolithic occurred around 40,000 years ago, some 100,000 years or so after the appearance of the first anatomically modern specimens in Africa. The Upper Paleolithic is known not only for a veritable explosion of tool industries, but also for clear artistic expression preserved in representative sculptures, paintings, and engravings (see Chapter 8). But the earliest anatomically modern humans, like the Neandertals and other archaic forms, used tools of the Middle Paleolithic traditions.

The relationship between cultural developments of the Upper Paleolithic and underlying biological differences between anatomically modern humans and archaic forms remains one of the most contentious debates in paleoanthropology. Discussions concerning the fate of the Neandertals and their cultural abilities are integral to this debate. Whether or not a new kind of human—anatomically modern with correspondingly superior intellectual and creative abilities—is responsible for the cultural explosion of the Upper Paleolithic is considered in Chapter 8.

CHAPTER CHECKLIST

What are the characteristics of the genus *Homo*?

● The genus *Homo* first appeared in East Africa and is marked by increasing cranial capacity and the earliest stone tools.

● Lumpers identify the first species as *Homo habilis* whereas splitters consider these fossils to be too varied to constitute a single species.

● *Homo erectus* appeared first in Africa around 1.9 million years ago and began spreading throughout the Old World.

● Cranial capacity in the genus *Homo* increased steadily from 2.5 million years ago until about 200,000 years ago when it reached modern proportions. Other trends include reduced jaws and teeth reduced sexual dimorphism, and an increase in overall body size.

How and when did stone tool industries develop for the genus *Homo*?

● The first evidence of stone tools is dated to about 2.6 million years ago from Gona, Ethiopia. Ancient toolmakers, presumably *Homo habilis*, used the percussion method of manufacture for these tools. The Lower Paleolithic or Lower Stone Age began with these early tools of the Oldowan tradition.

● *H. erectus* originated the hand-axe of the Acheulean tradition and exercised superior, more standardized craftsmanship compared to the preceding Oldowan tradition.

● Cranial capacity reached modern proportions between 200,000 and 400,000 years ago, roughly coincident with the Levalloisian tradition of stone tool manufacture and the practice of hafting.

● The Neandertal timespan coincides with the Mousterian tool era, although all the members of the genus *Homo* living at that time employed these methods. Together the Levalloisian and the Mousterian traditions constitute the Middle Paleolithic. It surpassed the Lower Paleolithic in variety and refinement, signifying our ancestors' developing reliance on cultural adaptation for survival.

What is the relationship between biological and cultural change among early *Homo*?

● Brain size increased over the course of 2.2 million years after the appearance of *H. habilis*, becoming the biological foundation for the cultural adaptation on which humans would rely for survival.

● As brain size reached modern proportions, the one-to-one correspondence between cultural innovation and larger brains no longer held.

● Meat eating satisfied the high-energy demands of larger brains and perhaps afforded leisure time for the development of culture and planning.

● Soft, cooked foods may have relaxed selection for large teeth and powerful jaws, permitting the cranium of *Homo erectus* to expand significantly.

● Increased overall size and decreased sexual dimorphism may have contributed to successful adaptation to bearing large-brained young.

● Fossil evidence indicates that early *Homo* was a scavenger rather than a hunter of big game, as the biases of Western tradition had suggested. Early tools were used to butcher scavenged carcasses in order to extract as much nutrition as possible.

How do we describe the history and lifeways of *Homo erectus*?

● *Homo erectus* appeared 1.8 million years ago, dispersing from Africa into Eurasia and Indonesia. A large cranial capacity, brow ridges, and a protruding mouth are some of the features that distinguish the *H. erectus* skull.

● Regional variation in fossils that are otherwise considered *Homo erectus* has led some scientists to create alternate species designations.

● Evidence of controlled use of fire dates to 1.3 million years ago. This skill presumably enabled *H. erectus* to expand into colder regions of Eurasia as well as to scavenge for frozen meat. Fire also provided the enormous nutritional benefits of cooked food.

● Evidence of handedness in tool manufacture and an enlarged hypoglossal canal support claims of late *H. erectus'* ability for language.

How do Neandertals compare to other members of *Homo*?

● Neandertal brains were larger than the modern average size, though their bulging facial features and muscular statures made them susceptible to derision by early Western scientists, especially before the theory of evolution was introduced.

● Aided by their implements and cognitive abilities, Neandertals could hunt large game effectively and relied upon it during the winter when vegetation was scarce.

● Neandertals practiced ritual burial and cared for ill and disabled members of their groups.

● Genetic, paleoneurological, anatomical, and artifact evidence all suggest Neandertals were capable of and used language, just as with other members of the genus *Homo* (generally classified as archaic *Homo sapiens*) who were living at that time.

QUESTIONS FOR REFLECTION

1. Members of the genus *Homo* draw upon integrated biological and cultural capabilities to face the challenges of existence. How do these factors play into the designation of species in the fossil record? How do paleoartists avoid introducing biases when they flesh out fossil species?

2. Paleoanthropologists can be characterized as lumpers or splitters depending upon their approach to the identification of species in the fossil record. Which of these approaches do you prefer and why?

3. In his 1871 book *Descent of Man, and Selection in Relation to Sex*, Charles Darwin stated, "Thus man has ultimately become superior to woman. It is indeed fortunate that the law of equal transmission of characters prevails with mammals. Otherwise it is probable that man would have become as superior in mental

endowment to woman as the peacock is in ornamental plumage to the peahen." How were the cultural norms of Darwin's time reflected in his statement? Can 21st-century paleoanthropologists speak about differences between the sexes in an evolutionary context without introducing their own cultural biases?

4. Life forms ranging from rabbits to plants have come to occupy new niches without the benefits of culture. Was the spread of *Homo* out of the African continent possible without the benefit of culture?

5. Though language itself does not "fossilize," the archaeological and fossil records provide some evidence of the linguistic capabilities of our ancestors. Using the evidence available, what sort of linguistic abilities do you think early *Homo* possessed?

ONLINE STUDY RESOURCES

CourseMate

Access chapter-specific learning tools, including learning objectives, practice quizzes, videos, flash cards, glossaries, and more in your Anthropology CourseMate.

Log into **www.cengagebrain.com** to access the resources your instructor has assigned and to purchase materials.

Challenge Issue

We all recognize this stencil of a hand, made by spraying paint on a cave wall, as human. Or is it? Scientists recently dated this ancient rock art from Spain's El Castillo Cave to 40,800 years ago, indicating that the outline may be of a Neandertal hand. Uranium-series techniques yielded these new dates in June 2012, making the cave art a good 10,000 years older than previously thought. What prompted this ancient being to venture deep into a pitch-black cave, guided perhaps by a burning flame for light, to leave a record of him- or herself or of another member of the group? Do these marks represent the urge of these ancient beings to connect people to one another across time and space? It these were made by Neandertals, are they speaking to us, directly asserting their humanity through the handprints they left behind? For many years, some paleoanthropologists have argued that a biological shift accounted for the creative urges, symbolic thought, and cultural sophistication necessary to execute such a stencil. They attribute the explosion of art and complex tool industries that begin to appear in the archaeological record from this point on to an intrinsic biological change, perhaps even a speciation event responsible for the appearance in the fossil record of anatomically modern humans. These ancient handprints challenge us to consider whether a biological change was at the root of this creative expression and whether biology separates us from these ancestors or other archaic forms that preceded them. These marks also suggest that humans, as a thoughtful and self-reflecting species, have always faced the challenge of understanding where and how we fit in the larger natural system of all life forms, past and present.

The Global Expansion of *Homo sapiens* and Their Technology

8

**IN THIS CHAPTER
YOU WILL LEARN TO**

- Describe the cultural and technological developments of the Upper Paleolithic era.

- Compare the multiregional continuity and recent African origins hypotheses for modern human origins.

- Identify the emerging diversity of human cultures during the Upper Paleolithic.

- Recognize the legacy of Upper Paleolithic peoples in modern times.

- Describe the evidence of symbolic thought and the expanding role of art in ancient peoples.

- Explain how humans came to inhabit the entire globe.

- Summarize the major biological and cultural features of human evolution.

In 1868, at the back of a rock shelter near the banks of the bucolic Vézère River, in a region of France now known for its delicious truffle mushrooms, the remains of eight ancient people were first discovered. These people, commonly referred to as **Cro-Magnons** after the rock shelter in which they were found (**Figure 8.1**), resembled contemporary Europeans more than Neandertals and were associated with tools of the **Upper Paleolithic**, the last part of the Old Stone Age. The Cro-Magnon name was extended to thirteen other specimens recovered between 1872 and 1902 in the caves of southwestern France and, since then, to Upper Paleolithic skeletons discovered in other parts of Europe.

Because Cro-Magnons were found with Upper Paleolithic tools and seemed to be responsible for the production of impressive works of art that abound in the caves of this region, scientists and laypeople alike considered them particularly clever when compared with the Neandertals. The idea of dimwitted Neandertals comfortably supported prevailing stereotypes based on their supposedly brutish appearance. Mousterian tools provided evidence of Neandertal cultural inferiority. Cro-Magnons, an anatomically modern people with a superior culture, swept into Europe and replaced a primitive local population. This idea mirrored the European conquest of other parts of the world during the colonial expansion that was concurrent with the discovery of these fossils.

With the invention of reliable dating techniques in the 20th century, we now know that many Neandertal specimens of Europe and the later Cro-Magnon specimens date from different time periods. The Middle Paleolithic Mousterian technology is associated with earlier fossil specimens, whereas the Upper Paleolithic technology and art belongs with later fossil specimens.

However, probably the most ethnocentric aspect of these beliefs is that the discussion focused on the

Cro-Magnons Europeans of the Upper Paleolithic after about 36,000 years ago.

Upper Paleolithic The last part (10,000 to 40,000 years ago) of the Old Stone Age, featuring tool industries characterized by long slim blades and an explosion of creative symbolic forms.

197

Figure 8.1 **Cro-Magnon** With a high forehead, the Cro-Magnon skull is more like contemporary Europeans compared to the prominent brow ridge and sloping forehead seen in the Neandertal skull. Whether these differences in skull shape account for their cultural differences rather than their relative age is hotly debated. The more recent Cro-Magnon skull even preserves evidence of continuity in diet with local contemporary French people because it exhibits signs of a fungal infection, perhaps caused by eating tainted mushrooms. Mushrooms are a delicacy in this region of France to this day.

those of modern Europeans, their brow ridges were a bit more prominent, and their teeth and jaws were as large as those of Neandertals. Some (a skull from the original Cro-Magnon site, for instance) even display the distinctive occipital bun of the Neandertals on the back of the skull. Nor were they particularly tall, as their average height of 5 feet 7 or 8 inches (170–175 centimeters) does not fall outside the Neandertal range. Similarly, early Upper Paleolithic skulls from Brno, Mladec, and Predmosti in the Czech Republic retain heavy brow ridges and Neandertal-like muscle attachments on the back of the skull.

Although paleoanthropologists routinely refer to the Cro-Magnons and Upper Paleolithic peoples from Africa and Asia as "anatomically modern," this definition lacks precision. We think of people with brains the size of modern people, but this had already been achieved by archaic *Homo sapiens*. Average brain size actually peaked in Neandertals at 10 percent larger than the contemporary human average. The reduction to today's average size correlates with a reduction in brawn, as bodies have become less massive overall. Living humans, in general, have faces and jaws smaller than those of Neandertals, but there are exceptions. For example, paleoanthropologists Milford Wolpoff and Rachel Caspari have pointed out that any definition of *modernity* that excludes Neandertals also excludes substantial numbers of recent and living Aborigines in Australia, although they are, quite obviously, a contemporary people (**Figure 8.2**). The fact is, no multidimensional diagnosis of anatomical modernity includes all living humans while excluding archaic populations (Wolpoff & Caspari, 1997).

Defining *modernity* in terms of culture also raises questions. The appearance of modern-sized brains in archaic *Homo* was related to increased reliance on cultural adaptation, but the Upper Paleolithic was a time of great technological innovation and a creative explosion. Upper Paleolithic toolkits contain a preponderance of blade tools, with flint flakes at least twice as long as they are wide. The earliest blade tools come from sites in Africa, but these tools do not make up the majority of the tool types until well into the Upper Paleolithic. The Upper Paleolithic archaeological record also contains a proliferation of expressive arts.

Technological improvements may have reduced the intensity of selective pressures that had previously favored especially massive robust bodies, jaws, and teeth. A marked reduction in overall muscularity accompanied the new emphasis on elongated tools with greater mechanical advantages, more effective techniques of hafting, a switch from thrusting to throwing spears, and the development of net hunting. A climate shift from the extreme cold that prevailed in Eurasia during the last Ice Age to milder conditions may have diminished selective pressure for short stature as an adaptation to conserve body heat.

European fossil evidence instead of incorporating evidence from throughout the globe. Recent fossil evidence for early anatomical modernity in Africa, evidence of regional continuity from Asia, new discoveries of earlier art such as that from the cave at El Castillo in Spain (Pike et al., 2012), and associated genetic studies (including the recent studies of the Denisovans) allow paleoanthropologists to develop more comprehensive theories for the origins of modern humans.

Upper Paleolithic Peoples: The First Modern Humans

What do we mean by *modernity*? Paleoanthropologists look at both skull shape and cultural practices, but still this is a difficult designation to make. Although Cro-Magnons resemble later populations of modern Europeans—in braincase shape, high broad forehead, narrow nasal openings, and common presence of chins—their faces were on average shorter and broader than

Michael Conye/Getty Images

Figure 8.2 A Problematic Definition Living people today such as Aborigines in Australia do not meet the definition of anatomical modernity proposed in the recent African origins model. Some paleoanthropologists suggest that this proves the definition itself is problematic. All living people are clearly full-fledged members of the species *Homo sapiens.*

The Human Origins Debate

On a biological level, the great human origins debate distills down to the question of whether one, some, or all populations of the archaic groups played a role in the evolution of modern *Homo sapiens.* Those supporting the multiregional hypothesis argue for a simultaneous local transition from *Homo erectus* to modern *Homo sapiens* throughout the parts of the world inhabited by members of the genus *Homo.* By contrast, those supporting a theory of recent African origins argue that all contemporary peoples derive from one single population of archaic *Homo sapiens* from Africa. This model proposes that the improved cultural capabilities of anatomically modern humans allowed this group to replace other archaic forms as they began to migrate out of Africa sometime after 100,000 years ago. Both theories are explored in detail following.

The Multiregional Hypothesis

Shared regional characteristics among African, Chinese, and southeastern Asian fossils of archaic *Homo sapiens* imply continuity within these respective populations,

from *H. erectus* through to modern *H. sapiens.* This observation in the fossil evidence strongly supported the interpretation that there was genetic continuity in these regions. For example, in China, Pleistocene fossils from the genus *Homo* consistently have small forward-facing cheeks and flatter faces than their contemporaries elsewhere, as is still true today. In Southeast Asia and Australia, by contrast, skulls are consistently robust, with huge cheeks and forward projection of the jaws. As new molecular research techniques have developed over the past two decades, scientists have amassed genetic data to support the physical evidence.

In this model, gene flow among populations keeps the human species unified throughout the Pleistocene. No speciation events remove ancestral populations such as Asian *H. erectus,* Denisovans, or Neandertals from the line leading to *H. sapiens.* Although proponents of the **multiregional hypothesis** accept the idea of continuity

---

multiregional hypothesis The hypothesis that modern humans originated through a process of simultaneous local transition from *Homo erectus* to *Homo sapiens* throughout the inhabited world.

from the earliest European fossils through the Neandertals to living people, many other paleoanthropologists reject the idea that Neandertals were involved in the ancestry of modern Europeans.

The Recent African Origins Hypothesis

The **recent African origins hypothesis** (also called the *Eve hypothesis* and the *out of Africa hypothesis*) states that anatomically modern humans descended from one specific population of *Homo sapiens*, replacing not just the Neandertals but other populations of archaic *H. sapiens* as our ancestors spread out from their original homeland. This idea did not originate from fossils but from a relatively new technique pioneered in the 1980s that uses mitochondrial DNA (mtDNA) to reconstruct family trees (**Figure 8.3**).

Unlike nuclear DNA (in the cell nucleus), mtDNA is located in the mitochondria, the cellular structures that produce the energy needed to keep cells alive. Because sperm contribute virtually no mtDNA to the fertilized egg, mtDNA is inherited essentially from one's mother and is not subject to recombination through meiosis and fertilization with each succeeding generation as is nuclear DNA. Therefore, changes in mtDNA over time occur only through mutation.

By comparing the mtDNA of living individuals from diverse geographic populations, anthropologists and molecular biologists seek to determine when and where modern *Homo sapiens* originated. As widely reported in the popular press (including cover stories in *Newsweek* and *Time*), preliminary results suggested that the mitochondrial DNA of all living humans could be traced back to a "mitochondrial Eve" who lived in Africa some 200,000 years ago. If so, all other populations of archaic *H. sapiens*, as well as non-African *H. erectus*, would have to be ruled out of the ancestry of modern humans.

For many years, the recent African origins theory has been weakened by the lack of good fossil evidence from Africa. In 2003, however, skulls of two adults and one child, discovered in Ethiopia in East Africa in 1997 (see Anthropologist of Note), were described as anatomically modern (**Figure 8.4**) and were reconstructed and dated to 160,000 years ago (White et al., 2003). The discoverers of these fossils called them *Homo sapiens idaltu* (meaning "elder" in the local Afar language). Although conceding that the skulls are robust, they believe that these skulls have conclusively proved the recent African origins hypothesis, relegating Neandertals to a side branch of human evolution.

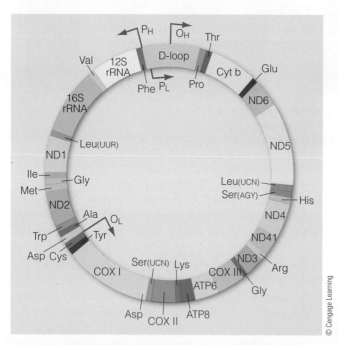

© Cengage Learning

Figure 8.3 Mitochondrial DNA The 16,569 bases in mitochondrial DNA (mtDNA) are organized into circular chromosomes present in large numbers in every cell. The human mtDNA sequence has been entirely sequenced, with functional genes identified. Because mtDNA is maternally inherited and not subject to recombination, it can be used to establish evolutionary relationships. However, population size impacts the preservation of variation in the mtDNA genome and complicates using contemporary mtDNA variation to calibrate a molecular clock.

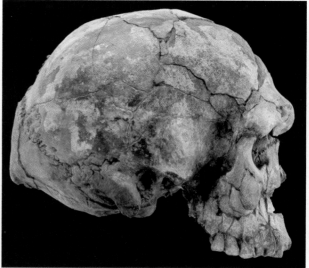

© David L. Brill

Figure 8.4 African Evidence for Anatomical Modernity The recently discovered well-preserved specimens from Herto, Ethiopia, provide the best fossil evidence in support of the recent African origins hypothesis. Though these fossils unquestionably possess an anatomically modern appearance, they are still relatively robust. In addition, it is not clear whether the higher skull and forehead indicate superior cultural abilities.

recent African origins hypothesis The theory that modern humans are all derived from one single population of archaic *Homo sapiens* who migrated out of Africa after 100,000 years ago, replacing all other archaic forms due to their superior cultural capabilities; also called the *Eve hypothesis* and the *out of Africa hypothesis*.

ANTHROPOLOGISTS OF NOTE

Berhane Asfaw (b. 1953) • Xinzhi Wu (b. 1928)

Born in Addis Ababa, Ethiopia, in 1953, **Berhane Asfaw** is a world-renowned paleoanthropologist leading major expeditions in Ethiopia. He is coleader of the international Middle Awash Research Project, the research team responsible for the discovery of spectacular ancestral fossils dating from the entire 6-million-year course of human evolutionary history, including *Ardipithecus ramidus, Australopithecus afarensis, Australopithecus garhi, Homo erectus,* and, most recently, the *Homo sapiens idaltu* fossils from Herto, Ethiopia.

© 1988 David L. Brill

Berhane Asfaw has been involved with most of the major recent finds in Ethiopia and has trained a generation of African paleoanthropologists.

At the June 2003 press conference, organized by Teshome Toga, Ethiopia's minister of culture, Asfaw described the Herto specimens as the oldest anatomically modern humans, likening Ethiopia to the Garden of Eden. This conference marked a shift in the Ethiopian government's stance toward the paleoanthropological research spanning Asfaw's career. Previous discoveries in the Middle Awash were also very important, but the government did not participate in or support this research.

Asfaw entered the discipline of paleoanthropology through a program administered by the Leakey Foundation providing fellowships for Africans to pursue graduate studies in Europe and the United States. Since this program's inception in the late 1970s, the Leakey Foundation has awarded sixty-eight fellowships totaling $1.2 million to Kenyans, Ethiopians, and Tanzanians to pursue graduate education in paleoanthropology.

Asfaw, mentored by U.S. paleoanthropologist Desmond Clark at the University of California, Berkeley, was among the earliest fellows in this program. They first met in 1979 when Asfaw was a senior studying geology in Addis Ababa. Asfaw obtained his doctorate in 1988 and returned to Ethiopia, where he had few Ethiopian anthropological colleagues, and the government had halted fossil exploration. Since that time, Asfaw has recruited and mentored many Ethiopian scholars and now has about a dozen on his team. Local scientists can protect the antiquities, keep fossils from disappearing, and mobilize government support. Asfaw's leadership in paleoanthropology has played a key role in helping the government recognize how important prehistory is for Ethiopia.

Xinzhi Wu is one of China's foremost paleoanthropological scholars, contributing to the development of the discipline for over a half-century. As with many other paleoanthropologists,

Xinzhi Wu pictured here at Zhoukoudian is one of the original formulators of the multiregional continuity hypothesis.

the study of human anatomy has been of vital importance to him.

He began his academic career with a degree from Shanghai Medical College followed by teaching in the Department of Human Anatomy at the Medical College in Dalian before beginning graduate studies in paleoanthropology. He is presently a professor at the Chinese Academy of Sciences Institute of Vertebrate Paleontology and Paleoanthropology in Beijing and the honorary president of the Chinese Society of Anatomical Sciences.

In addition to managing excavations in China and other parts of Asia, Wu has played a major role in the development of theories about modern human origins in cooperation with scholars internationally. He collaborated with Milford Wolpoff of the United States and Alan Thorne of Australia in the development of the theory of multiregional continuity for modern human origins. This theory fits well with the Asian fossil evidence proposing an important place for *Homo erectus* in modern human origins. Interestingly, it builds upon the model for human origins developed by Franz Weidenreich (see Chapter 7).

According to Wu, early humans from China are as old if not older than humans anyplace else. He suggests that the reason more fossils have been found in Africa recently is that Africa has been the site for more excavations.

Zhoukoudian remains a site of particular importance for Wu, as it documents continuous habitation of early humans and one of the earliest sites with evidence of controlled use of fire. Wu has predicted that more important discoveries will still be made at Zhoukoudian because a third of this site has still not been fully excavated. The Chinese government has responded to Wu's suggestions and is presently constructing a 2.4-square-kilometer Peking Man exhibition and paleoanthropology research area at Zhoukoudian.

Wu has welcomed many international scholars to China to study the Asian evidence. He also has led efforts to make descriptions of fossil material available in English. Collaborating with anthropologist Frank Poirier, he published the comprehensive volume *Human Evolution in China,* describing the fossil evidence and archaeological sites with great accuracy and detail.

Reconciling the Evidence

For many years, the recent African origins hypothesis has been the majority position among Western paleoanthropologists, but it does not prevail throughout the international scientific community. Chinese paleoanthropologists, for example, favor the multiregional hypothesis because it fits well with the fossil discoveries from Asia and Australia. By contrast, the recent African origins hypothesis depends more upon the interpretation of fossils and cultural remains from Europe, Africa, and Southwest Asia.

Recent sequencing of the entire human genome for a variety of contemporary populations—as well as for fossil hominins including Cro-Magnons, Neandertals, and Denisovans—has added substantially to the evidence. Genetic studies show that features unique to the Neandertal genome remain in contemporary humans, particularly those of regions inhabited by Neandertals in the past. Further, some contemporary Melanesians share 4 to 6 percent of their DNA with Denisovans, as will be discussed following.

As we have seen, paleoanthropologists on both sides of the modern human origins debate marshal genetic, anatomical, and cultural evidence to both support and critique each hypothesis.

The Genetic Evidence

Though genetic evidence had been the cornerstone of the recent African origins hypothesis, molecular evidence also provided the grounds to challenge it. For example, reanalysis of the original mtDNA data set showed that Africa was not the sole source of mtDNA in modern humans. In addition, because both theories propose African origins for the human line, the genetic evidence could also support the African origins of the genus *Homo* instead of the more recent species *Homo sapiens*. Each model assumes a distinct rate of molecular change. Both models place ultimate human origins firmly in Africa.

DNA analyses contain other problematic assumptions. For example, these models assume steady rates of mutation, when in fact they can be notoriously uneven. They also rely upon the assumption that selective pressures do not impact mtDNA, when in fact variants have been implicated in epilepsy and in a disease of the eye.

Another issue is that DNA is seen as traveling exclusively *from* Africa, when it is known that, over the past 10,000 years, there has been plenty of movement of humans *into* Africa as well. In fact, one study of DNA carried on the Y chromosome (the sex chromosome inherited exclusively in the male line) suggests that DNA on the Y chromosome of some Africans was introduced from Asia, where it originated some 200,000 years ago (Gibbons, 1997). Nevertheless, recent work on the Y chromosome by anthropologist and geneticist Spencer Wells traces the human lineage to a single population living in Africa about 60,000 years ago (Wells, 2002).

Despite the seeming conflict, these data all confirm the importance of gene flow in human evolutionary history. Where the hypotheses differ is in terms of whether this gene flow occurred over the course of 200,000 years or 2 million years.

Starting in 1997, molecular paleoanthropologists under the direction of Svante Pääbo of the Max Planck Institute, began to study the mitochondrial DNA of fossil specimens, starting with the extraction of mtDNA from the original German Neandertal remains, followed by two other Neandertals. Today, this work has expanded to nuclear DNA including the entire Neandertal genome in 2010 (Green et al., 2010), as well as that of the ancient Denisovans (Max Planck Institute for Evolutionary Anthropology, 2012), and Cro-Magnons. Now scientists can quantify how much of a genome the ancient peoples share with contemporary peoples. Neandertals seem to share about 1 percent with living Eurasian peoples, but not with Africans, whereas contemporary Melanesians share 4 to 6 percent genetic identity with ancient Denisovans. Both these observations support regional continuity, though the case might seem to be less strong in Neandertals.

Lower amounts of genetic identity, however, do not necessarily exclude hominin species from human ancestry. The amount of isolation and the inflow of new genes have an impact on the precise percentages of ancient molecular features retained. The Denisovan features may be better preserved in more isolated island populations compared to the Eurasian mainland, which was inhabited by Neandertals and where gene flow occurred more readily.

Further evidence from Australia illustrates that specific gene sequences can "go extinct" though the species itself does not. In this case, an mtDNA sequence present in a skeleton from Australia that is 40,000 to 62,000 years old (and that everyone agrees is anatomically modern) does not appear in recent native Australians (Gibbons, 2001). In short, the genetic evidence that was once the mainstay of the recent African origins hypothesis has now come to favor the multiregional continuity hypothesis.

The Anatomical Evidence

Though the recent fossil discoveries certainly provide evidence of the earliest anatomically modern specimens in Africa, they do not resolve the relationship between biological change in the shape of the skull and cultural change as preserved in the archaeological record (**Figure 8.5**). The changes in the archaeological record and the appearance of anatomically modern skulls are separated by some 100,000 years. The evidence from Southwest Asia is particularly interesting in this regard. Here, at a variety of sites dated to between 50,000 and 100,000 years ago, there are fossils described as both anatomically modern and Neandertal, and they are associated with Mousterian technology.

VISUAL COUNTERPOINT

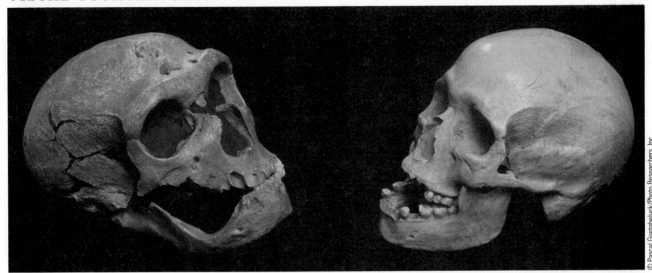

Figure 8.5 **Neandertals Compared to Recent *Homo sapiens*** A comparison of the Neandertal (*left*) and the contemporary *Homo sapiens* (*right*) shows that although both possess large brains, there are distinctive differences in the shape of the skull. The Neandertal has a large face, pronounced brow ridges, and a low, sloping forehead whereas the contemporary *H. sapiens* has a high forehead and a chin. The back of the Neandertal, though not visible from this angle, is robust (as seen in the Herto skull pictured in Figure 8.4). In what other ways is Herto like these two specimens? How do these three skulls compare to the Cro-Magnon skull pictured in Figure 8.1?

Nevertheless, recent African origins proponents argue that anatomically modern peoples coexisted for a time with other archaic populations until the superior cultural capacities of the "moderns" resulted in extinction of the archaic peoples. Especially clear evidence of this is said to exist in Europe, where Neandertals and moderns are said to have coexisted in close proximity between 30,000 and 40,000 years ago. However, defining fossils as either Neandertals or moderns illustrates the difficulty with defining a distinct biological species, given the presence of variation found in humans.

If we think in terms of varied populations, as seen in living humans today, we find that features reminiscent of modern humans can be discerned in some of the later Neandertals. A specimen from Saint Césaire in France, for example, has a higher forehead and a notable chin. A number of other Neandertals, too, show incipient chin development as well as reduced facial protrusion and smaller brow ridges. Conversely, the earliest anatomically modern human skulls from Europe often exhibit features reminiscent of Neandertals (see Chapter 7). In addition, some typical Neandertal features such as the occipital bun are found in diverse living populations today such as Bushmen from southern Africa, Finns and Saami from Scandinavia, and Australian Aborigines. Accordingly, we might view the population of this region between 30,000 and 40,000 years ago as a varied one, with some individuals retaining a stronger Neandertal heritage than others, in whom modern

characteristics are more prominent (**Figure 8.6**). If all these groups were members of the same species, gene flow would be expected, and individuals would express a mosaic of traits. The genetic evidence supports such blending.

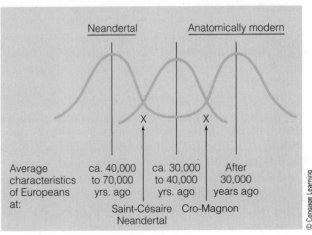

Figure 8.6 **Population Variation** This graph portrays a shift in average characteristics of an otherwise varied population over time from Neandertal to more modern features. Between 30,000 and 40,000 years ago, we would expect to find individuals with characteristics such as those of the Saint-Césaire Neandertal and the almost (but not quite) modern Cro-Magnon. Before and after this period of transition, both Neandertals and moderns had more classic features.

A mix of modern and Neandertal features is so strong in a child's skeleton found in Portugal as to lead several specialists to regard it as clear evidence of hybridization, or successful reproduction between the two groups. This would mean that the two forms are of a single species, rather than separate ones. Others, of course, argue that features interpreted as Neandertal-like might instead be related to this child's "chunky" build.

Scientists supporting the hypothesis that Neandertals are members of the species *Homo sapiens* suggest that the simplest explanation that accounts for all the evidence is that all of these fossils belong to a single varied population, with some individuals showing more typical Neandertal features than others. This accords with archaeological evidence that the intellectual abilities of late Neandertals were no different from those of early moderns.

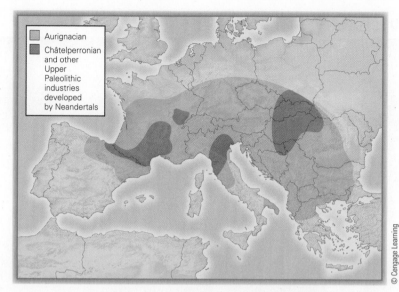

Figure 8.7 **Aurignacian and Châtelperronian Traditions** Between 30,000 and 36,500 years ago, Upper Paleolithic industries developed from the Mousterian tradition by European Neandertals coexisted with the Aurignacian industry, usually associated with anatomically modern humans.

The Cultural Evidence

In addition to the difficulties inherent with finding definitive fossil evidence that the physical or mental makeup of Neandertals would have prevented them from leading a typical Upper Paleolithic way of life, problems also exist with using technology to distinguish Neandertals from their contemporaries. Neandertals and anatomically modern humans alike used Mousterian toolkits during the Middle Paleolithic. At the time of the Upper Paleolithic transition, the latest Neandertals of Europe developed their own Upper Paleolithic technology (the Châtelperronian) comparable to the industries used by anatomically modern *Homo sapiens*. No earlier than 36,500 years ago (Zilhão, 2000), a new Upper Paleolithic technology known as the **Aurignacian tradition**— named after Aurignac, France, where tools of this sort were first discovered—appeared in Europe (**Figure 8.7**).

Though commonly considered to have spread from southwestern Asia, a recent reanalysis suggests instead that the Aurignacian developed exclusively in Europe (Clark, 2002). Although some paleoanthropologists consider anatomically modern humans the makers of Aurignacian tools, skeletal remains and tools are rarely found in association with one another. The central European site of Vindija, Croatia, is a notable exception to this observation because Neandertal remains were found there with an Aurignacian split-bone point (Karavanič & Smith, 2000).

Some have argued that the Upper Paleolithic technology of the Neandertals was a crude imitation of the true technological advancements practiced by anatomically modern humans. In some respects, however, Neandertals outdid their anatomically modern contemporaries, as in the use of red ochre, a substance less frequently used by Aurignacian peoples than by their late Neandertal neighbors. This cannot be a case of borrowing ideas and techniques from Aurignacians because these developments clearly predate the Aurignacian (Zilhão, 2000).

Coexistence and Cultural Continuity

Neandertals and anatomically modern humans also coexisted in Southwest Asia long before the cultural innovations of the Upper Paleolithic (**Figure 8.8**). Here neither the skeletal nor the archaeological evidence supports cultural difference between the fossil groups or absolute biological difference. Although Neandertal skeletons are clearly present at sites such as the caves of Kebara and Shanidar in Israel and Iraq, respectively, skeletons from some older sites have been described as anatomically modern.

At the cave site of Qafzeh near Nazareth in Israel, for example, 90,000-year-old skeletons show none of the Neandertal hallmarks; although their faces and bodies are large and heavily built by today's standards, they are nonetheless claimed to be within the range of living peoples. Yet, a statistical study comparing a number of measurements from among Qafzeh, Upper Paleolithic, and Neandertal skulls found those from Qafzeh to fall in between the anatomically modern and Neandertal norms, though slightly closer to the Neandertal. Nor is the

Aurignacian tradition Toolmaking tradition in Europe and western Asia at the beginning of the Upper Paleolithic.

Epoch
PLEISTOCENE

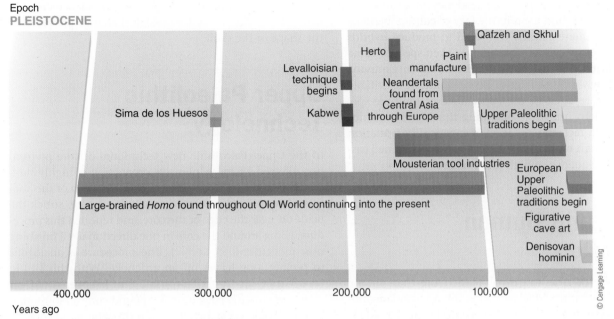

© Cengage Learning

Figure 8.8 **The Cultural Milestones in Human Evolution** Around 400,000 years ago, large-brained members of the genus *Homo* began to be found throughout Africa and Eurasia; corresponding cultural changes are evident as well. Analyses of DNA recovered from the Asian Denisova hominins and late Neandertals indicate a deeper time depth for these "sibling" fossil groups whose lines diverged around 640,000 ago. Large-brained members of the genus *Homo* continue into the present, of course, all members of the unified species *Homo sapiens*.

dentition functionally distinguishable when Qafzeh and Neandertal are compared (Brace, 2000).

Although skeletons from Skhul, a site on Mount Carmel of the same period, resemble those from Qafzeh, they were also part of a population whose continuous range of variation included individuals with markedly Neandertal characteristics. Furthermore, the idea of two distinctly different but coexisting populations receives no support from the archaeological evidence. Individuals living at Skhul and Qafzeh were making and using the same Mousterian tools as those at Kebara and Shanidar, a fact that undercuts the notion of biologically distinct groups with different cultural abilities. Indeed, recent genetic studies also support the notion that these were not biologically distinct groups.

The examination of sites continuously inhabited throughout the Upper Pleistocene provides no significant evidence for behavioral differences between the Middle Paleolithic and early Upper Paleolithic at these sites. For example, the Upper Paleolithic peoples who used Kebara Cave continued to live in exactly the same way as their Neandertal predecessors: They procured the same foods, processed them similarly, used comparable hearths, and disposed of their trash in the same way. The only evident difference is that the Neandertals did not use small stones or cobbles to bank their fires for warmth as did their Upper Paleolithic successors.

Nevertheless, by 28,000 years ago, many of the extreme anatomical features seen in archaic groups like

Neandertals seem to disappear from the European and Southwest and Central Asian fossil record. Instead, people with higher foreheads, smoother brow ridges, and distinct chins seemed to have Eurasia more or less to themselves. However, an examination of the full range of individual human variation across the globe and into the present reveals contemporary humans with skulls not meeting the anatomical definition of *modernity* proposed in the standard evolutionary arguments (recall Figure 8.2). Similarly, living people today possess many Neandertal features such as the occipital buns mentioned earlier. Human populations both now and during the Upper Paleolithic contain considerable physical variability.

Just how much gene flow took place among ancient human populations cannot be known precisely, but the sudden appearance of novel traits in one region later than their appearance elsewhere provides evidence of its occurrence. For example, some Upper Paleolithic remains from North Africa exhibit the kind of midfacial flatness previously seen only in East Asian fossils; similarly, various Cro-Magnon fossils from Europe show the short upper jaws, horizontally oriented cheekbones, and rectangular eye orbits previously seen in East Asians. Conversely, the round orbits, large frontal sinuses, and thin cranial bones seen in some archaic *H. sapiens* skulls from China represent the first appearance there of traits that have greater antiquity in Europe. The movement of these physical traits has a complex genetic basis that depends upon gene flow among populations.

Humans have a remarkable tendency to swap genes between populations, even in the face of cultural barriers. So do our primate cousins who tend to produce hybrids when two subspecies (and sometimes even species) come into contact either naturally or when bred in captivity. Moreover, without such gene flow, evolution inevitably would have resulted in the appearance of multiple species of modern humans, something that clearly has not happened. In fact, the low level of genetic differentiation among modern human populations can be explained easily as a consequence of high levels of gene flow.

Race and Human Evolution

The Neandertal question involves far more than simple interpretation of the fossil evidence. It raises fundamental issues about the relationship between biological and cultural variation. Can a series of biological features indicate particular cultural abilities?

As we examined the fossil record throughout this chapter and others, we made inferences about the cultural capabilities of our ancestors based on biological features in combination with archaeological features. The increased brain size of *Homo habilis* around 2.5 million years ago supported the notion that these ancestors were capable of more complex cultural activities than australopithecines, including the manufacture of stone tools. When we get closer to the present, can we make the same kinds of assumptions? Can we say that only the anatomically modern humans, with high foreheads and reduced brow ridges, and not archaic *Homo sapiens*, even with their modern-sized brains, were capable of making sophisticated tools and representational art?

Supporters of the multiregional hypothesis argue that we cannot. They suggest that using a series of biological features to represent a type of human being (Neandertals) with certain cultural capacities (inferior) is like making assumptions about cultural capabilities of living humans based on their appearance. In living peoples, such an assumption involves stereotyping or even racism. Supporters of the recent African origins hypothesis counter that because their theory embraces African human origins, it could hardly be considered prejudicial.

Although paleoanthropologists all acknowledge African origins for the first bipeds and the genus *Homo*, considerable disagreement exists with regard to the interpretation of the relationship between biological change and cultural change as we approach the present. The fossil and archaeological evidence from the Middle Paleolithic does

not indicate a simple one-to-one correspondence between cultural innovations and a biological change preserved in the shape of the skull.

Upper Paleolithic Technology

In the Upper Paleolithic new techniques of core preparation allowed for more intensive production of highly standardized blades and permitted the proliferation of this tool type. The toolmaker formed a cylindrical core, struck the blade off near the edge of the core, and repeated this procedure, going around the core in one direction until finishing near its center (**Figure 8.9**). The procedure is analogous to peeling long leaves off an artichoke. With this **blade technique**, an Upper Paleolithic flint-knapper could get 75 feet of working edge from a 2-pound core; a Mousterian knapper could get only 6 feet from the same-sized core.

Other efficient techniques of tool manufacture also came into common use at this time. One such method

Upper Paleolithic Tools

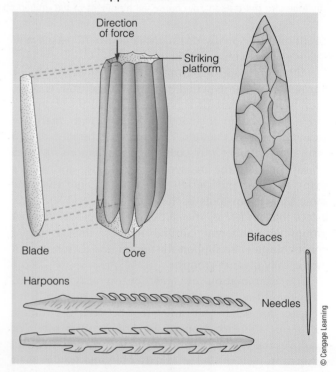

Figure 8.9 **Upper Paleolithic Industries** The techniques of the Upper Paleolithic allowed for the manufacture of a wide variety of tools including the efficient production of blade tools from carefully prepared cores. In addition, pressure-flaking techniques let toolmakers work with bone and antler, as well as stone, to produce finely shaped harpoons and eyed needles, and finely wrought leaf-shaped bifaces characteristic of the Solutrean industry of Europe.

blade technique A method of stone tool manufacture in which long, parallel-sided flakes are struck off the edges of a specially prepared core.

Courtesy of Willy Kemps

Figure 8.10 **Pressure Flaking** Flintknapper Willy Kemps, like others engaged in experimental archaeology, has mastered ancient toolmaking techniques such as pressure flaking, as well as an understanding of raw materials used at various sites. Here, he uses a moose-antler billet to press rather than strike small flakes off the edges of a core. This technique allows flint-knappers past and present to create tools far more intricate than those of the Mousterian, as you can see from his finished products.

is **pressure flaking**, in which a bone, antler, or wooden tool is used to press rather than strike off small flakes as the final step in stone tool manufacture (**Figure 8.10**). The advantage of this technique is that the toolmaker has greater control over the final shape of the tool than is possible with percussion flaking alone. The so-called Solutrean laurel leaf bifaces found in Spain and France are examples of this technique. The longest of these tools is 33 centimeters (13 inches) in length but less than a centimeter (about a quarter of an inch) thick. Through pressure flaking, tools could be worked with great precision into a variety of final forms, and worn tools could be effectively resharpened over and over until they were too small for further use.

Although invented in the Middle Paleolithic, the **burin**, a tool with a chisel-like edge, became more common in the Upper Paleolithic. Burins facilitated the working of bone, horn, antler, and ivory into such useful things as fishhooks, harpoons, and eyed needles. These implements made life easier for *Homo sapiens*, especially in colder northern regions where the ability to stitch together animal hides was particularly important for warmth.

The spear-thrower, also known by its Aztec (Nahuatl) name *atlatl*, appeared at this time as well. Atlatls are devices made of wood horn or bone, one end of which is gripped in the hunter's hand, while the other end has a hole or hook, in or against which the end of the spear is placed. It is held so as to effectively extend the length of the hunter's arm, thereby increasing the velocity of the spear when thrown. The greater thrust made possible through the use of a spear-thrower greatly added to the efficiency of the spear as a hunting tool (**Figure 8.11**). Ancient toolmakers often carved elaborate animal totems into the handles for their spear-throwers (**Figure 8.12**).

pressure flaking A technique of stone tool manufacture in which a bone, antler, or wooden tool is used to press, rather than strike off, small flakes from a piece of flint or similar stone.

burin A stone tool with chisel-like edges used for working bone, horn, antler, and ivory.

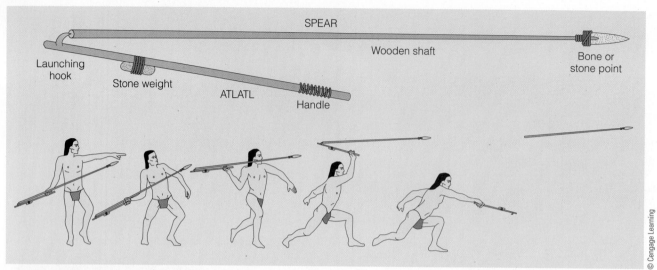

Figure 8.11 Spear-Throwers Spear-throwers (atlatls) allowed Upper Paleolithic individuals to throw spears at animals from a safe distance while still maintaining reasonable speed and accuracy. Upper Paleolithic artists frequently combined artistic expression with practical function, ornamenting their spear-throwers with animal figures.

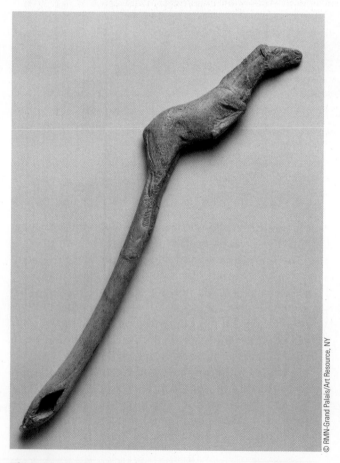

Figure 8.12 Early Production Art Some of the atlatl handles appear to have been relatively mass produced with the identical animal figure such as this 15,000-year-old horse appearing in the archaeological record multiple times. This could be the sign of an individual toolmaker or of a cultural group, or, in some cases, perhaps related to hunting a particular species of animal.

With handheld spears, hunters had to get close to their prey to make the kill. Because many of the animals they hunted were large and fierce, this was a dangerous business. The need to get within close striking range and the improbability of an instant kill exposed the hunter to considerable risk. But with the spear-thrower, the effective killing distance was increased; experiments demonstrate that the effective killing distance of a spear when used with a spear-thrower is between 18 and 27 meters as opposed to significantly less without.

Hunters can safely shorten the killing distance when their kill is assured. The use of poison on spear tips, as employed by contemporary hunters such as the Hadza of Tanzania, will decrease the risk to a hunter at shorter range. The archaeological record provides evidence of this innovation with the invention of tiny sharp stone blades that could possibly serve as dart tips and provide a vehicle for poison delivery. The earliest examples of these "micro-liths" began during the Upper Paleolithic in Africa but did not become widespread until the Mesolithic or Middle Stone Age, as will be described in detail in Chapter 9.

Another important innovation, net hunting, appeared sometime between 22,000 and 29,000 years ago. Knotted nets, made from the fibers of wild plants such as hemp or nettle, left their impression on the clay floors of huts when people walked on them. When the huts later burned, these impressions, baked into the earth, provide evidence that nets existed. Their use accounts for the high number of hare, fox, and other small mammal and bird bones at archaeological sites. Like historically known and contemporary net hunters, such as the Mbuti of the Congo, everyone—men, women, and children—probably participated, frightening animals with loud noises to drive them to where hunters were stationed with their nets.

This method lets hunters amass large amounts of meat without the requirement of great speed or strength.

The invention of the bow and arrow, which appeared first in Africa and arrived in Europe at the end of the Upper Paleolithic, marked another innovation in hunting techniques invented or adopted by some ancient peoples. The bow improves safety by increasing the distance between hunter and prey. Beyond 24 meters (79 feet), the accuracy and penetration of a spear thrown with a spear-thrower diminishes considerably whereas even a poor bow will shoot an arrow farther, with greater accuracy and penetrating power. With a good bow, effective even at nearly 91 meters (300 feet), hunters were able to maintain more distance between themselves and dangerous prey. This dramatically decreased both the risk to the hunter of being seriously injured by an animal fighting for survival and the chance of startling an animal and triggering its flight.

Upper Paleolithic peoples not only had better tools but also a greater diversity of tool types. The highly developed Upper Paleolithic toolkit included implements that varied seasonally as well as geographically. Thus, it is really impossible to speak of a single Upper Paleolithic culture even in Europe, a relatively small and isolated region compared to Asia and Africa. Geologic features such as mountain ranges, oceans, and glaciers isolated groups of people from one another.

Upper Paleolithic industries allowed past peoples to adapt specifically to the various environments in which they were living. Bone yards containing thousands of animal skeletons indicate just how proficient people had become at securing food. For example, at Solutré in France, over a period of many years, Upper Paleolithic hunters killed 10,000 horses; at Predmosti in the Czech Republic, they were responsible for the deaths of 1,000 mammoths. The favored big game of European hunters, however, was reindeer, which they killed in even greater numbers.

Upper Paleolithic Art

Although tools and weapons demonstrate the ingenuity of Upper Paleolithic peoples, artistic expression provides the best evidence of their creativity. Some have argued that this artistry was made possible by a newly evolved biological ability to manipulate symbols and make images. However, the modern-sized brains of archaic *Homo sapiens* and increasingly compelling evidence of the presence of language or behaviors involving symbolism—such as burials—undercut this notion. Like agriculture, which came later (see Chapter 9), the artistic explosion may have been no more than a consequence of innovations made by a people who already had possessed that capacity for tens of thousands of years.

In fact, just as many of the distinctive tools that were commonly used in Upper Paleolithic times first appear in the Middle Paleolithic, so too do objects of art. In Southwest Asia, a crude figurine of volcanic tuff is some 250,000 years old. Although some scholars contest whether this was carved, others believe that it indicates that people had the ability to carve all sorts of things from wood, a substance easier to fashion than volcanic tuff but rarely preserved for long periods of time. But with the Upper Paleolithic transition, the archaeological record becomes quite rich with figurative art that has no apparent utilitarian function. Most notable among these are the various Venus figurines found throughout Eurasia that will be discussed below (**Figure 8.13**).

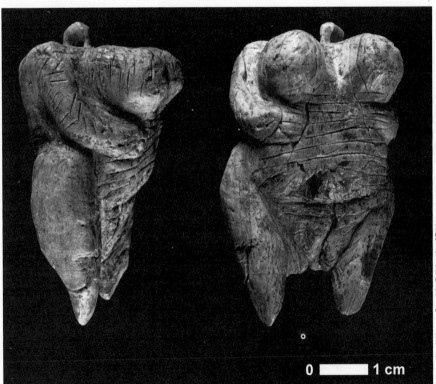

Photographer: H. Jensen; Copyright © University of Tübingen

Figure 8.13 The Hohle Fels Cave Venus This tiny 35,000-year-old Venus figurine (about the size and weight of a small cluster of grapes) was recently discovered in the archaeologically rich Hohle Fels Cave in southwestern Germany. Because it was associated with the assumed earliest presence of undisputed *Homo sapiens* in Europe, the piece changed paleoanthropological interpretations of the origins of figurative art. Prior to this discovery, the earliest figurative art had included only representations of animals; female figurines did not appear until about 30,000 years ago. The exaggerated breasts and vulva and stylized markings on this carving, as on similar prehistoric statuettes known as Venus figurines, indicate the importance of female fertility to our ancestors. Some suggest that these figurines demonstrate that our ancestors may have worshiped the power of females to give birth. Could this worship have predated the appearance of stone carved figurines?

Middle Paleolithic archaeological contexts in various parts of the world also included ochre "crayons" used by ancient peoples to decorate or mark. In southern Africa, for example, regular use of yellow and red ochre goes back 130,000 years, with some evidence as old as 200,000 years. Systematic production of paint took place by 100,000 years ago, as seen in the South African paint factory mentioned in Chapter 7 (Henshilwood et al., 2011). In that site, the Blombos Cave, archaeologists discovered large abalone shells and specialized stones used for grinding ochre pigment. They also found the shoulder bone of a seal from which marrow, a key ingredient in paint, had been removed. Ancient artists had apparently blended the pigment with the marrow, charcoal, and water to make paint. Associated artifacts at this site include large crosshatched chunks of ochre as well as beads smeared with ochre dating to 77,000 years ago.

Ancient people may well have used these pigmented paints on their bodies, as well as objects such as beads and the 50,000-year-old mammoth-tooth *churinga* described in Chapter 7. Recall as well, the use of ochre in burials in Mousterian contexts. The timeline in **Figure 8.14** shows some of the cultural events of the Upper Paleolithic and the years leading into it.

Music

Evidence that music played a role in the lives of Upper Paleolithic peoples is documented through the presence of bone flutes and whistles in various sites, the most recently discovered dated to 35,000 years old. But again, such instruments may have their origin in Middle Paleolithic prototypes, such as the probable Neandertal flute discussed in Chapter 7. Although we cannot know just where and when it happened, some genius discovered that bows could do more than kill prey. They could make music as well. Because the bow and arrow first appeared during the Upper Paleolithic, the musical bow likely got its start then as well. The oldest of the stringed instruments, the musical bow ultimately made possible the rich array of such instruments in use today.

Cave or Rock Art

The earliest evidence of cave art comes from Australia and dates back at least 45,000 years. This consists entirely of geometric patterns and repetitive motifs. Figurative pictures go back 40,000 years in Europe as seen at the cave at El Castillo pictured in the Challenge Issue at the opening of the chapter. Equally old evidence of both engravings and paintings come from rock shelters and outcrops in southern Africa. The 100,000-year-old paint factory in South Africa provides evidence that pictorial art may have appeared there even earlier. Bushmen peoples have continued to make various forms of rock art into the present. Scenes feature both humans and animals, depicted with extraordinary skill, often in association with geometric and other abstract motifs. Some sites reveal that ancient peoples had the seemingly irresistible urge to add to existing rock paintings, whereas others used new sites for creating what we today call graffiti.

The continuation of this rock art tradition, unbroken into the present, has allowed scientists to discover what this art means. Living peoples maintain a close connection between art and shamanism, with many scenes depicting visions seen in states of trance. Distortions in the art, usually of human figures, represent sensations felt by individuals in a state of trance, whereas the geometric designs depict illusions that originate in the central nervous system in altered states of consciousness. These

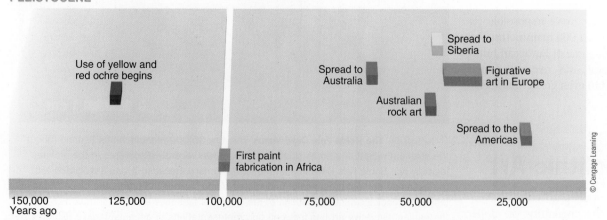

Epoch
PLEISTOCENE

Use of yellow and red ochre begins

Spread to Siberia

Spread to Australia

Figurative art in Europe

Australian rock art

First paint fabrication in Africa

Spread to the Americas

© Cengage Learning

150,000   125,000   100,000   75,000   50,000   25,000
Years ago

Figure 8.14 Cultural Innovation of the Upper Paleolithic This timeline indicates the dates for some for the cultural innovations associated with the Upper Paleolithic. Evidence exists to support the presence of other innovations such as deliberate burial and music during this time period.

Figure 8.15 **Entoptic Phenomena in Cave Art** These rock art paintings from the Kimberley Region of western Australia, depict things seen by dancers communicating with Wandjina (creation spirits) while in states of trance. Simple geometric designs such as zigzags, notches, dots, and spirals (as on the cave ceiling) as well as human and animal figures are common in these paintings.

entoptic phenomena are luminous grids, dots, zigzags, and other designs that seem to shimmer, pulsate, rotate, and expand and are seen as one enters a state of trance (**Figure 8.15**). Sufferers of migraines experience similar hallucinations. Entopic phenomena are typical of the Australian cave art mentioned previously.

In many recent cultures, geometric designs are used as symbolic expressions of genealogical patterns, records of origins, and the afterlife. The animals depicted in this art, often with startling realism, are not the ones most often eaten. Rather, they are powerful beasts like the eland (a large African antelope); this power is important to shamans—individuals skilled at manipulating supernatural forces and spirits for human benefit—who try to harness it for their rain-making, healing, and other rituals.

The most famous Upper Paleolithic art is that of Europe, largely because most researchers of prehistoric art are themselves of European background. Though the earliest of this art took the form of sculpture and engravings—often portraying such animals as reindeer, horses, bears, and ibexes—figurative art abounds in the spectacular paintings on the walls of 200 or so caves in southern France and northern Spain. Until El Castillo was recently dated, the oldest of these are from about 32,000 years ago (**Figure 8.16**). Visually accurate portrayals of Ice Age

mammals—including bison, aurochs, horses, mammoths, and stags—were often painted one on top of another.

Although well represented in other media, humans are not commonly portrayed in cave paintings; neither are scenes of events typical. Instead, the animals are often abstracted from nature and rendered two-dimensionally—no small achievement for these early artists. Sometimes the artists made use of bulges and other features of the rock to impart a more three-dimensional feeling. Frequently, the paintings are in hard-to-get-at places although suitable surfaces in more accessible locations remain untouched. In some caves, the lamps by which the artists worked have been found; these are spoon-shaped objects of sandstone in which animal fat was burned. Experimentation has shown that such lamps would have provided adequate illumination over several hours.

The techniques used by Upper Paleolithic peoples to create their cave paintings were unraveled a decade ago through the experimental work of Michel Lorblanchet. Interestingly, they turn out to be the same ones used by Aboriginal rock painters in Australia and in El Castillo. Lorblanchet's experiments are described in the following Original Study by science writer Roger Lewin.

entoptic phenomena Bright pulsating forms that are generated by the central nervous system and seen in states of trance.

Figure 8.16 Grotte de Chauvet
Ancestral humans painted these images of bison, panthers, and rhinoceroses some 32,000 years ago in the Chauvet Cave in France. These ancient paintings reflect a fundamental need to communicate, to record, and to share observations. Yet the ability to make these ancient paintings, like contemporary human culture, is rooted in the biology of the human hand, eye, and brain. Because these forms of expression appear in the Upper Paleolithic, does that provide evidence of a new species with such capabilities? Or does it simply demonstrate a cultural progression seen throughout the course of human evolutionary history? Do you think that our earlier ancestors made art that did not survive in the archaeological record?

AP Images/Jean Clottes

ORIGINAL STUDY

Paleolithic Paint Job BY ROGER LEWIN

© Cengage Learning

Lorblanchet's recent bid to recreate one of the most important Ice Age images in Europe was an affair of the heart as much as the head. "I tried to abandon my skin of a modern citizen, tried to experience the feeling of the artist, to enter the dialogue between the rock and the man," he explains. Every day for a week in the fall of 1990 he drove the 20 miles from his home in the medieval village of Cajarc into the hills above the river Lot. There, in a small, practically inaccessible cave, he transformed himself into an Upper Paleolithic painter.

And not just any Upper Paleolithic painter, but the one who 18,400 years ago crafted the dotted horses inside the famous cave of Pech Merle.

You can still see the original horses in Pech Merle's vast underground geologic splendor. You enter through a narrow passageway and soon find yourself gazing across a grand cavern to where the painting seems to hang in the gloom. "Outside, the landscape is very different from the one the Upper Paleolithic people saw," says Lorblanchet. "But in here, the landscape is the same as it was more than 18,000 years ago. You see what the Upper Paleolithic people experienced." No matter where you look in this cavern, the eye is drawn back to the panel of horses.

The two horses face away from each other, rumps slightly overlapping, their outlines sketched in black. The animal on the right seems to come alive as it merges with a crook in the edge of the panel, the perfect natural shape for a horse's head. But the impression of naturalism quickly fades as the eye falls on the painting's dark dots. There are more than 200 of them, deliberately distributed within and below the bodies and arcing around the right-hand horse's head and mane. More cryptic still are a smattering of red dots and half-circles and the floating outline of a fish. The surrealism is completed by six disembodied human hands stenciled above and below the animals.

Lorblanchet began thinking about recreating the horses after a research trip to Australia over a decade ago. Not only is Australia a treasure trove of rock art, but its aboriginal people are still creating it. "In Queensland I learned how people painted by spitting pigment onto the rock," he recalls. "They spat paint and used their hand, a piece of cloth, or a feather as a screen to create different lines and other effects. Elsewhere in Australia people used chewed twigs as paintbrushes, but in Queensland the spitting technique worked best." The rock surfaces there were too uneven for extensive brushwork, he adds—just as they are in Quercy.

An upper Paleolithic artist painted this spotted horse in the French cave of Pech Merle. Note the same hand motif as is seen at El Castillo.

© Bildarchiv/Preussischer Kulturbesitz/Art Resource, NY

When Lorblanchet returned home he looked at the Quercy paintings with a new eye. Sure enough, he began seeing the telltale signs of spit-painting—lines with edges that were sharply demarcated on one side and fuzzy on the other, as if they had been airbrushed—instead of the brushstrokes he and others had assumed were there. Could you produce lines that were crisp on both edges with the same technique, he wondered, and perhaps dots too? Archeologists had long recognized that hand stencils, which are common in prehistoric art, were produced by spitting paint around a hand held to the wall. But no one had thought that entire animal images could be created this way. Before he could test his ideas, however, Lorblanchet had to find a suitable rock face—the original horses were painted on a roughly vertical panel 13 feet across and 6 feet high. With the help of a speleologist, he eventually found a rock face in a remote cave high in the hills and set to work.

Following the aboriginal practices he had witnessed, Lorblanchet first made a light outline sketch of the horses with a charred stick. Then he prepared black pigment for the painting. "My intention had been to use manganese dioxide, as the Pech Merle painter did," says Lorblanchet, referring to one of the minerals ground up for paint by the early artists. "But I was advised that manganese is somewhat toxic, so I used wood charcoal instead." (Charcoal was used as pigment by Paleolithic painters in other caves, so Lorblanchet felt he could justify his concession to safety.) To turn the charcoal into paint, Lorblanchet ground it with a limestone block, put the powder in his mouth, and diluted it to the right consistency with saliva and water. For red pigment he used ochre from the local iron-rich clay.

He started with the dark mane of the right-hand horse. "I spat a series of dots and fused them together to represent tufts of hair," he says, unselfconsciously reproducing the spitting action as he talks. "Then I painted the horse's back by blowing the pigment below my hand held so"—he holds his hand flat against the rock with his thumb tucked in to form a straight line—"and used it like a stencil to produce a sharp upper edge and a diffused lower edge. You get an illusion of the animal's rounded flank this way."

He experimented as he went. "You see the angular rump?" he says, pointing to the original painting. "I reproduced that by holding my hand perpendicular to the rock, with my palm slightly bent, and I spat along the edge formed by my hand and the rock." He found he could produce sharp lines, such as those in the tail and in the upper hind leg, by spitting into the gap between parallel hands.

The belly demanded more ingenuity; he spat paint into a V-shape formed by his two splayed hands, rubbed it into a curved swath to shape the belly's outline, then finger-painted short protruding lines to suggest the animals' shaggy hair. Neatly outlined dots, he found, could not be made by blowing a thin jet of charcoal onto the wall. He had to spit pigment through a hole made in an animal skin. "I spent seven hours a day for a week," he says. "Puff . . . puff . . . puff. . . . It was exhausting, particularly because there was carbon monoxide in the cave. But you experience something special, painting like that. You feel you are breathing the image onto the rock—projecting your spirit from the deepest part of your body onto the rock surface."

Was that what the Paleolithic painter felt when creating this image? "Yes, I know it doesn't sound very scientific," Lorblanchet says of his highly personal style of investigation, "but the intellectual games of the structuralists haven't got us very far, have they? Studying rock art shouldn't be an intellectual game. It is about understanding humanity. That's why I believe the experimental approach is valid in this case."

Excerpted from Lewin, R. (1993). Paleolithic paint job. Discover 14 *(7), 67–69. Copyright ©1993 The Walt Disney Co. Reprinted with permission of* Discover Magazine.

Theories to account for the early European cave art often depend on conjectural and subjective interpretations. Some have argued that it is art for art's sake, but if that is so, why were animals often painted over one another, and why were they placed in inaccessible places? The latter might suggest that they served ceremonial purposes and that the caves were religious sanctuaries.

One suggestion is that the animals were drawn to ensure success in the hunt, another that their depiction was seen as a way to promote fertility and increase the size of the herds on which humans depended. In Altamira Cave in northern Spain, for example, the art shows a pervasive concern for the sexual reproduction of the bison. In cave art generally, though, the animals painted show little relationship to those most frequently hunted. Furthermore, cave art rarely includes depictions of animals being hunted, killed, copulating, birthing, or with exaggerated sexual parts, as is shown in the Venus figurines (Conard, 2009).

Another suggestion is that initiation rites, such as those marking the transition to adulthood, took place in the painted galleries. In support of this idea, footprints, most of which are small, have been found in the clay floors of several caves, and in one they even circle a modeled clay bison. As well, it appears that the small hands of ancient children created some of the finger "flutings," unpigmented grooves made into the soft surface of the cave walls (Sharpe & Van Gelder, 2006). The presence of children in the caves suggests that elders were transmitting knowledge to the new generation through painted animals and the countless "signs" and abstract designs that accompany much Upper Paleolithic art. Some have interpreted these markings as tallies of animals killed or as a reckoning of time according to a lunar calendar.

The abstract designs, including those such as the spots on the Pech Merle horses, suggest yet another possibility. For the most part, these are just like the entoptic designs seen by subjects in experiments dealing with altered states of consciousness and that are so consistently present in the rock art of southern Africa. Furthermore, the rock art of southern Africa shows the same painting of new images over older ones, as well as the same sort of fixation on large, powerful animals instead of the ones most often eaten. Thus, the cave art of Europe may well represent the same depictions of trance experiences, painted after the fact. Consistent with this interpretation, the isolation of the caves and the shimmering light on the cave walls themselves are conducive to the sort of sensory distortion that can induce trance.

Ornamental Art

Artistic expression, whatever its purpose may have been, was not confined to rock surfaces and portable objects. Upper Paleolithic peoples also ornamented their bodies with necklaces, rings, bracelets, and anklets made of perforated animal teeth, shells, and beads of bone, stone, and ivory. Clothing, too, was adorned with beads. Quite a lot of art was probably also executed in more delicate materials such as wood carving, painting on bark, and animal skins, which have not been preserved. Thus, the rarity of Upper Paleolithic art in some parts of the inhabited world may be due to the fact that some materials did not survive in the archaeological record, not that they never existed.

Gender and Art

As shown in Figure 8.13, the Upper Paleolithic also includes numerous portrayals of voluptuous women with body parts often described as exaggerated. Many appear to be pregnant, and some are shown in birthing postures. These so-called Venus figures have been found at sites from southwestern France to as far as Siberia. Made of stone, ivory, antler, or baked clay, they differ little in style from place to place, testifying to the sharing of ideas over vast distances. Although some have interpreted the Venuses as objects associated with a fertility cult, others suggest that they may have been exchanged to cement alliances between groups.

Art historian LeRoy McDermott has suggested that the Venus figurines are "ordinary women's views of their own bodies" and the earliest examples of self-representation (McDermott, 1996). He suggests that the distortions and exaggerations of the female form visible in the Venus figurines derive from the ancient artist looking down over her own pregnant body. Paleolithic archaeologist Margaret Conkey opened the door to such interpretations through her work combining gender theory and feminist theory with the science of archaeology.

With a particular interest in the Upper Paleolithic art of Europe, Conkey has spent decades challenging the traditional notion that Paleolithic art was made by male artists as an expression of spiritual beliefs related to hunting activities. She emphasizes that many reconstructions of behavior in the past rely upon contemporary gender norms to fill in blanks left in the archaeological record. Conkey, believing that today's stereotypes may be distorting our view of the past, seeks clues about the role of gender in the archaeological research she conducts (Gero & Conkey, 1991).

In this regard, note that current scientists tend to describe Venus figurines largely in sexual terms rather than in terms of fertility and birth. For example, in a commentary in the prestigious journal *Nature* that accompanied the description of the Hohle Fels Cave Venus, British archaeologist Paul Mellars states: "The figure is explicitly—and blatantly—that of a woman, with an exaggeration of sexual characteristics (large, projecting breasts, a greatly enlarged and explicit vulva, and bloated belly and thighs) that by twenty-first-century standards could be seen as bordering on the pornographic" (Mellars, 2009, p. 176).

Mellars's reaction to the Venus figurine reflects present-day attitudes toward the nude female form rather than the intent of an ancient artist. Perhaps the artist was a female, looking at her own pregnant form or remembering the experience of giving birth. Although the gender and the intention of the artist behind the Venus figurine cannot be known for sure, it is easy to imagine that pregnancy and the birth process were at least as awe-inspiring to Paleolithic peoples as were hunting experiences.

Human biology also provides us with some clues. Breasts and belly enlarge during pregnancy; the tissues around the vulva enlarge and stretch dramatically during the birth process. Breasts swell further with milk after a birth. Mellars's interpretation of the artistic depiction of these biological changes as "pornographic" derives from the gender norms of his particular culture. Many contemporary peoples with different worldviews would not react to the figurine in these terms.

© Goran Burenhult

Figure 8.17 **Upper Paleolithic Mammoth Bone Dwelling** Pictured is a reconstructed dwelling made from interlocked and lashed mammoth bones. These dwellings are typically round in form with a central hearth or several scattered hearths. Pits with bones and butchering areas and flint-knapping areas often surround the dwellings. They tend to be strategically built along old river terraces near migration pathways that grazing animals would take between steppes and rivers. Although most of these dwellings date to between 14,000 and 20,000 years ago, one from the site of Moldova dates back to 44,000 years ago and is associated with typical Neandertal tools. Others argue that the Moldova site represents the remains of a hunting blind.

Other Aspects of Upper Paleolithic Culture

Upper Paleolithic peoples lived not only in caves and rock shelters but also in structures built out in the open. In Ukraine, for example, remains of sizable settlements have been found in which huts were built on frameworks of intricately stacked mammoth bones (Figure 8.17). Where the ground was frozen, cobblestones were heated and placed in the earth to sink in, thereby providing sturdy, dry floors. Instead of shallow depressions or flat surfaces that radiated little heat, their hearths were stone-lined pits that conserved heat for extended periods and made for more efficient cooking.

For the outdoors, Upper Paleolithic peoples had the same sort of tailored clothing worn in historic times by Arctic and sub-Arctic peoples. Further, they engaged in long-distance trade, as indicated, for example, by the presence of seashells and amber from the Baltic Sea in northern Europe at sites several hundred kilometers

from the sources of these materials. Although Middle Paleolithic peoples also made use of rare and distant materials, these practices became far more regular in the Upper Paleolithic.

The Spread of Upper Paleolithic Peoples

Upper Paleolithic peoples expanded into regions previously uninhabited by their archaic forebears. Colonization of southern Siberia by the Denisovans dates back about 280,000 years, and it appears that the Denisovans were interbreeding with *Homo sapiens* there between 40,000 and 50,000 years ago. Upper Paleolithic peoples reached the northeastern part of that region about 10,000 years later. Although reaching this region did not involve crossing large bodies of water, inhabiting Greater Australia and the Americas did require such voyages.

The Sahul

Much earlier, possibly by at least 60,000 years ago, people managed to get to Australia, Tasmania, and New Guinea, then connected to one another in a single landmass called the **Sahul** (Rice, 2000). To do this, they had to use some kind of watercraft because the Sahul was separated from the islands (which are geologically a part of the Asian landmass) of Java, Sumatra, Borneo, and Bali. At times of maximum glaciation and low sea levels, these islands were joined to one another in a single landmass called **Sunda**, but a deep ocean trench (called the Wallace Trench, after Alfred Russel Wallace, who, as described in Chapter 2, discovered natural selection at the same time as Charles Darwin) always separated Sunda and Sahul (Figure 8.18).

Anthropologist Joseph Birdsell suggested several routes of island hopping and seafaring to make the crossing between these landmasses (Birdsell, 1977). Each of these routes involves crossing open water without land visible on the horizon. The earliest known site in New Guinea dates to 40,000 years ago. Sites in Australia are dated to even earlier, but these dates are especially contentious because they involve the critical question of the relationship between anatomical modernity and the presence of humanlike culture.

Early dates for habitation of the Sahul indicate that archaic *Homo* rather than anatomically modern forms possessed the cultural capacity for oceanic navigation. Evidence from a recent genetic analysis of a hair sample taken from an Australian Aborigine over a century ago indicates direct spread from Africa for some of these people (Rasmussen et al., 2011). Once in Australia, these people used ochre to create some of the world's earliest sophisticated rock art, perhaps even earlier than the more famous European cave paintings. One painting in the Arnhem Land plateau depicts a species of giant bird thought to have gone extinct around 40,000 years ago.

Interestingly, considerable physical variation is seen in Australian fossil specimens from this period. Some specimens have the high forehead characteristic of anatomical modernity whereas others possess traits providing excellent evidence of continuity between living Aborigines and the earlier *Homo erectus* and archaic *Homo sapiens* fossils from Indonesia. Willandra Lakes—the fossil lake region of southeastern Australia, far from where the earliest archaeological evidence of human habitation of the continent was found—is particularly rich with fossils. The variation present in these fossils illustrates the problems inherent with making a one-to-one correspondence between the skull of a certain shape and cultural capabilities.

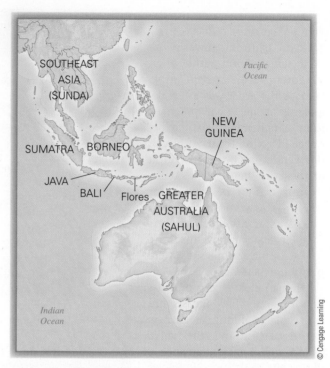

Figure 8.18 Sea Level and the Coastlines of Sunda and Sahul Habitation of Australia and New Guinea (joined together with Tasmania as a single landmass called Sahul) was dependent upon travel across the open ocean even at times of maximum glaciation when sea levels were low. This figure shows the coastlines of Sahul and Sunda (Southeast Asia plus the islands of Java, Sumatra, Borneo, and Bali) now and in the past. As sea levels rose with melting glaciers, sites of early human habitation were submerged under water.

Other evidence for sophisticated ritual activity in early Australia is provided by the burial of a man at least 40,000 and possibly 60,000 years ago from the Willandra Lakes region. His body was positioned with his fingers intertwined around one another in the region of his penis, and red ochre had been scattered over the body. It may be that this pigment had more than symbolic value; for example, its iron salts have antiseptic and deodorizing properties, and there are recorded instances in which red ochre is associated with prolonging life and is used medicinally to treat particular conditions or infections. One historically known Aborigine society is reported to have used ochre to heal wounds, scars, and burns and to use it for those in pain, covering the body with the substance and placing it in the sun to promote sweating. See this chapter's Globalscape to learn about the importance of Willandra Lakes to global and local heritage today.

As in many parts of the world, paleoanthropologists conducting research on human evolution in Australia are essentially constructing a view of history that conflicts with the beliefs of Aborigines. The story of human evolution is utterly dependent on Western conceptions of time, relationships established through genetics, and

---

Sahul The greater Australian landmass including Australia, New Guinea, and Tasmania. At times of maximum glaciation and low sea levels, these areas were continuous.

Sunda The combined landmass of the contemporary islands of Java, Sumatra, Borneo, and Bali that was continuous with mainland Southeast Asia at times of low sea levels corresponding to maximum glaciation.

Globalscape

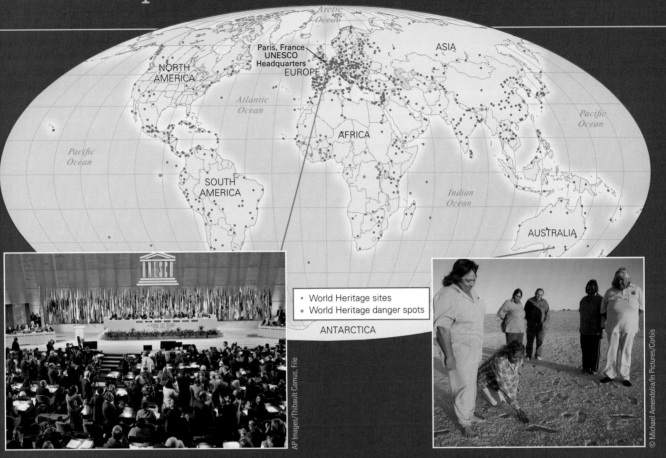

- • World Heritage sites
- • World Heritage danger spots

AP Images/Thibault Camus, File

© Michael Amendolia/In Pictures/Corbis

Whose Lakes Are These?

Paleoanthropologists regularly travel to early fossil sites and to museums where original fossil specimens are housed. Increasingly, these same destinations are becoming popular with tourists. Making sites accessible to everyone while protecting the sites requires considerable skill and knowledge. But most importantly, long before the advent of paleoanthropology or paleotourism, these sites were and are the homelands of living people.

Aboriginal people have lived along the shores of the Willandra Lakes region of Australia for at least 50,000 years. They have passed down their stories and cultural traditions even as the lakes dried up and a spectacular crescent-shaped, wind-formed dune (called a *lunette*) remained. The Mungo lunette has particular cultural significance to three Aboriginal tribal groups. Several major fossil finds from the region include cremated remains as well as an ochred burial, both dated to at least 40,000 years ago. Nearly 460 fossilized footprints dated to between 19,000 and 23,000 years ago were made by people of all ages who lived in the region when

the Willandra Lakes were still full of water. How can a place of local and global significance be appropriately preserved and honored?

Since 1972, UNESCO's World Heritage List has been an important part of maintaining places like Willandra Lakes, which was itself inscribed as a World Heritage Site in 1981. Individual states apply to UNESCO for site designation, and if approved they receive financial and political support for maintaining the site. When designated sites are threatened by natural disaster, war, pollution, or poorly managed tourism, they are placed on a danger list, indicated with a red dot on the map above, forcing the local governments to institute measures to protect the sites in order to continue receiving UNESCO support.

Each year approximately thirty new World Heritage sites are designated. In 2011 the list included 962 properties: 188 natural preserves, 745 cultural sites, and 29 mixed sites. Fossil and archaeological sites are well represented on the World Heritage List. The Willandra Lakes site is recognized for both natural and cultural value.

Although important to the world community, Willandra Lakes has particular meaning to the Aborigines. Aunty Beryl Carmichael, an elder of the Ngiyaampaa people, explains that this land is integrated with her culture:

> Because when the old people would tell the stories, they'd just refer to them as "marrathal warkan," which means long, long time ago, when time first began for our people, as people on this land after creation. We have various sites around in our country, we call them the birthing places of all our stories. And of course, the stories are embedded with the lore that governs this whole land. The air, the land, the environment, the universe, the stars.[a]

Not only are Aunty Beryl's stories and the land around Willandra Lakes critical for the Ngiyaampaa and other Aboriginal groups, but their survival ultimately contributes to all of us.

The following lists the sites considered endangered at the June 2011 meeting of the World Heritage Committee. Committee members included representatives from countries throughout the globe including: Australia, Bahrain, Barbados, Brazil, Cambodia, China, Egypt, France, Iraq, Jordan, Mali, Mexico, Nigeria, Russia, South Africa, Sweden, Switzerland, Thailand, and the United Arab Emirates.

Afghanistan
Cultural Landscape and Archaeological Remains of the Bamiyan Valley (2003)
Minaret and Archaeological Remains of Jam (2002)

Belize
Belize Barrier Reef Reserve System (2009)

Central African Republic
Manovo-Gounda St. Floris National Park (1997)

Chile
Humberstone and Santa Laura Saltpeter Works (2005)

Colombia
Los Katíos National Park (2009)

Côte d'Ivoire
Comoé National Park (2003)
Mount Nimba Strict Nature Reserve (1992)

Democratic Republic of the Congo
Garamba National Park (1996)
Kahuzi-Biega National Park (1997)
Okapi Wildlife Reserve (1997)
Salonga National Park (1999)
Virunga National Park (1994)

Egypt
Abu Mena (2001)

Ethiopia
Simien National Park (1996)

Georgia
Bagrati Cathedral and Gelati Monastery (2010)
Historical Monuments of Mtskheta (2009)

Guinea
Mount Nimba Strict Nature Reserve (1992)

Honduras
Río Plátano Biosphere Reserve (2011)

Indonesia
Tropical Rainforest Heritage of Sumatra (2011)

Iran, Islamic Republic of
Bam and Its Cultural Landscape (2004)

Iraq
Ashur (Qal'at Sherqat) (2003)
Samarra Archaeological City (2007)

Jerusalem (site proposed by Jordan)
Old City of Jerusalem and Its Walls (1982)

Madagascar
Rainforests of the Atsinanana (2010)

Niger
Air and Ténéré Natural Reserves (1992)

Pakistan
Fort and Shalamar Gardens in Lahore (2000)

Peru
Chan Chan Archaeological Zone (1986)

Philippines
Rice Terraces of the Philippine Cordilleras (2001)

Senegal
Niokolo-Koba National Park (2007)

Serbia
Medieval Monuments in Kosovo (2006)

Tanzania, United Republic of
Ruins of Kilwa Kisiwani and Ruins of Songo Mnara (2004)

Uganda
Tombs of Buganda Kings at Kasubi (2010)

United States of America
Everglades National Park (2010)

Venezuela
Coro and Its Port (2005)

Yemen
Historic Town of Zabid (2000)

Global Twister

The listing of endangered sites brings global pressure on a state to find ways to protect the natural and cultural heritage contained within its boundaries. Do you think this method of global social pressure is effective?

---

[a]"Why the stories are told," Aunty Beryl Carmichael. *Aboriginal Culture: Dreamtime Stories*. www.rmwebed.com.au/HSIE/y10/abc/dreamtime/dreamtime.htm

a definition of what it means to be human. All of these theories are at odds with Aboriginal beliefs about human origins. Still, while conducting their research on human evolution, paleoanthropologists working in Australia have advocated and supported the Aboriginal culture.

The Americas

Although scientists concur that American Indian ancestry can be traced ultimately back to Asian origins, just when people arrived in the Americas has been a matter of lively debate. This debate draws upon geographical, cultural, and biological evidence.

The conventional wisdom has long been that the first people migrated into North America over dry land that connected Siberia to Alaska. This land bridge was a consequence of the buildup of great continental glaciers. As the ice masses grew, there was a worldwide lowering of sea levels, causing an emergence of land in places like the Bering Strait where seas today are shallow. Thus, Alaska became, in effect, an eastward extension of Siberia (**Figure 8.19**). Climatic patterns of the Ice Age kept this land bridge, known as Beringia or the Bering Land Bridge, relatively ice free and covered instead with lichens and mosses that could support herds of grazing animals. It is possible that Upper Paleolithic peoples could have come to the Americas simply by following herd animals. The latest genetic evidence indicates movement took place back and forth across Beringia.

According to geologists, conditions were right for ancient humans and herd animals to traverse Beringia between 11,000 and 25,000 years ago. Though this land bridge was also open between 40,000 and 75,000 years ago, there is no evidence that conclusively confirms human migration at these earlier dates. As with the Sahul, early dates open the possibility of spread to the Americas by archaic *Homo*.

Although ancient Siberians did indeed spread eastward, it is now clear that massive glaciers blocked their way until 13,000 years ago at the earliest (Marshall, 2001). By then, people were already living farther south in the Americas. Thus, the question of how people first came to this hemisphere has been reopened. One possibility is that, like the first Australians, the first Americans may have come by boat or rafts, perhaps traveling between islands or ice-free pockets of coastline, from as far away as the Japanese islands and down North America's northwestern coast. Hints of such voyages are provided by a handful of North American skeletons (such as Kennewick Man) that bear a closer resemblance to the aboriginal Ainu people of northern Japan and their forebears than they do to other Asians or contemporary Native Americans. Unfortunately, because sea levels were lower than they are today, coastal sites used by early voyagers would now be under water.

Figure 8.19 **Land Bridge to the Americas** The Arctic conditions and glaciers in northeastern Asia and northwestern North America provided both opportunities and challenges for ancient peoples spreading to the Americas. On the one hand, the Arctic climate provided a land bridge (Beringia) between the continents, but on the other hand, the harsh environment posed considerable difficulties to humans. Ancient peoples may have also come to the Americas by sea. Once in North America, glaciers spanning a good portion of the continent determined the areas open to habitation.

Securely dated objects from Monte Verde, a site in south-central Chile, place people in southern South America by 14,500 years ago, if not earlier. Assuming the first populations spread from Siberia to Alaska, linguist Johanna Nichols suggests that the first people to arrive in North America did so by 20,000 years ago. She bases this estimate on the time it took various other languages to spread from their homelands—including Eskimo languages in the Arctic and Athabaskan languages from interior western Canada to New Mexico and Arizona (Navajo). Nichols's conclusion is that it would have taken at least 7,000 years for people to reach south-central Chile (Nichols, 2008). Others suggest people arrived in the Americas closer to 30,000 years ago or even earlier.

A recent genetic study using mitochondrial and nuclear DNA indicates that the American Indian Upper Paleolithic peoples separated from Asian peoples prior to 40,000 years ago and occupied Beringia for about 20,000 years with little population growth (Kitchen, Miyamoto, & Mulligan, 2008). Population size then expanded again as these peoples crossed Beringia between 15,000 and 17,000 years ago but then took different paths. One group traveled down the Pacific Coast and the other down the center of the continent. Although the dates generated in this study are as early as others have suggested, these findings support the notion that distinct language groups made separate migrations.

Another study suggests back and forth exchanges between Siberia and North America (Tamm et al., 2007). Yet a third study suggests three waves of migration across Beringia (Reich et al., 2012). As is the case with all investigations of the distant past, the narrative of how the Americas were peopled is under construction. Genetic data must be crosschecked with morphological data, linguistic data, and with the archaeological evidence. Each new discovery in the field or in the lab contributes to this chronicle. Careful verifications among various kinds of data allow for the eventual refinement of the account.

The picture currently emerging, then, is of people, who may not have looked like modern Native Americans, arriving by boats or rafts and spreading southward and eastward over time. In fact, contact back and forth between North America and Siberia never stopped. In all probability, it became more common as the glaciers melted away. As a consequence, through gene flow as well as later arrivals of people from Asia, people living in the Americas came to have the broad faces, prominent cheekbones, and round cranial vaults that tend to characterize the skulls of many Native Americans today. Still, Native Americans, like all human populations, are physically variable. The Kennewick Man controversy described in Chapter 5 illustrates the complexities of establishing ethnic identity based on the shape of the skull. In order to trace the history of the peopling of the Americas, anthropologists must combine archaeological, linguistic, and cultural information with evidence of biological variation.

Although the earliest technologies in the Americas remain poorly known, they gave rise in North America, about 12,000 years ago, to the distinctive fluted spear points of **Paleoindian** hunters of big game, such as mammoths, mastodons, caribou, and now extinct forms of bison. Fluted points are finely made, with large channel flakes removed from one or both surfaces. This thinned section was inserted into the notched end of a spear shaft for a sturdy haft. Fluted points are found from the Atlantic seaboard to the Pacific Coast, and from Alaska down into Panama. The efficiency of the hunters who made and used these points may have hastened the extinction of the mammoth and other large Pleistocene mammals. By driving large numbers of animals over cliffs, they killed

many more than they could possibly use, thus wasting huge amounts of meat.

This does not mean, however, that the first Americans were all big game hunters. Other Paleoindians, including those who inhabited Monte Verde in Chile, far distant from Beringia, provide evidence of a very different way of life. These people foraged for plants and seafood and consumed a variety of smaller mammals.

Upper Paleolithic peoples in Australia and the Americas, like their counterparts in Africa and Eurasia, possessed sophisticated technology that was efficient and appropriate for the environments they inhabited. As in other parts of the world, when a technological innovation such as the fluted points begins, this technology is rapidly disseminated among the people inhabiting the region.

Still, some innovations never became a part of a group's cultural repertoire. For example, Australian Aborigines retained the spear and spear-thrower, never adopting or inventing the bow and arrow. The bow and arrow was eventually widely used in the Americas, but it appeared there much later than it did in Africa and Eurasia. In each place, subsistence practices synchronized with the environment and other aspects of the local culture.

Major Paleolithic Trends

As we look at the larger picture, since the time the genus *Homo* appeared, evolving humans came to rely increasingly on cultural, as opposed to biological, adaptation. To handle environmental challenges, evolving humans developed appropriate tools, clothes, shelter, use of fire, and so forth rather than relying upon biological adaptation of the human organism. This was true whether human populations lived in regions that were hot or cold, wet or dry, forested or grassy. Though culture is ultimately based on what might loosely be called brainpower or, more formally, **cognitive capacity**, it is learned and not carried by genes. Therefore, cultural innovations may occur rapidly and can easily be transferred among individuals and groups.

Scientists have recently documented key differences in the proteins involved in brain metabolism in humans compared to other species that may account for some of this brainpower. Unfortunately, these metabolic changes are also associated with schizophrenia, indicating that there may have been some costs in the process. This study suggests that the cultural practice of cooking freed the body to devote more energy to brain metabolism. Although cooking was certainly an innovation of ancient *Homo*, the varied low-fat diet and high exercise of our ancestors were in general healthier than the dietary patterns prevailing in many parts of the world today. See this chapter's Biocultural Connection for a discussion of how a return to the diets and lifestyles of our forebears may improve human health.

Paleoindians The earliest inhabitants of North America.

cognitive capacity A broad concept including intelligence, educability, concept formation, self-awareness, self-evaluation, attention span, sensitivity in discrimination, and creativity.

BIOCULTURAL CONNECTION

Paleolithic Prescriptions for Diseases of Today

Throughout most of our evolutionary history, humans led more physically active lives and ate a more varied low-fat diet than we do now. Our ancestors did not drink alcohol or smoke. They spent their days scavenging or hunting for animal protein while gathering vegetable foods, with some insects thrown in for good measure. They stayed fit through traveling great distances each day over the savannah and beyond.

Though we hail increased life expectancy as one of modern civilization's greatest accomplishments, this phenomenon, brought about in part by the discovery and dissemination of antibiotics during the middle of the twentieth century, is quite recent. Anthropologists George Armelagos and Mark Nathan Cohen suggest that the downward trajectory for human health began when we left behind our Paleolithic lifeways and began farming instead of hunting and gathering and settled into permanent villages some 10,000 years ago.[a] The chronic diseases that linger—such as diabetes, heart disease, substance abuse, and high blood pressure—have their roots in this shift.

The prevalence of these "diseases of civilization" has increased rapidly over the past sixty-five years. Anthropologists Melvin Konner and Marjorie Shostak and physician Boyd Eaton have suggested that our Paleolithic ancestors left us with a prescription for a cure. They propose that as "stone-agers in a fast lane," people's health will improve by returning to the lifestyle to which their bodies are adapted.[b] Such Paleolithic prescriptions are an example of evolutionary medicine—a branch of medical anthropology that uses evolutionary principles to contribute to human health.

Evolutionary medicine bases its prescriptions on the idea that rate of cultural change exceeds the rate of biological change. Our food-forager physiology was shaped over millions of years, whereas the cultural changes leading to contemporary lifestyles have occurred rapidly. For example, tobacco was domesticated in the Americas only a few thousand years ago and was widely used as both a narcotic and an insecticide. Alcoholic beverages, which depend on the domestication of a variety of plant species such as hops, barley, and corn, also could not have arisen without village life, as the fermentation process requires time and watertight containers. However, the high-starch diets and sedentary lifestyle of village life contributes to diabetes and heart disease.

Our evolutionary history offers clues about the diet and lifestyle to which our bodies evolved. By returning to our ancient lifeways, we can make the diseases of civilization a thing of the past.

BIOCULTURAL QUESTION

Can you imagine what sort of Paleolithic prescriptions our evolutionary history would contribute for modern behaviors, such as childrearing practices, sleeping, and work patterns? Are there any ways that your culture or personal lifestyle is well aligned with past lifeways?

---

[a] Cohen, M. N., & Armelagos, G. J. (Eds.). (1984a). *Paleopathology at the origins of agriculture.* Orlando: Academic Press.

[b] Eaton, S. B., Konner, M., & Shostak, M. (1988). Stone-agers in the fast lane: Chronic degenerative diseases in evolutionary perspective. *American Journal of Medicine 84* (4), 739–749.

Certain trends stand out from the information anthropologists have gathered about the Old Stone Age in most parts of the world. One was toward increasingly more sophisticated, varied, and specialized toolkits. Tools became progressively lighter and smaller, resulting in the conservation of raw materials and a better ratio between length of cutting edge and weight of stone. Tools also became specialized according to region and function. Instead of crude all-purpose tools, more effective particularized devices were made to deal with the differing conditions of savannah, forest, and shore.

As humans came to rely increasingly on culture as a means to meet the challenges of existence, they were able to inhabit new environments. With more efficient tool technology, population size could increase, allowing humans to spill over into more diverse environments.

Improved cultural abilities may also have played a role in the reduction of heavy physical features, favoring instead decreased size and weight of face and teeth, the development of larger and more complex brains, and ultimately a reduction in body size and robustness. This dependence on intelligence rather than bulk provided the key for humans' increased reliance on cultural rather than physical adaptation. The development of conceptual thought can be seen in symbolic artifacts and signs of ritual activity throughout the world.

Through Paleolithic times, at least in the colder parts of the world, hunting became more important, and people became more proficient at it. Humans' intelligence enabled them to develop composite tools as well as the social organization and cooperation so important for survival and population growth. As discussed in the next chapter, this trend was reversed during the Mesolithic, when hunting lost its preeminence, and the gathering of wild plants and seafood became increasingly important.

As human populations grew and spread, cultural differences between regions also became more marked. Although some indications of cultural contact and intercommunication are evident in the development of long-distance trade networks, tool assemblages developed in response to the specific challenges and resources of specific environments.

As Paleolithic peoples eventually spread over all the continents of the world, including Australia and the Americas, changes in climate and environment called for new kinds of adaptations. In forest environments, people needed tools for working wood; on the open savannah and plains, humans began to use the bow and arrow to hunt the game they could not stalk closely; the people in settlements that grew up around lakes and along rivers and coasts developed harpoons and hooks; in the sub-Arctic regions, they needed tools to work the heavy skins of seals and caribou. Because culture is first and foremost a mechanism by which humans adapt, throughout the globe regional differentiations allowed Upper Paleolithic humans to face the challenges of their distinct environments.

CHAPTER CHECKLIST

What evidence supports the recent African origins hypothesis (or Eve hypothesis) for modern human origins? What are its assumptions?

● Evidence to support the recent African origins hypothesis originally came from the study of mitochondrial DNA of modern humans and extrapolating to the past based on an assumed rate of constant change.

● The earliest anatomically modern fossils have been found in Africa dating 160,000 old, relatively near in time to the estimation of when "Eve" should have existed.

● Issues with the recent African origins hypothesis include the movement of people into Africa, other geographical sources of mtDNA, and variable rates of molecular change.

● The recent African origins hypothesis supposes a strong connection between modern anatomy and cultural capacity that is inconsistent with findings on Neandertal culture.

What evidence supports the multiregional hypothesis for human origins? What are its assumptions?

● Modern humans retain certain anatomical characteristics of the *Homo erectus* fossils from the same region. This supports the idea that archaic humans all over the world simultaneously evolved into *Homo sapiens* and that gene flow kept humans connected as a single species.

● Distinguishing between various archaic and anatomically modern fossils poses a great challenge because many specimens and modern humans exhibit a mix of features.

● The anatomical variety of both archaic and modern humans and evidence of high levels of gene flow throughout human history support the multiregional hypothesis.

● Recent cultural innovations have no correspondence to changes in human appearance.

● Comparison of genomes of ancient peoples such as the Neandertals and the Denisovans with living human groups demonstrates genetic continuity.

What were the major technological developments of the Upper Paleolithic era?

● Throughout the globe blade tools became widespread along with an explosion of expressive arts. Spear throwing, the bow and arrow, and net hunting originated in this period. Hunting became a less dangerous and more effective manner of acquiring food.

● Pressure flaking gave toolmakers greater control over the shape of the tool whereas the blade technique yielded greater efficiency.

● In Europe Mousterian toolkits gave way to the earliest Upper Paleolithic industries—the Châtelperronian and Aurignacian traditions—shared by Neandertals and anatomically modern humans. Cultural distinction between the two groups in Europe does not clearly bear on either as superior.

How did the role of art in human societies evolve over this period?

● Starting 40,000 years ago, figurative art proliferated, including carved figurines, flutes, and cave art that most frequently depicted large mammals and abstract patterns seen perhaps in trance states.

● Evidence of paint manufacture goes back to 100,000 years ago when pigments were used as part of burial rituals and likely as body decoration. Figurative art that was not preserved in the archaeological record was also likely to have been created.

● Art began to be used in rituals and decorations, reflecting visions seen in altered states of consciousness known as entoptic phenomena.

● Interpretation of the artistic legacy of the Paleolithic remains subject to the biases of current social norms, as in the case of the Venus figurines.

How did humans spread throughout the globe during the Upper Paleolithic period?

● Spreading throughout the entire globe, Upper Paleolithic people built dwellings and tailored warm clothing that permitted habitation in harsh climates.

● Humans arrived in Australia at least 40,000 years ago by crossing wide bodies of open water. Original migration to North America may also have occurred by sea, with continued exchange happening while the Bering Land Bridge existed.

● Given their vast geographic distribution, disparate societies developed distinct art, technology, lifestyle, and anatomy.

QUESTIONS FOR REFLECTION

1. Upper Paleolithic art suggests that humans have always been challenged to understand where we fit in the larger system of life forms, past and present. What are your thoughts about how the impulse to create art relates to human efforts to make sense of our place in nature? What is your conception of the artist, a Neandertal perhaps, who had the impulse to create images of his or her hand shown in the chapter's Challenge Issue?

2. What does it mean to be "modern," biologically or culturally? How should we define *human*?

3. How do you feel personally about the possibility of having Neandertals as part of your ancestry?

How might you relate the Neandertal debates to stereotyping or racism in contemporary society?

4. Why do you think that most of the studies of prehistoric art have tended to focus on Europe? Do you think this focus reflects ethnocentrism or bias about the definition of *art* in Western cultures?

5. Do you think that gender has played a role in anthropological interpretations of the behavior of our ancestors and the way that paleoanthropologists and archaeologists conduct their research? Do you believe that feminism has a role to play in the interpretation of the past?

ONLINE STUDY RESOURCES

CourseMate

Access chapter-specific learning tools, including learning objectives, practice quizzes, videos, flash cards, glossaries, and more in your Anthropology CourseMate.

Log into **www.cengagebrain.com** to access the resources your instructor has assigned and to purchase materials.

Challenge Issue

With the start of the Neolithic some 10,000 years ago—when some humans shifted to farming and to the domestication of animals as they settled into village life—competition for critical resources began to intensify. Today, the competition set into motion at the start of the Neolithic takes place on a global scale and places untenable pressures on the world's natural resources. Consider potato farming, water, and a way of life in the Ica region of Peru, in the foothills of the Andes. Ancient peoples in the region domesticated numerous plants and animals including some 3,000 varieties of potato, cultivating different types at various elevations. According to legend, the gods gave potatoes to Andean peoples to help them overthrow invaders, who were led instead to the inedible leaves hiding the rich underground treasure. Potatoes also play a role in aboriginal peoples' marriage ceremonies and religious rituals because raw potatoes' natural alkaloids help healers in their communications with spirits. Today, this complete way of life is threatened by the large-scale industrial farming of asparagus, a water-intensive crop native to Europe, western Asia, and northern Africa. Over the past decade, Peru has become the largest global exporter of asparagus, earning about $500 million per year on this crop. In Peru's sunny Ica region where 95 percent of the asparagus is grown, the industrial farms are draining the aquifers at alarming rates, and nearby potato farmers are losing their livelihood. In such a competition for resources, global corporations are greatly advantaged over local inhabitants, but ultimately, for all of us to win, we need to implement strategies to ensure a planet in balance.

The Neolithic Revolution: The Domestication of Plants and Animals

9

IN THIS CHAPTER YOU WILL LEARN TO

- Identify the Mesolithic roots of farming and pastoralism.

- Describe the mechanisms of and evidence for plant and animal domestication.

- Compare theories about the reasons for this shift in lifeways.

- Identify the various centers of domestication globally.

- Examine the effects of food production on population size.

- Describe how the means of subsistence affect other aspects of social organization.

- Summarize the health consequences of the Neolithic revolution.

- Compare the cultural changes of the Neolithic to hunter-gatherer lifeways and to hierarchical notions of progress.

Throughout the Paleolithic, people depended exclusively on wild sources of food for their survival. They hunted and trapped wild animals, fished and gathered shellfish, eggs, berries, nuts, roots, and other plant foods, relying on their wits and muscles to acquire what nature provided. Whenever favored sources of food became scarce, people adjusted by increasing the variety of foods eaten and incorporating less desirable foods into their diets.

Over time, the subsistence practices of some peoples began to change in ways that radically transformed their way of life as they became food producers rather than food foragers. For some human groups, a more sedentary existence accompanied food production. This in turn permitted a reorganization of the workload in society: Some individuals could be freed from the food quest to devote their energies to other tasks. Over the course of thousands of years, these changes brought about an unforeseen way of life. With good reason, the **Neolithic** era (literally, the New Stone Age), when this change took place, has been called revolutionary in human history.

The Mesolithic Roots of Farming and Pastoralism

As seen in the previous chapter, by the end of the Paleolithic humans had spread throughout the globe. During this period glaciers covered much of the northern hemisphere. By 12,000 years ago, warmer climates prevailed, and these glaciers receded, causing changes in human habitats globally. Sea levels rose throughout the world, and areas flooded that had been dry land during periods of glaciation, such as the Bering Strait, parts of the North Sea, and an extensive land area that had joined the eastern islands of Indonesia to mainland Asia (recall Figure 8.19).

Neolithic The New Stone Age; a prehistoric period beginning about 10,000 years ago in which peoples possessed stone-based technologies and depended on domesticated crops and/or animals for subsistence.

In some northern regions, warmer climates brought about particularly marked changes, allowing the replacement of barren tundra with forests. In the process, the herd animals—upon which northern Paleolithic peoples had depended for much of their food, clothing, and shelter—disappeared from many areas. Some, like the caribou and musk ox, moved to colder climates; others, like the mammoths, died out completely. In the new forests, animals were often more solitary in their habits. As a result, large cooperative hunts were less productive than previously. Diets shifted to abundant plant foods as well as fish and other foods in and around lakes, bays, and rivers. In Europe, Asia, and Africa, anthropologists call this transitional period between the Paleolithic and the Neolithic the **Mesolithic**, or Middle Stone Age. In the Americas, comparable cultures are referred to as **Archaic cultures**.

New technologies accompanied the changed postglacial environment. Toolmakers began to manufacture ground stone tools, shaped and sharpened by grinding the tool against sandstone, often using sand as an additional abrasive. Once shaped and sharpened, these stones were set into wooden or sometimes antler handles to make effective axes and *adzes* (cutting tools with a sharp blade set at right angles to a handle). Though such implements take longer to make, with heavy-duty usage, they break less often than those made of chipped stone. Thus, they were helpful in clearing forest areas and in the woodwork needed for the creation of dugout canoes and skin-covered boats. Evidence of seaworthy watercraft at Mesolithic sites indicates that human foraging for food took place on the open water—coastal areas, rivers, and lakes—as well as on the land.

The **microlith**—a small, hard, sharp blade—tradition flourished in the Mesolithic. Although microlithic ("small stone") tools existed in Central Africa by about 40,000 years ago, they did not become common elsewhere until the Mesolithic. Microliths could be mass-produced because they were small, easy to make, and could be fashioned from sections of blades. This tool could be attached to an arrow or another tool shaft by using melted resin (from pine trees) as a binder.

Microliths provided Mesolithic people with an important advantage over their Upper Paleolithic forebears: The small size of the microlith enabled them to devise a wider array of composite tools made out of stone and wood or bone. Thus, they could make sickles, harpoons, arrows, knives, and daggers by fitting microliths into slots in wood, bone, or antler handles. Later experimentation with these forms led to more sophisticated tools and weapons, such as bows to propel arrows.

Dwellings from the Mesolithic provide evidence of a somewhat more settled lifestyle during this period. People subsisting on a dietary mixture of wild game, seafood, and plants in the now milder forested environments of the north did not need to move regularly over large geographic areas in pursuit of migratory herds. In the warmer parts of the world, wild plant foods were more readily available, and so collection already had complemented hunting in the Upper Paleolithic. Thus, in areas like Southwest Asia, the Mesolithic represents less of a changed way of life than was true in Europe. Here, the important **Natufian culture** flourished.

The Natufians lived between 10,200 and 12,500 years ago at the eastern end of the Mediterranean Sea in caves, rock shelters, and small villages with stone- and mud-walled houses. They are named after Wadi en-Natuf, a ravine near Jerusalem, Israel, where the remains of this culture were first found. Natufians buried their dead in communal cemeteries, usually in shallow pits without any other objects or decorations. One of their villages, a 10,500-year-old settlement at Jericho in the Jordan River Valley, contained a small shrine. Basin-shaped depressions in the rocks found outside homes and plastered pits beneath the floors of the houses indicate that the Natufians stored plant foods. Natufians also used sickles—small stone blades set in straight handles of wood or bone. The sickles were originally used to harvest sedge for baskets but later came to be used to cut grain (**Figure 9.1**).

© Erich Lessing/Art Resource, NY

Figure 9.1 **Tools of the Neolithic** The Neolithic gets its name from the polished stone tools that appeared during this period. Archaeologists have also recovered hafted sickles, mortars, and pestles as well as grain storage pits at some of the earliest Natufian settlements. The polished stone axes and hammerheads pictured here would have been hafted to handles made of wood. The handle would pass through the hole created in the tool or fitted up to the side of the polished stone and then secured with sinew and various glues.

Mesolithic The Middle Stone Age of Europe, Asia, and Africa beginning about 12,000 years ago.

Archaic cultures The term used to refer to Mesolithic cultures in the Americas.

microlith A small blade of flint or similar stone, several of which were hafted together in wooden handles to make tools; widespread in the Mesolithic.

Natufian culture A Mesolithic culture from the lands that are now Israel, Lebanon, and western Syria, between about 10,200 and 12,500 years ago.

The new way of life and abundant food supplies of the various Mesolithic and Archaic cultures permitted peoples in some parts of the world to live in larger and more sedentary groups. Some of these settlements went on to expand into the first farming villages, towns, and ultimately cities.

The Neolithic Revolution

The Neolithic, or New Stone Age, named for the polished stone tools characteristic of this period, represents a major cultural change. The transition from a foraging economy based on hunting, gathering, and fishing to one based on food production outweighs the importance of the tool type for which this period gets its name. Food foragers and village-dwellers alike used these Neolithic tools.

The **Neolithic revolution** (also known as the *Neolithic transition*) was by no means smooth or instantaneous; in fact, the switch to food production spread over many centuries—even millennia—and grew directly from the preceding Mesolithic. Where to draw the line between the two periods is not always clear. Food production in the early Neolithic included both **horticulture**, the cultivation of crops in food gardens carried out with simple hand tools such as digging sticks and stone- or bone-bladed hoes, and **pastoralism**, breeding and managing migratory herds of domesticated grazing animals, such as goats, sheep, cattle, llamas, and camels.

The ultimate source of all cultural change is **innovation**: any new idea, method, or device that gains widespread acceptance in society. **Primary innovation** refers to the creation, invention, or discovery by chance of a completely new idea, method, or device. For example, take the discovery that clay permanently hardens when exposed to high temperatures. Presumably, accidental firing of clay took place around numerous ancient campfires. This chance occurrence became a primary innovation when someone perceived its potential use. This perception allowed our ancestors to begin to make figurines of fired clay some 35,000 years ago.

A **secondary innovation** involves a deliberate application or modification of an existing idea, method, or device. For example, ancient peoples applied the knowledge about fired clay to make pottery containers and cooking vessels. Recent evidence from Yuchanyan Cave, located in the southwest of China's Hunan Province, indicates the presence of the earliest pottery vessels; these are radiocarbon dated to between 15,430 and 18,300 years ago.

The shift to relatively complete reliance on domesticated plants and

animals took several thousand years. Although this transition has been particularly well studied in Southwest Asia, archaeological evidence for food production also exists from other parts of the world, such as China and Central America and the Andes at similar or somewhat younger dates. Human groups throughout the globe independently, but more or less simultaneously, invented food production.

What Is Domestication?

Domestication takes place as humans modify, intentionally or unintentionally, the genetic makeup of a population of wild plants or animals, sometimes to the extent that members of the population are unable to survive and/or reproduce without human assistance. Domestication resembles the interdependence between different species frequently seen in the natural world, where one species depends on another (that feeds upon it) for its protection and reproductive success. For example, certain ants native to the American tropics grow fungi in their nests, and these fungi provide the ants with most of their nutrition. Like human farmers, the ants add manure to stimulate fungal growth and eliminate competing weeds, both mechanically and through use of antibiotic herbicides. The fungi are protected and ensured reproductive success while providing the ants with a steady food supply.

In plant–human interactions, domestication ensures the plants' reproductive success while providing humans with food. Selective breeding eliminates thorns, toxins, and bad-tasting chemical compounds, which in the wild had served to ensure a plant species' survival, at the same time producing larger, tastier edible parts attractive to humans. Environmentalist Michael Pollan suggests that domesticated plant species successfully exploit human desires so that they are able to outcompete other plant species; he has even proposed that agriculture is something the grasses did to people as a way to conquer trees (Pollan, 2001).

Neolithic revolution The domestication of plants and animals by peoples with stone-based technologies, beginning about 10,000 years ago and leading to radical transformations in cultural systems; sometimes referred to as the *Neolithic transition*.

horticulture The cultivation of crops in food gardens, carried out with simple hand tools such as digging sticks and hoes.

pastoralism The breeding and managing of migratory herds of domesticated grazing animals, such as goats, sheep, cattle, llamas, and camels.

innovation Any new idea, method, or device that gains widespread acceptance in society.

primary innovation The creation, invention, or chance discovery of a completely new idea, method, or device.

secondary innovation The deliberate application or modification of an existing idea, method, or device.

domestication An evolutionary process whereby humans modify, intentionally or unintentionally, the genetic makeup of a population of wild plants or animals, sometimes to the extent that members of the population are unable to survive and/or reproduce without human assistance.

© Cengage Learning

Evidence of Early Plant Domestication

Domesticated plants generally differ from their wild ancestors in ways favored by humans. These features include increased size, at least of edible parts; reduction or loss of natural means of seed dispersal; reduction or loss of protective devices such as husks or distasteful chemical compounds; loss of delayed seed germination (important to wild plants for survival in times of drought or other temporarily adverse conditions); and development of simultaneous ripening of the seed or fruit.

For example, wild cereals have a very fragile stem, whereas domesticated ones have a tough stem. Under natural conditions, plants with fragile stems scatter their seed for themselves, whereas those with tough stems do not. At harvest time, the grain stalks with soft stems would shatter at the touch of a sickle or flail, scattering the seeds to the wind. Inevitably, though unintentionally, most of the seeds that people were able to harvest would have come from the tough plants. Early domesticators probably also tended to select seed from plants having few husks or none at all—eventually breeding them out—because husking prior to pounding the grains into meal or flour required extra labor.

Many of the distinguishing characteristics of domesticated plants can be seen in remains from archaeological sites. One way that paleobotanists can often tell the fossil of a wild plant species from a domesticated one is by studying the shape and size of various plant structures (Figure 9.2).

Evidence of Early Animal Domestication

Domestication also produced changes in the skeletal structure of some animals. For example, the horns of wild goats and sheep differ from those of their domesticated counterparts. Some types of domesticated sheep have no horns at all. Similarly, the size of an animal or its parts can vary with domestication as seen in the smaller size of certain teeth of domesticated pigs compared to those of wild ones.

The age and sex ratios of butchered animals at an archaeological site can indicate the presence of animal domestication. For example, archaeologists found that the age and/or sex ratios at the 10,000-year-old site in the Zagros Mountains of Iran differed from those of wild herds. A sharp rise in the number of young male goats killed indicates that people were slaughtering the young males for food and saving the females for breeding. Although such herd management does not prove that the goats were fully domesticated, it indicates a step in that direction (Zeder & Hesse, 2000). Similarly, the archaeological sites in the Andean highlands, dating to around 6,300 years ago, contain evidence that animals were penned up, indicating the beginning of domestication.

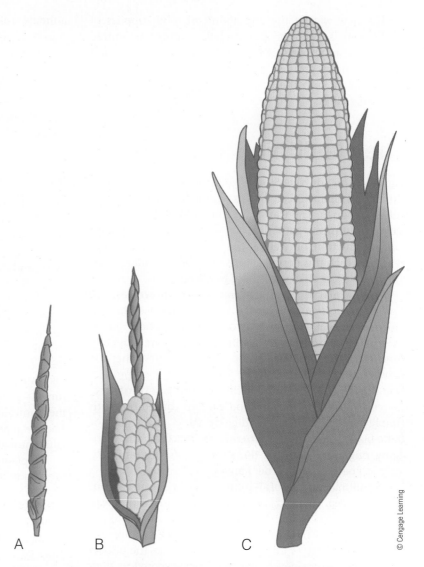

© Cengage Learning

A   B   C

Figure 9.2 Domestication of Maize Increased size of edible parts is a common feature of domestication. The large ear of corn or maize (C) that we know today is a far cry from the tiny ears (about an inch long) characteristic of 5,500-year-old maize (B). Maize may have arisen when a simple gene mutation transformed male tassel spikes of the wild grass called teosinte (A) into the small, earliest versions of the female maize ear. Teosinte, a wild grass from highland Mexico, is far less productive than maize and does not taste good. Like most plants that were domesticated, it was not a favored food for foraging peoples. Domestication transformed it into something highly desirable.

Why Humans Became Food Producers

Although it might seem that a sudden flash of insight about the human ability to control plants and animals underlies the rise of domestication, the evidence points us in different directions. Contemporary foragers, for example, choose to forgo food production, even though they know full well the role of seeds in plant growth and that plants grow better under certain conditions than others. In fact, Jared Diamond aptly describes contemporary food foragers as "walking encyclopedias of natural history with individual names for as many as a thousand or more plant and animal species, and with detailed knowledge of those species' biological characteristics, distribution, and potential uses" (Diamond, 1997, p. 143).

Food foragers clearly have the knowledge to undertake food production and frequently apply their expertise to actively manage the resources on which they depend. For example, indigenous peoples living in northern Australia deliberately alter the runoff channels of creeks to flood extensive tracts of land, converting them into fields of wild grain. Indigenous Australians choose to continue to forage while also managing the land.

Food foragers may avoid food production simply because of the hard work it involves. In fact, available ethnographic data indicate that farmers, by and large, work far longer hours compared to most food foragers. Also, food production is not necessarily a more secure means of subsistence than food foraging. Low species diversity makes highly productive seed crops—of the sort originally domesticated in Southwest Asia, Central America, and the Andean highlands—unstable from an ecological perspective. Without constant human attention, their productivity suffers.

For these reasons, contemporary food foragers do not necessarily regard farming and animal husbandry as superior to hunting, gathering, or fishing. Farming ushers in whole new systems of relationships that disturb an age-old balance between humans and nature. As long as existing practices work well, food foragers have no need to abandon them, especially if they provide an eminently satisfactory way of life. Noting that food foragers have more time for play and relaxation than food producers, anthropologist Marshall Sahlins has labeled hunter-gatherers the original "affluent society" (Sahlins, 1972). Nevertheless, as food-producing peoples (including postindustrial societies) have deprived them of more and more of the land base necessary for their way of life, foraging has become more difficult. The competition for resources ushered in during the Neolithic favors those cultures that develop concepts of land ownership.

Given this, we may well ask why any human group abandoned food foraging in favor of food production. Several theories account for this change in human subsistence practices. The desiccation or oasis theory, first championed by Australian archaeologist V. Gordon Childe in the mid-20th century, suggests environmental determinism. Glacial cover over Europe and Asia caused a shift in rain patterns from Europe to North Africa and Southwest Asia so that when the glaciers retreated northward, so did the rain. As a result, North Africa and Southwest Asia became drier, and people were forced to congregate at oases for water.

Relative food scarcity in such an environment drove people to collect the wild grasses and seeds growing around the oases, congregating in a part of Southwest Asia known as the Fertile Crescent (Figure 9.3). Eventually, they began to cultivate the grasses to provide enough food for the community. According to this theory, animal domestication began because the oases attracted hungry animals, such as wild goats, sheep, and cattle, which came to graze on the stubble of the grain fields and to drink. Finding that these animals were often too thin to kill for food, people began to fatten them up.

Although many other theories have been proposed to account for the shift to domestication, the oasis theory remains historically significant as the first scientifically testable explanation for the origins of food production. Childe's theory set the stage for the development of archaeology as a science. Later theories developed by archaeologists built on Childe's ideas.

The Fertile Crescent

Present evidence indicates that the earliest plant domestication took place gradually in the Fertile Crescent, the long arc-shaped sweep of river valleys and coastal plains extending from the Upper Nile (Sudan) to the Lower Tigris (Iraq). Archaeological data suggest the domestication of rye as early as 13,000 years ago by people living at a site (Abu Hureyra) east of Aleppo, Syria, although wild plants and animals continued to be their major food sources. Over the next several millennia they became full-fledged farmers, cultivating rye and wheat. By 10,300 years ago, crop cultivation spread to others in the region.

The domestication process was a consequence of a chance convergence of independent natural events and other cultural developments. The Natufians, whose culture we looked at earlier in this chapter, illustrate this process. These people lived at a time of dramatically changing climates in Southwest Asia. With the end of the last glaciation, temperatures not only became significantly warmer but markedly seasonal as well. Between 6,000 and 12,000 years ago, the region experienced the most extreme seasonality in its history, with dry summers significantly longer and hotter than today. As a consequence, many shallow lakes dried up, leaving just three in the Jordan River Valley.

At the same time, the region's plant cover changed dramatically. Among plants, the annuals, including wild cereal grains and legumes (such as peas, lentils, and chickpeas), adapt well to environmental instability and seasonal dryness. Because they complete their life cycle

Figure 9.3 The Fertile Crescent
This area of Southwest Asia and North Africa shows the Fertile Crescent, the site of the beginning of domestication.

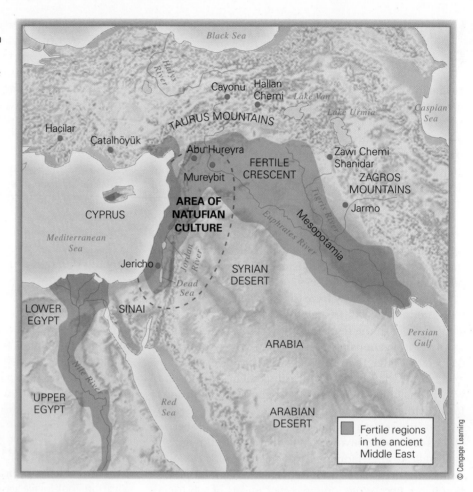

in a single year, annuals can evolve very quickly under unstable conditions. Moreover, they store their reproductive abilities for the next wet season in abundant seeds, which can remain dormant for prolonged periods.

The Natufians, who lived where these conditions were especially severe, adapted by modifying their subsistence practices in two ways: First, they probably burned the landscape regularly to promote browsing by red deer and grazing by gazelles, the main focus of their hunting activities. Second, they placed greater emphasis on the collection and storage of wild seeds from the annual plants that they used for food through the dry season. The importance of stored foods, coupled with the scarcity of reliable water sources, promoted more sedentary living patterns, reflected in the substantial villages of late Natufian times. Because they already possessed sickles (originally used to cut reeds and sedges for baskets) for harvesting grain and grinding stones to process a variety of wild foods, it was easier for the Natufians to shift to a reliance on seed.

The Natufians' use of sickles to harvest grain turned out to have important if unexpected consequences. In the course of harvesting, the easily dispersed seeds fell at the harvest site, whereas those that clung to the stems came back to the settlement where people processed and stored them. The periodic burning of vegetation carried

out to promote the deer and gazelle herds may have also affected the development of new genetic variation. Heat impacts mutation rates. Also, fire removes individuals from a population, which changes the genetic structure of a population drastically and quickly.

Inevitably, some seeds from nondispersing variants were carried back to settlements and germinated, growing on dump heaps and other disturbed sites (latrines, areas cleared of trees, or burned-over terrain). Certain variants known as *colonizers* do particularly well in disturbed habitats, making them ideal candidates for domestication. Sedentism itself disturbs habitats as resources closer to settlements become depleted over time. Thus, variants of plants particularly susceptible to human manipulation had more opportunities to flourish where people were living. Under such circumstances, humans began to actively promote the growth of these plants, even by deliberately sowing them. Ultimately, people realized that they could play a more active role in the process by deliberately trying to breed the strains they preferred. With this, domestication shifted from an unintentional to an intentional process.

The development of animal domestication in Southwest Asia seems to have proceeded along somewhat similar lines in the hilly country of southeastern Turkey, northern Iraq, and the Zagros Mountains of Iran. This region of rich environmental diversity contained large herds of wild sheep and goats. From the flood plains of the valley of the Tigris and Euphrates Rivers, for example, travel to the north or east takes one into high country through three other ecological zones: first steppe; then oak and pistachio woodlands; and finally high plateau country with grass, scrub, or desert vegetation. Valleys that run at right angles to the mountain ranges afford relatively easy access across these zones. Today, a number of peoples in the region still graze their herds of sheep and goats on the low steppe in the winter and move to high pastures on the plateaus in the summer.

Food foragers inhabited these regions prior to the domestication of plants and animals. Each ecological zone contained distinct plant species, and because of the variation in altitude, plant foods matured at different times in different zones. These ancient peoples hunted a variety of animal species for meat and hides. The bones of hoofed animals—deer, gazelles, wild goats, and wild sheep—dominate the human refuse piles from these periods. Most of these hoofed animals naturally move back and forth from low winter pastures to high summer pastures. People followed the animals in their seasonal migrations, eating and storing other wild foods as they passed through different zones: palm dates in the lowlands; acorns, almonds, and pistachios higher up; apples and pears higher still; wild grains maturing at different times in different areas; woodland animals in the forested region between summer and winter grazing lands. All in all, it was a rich, varied fare.

The archaeological record indicates that, at first, the people of the southwestern Asian highlands hunted animals of all ages and sexes. But, beginning about 11,000 years ago, the percentage of immature sheep consumed increased to about 50 percent of the total. At the same time, people ate fewer of the female animals. (Feasting on male lambs increases yields by sparing the females for breeding.) This marks the beginning of human management of sheep.

The human management of flocks shielded sheep from the effects of natural selection, affording the variants preferred by humans to have increased reproductive success. Variants attractive to humans did not arise out of need but randomly, as mutations do. But then humans selectively bred the varieties they favored. In such a way, those features characteristic of domestic sheep—such as greater fat and meat production, excess wool, and so on—began to develop (**Figure 9.4**). By 9,000 years ago, the shape and size of the bones of domestic sheep had become distinguishable from those of wild sheep. At about the same time and by similar means, ancient humans domesticated pigs in southeastern Turkey and the lower Jordan River Valley.

Some researchers link animal domestication to the development of fixed territories and settlements. They suggest that resource ownership promotes postponing the short-term gain of killing prey for the long-term gain of continued access to animals in the future (Alvard & Kuznar, 2001). Eventually, ancient peoples introduced animal species domesticated in one area to regions outside their natural habitat. However, not all scientists believe that domestication occurred in this way, with humans directing the process. Evolutionary anthropologist Brian Hare, featured in this chapter's Biocultural Connection, turns the theory around, arguing instead that animals (specifically, dogs) took advantage of new survival opportunities created by human settlements in the villages of the Neolithic.

The notion that dogs might have played a more active role in creating their own evolutionary relationship with humans underscores the fact that domestication took place as a series of interactions between species. Unaware of the long-term and revolutionary cultural consequences of their actions, the domesticators and domesticates alike sought only to maximize their available food sources. But as the domestication process continued, humans throughout the globe realized that the productivity of

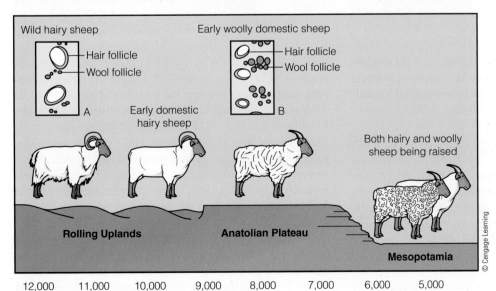

Figure 9.4 The Domestication of Sheep Domestication of sheep resulted in evolutionary changes that created more wool. Inset A shows a section of the skin of wild sheep, as seen through a microscope, with the arrangement of hair and wool follicles. Inset B shows how this arrangement changed with domestication so that the sheep produced more wool.

BIOCULTURAL CONNECTION

Dogs Get Right to the Point

Some dog breeds have a receptive vocabulary; that is, they can understand hundreds of words. How can they do this? In turn, do their soulful eyes, head tipped to the side, or wagging tail really speak of unconditional love? What if they could speak themselves? Would they say something different from what their bodies seem to tell us?

Poet Billy Collins reveals in the poem "The Revenant" what one cranky dog, just put to sleep by his owner, came back to tell him:

I never liked you—not one bit.

When I licked your face,
I thought of biting off your nose.[a]

Likewise, evolutionary anthropologist Brian Hare suggests that we view dog behavior, cognition, and communication through an anthropocentric lens.[b] He warns that these biases are in play when we speak of *Canis lupus familiaris*, a subspecies of wolf, as humankind's "best friend."

Hare came to this topic while researching chimpanzee cognition. Chimps, like the other great apes, can master human language at the level of a 2- to 3-year-old, and they can follow one another's gaze and figure out what might be in another chimp's

Dogs and humans are unique among mammals in their ability to interpret and act upon the meaning of pointing with a human hand.

line of sight. However, they struggle to comprehend the gesture of pointing.

Instead of relegating pointing to another area of human uniqueness, Hare thought of his own pet dogs, which, like all dogs, grasped this gesture immediately. Hare set about researching how and why dogs and humans, seemingly the lone species among mammals, understand the meaning of pointing. He conducted

pointing experiments using a "shell game" scenario, with dogs, chimps, wolves, and humans of all ages. Even puppies, like babies, understand pointing, which indicates that this ability is encoded in their genome and not a learned behavior. And like babies, they rely on social cues to interpret the meaning of a pointing finger.

The notion of a domesticated species, such as the dog, of course implies

the domestic species increased relative to the wild species. Thus, these species became increasingly more important to subsistence, resulting in further domestication and further increases in productivity (**Figure 9.5**).

Other Centers of Domestication

In addition to Southwest Asia, the domestication of plants and, in some cases, animals took place simultaneously in parts of the Americas (Central America, the Andean highlands, the tropical forests of South America, and eastern North America), northern China, and Africa (**Figure 9.6**). In China, domestication of rice was underway along the

middle Yangtze River by about 11,000 years ago. It took another 4,000 years, however, for domestic rice to dominate wild rice and become the dietary staple.

Similarly, decorations on pottery dated to between 5,000 and 8,800 years ago document rice as the earliest domesticated species of Southeast Asia. Other domesticates, particularly root crops such as yams and taro, dominate this region (**Figure 9.7**). Root crop farming, or **vegeculture**, typically involves growing many different species together in a single field. Because this approximates the complexity of the natural vegetation, vegeculture tends to be more stable than seed crop cultivation. Propagation or breeding of new plants usually occurs through vegetative means— the planting of cuttings—rather than the planting of seeds.

In the Americas, the domestication of plants began about as early as it did in these other regions. Evidence for one species of domestic squash appears as early as

vegeculture The cultivation of domesticated root crops, such as yams and taro.

that one species has effectively altered the genetic makeup of another. To avoid anthropocentrism, Hare has used a dog's eye view to think about domestication. Instead of seeing humans as the leaders in the process, he proposes that dogs domesticated themselves as humans began to live in discrete settlements during the Neolithic. Ancestral dogs, like wolves today, were probably partly scavengers and so came to orient to human habitations because of edible discarded material left by people. He suggests that those wolves that were least timid about humans had a selective advantage in the "human cohabitation" niche and eventually evolved into domesticated dogs.

Social acceptance of dogs by humans, and vice versa, has led to many interesting and humanlike behavioral adaptations in dogs. A dog "kissing" its owner's face may seem like love but really has its antecedents in the spitting up of prechewed food by wolves for their pack mates upon their return to the den. Although human owners do not spit up food for their dogs, they reward their dog's "love" through edible treats. Natural selection often produces such win–win scenarios among species—it's

just that when humans are involved, we call it domestication!

This reconstruction of the history of the canine–human partnership provides an interesting context to those who have had to clean up after their dog has upset the household trash bin. As the sequel to such an escapade, when the dog owner scolds his or her dog, the dog may show what we interpret as shame: head down, tail between the legs, body turned aside or walking away. Hare's experiments show that dogs will perform this behavior when scolded *even when they haven't broken any rule.* Their sensitivity to social judgment is so attuned that they can be in effect coerced into expressing what humans interpret as guilt when they are actually innocent. Evolutionary processes have favored dogs who could best manipulate humans.

Pointing has particular significance to a phenomenon in human psychology termed *joint attention*, which means that two individuals share an awareness that both are visually fixing on a common visual target. The connection of joint attention exists when a dog explores an area to which a human points or when one person "points out" a path to another. But most importantly,

joint attention lies at the heart of social awareness: Without it, we cannot function in groups. Interestingly, people with autism, who characteristically struggle with social cues and responses, also have a deficiency with pointing.

But not dogs. In the end they know just how to control us. The revenant dog from Billy Collins's poem gets the last laugh when he tells his owner about heaven:

> . . . that everyone here can read
> and write,
> the dogs in poetry, the cats and
> the others in prose.[c]

BIOCULTURAL QUESTION

Can you think of other examples of how we may impose human norms of behavior onto other species? How is this the same or different from imposing notions specific to one culture onto another?

———————

[a]Collins, B. (2005). The revenant. In *The trouble with poetry.* New York: Random House. Reprinted by permission of the Chris Calhoun Literary Agency.

[b]Hare, B., et al. (2002). The domestication of social cognition in dogs. *Science 298* (5598). 1634–1636.

[c]Collins, 2005.

© Wolfgang Flamisch/Corbis

Figure 9.5 Manufacturing Food Today, deliberate attempts to create new varieties of plants take place in many greenhouses, experiment stations, and labs. But when first begun, the creation of domestic plants was not deliberate; rather, it was the unforeseen outcome of traditional food-foraging activities. Today, genetic engineering creates crops (GMOs, or genetically modified organisms) designed to survive massive applications of herbicides and pesticides. The crops are also engineered to *not* produce viable seeds so that corporations can solidify their control of the food industry. Here researchers study a strain of genetically modified corn.

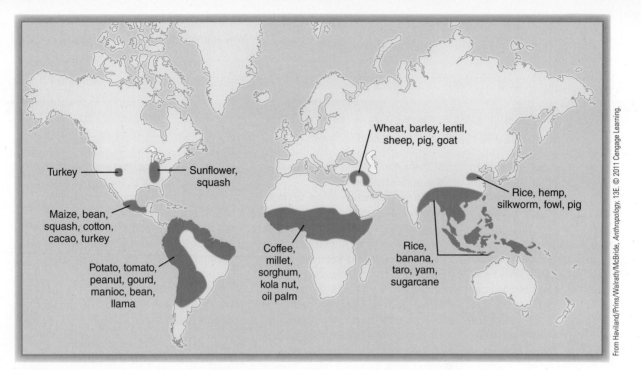

Turkey

Sunflower, squash

Wheat, barley, lentil, sheep, pig, goat

Rice, hemp, silkworm, fowl, pig

Maize, bean, squash, cotton, cacao, turkey

Coffee, millet, sorghum, kola nut, oil palm

Rice, banana, taro, yam, sugarcane

Potato, tomato, peanut, gourd, manioc, bean, llama

Figure 9.6 Early Plant and Animal Domestication Domestication of plants and animals took place in widely scattered areas more or less simultaneously. The figure indicates some of the domesticates typical to each area such as wheat and sheep in Southwest Asia; sorghum and millet in Central Africa, rice and pigs in China; taro and bananas in Southeast Asia; maize and dogs in Central America; potatoes and llamas in South America; and squash and sunflowers in North America. Although the domesticated plants and animals appeared independently in distinct regions, today humans use all of them throughout the globe.

Figure 9.7 Vegeculture The Dani people of Papua New Guinea, specialize in growing sweet potatoes through vegeculture, or root crop farming. Although vegeculture typically involves many species of root crop planted together in one area, the Dani fill vast irrigated fields exclusively with more than seventy varieties of sweet potato. The Dani have incorporated this important food into many of their rituals. Here, Dani women roast sweet potatoes on a fire as part of a ceremonial pig roast.

10,000 years ago in the coastal forests of Ecuador, the same time that another species independently appeared in an arid region of highland Mexico. The ecological diversity of the highland valleys of Mexico, like the hill country of Southwest Asia, provided an excellent environment for domestication (**Figure 9.8**). Movement of people through a variety of ecological zones as they changed altitude brought plant and animal species into new habitats, providing opportunities for "colonizing" species and humans alike.

Domestication in the Andean highlands of Peru, another environmentally diverse region, emphasized root crops, the best known being the thousands of varieties of potatoes discussed in the Challenge Issue at the opening of the chapter. They also domesticated plants for purposes other than eating, such as gourds (**Figure 9.9**) and cotton. South Americans also domesticated guinea pigs, llamas, alpacas, and ducks, whereas peoples in the Mexican highlands never did much with domestic livestock. They limited themselves to dogs, turkeys, and bees. American Indians living north of Mexico developed some of their own indigenous domesticates. These included local varieties of squash and sunflowers.

Ultimately, American Indians domesticated over 300 food crops, including two of the four most important ones in the

Figure 9.9 Domesticates for More than Food In coastal Peru, the earliest domesticates were the inedible bottle gourd (like the one shown here) and cotton. They were used to make nets and floats to catch fish, which was an important source of food.

world today: potatoes and maize (the other two are wheat and rice). In fact, America's indigenous peoples first cultivated 60 percent of the crops grown in the world today; they not only developed the world's largest array of nutritious foods but also are the primary contributors to the world's varied cuisines. After all, where would Italian cuisine be without tomatoes? Thai cooking without peanuts? Northern European cooking without potatoes? Small wonder American Indians have been called the world's greatest farmers.

The domestication of plant species brought about the development of horticultural societies. Using neither irrigation nor plows, small communities of gardeners worked together with simple hand tools. Horticulturists typically cultivate a variety of crops in small gardens they have cleared by hand. Indians in the Amazon rainforest used sophisticated farming methods, as is evident in the research conducted by an international team of archaeologists and other scientists. These ancient methods, which left behind rich dark soils, may have important current applications. Reviving these ancient soil-enrichment techniques could contribute to better global management of rainforests and climate today.

Although plant domestication took place independently across the globe, at the same time people everywhere developed the same categories of foods: starchy grains (or root crops) accompanied by one or more legumes. For example, people in Southwest Asia combined wheat and barley with peas, chickpeas, and lentils, and people in Mexico combined maize with various kinds of beans. Together, the amino acids (building blocks of proteins) in these starch

		PERCENTAGE			
CULTIGENS		Hunting	Horticulture	Wild plant use	Years ago
					3,000
Squash Chili Amaranth Avocado	Cotton Maize Beans Gourd Sapote	29%		31%	3,500
					4,000
					4,500
Squash Chili Amaranth Avocado	Maize Beans Gourd Sapote	25%		50%	5,000
					5,500
Squash Chili Amaranth Avocado	Maize Beans Gourd Sapote	34%		52%	6,000
					6,500
					7,000
Squash Chili Amaranth Avocado		54%		40%	7,500
					8,000
					8,500

Figure 9.8 Patterns of Neolithic Domestication in Mesoamerica Subsistence trends in Mexico's Tehuacan Valley show that here, as elsewhere, dependence of horticulture came about gradually, over a prolonged period of time.

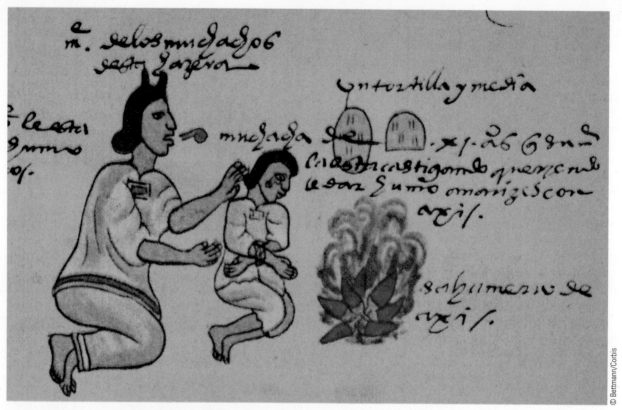

© Bettmann/Corbis

Figure 9.10 The Many Uses of Chilies Mexicans, have used chili peppers for millennia. Chili peppers enhance the flavors of food and aid in digestion by helping with the breakdown of cellulose in diets heavy in plant foods. Chilies have other uses as well: This illustration from a 16th-century Aztec manuscript shows a mother threatening to punish her child with the smoke from chili peppers. Chili smoke was also used as a chemical weapon in warfare.

and legume combinations provide humans with sufficient protein. The starchy grains eaten at every meal in the form of bread, some sort of food wrapper (like a tortilla), or a gruel or thickening agent in a stew along with one or more legumes form the core of the diet. Each culture combines these rather bland sources of carbohydrates and proteins with flavor-giving substances that help the food go down.

In Mexico, for example, the chili pepper serves as the flavor enhancer par excellence (**Figure 9.10**); in other cuisines bits of meat or fat, dairy products, or mushrooms add the flavor. Anthropologist Sidney Mintz refers to this as the *core-fringe-legume pattern* (CFLP), noting its stability until the recent worldwide spread of processed sugars and high-fat foods.

Food Production and Population Size

Human population size has grown steadily since the Neolithic. The exact relationship between population growth and food production resembles the old chicken and egg question: Does population growth create the pressures that result in innovations, such as food production, or is population growth a consequence of food production? As already noted, domestication inevitably leads to higher yields, and higher yields make it possible to feed more people, albeit at the cost of more work.

Across human populations, increased dependence on farming and increased fertility seem to go hand in hand: Farming populations tend to have higher rates of fertility compared to hunter-gatherers. Hunter-gatherer mothers have their children about four to five years apart while some contemporary farming populations not practicing any form of birth control have another baby every year and a half (**Figure 9.11**). A complex interplay between human biology and culture lies at the heart of this difference. Some researchers suggest that the availability of soft foods for infants brought about by farming promoted population growth. In humans, frequent breastfeeding has a dampening effect on mothers' ovulation, inhibiting pregnancy in nursing mothers who breastfeed exclusively. Because breastfeeding frequency declines when soft foods are introduced, fertility tends to increase.

However, many other pathways can also lead to fertility changes. For example, farming cultures tend to view numerous children as assets to help out with the many

VISUAL COUNTERPOINT

Figure 9.11 Diet and Fertility The higher fertility of the Amish, a religious farming culture in North America, compared to that of the Ju/'hoansi hunter-gatherers from the Kalahari Desert, was originally attributed to nutritional stress among the hunter-gatherers. We now know that childrearing beliefs and practices account for these differences. The Ju/'hoansi fertility pattern derives from the belief that a crying baby should be breastfed, an action that biologically suppresses fertility. In farming populations families view children as assets to help work the farm, and infant feeding practices reinforce high fertility rates. Children are weaned at young ages and transitioned to soft foods, a practice that promotes the next pregnancy. All human activity includes a complex interplay between human biology and culture.

household chores. Further, higher fertility rates among farmers might derive from higher mortality rates due to infectious diseases brought about by the sedentary lifestyles and narrow diets characteristic of the Neolithic. High infant mortality, in turn, could raise the cultural value placed on fertility.

In the past, biases contributed to oversimplified anthropological explanations of fertility differences among peoples. Early anthropologists viewed the hunter-gatherer lifestyle as inferior and interpreted the differences in fertility to be the consequence of nutritional stress among the hunter-gatherers. This theory was based in part on the observation that humans and many other mammals require a certain percentage of body fat in order to reproduce successfully (see Chapter 12 for more on this biological phenomenon).

However, detailed studies among the !Kung or Ju/'hoansi (pronounced "zhutwasi") of the Kalahari Desert in southern Africa disproved this nutritional theory. The low fertility among the Ju/'hoansi ultimately derives from cultural beliefs about the right way to handle a baby: The Ju/'hoansi mother responds rapidly to her baby, breastfeeding whenever the infant shows any signs of fussing, day or night. On a biological level, the Ju/'hoansi pattern of breastfeeding in short, very frequent bouts suppresses ovulation, or the release of a new egg into the womb for fertilization. Biology and culture interact in all aspects of the human experience.

The Spread of Food Production

Paradoxically, although domestication increases productivity, it also increases instability. As humans increasingly focus on varieties with the highest yields, other varieties become less valued and ultimately ignored. As a result, farmers depend on a rather narrow choice of resources, compared to the wide range utilized by food foragers.

Today, modern agriculturists rely on a mere dozen species for about 80 percent of the world's annual tonnage of all crops.

This dependence on fewer varieties means that when a crop fails, for whatever reason, farmers have less to fall back on compared to food foragers. Furthermore, the common farming practice of planting crops together in one locality increases the likelihood of failure because proximity promotes the spread of disease among neighboring plants. Moreover, by relying on seeds from the most productive plants of a species to establish next year's crop, farmers favor genetic uniformity over diversity. In turn, some virus, bacterium, or fungus could wipe out vast fields of genetically identical organisms all at once as in the terrible Irish potato famine of 1845–1850. This disaster caused the deaths of about 1 million people due to hunger and disease and forced another 2 million to abandon their homes and emigrate. The population of Ireland dropped from 8 million to 5 million as a result of the famine.

This concentration of domesticates and the consequent vulnerability to disease intensify with contemporary agribusiness and factory farming. This chapter's Globalscape examines the role of pig farming in the swine flu pandemic that began to sweep the world early in 2009.

The Irish potato famine illustrates how the combination of increased productivity and vulnerability may contribute to the geographic spread of farming. Time and time again in the past, population growth, followed by crop failure, has triggered movements of peoples from one place to another, where they have reestablished their familiar subsistence practices.

Once farming came into existence, its instability more or less guaranteed that it would spread to neighboring regions through such migrations. From Southwest Asia, for instance, farming spread northeastward eventually to all of Europe, westward to North Africa, and eastward to India. Domesticated variants also spread from China and Southeast Asia westward. Those who brought crops to new locations brought other things as well, including languages, beliefs, and new alleles for human gene pools. The spread of certain ideas, customs, or practices from one culture to another is termed **diffusion**.

A similar diffusion occurred from West Africa to the southeast, creating the modern far-reaching distribution of speakers of Bantu languages. Crops including sorghum (so valuable today it is grown in hot, dry areas on all continents), pearl millet, watermelon, black-eyed peas, African yams, oil palms, and kola nuts (the source of modern cola drinks) were first domesticated in West Africa but began spreading eastward by 5,000 years ago. Between 2,000 and 3,000 years ago, Bantu speakers with their crops reached the continent's east coast and a few centuries later reached its southern tip.

diffusion The spread of certain ideas, customs, or practices from one culture to another.

The Culture of Neolithic Settlements

Excavations of Neolithic settlements have revealed much about the daily activities of their former inhabitants. Archaeologists can reconstruct the business of making a living from structures, artifacts, and even the food debris found at these sites. Jericho, an early farming community located on the Jordan River's West Bank in the Palestinian territories, provides an excellent case in point.

Jericho: An Early Farming Community

Excavations at the Neolithic settlement that later grew to become the biblical city of Jericho have revealed the remains of a sizable farming community inhabited as early as 10,350 years ago. Here, in the Jordan River Valley, crops could be grown almost continuously due to the presence of a bounteous spring and the rich soils of an Ice Age lake that had dried up some 3,000 years earlier. In addition, waterborne deposits originating in the Judean highlands to the west regularly renewed the fertility of the soil.

To protect their settlement against floods and associated mudflows, as well as invaders, the people of Jericho built massive walls of stone around the settlement. Within these walls (6½ feet wide and 12 feet high), as well as a large rock-cut ditch (27 feet wide and 9 feet deep), an estimated 400 to 900 people lived in houses of mud brick with plastered floors arranged around courtyards.

Jericho's inhabitants also built a stone tower inside one corner of the wall, near the spring (**Figure 9.12**). It would have taken 100 people 104 days to build this tower. A staircase inside it probably led to a building on top. Recently archaeologists have suggested that this tower provides one of the earliest examples of an archaeological structure connected to the astronomical movement of the planet and seasonal cycles. The tower is oriented so that at the sunset of the summer solstice, the shadow of nearby mountains hit it first and then spread throughout the village (Barkai & Liran, 2008). The village also included storage facilities as well as ceremonial structures, all made of mud brick. A village cemetery also reflects the sedentary life of these early people. Nomadic groups, with few exceptions, rarely buried their dead in a single central location.

Common features in art, ritual, use of prestige goods, and burial practices indicate close contact between the farmers of Jericho and other nearby villages. Discovered inside the walls of Jericho, obsidian and turquoise from Sinai and marine shells from the coast document trade among neighboring villages.

Globalscape

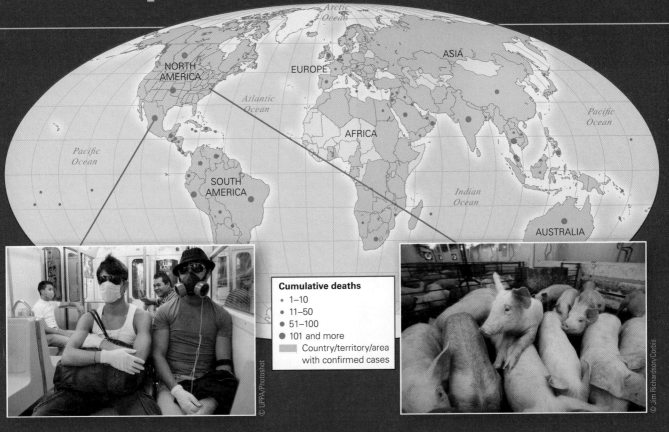

Cumulative deaths
- 1–10
- 11–50
- 51–100
- 101 and more
- Country/territory/area with confirmed cases

© UPPA/Photoshot

© Jim Richardson/Corbis

Factory Farming Fiasco?

In April 2009 protective masks and gloves were a common sight in Mexico City as the news of the first cases of swine flu pandemic appeared in the United States and Mexico. On June 11, 2009, the World Health Organization (WHO) made the pandemic official, and by July cases had been reported in three-quarters of the states and territories monitored by the WHO. Scientists across the world are examining the genetic makeup of the virus to determine its origins.

From the outset of the pandemic, many signs have pointed to a pig farming operation in Veracruz, Mexico, called Granjas Caroll, which is a subsidiary of Smithfield Foods, the world's largest pork producer. However, Ruben Donis, an expert virologist from the U.S. Centers for Disease Control and Prevention in Atlanta, Georgia, has come to a different conclusion based on genetic analysis. According to an article in the journal *Science*, Donis "suggests that the virus may have originated in a U.S. pig that traveled to Asia as part of the hog trade. The virus may have infected a human there, who then traveled back to North America, where the virus perfected human-to-human spread, maybe even moving from the United States to Mexico."[a] Another report has linked the current strain of swine flu to a strain that ran through factory farms in North Carolina in 1998 and to the avian flu that killed over 50 million people in 1918.[b]

While scientists examine the genetic evidence for swine flu, a look at factory farming shows how these practices facilitate the proliferation of disease. For example, the pig population of North Carolina numbers about 10 million, and most of these pigs are crowded onto farms of over 5,000 animals. These pigs travel across the country as part of farming operations. A pig may be born in North Carolina, then travel to the heartland of the United States to fatten up before a final trip to the slaughterhouses in California.

The crowded conditions in pig farms mean that if the virus enters a farm it quickly can infect many pigs, which are then shipped to other places spreading the virus further, with many opportunities for the virus to pass between species. Health risks of global food distribution have long been a concern, and the swine flu outbreak elevates these concerns to a new level.

Global Twister

Do you think the swine flu pandemic should lead to changes in meat production and distribution globally?

[a]Cohen, J. (2009). Out of Mexico? Scientists ponder swine flu's origin. *Science 324* (5928), 700–702.

[b]Trifonov, V., et al. (2009). The origin of the recent swine influenza A (H1N1) virus infecting humans. *Eurosurveillance 14* (17). www.eurosurveillance.org/ViewArticle.aspx?ArticleId=19193

© Nathan Benn/Ottochrome/Corbis

Figure 9.12 The Tower of Jericho The Natufian settlement of Jericho, located in the Palestinian West Bank of today's Israel, demonstrates that these ancient people had impressive social coordination, allowing them to build substantial structures. The defensive walls and the famous tower that stretched upward over 9 meters (28 feet) referenced in the Bible and gospel songs provide an example of cultural continuity in this region and beyond. The tower may have been part of a calendric ritual as the tower is built such that the shadows of mountains hit it first and then spread across the town at the sunset of the summer solstice.

Neolithic Material Culture

Life in Neolithic villages included various innovations in the realms of toolmaking, pottery, housing, and clothing. These aspects of material culture illustrate the dramatic social changes that took place during the Neolithic.

Toolmaking

Early harvesting tools consisted of razor-sharp flint blades inserted into handles of wood or bone. Later toolmakers added grinding and polishing the hardest stones to this toolmaking, technique. Scythes, forks, hoes, and simple plows replaced basic digging sticks. Later, when domesticated animals became available for use as draft animals, these early farmers redesigned their plows. Villagers used

mortars and pestles to grind and crush grain. Along with the development of diverse technologies, individuals acquired specialized skills for creating a variety of craft specialties including leatherwork, weavings, and pottery.

Pottery

Hard work on the part of those producing the food supported other members of the society who could then apply their skills and energy to various craft specialties such as pottery. In the Neolithic, different forms of pottery developed for transporting and storing food, water, and various material possessions (**Figure 9.13**). Impervious to damage by insects, rodents, and dampness, pottery vessels could be used for storing small grains, seeds, and other materials. Moreover, villagers could boil their food in pottery vessels directly over the fire instead of dropping fire-heated stones directly into food to cook it. Neolithic peoples used pottery for pipes, ladles, lamps, and other objects; some cultures even used large pottery vessels for disposal of the dead. Significantly, pottery containers remain important for much of humanity today.

Widespread use of pottery made of clay and fired in very hot ovens likely indicates a sedentary community. Archaeologists have found pottery in abundance in all but a few of the earliest Neolithic settlements. Its fragility and weight make it less practical for use by nomads and hunters, who more typically use woven bags, baskets, and containers made of animal hide. Nevertheless, some modern nomads make and use pottery, just as there are farmers today who do not. In fact, food foragers in East Asia were making pottery vessels by about 15,000 years ago, long before pottery appeared in Southwest Asia.

The manufacture of pottery requires artful skill and some technological sophistication. To make a useful vessel requires knowledge of clay: how to remove impurities from it, how to shape it into desired forms, and how to dry it in a way that does not cause cracking. Proper firing requires knowledge and care so that the clay heats enough to harden and resists future disintegration from moisture without cracking or even exploding as it heats and later cools down.

Neolithic peoples decorated their pottery in various ways. Some engraved designs on the vessel before firing whereas others shaped special rims, legs, bases, and other details separately and fastened them to the finished pot. Painting, the most common form of pottery decoration, accounts for literally thousands of unique designs found among the pottery remains of ancient cultures.

Housing

Food production and the new sedentary lifestyle brought about another technological development—house building. Because most food foragers move around frequently, they care little for permanent housing. Cave shelters, pits dug in the earth, and simple lean-tos made of hides and wooden poles serve the purpose of keeping the weather

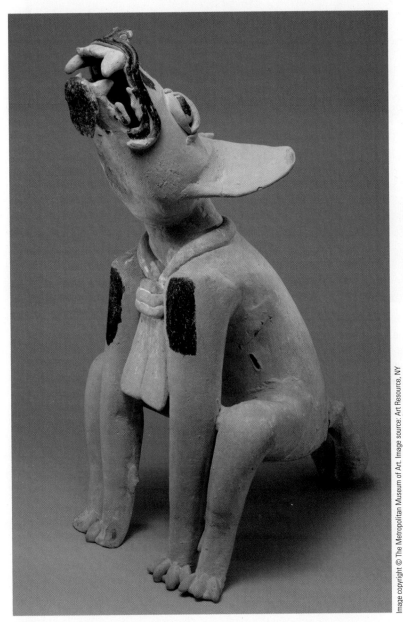

Image copyright © The Metropolitan Museum of Art. Image source: Art Resource, NY

Figure 9.13 Domesticated Art Ancient pottery provides evidence of animal domestication as well as the craft specializations that developed as a consequence of the Neolithic revolution. This howling canine came from Remojadas, a culture that flourished between 1,000 and 2,100 years ago along the Gulf Coast of present-day Mexico. Dogs, one of the few domesticated animal species found in Mesoamerica, were frequently incorporated into vessels or freestanding pieces such as this hollow ceramic figure. Throughout the world, species valued as domesticates appear in the ancient pottery and other decorative arts of the region. Rice appears in the pottery of East Asia, and pigs in the pottery of southeastern Turkey.

out. In the Neolithic, however, dwellings became more complex in design and more diverse in type. Some were constructed of wood, whereas others included more elaborate shelters made of stone, sun-dried brick, or branches plastered together with mud or clay.

Although permanent housing frequently goes along with food production, some cultures created substantial housing without shifting to food production. For example, on the northwestern coast of North America, people lived in sturdy houses made of heavy planks hewn from cedar logs, yet their food consisted entirely of wild plants and animals, especially salmon and sea mammals.

Clothing

Neolithic peoples were the first in human history to wear clothing made of woven textiles. The raw materials and technology necessary for the production of such clothing came from several sources: flax and cotton from farming; wool from domesticated sheep, llamas, or goats; silk from silkworms. Human invention contributed the spindle for spinning and the loom for weaving.

Social Structure

The economic and technological developments listed thus far enabled archaeologists to draw certain inferences concerning the organization of Neolithic societies. Although archaeological sites contain indications of ceremonial and spiritual activity, village life seemed to lack central organization and hierarchy. Burials, for example, reveal a marked absence of social differentiation. Only rarely did early Neolithic peoples use stone slabs to construct or cover graves or include elaborate objects with the dead. Evidently, no person had attained the kind of exalted status that required an elaborate funeral. The smallness of most villages and the absence of extravagant buildings suggest that the inhabitants knew one another very well and were even related, so that most of their relationships were probably highly personal ones, with equal emotional significance. Still, Neolithic peoples sometimes organized themselves to carry out impressive communal works preserved in the archaeological record, such as the site of Stonehenge in England (**Figure 9.14**).

© Cengage Learning

Figure 9.14 Druids of Stonehenge Sometimes Neolithic peoples organized themselves to carry out large projects, such as constructing Stonehenge, the famous ceremonial and astronomical center built in England some 4,500 years ago. Used as a burial ground long before the massive stone circle was erected, Stonehenge reflects the builders' understanding of the forces of nature and their impact upon food production. For instance, the opening of the stone circles aligns precisely with the sunset of the winter solstice. This careful alignment indicates that Neolithic peoples were paying close attention to the movement of the sun and to the seasonal growing cycle. Today people, such as the Wiltshire Druids pictured here, still gather at Stonehenge for rituals associated with the summer solstice.

In general, Neolithic social structure had minimal division of labor, but there is some evidence of new and more specialized social roles. In such **egalitarian societies** everyone has about the same rank and shares equally in the basic resources that support income, status, and power. Villages seem to have consisted of several households, each providing for most of its own needs. Kinship groups probably met the organizational needs of society beyond the household level.

Neolithic Cultures in the Americas

In the Americas the Neolithic revolution had a different shape and timing. For example, Neolithic farming villages were common in Southwest Asia between 8,000 and 9,000 years ago. But in **Mesoamerica**, the region from central Mexico to the northern regions of Central America, and in the Andean highlands, similar villages did not appear until about 4,500 years ago. Moreover, pottery, which developed in Southwest Asia shortly after plant and animal domestication, did not emerge in the Americas until about 4,500 years ago. Early Neolithic peoples in the Americas did not use the potter's wheel. Instead, they manufactured elaborate pottery by hand. Looms and the hand spindle appeared in the Americas about 3,000 years ago.

These absences do not indicate backwardness on the part of Native American peoples, many of whom, as we have already seen, were highly sophisticated farmers and plant breeders. Instead, we can surmise that Neolithic peoples in the Americas were satisfied with existing practices. Food production in Mesoamerica and the Andean highlands developed wholly independently from domestication in Eurasia and Africa, with different crops, animals, and technologies.

Outside Mesoamerica and the Andean highlands, hunting, fishing, and the gathering of wild plant foods remained important to the economy of Neolithic peoples in the Americas. Apparently, most American Indians continued to emphasize a food-foraging rather than a food-producing mode of life, even though maize and other domestic crops came to be cultivated just about everywhere that climate permitted. These groups, like hunter-gatherers in other parts of the world, opted not to take on the challenges of food production. These cultures remained stable until the arrival of European explorers, which instigated a pattern of disease and domination (Mann, 2005).

egalitarian societies Societies in which people have about the same rank, and share equally in the basic resources that support income, status, and power.

Mesoamerica The region extending from central Mexico to the northern regions of Central America.

The Neolithic and Human Biology

Although we tend to think of the invention of food production in terms of its cultural consequences, it had obvious biological impact as well. Physical anthropologists studying human skeletons from Neolithic burial grounds have found evidence for a somewhat lessened mechanical stress on peoples' bodies and teeth. Although exceptions exist, the teeth of Neolithic peoples generally show less wear, their bones are less robust, and compared to the skeletons of Paleolithic and Mesolithic peoples, they had less osteoarthritis (the result of stressed joint surfaces).

On the other hand, other skeletal features provide clear evidence for a marked deterioration in health and mortality. Skeletons from Neolithic villages show evidence of severe and chronic nutritional stress as well as pathologies related to infectious and deficiency diseases, as seen in this chapter's Original Study by Anna Roosevelt.

ORIGINAL STUDY

The History of Mortality and Physiological Stress

BY ANNA ROOSEVELT

Although there is a relative lack of evidence for the Paleolithic stage, enough skeletons have been studied that it seems clear that seasonal and periodic physiological stress regularly affected most prehistoric hunting-gathering populations, as evidenced by the presence of enamel hypoplasias [horizontal linear defects in tooth enamel] and Harris lines [horizontal lines near the ends of long bones].

What also seems clear is that severe and chronic stress, with high frequency of hypoplasias, infectious disease lesions, pathologies related to iron-deficiency anemia, and high mortality rates, is not characteristic of these early populations. There is no evidence of frequent, severe malnutrition, and so the diet must have been adequate in calories and other nutrients most of the time.

During the Mesolithic, the proportion of starch in the diet rose, to judge from the increased occurrence of certain dental diseases, but not enough to create an impoverished diet. At this time, diets seem to have been made up of a rather large number of foods, so that the failure of one food source would not be catastrophic. There is a possible slight tendency for Paleolithic people to be healthier and taller than Mesolithic people, but there is no apparent trend toward increasing physiological stress during the Mesolithic. Thus, it seems that both hunter-gatherers and incipient agriculturalists regularly underwent population pressure, but only to a moderate degree.

During the periods when effective agriculture first comes into use, there seems to be a temporary upturn in health and survival rates in a few regions: Europe, North America, and the eastern Mediterranean. At this stage, wild foods are still consumed periodically, and a variety of plants are cultivated, suggesting the availability of adequate amounts of different nutrients. Based on the increasing frequency of tooth disease related to high carbohydrate consumption, it seems that cultivated plants probably increased the storable calorie supply, removing for a time any seasonal or periodic problems in food supply. In most regions, however, the development of agriculture seems not to have had this effect, and there seems to have been a slight increase in physiological stress.

Stress, however, does not seem to have become common and widespread until after the development of high degrees of sedentism, population density, and reliance on intensive agriculture. At this stage in all regions the incidence of physiological stress increases greatly, and average mortality rates increase appreciably.

Most of these agricultural populations have high frequencies of porotic hyperostosis and cribra orbitalia [bone deformities indicative of chronic iron-deficiency anemia], and there is a substantial increase in the number and severity of enamel hypoplasias and pathologies associated with

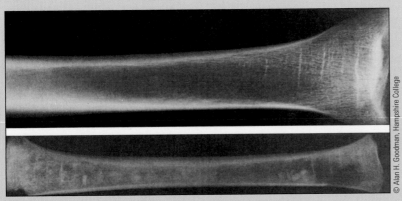

Harris lines near the ends of these youthful thighbones, found in a prehistoric farming community in Arizona, are indicative of recovery after growth arrest, caused by famine or disease.

© Alan H. Goodman, Hampshire College

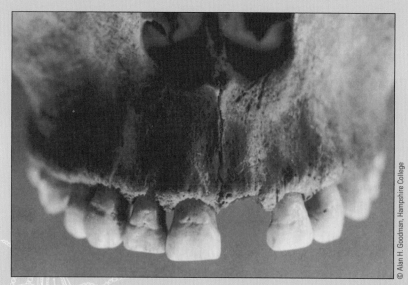

Enamel hypoplasias, such as those shown on these teeth, are indicative of arrested growth caused by famine or disease. These teeth are from an adult who lived in an ancient farming community in Arizona.

infectious disease. Stature in many populations appears to have been considerably lower than would be expected if genetically determined height maxima had been reached, which suggests that the growth arrests associated with pathologies were causing stunting.

Accompanying these indicators of poor health and nourishment, there is a universal drop in the occurrence of Harris lines, suggesting a poor rate of full recovery from the stress. Incidence of carbohydrate-related tooth disease increases, apparently because subsistence by this time is characterized by a heavy emphasis on a few starchy food crops. Populations seem to have grown beyond the point at which wild food resources could be a meaningful dietary supplement, and even domestic animal resources were commonly reserved for farm labor and transport rather than for diet supplementation.

It seems that a large proportion of most sedentary prehistoric populations under intensive agriculture underwent chronic and life-threatening malnutrition and disease, especially during infancy and childhood. The causes of the nutritional stress are likely to have been the poverty of the staple crops in most nutrients except calories, periodic famines caused by the instability of the agricultural system, and chronic lack of food due to both population growth and economic expropriation by elites. The increases in infectious disease probably reflect both a poorer diet and increased interpersonal contact in crowded settlements, and it is, in turn, likely to have aggravated nutritional problems.

Adapted from Roosevelt, A. C. (1984). Population, health, and the evolution of subsistence: Conclusions from the conference. In M. N. Cohen & G. J. Armelagos (Eds.), Paleopathology at the origins of agriculture *(pp. 572–574). Orlando: Academic Press.*

In addition to this evidence of stress preserved in Neolithic skeletons, dental decay increased during this period due to the high-starch diet. Scientists have recently documented dental drilling of teeth in a 9,000-year-old Neolithic site in Pakistan (Coppa et al., 2006). This resembles the high frequency of dental decay seen in contemporary populations when they switch from a varied hunter-gatherer diet to a high-starch diet.

Domestication encourages a sedentary lifestyle with the great potential for overpopulation relative to the resource base. Under these conditions, even minor environmental fluctuations can lead to widespread hunger and malnutrition. Evidence of stress and disease increased proportionally with population density and the reliance on intensive agriculture. Further, the crowded conditions in settlements led to competition for resources with other villages, increasing the mortality rate due to warfare.

For the most part, Neolithic peoples depended on crops selected for their higher productivity and storability rather than for nutritional balance. Moreover, as already noted, the crops' nutritional shortcomings would have been exacerbated by their susceptibility to periodic failure, particularly as populations grew in size. Thus, it comes as no surprise that Neolithic peoples experienced worsened health and higher mortality compared to their Paleolithic forebears. Some have gone so far as to assert that the switch from food foraging to food production was the worst mistake that humans ever made!

Sedentary life in fixed villages likely increased the incidence of disease and mortality characteristic of the Neolithic. With a sedentary, settled lifestyle come problems such as the accumulation of garbage and human waste. Small groups of people, who move about from one campsite to another, leave their waste behind. Moreover, transmission of airborne diseases increases where people are gathered into villages. As we saw in Chapter 2, farming practices also created the ideal environment for the species of mosquito that spreads malaria.

TABLE 9.1

Diseases Acquired from Domesticated Animals

Disease	Animal with Most Closely Related Pathogen
Measles	Cattle (rinderpest)
Tuberculosis	Cattle
Smallpox	Cattle (cowpox) or other livestock with related pox viruses
Influenza	Pigs, ducks
Pertussis (whooping cough)	Pigs, dogs

Close contact with animals provides a situation in which variants of animal pathogens may establish themselves in humans. For example, humans have developed symptoms from infection with avian influenza (bird flu) following contact with domesticated birds.

© Cengage Learning

Source: Diamond, J. (1997). *Guns, germs, and steel* (p. 207). New York: Norton.

The close association between humans and their domestic animals facilitated the transmission of some animal diseases to people. A host of life-threatening diseases—including smallpox, chicken pox, and in fact all of the infectious diseases of childhood, overcome by medical science only in the latter half of the 20th century—came to humans through their close association with domestic animals (Table 9.1). Again we see that domestication and the changes of the Neolithic revolution had unforeseen biological consequences to the human population.

The Neolithic and the Idea of Progress

Although the overall health of Neolithic peoples suffered as a consequence of this cultural shift, many view the transition from food foraging to food production as a great step upward on a ladder of progress. In part this interpretation derives from one of the more widely held beliefs of Western culture—that humans and their lifeways have progressed steadily over time. To be sure, farming allowed people to increase the size of their populations, to live together in substantial sedentary communities, and to reorganize the workload in ways that permitted craft specialization. However, this is not progress in a universal sense but, rather, a set of cultural beliefs about the nature of progress. Each culture defines *progress* (if it does so at all) in its own terms.

Whatever the benefits of food production, Neolithic humans paid a substantial price for the development of **agriculture**—intensive crop cultivation, employing plows, fertilizers, and/or irrigation. As anthropologists Mark Cohen and George Armelagos put it, "Taken as a whole, indicators fairly clearly suggest an overall decline in the quality—and probably in the length—of human life associated with the adoption of agriculture" (Cohen & Armelagos, 1984b, p. 594).

Rather than imposing ethnocentric notions of progress on the archaeological record, anthropologists view the advent of food production as part of the diversification of cultures, something that began in the Paleolithic. Although some societies continued to practice various forms of hunting, gathering, and fishing, others became horticultural. But the resource competition that began in the Neolithic has pushed hunter-gatherers into increasingly marginalized territories over time.

Some horticultural societies developed agriculture. Technologically more complex than horticultural societies, agriculturalists practice intensive crop cultivation, employing plows, fertilizers, and possibly irrigation. They may use a wooden or metal plow pulled by one or more harnessed draft animals, such as horses, oxen, or water buffaloes, to produce food on larger plots of land. At times, the distinction between horticulturalist and intensive agriculturalist blurs. For example, the Hopi Indians of the North American Southwest traditionally employed irrigation in their farming while at the same time using basic hand tools.

Pastoralism arose in environments that were too dry, too grassy, too steep, too cold, or too hot for effective horticulture or intensive agriculture. Pastoralists breed and manage migratory herds of domesticated grazing animals, such as goats, sheep, cattle, llamas, or camels. For example, without plows early Neolithic peoples could not farm the heavy grass cover of the Russian steppe, but they could graze their animals there. Thus, a number of peoples living in the arid grasslands and deserts that stretch from northwestern Africa into Central Asia kept large herds of domestic animals, relying on their neighbors for plant foods. Finally, some societies went on to develop civilizations—the subject of the next chapter.

agriculture Intensive crop cultivation, employing plows, fertilizers, and/or irrigation.

CHAPTER CHECKLIST

What is the Mesolithic?

⬤ The period between the Paleolithic and Neolithic, this period of warming after the last glacial period included rising sea levels, changes in vegetation, and the disappearance of herd animals from many areas.

⬤ The Mesolithic included a shift from the hunting of big game to hunting of smaller game and gathering a broad spectrum of plants and aquatic resources.

⬤ Increased reliance on seafood and plants allowed some people to become more sedentary.

⬤ Many Mesolithic tools in the Old World were made with microliths—small, hard, sharp blades of flint or similar stone that could be mass-produced and hafted. Mesolithic peoples also hafted larger blades to produce implements like sickles.

⬤ In the Americas, Archaic cultures are comparable to the Old World Mesolithic.

What is the Neolithic Revolution, and how did it come about?

⬤ A shift to food production through the domestication of plants and animals constitutes most of the change of this period.

⬤ Settlement in permanent villages accompanied food production in many cases, though some Neolithic peoples who depended on domesticated animals did not become sedentary. Still others maintained a hunter-gatherer lifestyle. The use of polished stone tools by all peoples of this period gives the Neolithic its name.

⬤ During the Neolithic, stone that was too hard to be chipped was ground and polished for tools. People developed scythes, forks, hoes, and plows to replace simple digging sticks. Axes and adzes made of polished stone were far stronger and less likely to chip than those with blades made of chipped stone.

⬤ Village life allowed for a reorganization of the workload, letting some individuals pursue specialized tasks.

⬤ The change to food production took place independently and more or less simultaneously in various regions of the world: Southwest and Southeast Asia, highland Mexico and Peru, South America's Amazon forest, eastern North America, China, and Africa. In all cases, people developed food complexes based on starchy grains and/or roots that were consumed with protein-containing legumes plus flavor enhancers.

⬤ Southwest Asia contains the earliest known Neolithic sites consisting of small villages of mud huts with individual storage pits and clay ovens along with evidence of food production and trade.

⬤ At ancient Jericho, remains of tools, houses, and clothing indicate Neolithic people occupied the oasis as early as 10,350 years ago. At its height, Neolithic Jericho had a population of 400 to 900 people. Comparable villages developed independently in Mexico and Peru by about 4,500 years ago.

⬤ The most probable theory to account for the Neolithic revolution is that domestication came about as a consequence of a chance convergence of separate natural events and cultural developments.

What is domestication, and how can we recognize it?

⬤ A domesticated plant or animal is one that has become genetically modified as an intended or unintended consequence of human manipulation.

⬤ Analysis of plant and animal remains at a site usually indicates whether its occupants were food producers. Wild cereal grasses, for example, typically have fragile stems, whereas cultivated ones have tough stems. Domesticated plants can also be identified because their edible parts are generally larger than those of their wild counterparts.

⬤ Domestication produces skeletal changes in some animals. The horns of wild goats and sheep, for example, differ from those of domesticated ones. Age and sex imbalances in herd animals may also indicate manipulation by human domesticators.

⬤ Domesticated crops are more productive but also more vulnerable. Food production also requires more labor compared to hunting and gathering.

How did the Neolithic revolution impact social structure?

⬤ Human population sizes have increased steadily since the Neolithic. Some scholars argue that pressure from increasing population size led to innovations such as intensive agriculture. Others suggest that these innovations allowed population size to grow.

⬤ Periodic crop failures forced Neolithic peoples to move into new regions, spreading farming from one region to another, as into Europe from Southwest Asia. Sometimes, food foragers will adopt the cultivation of crops from neighboring peoples in response to a shortage of wild foods.

⬤ Trade specializations came about due to the increased yields of food production. This included the extensive manufacture and use of pottery, the building of permanent houses, and the weaving of textiles.

● Archaeological evidence indicates that social organization was probably relatively egalitarian, with minimal division of labor and little development of specialized social roles.

● Neolithic peoples sometimes organized themselves to create monumental structures related to their belief systems, such as the ring of massive boulders at Stonehenge whose opening lines up precisely with the sunset of the winter solstice.

What were the biological consequences of the Neolithic revolution?

● New diets, living arrangements, and farming practices led to increased incidence of disease and higher mortality rates. Increased fertility, however, more than offset mortality, and globally human population has grown since the Neolithic.

● Many infectious diseases originated in the Neolithic because of close contact between humans and animal domesticates.

● Many of the health problems humans face today originated in the Neolithic.

● Increased competition for resources began in the Neolithic. Hunter-gatherers have become increasingly marginalized over time due to this competition.

QUESTIONS FOR REFLECTION

1. The changed lifeways of the Neolithic included the domestication of plants and animals as well as settlement into villages. This new way of life created a competition for resources. How is this competition manifest in the world today?

2. Why do you think some people of the past remained food foragers instead of becoming food producers? To what degree was the process of domestication conscious and deliberate? Were humans always directing this process?

3. Consider the reduction of diversity and the vulnerability to disease brought about by the domestication of wild species during the Neolithic. Are these same factors relevant to today's genetically modified foods? Who benefits most directly from these genetically engineered products?

4. Why are the changes of the Neolithic sometimes mistakenly associated with progress? Why have the social forms that originated in the Neolithic come to dominate the earth?

5. Although the archaeological record indicates some differences in the timing of domestication of plants and animals in different parts of the world, why is it incorrect to say that one region was more advanced than another?

ONLINE STUDY RESOURCES

CourseMate

Access chapter-specific learning tools, including learning objectives, practice quizzes, videos, flash cards, glossaries, and more in your Anthropology CourseMate.

Log into **www.cengagebrain.com** to access the resources your instructor has assigned and to purchase materials.

Challenge Issue

With the emergence of cities and states, human societies began to develop organized central governments and concentrated power that made it possible to build monumental structures such as the magnificent 12th-century Angkor Wat temple complex in Cambodia. But cities and states also ushered in a series of problems, many of which we still face today, such as large-scale warfare. Like monumental civic works, warfare requires elaborate organization under a centralized authority, both to mount attacks and for defense. Within decades of the dedication of this 500-acre temple to the Hindu god Vishnu, a neighboring group sacked it. The original Khmer rulers then took the temple back, restored it, ultimately dedicating the temple to Buddhism. In more recent times, this temple again was the site of violence when the army of Khmer Rouge, a murderous regime responsible for the deaths of at least 1.5 million Cambodians, retreated to the sacred ruins as they were ousted from power in 1979. Although the Khmer Rouge professed a doctrine of "complete eradication of the past" to justify their genocidal policies, in an ironic twist international concern for preservation of these sacred ruins protected the Khmer army from massive bombings. Today, peace has returned to Cambodia, and collective global infrastructure protects the temple of Angkor Wat for all of us.

The Emergence of Cities and States

A walk down a busy street in a city like New York or Cairo brings us into contact with numerous activities essential to life in contemporary urban society. People going to and from offices and stores fill crowded sidewalks. Heavy traffic of cars, taxis, and trucks periodically comes to a standstill. A brief two-block stretch may contain a grocery store; shops selling clothing, appliances, or books; a restaurant; a newsstand; a gasoline station; and a movie theater. Other neighborhoods may feature a museum, a police station, a school, a hospital, or a church.

Each of these services or places of business depends on others from outside this two-block radius. A butcher shop, for instance, depends on slaughterhouses and beef ranches. A clothing store could not exist without designers, farmers who produce cotton and wool, and workers who manufacture synthetic fibers. Restaurants rely on refrigerated trucking and vegetable and dairy farmers. Hospitals need insurance companies, pharmaceutical companies, and medical equipment industries to function. All institutions, finally, depend on the public utilities—the telephone, gas, water, and electric companies, not to mention the Internet. Although not perceptible at first glance, interdependence defines modern cities.

The interdependence of goods and services in a big city makes a variety of products readily available. But interdependence also creates vulnerability. If labor strikes, bad weather, or acts of violence cause one service to stop functioning, other services can deteriorate. At the same time, cities are resilient. When one service breaks down, others take over its functions. A long newspaper strike in New York City in the 1960s, for example, opened opportunities for several new newsmagazines as well as expanded television coverage of news and events. This phenomenon also occurred with the explosion of reality television programs in the United States during the 2007–2008 Hollywood writers' strike.

In many parts of the world, wars have caused extensive damage to basic infrastructure, leading to the development of alternative systems to cope with everything from the most basic tasks such as procuring food and water to communication

IN THIS CHAPTER YOU WILL LEARN TO

- Define *civilization*, *cities*, and *states* and identify their global origins.

- Identify the elements of archaeological exploration of ancient civilizations through a case study of the Maya city of Tikal.

- Examine the four major cultural changes that mark the transition from the Neolithic to life in urban centers.

- Compare theories for the development of states.

- Identify the problems that accompany the development of cities and states.

Figure 10.1 Urban Growth amid Destruction Decades of violence have severely compromised the infrastructure of Afghanistan, yet the size of Kabul, the fifth fastest-growing city in the world, has swelled to over 4 million people. Streets consist of rubble, and building facades stand as empty shells. Here children go to a public spigot to get their family's daily supply.

within global political systems (**Figure 10.1**). People coping with the aftermath of a natural disaster such as Hurricane Katrina in 2005 or the massive earthquake and tsunami that hit Japan in 2011 must also find such alternatives.

With the interconnectedness of modern life due to the Internet and globalization, the interdependence of goods and services transcends far beyond city limits. Social media such as Facebook and Twitter allow for instantaneous communication about geopolitical events and can mobilize global support, as occurred with the Arab Spring of 2011.

On the surface, city life seems so orderly that we take it for granted; but a moment's reflection reminds us that the intricate metropolitan fabric of life did not always exist, and the concentrated availability of diverse goods developed only very recently in human history.

Defining Civilization

The word *civilization* comes from the Latin *civis*, meaning "an inhabitant of a city," and *civitas*, "the urban community in which one dwells." In everyday North American and European usage, the word *civilization* connotes refinement and progress and may imply ethnocentric judgments about cultures. In anthropology, by contrast, the term has a more

precise meaning that avoids culture-bound notions. As used by anthropologists, **civilization** refers to societies in which large numbers of people live in cities, are socially stratified, and are governed by a ruling elite working through centrally organized political systems called states. We shall elaborate on all of these points in the course of this chapter.

As Neolithic villages grew into towns, the world's first cities developed (**Figure 10.2**). This happened between 4,500 and 6,000 years ago, first in Mesopotamia (modern-day Iraq and Syria), then in Egypt's Nile Valley and the Indus Valley (today's India and Pakistan). In China, civilization was underway by 5,000 years ago. Independent of these developments in Eurasia and Africa, the first American Indian cities appeared in Peru around 4,000 years ago and in Mesoamerica about 2,000 years ago.

What characterized these first cities? Why are they called the birthplaces of civilization? The most obvious feature of cities—and of civilization—is their large size and population. But cities include more than overgrown towns. Consider the case of Çatalhöyük, a compact 9,500-year-old settlement in south-central Turkey that, though well populated, was not a true city (Balter, 1998, 1999, 2001a; Kunzig, 1999). The tightly packed houses for its more than 5,000 inhabitants left no room for streets. People traversed the tops of neighboring houses and dropped through a hole in the roof to get into their own homes. Although house walls were covered with paintings and bas-reliefs, the houses were structurally similar to one another. People grew some crops and tended livestock but also collected significant amounts of food from wild plants and animals, never

civilization In anthropology, societies in which large numbers of people live in cities, are socially stratified, and are governed by a ruling elite working through centrally organized political systems called states.

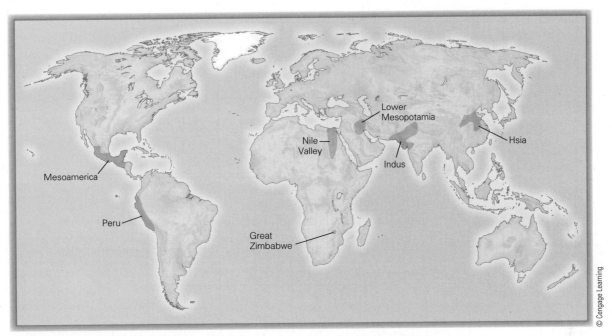

Figure 10.2 Early Civilizations The major early civilizations sprang from Neolithic villages in various parts of the world. Those of the Americas developed wholly independently of those in Africa and Eurasia. Chinese civilization seems to have developed independently of Southwest Asia, including the Nile and Indus civilizations. Although the Bantu city of Great Zimbabwe dates to later than some of these, it likewise was a major civilization that arose independently.

intensifying their agricultural practices. There is no evidence of public architecture and only minimal evidence of a division of labor or a centralized authority. It was as if several Neolithic villages were crammed together in one place at Çatalhöyük.

Archaeological evidence from early urban hubs, by contrast, demonstrates organized planning by a central authority, technological intensification, and social stratification. For example, flood control and protection were vital components of the great ancient cities of the Indus River Valley, located in today's India and Pakistan. Mohenjo-Daro, an urban center at its peak some 4,500 years ago with a population of at least 20,000, was built on an artificial mound, safe from floodwaters. The city streets were laid out in a grid pattern with sophisticated drainage systems for individual homes, indicating further centralized planning.

Ancient peoples incorporated their spiritual beliefs and social order into the cities they built. For example, the layout of the great Mesoamerican city Teotihuacan, founded 2,200 years ago, translated the solar calendar into a unified spatial pattern. Ancient city planners oriented the Street of the Dead—a grand north-south axis originating at the Pyramid of the Moon and bordered by the Pyramid of the Sun and the royal palace compound—to an astronomical marker, east of true north. They even channeled the San Juan River to conform to their pattern where it runs through the city (**Figure 10.3**). Thousands of apart-

ment compounds surrounded this core, separated from one another by a grid of narrow streets, maintaining the east-of-north orientation throughout the city. Archaeologists estimate that over 100,000 people inhabited this great city until its sudden collapse possibly in the 7th century.

Archaeologists have recovered clear evidence of both social and economic diversity in Teotihuacan. Variation in size and quality of apartment rooms indicates at least six levels of society. Those at the top of the social scale lived on or near the Street of the Dead (**Figure 10.4**). The Pyramid of the Sun, built along this avenue above a cave, was seen as a portal to the underworld and as the home of deities associated with death. Teotihuacan artisans worked

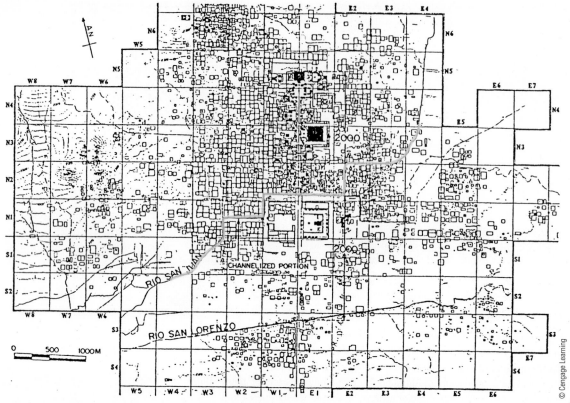

© Cengage Learning

Figure 10.3 Aztec City Planning The founders of Teotihuacan imposed an audacious plan on several square kilometers of landscape in central Mexico. At the center is the Street of the Dead, originating at the Pyramid of the Moon (*near top*) and running past the Pyramid of the Sun, and, south of the San Juan River (Rio), the palace compound. Note the gridded layout of surrounding apartment compounds and the channeled San Juan River.

VISUAL COUNTERPOINT

Figure 10.4 The Grand Avenues of Cities The view looking south down Teotihuacan's principal avenue, the Street of the Dead (*left*), was unequaled in scale until the construction of such modern-day avenues as the Champs-Élysées in Paris (*right*). Archaeologists estimate that 100,000 people lived in this city in various neighborhoods according to their social position. This major avenue was home to the elite.

on exotic goods and raw materials imported from distant regions, and at least two neighborhoods housed people with foreign affiliations: one for those from Oaxaca, the other (the "merchant's quarter") for those from the Gulf and Maya lowlands. Farmers, whose labor in fields (some of them irrigated) supplied the food to fellow city-dwellers, also resided in the city.

Mohenjo-Daro and Teotihuacan, like other early cities throughout the globe, represent far more than expanded Neolithic villages. Some consider the array of changes accompanying the emergence of urban living as one of the great developments in human culture. The following case study provides a glimpse into another of the world's ancient cities and reveals how archaeologists went about studying this city—from the first exploratory surveys, to the excavations, to the theories proposed about its development.

Tikal: A Case Study

The ancient city of Tikal, one of the largest lowland Maya centers in existence, is situated in Central America about 300 kilometers north of Guatemala City. Here, on a broad limestone terrace in a rainforest, the Maya settled 3,000 years ago. Because archaeologists have correlated the Maya calendar precisely with our own, we know that their civilization flourished until 1,100 years ago.

At its height, Tikal covered about 120 square kilometers (km²). The Great Plaza, a large paved area surrounded by about 300 major structures and thousands of houses, stood at Tikal's center, or nucleus (**Figure 10.5**). Starting from a small, dispersed population, Tikal swelled to at least

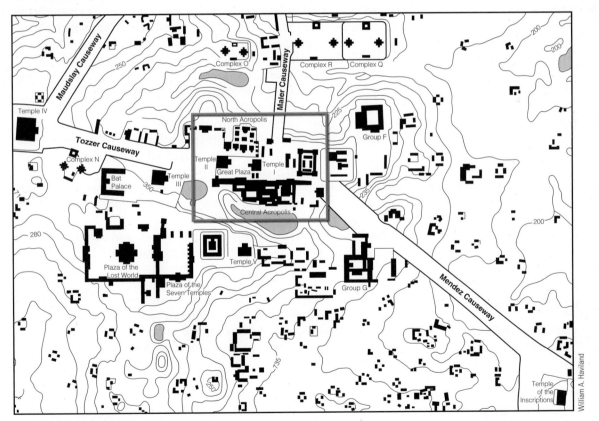

Figure 10.5 Layout of Tikal Tikal spreads far beyond the Great Plaza and the monumental buildings that have been excavated and are mapped here. Archaeologists used surveying techniques, test pits, and other strategies to define the city's boundaries and to understand the full spectrum of lifeways that took place there. The red outline in the center of the map delineates the royal court, royal burial ground, and central marketplace. In addition to what is pictured here, Tikal extends several kilometers outward in every direction. Those familiar with the original *Star Wars* movie will be interested to know that the aerial views of the rebel camp were filmed at Tikal, where monumental structures depicted in this map rise high above the forest canopy.

45,000 people. By 1,550 years ago, its population density had reached 600 to 700 persons per square kilometer, which was three times that of the surrounding region.

Archaeologists explored Tikal and the surrounding region under the joint auspices of the University of Pennsylvania Museum and the Guatemalan government from 1956 through the 1960s. At the time, it was the most ambitious archaeological project undertaken in the western hemisphere.

In the first few years of the Tikal Project, archaeologists investigated only the major temple and palace structures found in the vicinity of the Great Plaza, at the site's epicenter. But in 1959, aiming to gain a balanced view of Tikal's development and composition, they turned their attention to the hundreds of small mounds, thought to be the remains of dwellings that surrounded larger buildings. This represented a shift in the practice of archaeology toward studying the complexities of everyday life. Imagine trying to get a realistic view of life in a major city such as Chicago or Beijing by looking only at their monumental public buildings. Similarly, archaeologists realized that they needed to examine the full range of ruins at Tikal in order to accurately reconstruct past lifeways.

With data from the excavation of small structures, most of which were probably houses, archaeologists estimated Tikal's population size and density. In turn, this information allowed archaeologists to test the conventional assumption that the subsistence practices of the Maya inhabitants could not sustain large population concentrations.

Extensive excavation also provided a sound basis for a reconstruction of the everyday life and social organization of the Maya, a people who had been known almost entirely through the study of ceremonial remains. For example, differences in architecture, house construction, and associated artifacts and burials suggest differences in social class. Features of house distribution might reflect the existence of extended families or other types of kin groups. The excavation of both large and small structures revealed the social structure of the total population of Tikal (Haviland, 2002).

Surveying and Excavating the Site

Mapping crews extensively surveyed 6 square kilometers of forested land surrounding the Great Plaza, providing a preliminary map to guide the small-structure excavation process. The dense, tall rainforest canopy prevented the use of aerial photography for this mapping. Trees obscured all but the tallest temples. Many of the small ruins remain practically invisible even to observers on the ground. Four years of mapping revealed that ancient Tikal extended far beyond the original 6 km² surveyed. More time and money allowed continued surveying of the area in order to fully define the city's boundaries and calculate its overall size.

The initial excavation of six structures, two plazas, and a platform revealed new structures not visible before excavation, the architectural complexity of the structures, and an enormous quantity of artifacts. Some structures were partially excavated, and some remained uninvestigated. Following this initial work, the archaeological team excavated over a hundred additional small structures in different parts of the site in order to ensure investigation of a representative sample. The team also sank numerous test pits in various other small-structure groups to supplement the information gained from more extensive excavations. They also washed and catalogued every artifact recovered.

Evidence from the Excavation

Excavation at Tikal produced considerable evidence about the social organization, technology, and diversity in this ancient city, as well as the relationship between people in Tikal and other regions. For example, the site provides evidence of trade in nonperishable items. Granite, quartzite, hematite, pyrite, jade, slate, and obsidian all were imported, either as raw materials or finished products. Marine materials came from Caribbean and Pacific coastal areas. In turn, Tikal residents exported chert (a flintlike stone used to manufacture tools) both in its raw form and as finished objects. Tikal's location between two river systems may have facilitated an overland trade route. Evidence of trade in perishable goods—such as textiles, feathers, salt, and cacao—indicated the presence of full-time traders among the Tikal Maya.

In the realm of technology, archaeologists found specialized woodworking, pottery, obsidian, and shell workshops. The skillful carving displayed on stone monuments suggests that occupational specialists did this work. Similarly, the fine artwork glazed into ceramic vessels demonstrates that ancient artists could envision the transformation of their pale, relatively colorless ceramics into their finished fired form.

To control the large population, some form of bureaucratic organization must have existed in Tikal. From Maya written records (glyphs), we know that the government was headed by a hereditary ruling dynasty with sufficient power to organize massive construction and maintenance (Figure 10.6). This included a system of defensive ditches and embankments on the northern and southern edges of the city. The longest of these ran for a distance of perhaps 19 to 28 kilometers. We also know that astrological experts constructed detailed and accurate calendars for tracking the dynasties and their conquests (Figure 10.7). Although we do not have direct evidence, clues indicate the presence of textile workers, dental workers, makers of bark cloth "paper," scribes, masons, astronomers, and other occupational specialists.

Archaeologists suggest that the religion of the Tikal Maya developed initially as a means to cope with the uncertainties of agriculture. With thin soils and no streams, Tikal residents

© Anita de Laguna Haviland

Figure 10.6 Stone Documents Carved monuments like this were commissioned by Tikal's rulers to commemorate important events in their regions. Archaeologists have deciphered the glyphs or written language chiseled into the stone. This monument portrays the reign of a king who ruled about 1,220 years ago. Only a specialist could have accomplished such skilled stone carvings. The glyphs also provide indirect evidence of writing specialists or scribes who may have kept records on perishable materials such as bark cloth paper. (For a translation of the inscription on the monument's left side, see Figure 10.13.)

depended on rainwater collected in reservoirs. Rain is abundant in season, but its onset is unreliable. The ancient Maya may have perceived Tikal, with a high elevation relative to surrounding terrain, as a "power place," especially suited for making contact with supernatural forces and beings (**Figure 10.8**).

The Maya priests tried not only to win over and please the deities in times of drought but also to honor them in times of plenty. Priests—experts on the Maya calendar—determined the most favorable time to plant crops and were involved with other agricultural matters. This tended to keep people in or near the city so that they could receive guidance on their crops. The population in and around Tikal depended upon their priests to influence supernatural beings and forces on their behalf.

As the population increased, land for agriculture became scarce, forcing the Maya to find new methods of food production that could sustain Tikal's dense population. They added the planting and tending of fruit trees and other crops that could be grown around their houses in soils enriched by human waste. (Unlike houses at Teotihuacan, those at Tikal were not built close to one another.) Along with increased reliance on household gardening, the Maya constructed artificially raised fields in areas that flooded during the rainy season. Careful maintenance allowed for intensive cultivation of these raised fields, year after year. By converting low areas into reservoirs and constructing channels to carry runoff from plazas and other architecture into these reservoirs, the Maya at Tikal maximized the collection of water for the dry season.

As these agricultural changes took place, a class of artisans, craftspeople, and other occupational specialists emerged to serve the needs of an elite consisting of the priesthood and a ruling dynasty. The Maya built numerous

Tyrone Turner/National Geographic Stock

Figure 10.7 Maya Calendar Mesoamerican cultures like the Maya and the Olmec used a nonrepeating "long count" calendar system that tallied the number of days that had passed since a mythical creation date, corresponding to August 11, 3114 BCE. According to Mayan mythology, we live in the fourth world, the first three creations having been failed attempts by the gods. The end of the current long count on December 12, 2012, caused numerous doomsday predictions. Also, in 2012, a team of archaeologists lead by William Saturno of Boston Univeristy uncovered a remarkable series of glyphs at the Guatemalan site of Xultun that confirmed the astronomically accurate Maya calendars extend far into the future.

Figure 10.8 **Modern Maya at Tikal** Archaeologists have proposed that Tikal emerged as an important religious center due to its relative altitude in the region. Altitude may have created a perception of power and access to supernatural forces. Today, Tikal remains an important religious center for local Maya, who gather in front of the acropolis for a traditional ceremony.

temples, public buildings, and various kinds of houses appropriate to the distinct social classes of their society.

For several hundred years, Tikal sustained its ever-growing population. When the pressure for food and land reached a critical point, population growth stopped. At the same time, warfare with other cities had increasingly destructive effects on Tikal. Archaeologists diagnosed the damage caused by warfare from abandoned houses situated on prime lands in rural areas, from nutritional problems visible in skeletons recovered from burials, and from construction of the previously mentioned defensive ditches and embankments. The archaeological record shows that there was a period of readjustment directed by an already strong central authority. Activities then continued as before, but without further population growth for another 250 years or so.

As this case study shows, excavations at Tikal demonstrated the splendor, the social organization, the belief systems, and the agricultural practices of the ancient Maya civilization. This chapter's Original Study illustrates a very different Maya site just a day's walk from Tikal.

Action Archaeology and the Community at El Pilar BY ANABEL FORD

Resource management and conservation are palpable themes of the 21st century. Nowhere is this more keenly felt than in the tropics, seemingly our last terrestrial frontier. The Maya forest, one of the world's most biodiverse areas, is experiencing change at a rapid rate. Over the next two decades this area's population will double, threatening the integrity of the tropical ecosystems with contemporary development strategies that are at odds with the rich biodiversity of the region.

Curiously, in the past the Maya forest was home to a major civilization with at least three to nine times the current population of the region. The prosperity of the Classic Maya civilization has been touted for the remarkable quality of their unique hieroglyphic writing; the beauty of their art expressed in stone, ceramics, and plaster; and the precision of their mathematics and astronomy. What was the secret

of Maya conservation and prosperity? How can archaeology shed light on the conservation possibilities for the future? These are the questions I address in my research at El Pilar.

I began my work as an archaeologist in the Maya forest in 1972. Eschewing the monumental civic centers that draw tourist and scholar alike, I was interested in the everyday life of the Maya through the study of their cultural ecology—the multifaceted relationships of humans and their environment. Certainly, the glamorous archaeological centers intrigued me; they were testaments to the wealth of the

Maya civilization. Yet, it seemed to me that an understanding of the ancient Maya landscape would tell us more about the relationship of the Maya and their forest than yet another major temple. After all, the Maya were an agrarian civilization.

The ancient Maya agricultural system must be the key to their growth and accomplishments. With more than a century of exploration of the temple centers, we know that the civic centers were made for the ceremonial use of the ruling elite, that the temples would hold tombs of the royals and would include dedications of some of the most astounding artworks of the ancient world. Centers, too, would present stone stele erected in commemoration of regal accomplishments with hieroglyphic writing that is increasingly understood as codification of the Mayan language. These facts about the Maya point to successful development founded in their land use strategies that supported the increasing populations, underwrote the affluent elite glamor, and allowed for the construction of major civic centers over 2 millennia. The Maya farmers were at the bottom of this astounding expansion, and that is where I thought there could be a real discovery.

Because agriculture figures so importantly in preindustrial agrarian societies, such as the Maya, we would expect that the majority of the settlements would be farming ones. But how can we understand the farming techniques and strategies? Our appreciation of the traditional land use methods has been subverted with technology and a European ecological imperialism that inhibits a full understanding of other land use systems.

During the conquest of the Maya area, Spaniards felt there was nothing to eat in the forest; presented with a staggering cornucopia of fruits and vegetables that could fill pages, they asserted they were starving because there was no grain or cattle. Today, we use European terms to describe agricultural lands around the world that are in many ways inappropriate to describe traditional systems. The word *arable* specifically means "plowable" and is derived from the Egyptian word *Ard*, or "plow." *Arable* is equated with *cultivable* by the United Nations Food and Agriculture Organization, and by doing so eliminates realms of land use and management that have a subtler impact on the environment. *Fallow* is loosely used to indicate abandoned fields, but really *fallow* means "unseeded plowed field." For European eyes, plowing was equivalent to cultivating, but in the New World cultivating embraced a much broader meaning that included fields of crops, selective succession, diverse orchards, and managed forests. In fact, it meant the entire landscape mosaic.

It is important to remember that the Maya, like all Native Americans prior to the tumultuous conquest 500 years ago, lived in the Stone Age without metal tools and largely without domesticated animals. This was not a hindrance, as it would seem today, but a fact that focused land use and intensification in other realms. Farmers were called upon to use their local skill and knowledge to provide for daily needs. And, as with all Native Americans, this skill would involve the landscape and most particularly the plants.

Reports of yields of grain from the Mesoamerican maize fields, or *milpas*, suggest that they were more than two to three times as productive as the fertile fields of the Seine River near Paris of the 16th century, the time of the conquest. The Maya farmed in cooperation with the natural environment. Like the Japanese rice farmer Masanubu Fukuoka describes in his book *One Straw Revolution*, Maya farmers today use their knowledge of the insects to ensure pollination, their understanding of animals to promote propagation, their appreciation of water to determine planting, and their observations of change and nuance to increase their yields. This is not at all like the current agricultural development models that rely on increasingly complex techniques to raise production, disregarding nature in the process.

My focus on the patterns of the ancient Maya settlements has guided me along a path that I believe can provide important answers to questions of how the Maya achieved their success. The answers lie in finding where the everyday Maya lived, when they lived there, and what they did there. Although popular notions would have you think that the Maya were a seething sea of humanity displacing the forest for their cities, I have discovered patterns on the landscape indicating that at their height in the Late Classic from 600 to 900 CE, the Maya occupied less than two-thirds of the landscape. More than 80 percent of the settlements were concentrated into less than 40 percent of the area, whereas another 40 percent of the region was largely unoccupied.

This diversity of land use intensity created a patchwork of stages of what traditional farmers see as a cycle from forest to field and from field to orchard and back to forest again. The result in the Maya forest garden was an economic landscape that supported the ancient Maya, fueled wealth in the colonial and independence eras with lumber, and underwrote capitalism with the natural gum chicle. Today, more than 90 percent of the dominant trees of the forest are of economic value. The Maya constructed this valuable forest over the millennia.

Despite my interest in daily life in the forest, monumental buildings became a part of my work. While conducting a settlement survey in the forest, I uncovered and mapped El Pilar, a major ancient Maya urban center with enormous temples towering more than 22 meters high and plaza expanses greater than soccer fields. The whole center of civic buildings covers more than 50 hectares. El Pilar is the largest center in the Belize River area and is located only 50 kilometers from Tikal. This center was bound to become a tourist destination, presenting an opportunity to explore new ways to tell the Maya story. My observation that the ancient Maya evolved a sustainable economy in the tropics of Mesoamerica led my approach to developing El Pilar.

Astride the contemporary border separating Belize from Guatemala, El Pilar has been the focus of a bold conservation design for an international peace park on a long-troubled border. The vision for El Pilar is founded on the preservation of cultural heritage in the context of the natural environment. With a collaborative and interdisciplinary team of local villagers, government administrators, and scientists, we have established the El Pilar Archaeological Reserve for Maya Flora and Fauna. Since 1993, the innovations of the El Pilar program have forged new ground in testing novel strategies for community participation in the conservation development of the El Pilar Archaeological Reserve.

This program touches major administrative themes of global importance: tourism, natural resources, foreign affairs, agriculture, rural development, and education. Yet the program's impact goes further. Working with traditional forest gardeners affects agriculture, rural enterprise, and capacity building. There are few areas untouched by the program's inclusive sweep, and more arenas can contribute to its evolution.

At El Pilar, I practice what I call "action archaeology," a pioneering conservation model that draws on lessons learned from the recent and distant past to benefit contemporary populations. For example, the co-evolution of Maya society and the environment provide clues about sustainability in this region today. At El Pilar we have advanced programs that will simulate Maya forest gardens as an alternative to resource diminishing plow-and-pasture farming methods. Working with the traditional farmers, school models are being established. These models will help to transfer knowledge to the younger generation and carry on important conservation strategies. The forest survives and demonstrates resilience to impacts brought on by human expansion. The ancient Maya lived with this forest for millennia, and the El Pilar program argues there are lessons to be learned from that past.

The El Pilar program recognizes the privilege it has enjoyed in forging an innovative community participatory process, in creating a unique management planning design, and in developing a new tourism destination. The success of local outreach at El Pilar can best be seen in the growth of the community organizations such as the El Pilar Forest Garden Network and Amigos de El Pilar (Friends of El Pilar). With groups based in both Belize and Guatemala working together, the El Pilar program can help build an inclusive relationship between the community and the reserve that is mutually beneficial. The development of this dynamic relationship lies at the heart of the El Pilar philosophy—resilient and with the potential to educate communities, reform local-level resource management, and inform conservation designs for the Maya forest.

Written expressly for this text, 2005. Anabel Ford is the director of the Mesoamerican Research Center, University of California, Santa Barbara, and president of the nonprofit Exploring Solutions Past: The Maya Forest Alliance. www.marc.ucsb.edu/elpilar/. Reprinted by permission of Professor Anabel Ford.

Archaeologist Anabel Ford at work in El Pilar.

© Rolox Awards for Excellence, Susan Gray

Cities and Cultural Change

If a person who grew up in a rural North American village today moved to Philadelphia, Montreal, or Los Angeles, she or he would experience a very different way of life. The same would be true for a Neolithic village-dweller who moved into one of the world's first cities in Mesopotamia 5,500 years ago. Because cultures are dynamic and integrated systems of adaptation that respond to external and internal factors, a shift from food production to living in urban centers also includes changes in the social structure and ideology. Four basic changes mark the transition from Neolithic village life to life in the first urban centers: agricultural innovation, diversification of labor, central government, and social stratification.

Agricultural Innovation

Changes in farming methods distinguished early civilizations from Neolithic villages. The ancient Sumerians, for example, built an extensive system of dikes, canals, and reservoirs to irrigate their farmlands. With such a system, they could control water resources at will; water could be held and then run off into the fields as necessary. Such innovations also contributed to large-scale production and management of animals needed to sustain large populations. As described in this chapter's Anthropology Applied feature, an understanding of these ancient techniques can provide models for effective land use in the present.

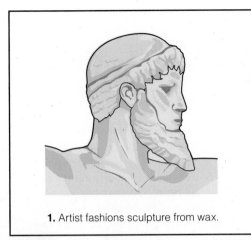

1. Artist fashions sculpture from wax.

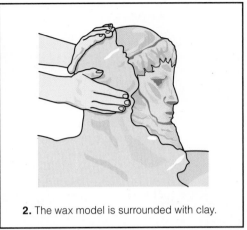

2. The wax model is surrounded with clay.

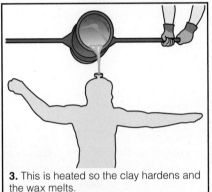

3. This is heated so the clay hardens and the wax melts.
4. The now hollow mold is inverted, and molten bronze metal is poured into it.

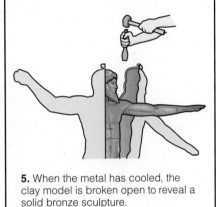

5. When the metal has cooled, the clay model is broken open to reveal a solid bronze sculpture.

© Cengage Learning

Figure 10.9 Lost Wax Casting Method The Bronze Age included manufacture of wholly practical metal items such as knives and plows, but it also contributed symbolically to maintaining the power of the ruling elite. Elaborate lifelike, large-scale sculptures of deities—such as the 3,000-year-old bronze Zeus, from the National Museum of Archaeology in Athens, Greece—or of the rulers themselves, demonstrated their power. This cultural tradition has continued into the present. Artists today employ the same methods of lost wax casting.

Irrigation improved crop yield: Not having to depend upon the seasonal rain cycles allowed farmers to harvest more crops in one year. Increased crop yields, resulting from agricultural innovations, contributed to the high population densities of ancient civilizations.

Diversification of Labor

Diversified labor activity also characterized early civilizations. In a Neolithic village without irrigation or plow farming, every family member participated in the raising of crops. In contrast, the high crop yields made possible by new farming methods and the increased population of civilizations permitted a sizable number of people to pursue nonagricultural activities on a full-time basis.

Ancient public records document a variety of specialized workers. For example, an early Mesopotamian document from the old Babylonian city of Lagash (modern-day Tell al-Hiba, Iraq) lists the artisans, craftspeople, and others paid from crop surpluses stored in the temple granaries. These lists included coppersmiths, silversmiths, sculptors, merchants, potters, tanners, engravers, butchers, carpenters, spinners, barbers, cabinetmakers, bakers, clerks, and brewers.

With specialization came the expertise that led to the invention of new ways of making and doing things. In Eurasia and Africa, civilization ushered in the **Bronze Age**, a period marked by the production of tools, ornaments, and monuments made of this metal alloy **(Figure 10.9)**. Metals were in great demand for the manufacture of farmers' and artisans' tools, as well as for weapons. Copper and tin (the raw materials from which bronze is made) were smelted, or separated from their ores, then purified and cast to make plows, swords, axes, and shields.

Bronze Age In the Old World, the period marked by the production of tools and ornaments of bronze; began about 5,000 years ago in China, the Mediterranean, and South Asia and about 500 years earlier in Southwest Asia.

ANTHROPOLOGY APPLIED

Pre-Columbian Fish Farming in the Amazon

By Clark L. Erickson

Popular images associated with the Amazon today include the towering continuous green forest canopy, Day-Glo poison dart frogs, and natives' faces painted red. These potent images have been used to raise funds for conservation, educate the public in "green" politics, and promote ecotourism. Two themes have long dominated the popular and scientific literature on the Amazon: (1) the Myth of the Pristine Environment and (2) the Myth of the Noble Savage. The Myth of the Pristine Environment is the belief that the landscapes of the Americas were largely undisturbed Nature until the arrival of Europeans, who have destroyed the environment with their agriculture, mining, urbanism, and

industry. The Myth of the Noble Savage posits that indigenous peoples of the past and present exist as a harmonious part of an undisturbed Nature. We now know that much of what has been traditionally recognized as Wilderness in the Amazon is the indirect result of massive depopulation after the arrival of Europeans. The introduction of Old World diseases, slavery, missionization, resettlement, and warfare removed most of the native peoples from the land within 100 years. Many areas of Amazonia were not repopulated until this century, and many still remain underpopulated.

My colleagues and I are documenting numerous cases of how native peoples of the Amazon (past and present) transformed, shaped, and in some cases, constructed what is often misidentified as pristine "wilderness." We find that high biodiversity is clearly related to past human activities such as gap formation, burning, and gardening. Our approach, called historical ecology or the archaeology of landscapes, assumes that all landscapes have long, complex histories. We find that high biodiversity is clearly related to past human activities such as opening up the forest, burning, and gardening. Since 1990, my research team has studied the vast networks of earthworks in the Bolivian Amazon

built before the arrival of Europeans. These features include causeways of earth, artificial canals for canoe traffic, raised fields for growing crops in the savannahs, and settlement mounds of urban scale.

In 1995, we were invited by the local governor to begin archaeological investigations in Baures, a remote region of seasonally flooded savannahs, wetlands, and forest islands in northeast Bolivia. He loaned us his Cessna and pilot for an initial aerial survey of the region. As the plane circled the landscape, we saw an amazingly complex web of straight roads, canals, and moated earthwork enclosures below. During the dry season of 1996, I surveyed the area accompanied by a group of local hunters.

One artificial feature, referred to as a zigzag earthwork, particularly intrigued me. Low earthen walls zigzag across the savannahs between forest islands. Because of their changing orientations, they did not make sense as roads between settlements. As we mapped them with tape measure and compass, I noted that there were small funnel-like openings where the earthworks changed direction. I immediately realized that these matched the description of fish weirs that are reported in the ethnographic and historical literature on Amazonian peoples.

Later, such tools were made from smelted iron. In wars, stone knives, spears, and slings could not stand up against metal spears, arrowheads, swords, helmets, and armor.

The indigenous civilizations of the Americas also used metals. South American peoples used copper, silver, and gold for tools as well as for ceremonial and ornamental objects. The Aztecs and Maya used the same soft metals for ritual and decorative objects while continuing to rely on stone for their everyday tools. To those who assume the inherent superiority of metal, this seems puzzling. However, the ready availability of obsidian (a glass formed

by volcanic activity), its extreme sharpness (many times sharper than the finest steel), and the ease with which toolmakers can work it made it perfectly suited to their needs. Moreover, unlike bronze—and especially iron— copper, silver, and gold are soft metals and have limited practical use. Obsidian tools provide some of the sharpest cutting edges ever made (recall Chapter 7's Anthropology Applied, "Stone Tools for Modern Surgeons").

Early civilizations developed extensive trade systems to procure the raw materials needed for their technologies. In many parts of the world, boats provided greater

Working with archaeologist Clark Erickson, artist Dan Brinkmeier of the Field Museum of Natural History has illustrated the fish weirs and ponds of ancient Baures, Bolivia.

season. I believe that in the past these were used to store live fish until needed. Our studies show that the weirs were used before the arrival of Europeans to the region.

The scale of the fish weir complex is larger than any previously reported. The native peoples of Baures shaped the environment into a productive landscape capable of providing sufficient protein to sustain large populations. The people responsible for this impressive land management are long gone or have forgotten the technology. Archaeology provides the only means of documenting this important lost knowledge. As politicians, conservationists, and aid agencies seek sustainable solutions to both develop and conserve the Amazon, archaeologists can play a key role by providing time-tested models of land use.

Fish weirs are fences made of wood, brush, basketry, or stones with small openings that extend across bodies of water. Baskets or nets are placed in the openings to trap migrating fish. Although most fish weirs are simple ephemeral structures crossing a river or shallow lake, those of Baures are permanent earthen features covering more than 500 square kilometers. In addition, small artificial ponds are associated with the fish weirs. Today, these ponds are filled with fish as the floodwaters recede in the dry

Adapted from Erickson, C. L. (2001). Pre-Columbian fish farming in the Amazon. Expedition 43 (3), 7–8. Copyright © 2001 Clark L. Erickson. Reprinted by permission of the author.

access to trade centers, transporting large loads of imports and exports between cities at lower costs than if they had been carried overland. A one-way trip from the ancient Egyptian cities along the Nile River to the Mediterranean port city of Byblos in Phoenicia (not far from today's Beirut, Lebanon) took far less time by rowboat compared to the overland route. With a sailboat, it was even faster.

Egyptian kings, or pharaohs, sent expeditions in various directions for prized resources: south to Nubia (northern Sudan) for gold; east to the Sinai Peninsula for copper; to Arabia for spices and perfumes; to Asia for lapis lazuli (a blue semiprecious stone) and other jewels; north to Lebanon for cedar, wine, and funerary oils; and southwest to Central Africa for ivory, ebony, ostrich feathers, leopard skins, cattle, and the captives they enslaved. Evidence of trading from Great Zimbabwe (**Figure 10.10**) in southern Africa indicates that by the 11th century these trading networks extended throughout the Old World. Increased contact with foreign peoples through trade brought new information to trading economies, furthering the spread of innovations and bodies of knowledge such as geometry and astronomy.

Figure 10.10 **Great Zimbabwe** The construction of elliptical granite walls held together without any mortar at Great Zimbabwe in southern Zimbabwe, Africa, attests to the skill of the people who built these structures. When European explorers, unwilling to accept the notion of civilization in sub-Saharan Africa, discovered these magnificent ruins, they wrongly attributed them to white non-Africans. This false notion persisted until archaeologists demonstrated that these structures were part of a city with 12,000 to 20,000 inhabitants that served as the center of a medieval Bantu state.

Central Government

A governing elite also emerged in early civilizations. The challenges new cities faced because of their size and complexity required a strong central authority. The governing elite saw to it that different interest groups, such as farmers or craft specialists, provided their respective services and did not infringe on one another.

Just as they do today, governments of the past ensured that cities were safe from their enemies by constructing fortifications and raising an army. They levied taxes and appointed tax collectors so that construction workers, the army, and other public expenses could be paid. They saw to it that merchants, carpenters, or farmers who made legal claims received justice according to their legal system's standards. They guaranteed safety for the lives and property of ordinary people and assured them that any harm done to one person by another would be justly handled. In addition, they arranged for storage of surplus food

for times of scarcity and supervised public works such as extensive irrigation systems and fortifications.

Evidence of Centralized Authority

Evidence of centralized authority in ancient civilizations comes from sources such as law codes, temple records, monuments, and royal chronicles. Excavation of the city structures themselves provides additional evidence because these remains can show definitive signs of city planning. The precise astronomical layout of the Mesoamerican city of Teotihuacan, described earlier, attests to strong, centralized control.

Monumental buildings and temples, palaces, and large sculptures are usually found in ancient civilizations. For example, the Great Pyramid for the tomb of Khufu, the Egyptian pharaoh, is 755 feet long (236 meters) and 481 feet high (147 meters); it contains about 2.3 million stone blocks, each with an average weight of 2.5 tons. The Greek historian Herodotus reports that it took 100,000 men twenty years to build this tomb. Such gigantic structures could be built only because a powerful central authority was able to harness the considerable labor force, engineering skills, and raw materials necessary for their construction.

Writing or some form of recorded information provides another indicator of the existence of centralized authority. With writing, governors could disseminate information and store, systematize, and deploy written records for political, religious, and economic purposes. Of course, the development of writing went hand in hand with the development of specialized laborers: scribes responsible for physically creating the centralized authorities' records.

Scholars attribute the initial motive for the development of writing in Mesopotamia to recordkeeping of state affairs. Writing allowed early governments to track accounts of their food surplus, tribute records, and other business receipts. Some of the earliest documents appear to be just such records—lists of vegetables and animals bought and sold, tax lists, and storehouse inventories.

Before 5,500 years ago, records consisted initially of "tokens," ceramic pieces with different shapes indicative of different commercial objects. Thus, a cone shape could represent a measure of grain or a cylinder could be an animal. As the system became more sophisticated, tokens came to represent different animals, as well as processed foods (such as oil, trussed ducks, or bread) and manufactured or imported goods (such as textiles and metal) (Lawler, 2001). Ultimately, clay tablets with impressed marks representing objects replaced these tokens.

By 5,000 years ago, in the Mesopotamian city of Uruk in Iraq (which likely derives its modern country name

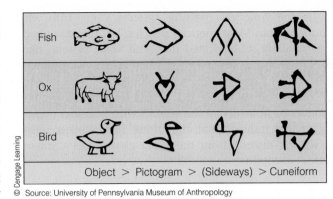

Figure 10.11 Cuneiform Cuneiform writing developed from representational drawings of objects. Over time the drawings became simplified and more abstract, as well as being wedge-shaped so that they could be cut into a clay tablet with a stylus.

from this ancient place), a new writing technique emerged. Writers would use a reed stylus to make wedge-shaped markings on a tablet of damp clay. Originally, each marking stood for a word. Because most words in this language were monosyllabic, over time the markings came to stand for syllables, and cuneiform writing developed (**Figure 10.11**).

Controversy surrounds the question of the earliest evidence of writing (**Figure 10.12**). Traditionally, the earliest writing was linked to Mesopotamia. However, in 2003 archaeologists working in the Henan Province of central China discovered signs carved into 8,600-year-old tortoise shells; these markings resemble later-written characters and predate the Mesopotamian evidence by about 2,000 years (Li et al., 2003).

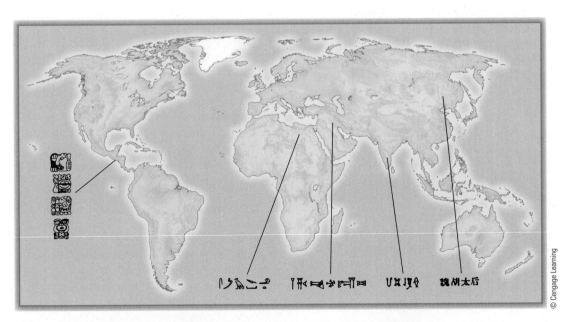

Figure 10.12 The Birthplaces of Writing The transience of spoken words contrasts with the relative permanence of written records. In all of human history, writing has been independently invented at least five times.

In the Americas, writing systems came into use among various Mesoamerican peoples, but the Maya had a particularly sophisticated one. The Maya system, like other aspects of that culture, first appeared to be rooted in the earlier writing system of the Olmec civilization (Pohl, Pope, & von Nagy, 2002). However, discoveries announced in 2006 of a stone tablet with a different writing system indicate that the Olmec had another form of writing distinct from the Maya glyphs (del Carmen Rodríguez Martínez et al., 2006).

The Maya hieroglyphic system had less to do with keeping track of state properties than with extravagant celebrations of the accomplishments of their rulers (**Figure 10.13**). Maya lords glorified themselves by recording their dynastic genealogies, important conquests, and royal marriages; by using grandiose titles to refer to themselves; and by associating their actions with important astronomical events. Different though this may be from the recordkeeping of ancient Mesopotamia, all writing systems share a concern with political power and its maintenance.

The Earliest Governments

A king and his advisors typically headed the earliest city governments although a few ancient queens also ruled. Of the many ancient kings known, one stands out as truly remarkable for the efficient government organization and highly developed legal system characterizing his reign: Hammurabi, the Babylonian king who lived in Mesopotamia (modern Iraq) between 3,700 and 3,950 years ago. From Babylon, the capital of his empire, he issued a set of laws now known as the Code of Hammurabi, notable for its thorough detail and standardization. In 1901, a French archaeological team first discovered this code, entirely inscribed in stone with cuneiform writing. It prescribed the correct form for legal procedures and determined penalties for perjury and false accusation. It contained laws applying to property rights, loans and debts, family rights, and even damages paid for malpractice by a physician. It defined fixed rates to be charged in various trades and branches of commerce, and it instituted mechanisms to protect vulnerable people—the poor, women, children, and slaves—from injustice.

Officials ordered that the code be publicly displayed on huge stone slabs so that no one could plead ignorance. Even the neediest citizens were supposed to know their rights and responsibilities. Distinct social classes were clearly

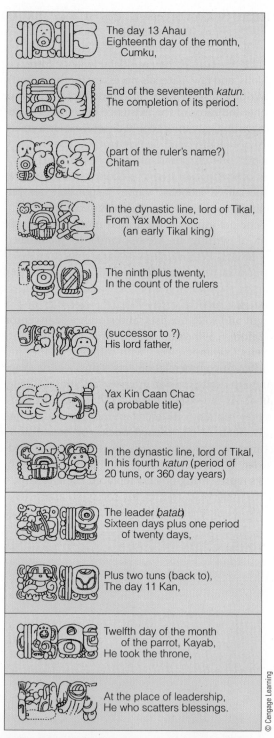

	The day 13 Ahau Eighteenth day of the month, Cumku,
	End of the seventeenth *katun*. The completion of its period.
	(part of the ruler's name?) Chitam
	In the dynastic line, lord of Tikal, From Yax Moch Xoc (an early Tikal king)
	The ninth plus twenty, In the count of the rulers
	(successor to ?) His lord father,
	Yax Kin Caan Chac (a probable title)
	In the dynastic line, lord of Tikal, In his fourth *katun* (period of 20 tuns, or 360 day years)
	The leader (*batab*) Sixteen days plus one period of twenty days,
	Plus two tuns (back to), The day 11 Kan,
	Twelfth day of the month of the parrot, Kayab, He took the throne,
	At the place of leadership, He who scatters blessings.

Figure 10.13 Maya Writing The translation of the text on the monument in Figure 10.6 gives some indication of the importance of dynastic genealogy to Maya rulers. The "scattering" mentioned may refer to bloodletting as part of the ceremonies associated with the end of one twenty-year period, or *katun*, and the beginning of the next. Archaeologists cracked the meaning of these glyphs over the course of many decades of intense study. The base 20 numerical system of bars and dots was the first breakthrough followed by the realization that the symbols represented syllables instead of an alphabet.

reflected in the law ("rule of law" does not necessarily mean "equality before the law"). For example, if an aristocrat put out the eye of a fellow aristocrat, the law required that his own eye be put out in turn; hence the saying "an eye for an eye." However, if the aristocrat put out the eye of a commoner, he simply owed this person a payment of silver.

Although some civilizations flourished under a single ruler with extraordinary governing abilities, other civilizations prospered with a widespread governing bureaucracy that was very efficient at every level. The government of the Inca empire is one such example.

The Inca civilization of Peru (Figure 10.14) and its surrounding territories reached its peak 500 years ago, just before the arrival of the Spanish invaders. By 1525, it stretched 4,000 kilometers (2,500 miles) from north to south and 800 kilometers (500 miles) from east to west, making it one of the largest empires of its time. Its population, which numbered in the millions, was composed of people of many different ethnic groups. In the achievements of its governmental and political system, Inca

civilization surpassed every other civilization of the Americas and most of those of Eurasia. An emperor, regarded as the divine son of the Sun God, headed the government. Below him came the royal family, the aristocracy, imperial administrators, and lower nobility. Below them were the masses of artisans, craftspeople, and farmers.

The empire was divided into four administrative regions, further subdivided into provinces, and so on down to villages and families. Governmental agriculture and tax officials closely supervised farming activities such as planting, irrigation, and harvesting. Teams of professional relay runners could carry messages

Figure 10.14 Machu Picchu The Inca civilization spanned a vast territory and was responsible for monumental structures such as Machu Picchu, located high in the Andes Mountains at an altitude of almost 2,500 meters (nearly 8,000 feet). Scholars believe that the monument was built for the Inca ruler Pachacuti (1438–1472). The archaeological record indicates Machu Picchu may have been a sacred site as well. By the time of the Spanish conquistadores, the Inca people had abandoned the site, possibly because of a smallpox epidemic that had been brought to the Americas by Europeans.

Figure 10.15 Terra Cotta Warriors Grave goods frequently indicate the status of deceased individuals in stratified societies. For example, China's first emperor was buried with 7,000 life-sized terra cotta figures of warriors complete with chariots and horses. In fact, an entire necropolis or "dead city" was built for the emperor, which, according to some historians, required 700,000 workers to complete.

up to 400 kilometers (250 miles) in a single day over a network of roads and bridges that remains impressive even today.

Despite the complexity of the Inca civilization, they had no known form of conventional writing. Instead, they used an ingenious coding system of colored strings with knots known as *quipus* (the Quechua word for "knot") to keep public records and historical chronicles.

Social Stratification

The rise of large, economically diversified populations presided over by centralized governing authorities brought with it the fourth cultural change characteristic of civilization: social stratification, or the emergence of social classes. With social stratification, symbols of special status and privilege that ranked people according to the kind of work they did or the family into which they were born appeared in the ancient cities of Mesopotamia.

A social position at or near the head of government conferred high status. Although specialists—metalworkers, tanners, traders, or the like—generally outranked farmers, the people engaged in these kinds of economic activities were either members of the lower classes or outcasts.

Merchants of the past could sometimes buy their way into a higher class. With time, the possession of wealth and the influence it could buy became their own prerequisite for high status, as seen in some contemporary cultures.

How do archaeologists know that different social classes existed in ancient civilizations? As described earlier, laws and other written documents, as well as archaeological features including dwelling size and location, can reflect social stratification. Burial customs also provide evidence of social stratification. Graves excavated at early Neolithic sites consist mostly of simple pits dug in the ground. They contained few, if any, **grave goods**—utensils, figurines, and personal possessions, symbolically placed in the grave for the deceased person's use in the afterlife (Figure 10.15).

The uniformity of early Neolithic gravesites indicates essentially classless societies. In contrast, graves excavated in civilizations vary widely in size, mode of burial, and the number and variety of grave goods. This reflects a stratified society, divided into social classes. The graves of important people contain not only various artifacts made from precious materials, but sometimes, as in some early Egyptian burials, the remains of servants evidently killed to serve their master in the afterlife.

Skeletons from the gravesites also provide evidence of stratification. Age at death, nutritional stress during childhood, as well as presence of certain diseases can be determined from skeletal remains. In stratified societies of the past, the dominant groups usually lived longer, ate better, and enjoyed an easier life than lower-ranking members of society, just as they do today.

grave goods Items such as utensils, figurines, and personal possessions, symbolically placed in the grave for the deceased person's use in the afterlife.

The Making of States

From Africa to China to the South American Andes, ancient civilizations have created magnificent palaces built high above the ground, sculptures beautifully rendered using techniques that continue into the present, and vast, awe-inspiring engineering projects. These impressive accomplishments could indicate the superiority of civilization compared to other cultural forms, particularly when civilizations have come to dominate other social systems. But domination reflects aggression, size, and power—not cultural superiority. In other words, the emergence of centralized governments, characteristic of civilizations, has allowed some cultures to dominate others and for civilizations to flourish. Anthropologists have proposed several theories to account for the transition from small, egalitarian farming villages to large urban centers in which population density, social inequality, and diversity of labor required a centralized government.

Figure 10.16 **Policing Ancient Cities** To build a monument such as the Great Ziggurat of Ur, a temple in the ancient Mesopotamian city, a centralized authority needed to be able to mobilize the laborers to build the structures and to amass defensive armies. In the present, centralized authorities such as the U.S. military turn to archaeologists at times of war in order to protect cultural resources. The Archaeological Institute of America instituted an innovative program to educate troops before their deployment. For example, the mandatory class taken by both officers and enlisted men and women heading to Iraq included topics such as Mesopotamia's role in the development of writing, schools, libraries, law codes, calendars, and astronomy. Archaeologists taught troops basic archaeological techniques including effective strategies to protect sites against looters. Similar courses appropriate to each region will accompany future U.S. military deployments.

Ecological Theories

Ecological approaches emphasize the role of the environment in the development of states. Among these, the **hydraulic theory**, or *irrigation theory*, holds that civilizations developed when Neolithic peoples realized that the best farming occurred in the fertile soils of river valleys, provided that they could control the periodic flooding. The centralized effort to control the irrigation process blossomed into the first governing body, elite social class, and civilization.

Another theory suggests that in regions of ecological diversity, procuring scarce resources requires trade networks. In Mexico, for example, trade networks distributed chilies grown in the highlands, cotton and beans from intermediate elevations, and salt from the coasts to people throughout the region. Some form of centralized authority developed to organize the procurement and redistribution of these commodities.

A third theory developed by anthropologist Robert Carneiro (1970) suggests that states develop where populations are hemmed in by environmental barriers such as mountains, deserts, seas, or other human populations as an outcome of warfare and conflict in these circumscribed regions. As these populations grow, they have no space in which to expand, and so they begin to compete for increasingly scarce resources. Internally, this may result in the development of social stratification, in which an elite controls important resources to which lower classes have limited access. Externally, this leads to warfare and even conquest, which, to be successful, requires elaborate organization under a centralized authority (Figure 10.16). See this chapter's Globalscape for an example of warfare's current impact on archaeology.

Each of these ecological theories has limitations. Across the globe and through time, anthropologists find cultures

---

hydraulic theory The theory that explains civilization's emergence as the result of the construction of elaborate irrigation systems, the functioning of which required full-time managers whose control blossomed into the first governing body and elite social class; also known as *irrigation theory*.

Globalscape

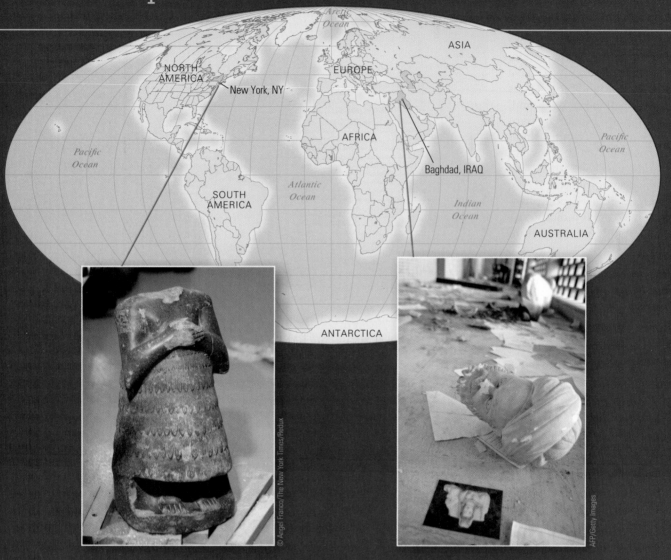

NORTH AMERICA

New York, NY

SOUTH AMERICA

Pacific Ocean

EUROPE

ASIA

AFRICA

Baghdad, IRAQ

Atlantic Ocean

Indian Ocean

Pacific Ocean

AUSTRALIA

ANTARCTICA

© Angel Franco/The New York Times/Redux

AFP/Getty Images

Iraqi Artifacts in New York City?

A clandestine operation carried out by the U.S. government led to the recovery in New York City of a priceless (though headless) 4,400-year-old stone statue of the Sumerian King Entemena of Lagash. The statue was returned to its rightful place in the center of the Sumerian Hall of the Iraqi National Museum in Baghdad.

The modern-day state of Iraq, located in an area known as the cradle of civilization, is home to 10,000 archaeological sites preserving evidence of the earliest cities, laws, and civilizations. Though many Mesopotamian artifacts were brought to museums in Europe and the United States in the 19th and early 20th centuries, the Iraqi National Museum in Baghdad still housed an extraordinary collection of priceless artifacts.

That was the case until the weeks following the U.S. invasion in 2003, when several waves of looters removed tens of thousands of artifacts. According to Matthew Bogdanos, the Marine colonel who led the task force to track down and recover these artifacts, "The list of missing objects read like a 'who's who' of Near Eastern archaeology." Ironically, looting during the first Gulf War had led local archaeologists to move artifacts from regional museums to the National Museum of Baghdad for safekeeping.

This statue, like many other stolen artifacts, was first taken across the border into Syria and then made its way into the international black market in antiquities. Many artifacts have been returned to the museum through a no-questions-asked amnesty program. Others have required a combination of international cooperation and investigation, along with raids and seizures once artifacts have been tracked down.

Global Twister

If artifacts from ancient civilizations from throughout the world represent our shared global heritage, how can such treasures be kept safe from the chaos and desperation that result from war?

Figure 10.17 **Mesa Verde** Although the Ancient Pueblo cultures did not develop sprawling, crowded cities with vast monumental structures, their housing and farming methods demonstrate remarkable sophistication. They built a series of linked enclaves, with about 100 inhabitants each, into the dramatic cliff faces and farmed the top of the mesa they inhabited by using reservoirs and irrigation channels. They also built shrines within their villages of the sort still used by their descendants in the U.S. Southwest today. Other native North Americans built large cities such as Cahokia, a city with an estimated population of 40,000 people dating from 650 to 1400, located in southern Illinois. Until 1800, when Philadelphia surpassed it, Cahokia was the largest city in the land that is now the United States. The development of civilization does not make a people better—just better able to dominate.

that do not fit these models. For example, some of the earliest large-scale irrigation systems developed in highland New Guinea, where strong centralized governments never emerged. North American Indians (**Figure 10.17**) possessed trade networks that extended from Labrador in northeastern Canada to the Gulf of Mexico and the Yellowstone region of the Rocky Mountains and even to the Pacific—all without centralized control. And in many of the cultures that do not fit the theories of ecological determinism, neighboring cultures learned to coexist rather than pursuing warfare to the point of complete conquest.

Although few anthropologists would deny the importance of the human–environment relationship, many are dissatisfied with approaches that do not take into account beliefs and values (Adams, 2001). For example, as described in the case study of Tikal, even though their religion had some ties to natural cycles and the Maya astronomers created elaborate and accurate calendars, the beliefs and power relations that developed within Maya culture were not environmentally determined. Human societies past and present bring their beliefs and values into their interactions with the environment.

Action Theory

Scholars have criticized the aforementioned theories because they fail to recognize the capacity of ambitious, charismatic leaders to shape the course of human history. Accordingly, U.S. anthropologists Joyce Marcus and Kent Flannery (1996) have developed what they call **action theory**. This theory acknowledges the relationship of society to the environment in shaping social and cultural behavior, but it also recognizes that forceful leaders strive to advance their positions through self-serving actions. In so doing, they may create change.

In the case of Maya history, for example, local leaders, who once relied on personal charisma for the economic and political support needed to sustain them in their positions, may have seized upon religion to solidify their power. Through religion they developed an ideology that endowed them and their descendants with supernatural

action theory The theory that self-serving actions by forceful leaders play a role in civilization's emergence.

ancestry and gave them privileged access to the gods, on which their followers depended. In this case, certain individuals could monopolize power and emerge as divine kings, using their power to subjugate any rivals.

This example demonstrates the importance of the context in which a forceful leader operates. In the case of the Maya, the combination of existing cultural and ecological factors opened the way to the emergence of political dynasties. Thus, explanations of civilization's emergence tend to involve multiple causes, rather than just one. Furthermore, we may have the cultural equivalent of what biologists call *convergence*, where similar societies come about in different ways. Consequently, a theory that accounts for the rise of civilization in one place may not account for its rise in another.

Civilization and Its Discontents

Living in the context of civilization ourselves, we are inclined to view its development as a great step up on a so-called ladder of progress. Whatever benefits civilization has brought, these cultural changes have produced new problems. Among them is the challenge of waste disposal and its consequences. In fact, waste disposal probably began to be a difficulty in settled farming communities even before civilizations emerged. But as villages grew into towns and towns grew into cities, the situation became far more serious, as crowded conditions and the buildup of garbage and sewage created optimal environments for infectious diseases such as bubonic plague, typhoid, and cholera. As a result, early cities were disease-ridden places, with relatively high death rates.

Genetic adaptation to urban disease has influenced the course of history globally. Among northern Europeans, for example, the mutation of a gene on chromosome 7 makes carriers resistant to cholera, typhoid, and other bacterial diarrheas, all of which spread easily in urban environments. Because of the mortality caused by these diseases, selection favored spread of this allele among northern Europeans. But, as with sickle-cell anemia, protection comes at a price: cystic fibrosis, a usually fatal disease present in people who are homozygous for the altered gene.

Other acute infectious diseases accompanied the rise of towns and cities. In a small population, diseases such as chicken pox, influenza, measles, mumps, pertussis, polio, rubella, and smallpox will kill or immunize so high a proportion of the population that the virus cannot continue to propagate. Measles, for example, tends to die out in any human population with fewer than half a million people. The continued existence of such diseases depends upon the presence of a large population, as is found in cities. Survivors possessed immunity to these deadly diseases.

Other conditions unique to cities also promote disease. For example, the bacteria that cause tuberculosis (TB) cannot survive in the presence of sunlight and fresh air.

Before people began working and living in dark, crowded urban centers, if an infected individual coughed and released the TB bacteria into the air, sunlight would prevent the spread of infection. TB, like many other sicknesses, can be called a disease of civilization.

Social Stratification and Disease

Civilization affects disease in another powerful way. Social stratification impacts who gets sick as much as any bacterium, past and present. For example, Ashkenazi Jews of eastern Europe were forced into urban ghettos over several centuries, becoming especially vulnerable to the TB thriving in crowded, dark, confined neighborhoods. As with the genetic response to malaria (the sickle-cell allele) and bacterial diarrheas (the cystic fibrosis gene), TB triggered a genetic response in the form of the Tay-Sachs allele, which protects heterozygous individuals from TB.

Unfortunately, homozygotes for the Tay-Sachs allele develop a lethal, degenerative condition that remains common in Ashkenazi Jews. Without the selective pressure of TB, the frequency of the Tay-Sachs allele would never have increased. Similarly, without the strict social rules confining poor Jews to the ghettos (compounded by social and religious rules about marriage), the frequency of the Tay-Sachs allele would never have increased.

Today, not only are poor individuals more likely to become infected with TB, they are also less likely to be able to afford the medicines to treat this disease. For people in poor countries and for disadvantaged people in wealthier countries, tuberculosis, like AIDS, can be an incurable, fatal, infectious disease. As Holger Sawert from the World Health Organization has said, both TB and HIV thrive on poverty (Sawert, 2002). The poor of the world have borne a higher disease burden since the development of stratified societies characteristic of cities and states.

Colonialism and Disease

Infectious disease played a major role in European colonization of the Americas. When Europeans with immunity to so-called Old World diseases came to the Americas for the first time, they brought these devastating diseases with them. Millions of Native Americans—who had never been exposed to influenza, smallpox, typhus, and measles—died as a result. The microbes causing these diseases and the human populations upon which they depend developed in tandem over thousands of years of urban life in Eurasia, and before that in village life with a variety of domesticated animal species. Thus, anyone who survived had acquired immunity in the process. See this chapter's Biocultural Connection for more on the death and disease Europeans brought with them when they colonized the Americas.

Very few diseases traveled back to Europe from the Americas. Instead, these colonizers brought back the riches that they had pillaged and papers that gave them ownership of the lands they had claimed.

BIOCULTURAL CONNECTION

Perilous Pigs: The Introduction of Swine-Borne Disease to the Americas

By Charles C. Mann

On May 30, 1539, Hernando de Soto landed his private army near Tampa Bay, in Florida. . . . Half warrior, half venture capitalist, Soto had grown very rich very young by becoming a market leader in the nascent trade for Indian slaves. The profits had helped to fund Pizarro's seizure of the Incan empire, which had made Soto wealthier still. Looking quite literally for new worlds to conquer, he persuaded the Spanish Crown to let him loose in North America. . . . He came to Florida with 200 horses, 600 soldiers, and 300 pigs.

From today's perspective, it is difficult to imagine the ethical system that would justify Soto's actions. For four years his force, looking for gold, wandered through what is now Florida, Georgia, North and South Carolina, Tennessee, Alabama, Mississippi, Arkansas, and Texas, wrecking almost everything it touched. The inhabitants often fought back vigorously, but they had never before encountered an army with horses and guns. . . . Soto's men managed to rape, torture, enslave, and kill countless Indians. But the worst thing the Spaniards did, some researchers say, was entirely without malice— bring the pigs.

According to Charles Hudson, an anthropologist at the University of Georgia, . . . [t]he Spaniards approached a cluster of small cities, each protected by earthen walls, sizeable moats, and deadeye archers. In his usual fashion, Soto brazenly marched in, stole food, and marched out.

After Soto left, no Europeans visited this part of the Mississippi Valley for more than a century. Early in 1682 whites appeared again, this time Frenchmen in canoes. . . area[s] where Soto had found cities cheek by jowl . . . [were] deserted [without an] Indian village for 200 miles. About fifty settlements existed in this strip of the Mississippi when Soto showed up, according to Anne Ramenofsky, an anthropologist at the University of New Mexico. . . . Soto "had a privileged glimpse" of an Indian world,

Hudson says. "The window opened and slammed shut. When the French came in and the record opened up again, it was a transformed reality. A civilization crumbled. The question is, how did this happen?"

The question is even more complex than it may seem. Disaster of this magnitude suggests epidemic disease. In the view of Ramenofsky and Patricia Galloway, an anthropologist at the University of Texas, the source of the contagion was very likely not Soto's army but its ambulatory meat locker: his 300 pigs. Soto's force itself was too small to be an effective biological weapon. Sicknesses like measles and smallpox would have burned through his 600 soldiers long before they reached the Mississippi. But the same would not have held true for the pigs, which multiplied rapidly and were able to transmit their diseases to wildlife in the surrounding forest. When human beings and domesticated animals live close together, they trade microbes with abandon. Over time mutation spawns new diseases: Avian influenza becomes human influenza, bovine rinderpest becomes measles. Unlike Europeans, Indians did not live in close quarters with animals—they domesticated only the dog, the llama, the alpaca, the guinea pig, and, here and there, the turkey and the Muscovy duck. . . . [W]hat scientists call zoonotic disease was little known in the Americas. Swine alone can disseminate anthrax, brucellosis, leptospirosis, taeniasis, trichinosis, and tuberculosis. Pigs breed exuberantly and can transmit diseases to deer and turkeys. Only a few of Soto's pigs would have had to wander off to infect the forest.

Indeed, the calamity wrought by Soto apparently extended across the whole Southeast. The Coosa city-states, in western Georgia, and the Caddoan-speaking civilization, centered on the Texas-Arkansas border, disintegrated soon after Soto appeared. The Caddo had had a taste for monumental architecture: public plazas, ceremonial platforms, mausoleums. After Soto's army

left, notes Timothy K. Perttula, an archaeological consultant in Austin, Texas, the Caddo stopped building community centers and began digging community cemeteries. . . . [After] Soto's . . . visit, Perttula believes, the Caddoan population fell from about 200,000 to about 8,500—a drop of nearly 96 percent. . . . "That's one reason whites think of Indians as nomadic hunters," says Russell Thornton, an anthropologist at the University of California at Los Angeles. "Everything else—all the heavily populated urbanized societies—was wiped out."

How could a few pigs truly wreak this much destruction? . . . One reason is that Indians were fresh territory for many plagues, not just one. Smallpox, typhoid, bubonic plague, influenza, mumps, measles, whooping cough—all rained down on the Americas in the century after Columbus. . . .

To Elizabeth Fenn, the smallpox historian, the squabble over numbers obscures a central fact. Whether one million or 10 million or 100 million died, . . . the pall of sorrow that engulfed the hemisphere was immeasurable. Languages, prayers, hopes, habits, and dreams— entire ways of life hissed away like steam. . . . In the long run, Fenn says, the consequential finding is not that many people died but that many people once lived. The Americas were filled with a stunningly diverse assortment of peoples who had knocked about the continents for millennia. "You have to wonder," Fenn says. "What were all those people *up to* in all that time?"

BIOCULTURAL QUESTION

Does the history of the decimation of American Indians through infectious disease have any parallels in the contemporary globalized world? Do infectious diseases impact all peoples equally?

Adapted from Mann, C. C. (2005). 1491: New revelations of the Americas before Columbus. New York: Knopf.

Anthropology and Cities of the Future

Not until relatively recent times did public health measures reduce the risk of living in cities, and had it not been for a constant influx of rural peoples, areas of high population density might not have persisted. Europe's urban population, for example, did not become self-sustaining until early in the 20th century.

What led humans to live in such unhealthy places? Most likely, our ancestors were attracted by the same things that lure people to cities today. Cities are vibrant, exciting places that provide new opportunities and protection in times of warfare. Of course, people's experience in the cities did not always live up to expectations, particularly for the poor.

In addition to health problems, many early cities faced social problems strikingly similar to those found in contemporary cities all over the world. Dense population and the inequalities of class systems and oppressive centralized governments created internal stress. The poor saw that the wealthy had all the things that they themselves lacked. It was not just a question of luxury items; the poor did not have enough food or space in which to live with comfort, dignity, and health (Figure 10.18).

In addition to these challenges, abundant archaeological evidence also documents warfare in early civilizations. Cities were fortified. Ancient documents list battles, raids, and wars between groups. Cylinder seals, paintings, and sculptures depict battle scenes, victorious kings, and captured prisoners of war. Increasing population and the accompanying scarcity of fertile farmland often led to boundary disputes and quarrels between civilized states or between so-called tribal peoples and a state. When war broke out, people crowded into walled cities for protection and for access to irrigation systems.

It is discouraging to note that many of the problems associated with the first civilizations are still with us. Waste disposal, pollution-related health problems, crowding, social inequities, and warfare continue to challenge humanity. Through the study of past civilizations, and through comparison of contemporary societies, we now stand a chance of understanding these problems. Such understanding represents a central part of the anthropologist's mission and can contribute to the ability of our species to transcend human-made problems.

AP Images Kahlil Hamra

Figure 10.18 **"City of the Dead," Cairo, Egypt** One of Cairo's poorest neighborhoods, the "City of the Dead" is actually a cemetery. Thousands of poor families use centuries-old mausoleums, built for some of Cairo's wealthy inhabitants, as makeshift homes. For the poor, a gravestone might serve as a table or a bed. Children play among the graves. Because the land on which these families live is officially a cemetery, this neighborhood lacks basic services such as running water and a sewer system.

CHAPTER CHECKLIST

When did the first cities and states develop, and how did this occur?

● The world's first cities grew out of Neolithic villages between 4,500 and 6,000 years ago—first in Mesopotamia, then in Egypt and the Indus Valley. In China, the process was underway by 5,000 years ago. Somewhat later, and completely independently,

similar changes took place in Mesoamerica and the central Andes.

● Four basic cultural changes mark the transition from Neolithic village life to life in civilized urban centers: agricultural innovation, diversification of labor, emergence of centralized government, and social stratification.

What characteristics distinguished the four cultural changes leading to the development of urban centers?

● Agricultural innovation involved the development of new farming methods such as irrigation that increased crop yields. Agricultural innovations brought about other changes such as increased population size.

● Diversification of labor occurred as a result of population growth in cities. Some people could provide sufficient food for everyone so that others could devote themselves to specialization as artisans and craftspeople. Specialization led to the development of new technologies and the beginnings of extensive trade systems.

● The emergence of a central government provided an authority to deal with the complex problems associated with cities and permitted governors to mobilize workers to erect monumental structures. With the invention of writing, governments began keeping records and boasting of their own power and glory.

● Symbols of status and privilege appeared with the emergence of social classes, as individuals were ranked according to the work they did or the position of their families. Graves, burial customs, grave goods, dwelling size, and records in documents and art provide evidence of social stratification.

Why did cities and states develop?

● Ecological theories emphasize the interrelation of the actions of ancient peoples with their environment. According to these theories, civilizations developed as centralized governments began to control irrigation systems, trade networks, and scarce resources.

● These theories omit the importance of the beliefs and values of the cultures of the past as well as the actions of forceful, dynamic leaders, whose efforts to promote their own interests may play a role in social change.

● Several factors probably acted together to bring about the emergence of cities and states.

What problems beset early cities?

● Poor sanitation in early cities, coupled with large numbers of people living in close proximity, created environments in which infectious diseases were rampant.

● Early urban centers also faced social problems strikingly similar to those persisting in the world today. Dense population, class systems, and a strong centralized government created internal stress.

● Warfare was common; cities were fortified, and armies served to protect the state.

● European city-dwellers had already adapted to urban diseases that decimated both urban and rural Indian populations when the European colonial explorers arrived in the Americas.

QUESTIONS FOR REFLECTION

1. Since the origins of cities and states, humans have engaged in large-scale elaborate warfare. Is warfare an inevitable outcome to this form of social organization?

2. In large-scale societies of the past and present, elite classes have disproportionate access to and control of all resources. Is this social stratification an inevitable consequence of the emergence of cities and states? How can the study of social stratification in the past contribute to the resolution of contemporary issues of social justice?

3. What are some of the ways that differences in social stratification are expressed where you live? Does your community have any traditions surrounding death that serve to restate the social differentiation of individuals?

Are there local traditions that serve to redistribute the wealth so that it is shared more evenly?

4. With today's global communication and economic networks, will it be possible to shift away from social systems involving centralized governments, or is a global, centralized authority inevitable?

5. With many archaeological discoveries, there is a value placed on "firsts," such as the earliest writing, the first city, or the earliest government. Given the history of the independent emergence of cities and states throughout the world, do you think that scientists should place more value on these events just because they are older?

ONLINE STUDY RESOURCES

CourseMate

Access chapter-specific learning tools, including learning objectives, practice quizzes, videos, flash cards, glossaries, and more in your Anthropology CourseMate.

Log into **www.cengagebrain.com** to access the resources your instructor has assigned and to purchase materials.

Chris Trotman/Getty Images

Challenge Issue

The biological forces of evolution have resulted in a unified but pheno-typically diverse human species. Yet social factors impact how people think about this diversity. In some societies, the false belief that there are natural and separate divisions within our species fuels racism, a doctrine of superiority by which one group justifies the dehumanization of others based on their distinctive physical characteristics. Although there are obvious physical differences among humans, biological evidence demonstrates unequivocally that separate races do not exist. No human subspecies exists that would indicate distinct biological races, and far more genetic diversity exists within a single so-called racial category than between any two. However, racism and its vocabulary continually surface in different cultures, whether in security profiling, wage disparities, or media commentary. When basketball's Jeremy Lin moved from the bench to stardom in the NBA, sports reporters everywhere spoke about the new Asian American phenomenon in terms of breaking cultural barriers. Critics of "Linsanity" thought of Lin as a middle-range player who received undue attention only because of his Chinese ancestry. But when ESPN posted a photo of Lin alongside the headline "Chink in the Armor," uproar ensued: One reporter was fired and another suspended. The challenge for all of us is to under-stand that although distinct biological races do not exist, the social and political reality of race impacts, if not determines, the human experience in some societies including the United States.

Modern Human Diversity: Race and Racism

11

From male to female, short to tall, light to dark, we can categorize biological variation in a number of ways, but in the end we are all members of the same species. Minute variations of our DNA give each of us a unique genetic fingerprint, yet this variation remains within the bounds of being genetically human. Any visible differences among modern humans exist within the framework of biological features shared throughout the species, and as a species, humans vary. Although we use the terms *black*, *white*, and *race* in this chapter, they signify purely cultural concepts.

Human genetic variation generally is distributed across the globe in a continuous fashion. From a biological perspective, this variation sometimes follows a pattern imposed by interaction with the environment through the evolutionary process of natural selection. Random genetic drift accounts for the remainder. But the significance we give our biological variation is anything but random because cultures determine the way we perceive variation—in fact, whether we perceive it at all. For example, in many Polynesian cultures, where skin color bears no relationship to social status, people pay little attention to this physical characteristic. By contrast, people in countries such as the United States, Brazil, and South Africa notice skin color immediately because it remains a significant social and political category. The study of biological diversity, therefore, requires an awareness of the cultural dimensions that shape the questions asked about diversity as well as an understanding of how this knowledge has been used historically.

When European scholars first began their systematic study of human variation in the 18th and 19th centuries, they focused on documenting differences among human groups in order to divide them hierarchically into progressively "better types" of humans. Today, this hierarchical approach has been appropriately abandoned. Before exploring how we study contemporary biological variation today, let's examine the effects of social ideas about race and racial hierarchy on the interpretation of biological variation, past and present.

IN THIS CHAPTER YOU WILL LEARN TO

- Examine the history of human classification.

- Describe how the biological concept of race cannot be applied to humans.

- Recognize the conflation of biological race into cultural race in theories that attempt to link race to behavior and intelligence.

- Discuss physical anthropological approaches to the study of human biological variation.

- Describe the role of adaptation in human variation in skin color.

- Examine the interaction between biological and cultural components of the human adaptive complex.

The History of Human Classification

Early European scholars tried to systematically classify *Homo sapiens* into subspecies, or races, based on geographic location and phenotypic features such as skin color, body size, head shape, and hair texture. The 18th-century Swedish naturalist Carolus Linnaeus (recall him from Chapter 2) originally divided humans into subspecies based on geographic location and classified all Europeans as white, Africans as black, American Indians as red, and Asians as yellow.

The German physician Johann Blumenbach (1752–1840) introduced some significant and pernicious changes to this four-race scheme in the 1795 edition of his book *On the Natural Variety of Mankind*. Most notably, this book formally introduced a hierarchy of human types (**Figure 11.1**). Blumenbach considered the skull of a woman from the Caucasus Mountains (located between the Black and Caspian Seas of southeastern Europe and southwestern Asia) the most beautiful in his collection. More symmetrical than the others, he saw it as a reflection of nature's ideal form: the circle. Surely, Blumenbach reasoned, this "perfect" specimen resembled God's original creation. Moreover, he thought that the living inhabitants of the Caucasus region were the most beautiful in the world. Based on these criteria, he concluded that this high

mountain range, not far from the lands mentioned in the Bible, was the place of human origins.

Blumenbach concluded that all light-skinned peoples in Europe and adjacent parts of western Asia and northern Africa belonged to the same race. On this basis, he dropped the "European" race label and replaced it with "Caucasian." Although he continued to distinguish American Indians as a separate race, he regrouped dark-skinned Africans as "Ethiopian" and split those Asians not considered Caucasian into two separate races: "Mongolian" (referring to most inhabitants of Asia, including China and Japan) and "Malay" (indigenous Australians, Pacific Islanders, and others).

Convinced that Caucasians were closest to the original ideal humans supposedly created in God's image, Blumenbach ranked them as superior. The other races, he argued, were the result of "degeneration"; by moving away from their place of origin and adapting to different environments and climates, they had degenerated physically and morally into what many Europeans came to think of as inferior races (Gould, 1994).

We now clearly recognize the factual errors and ethnocentric prejudices embedded in Blumenbach's work, as well as others, with respect to the concept of race. Political leaders have used this notion of superior and inferior races to justify brutalities ranging from repression to slavery to mass murder to genocide. The tragic story of

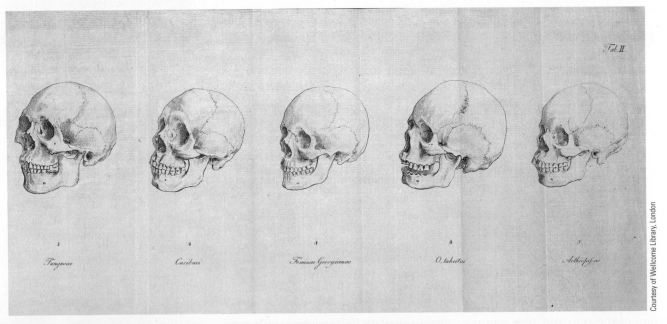

Tab. II.

Tungusae   *Caribaei*   *Feminae Georgianae*   *O. tahaitae*   *Aethiopissae*

Courtesy of Wellcome Library, London

Figure 11.1 Blumenbach's Skulls Johann Blumenbach ordered humans into a hierarchical series with Caucasians (his own group) ranked the highest and created in God's image. He suggested that the variation seen in other races was a result of "degeneration" or movement away from this ideal type. (The five types he identified from left to right are: Mongolian, American Indian, Caucasian, Malay, and Ethiopian.) This view is both racist and an oversimplification of the expression of human variation in the skeleton. Although people from one part of the world might be more likely to possess a particular nuance of skull shape, within every population there is significant variation. Humans do not exist as discrete types.

Missouri History Museum, St. Louis

Figure 11.2 Ota Benga The placement of Ota Benga on display in the Bronx Zoo illustrates the depths of racism in the early 20th century. Here's Ota Benga posing for the camera when he was part of the African Exhibit at the St. Louis World's Fair.

Ota Benga, a Twa Pygmy man who in the early 1900s was caged in a New York zoo with an orangutan, painfully illustrates the disastrous impact of this dogma (Figure 11.2).

Captured in a raid in Congo, Ota Benga came into the possession of North American businessman Samuel Verner, who was looking for exotic "savages" for exhibition in the United States. In 1904, Ota and a group of fellow Twa were shipped across the Atlantic and exhibited at the World's Fair in St. Louis, Missouri. About 23 years old at the time, Ota was 4 feet 11 inches in height and weighed 103 pounds. Throngs of visitors came to see displays of dozens of indigenous peoples from around the globe, shown in their traditional dress and living in replica villages doing their customary activities. The fair was a success for the organizers, and all the Twa Pygmies survived to be shipped back to their homeland. Verner also returned to Congo and with Ota's help collected artifacts that he intended to sell to the American Museum of Natural History in New York City.

In the summer of 1906, Ota came back to the United States with Verner, who soon went bankrupt and lost his entire collection. Left stranded in the big city, Ota was placed in the care of the museum and then taken to the Bronx Zoo and exhibited in the monkey house, with an orangutan as company. Ota's sharpened teeth (a cultural practice among his people) were seen as evidence of his supposedly cannibal nature. After intensive protest, zoo officials released Ota

from his cage and during the day let him roam free in the park, where teasing visitors often harassed him. Ota (usually referred to as a "boy") was then turned over to an orphanage for African American children. In 1916, upon hearing that he would never return to his homeland, he took a revolver and shot himself through the heart (Bradford & Blume, 1992).

The racist display at the Bronx Zoo a century ago was by no means unique. Ota Benga's tragic life was the manifestation of a powerful ideology in which one small part of humanity sought to demonstrate and justify its claims of biological and cultural superiority. Indeed, such claims, based on false notions of race, have resulted in the oppression and genocide of millions of humans because of the color of their skin or the shape of their skull. This ideology had particular resonance in North America, where people of European descent colonized lands originally inhabited by Native Americans and then went on to exploit African slaves and (later) Asians imported as a source of cheap labor.

According to U.S. anthropologist Audrey Smedley, the earliest settlers who came over from England had already refined this ideology of dehumanization and the practice of slavery in their dealings with the Irish (Smedley, 2007). They even imported Irish slaves and indentured servants. Indeed, in Bacon's Rebellion of 1676, Irish and African slaves fought side by side. Only later did North American slavery become the exclusive burden of Africans.

Although the Emancipation Proclamation ended slavery in 1863, dismantling its pseudoscientific bases took much longer. In the early 20th century, some scholars began to challenge the concept of racial hierarchies. Among the strongest critics was Franz Boas (1858–1942), a Jewish scientist who immigrated to the United States because of rising anti-Semitism in his German homeland and who became a founder of North America's four-field anthropology. As president of the American Association for the Advancement of Science, Boas criticized false claims of racial superiority in an important speech titled "Race Problems in America," published in the prestigious journal *Science* in 1909. Boas's scholarship in both cultural and biological anthropology contributed to the depth of his critique.

Ashley Montagu (1905–1999), a student of Boas and one of the best-known anthropologists of his time, devoted much of his career to combating scientific racism. Born Israel Ehrenberg to a working-class Jewish family in England, he also felt the sting of anti-Semitism. After changing his name in the 1920s, he immigrated to the United States, where he went on to fight racism in his writing and in academic and public lectures. His book *Man's Most Dangerous Myth: The Fallacy of Race*, published in 1942, took the lead in debunking the concept of clearly bounded races as a "social myth." The book has since gone through six editions, the last in 1998. Montagu's once controversial ideas have now become mainstream, and his text remains one of the most comprehensive treatments of its subject. (For a contemporary approach to human biological variation, see this chapter's Anthropologist of Note.)

ANTHROPOLOGIST OF NOTE

Fatimah Jackson 1950

Although at first glance **Fatimah Jackson**'s research areas seem quite diverse, they are unified by consistent representation of African American perspectives in biological anthropological research.

With a keen awareness of how culture determines the content of scientific questions, Jackson chooses hers carefully. One of her earliest areas of research concerned the use of

Fatimah Jackson, a leader in the investigations of human biological diversity, emphasizes the social and political reality of race in her work.

© Courtesy of Robert T. Jackson

common African plants as foods and medicines. She has examined the coevolution of plants and humans and the ways plant compounds serve to modify human biology and behavior. Through laboratory and field research, she has documented that cassava, a New World root crop providing the major source of dietary energy for over 500 million people, also helps protect against malaria. This crop has become a major food throughout Africa in areas where malaria is common.

Jackson, who received her PhD from Cornell in 1981, is also the genetics group leader for the African Burial Ground Project (mentioned in Chapter 1). In a small area uncovered during a New York City construction project, scientists found the remains of thousands of Africans and people of African descent. Jackson is recovering DNA from skeletal remains and attempting to match the dead with specific regions of Africa through the analysis of genetic markers in living Africans.

Jackson, one of the early advocates for appropriate ethical treatment of minorities in the human genome project, is concerned with ensuring that the genetic work for the African Burial Ground Project is conducted with sensitivity to African people. She has worked to establish genetic repositories in Africa that capture both environmental and genetic data on local groups. For Jackson, these laboratories are symbolic of the fact of human commonality and that all humans today have roots in Africa.

Jackson has also developed models to better understand the biological and cultural substructure of peoples of African descent worldwide. Using these models, she has been able to link certain subgroups of African descended peoples to increased risk for certain diseases, including breast cancer and hypertension.

Race as a Biological Concept

To understand why the racial approach to human variation has been so unproductive and even damaging, we must first understand the race concept in strictly biological terms. Biologists define **race** as a subspecies,

or a population of a species differing geographically, morphologically, or genetically from other populations of the same species.

As simple and straightforward as such a definition may seem, there are three very important things to note about it. First, it is arbitrary; no scientific criteria exist on how many differences it takes to make a race. For example, if one researcher emphasizes skin color while another emphasizes fingerprint differences, they will not classify people in the same way (**Figure 11.3**).

Second, this biological definition of race does not mean that any one race has exclusive possession of any particular variant of any gene or genes. In human terms, the frequency of a trait like the type O blood

race In biology, the taxonomic category of subspecies that is not applicable to humans because the division of humans into discrete types does not represent the true nature of human biological variation. In some societies race is an important social category.

Figure 11.3 An Alternative Grouping Fingerprint patterns of loops, whorls, and arches are genetically determined. Grouping people on this basis would place most Europeans, sub-Saharan Africans, and East Asians together as "loops." Australian Aborigines and the people of Mongolia would be together as "whorls." The Bushmen of southern African would be grouped as "arches."

group, for example, may be high in one population and low in another, but it is present in both. In other words, populations are genetically "open," meaning that genes flow between them (**Figure 11.4**). The only reproductive barriers that exist for humans are the cultural rules some societies impose regarding appropriate mates.

As President Obama's family illustrates (Luo father from western Kenya and Anglo-American mother born in Kansas, who, incidentally, was an anthropologist), these social barriers change through time. As well, in July 2012, Ancestry.com, a genealogy business, released a report indicating that the president's mother, like so many white Americans, was descended from a slave ancestor ("President Obama descends from the first African enslaved for life in America," 2012). This news made a splash, particularly because the ancestor was a man named John Punch, one of the first African slaves to be documented in this country (Thompson, 2012). This chapter's Original Study by biological anthropologist Jonathan Marks explores the hype and folk appeal of such genealogical analyses and the ultimate biological truth: We are all related.

Figure 11.4 Jefferson's Family Many people have become accustomed to viewing racial groups as natural and separate divisions within our species based on visible physical differences. However, these groups differ from one another in only 7 percent of their genes. For many thousands of years, individuals belonging to different human social groups have been in sexual contact. Exchanging their genes, they maintained the human species in all its colorful variety and prevented the development of distinctive subspecies (biologically defined races). This continued genetic mixing is effectively illustrated by the above photo of distant relatives, all of whom are descendants of Sally Hemings, an African American slave, and Thomas Jefferson, the Anglo-American gentleman-farmer who had 150 slaves working for him at his Virginia plantation and served as third U.S. president (1801–1809).

ORIGINAL STUDY

Caveat Emptor: Genealogy for Sale BY JONATHAN MARKS

We are related, you and I.

Darwin says so. The Bible says so. Not much controversy about it.

The question is, How related? If we're too close, there will be restrictions on our sexual behavior toward one another. If we're too distant—that is to say, if you're a chimpanzee—there will be restrictions as well, of a different sort.

But the middle ground is very large—about seven billion people large—and we all form a network of biological kin (if not social kin). The structure of that network is the domain of human population genetics, a field newly reinvigorated by free-market genomics.

The power of molecular genetic data to address issues of identity and relatedness with scientific authority has been appreciated for decades, particularly in the domains of paternity, genealogy, and forensics. Only recently, however, has the field branched out, so to speak, into the field of family trees, and what is now often called "recreational ancestry," tapping into a universal human desire to situate ourselves within a complex social universe. The math is simple: genomic data + folk ideology = profits, and tests have been available for several years purporting to match your Y chromosome with Genghis Khan or Moses, or your mitochondrial DNA with any of seven imaginary European "clan mothers" who lived 15,000 years ago.

The commercial success of these tests lies in how successfully they can represent biological relatedness to be the equivalent of meaningful relatedness. In fact, the two never map on to one another particularly well, as anthropologists have long appreciated. Kinship (meaningful relatedness) is constructed by human societies from a locally particular calculus combining biological ties of heredity and legal ties of marriage and adoption. Your mother's sister's child and mother's brother's child are genetically equivalent, but the first is widely considered an incestuous relationship, while the second may be a preferred spouse across diverse cultures and eras. Charles Darwin, for example, married his mother's brother's daughter, yet his face nevertheless graces the English £10 note.

The mode of transmission of mitochondrial DNA makes it particularly vexing as a surrogate for biological ancestry. Most DNA, the nuclear human genome, is transmitted probabilistically; you have a 50% chance of having inherited any particular DNA segment from any particular parent. MtDNA, however, is inherited only through the maternal line: Thus, you are a mitochondrial clone of your mother and mitochondrially unrelated to your father.

Such a fundamental discrepancy between the heredity of mtDNA and our understandings of heredity ought to raise caution about glibly confounding the two. A generation further removed, the discrepancy becomes more glaring: You are equally descended from all four grandparents, but only mitochondrially descended from one of them (your mother's mother). And of your eight great-grandparents, only one is your mitochondrial ancestor.

In general terms, as you proceed upward in your genealogical tree, the number of ancestors you have in every generation increases exponentially (every ancestor had two parents), whereas the number of mitochondrial ancestors remains constant (one—your mother's mother's . . . mother). From a different angle, 75 percent of your grandparents are invisible to an mtDNA analysis—and every generation back, that percentage increases.

Or from yet another angle, a test for relatedness derived from mtDNA carries a risk of producing a false negative result that is incalculably high. A mitochondrial match is good evidence that the two bearers are genealogically linked, but a nonmatch means nothing at all. Moreover, there is a wide zone between a match and a nonmatch: Geneticists can cluster mtDNA sequences by their degrees of similarity to one another. Thus, the coalescence of the mtDNA sequences of a large population into a small number of basic groups can suggest a founder—a mother—for each of those groups.

Consider, though, what being a "member" of a 15,000-year-old mitochondrial "clan" actually implies. How many ancestors did you actually have 15,000 years ago? Conservatively assuming 25 years per generation yields 600 generations, and your 2-to, the-six-hundredth-power ancestors comprise a number with 180 zeroes, or about 173 orders of magnitude larger than the number of people alive at the time, and effectively beyond the power of language to express.

Let us call this a squijillion.

Not only do you have a squijillion ancestors 15,000 years ago, but so does everybody else. How could you have so many ancestors? Many of them are the same people—specific ancestors recur in your own tree, and many of your ancestors are other people's ancestors as well. That is to say, to some extent you are inbred, and to some extent you are related to everyone else. And of those squijillion ancestors distributed among the 10,000,000 or so people alive back then—the ones who all contributed nuclear DNA to your genome—how many are being detected by your mtDNA? One.

Here the tenuous connection between meaningful relatedness and biological relatedness becomes helpful. There is almost nothing biological there, but the cultural associations of DNA give these data the appearance of familial association, of science, of reality. The mtDNA similarity is symbolically powerful in spite of being biologically trivial in this context.

The intersection of that symbolic power with the free market has created a hybrid nature for the science of human population genetics: partly derived from Watson and Crick, that is to say, from molecular genetics; and partly derived from P. T. Barnum, that is to say, from the fellow who said epigrammatically, "There's a sucker born every minute."

Suppose there were a scientific test that allowed you to identify all of your family members and distinguish them from people to whom you were not related? You might find distant relatives you never knew you had; you might find that you are descended from someone noteworthy; you might find something exotic, romantic, interesting, or even admirable in your DNA. You might even be able to fill in gaps in your self-identity and find out who you "really" are and where you "really" come from. That is, after all, the source of a classic dramatic arc, from Oedipus to Skywalker.

But what would such a test entail? After all, heredity is probabilistic. You have, on the average, 25 percent of your DNA from each of your grandparents. Or more to the point, any bit of any grandparent's DNA has a 25 percent chance of showing up in your genome. Consequently, you may not necessarily match any specific bit of your grandfather's DNA—given you have three other grandparents and only two sets of DNA.

Moreover, because you are related to every other human being, there is no qualitative break between your family members and nonrelatives that a genetic test could detect. That is the "constructedness" of human kinship systems: Some people are defined as relatives and some people are not, regardless of their biological relationships. The only kind of test that can reliably sort people into your relatives and your nonrelatives would be a magic test.

In America, hardly any social fact can be understood outside the historical context of slavery. One modern legacy is the obliteration of the preslavery ancestry of African Americans. But what if your DNA matched that of an African tribe? Would that not provide a grounding in African soil and establish African kin? For a few hundred dollars, indeed that service is now provided.

One pioneering company's website "allows you to reconnect to your ancestral past—easily, accurately and profoundly" and will "connect your ancestry to a specific country in Africa and often to a specific African ethnic group." And there is no doubt that it does what it promises—it connects black Americans to black Africa. But of course, that is a sloppy term—"connects"—sounding as if it has profound biological meaning, when the profound connection it provides may be more emotional than genetic. After all, of the literally thousands of genetic ancestors you had 12 generations ago—say, about the year 1700—mtDNA is connecting you with only one. On the other hand, isn't that better than nothing?

Well, when you consider the fact that all of these mtDNA forms are polymorphic—that is to say, varying within any population, and that the sampling of Africans is very poor, you have to begin to wonder whether a mitochondrial DNA match to a Yoruba may actually be worse than nothing. Being biologically meaningless, yet mimicking a hereditary identity, the mtDNA match might well be giving you a false identity in the name of science.

As the classic 1973 film *The Sting* showed clearly, the best scams are the ones in which the victim does most of the work. You give them the dots, and they connect them—to your advantage. In this case, the clients are paying for science and are getting it. They are getting accurate DNA results and true matches. The companies certify the match, and allow their clients to make the meaningful "connection."

Testimonials vouch for the lives thereby changed, and why shouldn't they? The only problem might be if you confuse them for scientific evidence.

Ultimately, this essay is not intended as a public service or a whistle-blowing venture. Nothing illegal or even necessarily immoral is going on. Instead, this is an illustration of the way in which science has changed during our lifetimes. Science—and in particular, genetics—may never have been "pure," but until quite recently it never had to compete seriously with the profit motive for its public credibility.

In short, this isn't your grandfather's genetics.

Adapted from Marks, J. (2008). Caveat emptor: Genealogy for sale. Newsletter of the ESRC Genomics Network 7, 23. Reprinted by permission.

In addition to the genetic openness of populations, and the arbitrary nature of criteria, a third problem with applying the biological definition of *race* to humans exists: The differences among individuals within a so-called racial population are greater than the differences among separate populations. Evolutionary biologist Richard Lewontin demonstrated this in the 1970s. He compared the amount of genetic variation within populations and among racial groups, finding a mere 7 percent of human variation existing among groups (Lewontin, 1972). Instead, the vast majority of genetic variation exists *within* groups. As the science writer James Shreeve puts it, "Most of what separates me genetically from a typical African or Eskimo also separates me from another average American of European ancestry" (Shreeve, 1994, p. 60). In other words, no one race has an exclusive claim to any particular form of a gene or trait.

The Conflation of the Biological into the Cultural Category of Race

Although the biological race concept does not pertain to human variation, race remains a significant cultural category. Human groups frequently insert a false notion of biological difference into the cultural category of race to make it appear more factual and objective. In various ways, cultures define religious, linguistic, and ethnic groups as races, thereby confusing linguistic and cultural traits with physical traits.

For example, people in many Latin American countries classify one another as Indian, Mestizo (mixed), or Ladino (of Spanish descent). But despite the biological connotations of these terms, the criteria used for assigning individuals to these categories are determined by whether they wear shoes, sandals, or go barefoot; speak Spanish or an Indian language; live in a thatched hut or a European-style house; and so forth. By speaking Spanish, wearing Western-style clothes, and living in a house in a non-Indian neighborhood, Indian people shed their indigenous identity and acquire a national identity as citizens of the country.

Similarly, the ever-changing racial categories used by the U.S. Census Bureau both reflect and reinforce the conflation of the biological and the cultural. The 2010 list includes large catchall political categories such as white and black as well as specific tribal affiliations of American Indians or Alaskan Natives, a designation that comes much closer to a population in the biological sense. The Census Bureau asks people to identify Hispanic ethnicity, independent of the category of race, but considers Arabs and Christians of Middle Eastern ancestry as white (Caucasian) despite the political relevance of their ancestry. The observation that the purported race of an individual can vary over the course of his or her lifetime speaks to the fact that cultural forces shape the designation of membership in a particular racial category (Hahn, 1992).

The Census Bureau gathers health statistics by racial categories for the purposes of correcting health disparities among social groups. Unfortunately, the false biological concept of race gets inferred in these analyses. As a result, the increased risk of dying from a heart attack for African Americans compared to whites is falsely attributed to biological differences rather than to health-care disparities or other social factors.

Similarly, medical genetics research is regularly oversimplified into comparisons of the racial types defined in the 18th and 19th centuries. Whether this genetic research will avoid the trap of recreating false genetic types that do not reflect the true nature of human variation remains to be seen. The recent claims made for race-specific drugs and vaccines based on limited scientific data indicate that the social category of race may again be interfering with our understanding of the true nature of human genetic diversity.

Against a backdrop of prejudice, the conflation of the social with the biological has historically provided a "scientific" justification for the exclusion of whole categories of people from certain roles or positions in society. For example, in colonial North America, a racial worldview assigned American Indians and Africans imported as slaves to perpetual low status. A supposed biological inferiority was used to justify this low status, whereas access to privilege, power, and wealth was reserved for favored groups of European descent (American Anthropological Association, 1998). Before the civil rights era brought equal legal rights to all U.S. citizens, the "one drop rule," also known as *hypodescent*, would assign individuals with mixed ethnicity or socioeconomic class to the subordinate group in the hierarchy. Similarly, the historical caste system in Mexico took into account intermarriage between various groups to position people within the hierarchical order (**Figure 11.5**).

Because of the colonial association of lighter skin with greater power and higher social status, people whose history includes domination by lighter-skinned Europeans have sometimes valued this phenotype. In Haiti, for example, the "color question" has been the dominant force in social and political life. Skin texture, facial features, hair color, and socioeconomic class collectively play a role in the ranking. According to Haitian anthropologist Michel-Rolph Trouillot, "a rich black becomes a mulatto, a poor mulatto becomes black" (Trouillot, 1996).

The Nazis in Germany elevated a racialized worldview to state policy, with particularly evil consequences. Hitler's agenda was inspired by the American eugenics movement of the early 20th century. He considered a 1916 book by Madison Grant, from the American Museum of Natural History, titled *The Passing of the Great Race*, his bible. The Nuremberg race laws of 1935 codified the superiority of the Aryan race and the inferiority of the Gypsy and Jewish races (**Figure 11.6**). The Nazi doctrine justified, on supposed biological grounds, political repression and extermination. In all, 11 million people (Jews, Gypsies, homosexuals, and other so-called inferior people, as well as political opponents of the Nazi regime) were deliberately put to death or died from starvation, disease, and exposure in labor camps.

Tragically, human history contains many atrocities on the scale of the Nazi Holocaust (from the Greek word for "wholly burnt" or "sacrificed by fire"). Such **genocides**, programs of extermination of one group by another, have a long history that predates World War II and continues today. From the massacre of 1.5 million Armenians during WWI, to the slaughter of 1.7 million Cambodians in the 1970s, to selective elimination of indigenous Guatemalans in the 1980s, to the massacre of nearly a million Tutsis by Hutus in the 1994, an estimated 83 million people died from genocides in the 20th century (White, 2001). A rhetoric of dehumanization and a depiction of the people being exterminated as a lesser type of human has accompanied each of these (**Figure 11.7**).

---

genocide The physical extermination of one people by another, either as a deliberate act or as the accidental outcome of activities carried out by one people with little regard for their impact on others.

Español con India.
Mestizo.

Mestizo con Española
Castizo.

Castizo con Española
Español.

Español con Nora.
Mulato.

Mulato con Española.
Morisco.

Morisco con Española
Chino.

Chino con India.
Salta atras.

Salta atras con Mulata.
Lobo.

Lobo con China
Gibaro.

Gibaro con Mulata
Albarazado.

Albarazado con Negra
Canbujo.

Canbujo con India.
Sanbaigo.

Sanbaigo con Loba
Calpamulato.

Calpamulato con Canbuja
Tente en elAire.

Tente enelAire. con Mulata
Note entiendo.

Noteentiendo con India.
Tornaatras.

© Schalkwijik/Art Resource, NY

Figure 11.5 Castas In colonial Mexico, sixteen different *castas* ("castes") were designated, giving specific labels to individuals who were various combinations of Spanish, Indian, and African ancestry. These paintings of *castas* are traditionally arranged from light to dark as a series and reflect an effort to impose hierarchy despite the fluid social system in place. In the United States, despite the use of descriptors such as *quadroon, octoroon, sambo,* and *mulatto* that attempt to quantify the amount of mixture among races, the hierarchy was more rigid; the "one drop rule" would ascribe individuals to a subordinate position within the hierarchy if they had even one drop of blood from a "lower" ranking group.

Figure 11.6 **The Aryan Race** Members of the SS Tibet expedition team sit with local people at a banquet in Lhasa, Tibet, in 1939. Second from the left is anthropologist Bruno Beger, whose work for the German SS on this expedition included measuring skulls and cataloguing the physical traits of Tibetans as part of a search for the origins of the purportedly superior Aryan Race. After this expedition, Beger continued an even darker side of this racialized agenda at Auschwitz. There, through measurement of physical characteristics, he selected and prepared individuals for lethal experimentation, and for death in order to be included in the Jewish skeletal collection. Though a West German court found Beger guilty as an accessory to murder for his role at Auschwitz, he never served time.

Figure 11.7 **Victims of Genocide** These skulls, from the genocide war memorial in Rwanda, record some of the horror that took place in this Central African country in 1994. Over the course of only about a hundred days, a militia of the ruling Hutu majority brutally murdered close to 1 million ethnic Tutsis. With clear genocidal intent, systematic organization, and intense speed, Hutu actions, resembling those of the Nazi regime, remind us that genocide is far from a thing of the past. The global effects of the Rwandan genocide have been massive. Millions of Rwandans, both refugees and killers, now live in neighboring regions, disrupting the stability of these states. Through the United Nations and individual governments, the international community has recognized that it failed to act to prevent this genocide and collectively has taken steps toward maintaining peace in the region. The parallels between Rwanda and current conflicts in Congo, Burundi, and Sudan are chilling.

The Social Significance of Race: Racism

Scientific facts, unfortunately, have been slow to change what people think about race. **Racism**, a doctrine of superiority by which one group justifies the dehumanization of others based on their distinctive physical characteristics, persists as a major political problem. Indeed, politicians have often exploited this concept as a means of mobilizing support, demonizing opponents, and eliminating rivals. Racial conflicts result from social stereotypes, not scientific facts.

Race and Behavior

The assumption that behavioral differences exist among human races remains an issue to which many people still cling tenaciously. Throughout history, certain characteristics have been attributed to groups of people under a variety of names—national character, spirit, temperament—all of them vague and standing for concepts unrelated to any biological phenomena. Common myths involve the coldness of Scandinavians or the rudeness of Americans or the fierceness of the Yanomami Indians. Such unjust characterizations rely upon a false notion of biological difference.

To date, no inborn behavioral characteristic can be attributed to any group of people (which the nonscientist might call a race) that cannot be explained in terms of cultural practices. If the Chinese happen to exhibit exceptional visual-spatial skills, it is probably because the business of learning to read Chinese characters requires a visual-spatial mastery that Western alphabets do not (Chan & Vernon, 1988). Similarly, the almost complete exclusion of non-whites from achievements in the sport of golf (until Tiger Woods) had everything to do with the social rules of country clubs and the sport's expense.[1] All such differences or characteristics can be explained in terms of culture.

In the same vein, high crime rates, alcoholism, and drug use among certain groups can be explained with reference to culture rather than biology. Individuals alienated and demoralized by poverty, injustice, and unequal opportunity tend to abandon the traditional paths to success of the dominant culture because these paths are blocked. In a racialized society, poverty and all its ill consequences affect some groups of people much more severely than others.

Slowly, some of this systemic racism, a form of **structural violence**—physical and/or psychological harm caused by impersonal, exploitative, and unjust social, political and economic systems—has been rectified. For example in 2010 the U.S. Congress passed the Fair Sentencing Act, legislation aimed at redressing many years of harsher penalties associated with crack cocaine use; crack is primarily associated with African Americans, as compared to the more expensive and equally potent powdered form of cocaine more often associated with white drug users. Before this legislation, the typical white user would have to possess 100 times the amount of powdered cocaine to receive the same sentence as his or her African American crack-using counterpart (King, 2010).

Race and Intelligence

Scholars and laypeople alike, unfamiliar with the fallacy of biological race in humans, have asked whether some races are inherently more intelligent than others. To address this issue requires, first, clarification of the term *intelligence*. Unfortunately, deciding what abilities or talents actually make up what we call intelligence remains contentious, even though some psychologists insist that it is a single quantifiable thing measured by IQ tests. Many more psychologists consider intelligence to be the product of the interaction of different sorts of cognitive abilities: verbal, mathematical-logical, spatial, linguistic, musical, bodily-kinesthetic, social, and personal (Jacoby & Glauberman, 1995). Each of these kinds of intelligence seems unrelated to the others in that individuals possess unique combinations of strengths in each of these areas. Just as humans inherit height, blood type, skin color, and so forth independently, it seems likely that to the degree that intelligence is heritable, each of these kinds of intelligence would be inherited independently.

Furthermore, scholars have shown the limits of IQ tests as a fully valid measure of inborn intelligence. An IQ test measures *performance* (something that one does) rather than *genetic disposition* (something that the individual is born with). Performance reflects past experiences and present motivational state, as well as innate ability.

Despite these limits, for at least a century some researchers have used IQ tests to try to prove the existence of significant differences in intelligence among human populations. In the United States, systematic comparisons of intelligence between whites and blacks began in the early 20th century and were frequently combined with data gathered by physical anthropologists about skull shape and size.

During World War I, for example, draftees were regularly given a series of IQ tests, known as Alpha and Beta. The results showed that on average white Americans attained higher scores compared to African Americans. Even though African Americans from the urban northern states scored higher than white Americans from the rural South, and some African Americans scored higher than most white Americans, many people took this as proof of the intellectual superiority of white people. But all the tests really showed was that, on

---

[1] Before Tiger Woods came Charles Sifford (b. 1922), the first African American to win honors in golf. Sifford did so at a time when desegregating the sport meant being subjected to threats and racial abuse. In 2004, the World Golf Hall of Fame inducted him as their first African American member.

racism A doctrine of superiority by which one group justifies the dehumanization of others based on their distinctive physical characteristics.
structural violence Physical and/or psychological harm caused by impersonal, exploitative, and unjust social, political, and economic systems.

the average, whites outperformed blacks in the social situation of IQ testing. The tests did not measure intelligence per se, but the ability, conditioned by culture, of certain individuals to respond appropriately to certain questions conceived by Americans of European descent for comparable middle-class whites. These tests frequently require knowledge of white middle-class values and linguistic behavior.

For such reasons, intelligence tests continue to be the subject of controversy. Many psychologists as well as anthropologists have shown that the tests have only limited application in particular cultural circumstances. In turn, holding cultural and environmental factors constant results in African and European Americans scoring equally well (Sanday, 1975).

Nevertheless, some researchers still insist that there are significant differences in intelligence among human populations. Richard Herrnstein, a psychologist, and Charles Murray, a political scientist and longtime fellow of a conservative think tank called the American Enterprise Institute, are among these researchers. In a lengthy and highly publicized book entitled *The Bell Curve*, they argue for immutable genetic origins for the difference in IQ scores between Americans of African, Asian, and European descent.

Scholars have criticized Herrnstein and Murray's book on many grounds, including violation of basic rules of statistics and their practice of utilizing studies, no matter how flawed, that appear to support their thesis while ignoring or barely mentioning those that contradict it. In addition, the basic laws of heredity also discredit their argument. As Mendel discovered with his pea plants back in the late 19th century, genes are inherited independently of one another. Whatever the alleles that may be associated with intelligence, they bear no relationship with the ones for skin pigmentation or with any other aspect of human variation such as blood type. Further, the expression of genes always occurs in an environment, and among humans culture shapes all aspects of the environment.

Separating genetic components of intelligence (or any other continuous trait) from environmental contributors poses enormous problems (Andrews & Nelkin, 1996). Most studies of intelligence rely on comparisons between identical twins, genetically identical individuals raised in the same or different environments. A host of problems plague twin studies: inadequate sample sizes, biased subjective judgments, failure to make sure that "separated" twins really were raised separately, unrepresentative samples of adoptees to serve as controls, untested assumptions about similarity of environments. In fact, children reared by the same mother resemble her in IQ to the same degree, whether or not they share her genes (Lewontin, Rose, & Kamin, 1984). Clearly, the degree to which intelligence is inherited through genes is far from understood.

Undoubtedly, the social environment contributes substantially to intelligence. This should not surprise us, as environmental factors influence other genetically determined traits. Height in humans, for example, has a

genetic basis, but it also depends upon both nutrition and health status (severe illness in childhood arrests growth, and renewed growth never makes up for this loss).

Moreover, scientists have not yet teased apart the exact relative contributions of genetic and environmental factors on either the height or the intelligence of an individual (Figure 11.8). Although the burgeoning field of epigenetics has begun to unravel these interactions, the work is meaningful only in the context of individuals and discrete populations, not in the biologically false category of race (Marks, 2008b; Rose, 2009).

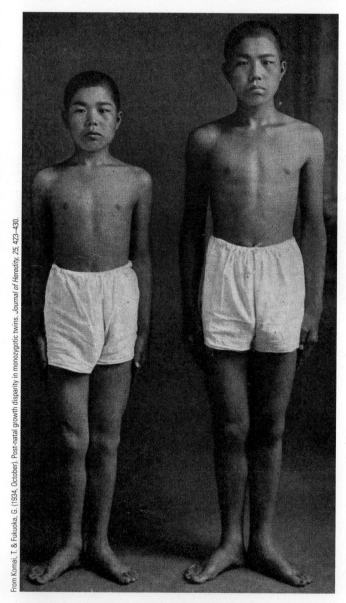

From Komai, T. & Fukuoka, G. (1934, October). Post-natal growth disparity in monozygotic twins. *Journal of Heredity, 25,* 423–430.

Figure 11.8 Duplicate Genes, Unique Experiences Differences in the growth process can lead to very different outcomes in terms of size as seen in these twins, who are genetically identical. Starting from inside their mother's womb, twins may experience environmental differences in terms of blood and nutrient supply. This can impact not only size but cognitive development.

Research on the importance of the environment in the expression of intelligence further exposes the problems with generalizations about IQ and race. For example, IQ scores of all groups in the United States, as in most industrial and postindustrial countries, have risen some 15 points since World War II. In addition, the gap between Americans of African and European descent has narrowed in recent decades. Other studies show impressive IQ scores for African American children from socially deprived and economically disadvantaged backgrounds who have been adopted into highly educated and prosperous homes. Studies have shown that underprivileged children adopted into such privileged families can boost their IQs by 20 points. Also, IQ scores rise in proportion to the test-takers' amount of schooling.

More such cases could be cited, but these suffice to make the point and lead to three conclusions. First, there is a bias in IQ testing based on social class. Second, the assertion that IQ is biologically fixed and immutable is clearly false. Third, ranking human beings with respect to their intelligence scores in terms of racial difference is doubly false.

Over the past 2.5 million years, all populations of the genus *Homo* have adapted primarily through culture—actively inventing solutions to the problems of existence rather than relying only on biological adaptation. Thus, we would expect a comparable degree of intelligence in all present-day human populations. The only way to be sure that individual human beings develop their innate abilities and skills to the fullest is to make sure they all have access to the necessary resources and the opportunity to do so (**Figure 11.9**).

Figure 11.9 **The Legacy of Slavery** Any discussion of race and behavior or intelligence in the United States must include the history of slavery and of legal segregation in the South, as well as other forms of structural violence that favored the white race at the expense of minorities. These social, political, and historical facts influence race relations in the United States today far more than minute genetic differences.

Studying Human Biological Diversity

Considering the problems, confusion, and horrendous consequences, anthropologists have abandoned the race concept as being of no utility in understanding human biological variation. Instead, they have found it more productive to study *clines*, the distribution and significance of single, specific, genetically based characteristics and continuous traits related to adaptation.

The physical characteristics of both populations and individuals derive from the interaction between genes and environments. For example, genes predispose people to a particular skin color, but the color of an individual's skin is also influenced by cultural and environmental factors. The skin of sailors, for example, darkens or burns after many hours of exposure to the sun, depending on not only genetic predisposition but cultural practices regarding exposure to the sun. In other cases, such as A-B-O blood type, phenotypic expression closely reflects genotype.

For characteristics controlled by a single gene, different versions of that gene, known as alleles (see Chapter 2), also mediate variation. Such traits are called **polymorphic** (meaning "many shapes"). Our blood types—determined by the alleles for types A, B, and O blood—are an example of polymorphism and may appear in any of four distinct phenotypic forms (A, B, O, and AB).

A species can also be considered polymorphic, meaning that there is wide variation among individuals (beyond differences between males and females). Here *polymorphic* refers to continuous phenotypic variation that may be genetically controlled by interactions among multiple different genes, in addition to the allelic variation described previously. When a polymorphic species faces changing

polymorphic Describing species with alternative forms (alleles) of particular genes.

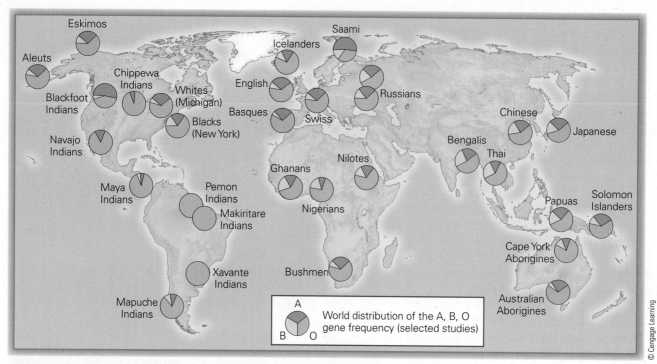

Figure 11.10 **Blood Types** Frequencies of the three alleles for the A, B, and O blood groups for selected samples around the world illustrate the polytypic nature of *Homo sapiens*. The frequency of the alleles differs among "populations." Which of the groups here best represent populations (a group of individuals within which breeding takes place) in the biological sense?

environmental conditions, the variation it has within its gene pool fosters survival of the species because some of those individuals may possess traits that prove adaptive in the altered environment. Individuals whose physical characteristics enable them to do well in the new environment will usually reproduce more successfully, so that their genes become more common in subsequent generations. Similarly, the polymorphism of the human species has allowed us to thrive in a wide variety of environments.

When polymorphisms are distributed into geographically dispersed populations, biologists describe this species as **polytypic** ("many types") for that feature; that is, uneven distribution of genetic variability among populations. For example, consider the polytypic distribution of the polymorphism for blood type (four distinct phenotypic groups: A, B, O, or AB). American Indian populations possess the highest frequency of the O allele, especially some populations native to South America; certain European populations have the highest frequencies of the allele for type A blood (although the highest frequency is found among the Blackfoot Indians of the northern Plains in North America); some Asian populations have the highest frequencies of the B allele (**Figure 11.10**). Even though single traits may be grouped within specific geographic regions, when a greater number of traits are considered,

specific human "types" cannot be identified. Instead, evolutionary forces work independently on each of these traits.

Scientists also use clinal analyses to examine continuous traits such as body shape. These studies have allowed anthropologists to interpret human global variation in body build as an adaptation to climate as we will explore in the next chapter. Relevant to the false notion of biological race, some anthropologists have also suggested that variation in features such as face and eye shape relate to climate. For example, some early biological anthropologists once proposed that the "Mongoloid" face, common in populations native to East and Central Asia, as well as Arctic North America, exhibits features adapted to life in very cold environments (Coon, 1962). The **epicanthic eye fold** (which minimizes the eye's exposure to the cold), a flat facial profile, and extensive fatty deposits may help to protect the face against frostbite.

Although experimental studies have failed to sustain the frostbite hypothesis, a flat facial profile generally goes with a round head. Because a significant percentage of body heat may be lost from the head, a round-shaped head, with less surface area relative to volume, loses less heat than a longer, more elliptical-shaped head. Predictably, populations with more elliptical-shaped heads are generally found in hotter climates; those with rounder-shaped heads are more common in cold climates. However, these same features also could be present in populations due to genetic drift. This chapter's Biocultural Connection on ethnic plastic surgery illustrates a very different approach to phenotypic variation in which individuals undergo elective surgery to attain the phenotype of the dominant culture.

polytypic Describing the expression of genetic variants in different frequencies in different populations of a species.
epicanthic eyefold A fold of skin at the inner corner of the eye that covers the true corner of the eye; common in Asian populations.

BIOCULTURAL CONNECTION

Beauty, Bigotry, and the Epicanthic Eyefold of the Beholder

One need look no farther than the magazines displayed at a store's checkout aisle to determine that appearance matters in the United States. It is not surprising that a society that once used skin color to determine social status should continue to emphasize the superiority of specific physical traits and to encourage people to acquire these desired traits through plastic surgery.

Plastic surgery began in the United States during World War I, as medical doctors developed procedures to reconstruct disfigured soldiers. Soon doctors began finding other applications for these new techniques. The physical traits associated with ethnic groups considered inferior provided new work for the fledgling medical specialty. Rhinoplasty, or the nose job, was originally a surgical procedure used to treat the "deformity" referred to in scientific literature as "Jewish nose," an angular prominence of the nose. Doctors considered this a medical condition that affected the entire well-being of the patient and demanded intervention. The modern plastic surgery literature still refers to various aspects of human variation as "deformities" that cause psychological and physical impairment to the patient.

For immigrant groups, including European Jews who endured significant psychological scarring as a result of discrimination and racism, cosmetic surgery provided one means of gaining acceptance into this new culture promising the American Dream. Cosmetic procedures offered a way to adapt to the stressor of discrimination. As a result, the United States, with its history of racism and discrimination, inherited a significant market for dealing in certain phenotypic traits. In this sense, plastic surgery continues the work of the eugenics movement by eliminating undesirable phenotypes.

Of course, plastic surgeons maintain that individual pursuit of beauty and a natural desire to look one's best motivate their practice and that it has nothing to do with race. Yet, roughly 30 percent of all cosmetic procedures occur in minority populations—a relatively high proportion. Many of these procedures, especially ones that alter features strongly identified with a particular ethnic group, have been criticized as a means of "occidentalizing" ethnic populations.

In response to the controversy, plastic surgeons published *Ethnic Considerations in Facial Aesthetic Surgery*, with the goal of outlining a "universal standard of beauty" while making considerations for each ethnic group. This difficult task quickly unraveled as the authors relied heavily on Western aesthetic principles derived from classical Greek concepts of beauty. The so-called universal standard was criticized as no more than a Western standard written in a politically correct style.

Double eyelid surgery, a procedure that removes the epicanthic eyefold common in people with East Asian ancestry, is at the center of the debate. The procedure gives the eyes a rounder look and occurs among East Asian almost exclusively. It is the third most common cosmetic procedure—after breast augmentation and nose reshaping.

Imagine a commercial in which a man with an epicanthic eyefold continually struggles to find employment. He comes home to his family after job searching, anxious and insecure. Then he gets double eyelid surgery, giving his eyes a rounder, more European look. His anxiety suddenly is transformed into confidence, and his wife embraces him as he proudly declares "I got the job, honey." A doctor writing in 1954 in the *American Journal of Ophthalmology* described a patient whose story almost exactly mirrors such a tale. The social pressures in a racialized society had already persuaded this patient to have the surgery. The patient, a Chinese American, recounted people consistently mocking the shape of his eyes, saying that he looked sleepy so his business must be sleepy too. After double eyelid surgery, he found both that he was treated more respectfully and that his business became more successful.[a] This account tells of no individual pursuit of beauty or natural desire to look one's best. Instead, it illustrates how years of persecution

REUTERS/Nir Elias/Landov

Here a plastic surgeon explains to a patient how double eyelid surgery could remove the epicanthic eyefold of her eye (*top*) and give her eyes a rounder and more Western look.

BIOCULTURAL CONNECTION (CONTINUED)

become internalized, only to morph into an expression of aesthetic preference.

Regardless of its cultural consequences, cosmetic surgery—whether chosen for its aesthetic properties or for the perceived social advantages of fitting in with a specific race—demonstrates the high value still attached to certain phenotypic traits. Yet the very ability to manipulate these traits illustrates both their superficiality and the fundamental

flaws in the concept of discrete biological races. Ethnic plastic surgery, at best a harmless pursuit to look good and at worst a subversive continuation of racism's grip on society, shows us that the cost of beauty, or at least an idea of it, can be high indeed.

BIOCULTURAL QUESTION

Where would you draw the line for determining when plastic surgery was

medically required and when it was a luxury item? Are there any aspects of your own appearance about which you have internalized a negative perception on account of the social value of this characteristic?

———

[a]Kaw, E. (1993). Medicalization of racial features: Asian American women and cosmetic surgery. *Medical Anthropology Quarterly* 7 (1), 74–89.

In contrast to facial features and shape, skin color—the trait so often used to separate people into groups—provides an excellent example of the role of natural selection in shaping human variation.

Skin Color: A Case Study in Adaptation

Several key factors impact variation in skin color: the transparency or thickness of the skin; a copper-colored pigment called carotene; reflected color from the blood vessels (responsible for the rosy color of lightly pigmented people); and, most significantly, the amount of **melanin** (from *melas*, a Greek word meaning "black")—a dark pigment in the skin's outer layer. People with dark skin have more melanin-producing cells than those with light skin, but everyone (except albinos) has a measure of melanin. Exposure to sunlight increases melanin production, causing skin color to deepen.

Melanin protects skin against damaging ultraviolet solar radiation conferring less susceptibility to skin cancers and sunburn on dark-skinned peoples compared to those with less melanin. Dark skin also helps to prevent the destruction of certain vitamins under intense exposure to sunlight. Because the highest concentrations of dark-skinned people tend to be found in the tropical regions of the world, it appears that natural selection has favored heavily pigmented skin as a protection against exposure where ultraviolet radiation is most constant.

The inheritance of skin color involves several genes (rather than variants of a single gene), each with several alleles, thus creating a continuous range of expression for this trait. In addition, the geographic distribution of skin color tends to be continuous (**Figure 11.11** and **Figure 11.12**). In northern latitudes, light skin has an adaptive advantage related to the skin's important biological function as the manufacturer of vitamin D through a chemical reaction dependent upon sunlight. Vitamin D maintains the balance of calcium in the body essential for healthy bones and balance in the nervous system. In northern climates with little sunshine, light skin allows enough sunlight to penetrate the skin and stimulate the formation of vitamin D. Dark pigmentation interferes with this process in environments with limited sunlight.

Cultural practices can contribute to avoiding the severe consequences of vitamin D deficiency (**Figure 11.13**). Only about 50 years ago, parents in northern Europe and northern North America fed their children a spoonful of cod liver oil, rich in vitamin D, during the dark winter months. Today, pasteurized milk is fortified with vitamin D.

Culture and Biological Diversity

Although cultural adaptation has reduced the importance of biological adaptation and physical variation, at the same time cultural forces impose their own selective pressures. For example, take the reproductive fitness of individuals with diabetes—a disease with a known genetic predisposition. Ready medication in North America and Europe makes people with diabetes as biologically fit as anyone else. However, without access

---

melanin A dark pigment produced in the outer layer of the skin that protects against damaging ultraviolet solar radiation.

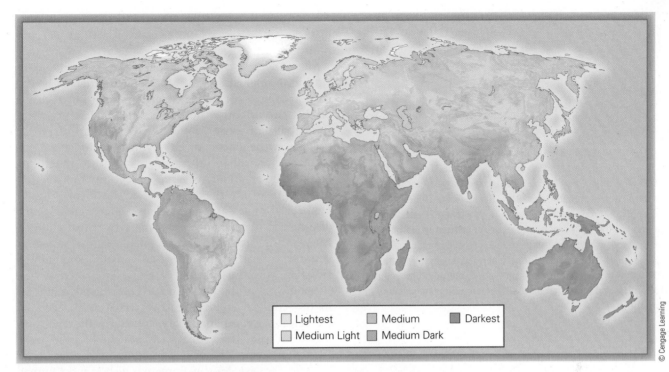

Lightest   Medium   Darkest
Medium Light   Medium Dark

Figure 11.11 Global Distribution of Skin Pigmentation This map illustrates the distribution of dark and light human skin pigmentation before 1492. The earliest members of the genus *Homo*, who inhabited the tropics, likely had dark skin, which is protective from UV radiation. In the tropics and at high altitudes, darker skin has selective advantages. As humans spread to regions with less UV exposure, some pigmentation was lost. Medium-light skin color in Southeast Asia reflects the spread into that region of people from southern China, whereas the medium darkness of people native to southern Australia is a consequence of their tropical Southeast Asian ancestry. Lack of dark skin pigmentation among tropical populations of Native Americans reflects their more recent ancestry in northeastern Asia a mere 20,000 or so years ago.

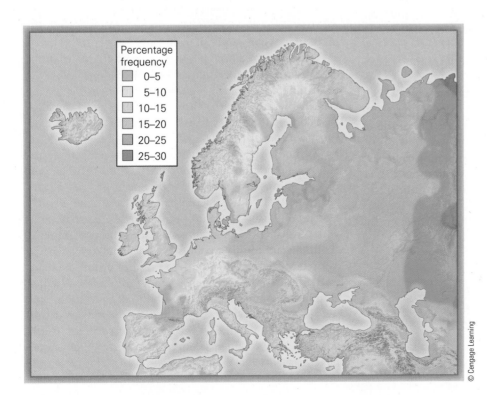

Percentage
frequency
0–5
5–10
10–15
15–20
20–25
25–30

Figure 11.12 Distribution of Type B Blood in Europe The east-west gradient in the frequency of type B blood in Europe contrasts with the north-south gradient in skin color shown in Figure 11.11. Just as the clines for skin color and blood type must be considered independently, so too must be whatever genes are involved in the complex of abilities known as intelligence.

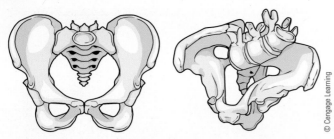

Figure 11.13 When Skin Color Counts Bone diseases such as osteomalacia and rickets caused by vitamin D deficiency can deform the birth canal of the pelvis to the degree that it can interfere with successful childbirth. Because sunshine is vital to the body's production of vitamin D, this disease was very common in the past among the poor in northern industrial cities because they had limited exposure to sunlight. Dietary supplements have reduced the impact of bone diseases, such as rickets, although they continue to be a problem in cultures that require women and girls to dress so that they are completely veiled from the sun.

to the needed medication, a situation all too common globally, diabetes results in death. In fact, one's financial status affects one's access to medication, and so, however unintentional it may be, financial status determines biological fitness.

Culture can also contribute directly to the development of disease. For example, one type of diabetes very common among overweight individuals who get little exercise—a combination that describes 61 percent of people from the United States today—disproportionately affects the poor. Further, when people from traditional cultures adopt the Western high-sugar diet and low activity pattern, the incidence of diabetes and obesity skyrockets.

For years scientists attributed a tendency toward diabetes among American Indians to their **thrifty genotype**, a genotype thought to characterize all humans until about 6,000 years ago (Allen & Cheer, 1996). The thrifty genotype permitted efficient storage of fat to draw on in times of food shortage. In times of scarcity, individuals with the thrifty genotype conserve glucose (a simple sugar) for use in brain and red blood cells (as opposed to other tissues such as muscle), as well as nitrogen (vital for growth and health). Among Europeans, regular access to glucose particularly through the lactose in milk led to selection for

the nonthrifty genotype as protection against adult-onset diabetes, or at least its onset relatively late in life (at a nonreproductive age).

Recently, conservation biologist Gary Nabhan and his wife, anthropologist Laurie Monti, have enriched the discussion of diabetes among American Indians by focusing on diet and activity instead of a genetic difference. They show that native "slow release foods" such as the prickly pear lower the glucose levels of American Indians prone to diabetes (Nabhan, 2004). They chronicle the ability of these desert foods to sustain American Indians during long treks into the desert. These "treatments," unlike biomedical shots and pills, predate the appearance of the disease and also empower and preserve native cultures. Each culture developed as a complete adaptive system so it stands to reason that biological variation and cultural variation would be linked.

And what of the northern European adaptive system? In this context, cultural practices acted as an agent of biological selection for lactose tolerance: the ability to digest **lactose**, the primary constituent of fresh milk. This ability depends on the capacity to make a particular enzyme, **lactase**. Most mammals as well as most human populations—especially Asian, Native Australian, Native American, and many African populations—do not continue to produce lactase into adulthood. Adults with lactose intolerance suffer from gas pains and diarrhea when they consume milk or milk products. Only 10 to 30 percent of Americans of African descent and 0 to 30 percent of adult Asians are lactose tolerant. By contrast, lactase retention and lactose tolerance are normal for over 80 percent of adults of northern European descent. Eastern Europeans, central Asians, Arabs, and some East Africans resemble northern Europeans in lactase retention more than Asians and other Africans (**Figure 11.14**).

Generally speaking, populations with a long tradition of dairying tend to retain lactase into adulthood. With fresh milk contributing significantly to their diets, selection in the past favored those individuals with the allele that confers the ability to assimilate lactose, selecting out those without this allele.

At times, the usual synchronicity between genetic and cultural adaptations goes awry. Interactions between populations whose histories have produced distinct genetic adaptations illustrate such clashes. For example, because North American and European societies associate milk with health, powdered milk has long been a staple of economic aid to other countries. But populations who do not retain lactase into adulthood cannot utilize the many nutrients in milk. Frequently, they also suffer diarrhea, abdominal cramping, and even bone degeneration, with serious results. In fact, the shipping of powdered milk to earthquake victims in the 1960s caused many deaths among South Americans. Since this tragedy, relief workers have learned to take global variation of lactase retention into account.

thrifty genotype Human genotype that permits efficient storage of fat to draw on in times of food shortage and conservation of glucose and nitrogen.
lactose A sugar that is the primary constituent of fresh milk.
lactase An enzyme in the small intestine that enables humans to assimilate lactose.

form of cultural practices such as local cuisine. Biological and dietary adaptations to malaria converge with the interaction between one form of the glucose-6-phosphate-dehydrogenase (G-6-PD) enzyme and fava bean consumption.

The broad, flat fava bean (*Vicia faba*) is a dietary staple in malaria-endemic areas along the Mediterranean coast (**Figure 11.15**). G-6-PD is an enzyme that serves to reduce one sugar, glucose-6-phosphate, to another sugar—in the process releasing an energy-rich molecule. The malaria parasite lives in red blood cells off of energy produced via G-6-PD. Individuals with a mutation in the G-6-PD gene, so-called G-6-PD deficiency, produce energy by an alternate pathway not involving this enzyme that the parasite cannot use. Furthermore, G-6-PD-deficient red blood cells seem to turn over more quickly, thus allowing less time for the parasite to grow and multiply. Although a different form of G-6-PD deficiency is also found in some sub-Saharan African populations, the form found in Mediterranean populations is at odds with an adaptation embedded in the cuisine of the region.

Enzymes naturally occurring in fava beans also contain substances that interfere with the development of the malarial parasite. In cultures around the Mediterranean Sea where malaria is common, fava beans are incorporated into the diet through foods eaten at the height of the malaria season. However, if an individual with G-6-PD deficiency eats fava beans, the substances toxic to the parasite become toxic to humans. With G-6-PD deficiency, fava bean consumption leads to *hemolytic crisis* (Latin for "breaking of red blood cells") and a series of chemical reactions that release free radicals and hydrogen peroxide into the bloodstream. This condition is known as *favism*.

Figure 11.14 Got Milk? The "Got Milk?" campaign emphasizes the health benefits of milk for all people, yet globally, the vast majority of adults cannot digest milk. Instead it makes them quite sick. Mexican born Academy Award–nominated actress Salma Hayek, whose parents are of Lebanese and Spanish descent, can "get milk" because some of her ancestors had a tradition of dairying. Only populations with long traditions of dairying have high frequencies of the alleles for this biological capacity.

Beans, Enzymes, and Adaptation to Malaria

We have already explored some of the human biological adaptations to the deadly malarial parasite through the sickle-cell allele. Other adaptations to malaria take the

Figure 11.15 Fava Beans at Market Fava beans, a dietary staple in the countries around the Mediterranean Sea, also provide some protection against malaria. However, in individuals with G-6-PD deficiency, the protective aspects of fava beans turn deadly. This dual role has led to a rich folklore surrounding fava beans.

© Charles O. Cecil/Alamy

Unfortunately, apprehension about the fava bean has sometimes generalized to fear about many excellent sources of protein such as peanuts, lentils, chickpeas, soybeans, and nuts. Language accounts for this unnecessary deprivation. The Arabic name for fava beans is *foul* (pronounced "fool"), and the soybeans are called *foul-al-Soya*, and peanuts are *foul-al-Soudani*; in other words, the plants are linked linguistically even though they are unrelated biologically (Babiker et al., 1996).

An environmental stressor as potent as malaria has led to a number of human adaptations. In the case of fava beans and G-6-PD deficiency, these adaptations can work at cross-purposes. Just as understanding the history of lactose tolerance and intolerance has improved global health, cultural knowledge of the biochemistry of these interactions will allow humans to adapt, regardless of their genotype. The complexity of ongoing genetic and cultural adaptations highlights the flaws of a strictly biological definition of *race*.

Race and Human Evolution

Throughout this chapter we have explored the fallacy of the biological category of race when applied to the human species. Generalizations cannot be made about types of humans because no discrete types of humans exist. By contrast, the paleoanthropological analysis of the fossil record

The toxic effect of fava bean consumption in G-6-PD individuals has prompted a rich folklore around this simple food, including the ancient Greek belief that fava beans contain the souls of the dead. The link between favism and G-6-PD deficiency has led parents of children with this condition to limit their consumption of this favorite dietary staple.

explored in previous chapters includes defining specific types of ancestors based on biological and cultural capacities that go hand in hand.

The increased brain size of *Homo habilis* noted around 2.5 million years ago supports the notion that these ancestors were capable of more complex cultural activities than australopithecines, including the manufacture of stone tools. Closer to the present, the same assumptions do not hold. At some point in our evolutionary history we became a single, unified global species. Bearing this in mind, we can frame the modern human origins debate in the terms of the content of this chapter.

The modern human origins debate hinges on the question of whether cultural abilities and intelligence can be inferred from details of skull and skeletal shape and size. Supporters of the multiregional hypothesis argue that they cannot. They suggest that using a series of biological features to represent a type of human being (Neandertals) with certain cultural capacities (inferior) is like making assumptions about the cultural capabilities of living humans based on their appearance. In living people, such assumptions are considered stereotypes or racism. By arguing that ancient groups like Neandertals represent a distinct species, supporters of the recent African origins hypothesis bypass the potential prejudice inherent in these assumptions. Both theories embrace African human origins, and in doing so they confront the issue of skin color—the physical feature with extreme political significance today.

Given what we know about the adaptive significance of human skin color, and the fact that, until 800,000 years ago, members of the genus *Homo* were exclusively creatures of the tropics, lightly pigmented skins are likely a recent development in human history. Conversely, and consistent with humanity's African origins, darkly pigmented skins are likely quite ancient. Lightly pigmented peoples possess the enzyme tyrosinase, which converts the amino acid tyrosine into the compound that forms melanin, in sufficient quantity to make them very black. But they also possess genes that inactivate or inhibit it (Wills, 1994).

Human skin, more liberally endowed with sweat glands and lacking heavy body hair compared to other primates, effectively eliminates excess body heat in a hot climate. This would have been especially advantageous to our ancestors on the savannah, who could have avoided confrontations with large carnivorous animals by carrying out most of their activities in the heat of the day. For the most part, tropical predators rest during this period, hunting primarily from dusk until early morning. Without much hair to cover their bodies, selection would have favored dark skin in our human ancestors. In short, based on available scientific evidence, all humans appear to have a black ancestry, no matter how white some of them may appear to be today.

Light pigmentation developed later in populations living outside the tropics; exactly when this occurred remains an interesting question. Whether one subscribes to the multiregional continuity model or to the recent African origins hypothesis, the settling of Greater Australia helps answer this question, as we know that the first people to

reach Australia did so sometime between 40,000 and 60,000 years ago. These people came there from tropical Southeast Asia, spreading throughout Australia eventually to what is now the island of Tasmania, with the latitude and levels of ultraviolet radiation similar to New York City, Rome, or Beijing. Multiregionalists see

these earliest Australians as direct ancestors of early *Homo* in Asia. The recent Denisova fossils and associated genetic studies support this notion.

As Aboriginal Australians originally came from the tropics, we would expect them to have had darkly pigmented skin. In Australia, those populations that spread south of the tropics (where, as in northern latitudes, ultraviolet radiation is less intense) underwent some reduction of pigmentation. But for all that, their skin color is still far darker than that of Europeans or East Asians (recall Figure 11.11). Most of today's Southeast Asian population spread there from southern China following the invention of farming. This expansion of lighter-skinned populations effectively "swamped" the original populations of this region, except in a few out-of-the-way places like the Andaman Islands, in the Bay of Bengal between India and Thailand (Diamond, 1996).

The obvious conclusion is that 40,000 to 60,000 years is not enough to produce significant depigmentation (Ferrie, 1997). These observations also suggest that Europeans and East Asians may have lived outside the tropics for far longer than the people of Tasmania or that settlement in latitudes even more distant from the equator were required for depigmentation to occur.

One should not conclude that because it is relatively new lightly pigmented skin is better or more highly evolved. Darker skin better suits the conditions of life in the tropics or at high altitudes, although with cultural adaptations like protective clothing, hats, and more recently invented sunscreen lotions lightly pigmented people can survive there. Conversely, the availability of supplementary sources of vitamin D allows more heavily pigmented people to do quite well far away from the tropics. In both cases, culture has rendered skin color differences largely irrelevant from a purely biological perspective. With time and effort, skin color may eventually lose its social significance as well.

CHAPTER CHECKLIST

Does the biological concept of race apply to human variation?

● Humans are a single, highly variable species inhabiting the entire globe. Though biological processes are responsible for human variation, the biological concept of race or subspecies cannot be applied to human diversity. No discrete racial types exist.

● Scientists of the past placed humans into discrete races and then ordered them hierarchically. This work was dismantled and discredited beginning in the early 20th century.

● Individual traits appear in continuous gradations (clines) from one population to another without sharp breaks. Traits are inherited independently, and populations are genetically open.

● The vast majority of human variation exists within single populations rather than across different populations.

How does the race concept function within cultures?

● In many countries such as the United States, Haiti, Brazil, and South Africa, the sociopolitical category of race significantly impacts social identity and opportunity.

● Racial conflicts result from social stereotypes and not scientific facts.

● Racists of the past and present frequently invoke the notion of biological difference to support unjust social practices.

● Behavioral characteristics attributed to race can be explained in terms of experience as well as a hierarchical social order affecting the opportunities and challenges faced by different groups of people, rather than biology.

What are the flaws with studies that attempt to link race and intelligence?

● These studies imply a biological basis and do not take into account that biological race does not exist.

● The inherited components of intelligence cannot be separated from those that are culturally acquired.

● There is still no consensus on what intelligence really is, but it is generally agreed that intelligence is made up of several different talents and abilities, each of which would be separately inherited.

● The cultural and environmental specificity of IQ testing makes it invalid for broad comparisons.

Why does human skin color vary across the globe?

● Subject to tremendous variation, skin color is a function of several factors: transparency or thickness of the skin, distribution of blood vessels, and amount of carotene and melanin in the skin.

● Exposure to sunlight increases the amount of melanin, darkening the skin.

● Natural selection has favored heavily pigmented skin as protection against the strong solar radiation of equatorial latitudes.

● In northern latitudes, natural selection has favored relatively depigmented skin, which can utilize relatively weak solar radiation in the production of vitamin D.

● Cultural factors such as social rules about mating and slavery play a part in contemporary skin color distribution globally.

How have human cultures shaped human biology?

● Cultural practices shape human environments, which in turn can act on gene pools.

● Peoples with a dairying tradition possess the ability to digest milk sugars (lactose) into adulthood.

● Foods and activity patterns are a complete adaptive package.

● Western-style lifeways, which are characterized by diets high in sugar and low levels of activity, produce a greater incidence of obesity and diabetes. These diseases skyrocket in populations with dietary traditions of "slow release" foods and high activity.

● The cline of global variation in skin color derives from a balance between selective pressures: synthesis of vitamin D through the skin and protection from solar ultraviolet radiation.

● Cultural and biological adaptations at times work at cross-purposes as seen with the example of G-6-PD deficiency and fava beans as adaptations to malaria.

What is the relationship between race and human evolution?

● The one-to-one correspondence between phenotype and cultural capacity that pertains to early human evolution is problematic when applied to modern human origins and contemporary human variation.

● Light pigment appeared relatively late in the course of human evolution.

● All humans have black ancestry no matter how white they might appear today.

QUESTIONS FOR REFLECTION

1. As a species humans are extremely diverse, and yet our biological diversity cannot be partitioned into discrete types, subspecies, or races. At the same time, race functions as a social and political category, imposing inequality in some societies. How did so-called biological race and very real sociopolitical race play out in the "Linsanity" of the spring of 2012? What are the beliefs about biological diversity and race in your community today?

2. Although we can see and scientifically explain population differences in skin color, why is it invalid to use the biological concept of subspecies or race when referring to humans? Can you imagine another species of animal, plant, or microorganism for which the subspecies concept makes sense?

3. Globally, health statistics are gathered by country. In addition, some countries such as the United States gather health statistics by so-called racial categories. How are these two endeavors different and similar? Should health statistics be gathered by group?

4. How do you define the concept of intelligence? Do you think scientists will ever be able to discover the genetic basis of intelligence?

5. Cultural practices affect microevolutionary changes in the human species and often have dramatic effects on human health. Do you see examples of structural violence in your community that make some individuals more vulnerable to disease than others? Do you see examples globally?

ONLINE STUDY RESOURCES

CourseMate

Access chapter-specific learning tools, including learning objectives, practice quizzes, videos, flash cards, glossaries, and more in your Anthropology CourseMate.

Log into **www.cengagebrain.com** to access the resources your instructor has assigned and to purchase materials.

Challenge Issue

In the early 21st century, the human species faces novel challenges due to the massive changes our societies have imposed on the world. An ever-expanding population size consumes the earth's natural resources leaving humans to compete for everything from water to fossil fuels to antiretroviral therapy for HIV and AIDS. But, just as we have done over the course of human evolutionary history, our entwined cultural and biological capabilities help us to adapt as a species. In South Africa, for example, a group from the Bambanani Women's Group—HIV-positive women who receive therapy through Doctors Without Borders—have turned to making body maps that convey their experiences and to show the privilege inherent in access to medical treatment. In her body map, a life-sized tracing made with the help of Cape Town artist Jane Solomon, each woman includes her name, a personal symbol of power, her hand- and footprints, and her own visualization of her biological and life history. Here, Nondomiso Hlwele stands outside of her mother's house in Khayelitsha township with the body map she made. These maps become objects of hope and inspiration for the makers and a means for these women to transfer their personal stories to their children. The maps in turn challenge us to directly engage with the individual suffering of others. Only through such engagement—through awareness of how social and biological processes shape one another and through recognition of our shared humanity—can we ensure the future of our species and our planet.

Human Adaptation to a Changing World

12

IN THIS CHAPTER YOU WILL LEARN TO

- Recognize old and new pressures to human survival across the globe.

- Describe human biological adaptations to high altitude, cold, and heat.

- Identify patterns of human growth and how the process allows humans to adapt.

- Explain the challenges that we humans have created for ourselves and how their effects fall upon distinct yet interconnected communities.

- Describe modern humans' variety of coping methods and treatments for health issues.

- Define *disease* versus *illness*, and discuss cultural attitudes about both.

- Investigate the multiple causes of health problems from a medical anthropological perspective.

Throughout millions of years of human evolutionary history, biology and culture interacted to make humans the species we are today. The archaeological record and contemporary human variation reveal that biology and culture continue to shape all areas of human experience, including health and disease. Indeed, an inside joke among anthropologists is that if you do not know the answer to an exam question about biology and culture, the answer is either "both" or "malaria." Our current understanding of malaria, as explained in previous chapters, illustrates how answering "malaria" is just like answering "both." Farming practices (culture) of the past created the perfect environment for the malarial parasite. The genetic response (biology) to this environmental change was increased frequencies of the sickle-cell allele.

To add a few more biocultural layers closer to the present, think about how contemporary global inequalities contribute to the continuing devastation of malaria in poorer countries today. If malaria were a problem plaguing North America or Europe, would most citizens of these countries still be without adequate treatment or cure? Similarly, African Americans, who have experienced racism rooted in a false message of biological difference, have distrusted the public health initiatives for genetic counseling to reduce frequencies of sickle-cell anemia in the United States (Tapper, 1999; Washington, 2006). Would average Americans of European descent feel comfortable with genetic testing to eliminate a disease gene if they had experienced the wrongs underprivileged ethnic minorities have experienced in the name of science?

Consider, for example, the Tuskegee Syphilis Study, carried out by the U.S. Public Health Service in Macon County, Alabama, from 1932 to 1972. This study involved withholding syphilis medication from a group of poor African American men without their knowledge, so that the scientists could learn more about the biology of syphilis in the "Negro" (**Figure 12.1**). Today, this could not happen. Any kind of biological research on human subjects without informed consent is illegal in the United States and in many other countries.

Figure 12.1 The Tuskegee Experiments The Tuskegee Syphilis Study denied appropriate medical treatment to African American men in order to study the supposed differences in the biology of the disease in the "Negro." This human experimentation was not only false from a biological perspective but represented a moral breach in research conduct. Public outcry about this experiment led to regulations that protect all human subjects in biomedical research. Today, laws in the United States and in many other countries require informed consent of study participants for all research on human subjects.

When examining a seemingly biological phenomenon such as disease, cultural factors must be considered at every level—from how that phenomenon is represented in social groups (reflected in this case in the false notion that the biology of syphilis would differ between people of different skin colors) to how biological research is conducted.

The integration of biology and culture is the hallmark of anthropology. Throughout this book we have emphasized biocultural connections in examples ranging from infant feeding and sleeping practices to the relationship between poverty and tuberculosis. In this chapter, we take a deeper look at this connection and examine some of the theoretical approaches biological and medical anthropologists use to examine the interaction of biology and culture.

Although humans possess a number of exquisite biological mechanisms through which they have adapted to the natural environment, these mechanisms can fall short in a globalizing world. But before turning to the challenges we face from the dramatic changes in the human-made environments of today, we will explore the biological mechanisms people have used over millennia to adapt to three naturally occurring environmental extremes: high altitude, cold, and heat.

Human Adaptation to Natural Environmental Stressors

Studies of human adaptation traditionally focus on the capacity of humans to adapt or adjust to their environment through biological and/or cultural mechanisms. Darwin's theory of natural selection accounts for **genetic adaptations**—discrete genetic changes built into the allele frequencies of populations, such as the various adaptations to malaria that we have examined. It also provides the mechanism for understanding that adaptations, evident in population variation of continuous phenotypic traits, depend upon multiple interacting genes.

genetic adaptations Discrete genetic changes built into the allele frequencies of populations or microevolutionary change brought about by natural selection.

Figure 12.2 Twins Diana Bozza and her identical twin, Deborah Faraday, share 100 percent genetic identity. Yet only Deborah suffers from early onset Alzheimer's disease. Here Diana comforts Deborah at an assisted living facility in Front Royal, Virginia. Diagnosed in 2004, Deborah is completely disabled while Diana has no symptoms of Alzheimer's. Though identical twins share 100 percent of their genetic material, their phenotypes can be distinct because of interactions between these genes and the environment over the course of each individual's distinct life.

Jodi Cobb/National Geographic Stock

Even without knowing the precise genetic bases to these adaptations (such as skin color or body build), scientists can study them through comparative measurement of the associated phenotypic variation. In both these cases, differential reproductive success accounts for differences in allele frequency.

Humans possess two additional biological mechanisms through which they can adapt. The first of these, **developmental adaptation**, also produces permanent phenotypic variation through environmental shaping of individual gene expression **(Figure 12.2)**. The extended period of growth and development characteristic of humans allows for a prolonged time period during which the environment can exert its effects on the developing organism. Humans inherit this capacity to adapt through the process of growth and development, but the specific permanent phenotypic changes brought about through environmental interaction do not get directly passed onto future generations. Even after most physical growth ceases, our genomes interact with the environment, producing discrete biological changes.

The anthropological focus on growth and development has a long history dating back to the work of Franz Boas, the founder of American four-field anthropology. Boas is credited with discovering the features of the human growth curve **(Figure 12.3)**. He demonstrated that the rate of human growth varies in typical patterns until adulthood, when physical growth ceases. Humans experience a period of very rapid growth after birth through infancy, followed by a gradually slower rate of growth during childhood. At adolescence, the rate of growth increases again during the adolescent growth spurt. Growth in height or stature results from the addition of

new cells throughout the body, but particularly in the bones where growth takes place at specific growth plates **(Figure 12.4)**.

In addition to describing the long-term pattern of human growth, anthropologists have also demonstrated that within periods of growth, the actual process proceeds as a series of alternating bursts and relative quiet (Lampl, Velhuis, & Johnson, 1992). When challenged by malnutrition, physical growth slows to permit immediate survival at the expense of height in adulthood. This adaptive mechanism may have negative consequences for subsequent generations given individuals who were malnourished as children have been shown to experience reduced reproductive success as adults (Martorell, 1988).

Boas also demonstrated differences in the growth of immigrant children in the United States compared to their parents. This work was the earliest documentation of the variable effects of different environments on the growth process. Presumably, immigrant children resemble their parents genetically; therefore, size differences between immigrant children and their parents could be attributed to the environment alone. This kind of difference, known as a **secular trend**, allows anthropologists to make inferences about environmental effects on growth and development.

---

developmental adaptation A permanent phenotypic variation derived from interaction between genes and the environment during the period of growth and development.

secular trend A physical difference among related people from distinct generations that allows anthropologists to make inferences about environmental effects on growth and development.

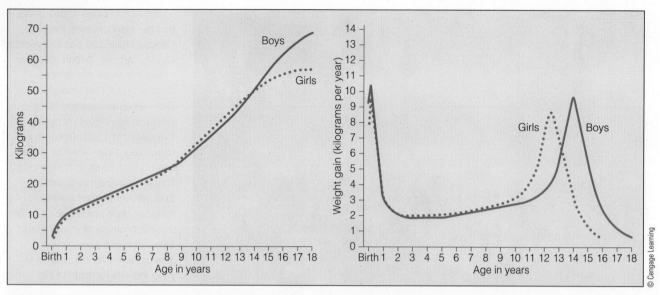

Figure 12.3 Human Growth Curves Franz Boas defined the features of the human growth curve. The graph on the left depicts distance, or the amount of growth attained over time, and the graph on the right shows the velocity, or rate of growth over time. These charts are widely used throughout the globe to determine the health status of children.

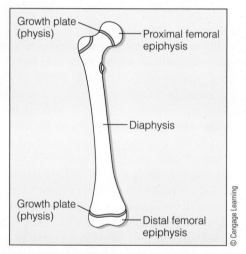

Figure 12.4 Long Bone Growth Each long bone has specific regions (in red) of cartilage where growth occurs; these are called growth plates. This allows the harder bony tissue of the diaphysis to support the body and for the epiphyses to function within the joint while an individual is developing. This thighbone, or femur, has four distinct areas of growth. In an x-ray of a child who is still growing, the cartilage does not appear white like bone. Each bone has a particular sequence of maturation that is regulated by hormones. Growth stops when the epiphyses fuse with the rest of the bone, a process regulated by estrogens in both males and females. In males, the clavicle or collarbone is one of the last bones to fuse. In females, the pubic bone of the pelvis is one of the last bones to fuse.

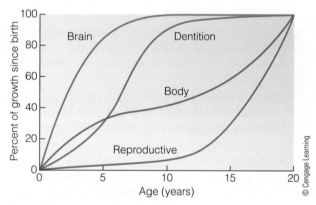

Figure 12.5 Development Trajectories The various systems of the human body each follow their own trajectory of growth. Brain growth is most rapid in the first five years of life but continues at a slower pace into young adulthood. Children's immune systems also undergo rapid development early in life. Human children acquire most of their permanent dentition by the time their reproductive systems start to mature at adolescence; their 12-year molars have emerged, and only the wisdom teeth have not yet erupted. The pace of growth for the reproductive system and the body both increase rapidly at adolescence.

The various systems of the human body have their own trajectory of growth and development (**Figure 12.5**). Over the past sixty years, a downward secular trend in the age at **menarche** (first menstruation) has become evident in North America. Whether this secular trend is attributable to healthy or problematic stimuli (such as childhood obesity or hormones in the environment) has yet to be determined. Likewise, age at menarche varies tremendously across the globe. Genetic differences from population to population

menarche First menstruation in the maturation of a human female.

Figure 12.6 Nutrition and Fertility The theory that human females require a minimum percentage of body fat in order to attain menarche accounts for some of the global variation in the age at which this occurs. Around the world, many women stay incredibly lean through a combination of hard labor and limited food availability, a condition that limits their fertility. Further, sufficient body fat maintains menstrual cycles throughout adulthood. Thus, female bodies regulate their potential pregnancies in times of limited food because successful pregnancy and breastfeeding require extra nutrition. In postindustrial societies, loss of periods, or amenorrhea, is common among athletes and among women with anorexia nervosa, a disorder in which individuals starve themselves.

account for some of this variation, and environmental effects account for the remainder. The Bundi of New Guinea have the oldest average age (18) at menarche. By comparison, U.S. girls reach menarche on average at the age of 12.4 years.

An important theory accounting for the timing of sexual maturation ties age at menarche to the percentage of body fat possessed by growing individuals as a regulator of hormonal production (Frisch, 2002). Most female bodies seem to require a minimum ratio of 17 percent body fat to lean mass for menarche to occur (Figure 12.6). This body fat helps with the conversion of androgens (the male hormones) to the female hormonal counterpart, estrogens. Highly active lean women, whether from athletics or some kind of labor, may experience a delayed menarche or a secondary loss of menstruation. Starvation has the same effect. A massive excess of body fat also interferes with fertility.

Hormones impact fertility into adulthood, but teasing apart the role of biology and culture with respect to hormones has proven to be complex. Take, for example, the case of androgen hormone levels, waist-to-hip ratio, and fertility

levels of women in high-powered careers. These women tend to have a more cylindrical shape, which could be because their bodies produce relatively more androgen than hourglass-shaped women. A higher androgen level, however, may be the reason for lower fertility among these women. High androgen levels may also represent a biological response to a specific work environment that ultimately impedes the fertility of women in high-powered careers (Cashdan, 2008). Similarly, diminishing estrogens after **menopause** (the cessation of menstrual cycles) causes female body fat distribution patterns to shift to a more male pattern.

The bottom line is that human hormonal systems are highly sensitive to a variety of environmental stimuli. Biological anthropologist Peter Ellison works extensively on the connections between hormones and the environment—a subspecialty defined as reproductive ecology (see the Anthropologist of Note).

menopause The cessation of menstrual cycles.

ANTHROPOLOGIST OF NOTE

Peter Ellison

Reproductive biology and human health across cultures have been the focus of the work of biological anthropologist **Peter Ellison**. In the 1970s, Ellison first read Darwin's *Origin of Species* as a college student at St. John's College in Annapolis, Maryland. He found Darwin's text transformative and went to the University of Vermont to study biology; later he earned a doctorate in biological anthropology from Harvard, where he now runs a comprehensive program in reproductive ecology.

Ellison has pioneered techniques for hormonal analysis from saliva, and he uses this technique to monitor individuals' hormonal response to a variety of environmental stressors. This noninvasive technique has allowed Ellison to conduct hormonal studies throughout the world and to correlate hormonal levels with social events. People from long-term field sites in Congo, Poland, Japan, Nepal, and Paraguay have participated in this research, allowing Ellison to document the hormonal variation around biological events, such as egg implantation and breastfeeding, as well as cultural factors such as farm work or foraging.

Dr. Ellison is especially interested in how behavior and social stimuli affect reproductive physiology. In Western societies, he has explored hormonal levels of males and females in response to stimuli, such as winning a championship or taking a stressful exam. He has also studied the relationship between cancer development and exercise and stress. In his book *On Fertile Ground*, Ellison illustrates how evolutionary forces have shaped human reproductive physiology into a system capable of precise responses to environmental stimuli.

© Kris Snibbe/Staff Photo Harvard News Office

Peter Ellison (*left*) and Peter Gray discuss how male testosterone levels differ between married and single men and among men of different cultures.

Although genetic and developmental adaptations become permanent parts of an adult's phenotype, **physiological adaptations** come and go in response to a specific environmental stimulus. Along with cultural adaptations, these various biological mechanisms allow humans to be the only primate species to inhabit the entire globe. Over the course of our evolutionary history, most environmental stressors were climatic and geographic. Today, humans face a series of new environmental stressors of their own making.

Adaptation to High Altitude

High altitude differs from other natural environmental stressors because it is the least amenable to cultural adaptation. Humans can heat the cold and cool the heat, but the reduced availability of oxygen at high altitude poses more of a challenge. At a cellular level, this results in reduced oxygen availability, or **hypoxia** (from the Greek *hypo*, for "low" or "under" and the word *oxygen*). Before

physiological adaptation A short-term physiological change in response to a specific environmental stimulus. An immediate short-term response is not very efficient and is gradually replaced by a longer-term response; see *acclimatization*.

hypoxia The reduced availability of oxygen at a cellular level.

the invention of oxygen masks and pressurized cabins in airplanes, there was no way to modify this environmental stressor via culture.

When people speak of the air being "thinner" at high altitude, they are referring to the concentration (partial pressure) of oxygen available to the lungs, and so to the circulatory system. At high altitudes, the partial pressure of oxygen is sufficiently reduced so that most lowlanders experience severe oxygen deprivation (Figure 12.7).

Populations that have lived at high altitudes for generations, such as the Quechua Indians of the highlands of Peru and the Sherpa native to the Himalaya Mountains, possess a remarkable ability to tolerate oxygen deprivation, living and working at altitudes as high as 20,000 feet above sea level. Some of these abilities have been encoded in the genetic makeup of these populations. In addition, developmental and physiological adaptations to the lower partial pressure of oxygen in the environment have rendered their body tissues resistant to oxygen deprivation (Figure 12.8).

Typical lowlanders can make both short- and long-term physiological adjustments to high altitude. In general, short-term changes help an individual avoid an immediate crisis, but the poor efficiency of these changes makes them difficult to sustain. Instead, long-term responses take over as the individual's physiological

Kyodo/Landov

Figure 12.8 Born to Run Observing that East African runners, like Ethiopian Tiki Gelana crossing the women's marathon finish line at the 2012 Olympics, have won most of the major marathon competitions over the past several decades, coaches have emulated the East African approach. Adaptation to the hot, dry yet mountainous region leads to a long, lean build (a product of the heat adaptation) and increased oxygen-carrying capacity. Although runners worldwide tend to be long and lean, many athletes now train at high altitude so that when race day comes, their red blood cell count and hemoglobin levels allow them to carry more oxygen.

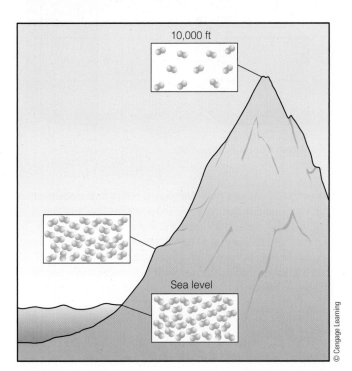

© Cengage Learning

Figure 12.7 Atmospheric Pressure The amount of atmosphere above us determines the amount of pressure being exerted on oxygen molecules in the air. At sea level, the pressure of the atmosphere packs oxygen molecules more tightly together compared to the density of oxygen molecules at higher altitudes. This in turn impacts the ease at which oxygen can enter the lungs when we breathe.

responses attain equilibrium with the environment. This process is known as **acclimatization**. Most lowlanders stepping off an airplane in Cuzco, Peru, for example will experience increased respiratory rate, cardiac output, and pulse rate. Their arteries will expand as blood pressure increases in order to get oxygen to the tissues. This kind of response cannot be maintained indefinitely. Instead, lowlanders acclimatize as their bodies begin to produce more red blood cells and hemoglobin in order to carry more oxygen. Because of differences in genetic makeup, individuals' physiological responses begin at varying altitudes.

Developmental adaptations are seen in individuals who spend their childhood years of growth and development at high altitude. Among the highland Quechua, for

acclimatization Long-term physiological adjustments made in order to attain equilibrium with a specific environmental stimulus.

example, both the chest cavity and the right ventricle of the heart (which pushes blood to the lungs) are enlarged compared to lowland Quechua. This may have genetic underpinnings in that all Quechua experience a long period of growth and development compared to the average person in the United States.

The process of growth and development begins with reproduction, and high altitude has a considerable impact on this process. For populations that have not adapted to high altitude, successful reproduction requires some cultural interventions. For example, take the case of fertility among Spanish colonialists in the city of Potosi high in the Andes. For the first fifty-four years of this city's existence, founded to mine the "mountain of silver" that towers above the community, no Spanish child was born who survived childhood. Indigenous populations did not have this problem. To ensure reproductive success, Spanish women began the cultural practice of retreating to lower altitude for their pregnancy and the first year of their child's life (Wiley, 2004).

At high altitudes cold stress is also a problem. A stocky body and short limbs help individuals conserve heat whereas the opposite facilitates heat loss. We dissipate heat through the surface of our bodies. A stocky build has a lower surface area to volume ratio compared to a long, linear build. Small body size also results in a higher surface area to volume ratio. These phenomena have been formalized into two rules named after the naturalists who made such observations in mammals. **Bergmann's rule** refers to the tendency for the bodies of mammals living in cold climates to be more massive than members of the same species living in warm climates (**Figure 12.9**). **Allen's rule** refers to the tendency of mammals living in cold climates to have shorter appendages (arms and legs) than members of the same species living in warm climates (**Figure 12.10**).

Adaptation to Cold

Cold stress can exist without high altitude, as it does in the Arctic. In addition to the previously mentioned patterns of body and limb shape and size, other cold responses are also evident in Arctic populations.

In extreme cold, the limbs need enough heat to prevent frostbite, but giving up heat to the periphery takes it away from the body core. Humans balance this through

Bergmann's rule The tendency for the bodies of mammals living in cold climates to be shorter and rounder than members of the same species living in warm climates.

Allen's rule The tendency for the bodies of mammals living in cold climates to have shorter appendages (arms and legs) than members of the same species living in warm climates.

hunting response A cyclic expansion and contraction of the blood vessels of the limbs that balances releasing enough heat to prevent frostbite with maintaining heat in the body core.

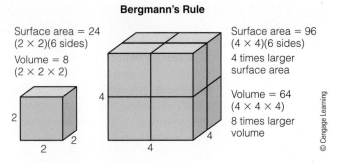

Bergmann's Rule

Surface area = 24
(2 × 2)(6 sides)
Volume = 8
(2 × 2 × 2)

Surface area = 96
(4 × 4)(6 sides)
4 times larger surface area

Volume = 64
(4 × 4 × 4)
8 times larger volume

© Cengage Learning

Figure 12.9 Bergmann's Rule Bergmann's rule refers to the observation that as overall body size increases, the amount of surface area increases less rapidly than the amount of volume. This accounts for the tendency for mammals living in cold climates to be more massive than members of the same species living in warmer climates. This allows for the conservation of heat in cold climates and its dissipation in warm climates.

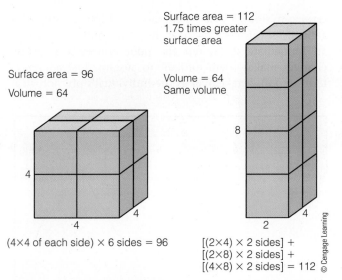

Allen's Rule

Surface area = 96
Volume = 64

Surface area = 112
1.75 times greater surface area

Volume = 64
Same volume

(4×4 of each side) × 6 sides = 96

[(2×4) × 2 sides] +
[(2×8) × 2 sides] +
[(4×8) × 2 sides] = 112

© Cengage Learning

Figure 12.10 Allen's Rule Allen's rule refers to the observation that in two bodies that have the same volume, the one that is long and lean rather than short and squat will have a greater surface area. This accounts for the tendency for mammals living in cold climates to have shorter appendages (arms and legs) than the same species living in warmer climates. Heat can be dissipated through long limbs or conserved through short ones.

a cyclic expansion and contraction of the blood vessels of their limbs called the **hunting response**. Blood vessels oscillate between closing down to prevent heat loss and opening up to warm the hands and feet. When first exposed to cold as gloves are taken off, blood vessels immediately constrict. Initial alternations between open (warm) and shut (cold) and the corresponding temperature of the skin range dramatically. But the oscillations become smaller and more rapid, allowing a hunter to

Flip Nicklin/National Geographic Stock

Figure 12.11 Whale Hunting Arctic populations adapt to frigid conditions through a variety of biological and cultural adaptations. Often biology and culture interact. The high-energy readily available whale blubber diet, integral to Eskimo cultural systems, also stimulates the body to burn this energy at a high metabolic rate. A high metabolic rate, in turn, helps the body stay warm in very cold climates.

maintain the warmth-derived manual dexterity required for tying knots or positioning arrows.

Eskimos (including the Inuit) also deal with cold through a high **metabolic rate**: the rate at which their bodies burn energy. This may result from a diet high in protein and fat (whale blubber is the common food; see **Figure 12.11**). In addition, genetic factors likely also contribute to Eskimos' high metabolic rate.

Shivering provides a short-term physiological response to cold. Shivering quickly generates heat for the body but cannot be maintained for long periods of time. Instead, as an individual acclimatizes to the cold, adjustments to diet, activity pattern, metabolic rate, and the circulatory system must occur.

Adaptation to Heat

Sweating or perspiring provides the human body's primary physiological mechanism for coping with extreme heat. Through sweating, the body gives up heat as water released from sweat glands evaporates (**Figure 12.12**).

Without water, exposure to heat can be fatal. We must drink enough water to replace whatever we lose through sweating.

Each human has roughly 2 million sweat glands though this number varies among individuals and populations. Sweat glands spread out over a greater surface area on tall, thin bodies, facilitating water evaporation and heat loss. Thus, Bergmann's and Allen's rules also apply to heat adaptation. The more surface area a body has, the more surface for the sweat glands. In addition, because heat is produced by unit of volume, having a high surface area to volume ratio is beneficial for heat loss. Long, slender bodies dissipate heat best. In hot and humid environments such as rainforests, water evaporation poses a challenge. In this environment, human populations have adapted to minimize heat production through a reduction in overall size while keeping a slender, lean build.

metabolic rate The rate at which bodies burn energy (food) to function.

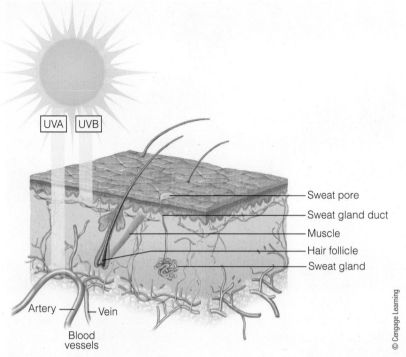

Figure 12.12 Cross-Section of Human Skin Skin—a sensitive, functional, and highly diffuse organ of the human body—responds exquisitely to the environment. As described in Chapter 11, vitamin D is synthesized here. In addition, skin regulates our adaptive response to heat through sweating. Blood vessels carry heat to the surface of the body. Water released through the sweat glands onto the surface of the skin through pores will evaporate and dissipate this body heat. Individuals who spend their growth and development in hotter climates possess more sweat glands as a developmental adaptation to heat. In addition, body build impacts heat dissipation. More skin or surface area allows an individual to dissipate heat more easily because of the increased number of sweat glands distributed on the skin.

Human-Made Stressors of a Changing World

Traditionally, culture has allowed humans to modify natural stressors such as heat and cold through means such as housing, diet, and clothing. But in today's globalizing world, the effects of culture are much more complex. Rather than simply alleviating physical stressors, cultural processes can *add* new stressors such as pollution, global warming, and exhaustion of the world's natural resources. Indeed, as you will recall from Chapter 5, geologists have added "Anthropocene" to the geological epochs to reflect the profound human modification of the earth since the industrial revolution.

Biological adaptation to these human-made stressors cannot keep pace with the rapid rate at which humans are changing the earth. Biological adaptation still occurs, but it takes many generations for beneficial alleles and phenotypes to be incorporated into a population's genome. Until human cultures cooperate to collectively address these global challenges, unnatural stressors will inevitably lead to sickness and suffering. An integrated, holistic anthropological perspective has much to contribute to alleviating if not eliminating these human-made stressors.

The Development of Medical Anthropology

Medical anthropology, a specialization that cuts across all four fields of anthropology, contributes significantly to the understanding of sickness and health in the 21st century. Some of the earliest medical anthropologists were individuals trained as physicians and ethnographers who investigated the health beliefs and practices of peoples in "exotic" places while also providing them with Western medicine. Medical anthropologists during this early period translated local experiences of sickness into

VISUAL COUNTERPOINT

Figure 12.13 **Cultural Symbols of Authority** Shamans and biomedical doctors both rely upon symbols to heal their patients. The physician's white coat is a powerful symbol of medical knowledge and authority that communicates to patients just as clearly as does the pattern on the skin of the shaman's drum. Interestingly, medical schools in the United States are increasingly incorporating a "white coat" ceremony into medical education, conferring the power of the white coat onto new doctors.

the scientific language of Western biomedicine. Following a reevaluation of this ethnocentric approach in the 1970s, medical anthropology emerged as a specialization that brings theoretical and applied approaches from cultural and biological anthropology to the study of human health and sickness.

Medical anthropologists study **medical systems**, or patterned sets of ideas and practices relating to illness. Medical systems are cultural systems, similar to any other social institution. Medical anthropologists examine healing traditions and practices cross-culturally and the qualities all medical systems have in common. For example, the terms used by French cultural anthropologist Claude Lévi-Strauss to describe the healing powers of *shamans* (the name for indigenous healers, originally from Siberia, and now applied to many traditional healers) also apply to medical practices in Europe and North America (Lévi-Strauss, 1963). In both situations, the healer has access to a world of restricted knowledge (spiritual or scientific) from which the average community member is excluded (**Figure 12.13**).

Medical anthropologists also use scientific models drawn from biological anthropology, such as evolutionary theory and ecology, to understand and improve

human health. Moreover, they have turned their attention to the connections between human health and political and economic forces, both globally and locally. Because global flows of people, germs, cures, guns, and pollution underlie the distribution of sickness and health in the world today, a broad anthropological understanding of the origins of sickness is vital for alleviating human suffering.

The medical anthropological perspective recognizes poverty as one of the major determinants of sickness; anthropologists throughout the globe have demonstrated this connection and worked to improve health through social justice. This perspective has gained support from the World Bank, a global financial institution that provides loans to developing countries, with U.S. medical anthropologist and physician Jim Yong Kim as its new president. Kim, the cofounder (with physician-anthropologist Paul Farmer) of Partners in Health, has spent his career improving human health through the eradication of poverty.

medical system A patterned set of ideas and practices relating to illness.

Science, Illness, and Disease

During the course of medical anthropology's development as a distinct specialty within anthropology, there was a concurrent transformation in the relationship between biological and cultural knowledge. The earliest research on medical systems was carried out by physician-anthropologists— individuals trained as medical doctors and as anthropologists who participated in the international public health movement emerging early in the 20th century. While delivering the medical care developed in Europe and North America, these physician-anthropologists simultaneously studied the health beliefs and practices of the cultures they were sent to help. Local cultural categories about sickness were translated into Western biomedical terms.

Initially, these Western approaches were thought to be culture-free depictions of human biology and were therefore used as an interpretive framework for examining the medical beliefs and practices of other cultures. Implicit in this work was the notion that the Western approach, with its supposed objectivity, was superior. Fieldwork conducted by cultural anthropologists, however, has shown that medical categories, like other aspects of a people's unique worldview, reflect the value system of their particular culture. For example, the Subanun people of Mindinao, one of the large islands of the Philippines, give different names to fungal infections of the skin depending on whether the infection is openly visible or hidden under clothes. In contrast, the biomedical and scientific categorization of fungal infections refers only to genus and species of the fungus.

In the 1970s the place of biological and cultural knowledge in medical anthropology was dramatically reorganized. The admission of the People's Republic of China to the United Nations in 1971, and the subsequent improvement of diplomatic and other relationships between that communist country and Western powers, played a role in this theoretical shift. Cultural exchanges revealed a professional medical system in the East rivaling that of Western biomedicine in its scientific basis and technical feats. For example, the practice of open-heart surgery in China, using only acupuncture needles as an anesthetic, challenged the assumption of biomedical superiority within anthropological thought. Scholars began proposing that biomedicine is a cultural system, just like the medical systems in other cultures, and that it, too, is worthy of anthropological study.

To effectively compare medical systems and health cross-culturally, medical anthropologists have made a theoretical distinction between the terms *disease* and *illness*. **Disease** refers to a specific pathology: a physical or biological abnormality. **Illness** refers to the meanings and elaborations given to particular physical states. Disease and illness do not necessarily overlap. An individual may experience illness without having a disease, or a disease may occur in the absence of illness.

In cultures with scientific medical systems, a key component of the social process of illness involves delineating human suffering in terms of biology. At times this extends to labeling an illness as a disease even though the biology is poorly understood. Think about alcoholism in the United States, for example. A person who is thought of as a drunk, partier, barfly, or boozer tends not to get sympathy from the rest of society. By contrast, a person struggling with the disease of alcoholism receives cultural help from physicians, support from groups such as Alcoholics Anonymous, and financial aid from health insurance covering medical treatment. It matters little that the biology of this "disease" is still poorly understood and that alcoholism is treated through social support rather than expert manipulation of biology. By calling alcoholism a disease, it becomes a socially sanctioned and recognized illness within the dominant medical system of the United States. See this chapter's Globalscape for an innovative method of reducing the stigma and improving health through a focus on the social aspects of sickness.

Disease can also exist without illness. Schistosomiasis, infection with a kind of parasitic flatworm called a blood fluke, is an excellent example. Scientists have fully documented the life cycle of this parasite that alternates between water snail and human hosts. The adult worms live for many years inside human intestine or urinary tract. Human waste then spreads the mobile phase of the parasite to freshwater snails. Inside the snails, the parasite develops further to a second mobile phase of the flatworm life cycle, releasing thousands of tiny creatures into freshwater. If humans swim, wade, or do household chores such as laundry in this infested water, the parasite can bore its way through the skin, traveling to the intestine or bladder where the life cycle continues.

The idea of parasites boring through the skin and living permanently inside the bladder or intestine may well be revolting; ingesting poisons to rid the body of these parasites is an acceptable treatment for people at certain social and economic levels. But to people living where schistosomiasis is **endemic** (the public health term for a disease that is widespread in the population), this disease state is normal, and thus they seek no treatment. In other words, schistosomiasis is not an illness. Individuals may know about expensive effective biomedical treatments, but given the likelihood of reinfection and the inaccessibility of the drugs, they tend not to seek treatment with pharmaceutical agents.

Over time, the forces of evolution generally lead to a tolerance between parasite and host so that infected

disease A specific pathology; a physical or biological abnormality.

illness The meanings and elaborations given to a particular physical state.

endemic The public health term for a disease that is widespread in a population.

Globalscape

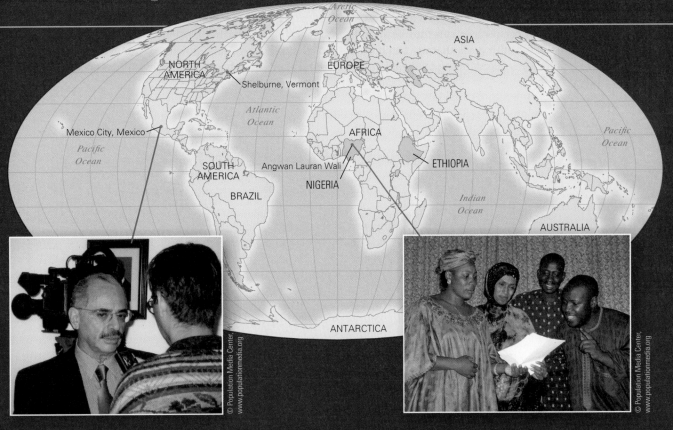

NORTH AMERICA
Shelburne, Vermont
Mexico City, Mexico
SOUTH AMERICA
BRAZIL
EUROPE
ASIA
AFRICA
Angwan Lauran Wali
NIGERIA
ETHIOPIA
AUSTRALIA
ANTARCTICA
Arctic Ocean
Atlantic Ocean
Pacific Ocean
Pacific Ocean
Indian Ocean

© Population Media Center, www.populationmedia.org

© Population Media Center, www.populationmedia.org

From Soap Opera to Clinic?

When Hajara Nasiru in Angwan Lauran Wali, Nigeria, listened to the radio soap opera *Gugar Goge* (*Tell It to Me Straight*), she learned something that changed her life. Created in Nigeria using a methodology developed originally in Mexico, the radio drama tells the story of 12-year-old Kande, who is forced to marry a man more than twice her age. She soon becomes pregnant. After a prolonged labor, her baby dies, and Kande develops an obstetric fistula (a hole between either the rectum and vagina or the bladder and vagina) leading to incontinence, infection, and nerve damage. Kande's husband abandons her, but a neighbor brings her to the hospital in the nearby city of Zaira. After the fistula is repaired, Kande is able to return to her father's home in full health.

Like Kande, Hajara married young (at 15), and by the age of 25 she had experienced eight labors, lost five children, and developed a fistula with her last labor. After living with the debilitating discomfort for nine weeks, she invited her husband to listen to the soap opera too. *Gugar Goge* gave Hajara and her husband the information they needed. From the show, they learned that the fistula could be repaired and that Hajara need not suffer.

This radio drama is one of many created by the local branches of the Population Media Center (PMC), a U.S.-based international nongovernmental organization, headquartered in Shelburne, Vermont, that uses "entertainment-education for social change." Mexican television producer Miguel Sabido, pictured above, developed PMC's methodology and created *telenovelas* that prompted dramatic social change across Mexico during the 1970s. For example, one program resulted

in an eightfold increase in adult education, and another led to a 50 percent increase in contraceptive use.

Population Media Center is bringing the Sabido methodology to the world, through work with local radio and television broadcasters, appropriate government ministries, and nongovernmental organizations. Their goal is to design and implement a comprehensive media strategy for addressing family and reproductive health issues. This collaborative process takes place with local constituents, identifying and addressing various health issues. Transformed into a radio drama such as *Guga Goge* and performed by professional radio actors, the issues gain broad attention.

In addition to the individual success stories like Hajara's, success can be measured quantitatively at the countrywide level. For example, radio programs broadcast in Ethiopia in two different languages between 2002 and 2004 changed the reproductive health behavior in that region. The percentage of married women using contraception increased from 23 percent to 79 percent, and the birth rates for Ethiopia decreased. Reduction in fertility is a vital part of the transition each society must make to achieve better overall health. In exit interviews at family planning clinics, one-fourth of the 14,000 people surveyed cited the radio drama as their reason for coming.

Global Twister

Would the Sabido method work in your community? Is it already at work? What health issues would you like to see embedded in soap operas?

individuals can live normal lives. Some peoples are so accustomed to this parasitic infection that they regard the appearance of bloody urine in a teenage boy (due to a sufficient parasite load to cause this symptom) as a male version of menstruation. Cultural perspectives can thus be at odds with international public health goals that are based on a strictly Western biomedical understanding of disease.

Medical anthropologists working on global public health issues are careful to not impose their own interpretations and meanings as they work to improve the health of others. In the following Original Study, biological anthropologist Katherine Dettwyler explains how she was challenged to rethink Down syndrome as she worked on childhood growth and health in Mali.

Dancing Skeletons: Life and Death in West Africa BY *KATHERINE DETTWYLER*

I stood in the doorway, gasping for air, propping my arms against the door frame on either side to hold me up. I sucked in great breaths of cool, clean air and rested my gaze on the distant hills, trying to compose myself. Ominous black thunderclouds were massed on the horizon and moved rapidly toward the schoolhouse. . . .

The morning had begun pleasantly enough, with villagers waiting patiently under the huge mango tree in the center of the village. But before long, the approaching storm made it clear that we would have to move inside. The only building large enough to hold the crowd was the one-room schoolhouse, located on the outskirts of the village. . . .

Inside the schoolhouse, chaos reigned. It was 20 degrees hotter, ten times as noisy, and as dark as gloom. What little light there was from outside entered through the open doorway and two small windows. The entire population of the village crowded onto the rows of benches, or stood three deep around the periphery of the room. Babies cried until their mothers pulled them around front where they could nurse, children chattered, and adults seized the opportunity to converse with friends and neighbors. It was one big party, a day off from working in the fields, with a cooling rain thrown in for good measure. I had to shout the measurements out to Heather, to make myself heard over the cacophony of noise. . . .

A middle-aged man dressed in a threadbare pair of Levis shoved a crying child forward. I knelt down to encourage the little boy to step up onto the scales and saw that his leg was wrapped in dirty bandages. He hesitated before lifting his foot and whimpered as he put his weight onto it. . . .

"What's the matter with his leg?" I asked his father.

"He hurt it in a bicycle accident," he said.

I rolled my eyes at Heather. "Let me guess. He was riding on the back fender, without wearing long pants, or shoes, and he got his leg tangled in the spokes." Moussa translated this aside into Bambara, and the man acknowledged that was exactly what had happened. . . .

The festering wound encompassed the boy's ankle and part of his foot, deep enough to see bone at the bottom. His entire lower leg and foot were swollen and putrid; it was obvious that gangrene had a firm hold. . . .

"You have to take him to the hospital in Sikasso immediately," I explained.

"But we can't afford to," he balked.

"You can't afford not to," I cried in exasperation, turning to Moussa. "He doesn't understand," I said to Moussa. "Please explain to him that the boy is certain to die of gangrene poisoning if he doesn't get to a doctor right away. It may be too late already, but I don't think so. He may just lose his leg." Moussa's eyes widened with alarm. Even he hadn't realized how serious the boy's wounds were. As the father took in what Moussa was saying, his face crumpled. . . . Father and son were last seen leaving Merediela, the boy perched precariously on the back of a worn-out donkey hastily borrowed from a neighbor, while the father trotted alongside, shoulders drooping, urging the donkey to greater speed. . . .

Lunch back at the animatrice's compound provided another opportunity for learning about infant feeding beliefs in rural Mali, through criticism of my own child feeding practices. This time it was a chicken that had given its life for our culinary benefit. As we ate, without even thinking, I reached into the center pile of chicken meat and pulled pieces of meat off the bone. Then I placed them over in Miranda's section of the communal food bowl and encouraged her to eat.

"Why are you giving her chicken?" Bakary asked.

"I want to make sure she gets enough to eat," I replied. "She didn't eat very much porridge for breakfast because she doesn't like millet."

"But she's just a child. She doesn't need good food. You've been working hard all morning, and she's just been lying around. Besides, if she wanted to eat, she would," he argued.

"It's true that I've been working hard," I admitted, "but she's still growing. Growing children need much more food, proportionately, than adults. And if I didn't encourage her to eat, she might not eat until we get back to Bamako."

Bakary shook his head. "In Dogo," he explained, "people believe that good food is wasted on children. They don't appreciate its good taste or the way it makes you feel. Also, they haven't worked hard to produce the food. They have their whole lives to work for good food for themselves, when they get older. Old people deserve the best food because they're going to die soon." . . .

. . . In rural southern Mali, "good food" (which included all the high protein/high calorie foods) was reserved for elders and other adults. Children subsisted almost entirely on the carbohydrate staples, flavored with a little sauce. My actions in giving Miranda my share of the chicken were viewed as bizarre and misguided. I was wasting good food on a mere child, and depriving myself. . . .

In N'tenkoni the next morning, we were given use of the men's sacred meeting hut for our measuring session. A round hut about 20 feet in diameter, it had a huge center pole made from the trunk of a tree that held up the thatched roof. Because it had two large doorways, it was light and airy and would provide protection in the event of another thunderstorm. . . .

There was some initial confusion caused by the fact that people outside couldn't really see what we were doing, and everyone tried to crowd in at once. That was straightened out by the chief, however, and measuring proceeded apace, men, women, children, men, women, children. One family at a time filed into the hut through one door, had their measurements taken, and departed through the other door. It was cool and pleasant inside the hut, in contrast to the hot sun and glare outside. Miranda sat off to one side, reading a book, glancing up from time to time, but generally bored by the whole thing.

"Mommy, look!" she exclaimed in mid-morning. "Isn't that an *angel*?" she asked, using our family's code word for a child with Down syndrome. Down syndrome children are often (though not always!) sweet, happy, and affectionate kids, and many families of children with Down syndrome consider them to be special gifts from God and refer to them as angels. I turned and followed the direction of Miranda's gaze. A little girl had just entered the hut, part of a large family with many children. She had a small round head, and all the facial characteristics of a child with Down syndrome—Oriental-shaped eyes with epicanthic folds, a small flat nose, and small ears. There was no mistaking the diagnosis. Her name was Abi, and she was about 4 years old, the same age as Peter.

I knelt in front of the little girl. "Hi there, sweetie," I said in English. "Can I have a hug?" I held out my arms, and she willingly stepped forward and gave me a big hug.

I looked up at her mother. "Do you know that there's something 'different' about this child?" I asked, choosing my words carefully.

"Well, she doesn't talk," said her mother, hesitantly, looking at her husband for confirmation. "That's right," he said. "She's never said a word."

"But she's been healthy?" I asked.

"Yes," the father replied. "She's like the other kids, except she doesn't talk. She's always happy. She never cries. We know she can hear because she does what we tell her to. Why are you so interested in her?"

"Because I know what's the matter with her. I have a son like this." Excitedly, I pulled a picture of Peter out of my bag and showed it to them. They couldn't see any resemblance, though. The difference in skin color swamped the similarities in facial features. But then, Malians think all white people look alike. And it's not true that all kids with Down syndrome look the same. They're "different in the same way," but they look most like their parents and siblings.

"Have you ever met any other children like this?" I inquired, bursting with curiosity about how rural Malian culture dealt with a condition as infrequent as Down syndrome. Children with Down syndrome are rare to begin with, occurring about once in every 700 births. In a community where thirty or forty children are born each year at the most, a child with Down syndrome might be born only once in twenty years. And many of them would not survive long enough for anyone to be able to tell that they were different. Physical defects along the midline of the body (heart, trachea, intestines) are common among kids with Down syndrome; without immediate surgery and neonatal intensive care, many would not survive. Such surgery is routine in American children's hospitals, but nonexistent in rural Mali. For the child without any major physical defects, there are still the perils of rural Malian life to survive: malaria, measles, diarrhea, diphtheria, and polio. Some, like Peter, have poor immune systems, making them even more susceptible to childhood diseases. The odds against finding a child with Down syndrome, surviving and healthy in a rural Malian village, are overwhelming.

Not surprisingly, the parents knew of no other children like Abi. They asked if I knew of any medicine that could cure her. "No," I explained, "this condition can't be cured. But she will learn to talk, just give her time. Talk to her a lot. Try to get her to repeat things you say. And give her lots of love and attention. It may take her longer to learn some things, but keep trying. In my country, some people say these children are special gifts from God." There was no way I could explain cells and chromosomes and nondisjunction to them, even with Moussa's help. And how, I thought to myself, would that have helped them anyway? They just accepted her as she was.

We chatted for a few more minutes, and I measured the whole family, including Abi, who was, of course, short for her age. I gave her one last hug and a balloon and sent her out the door after her siblings. . . .

I walked out of the hut, . . . trying to get my emotions under control. Finally I gave in, hugged my knees close to my chest, and sobbed. I cried for Abi—what a courageous heart she must have; just think what she might have achieved given all the modern infant stimulation programs available in the West. I cried for Peter—another courageous heart; just think of what he might achieve given the chance to live in a culture that simply accepted him, rather than stereotyping and pigeonholing him, constraining him because people didn't think he was capable of more. I cried for myself—not very courageous at all; my heart felt as though it would burst with longing for Peter, my own sweet angel.

There was clearly some truth to the old adage that ignorance is bliss. Maybe pregnant women in Mali had to worry about evil spirits lurking in the latrine at night, but they didn't spend their pregnancies worrying about chromosomal abnormalities, the moral implications of amniocentesis, or the heart-wrenching exercise of trying to evaluate handicaps, deciding which ones made life not worth living. Women in the United States might have the freedom to choose not to give birth to children with handicaps, but women in Mali had freedom from worrying about it. Children in the United States had the freedom to attend special programs to help them overcome their handicaps, but children in Mali had freedom from the biggest handicap of all—other people's prejudice.

I had cried myself dry. I splashed my face with cool water from the bucket inside the kitchen and returned to the task at hand.

Adapted from Dettwyler, K. A. (1994). Dancing skeletons: Life and death in West Africa (ch. 8). Long Grove, IL: Waveland Press, Inc. All rights reserved.

Although diseases are generally described in biological terms as understood through scientific investigation, the medical anthropological framework admits that these notions are not universal. Each culture's medical system provides individuals with a map of how to think about themselves in sickness and health, and each system defines specific terms and mechanisms for thinking about, preventing, and managing illness.

Evolutionary Medicine

Evolutionary medicine—an approach to human sickness and health combining principles of evolutionary theory and human evolutionary history—draws from both scientific medicine and anthropology. Although it may seem at first to concentrate on human biological mechanisms, evolutionary medicine emphasizes the biocultural integration characteristic of anthropology: Humans give cultural meaning to biological processes, and cultural practices impact human biology.

As with evolutionary theory in general, it is difficult to prove conclusively that specific ideas and theories from evolutionary medicine are indeed beneficial to human health. Instead, scientists work to amass a sufficient body of knowledge that supports their theories. Where appropriate, the theories can lead to hypotheses that can be tested experimentally. Frequently, treatments derived from evolutionary medicine lead to alterations in cultural practices and to a return to a more natural state

in terms of human biology. As described in the Biocultural Connection on Paleolithic prescriptions, evolutionary medicine has contributed to current attitudes about the diseases of civilization.

The work of biological anthropologist James McKenna mentioned in our opening chapter provides an excellent example of evolutionary medicine. McKenna has suggested that the human infant, immature compared to some other mammals, has evolved to co-sleep with adults who provide breathing cues to the sleeping infant, protecting the child from sudden infant death syndrome (SIDS) (McKenna, Ball, & Gettler, 2007). He has used cross-cultural data of sleeping patterns and rates of SIDS to support his claim.

McKenna conducted a series of experiments documenting differences between the brainwave patterns of mother–infant pairs who co-sleep compared to mother–infant pairs who sleep in separate rooms. These data fit McKenna's theory, challenging the cultural practice of solitary sleeping that predominates in North America. Further, McKenna showed how the cultural pattern of sleeping directly impacts infant feeding practices, demonstrating that co-sleeping and breastfeeding are mutually reinforcing behaviors.

Evolutionary medicine suggests that cultural practices in industrial and postindustrial societies promote a variety of other biomedically defined diseases, ranging from psychological disorders to hepatitis (inflammation of the liver).

Symptoms as Defense Mechanisms

Scientists have documented that when faced with infection from a bacterium or virus, the human body mounts a series of physiological responses. For example, as a young individual learns the culture's medical system, the person

evolutionary medicine An approach to human sickness and health combining principles of evolutionary theory and human evolutionary history.

might learn to recognize an illness as a cold or flu by responses of the body, such as fever, aches, runny nose, sore throat, vomiting, or diarrhea.

Think of how you may have learned about sickness as a young child. A caregiver or parent might have touched your forehead or neck with the back of the hand or lips to gauge your temperature. Maybe you had a thermometer placed under your arm, in your mouth, or in your ear to see if you had an elevated temperature or fever. (In the past, young children's temperatures were usually taken rectally in North America.) If any of these methods revealed a temperature above the value defined as normal, a medicine might have been given to lower the fever.

Evolutionary medicine proposes that many of the symptoms that biomedicine treats are themselves nature's treatments developed over millennia. Some of these symptoms, such as fever, perhaps should be tolerated rather than suppressed, so the body can heal itself. An elevated temperature is part of the human body's response to infectious particles, whereas eliminating the fever provides favorable temperatures for bacteria or viruses. Further, within some physiological limits, vomiting, coughing, and diarrhea may be adaptive because they remove harmful substances and organisms from the body. In other words, the cultural prescription to lower a fever or suppress a cough might actually prolong the disease.

Similarly, the nausea and vomiting during early pregnancy may also represent an adaptive mechanism to avoid toxins during this most sensitive phase of fetal development. Many plants, particularly those in the broccoli and cabbage family, naturally contain toxins developed through the plants' evolutionary process to prevent them from being eaten by animals. Eating these plants during the first weeks of pregnancy, when the developing embryo is rapidly creating new cells through mitosis and differentiating into specific body parts, makes the embryo vulnerable to mutation. Therefore, a heightened sense of smell and lowered nausea threshold serve as natural defenses for the body. Pregnant women tend to avoid these foods, thus protecting the developing embryo.

Evolution and Infectious Disease

In a globalizing world where people, viruses, and bacteria cross national boundaries freely, evolutionary medicine provides key insights with regard to infectious disease.

First, if infectious disease is viewed as competition between microorganisms and humans—as it is in biomedicine where patients and doctors "fight" infectious disease—microorganisms possess one very clear advantage (**Figure 12.14**). Viruses, bacteria, fungi, and parasites all have very short life cycles compared to humans. Therefore, when competing on an evolutionary level, they will continue to pose new threats to health because any new genetic variants appearing through a random mutation will quickly become incorporated in the population's

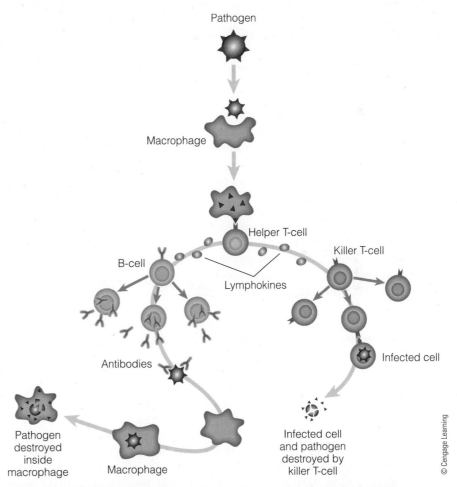

© Cengage Learning

Figure 12.14 The Immune System Biomedical descriptions of the human immune system concentrate on "invading" pathogens, "triggering" the immune response, and "killer T-cells" that destroy the pathogens, as shown in this image introducing the fundamentals of the immune response. Medical anthropologist Emily Martin (1994, 1999) has shown that scientific depictions of infectious disease draw upon violent imagery common to the culture of the United States. Biomedical treatments involve taking antibiotics to kill "invading" organisms adding additional weapons to the "natural" human defenses. An evolutionary perspective suggests that the quick life cycle of microorganisms makes this "battle" a losing proposition for humans.

From *A Positron Named Priscilla: Scientific Discovery at the Frontier*, 1994. Reprinted with permission from National Academies Press, Washington, D.C.

genome. This notion is of particular importance with regard to the use of antibiotics to fight infectious disease.

Although antibiotics do kill many bacteria, increasingly resistant strains are becoming more common. *Resistant strains* refers to genetic variants of a specific bacterium that are not killed by antibiotics. If a resistant strain appears in an infected individual who is being treated with antibiotics, the removal of all the nonresistant strains essentially opens up an entire ecological niche for that resistant strain inside the infected human. Here, without competition from the original form of the bacterium wiped out by the antibiotic, this mutant can proliferate easily and then spread to other individuals. The practice of taking antibiotics artificially alters the environment inside the human body.

In order to avoid the development of resistant strains, complex lengthy treatment regimes, often of multiple drugs, must be followed exactly. These treatments are prohibitively expensive in many parts of the world. The unfortunate result is not only increased human suffering but also the possibility of creating environments for the development of resistant strains as individuals receive partial treatments.

Another problem is that although individuals seek treatment within their own country's health-care system, infectious microbes do not observe national boundaries. To eradicate or control any infectious process, the world has to be considered in its entirety.

Evolutionary process provides a long-term natural mechanism for fighting infectious disease: Those individuals who survive the infection possess genes that provide them with immunity. At times these same genes also have potentially lethal consequences, as seen with the examples of sickle-cell anemia and malaria, cystic fibrosis and cholera, and Tay-Sachs disease and tuberculosis. An interesting recent example of population-based resistance to disease is that of a group of sex workers in Kenya who escape the HIV infection despite constant exposure (Fowke et al., 1996; Songok et al., 2012). This may represent a case of hosts and microbes adjusting to one another through the process of evolution. In order to survive, microbes cannot afford to eliminate all their hosts. Thus, over time a population and a microbe will become balanced, with the host population better able to resist and the microbe less virulent.

One positive note is that treatments can also be allowed to flow freely across the globe. For example, Brazil's HIV/AIDS program is internationally recognized as a model for prevention, education, and treatment for several reasons. Through a national policy of developing alternative generic antiretroviral agents and negotiating for reduced prices on patented agents, in 1996 Brazil became the first country to guarantee free antiretroviral access to all its citizens. At the same time, Brazilian public health officials developed counseling and prevention programs in collaboration with community groups and religious organizations. Their AIDS program's success derives, in part, from the candid public education on disease transmission targeted at heterosexual women and young people, who are now the fastest-growing groups affected by HIV.

In 2004, Brazil continued its innovations with the South to South Initiative providing assistance to the HIV and AIDS programs in the Portuguese-speaking African countries of Mozambique and Angola. These African countries directly replicate the Brazilian approach of providing free antiretroviral agents and collaborating with civil and religious groups to develop appropriate counseling, education, and prevention programs (D'Adesky, 2004).

Vaccines are another method for fighting infectious disease. Vaccines stimulate the body to mount its own immune response that will protect the individual from the real infectious agent if the individual is exposed at a later date. Vaccinations have been responsible for major global reduction of disease, as in the case of smallpox.

Historical records show that people in Asia, Africa, Europe, and the colonizers of North America practiced a form of vaccination for this deadly disease through what were known as "pox parties." Parents in recent years have revived this tradition, deliberately exposing their children to chicken pox rather than opt for the vaccine.

Despite numerous medical reports to the contrary, some parents believe that vaccinations may lead to other health problems. Although the vaccine to eradicate smallpox—a disease that killed 300 million people in the 20th century alone—is clearly beneficial, it is harder to convince parents of the need for vaccines for less fatal, although still serious, childhood diseases. But opting out has had grim consequences: The rates of pertussis (whooping cough) have reached epidemic proportions in some parts of the United States, and other regions are not far behind. The pertussis problem has become so severe that a booster for it is now routinely added to tetanus shots.

Vaccinations, like all medical procedures, change the social fabric. The vaccine for chicken pox in the United States provides an interesting case in point. Before this vaccination became standard care, most American children experienced chicken pox as a rite of childhood. Parents watched their children become covered with ugly poxes that then disappeared. This experience modeled for parents that intense sickness can be followed by full recovery, which, in and of itself, can provide some comfort. Only extremely rarely is chicken pox fatal.

Infectious disease and the human efforts to stop it always occur in the context of the human-made environment. Humans have been altering their external environments with increasing impact since the Neolithic revolution, resulting in an increase in a variety of infectious diseases. In this regard, evolutionary medicine shares much with political ecology—a discipline closely related to medical anthropology and described next.

The Political Ecology of Disease

An ecological perspective considers organisms in the context of their environment. Because human environments are shaped not only by local culture but by global political and economic systems, these features must all be included in a comprehensive examination of human disease. Simply describing disease in terms of biological processes leaves out the deeper, ultimate reasons that some individuals are likelier than others to become sick. A strictly biological approach also leaves out differences in the resources available to individuals, communities, and states to cope with disease and illness. Prion diseases provide excellent illustrations of the impact of local and global factors on the social distribution of disease.

Prion Diseases

In 1997 physician-scientist Stanley Prusiner won the Nobel Prize in medicine for his discovery of an entirely new disease agent called a **prion**—a protein lacking any genetic material that behaves as an infectious particle. Prions are a kind of protein that can cause the reorganization and destruction of other proteins, which may result in neurodegenerative disease as brain tissue and the nervous system are destroyed.

This discovery provided a mechanism for understanding mad cow disease, a serious problem in postindustrial societies. But knowing the biological mechanism alone is not enough to truly grasp how this disease spreads. The beef supply of several countries in Europe and North America became tainted by prions introduced through the cultural practice of grinding up sheep carcasses and adding them to the commercial feed of beef cattle. This practice began before prions were discovered, but postindustrial farmers were aware that these sheep had a condition known as *scrapie*; they just did not know that this condition was infectious. Through the wide distribution of tainted feed, prion disease spread from sheep to cows, and then to humans who consumed tainted beef. Today, countries without confirmed mad cow disease ban the importation of beef from neighboring countries with documented prion disease. Such bans have a tremendous negative impact on the local economies.

Mad cow disease is not new. This type of disease was a major concern for the Fore (pronounced "foray") people of Papua New Guinea during the middle of the 20th century. The Fore gave the name *kuru* to the prion disease that claimed the lives of great numbers of women and children in their communities. To deal with the devastation, the Fore welcomed assistance provided by an international team of health workers led by a physician from the United States, Carleton Gajdusek. As with mad cow disease, local

and global cultural processes affected both the transmission of kuru and the measures taken to prevent its spread long before prion biology was understood.

Kuru did not fit neatly into any known biomedical categories. Because the disease seemed to be limited to families of related individuals, cultural anthropologists Shirley Lindenbaum from Australia and Robert Glasse from the United States, who were doing fieldwork in the region, were recruited to contribute documentation of Fore kinship relationships. It was hoped this knowledge would reveal an underlying genetic mechanism for the disease.

When kinship records did not reveal a pattern of genetic transmission, the medical team turned instead to the notion of infectious disease, even though the slow progression of kuru seemed to weigh against an infectious cause. Material derived from infected individuals was injected into chimpanzees (recall Chapter 4's discussion of the ethics of this practice) to see whether they developed the disease. After 18 months, injected chimpanzees succumbed to the classic symptoms of kuru, and their autopsied brains indicated the same pathologies as seen in humans with kuru. At this point, the disease was defined as infectious (garnering Gajdusek a Nobel Prize). Because prions had not yet been discovered, scientists defined this infectious agent as an unidentified "slow virus."

Scientists knew that kuru is infectious, but they still did not understand why some individuals were infected but not others. The explanation requires a wider anthropological perspective, as Lindenbaum explains in her book *Kuru Sorcery*. Lindenbaum demonstrates that kuru is related to cultural practices regarding the bodies of individuals who have died from kuru and the way global factors impacted local practices.

Culturally, Fore women are responsible for preparing the bodies of their loved ones for the afterlife. This practice alone put women at a greater risk for exposure to kuru. Lindenbaum also discovered that women and children were at risk due to a combination of these local practices with global economic forces. In Fore society, men were responsible for raising pigs and slaughtering and distributing meat. The middle of the 20th century was a time of hardship and transition for the Fore people. Colonial rule by Australia had changed the fabric of

prion An infectious protein lacking any genetic material but capable of causing the reorganization and destruction of other proteins.

society, threatening traditional subsistence patterns and resulting in a shortage of protein in the form of pigs. Fore men preferentially distributed the limited amount of pig meat available to other men.

Fore women told Lindenbaum that, as a practical solution to their hunger, they consumed their own dead. Fore women preferred eating their loved ones who had died in a relatively "meaty" state from kuru compared to eating individuals wasted away from malnutrition. This temporary practice was abandoned as the Fore subsistence pattern recovered, and the Fore learned of the biological mechanisms of kuru transmission.

Medical Pluralism

The Fore medical system had its own explanations for the causes of kuru, primarily involving sorcery, that were compatible with biomedical explanations for the mechanisms of disease. Such blending of medical systems is common throughout the globe today.

Medical pluralism refers to the practice of multiple medical systems, each with its own techniques and beliefs, in a single society. As illustrated with the Fore, individuals generally can reconcile conflicting medical systems and incorporate diverse elements from a variety of systems to ease their suffering. Although Western biomedicine has contributed some spectacular treatments and cures for a variety of diseases, many of its practices and values are singularly associated with the European and North American societies in which they developed. The international public health movement attempts to bring many of the successes of biomedicine based on the scientific understanding of human biology to the rest of the world. But to do so successfully, local cultural practices and beliefs must be taken into account.

Both mad cow disease and kuru illustrate that no sickness in the 21st century can be considered in isolation; an understanding of these diseases must take into account political and economic influences as well as how these forces affect the ability to treat or cure.

Globalization, Health, and Structural Violence

One generalization that can be made with regard to most diseases is that wealth means health. In 1948, the World Health Organization defined *health* as "a complete state of physical, mental, and social well-being and not merely

the absence of disease or infirmity," a definition that has never been amended (World Health Organization, 1948). While the international public health community works to improve health throughout the globe, heavily armed states, megacorporations, and very wealthy elites are using their powers to rearrange the emerging world system to their own competitive advantage. When such power relationships undermine the well-being of others, we are witnessing the *structural violence* we discussed in Chapter 11.

Health disparities, or differences in the health status between the wealthy elite and the poor in stratified societies, are nothing new. Globalization has expanded and intensified structural violence, leading to enormous health disparities among individuals, communities, and even states. Medical anthropologists have examined how structural violence leads not only to unequal access to treatment but also to the likelihood of contracting disease through exposure to malnutrition, crowded conditions, and toxins.

Population Size and Health

At the time of the speciation events of early human evolutionary history, population size was extraordinarily small compared to what it is today. With human population size at over 7 billion and still climbing, we are reaching the carrying capacity of the earth (**Figure 12.15**). India and China alone have well over 1 billion inhabitants each. And population growth is still rapid in South Asia, which will become even more densely populated in the 21st century. Population growth threatens to increase the scale of hunger, poverty, and pollution—and the many problems associated with these issues.

Although human population growth must be curtailed, government-sponsored programs to do so have posed new problems. For example, China's much-publicized "one child" policy, introduced in 1979 to control its soaring population growth, led to sharp upward trends in sex-selective abortions, female infanticide, and female infant mortality due to abandonment and neglect. The resulting imbalance in China's male and female populations is referred to as the "missing girl gap." One study reported that China's male-to-female ratio has become so distorted that 111 million men would not be able to find a wife. Government regulations softened slightly in the 1990s, when it became legal for rural couples to have a second child if their first was a girl—and if they paid a fee. Millions of rural couples have circumvented regulations by not registering births—resulting in millions of young people who do not officially exist (Bongaarts, 1998).

But human cultures adapt and change. Some rural families in northeastern China have instead chosen to have only one daughter, reshaping the culture's gender norms (Shi, 2009).

---

medical pluralism The practice of multiple medical systems, each with its own techniques and beliefs, in a single society.

health disparity A difference in the health status between the wealthy elite and the poor in stratified societies.

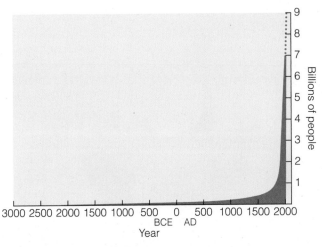

Figure 12.15 **World Population** Human population size grew at a relatively steady pace until the industrial revolution, when a geometric pattern of growth began. Since that time, human population size has been doubling at an alarming rate. The earth's natural resources will not be able to accommodate the ever-increasing human population if the rates of consumption seen in Western industrialized nations, particularly in the United States, persist. Notice, as well, that human populations are not distributed evenly across the globe; the highest concentrations are in urban centers and regions with fertile land. Climatic extremes and lack of natural resources like water characterize the sparsely populated areas, such as the Sahara Desert and Greenland.

Poverty and Health

With an ever-expanding population, a shocking number of people worldwide face hunger on a regular basis, leading to a variety of health problems including premature death. It is no accident that poor countries and poorer citizens of wealthier countries are disproportionately malnourished. All told, about 1 billion people in the world are undernourished. Some 7.6 million children age 5 and under die every year due to hunger, and those who survive often suffer from physical and mental impairment (World Health Organization, 2012).

In wealthy industrialized countries, obesity, a particular version of malnourishment, is becoming increasingly common (**Figure 12.16**). Obesity primarily affects poor working-class people who are no longer physically active

VISUAL COUNTERPOINT

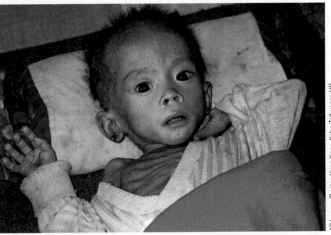

Figure 12.16 **Extremes of Malnutrition** The scientific definition of *malnutrition* includes undernutrition as well as excess consumption of foods, healthy or otherwise. Malnutrition leading to obesity is increasingly common among poor working-class people in industrialized countries. Obesity and Type 2 diabetes, previously degenerative diseases of adulthood only, now occur at alarming rates among children in the United States. Starvation is more common in poor countries or in those facing years of political turmoil, as is evident in this emaciated North Korean child.

at their work (because of increasing automation) and who cannot afford more expensive, healthy foods to stay fit. High sugar and fat content of mass-marketed foods and "super-sized" portions underlie this dramatic change. Obesity also greatly increases the risk of diabetes, heart disease, and stroke. High rates of obesity among American youth have led U.S. public health officials to project that the current generation of adults may be the first generation to outlive their children due to a cause other than war.

Environmental Impact and Health

Just as the disenfranchised experience a disproportionate share of famine and associated death, this same population also must contend with the lion's share of contaminants and pollution (Figure 12.17). The industries of wealthier communities and states create the majority of the pollutants that are changing the earth today. Yet those who do not have the resources to consume and thus pollute the earth at high rates often feel the impact of these pollutants most keenly.

For example, increasing emissions of greenhouse gases, as a consequence of deforestation and human industrial activity, have resulted in global warming. As the carbon emissions from the combustion of petroleum in wealthy nations warm the climate globally, the impact will be most severe for individuals in the tropics because these populations must contend with increases in deadly infectious diseases such as malaria.

Experts predict that global warming will lead to an expansion of the geographic ranges of tropical diseases and to an increase in the incidence of respiratory diseases due to additional smog caused by warmer temperatures. Similarly, the summer of 2012 included record heat waves, fires, and fatalities. To solve the problem of global warming, our species needs to evolve new cultural tools in order to anticipate environmental consequences that eventuate over decades. Regulating human population size globally and using the earth's resources more conservatively are necessary to ensure our survival.

© Ian Berry/Magnum Photos

Figure 12.17 Ship-Breakers For wages of about a dollar a day, workers at the ship-breaking yards of Bangladesh risk their health if not their lives as they toil in conditions of extreme heat, humidity, and exposure to a wide variety of toxins. Here, the large rusty tankers that have transported everything from crude oil to passengers throughout the globe are broken apart for recycling in an area that was pristine beach just decades ago. Workers dismember these ships by hand and are often barefoot; they have very little in the way of protective gear. Explosions and other accidents kill on average one worker a week. The long-term effects of toxins from the ships set other disease processes in motion. Some individuals might possess genotypes that can better process the toxins (comparable to the 90-year-old who has smoked two packs of cigarettes a day for over seventy years). And over time a population might become better able to tolerate these poisons through the process of biological adaptation. But in this case, a cultural solution—environmental regulation of the ship-breaking process—would protect these workers and our oceans and beaches and is a requirement for our collective human survival. As well, our global health requires addressing the social justice issues inherent in poor countries taking on the health burden of privileges enjoyed by the wealthy.

Global warming is merely one of a host of problems today that will ultimately have an impact on human gene pools. In view of the consequences for human biology of seemingly benign innovations such as dairying or farming (as discussed in Chapter 9), we may wonder about many recent practices—for example, the effects of increased exposure to radiation from use of x-rays, nuclear accidents, production of radioactive waste, ozone depletion (which increases human exposure to solar radiation), and the like.

Again the impact is often most severe for those who have not generated the pollutants in the first place. Take, for example, the flow of industrial and agricultural chemicals via air and water currents to Arctic regions. Icy temperatures allow these toxins to enter the food chain. As a result toxins generated in temperate climates end up in the bodies (and breast milk) of Arctic peoples who do not produce the toxins but who eat primarily foods that they hunt and fish.

In addition to exposure to radiation, humans also face increased exposure to other known mutagenic agents, including a wide variety of chemicals, such as pesticides. Despite repeated assurances about their safety, there have been tens of thousands of cases of poisonings in the United States alone and thousands of cases of cancer related to the manufacture and use of pesticides. The impact may be greater in so-called underdeveloped countries, where substances banned in the United States are routinely used.

Pesticides are responsible for millions of birds being killed each year (which would have been happily gobbling down bugs and other pests), serious fish kills, and decimation of honeybees (bees are needed for the efficient pollination of many crops). In all, pesticides alone (not including other agricultural chemicals) are responsible for billions of dollars of environmental and public health damage in the United States each year. Anthropologists document the effects on individuals, as described in the Biocultural Connection feature.

The shipping of pollutant waste between countries represents an example of structural violence. Individuals in the government or business sector of either nation may profit from these arrangements, creating another obstacle to addressing the problem. Similar issues may arise within countries, when authorities attempt to coerce ethnic minorities to accept disposal of toxic waste on their lands.

In particular, hormone-disrupting chemicals raise serious concerns because they interfere with the reproductive process. For example, in 1938 a synthetic estrogen known as DES (diethylstilbestrol) was developed and subsequently prescribed for a variety of ailments ranging from acne to prostate cancer. Moreover, DES was routinely added to animal feed. But, in 1971 researchers realized that DES causes vaginal cancer in young women. Subsequent studies have shown that DES causes problems with the male reproductive system and can produce deformities of the female reproductive tract of individuals exposed to DES in utero. DES mimics the natural hormone, binding with appropriate receptors in and on cells, and thereby turns on biological activity associated with the hormone (Colborn, Dumanoski, & Myers, 1996).

DES is not alone in its effects: Scientists have identified at least fifty-one chemicals—many of them in common use—that disrupt hormones, and even this could be the tip of the iceberg. Some of these chemicals mimic estrogens in the manner of DES, whereas others interfere with other parts of the endocrine system, such as thyroid and testosterone metabolism. The list includes such supposedly benign and inert substances as plastics widely used in laboratories and chemicals added to polystyrene and polyvinyl chloride (PVCs) to make them more stable and less breakable. These plastics are widely used in plumbing, food processing, and food packaging.

In addition, many detergents and personal care products, contraceptive creams, the giant jugs used to bottle drinking water, and plastic linings in cans contain hormone-disrupting chemicals. Plastics line about 85 percent of food cans in the United States. Similarly, after years of plastics use in microwave ovens, the deleterious health consequences of the release of compounds from plastic wrap and plastic containers during microwaving have come to light. Most concerning is bisphenol-A (BPA)—a chemical widely used in the manufacturing of water bottles and baby bottles (hard plastics). Researchers have documented an association between BPA and higher rates of chronic diseases such as heart disease and diabetes. It also disrupts a variety of other reproductive and metabolic processes. Infants and fetuses are at the greatest risk from exposure to BPA.

Consensus in the scientific community has led governments to start taking action (the Canadian government declared BPA a toxic compound). However, removing this compound from the food industry may be easier than ridding the environment of this contaminant. For decades billions of pounds of BPA have been produced each year, and in turn it has been dumped into landfills and into bodies of water. As with the Neolithic revolution and the development of civilization, each invention creates new challenges for humans.

The Future of *Homo sapiens*

One of the difficulties with managing environmental and toxic health risks is that serious consequences of new cultural practices often do not appear until years or even decades later. By then, of course, the cultural system has fully absorbed these practices, and huge financial interests function to keep them there. Today, cultural practices, probably as never before, impact human gene pools. The long-term effects on the human species as a whole remain to be seen, but as with disease today, poor people and people of color will bear a disproportionate burden for these practices.

BIOCULTURAL CONNECTION

Picturing Pesticides

The toxic effects of pesticides have long been known. After all, these compounds are designed to kill bugs. However, documenting the toxic effects of pesticides on humans has been more difficult, because they are subtle—sometimes taking years to become apparent.

Anthropologist Elizabeth Guillette, working in a Yaqui Indian community in Mexico, combined ethnographic observation, biological monitoring of pesticide levels in the blood, and neurobehavioral testing to document the impairment of child development by pesticides.[a] Working with colleagues from the Technological Institute of Sonora in Obregón, Mexico, Guillette compared children and families from two Yaqui communities: one living in a valley farm who was exposed to large doses of pesticides and one living in a ranching village in the foothills nearby.

Guillette documented the frequency of pesticide use among the farming Yaqui to be forty-five times per crop cycle with two crop cycles per year. In the farming valleys she also noted that families tended to use household bug sprays on a daily basis, thus increasing their exposure to toxic pesticides. In the foothill ranches, she found that the only pesticides that the Yaqui were exposed to consisted of DDT sprayed by the government to control malaria. In these communities, indoor bugs were swatted or tolerated.

Pesticide exposure was linked to child health and development through two sets of measures. First, levels of pesticides in the blood of valley children at birth and throughout their childhood were examined and found to be far higher than in the children from the foothills. Further, the presence of pesticides in breast milk of nursing mothers from the valley farms was also documented.

Second, children from the two communities were asked to perform a variety of normal childhood activities, such as jumping, memory games, playing catch, and drawing pictures. The children exposed to high doses of pesticides had significantly less stamina, eye–hand coordination, large motor coordination, and drawing ability compared to the Yaqui children from the foothills. These children exhibited no overt symptoms of pesticide poisoning—instead exhibiting delays and impairment in their neurobehavioral abilities that may be irreversible.

Though Guillette's study was thoroughly embedded in one ethnographic community, she emphasizes that the exposure to pesticides among the Yaqui farmers is typical of agricultural communities globally and has significance for changing human practices regarding the use of pesticides everywhere.

BIOCULTURAL QUESTION

Given the documented developmental damage these pesticides have inflicted on children, should their sale and use be regulated globally? Are there potentially damaging toxins in use in your community?

———

[a]Guillette, E. A., et al. (1998, June). An anthropological approach to the evaluation of preschool children exposed to pesticides in Mexico. *Environmental Health Perspectives 106*(6), 347–353. Courtesy of Dr. Elizabeth A. Guillette.

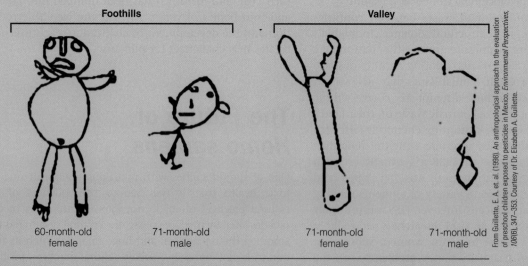

Foothills		Valley	
60-month-old female	71-month-old male	71-month-old female	71-month-old male

From Guillette, E. A. et al. (1998). An anthropological approach to the evaluation of preschool children exposed to pesticides in Mexico. *Environmental Perspectives, 106*(6), 347–353. Courtesy of Dr. Elizabeth A. Guillette.

Compare the drawings typically done by Yaqui children heavily exposed to pesticides (*right, valley*) to those made by Yaqui children living in nearby areas who were relatively unexposed (*left, foothills*).

Further, with globalization, the values of wealthy consumers living in industrialized countries have spread to the inhabitants of poorer and developing countries, influencing their expectations and dreams. Of course, a luxurious standard of living requires a disproportionate share of the earth's limited resources. Instead of globalizing a standard of living that the world's natural resources cannot meet, it is time for all of humanity to use today's global connections to learn how to live within the carrying capacity of the earth (**Figure 12.18**).

We are a social species with origins on the African continent over 5 million years ago. Over the course of our evolutionary history, we came to inhabit the entire globe. From cities, to deserts, to mountaintops, to grassy plains, to rich tropical forests, human cultures in these varied places became distinct from one another. In each environment, human groups devised their own specific beliefs and practices to meet the challenges of survival. In the future, dramatic changes in cultural values will be required if our species is to thrive. "New, improved" values might, for example, include a worldview that sees humanity as *part of* the world, rather than as *master over* it, as it is in many of the world's cultures today. Included, too, might be a sense of social responsibility that recognizes and affirms respect among ethnic groups as well as our collective stewardship of the earth we inhabit.

Our continued survival will depend on our ability to cultivate positive social connections among all kinds of people and to recognize the ways we impact one another in a world interconnected by the forces of globalization. Together, we can use the adaptive faculty of culture, the hallmark of our species, to ensure our continued survival.

Lok Samiti (translation: People's Committee) of Mehdiganj, India. Photograph by Nandal Master

Figure 12.18 Water Troubles Women in Mehdiganj, India, hold water urns called *gharas* with the words "Water Is Life" written on them to protest the nearby Coca-Cola bottling plant. Because the plant uses up the local water, nearby farmers lose their livelihood and way of life. In a competition for resources such as this, global corporations like Coca-Cola have advantages over local inhabitants.

CHAPTER CHECKLIST

What biological mechanisms allow humans to adapt to a variety of environments?

● Genetic adaptations such as shorter limbs and stocky build for colder climates and long linear builds for hotter climates have developed in regions where continuous experience over generations has allowed for reproductive selection of such traits.

● Developmental adaption in response to an individual's environment occurs over the growth stages of life to shape gene expression in the way that best suits that individual to that specific environment.

● Developmental adaptations become permanent parts of an individual's phenotype, but they are not encoded directly into the genome and therefore do not get passed on directly to the next generation. Examples include growth stunting due to malnutrition, and the increased number of sweat glands in hot environments.

● Physiological adaptation allows the body to accustom itself to environmental stressors, such as low partial pressure of oxygen at high altitude or extremes of temperature.

● Individuals first experience short-term physiological responses that cannot be sustained indefinitely. *Acclimatization* refers to reversible long-term adaptations in the form of modulation of ongoing bodily processes such as metabolism rates or hemoglobin production.

● The human biological adaption cannot keep pace with the environmental changes impacting global environments today.

What are medical systems, and how do they vary across cultures?

● Medical systems are the idea patterns and practices relating to illness. Medical anthropologists study them cross-culturally, including western biomedicine.

● Medical systems globally are all alike in that they include a healer who possesses specialized, restricted knowledge from which others are excluded. Where multiple medical systems coexist (medical pluralism), individuals freely use what works from the various systems in order to alleviate their suffering.

● Medical systems define whether a given pathophysio-logical state (a disease) will be defined as an illness. For example, in regions where schistosomiasis is endemic, it may not be considered an illness. Without access to costly medicine or parasite free water, people tolerate a moderate parasite load.

What health hazards are attributable to the global political economy and population size?

● Privileged states, corporations, and individuals maintain systems that exercise structural violence upon the poor worldwide resulting in an unequal distribution of disease.

● Hunger and obesity both impact poor communities and cause chronic health problems and early mortality.

● Environmental contaminants such as carcinogenic pesticides and plastics or byproducts created by wealthier communities also affect the poor disproportionately.

● The effects of global warming, largely caused by pollution from industries to supply rich nations, will increase the incidence of tropical disease.

● With a global human population of over seven billion and rising, the carrying capacity of the earth may soon max out. Wealthy nations use a disproportionate portion of resources.

How have humans responded to the widening array of health threats?

● Evolutionary medicine emphasizes the importance of a body's natural responses to disease and recreation of lifestyle conditions that led to our current evolutionary state as methods of health care.

● Western scientific medicine has effectively introduced pharmaceutical and procedural innovation to fight pathogens, but it often ignores deeper reasons for the causes of sickness and the levels of resource availability in other communities.

● Analysis of the political and economic causes of sickness has led to successful treatment and prevention of diseases such as AIDS, kuru, and mad cow disease.

● Recognition of the political and economic causes of disease can lead to cooperation on global health issues with the effect of mitigating suffering worldwide.

QUESTIONS FOR REFLECTION

1. If you were to create a body map of yourself, what would you include to show aspects of your biology, health, and your place in the global political economy?

2. The anthropological distinction between illness and disease provides a way to separate biological states from cultural elaborations given to those biological states. Can you think of some examples of illness without disease and disease without illness?

3. What do you think of the notion of letting a fever run its course instead of taking a medicine to lower it? Do these prescriptions suggested by evolutionary medicine run counter to your own medical beliefs and practices?

4. Are there any examples in your experience of how the growth process or human reproductive physiology helped you adapt to environmental stressors? Does this ability help humans from an evolutionary perspective?

5. Do you see examples of structural violence in your community that make some individuals more vulnerable to disease than others?

ONLINE STUDY RESOURCES

CourseMate

Access chapter-specific learning tools, including learning objectives, practice quizzes, videos, flash cards, glossaries, and more in your Anthropology CourseMate.

Log into **www.cengagebrain.com** to access the resources your instructor has assigned and to purchase materials.

Glossary

abduction Movement away from the midline of the body or from the center of the hand or foot.

absolute dating In archaeology and paleoanthropology, dating archaeological or fossil materials in units of absolute time using scientific properties such as rates of decay of radioactive elements; also known as *chronometric dating.*

acclimatization Long-term physiological adjustments made in order to attain equilibrium with a specific environmental stimulus.

acculturation The massive cultural change that occurs in a society when it experiences intensive firsthand contact with a more powerful society.

Acheulean tool tradition The prevalent style of stone tools associated with *Homo erectus* remains and represented by the hand-axe.

action theory The theory that self-serving actions by forceful leaders play a role in civilization's emergence.

adaptation A series of beneficial adjustments to a particular environment.

adaptive radiation The rapid diversification of an evolving population as it adapts to a variety of available niches.

adduction Movement toward the midline of the body or to the center of the hand or foot.

affiliative Behaving in a manner that tends to promote social cohesion.

agriculture Intensive crop cultivation, employing plows, fertilizers, and/or irrigation.

alleles Alternate forms of a single gene.

Allen's rule The tendency for the bodies of mammals living in cold climates to have shorter appendages (arms and legs) than members of the same species living in warm climates.

altruism Concern for the welfare of others expressed as increased risk undertaken by individuals for the good of the group.

anagenesis A sustained directional shift in a population's average characteristics.

analogies In biology, structures possessed by different organisms that are superficially similar due to similar function but that do not share a common developmental pathway or structure.

ancestral Characteristics that define a group of organisms that are due to shared ancestry.

anthropoids The suborder of primates that includes New World monkeys, Old World monkeys, and apes (including humans).

anthropology The study of humankind in all times and places.

applied anthropology The use of anthropological knowledge and methods to solve practical problems, often for a specific client.

arboreal Living in the trees.

arboreal hypothesis A theory for primate evolution that proposes that life in the trees was responsible for enhanced visual acuity and manual dexterity in primates.

archaeology The study of cultures through the recovery and analysis of material remains and environmental data.

Archaic cultures The term used to refer to Mesolithic cultures in the Americas.

archaic *Homo sapiens* A loosely defined group within the genus *Homo* that "lumpers" use for fossils with the combination of large brain size and ancestral features on the skull.

Ardipithecus One of the earliest genera of bipeds that lived in eastern Africa. *Ardipithecus* is actually divided into two species: the older, *Ardipithecus kadabba,* which dates to between 5.2 and 5.8 million years ago, and the younger, *Ardipithecus ramidus,* which dates to around 4.4 million years ago.

artifact Any object fashioned or altered by humans.

Aurignacian tradition Toolmaking tradition in Europe and western Asia at the beginning of the Upper Paleolithic.

Australopithecus The genus including several species of early bipeds from southern and eastern Africa living between about 1.1 and 4.3 million years ago, one of whom was directly ancestral to humans.

Australopithecus sebida A newly identified species of South African gracile australopithecine dated precisely to between 1.97 and 1.98 million years ago, with derived *Homo*-like characteristics in the hands and pelvis.

Bergmann's rule The tendency for the bodies of mammals living in cold climates to be shorter and rounder than members of the same species living in warm climates.

binocular vision Vision with increased depth perception from two eyes set next to each other, allowing their visual fields to overlap.

bioarchaeology The archaeological study of human remains—bones, skulls, teeth, and sometimes hair, dried skin, or other tissue—to determine the influences of culture and environment on human biological variation.

biocultural An approach that focuses on the interaction of biology and culture.

biological anthropology The systematic study of humans as biological organisms; also known as *physical anthropology.*

bipedalism A special form of locomotion, distinguishing humans and their ancestors from the African great apes, in which the organism walks upright on two feet; also called *bipedality.*

blade technique A method of stone tool manufacture in which long, parallel-sided flakes are struck off the edges of a specially prepared core.

brachiation Moving from branch to branch using the arms, with the body hanging suspended below.

Bronze Age In the Old World, the period marked by the production of tools and ornaments of bronze; began about 5,000 years ago in China, the Mediterranean, and Southwest Asia, and about 500 years earlier in Southeast Asia.

burin A stone tool with chisel-like edges used for working bone, horn, antler, and ivory.

cartography The craft of making maps of remote regions.

catarrhines The primate infraorder that includes Old World monkeys, apes, and humans.

chromatid One half of the X shape of chromosomes visible once replication is complete. Sister chromatids are exact copies of each other.

chromosomes In the cell nucleus, the structures visible during cellular division containing long strands of DNA combined with a protein.

chronometric dating In archaeology and paleoanthropology, dating archaeological or fossil materials in units of absolute time using scientific properties such as rates of decay of radioactive elements; also known as *absolute dating*.

civilization In anthropology, societies in which large numbers of people live in cities, are socially stratified, and are governed by a ruling elite working through centrally organized political systems called states.

clade A taxonomic grouping that contains a single common ancestor and all of its descendants.

cladogenesis Speciation through a branching mechanism whereby an ancestral population gives rise to two or more descendant populations.

clavicle The collarbone connecting the sternum (breastbone) with the scapula (shoulder blade).

clines The gradual changes in the frequency of an allele or trait over space.

codon Three-base sequence of a gene that specifies a particular amino acid for inclusion in a protein.

cognitive capacity A broad concept including intelligence, educability, concept formation, self-awareness, self-evaluation, attention span, sensitivity in discrimination, and creativity.

community In primatology, a unit of primate social organization composed of fifty or more individuals who collectively inhabit a large geographic area.

continental drift According to the theory of plate tectonics, the movement of continents embedded in underlying plates on the earth's surface in relation to one another over the history of life on earth.

convergent evolution In biological evolution, a process by which unrelated populations develop similarities to one another due to similar function rather than shared ancestry.

coprolites Preserved fecal material providing evidence of the diet and health of past organisms.

cranium The braincase of the skull.

Cro-Magnons Europeans of the Upper Paleolithic after about 36,000 years ago.

cultural anthropology The study of patterns in human behavior, thought, and emotions, focusing on humans as culture-producing and culture-reproducing creatures. Also known as *social* or *sociocultural anthropology*.

cultural resource management A branch of archaeology concerned with survey and/or excavation of archaeological and historical remains that might be threatened by construction or development; also involved with policy surrounding protection of cultural resources.

culture A society's shared and socially transmitted ideas, values, emotions, and perceptions, which are used to make sense of experience and generate behavior and are reflected in that behavior.

culture-bound A perspective that produces theories about the world and reality that are based on the assumptions and values from the researcher's own culture.

culture shock In fieldwork, the anthropologist's personal disorientation and anxiety that may result in depression.

datum point The starting point or reference for a grid system.

demographics Population characteristics such as the number of individuals of each age and sex.

dendrochronology In archaeology and paleoanthropology, a technique of chronometric dating based on the number of rings of growth found in tree trunks.

Denisovans A newly discovered group of archaic *Homo sapiens* from southern Siberia dated to between 30,000 and 50,000 years ago.

dental formula The number of each tooth type (incisors, canines, premolars, and molars) on one half of each jaw. Unlike other mammals, primates possess equal numbers on their upper and lower jaws so the dental formula for the species is a single series of numbers.

derived Characteristics that define a group of organisms and that did not exist in ancestral populations.

developmental adaptation A permanent phenotypic variation derived from interaction between genes and the environment during the period of growth and development.

diastema A space between the canines and other teeth allowing the large projecting canines to fit within the jaw.

diffusion The spread of certain ideas, customs, or practices from one culture to another.

disease A specific pathology; a physical or biological abnormality.

diurnal Active during the day and at rest at night.

DNA (deoxyribonucleic acid) The genetic material consisting of a complex molecule whose base structure directs the synthesis of proteins.

doctrine An assertion of opinion or belief formally handed down by an authority as true and indisputable.

domestication An evolutionary process whereby humans modify, intentionally or unintentionally, the genetic makeup of a population of wild plants or animals, sometimes to the extent that members of the population are unable to survive and/or reproduce without human assistance.

dominance hierarchy An observed ranking system in primate societies, ordering individuals from high (alpha) to low standing corresponding to predictable behavioral interactions including domination.

dominant In genetics, a term to describe the ability of an allele for a trait to mask the presence of a recessive allele.

ecological niche A species' way of life considered in the full context of its environment including factors such as diet, activity, terrain, vegetation, predators, prey, and climate.

egalitarian societies Societies in which people have about the same rank and share equally in the basic resources that support income, status, and power.

empirical Research based on observations of the world rather than on intuition or faith.

endemic The public health term for a disease that is widespread in a population.

endocast A cast of the inside of a skull; used to help determine the size and shape of the brain.

entoptic phenomena Bright pulsating forms that are generated by the central nervous system and seen in states of trance.

enzymes Proteins that initiate and direct chemical reactions.

epicanthic eyefold A fold of skin at the inner corner of the eye that covers the true corner of the eye; common in Asiatic populations.

estrus In some primate females, the time of sexual receptivity during which ovulation is visibly displayed.

ethnocentrism The belief that the ways of one's own culture are the only proper ones.

ethnocide The violent eradication of an ethnic group's collective cultural identity as a distinctive people; occurs when a dominant society deliberately sets out to destroy another society's cultural heritage.

ethnography A detailed description of a particular culture primarily based on fieldwork.

ethnology The study and analysis of different cultures from a comparative or historical point of view, utilizing ethnographic accounts and developing anthropological theories that help explain why certain important differences or similarities occur among groups.

Eve hypothesis The theory that modern humans are all derived from one single population of archaic *Homo sapiens* who migrated out of Africa after 100,000 years ago, replacing all other archaic forms due to their superior cultural capabilities; also known as the *recent African origins hypothesis* or the *out of Africa hypothesis*.

evolution The changes in allele frequencies in populations; also known as *microevolution*.

evolutionary medicine An approach to human sickness and health combining principles of evolutionary theory and human evolutionary history.

experimental archaeology The recreation of ancient lifeways by modern paleoanthropologists in order to test hypotheses, interpretations, and assumptions about the past.

fieldwork The term anthropologists use for on-location research.

flotation An archaeological technique employed to recover very tiny objects by immersion of soil samples in water to separate heavy from light particles.

fluorine dating In archaeology or paleoanthropology, a technique for relative dating based on the fact that the amount of fluorine in bones is proportional to their age.

foramen magnum A large opening in the skull through which the spinal cord passes and connects to the brain.

forensic anthropology The identification of human skeletal remains for legal purposes.

fossil The preserved remains of past life forms.

founder effects A particular form of genetic drift deriving from a small founding population not possessing all the alleles present in the original population.

fovea centralis A shallow pit in the retina of the eye that enables an animal to focus on an object while maintaining visual contact with its surroundings.

gender The cultural elaborations and meanings assigned to the biological differentiation between the sexes.

gene flow The introduction of alleles from the gene pool of one population into that of another.

gene pool All the genetic variants possessed by members of a population.

genes The portions of DNA molecules that direct the synthesis of specific proteins.

genetic adaptations Discrete genetic changes built into the allele frequencies of populations or microevolutionary change brought about by natural selection.

genetic code The sequence of three bases (a codon) that specifies the sequence of amino acids in protein synthesis.

genetic drift The chance fluctuations of allele frequencies in the gene pool of a population.

genocide The physical extermination of one people by another, either as a deliberate act or as the accidental outcome of activities carried out by one people with little regard for their impact on others.

genome The complete structure sequence of DNA for a species.

genotype The alleles possessed for a particular trait.

genus (genera) In the system of plant and animal classification, a group of like species.

globalization Worldwide interconnectedness, evidenced in rapid global movement of natural resources, trade goods, human labor, finance capital, information, and infectious diseases.

gracile australopithecines Members of the genus *Australopithecus* possessing a more lightly built chewing apparatus; likely had a diet that included more meat than that of the robust *australopithecines*; best represented by the South African species *A. africanus*.

grade A general level of biological organization seen among a group of species; useful for constructing evolutionary relationships.

grave goods Items such as utensils, figurines, and personal possessions, symbolically placed in the grave for the deceased person's use in the afterlife.

grid system A system for recording data in three dimensions from an archaeological excavation.

grooming The ritual cleaning of another animal's coat to remove parasites and other matter.

haplorhines The subdivision within the primate order based on shared genetic characteristics; includes tarsiers, New World monkeys, Old World monkeys, and apes (including humans).

Hardy-Weinberg principle The concept that demonstrates algebraically that the percentages of individuals that are homozygous for the dominant allele, homozygous for the recessive allele, and heterozygous should remain constant from one generation to the next, provided that certain specified conditions are met.

health disparity A difference in the health status between the wealthy elite and the poor in stratified societies.

hemoglobin The protein that carries oxygen in red blood cells.

heterozygous Refers to a chromosome pair that bears different alleles for a single gene.

historical archaeology The archaeological study of places for which written records exist.

holistic perspective A fundamental principle of anthropology: The various parts of human culture and biology must be viewed in the broadest possible context in order to understand their interconnections and interdependence.

homeotherm An animal that maintains a relatively constant body temperature despite environmental fluctuations.

home range The geographic area within which a group of primates usually moves.

hominid African hominoid family that includes humans and their ancestors. Some scientists, recognizing the close relationship of humans, chimps, bonobos, and gorillas, use the term *hominid* to refer to all African hominoids. They then divide the hominid family into two subfamilies: the Paninae (chimps, bonobos, and gorillas) and the Homininae (humans and their ancestors).

hominin The taxonomic subfamily or tribe within the primates that includes humans and our ancestors.

hominoid The taxonomic division superfamily within the Old World primates that includes gibbons, siamangs, orangutans, gorillas, chimpanzees, bonobos, and humans.

Homo The genus of bipeds that appeared 2.5 million years ago, characterized by increased brain size compared to earlier bipeds. The genus is divided into various species based on features such as brain size, skull shape, and cultural capabilities.

Homo erectus "Upright man." A species within the genus *Homo* first appearing just after 2 million years ago in Africa and ultimately spreading throughout the Old World.

Homo habilis "Handy man." The first fossil members of the genus *Homo* appearing 2.5 million years ago, with larger brains and smaller faces than australopithecines.

homologies In biology, structures possessed by two different organisms that arise in similar fashion and pass through similar stages during embryonic development, although they may have different functions.

homozygous Refers to a chromosome pair that bears identical alleles for a single gene.

horticulture The cultivation of crops in food gardens, carried out with simple hand tools such as digging sticks and hoes.

hunting response A cyclic expansion and contraction of the blood vessels of the limbs that balances releasing enough heat to prevent frostbite with maintaining heat in the body core.

hydraulic theory The theory that explains civilization's emergence as the result of the construction of elaborate irrigation systems, the functioning of which required full-time managers whose control blossomed into the first governing body and elite social class; also known as *irrigation theory*.

hypoglossal canal The opening in the skull that accommodates the tongue-controlling hypoglossal nerve.

hypothesis A tentative explanation of the relationships between certain phenomena.

hypoxia The reduced availability of oxygen at the cellular level.

illness The meanings and elaborations given to a particular physical state.

informed consent A formal recorded agreement between the subject and the researcher to participate in the research.

innovation Any new idea, method, or device that gains widespread acceptance in society.

irrigation theory The theory that explains civilization's emergence as the result of the construction of elaborate irrigation systems, the functioning of which required full-time managers whose control blossomed into the first governing body and elite social class; also known as *hydraulic theory*.

ischial callosities Hardened, nerveless pads on the buttocks that allow baboons and other primates to sit for long periods of time.

isotherm An animal whose body temperature rises or falls according to the temperature of the surrounding environment.

karyotype The array of chromosomes found inside a single cell.

Kenyanthropus platyops A proposed genus and species of biped contemporary with early australopithecines; may not be a separate genus.

k-selected Reproduction involving the production of relatively few offspring with high parental investment in each.

lactase An enzyme in the small intestine that enables humans to assimilate lactose.

lactose A sugar that is the primary constituent of fresh milk.

law of competitive exclusion When two closely related species compete for the same niche, one will out-compete the other, bringing about the latter's extinction.

law of independent assortment The Mendelian principle that genes controlling different traits are inherited independently of one another.

law of segregation The Mendelian principle that variants of genes for a particular trait retain their separate identities through the generations.

Levalloisian technique Toolmaking technique by which three or four long triangular flakes are detached from a specially prepared core; developed by members of the genus *Homo* transitional from *H. erectus* to *H. sapiens*.

linguistic anthropology The study of human languages—looking at their structure, history, and relation to social and cultural contexts.

Lower Paleolithic The first part of the Old Stone Age beginning with the earliest Oldowan tools spanning from about 200,000 or 250,000 to 2.6 million years ago.

macroevolution Evolution above the species level or leading to the formation of new species.

mammals The class of vertebrate animals distinguished by bodies covered with hair or fur, self-regulating temperature, and in females, milk-producing mammary glands.

marrow The fatty nutritious tissue inside of long bones where blood cells are produced.

material culture The durable aspects of culture such as tools, structures, and art.

medical anthropology A specialization in anthropology that brings theoretical and applied approaches from cultural and biological anthropology to the study of human health and disease.

medical pluralism The practice of multiple medical systems, each with its own techniques and beliefs, in a single society.

medical system A patterned set of ideas and practices relating to illness.

meiosis A kind of cell division that produces the sex cells, each of which has half the number of chromosomes found in other cells of the organism.

melanin A dark pigment produced in the outer layer of the skin that protects against damaging ultraviolet solar radiation.

menarche First menstruation in the maturation of a human female.

menopause The cessation of menstrual cycles.

Mesoamerica The region extending from central Mexico to northern Central America.

Mesolithic The Middle Stone Age of Europe, Asia, and Africa beginning about 12,000 years ago.

metabolic rate The rate at which bodies burn energy (food) to function.

microevolution The changes in allele frequencies in populations; also known as *evolution*.

microlith A small blade of flint or similar stone, several of which were hafted together in wooden handles to make tools; widespread in the Mesolithic.

middens A refuse or garbage disposal area in an archaeological site.

Middle Paleolithic The middle part of the Old Stone Age characterized by the development of the Mousterian tool tradition and the earlier Levalloisian techniques.

mitosis A kind of cell division that produces new cells having exactly the same number of chromosome pairs, and hence copies of genes, as the parent cell.

molecular anthropology The anthropological study of genes and genetic relationships, which contributes significantly to our understanding of human evolution, adaptation, and diversity.

molecular clock The hypothesis that dates of divergences among related species can be calculated through an examination of the genetic mutations that have accrued since the divergence.

money A means of exchange used to make payments for other goods and services as well as to measure their value.

monogamous In primatology, mating for life with a single individual of the opposite sex.

Mousterian tool tradition The tool industry of the Neandertals and their contemporaries of Europe, Southwest Asia, and North Africa from 40,000 to 125,000 years ago.

multiregional hypothesis The hypothesis that modern humans originated through a process of simultaneous local transition from *Homo erectus* to *Homo sapiens* throughout the inhabited world.

mutation The chance alteration of genetic material that produces new variation.

natal group The group or the community an animal has inhabited since birth.

Natufian culture A Mesolithic culture from the lands that are now Israel, Lebanon, and western Syria, between about 10,200 and 12,500 years ago.

natural selection The evolutionary process through which factors in the environment exert pressure, favoring some individuals over others to produce the next generation.

Neandertals A distinct group within the genus *Homo* inhabiting Europe and Southwest Asia from approximately 30,000 to 125,000 years ago.

Neolithic The New Stone Age; a prehistoric period beginning about 10,000 years ago in which peoples possessed stone-based technologies and depended on domesticated crops and/or animals for subsistence.

Neolithic revolution The domestication of plants and animals by peoples with stone-based technologies, beginning about 10,000 years ago and leading to radical transformations in cultural systems; sometimes referred to as the *Neolithic transition*.

nocturnal Active at night and at rest during the day.

notochord A rodlike structure of cartilage that, in vertebrates, is replaced by the vertebral column.

Oldowan tool tradition The first stone tool industry, beginning between 2.5 and 2.6 million years ago.

Old Stone Age A period of time beginning with the earliest Oldowan tools, spanning from about 200,000 to 2.6 million years ago; also known as the *Lower Paleolithic*.

opposable Having the ability to bring the thumb or big toe in contact with the tips of the other digits on the same hand or foot in order to grasp objects.

out of Africa hypothesis The theory that modern humans are all derived from one single population of archaic *Homo sapiens* who migrated out of Africa after 100,000 years ago, replacing all other archaic forms due to their superior cultural capabilities; also known as the *recent African origins hypothesis* or the *Eve hypothesis*.

ovulation The moment when an egg released from an ovary into the womb is receptive for fertilization.

paleoanthropology The anthropological study of biological changes through time (evolution) to understand the origins and predecessors of the present human species.

Paleoindians The earliest inhabitants of North America.

palynology In archaeology and paleoanthropology, a technique of relative dating based on changes in fossil pollen over time.

participant observation In ethnography, the technique of learning a people's culture through social participation and personal observation within the community being studied, as well as interviews and discussion with individual members of the group over an extended period of time.

pastoralism The breeding and managing of migratory herds of domesticated grazing animals, such as goats, sheep, cattle, llamas, and camels.

percussion method A technique of stone tool manufacture performed by striking the raw material with a hammerstone or by striking raw material against a stone anvil to remove flakes.

phenotype The observable or testable appearance of an organism that may or may not reflect a particular genotype due to the variable expression of dominant and recessive alleles.

physical anthropology The systematic study of humans as biological organisms; also known as *biological anthropology*.

physiological adaptation A short-term physiological change in response to a specific environmental stimulus. An immediate short-term response is not very efficient and is gradually replaced by a longer-term response; see *acclimatization*.

platyrrhines The primate infraorder that includes New World monkeys.

polygenetic inheritance Two or more genes contributing to the phenotypic expression of a single characteristic.

polymerase chain reaction (PCR) A technique for amplifying or creating multiple copies of fragments of DNA so that it can be studied in the laboratory.

polymorphic Describing species with alternative forms (alleles) of particular genes.

polytypic Describing the expression of genetic variants in different frequencies in different populations of a species.

population In biology, a group of similar individuals that can and do interbreed.

potassium-argon dating In archaeology and paleoanthropology, a technique of chronometric dating that measures the ratio of radioactive potassium to argon in volcanic debris associated with human remains.

preadapted Possessing characteristics that, by chance, are advantageous in future environmental conditions.

prehensile Having the ability to grasp.

prehistory A conventional term used to refer to the period of time before the appearance of written records; does not deny the existence of history, merely of *written* history.

pressure flaking A technique of stone tool manufacture in which a bone, antler, or wooden tool is used to press, rather than strike off, small flakes from a piece of flint or similar stone.

primary innovation The creation, invention, or chance discovery of a completely new idea, method, or device.

primates The group of mammals that includes lemurs, lorises, tarsiers, monkeys, apes, and humans.

primatology The study of living and fossil primates.

prion An infectious protein lacking any genetic material but capable of causing the reorganization and destruction of other proteins.

projection In cartography, refers to the system of intersecting lines (of longitude and latitude) by which part or all of the globe is represented on a flat surface.

prosimians The suborder of primates that includes lemurs, lorises, and tarsiers.

punctuated equilibria A model of macroevolutionary change that suggests evolution occurs via long periods of stability or stasis punctuated by periods of rapid change.

race In biology, the taxonomic category of subspecies that is not applicable to humans because the division of humans into discrete types does not represent the true nature of human biological variation. In some societies race is an important social category.

racism A doctrine of superiority by which one group justifies the dehumanization of others based on their distinctive physical characteristics.

radiocarbon dating In archaeology and paleoanthropology, a technique of chronometric dating based on measuring the amount of radioactive carbon (^{14}C) left in organic materials found in archaeological sites.

recent African origins hypothesis The theory that modern humans are all derived from one single population of archaic *Homo sapiens* who migrated out of Africa after 100,000 years ago, replacing all other archaic forms due to their superior cultural capabilities; also known as the *Eve hypothesis* or the *out of Africa hypothesis*.

recessive In genetics, a term to describe the inability of an allele for a trait to mask the presence of a dominant allele.

reconciliation In primatology, a friendly reunion between former opponents not long after a conflict.

relative dating In archaeology and paleoanthropology, designating an event, object, or fossil as being older or younger than another by noting the position in the earth, by measuring the amount of chemicals contained in fossil bones and artifacts, or by identifying its association with other plant, animal, or cultural remains.

reproductive success The relative production of fertile offspring by a genotype. In practical terms, the number of offspring produced by individual members of a population is tallied and compared to that of others.

ribosomes Structures in the cell where translation occurs.

rifting In geology, the process by which a rift, or a long narrow zone of faulting, results when two geological plates come together.

RNA (ribonucleic acid) Similar to DNA but with uracil substituted for the base thymine. Transcribes and carries instructions from DNA from the nucleus to the ribosomes, where it directs protein synthesis. Some simple life forms contain RNA only.

robust australopithecines Several species within the genus *Australopithecus*, who lived from 1.1 to 2.5 million years ago in eastern and southern Africa; known for the rugged nature of their chewing apparatus (large back teeth, large chewing muscles, and a bony ridge on their skull tops to allow for these large muscles).

r-selected Reproduction involving the production of large numbers of offspring with relatively low parental investment in each.

sagittal crest A crest running from front to back on the top of the skull along the midline to provide a surface of bone for the attachment of the large temporal muscles for chewing.

Sahul The greater Australian landmass including Australia, New Guinea, and Tasmania. At times of maximum glaciation and low sea levels, these areas were continuous.

savannah Semi-arid plains environment as in eastern Africa.

scapula The shoulder blade.

secondary innovation The deliberate application or modification of an existing idea, method, or device.

secular trend A physical difference among related people from distinct generations that allows anthropologists to make inferences about environmental effects on growth and development.

seriation In archaeology and paleoanthropology, a technique for relative dating based on putting groups of objects into a sequence in relation to one another.

sexual dimorphism Within a single species, differences between males and females in the shape or size of a feature not directly related to reproduction, such as body size or canine tooth shape and size.

sickle-cell anemia An inherited form of anemia produced by a mutation in the hemoglobin protein that causes the red blood cells to assume a sickle shape.

soil marks The stains that show up on the surface of recently plowed fields that reveal an archaeological site.

speciation The process of forming new species.

species The smallest working units in biological classificatory systems; reproductively isolated populations or groups of populations capable of interbreeding to produce fertile offspring.

stabilizing selection Natural selection acting to promote stability rather than change in a population's gene pool.

stereoscopic vision Complete three-dimensional vision, or depth perception, from binocular vision and nerve connections that run from each eye to both sides of the brain, allowing nerve cells to integrate the images derived from each eye.

stratified In archaeology, a term describing sites where the remains lie in layers, one upon another.

stratigraphy In archaeology and paleoanthropology, the most reliable method of relative dating by means of strata.

strepsirhines The subdivision within the primate order based on shared genetic characteristics; includes lemurs and lorises.

structural power Power that organizes and orchestrates the systemic interaction within and among societies, directing economic and political forces on the one hand and ideological forces that shape public ideas, values, and beliefs on the other.

structural violence Physical and/or psychological harm (including repression, environmental destruction, poverty, hunger, illness, and premature death) caused by impersonal, exploitative, and unjust social, political, and economic systems.

Sunda The combined landmass of the contemporary islands of Java, Sumatra, Borneo, and Bali that was continuous with mainland Southeast Asia at times of low sea levels corresponding to maximum glaciation.

suspensory hanging apparatus The broad powerful shoulder joints and muscles found in all the hominoids, allowing these large-bodied primates to hang suspended below the tree branches.

taxonomy The science of classification.

tertiary scavenger In a food chain, the third animal group (second to scavenge) to obtain meat from a kill made by a predator.

theory A coherent statement that provides an explanatory framework for understanding; an explanation or interpretation supported by a reliable body of data.

thrifty genotype Human genotype that permits efficient storage of fat to draw on in times of food shortage and conservation of glucose and nitrogen.

tool An object used to facilitate some task or activity. Although toolmaking involves intentional modification of the material of which it is made, tool use may involve objects either modified for some particular purpose or completely unmodified.

transcription The process of conversion of instructions from DNA into RNA.

translation The process of conversion of RNA instructions into proteins.

Upper Paleolithic The last part (10,000 to 40.000 years ago) of the Old Stone Age, featuring tool industries characterized by long, slim blades and an explosion of creative symbolic forms.

vegeculture The cultivation of domesticated root crops, such as yams, manioc, and taro together in a single field, generally by planting cuttings instead of seeds.

vertebrates Animals with a backbone, including fish, amphibians, reptiles, birds, and mammals.

visual predation hypothesis A theory for primate evolution that proposes that hunting behavior in tree-dwelling primates was responsible for their enhanced visual acuity and manual dexterity.

worldview The collective body of ideas that members of a culture generally share concerning the ultimate shape and substance of their reality.

References

Adams, R. M. (2001). Scale and complexity in archaic states. *Latin American Antiquity 11*, 188.

Allen, J. S., & Cheer, S. M. (1996). The non-thrifty genotype. *Current Anthropology 37*, 831–842.

Alvard, M. S., & Kuznar, L. (2001). Deferred harvest: The transition from hunting to animal husbandry. *American Anthropologist 103* (2), 295–311.

Amábile-Cuevas, C. F., & Chicurel, M. E. (1993). Horizontal gene transfer. *American Scientist 81*, 338.

Ambrose, S. H. (2001). Paleolithic technology and human evolution. *Science 291*, 1748–1753.

American Anthropological Association. (1998). Statement on "race." www.aaanet.org/stmts/racepp .htm (retrieved August 1, 2012)

Andrews, L. B., & Nelkin, D. (1996). The Bell Curve: A statement. *Science 271*, 13.

Arnold, F., Kishor, S., & Roy, T. K. (2002). Sex-selective abortions in India. *Population and Development Review 28* (4), 759–785.

Aureli, F., & de Waal, F. B. M. (2000). *Natural conflict resolution*. Berkeley: University of California Press.

Babiker, M. A., et al. (1996). Unnecessary deprivation of common food items in glucose-6-phosphate dehydrogenase deficiency. *Annals of Saudi Arabia 16* (4), 462–463.

Balter, M. (1998). Why settle down? The mystery of communities. *Science 282*, 1442–1444.

Balter, M. (1999). A long season puts Çatalhöyük in context. *Science 286*, 890–891.

Balter, M. (2001). In search of the first Europeans. *Science 291*, 1724.

Balter, M. (2001a). Did plaster hold Neolithic society together? *Science 294*, 2278–2281.

Barkai, R., & Liran, R. (2008). Midsummer sunset at Neolithic Jericho. *Time and Mind: The Journal of Archaeology, Consciousness, and Culture 1* (3), 273–284.

Barr, R. G. (1997, October). The crying game. *Natural History*, 47.

Barrett, L., et al. (2004). Habitual cave use and thermoregulation in chacma baboons (*Papio hamadryas ursinus*). *Journal of Human Evolution 46* (2), 215–222.

Birdsell, J. H. (1977). The recalibration of a paradigm for the first peopling of Greater Australia. In J. Allen, J. Golson, & R. Jones (Eds.), *Sunda and Sahul: Prehistoric studies in Southeast Asia, Melanesia, and Australia* (pp. 113–167). New York: Academic Press.

Blom, A., et al. (2004). Behavioral responses of gorillas to habituation in the Dzanga-Ndoki National Park, Central African Republic. *International Journal of Primatology 25*, 179–196.

Blumberg, R. L. (1991). *Gender, family, and the economy: The triple overlap*. Newbury Park, CA: Sage.

Boas, F. (1909, May 28). Race problems in America. *Science 29* (752), 839–849.

Bodley, J. H. (2007). *Anthropology and contemporary human problems* (5th ed.). Lanham, MD: AltaMira Press.

Boehm, C. (2000). The evolution of moral communities. *School of American Research, 2000 Annual Report, 7.*

Bongaarts, J. (1998). Demographic consequences of declining fertility. *Science 182*, 419.

Brace, C. L. (2000). *Evolution in an anthropological view*. Walnut Creek, CA: AltaMira Press.

Bradford, P. V., & Blume, H. (1992). *Ota Benga: The Pygmy in the zoo*. New York: St. Martin's Press.

Brunet, M., et al. (2002). A new hominid from the Upper Miocene of Chad, Central Africa. *Nature 418*, 145–151.

Carbonell, E., et al. (2008). The first hominin of Europe. *Nature 452* (7186), 465–469.

Carneiro, R. L. (1970). A theory of the origin of the state. *Science 169*, 733–738.

Cashdan, E. (2008). Waist-to-hip ratio across cultures: Trade-offs between androgen- and estrogen-dependent traits. *Current Anthropology 49* (6).

Chan, J. W. C., & Vernon, P. E. (1988). Individual differences among the peoples of China. In J. W. Berry (Ed.), *Human abilities in cultural context* (pp. 340–357). Cambridge, UK: Cambridge University Press.

Chicurel, M. (2001). Can organisms speed their own evolution? *Science 292*, 1824–1827.

Clark, E. E. (1966). *Indian legends of the Pacific Northwest*. Berkeley: University of California Press.

Clark, G. A. (2002). Neandertal archaeology: Implications for our origins. *American Anthropologist 104* (1), 50–67.

Clarke, R. J., & Tobias, P. V. (1995). Sterkfontein Member 2 foot bones of the oldest South African hominid. *Science 269*, 521–524.

Cohen, J. (2009). Out of Mexico? Scientists ponder swine flu's origin. *Science 324* (5928), 700–702.

Cohen, M. N., & Armelagos, G. J. (1984a). *Paleopathology at the origins of agriculture*. Orlando: Academic Press.

Cohen, M. N., & Armelagos, G. J. (1984b). Paleopathology at the origins of agriculture: Editors' summation. In *Paleopathology at the origins of agriculture*. Orlando: Academic Press.

Colborn, T., Dumanoski, D., & Myers, J. P. (1996). Hormonal sabotage. *Natural History 3*, 45–46.

Collins, B. (2005). *The trouble with poetry*. New York: Random House.

Conard, N. J. (2009). A female figurine from the basal Aurignacian deposits of Hohle Fels Cave in southwestern Germany. *Nature 459* (7244), 248.

Coon, C. S. (1962). *The origins of races*. New York: Knopf.

Copeland, S. R., et al. (2011, June 2). Strontium isotope evidence for landscape use by early hominins. *Nature 474*, 76–78. doi: 10.1038/nature10149

Coppa, A., et al. (2006). Early Neolithic tradition of dentistry. *Nature 440*, 755–756.

Crystal, D. (2002). *Language death*. Cambridge, UK: Cambridge University Press.

Culotta, E., & Koshland, D. E., Jr. (1994). DNA repair works its way to the top. *Science 266*, 1926.

D'Adesky, A.-C. (2004). *Moving mountains: the race to treat global AIDS*. New York: Verso.

Dalton, R. (2009). Fossil primate challenges Ida's place: Controversial German specimen is related to lemurs, not humans, analysis of an Egyptian find suggests. *Nature 461*, 1040.

Darwin, C. (1859). *On the origin of species*. New York: Atheneum.

Darwin, C. (1871). *The descent of man and selection in relation to sex*. New York: Random House (Modern Library).

Darwin, C. (1887). *Autobiography*. Reprinted in *The life and letters of Charles Darwin* (1902). F. Darwin (Ed.), London: John Murray.

Deetz, J. (1977). *In small things forgotten: The archaeology of early American life*. Garden City, NY: Doubleday/ Anchor.

de la Torre, S., & Snowden, C. T. (2009). Dialects in pygmy marmosets? Population variation in call structure. *American Journal of Primatology 71* (5), 333–342.

del Carmen Rodríguez Martínez, M., et al. (2006). Oldest writing in the New World. *Science 313* (5793), 1610–1614.

DeSilva, J. M. (2009). Functional morphology of the ankle and the likelihood of climbing in early hominins. *Proceeding of the National Academy of Sciences USA 106,* 6567–6572.

Dettwyler, K. A. (1994). *Dancing skeletons: Life and death in West Africa.* Prospect Heights, IL: Waveland Press.

de Waal, F. B. M. (2000). Primates: A natural heritage of conflict resolution. *Science 28,* 586–590.

de Waal, F. B. M. (2001). Sing the song of evolution. *Natural History 110* (8), 77.

de Waal, F. B. M., Kano, T., & Parish, A. R. (1998). Comments. *Current Anthropology 39,* 408, 413.

Diamond, J. (1996). Empire of uniformity. *Discover 17* (3), 83–84.

Diamond, J. (1997). *Guns, germs, and steel.* New York: Norton.

Dorit, R. (1997). Molecular evolution and scientific inquiry, misperceived. *American Scientist 85,* 475.

Durant, J. C. (2000, April 23). Everybody into the gene pool. *New York Times Book Review,* 11.

Eaton, S. B., Konner, M., & Shostak, M. (1988). Stone-agers in the fast lane: Chronic degenerative diseases in evolutionary perspective. *American Journal of Medicine 84* (4), 739–749.

Ehrlich, P. R., & Ehrlich, A. H. (2008). *The dominant animal: Human evolution and the environment.* Washington, DC: Island Press.

Ellison, P. T. (2003). *On fertile ground: A natural history of human reproduction.* Cambridge, MA: Harvard University Press.

Erickson, C. L. (2001). Pre-Columbian fish farming in the Amazon. *Expedition 43* (3), 7–8.

Fagan, B. M. (1995). *People of the earth* (8th ed., p. 19). New York: HarperCollins.

Farmer, P. (2001). *Infections and inequalities: The modern plagues.* Berkeley: University of California Press.

Fedigan, L. M. (1992). *Primate paradigms: Sex roles and social bonds.* Chicago: University of Chicago Press.

Fernandez-Carriba, S., & Loeches, A. (2001). Fruit smearing by captive chimpanzees: A newly observed food-processing behavior. *Current Anthropology 42,* 143–147.

Ferrie, H. (1997). An interview with C. Loring Brace. *Current Anthropology 38,* 851–869.

Folger, T. (1993). The naked and the bipedal. *Discover 14* (11), 34–35.

Ford, A. The BRASS/El Pilar Program. www.marc.ucsb.edu/elpilar/ (retrieved November 15, 2012)

Fowke, K. R., Nagelkerke, N. J., Kimani, J., Simonsen, J. N., Anzala, A. O., Bwayo, J. J., MacDonald, K. S., Ngugi, E. N., & Plummer, F. A. (1996). Resistance to HIV-1 infection among persistently seronegative prostitutes in Nairobi, Kenya. *Lancet 348* (9038), 1347–1351.

Franzen, J. L., et al. (2009). Complete primate skeleton from the middle Eocene of Messel in Germany: Morphology and paleobiology. *PLoS One 4* (5), e5723.

Frisch, R. (2002). *Female fertility and the body fat connection,* Chicago: University of Chicago Press.

Gebo, D. L., Dagosto, D., Beard, K. C., & Tao, Q. (2001). Middle Eocene primate tarsals from China: Implications for haplorhine evolution. *American Journal of Physical Anthropology 116,* 83–107.

"Gene study suggests Polynesians came from Taiwan." (2005, July 4). Reuters. www.freerepublic.com/focus/f-news/1436791/posts (retrieved November 15, 2012)

Gero, J. M., & Conkey, M. W. (Eds.). (1991). *Engendered archaeology: Women and prehistory.* New York: Wiley-Blackwell.

Gibbons, A. (1997). Ideas on human origins evolve at anthropology gathering. *Science 276,* 535–536.

Gibbons, A. (1998). Ancient island tools suggest *Homo erectus* was a seafarer. *Science 279,* 1635.

Gibbons, A. (2001). The riddle of coexistence. *Science 291,* 1726.

Gibbons, A. (2001a). Studying humans—and their cousins and parasites. *Science 292,* 627.

Goldsmith, M. L. (2005). Habituating primates for field study: Ethical considerations for great apes. In T. Turner (Ed.), *Biological anthropology and ethics: From repatriation to genetic identity* (pp. 49–64). New York: SUNY Press.

Goldsmith, M. L., Glick, J., & Ngabirano, E. (2006). Gorillas living on the edge: Literally and figuratively. In N. E. Newton-Fisher, et al. (Eds.), *Primates of western Uganda* (pp. 405–422). New York: Springer.

Goodall, J. (1986). *The chimpanzees of Gombe: Patterns of behavior.* Cambridge, MA: Belknap Press.

Goodall, J. (1990). *Through a window: My thirty years with the chimpanzees of Gombe.* Boston: Houghton Mifflin.

Goodman, M., et al. (1994). Molecular evidence on primate phylogeny from DNA sequences. *American Journal of Physical Anthropology 94,* 7.

Gould, S. J. (1989). *Wonderful life.* New York: Norton.

Gould, S. J. (1991). *Bully for brontosaurus.* New York: Norton.

Gould, S. J. (1994). The geometer of race. *Discover 15* (11), 65–69.

Green, R. E., et al. (2010, May 7). A draft sequence of the Neandertal genome. *Science 328* (5979), 710–722.

Griffin, D., & Fitzpatrick, D. (2009, September 1). Donor says he got thousands for his kidney. *CNNWorld.com.* http://articles.cnn.com/2009-09-01/world/blackmarket.organs_1_kidney-transplants-kidney-donor-kidney-specialist?_s=PM:WORLD (retrieved June 10, 2012)

Guillette, E. A., et al. (1998, June). An anthropological approach to the evaluation of preschool children exposed to pesticides in Mexico. *Environmental Health Perspectives 106,* 347.

Haglund, W. D., Conner, M., & Scott, D. D. (2001). The archaeology of contemporary mass graves. *Historical Archaeology 35* (1), 57–69.

Hahn, R. A. (1992). The state of federal health statistics on racial and ethnic groups. *Journal of the American Medical Association 267* (2), 268–271.

Hale, C. (2004). *Himmler's crusade: The true story of the 1938 Nazi expedition into Tibet.* New York: Bantam.

Handwerk, B. (2005, March 8). King Tut not murdered violently, CT scans show. *National Geographic News,* 2.

Harcourt-Smith, W. E. H., & Aiello, L. C. (2004). Fossils, feet and the evolution of human bipedal locomotion. *Journal of Anatomy 204,* 412.

Hare, B., Brown, M., Williamson, C., & Tomasello, M. (2002). The domestication of social cognition in dogs. *Science 298* (5598). 1634–1636.

Hart, D. (2006, April 21). Humans as prey. *Chronicle of Higher Education.*

Hart, D., & Sussman, R. W. (2005). *Man the hunted: Primates, predators, and human evolution.* Boulder, CO: Westview Press.

Haviland, W. A. (2002). Settlement, society and demography at Tikal. In J. Sabloff (Ed.), *Tikal.* Santa Fe: School of American Research.

Hawks, J. (2009). Ankles of the Australopithecines. *John Hawks Weblog.* http://johnhawks.net/weblog/reviews/early_hominids/anatomy/desilva-2009-chimpanzee-climbing-talus.html (retrieved July 5, 2012)

Heita, K. (1999). Imanishi's world view. *Journal of Japanese Trade and Industry 18* (2), 15.

Helman, C. B. (2007). *Culture, health, and illness: An introduction for health professionals* (5th ed.). New York: Trans-Atlantic Publications.

Henry, S., & Porter, D. (2011, October 27). Levy Izhak Rosenbaum pleads guilty to selling black market kidneys. *Huffingtonpost.com.* www.huffingtonpost.com/2011/10/27/levy-izhak-rosenbaum-plea_n_1035624.html (retrieved June 10, 2012)

Henshilwood, C. S., d'Errico, F., van Niekerk, K. L., Coquinot, Y., Jacobs, Z., Lauritzen, S.-E., Menu, M., & Garcia-Moreno. R. (2011). A 100,000-year-old ochre-processing workshop at Blombos Cave, South Africa. *Science 334* (6053), 219. doi:10.1126/science.1211535

Herrnstein, R. J., & Murray, C. (1994). *The bell curve.* New York: Free Press.

Hole, F., & Heizer, R. F. (1969). *An introduction to prehistoric archeology.* New York: Holt, Rinehart & Winston.

Ingmanson, E. J. (1998). Comment. *Current Anthropology 39,* 409.

Inoue, S., & Matsuzawa, T. (2007). Working memory of numerals in chimpanzees. *Current Biology 17,* 23, 1004–1005.

Jacoby, R., & Glauberman, N. (Eds.). (1995). *The Bell Curve debate.* New York: Random House.

Jane Goodall Institute. www.janegoodall.org/janes-story (retrieved June 15, 2012)

Kaiser, J. (1994). A new theory of insect wing origins takes off. *Science 266,* 363.

Kaplan, M. (2007, May 31). Upright orangutans point way to walking. *Nature.* doi:10.1038/news070528–8.

Kaplan, M. (2008, August 5). Almost half of primate species face extinction. *Nature.* doi:10.1038/news.2008.1013 (retrieved June 23, 2012)

Karavanić, I., & Smith, F. H. (2000). More on the Neanderthal problem: The Vindija case. *Current Anthropology 41*, 839.

Kaw, E. (1993). Medicalization of racial features: Asian American women and cosmetic surgery. *Medical Anthropology Quarterly 7* (1), 74–89.

Kay, R. F., Fleagle, J. G., & Simons, E. L. (1981). A revision of the Oligocene apes of the Fayum Province, Egypt. *American Journal of Physical Anthropology 55*, 293–322.

Kibii, J. M., et al. (2011, September 9). A partial pelvis of *Australopithecus sebida*. *Science 333* (6048), 1407–1411.

King, J. (2010, July 28). Reducing the crack and powder cocaine sentencing disparity should also reduce racial disparities in sentences and prisons. *NACDL news release*. www.nacdl.org/newsreleases.aspx?id=19533 (retrieved August 2, 2012)

Kitchen, A., Miyamoto, M. M., & Mulligan, C. J. (2008). A three-stage colonization model for the peopling of the Americas. *PLoS One 3* (2), e1596. doi:10.1371/journal.pone.0001596

Knight, C., Studdert-Kennedy, M., & Hurford, J. (Eds.). (2000). *The evolutionary emergence of language: Social function and the origins of linguistic form*. Cambridge, UK: Cambridge University Press.

Komai, T., & Fukuoka, G. (1934, October). Post-natal growth disparity in monozygotic twins. *Journal of Heredity 25*, 423–430.

Kunzig, R. (1999). A tale of two obsessed archaeologists, one ancient city and nagging doubts about whether science can ever hope to reveal the past. *Discover 20* (5), 84–92.

Lai, C. S. L., et al. (2001). A forkhead-domain gene is mutated in severe speech and language disorder. *Nature 413*, 519–523.

Lampl, M., Velhuis, J. D., & Johnson, M. L. (1992). Saltation and stasis: A model of human growth. *Science 258* (5083), 801–803.

Landau, M. (1991). *Narratives of human evolution*. New Haven, CT, & London: Yale University Press.

Lawler, A. (2001). Writing gets a rewrite. *Science 292*, 2419.

Leakey, M. G., Spoor, F., Brown, F. H., Gathogo, P. N., Kiare, C., Leakey, L. N., & McDougal, I. (2001). New hominin genus from eastern Africa shows diverse middle Pliocene lineages. *Nature 410*, 433–440.

Leclerc-Madlala, S. (2002). Bodies and politics: Healing rituals in the democratic South Africa. In V. Faure (Ed.), *Les cahiers de 'l'IFAS*, no. 2. Johannesburg: The French Institute.

Lestel, D. (1998). How chimpanzees have domesticated humans. *Anthropology Today 12* (3).

Leth, P. M. (2007). The use of CT scanning in forensic autopsy. *Forensic Science, Medicine, and Pathology 3* (1), 65–69.

Lévi-Strauss, C. (1963). The sorcerer and his magic. In *Structural anthropology*. New York: Basic Books. (orig. 1958)

Lewin, R. (1993). Paleolithic paint job. *Discover 14* (7), 64–70.

Lewontin, R. C. (1972). The apportionment of human diversity. In T. Dobzhansky et al. (Eds.), *Evolutionary biology* (pp. 381–398). New York: Plenum Press.

Lewontin, R. C., Rose, S., & Kamin, L. J. (1984). *Not in our genes*. New York: Pantheon.

Li, X., Harbottle, G., Zhang, J., & Wang, C. (2003). The earliest writing? Sign use in the seventh millennium BC at Jiahu, Henan Province, China. *Antiquity 77*, 31–44.

Lindenbaum, S. (1978). *Kuru sorcery: Disease and danger in the New Guinea highlands*. New York: McGraw-Hill.

Lock, M. (2001). *Twice dead: Organ transplants and the reinvention of death*. Berkeley: University of California Press.

Maggioncalda, A. N., & Sapolsky, R. M. (2002). Disturbing behaviors of the orangutan. *Scientific American 286* (6), 60–65.

Mann, C. C. (2002). The real dirt on rainforest fertility. *Science 297*, 920–923.

Mann, C. C. (2005). *1491: New revelations of the Americas before Columbus*. New York: Knopf.

Marcus, J., & Flannery, K. V. (1996). *Zapotec civilization: How urban society evolved in Mexico's Oaxaca Valley*. New York: Thames & Hudson.

Marks, J. (2000, May 12). 98% alike (what our similarity to apes tells us about our understanding of genetics). *Chronicle of Higher Education*, B7.

Marks, J. (2008a). Caveat emptor: Genealogy for sale. *Newsletter of the ESRC Genomics Network 7*, 22–23.

Marks, J. (2008b). Race: Past, present, and future. In B. Koenig, S. Lee, & S. Richardson (Eds.), *Revisiting race in a genomic age* (pp. 21–38). New Brunswick, NJ: Rutgers University Press.

Marshack, A. (1989). Evolution of the human capacity: The symbolic evidence. *Yearbook of physical anthropology* (vol. 32, pp. 1–34). New York: Alan R. Liss.

Marshall, E. (2001). Preclovis sites fight for acceptance. *Science 291*, 1732.

Martin, E. (1994). *Flexible bodies: Tracking immunity in American culture from the days of polio to the age of AIDS*. Boston: Beacon Press.

Martin, E. (1999). Flexible survivors. *Anthropology News 40* (6), 5–7.

Martorell, R. (1988). Body size, adaptation, and function. *GDP*, 335–347.

Max Planck Institute of Evolutionary Anthropology. (2012). Denisova genome. Public data set: http://aws.amazon.com/datasets/2357 (retrieved July 19, 2012)

McDermott, L. (1996). Self-representation in Upper Paleolithic female figurines. *Current Anthropology 37*, 227–276.

McElroy, A., & Townsend, P. K. (2003). *Medical anthropology in ecological perspective*. Boulder, CO: Westview Press.

McGrew, W. C. (2000). Dental care in chimps. *Science 288*, 1747.

McHenry, H. M., & Jones, A. L. (2006). Hallucific convergence in early hominids. *Journal of Human Evolution 50*, 534–539.

McKenna, J. J., Ball, H., & Gettler, L. T. (2007). Mother–infant cosleeping, breastfeeding and SIDS: What biological anthropology has discovered about normal infant sleep and pediatric sleep medicine. *Yearbook of Physical Anthropology 50*, 133–161.

McKenna, J. J., & McDade, T. (2005, June). Why babies should never sleep alone: A review of the co-sleeping controversy in relation to SIDS, bedsharing, and breastfeeding. *Pediatric Respiratory Reviews 6* (2), 134–152.

"Media frenzy." (2009, May 27). Editorial. *Nature 459*, 484.

Mellars, P. (2009). Archaeology: Origins of the female image. *Nature 459*, 176–177.

Miles, H. L. W. (1993). Language and the orangutan: The "old person" of the forest. In P. Cavalieri & P. Singer (Eds.), *The great ape project* (pp. 45–50). New York: St. Martin's Press.

Montagu, A. (1998). *Man's most dangerous myth: The fallacy of race* (6th ed.). Lanham, MD: Rowman & Littlefield.

Moore, J. (1998). Comment. *Current Anthropology 39*, 412.

Mydens, S. (2001, August 12). He's not hairy, he's my brother. *New York Times*. www.nytimes.com/2001/08/12/weekinreview/ideas-trends-he-s-not-hairy-he-s-my-brother.html (retrieved June 25, 2012)

Nabhan, G. P. (2004). *Why some like it hot: Food, genes, and cultural diversity*. Washington, DC: Island Press.

Nichols, J. (2008). Language spread rates as indicators of glacial-age peopling of the Americas. *Current Anthropology 49* (6), 1109–1117.

Normile, D. (1998). Habitat seen as playing larger role in shaping behavior. *Science 279*, 1454.

Nunney, L. (1998). Are we selfish because we are nice, or are we nice because we are selfish? *Science 281*, 1619.

O'Carroll, E. (2008, June 27). Spain to grant some human rights to apes. *Christian Science Monitor*.

Otte, M. (2000). On the suggested bone flute from Slovenia. *Current Anthropology 41*, 271.

Parés, J. M., et al. (2000). On the age of hominid fossils at the Sima de los Huesos, Sierra de Atapuerca, Spain: Paleomagnetic evidence. *American Journal of Physical Anthropology 111*, 451–461.

Parish, A. (1998). Comment. *Current Anthropology 39*, 414.

Parnell, R. (1999). Gorilla exposé. *Natural History 108* (8), 43.

Pickering, R., et al. (2011). *Australopithecus sediba* at 1.977 ma and implications for the origins of the genus *Homo*. *Science 333* (6048), 1421–1423.

Pike, A. W. G., et al. (2012). U-series dating of Paleolithic art in 11 caves in Spain. *Science 336*, 1409–1413.

Pohl, M. E. D., Pope, K. O., & von Nagy, C. (2002). Olmec origins of Mesoamerican writing. *Science 298*, 1984–1987.

Pollan, M. (2001). *The botany of desire: A plant's-eye view of the world*. New York: Random House.

Power, M. G. (1995). Gombe revisited: Are chimpanzees violent and hierarchical in the "free" state? *General Anthropology 2* (1), 5–9.

"President Obama descends from the first African enslaved for life in America." (2012, July). *Ancestry .com*. www.ancestry.com/obama (retrieved August 10, 2012)

Pruetz, J. D., & Bertolani, P. (2007, March 6). Savanna chimpanzees, *Pan troglodytes verus*, hunt with tools. *Current Biology 17*, 412–417.

Rapp, R. (1999). *Testing women, testing the fetus: The social impact of amniocentesis in America (The Anthropology of Everyday Life)*. New York: Routledge.

Rasmussen, M., et al. (2011). An aboriginal Australian genome reveals separate human dispersals into Asia, *Science 334* (6052), 94–98. doi: 10.1126/science.1211177

Rathje, W., & Murphy, C. (2001). *Rubbish!: The archaeology of garbage.* Tucson: University of Arizona Press.

Recer, P. (1998, February 16). Apes shown to communicate in the wild. *Burlington Free Press*, 12A.

Reich, D., et al. (2010, December 23). Genetic history of an archaic hominin group from Denisova Cave in Siberia. *Nature 468*, 1053–1060.

Reich, D., et al. (2012). Reconstructing Native American population history. *Nature*. doi: 10.1038/nature11258

Relethford, J. H. (2001). Absence of regional affinities of Neandertal DNA with living humans does not reject multiregional evolution. *American Journal of Physical Anthropology 115*, 95–98.

Relethford, J. H., & Harpending, H. C. (1994). Craniometric variation, genetic theory, and modern human origins. *American Journal of Physical Anthropology 95*, 249–270.

Rice, P. (2000). Paleoanthropology 2000—part 1. *General Anthropology 7* (1), 11.

Ridley, M. (1999). *Genome: The autobiography of a species in 23 chapters.* New York: HarperCollins.

Rightmire, G. P. (1998). Evidence from facial morphology for similarity of Asian and African representatives of *Homo erectus. American Journal of Physical Anthropology 106*, 61–85.

Rogers, J. (1994). Levels of the genealogical hierarchy and the problem of hominoid phylogeny. *American Journal of Physical Anthropology 94*, 81–88.

Romer, A. S. (1945). *Vertebrate paleontology.* Chicago: University of Chicago Press.

Roosevelt, A. C. (1984). Population, health, and the evolution of subsistence: Conclusions from the conference. In M. N. Cohen & G. J. Armelagos (Eds.), *Paleopathology at the origins of agriculture* (pp. 572–574). Orlando: Academic Press.

Rose, S. (2009). Darwin 200: Should scientists study race and IQ? NO: Science and society do not benefit. *Nature 457*, 786–788.

Sacks, O. (1998). *Island of the colorblind.* New York: Knopf.

Sahlins, M. (1972). *Stone Age economics.* Chicago: Aldine.

Sanday, P. R. (1975). On the causes of IQ differences between groups and implications for social policy. In M. F. A. Montagu (Ed.), *Race and IQ* (pp. 232–238). New York: Oxford University Press.

Sapolsky, R. (2002). *A primate's memoir: Love, death, and baboons in East Africa.* New York: Vintage.

Savage-Rumbaugh, S., & Lewin, R. (1994). *Kanzi: The ape at the brink of the human mind.* New York: Wiley.

Sawert, H. (2002, October 11–12). *TB and poverty in the context of global TB control.* World Health Organization. Satellite Symposium on TB & Poverty. www.stoptb.org/assets/documents/resources/publications/acsm/H.RightsReport2001.pdf

Schuster, C., & Carpenter, E. (1996). *Patterns that connect: Social symbolism in ancient and tribal art.* New York: Abrams.

Scully, T. (2008). Online anthropology draws protest from aboriginal group. *Nature 453*, 1155. doi:10.1038/4531155a.

Seiffert, E. R., et al. (2009). Convergent evolution of anthropoid-like adaptations in Eocene adapiform primates. *Nature 461*, 1118–1121.

Semenov, S. A. (1964). *Prehistoric technology.* New York: Barnes & Noble.

Senut, B., et al. (2001). First hominid from the Miocene (Lukeino formation, Kenya). *C. R. Academy of Science, Paris 332*, 137–144.

Seyfarth, R. M., Cheney, D. L., & Marler, P. (1980). Vervet monkey alarm calls: Semantic communication in a free-ranging primate. *Animal Behavior 28* (4), 1070–1094.

Sharpe, K., & Van Gelder, L. (2006). Evidence of cave marking by Paleolithic children. *Antiquity 80* (310), 937–947.

Sheets, P. D. (1993). Dawn of a New Stone Age in eye surgery. In R. J. Sharer & W. Ashmore (Eds.), *Archaeology: Discovering our past.* Palo Alto, CA: Mayfield.

Shi, L. (2009). Little quilted vests to warm parents' hearts: Redefining the gendered practice of filial piety in rural north-eastern China. *China Quarterly 198*, 348–363.

Shreeve, J. (1994). Terms of estrangement. *Discover 15* (11), 60.

Shreeve, J. (1995). *The Neandertal enigma: Solving the mystery of modern human origins.* New York: William Morrow.

Silverstein, J. (2012). Bonds beyond blood: DNA testing and refugee family resettlement. *Anthropology News 53* (4), 11.

Simons, E. L., et al. (2009, July 22). Outrage at high price paid for a fossil. Correspondence. *Nature 460*, 456.

Simpson, S. (1995, April). Whispers from the ice. *Alaska*, 23–28.

Simpson, S. W., et al. (2008). A female *Homo erectus* pelvis from Gona, Ethiopia. *Science 322* (5904), 1089–1092.

Small, M. F. (2008, August 15). Why red is such a potent color. *Live Science.* www.livescience.com/5043-red-potent-color.html (retrieved June 20, 2012)

Small, M. F. (2009, May 15). Why "Ida" inspires navel-gazing at our ancestry. *Live Science.* www.livescience.come/history/090520-hn-ida.html

Smedley, A. (2007). *Race in North America: Origin and evolution of a worldview.* Boulder, CO: Westview Press.

Songok, E. M., Luo, M., Liang, B., Mclaren, P., Kaefer, N., Apidi, W., Boucher, G., Kimani, J., Wachihi, C., Sekaly, R., Fowke, K., Ball, B. T., &

Plummer, F. A. (2012). Microarray analysis of HIV resistant female sex workers reveal a gene expression signature pattern reminiscent of a lowered immune activation state. *PLoS One 7* (1), e30048.

Stedman, H. H., et al. (2004). Myosin gene mutation correlates with anatomical changes in the human lineage. *Nature 428*, 415–418.

Strier, K. (1993, March). Menu for a monkey. *Natural History*, 42.

Strum, S., & Mitchell, W. (1987). Baboon models and muddles. In W. Kinsey (Ed.), *The evolution of human behavior: Primate models.* Albany: SUNY Press.

Tamm, E., et al. (2007). Beringian standstill and spread of Native American frontiers. *PLoS One 2* (9), e829. doi: 10.1371/journal/pone.0000829

Tapper, M. (1999). *In the blood: Sickle-cell anemia and the politics of race.* Philadelphia: University of Pennsylvania Press.

Thompson, K. (2012, July 30). Obama's purported link to early American slave is latest twist in family tree. *Washington Post.* www.washingtonpost.com/politics/purported-obama-link-to-first-american-slave-is-latest-twist-in-presidents-family-tree/2012/07/30/gJQAYuG1KX_story.html?hpid=z4 (retrieved August 10, 2012)

Thomson, K. S. (1997). Natural selection and evolution's smoking gun. *American Scientist 85*, 516.

Thorpe, S. K. S., Holder, R. L., & Crompton, R. H. (2007). Origin of human bipedalism as an adaptation for locomotion on flexible branches. *Science 316*, 1328–1331.

Toth, N., et al. (1993). Pan the tool-maker: Investigations in the stone tool-making and tool-using capabilities of a bonobo (*Pan paniscus*). *Journal of Archaeological Science 20* (1), 81–91.

Tracy, J. L., & Matsumoto, D. (2008). The spontaneous expression of pride and shame: Evidence for biologically innate nonverbal displays. *Proceedings of the National Academy of Sciences 105* (33), 11655–11660.

Trevathan, W., Smith, E. O., & McKenna, J. J. (Eds.). (1999). *Evolutionary medicine.* London: Oxford University Press.

Trifonov, V., Khiabanian, H., Greenbaum, B., & Rabadan, R. (2009). The origin of the recent swine influenza A (H1N1) virus infecting humans. *Eurosurveillance 14* (17). www.eurosurveillance.org/ViewArticle.aspx?ArticleId=19193 (retrieved July 16, 2012)

Trouillot, M. R. (1996). Culture, color, and politics in Haiti. In S. Gregory & R. Sanjek (Eds.), *Race.* New Brunswick, NJ: Rutgers University Press.

Vidya, R. (2002). Karnataka's unabating kidney trade. *Frontline.* www.frontlineonnet.com/fl1907/19070610.htm (retrieved June 10, 2012)

Washington, H. (2006) *Medical apartheid: The dark history of medical experimentation on black Americans from colonial times to the present,* New York: Anchor.

Weatherford, J. (1988). *Indian givers: How the Indians of the Americas transformed the world.* New York: Ballantine.

Wells, S. (2002). *The journey of man: A genetic odyssey.* Princeton, NJ: Princeton University Press.

White, M. (2001). *Historical atlas of the twentieth century.* http://users.erols.com/mwhite28/20century.htm (retrieved August 28, 2012)

White, T., Asfaw, B., Degusta, D., Gilbert, H., Richards, G., Suwa, G., & Howell, F. C. (2003). Pleistocene *Homo sapiens* from the Middle Awash, Ethiopia. *Nature 423,* 742–747.

White, T. D. (2003). Early hominids—diversity or distortion? *Science 299,* 1994–1997.

White, T. D., & Toth, N. (2000). Cutmarks on a Plio-Pleistocene hominid from Sterkfontein, South Africa. *American Journal of Physical Anthropology 111,* 579–584.

White, T. D., et al. (2009, October). *Ardipithecus ramidus* and the paleobiology of early hominoids. *Science 326* (5949), 64, 75–86.

"Why the stories are told," Aunty Beryl Carmichael. *Aboriginal culture: Dreamtime stories.* www.rmwebed.com.au/HSIE/y10/abc/dreamtime/dreamtime.htm (retrieved November 15, 2012)

Wiley, A. S. (2004). *An ecology of high-altitude infancy: A biocultural perspective.* Cambridge, UK: Cambridge University Press.

Wills, C. (1994). The skin we're in. *Discover 15* (11), 79.

Wolpoff, M., & Caspari, R. (1997). *Race and human evolution.* New York: Simon & Schuster.

Woodford, M. H., Butynski, T. M., & Karesh W. (2002). Habituating the great apes: The disease risks. *Oryx 36,* 153–160.

World Health Organization, Preamble to the Constitution. (1948). www.who.int/about/definition/en/print.html (retrieved November 15, 2012)

World Health Organization. (2012, June). Children: Reducing mortality. Fact sheet no. 178. www.who.int/mediacentre/factsheets/fs178/en/index.html (retrieved August 11, 2012)

Wu, X., & Poirier, F. E. (1995). *Human evolution in China.* New York: Oxford University Press.

Zeder, M. A., & Hesse, B. (2000). The initial domestication of goats (*Capra hircus*) in the Zagros Mountains 10,000 years ago. *Science 287,* 2254–2257.

Zeresenay, A., et al. (2006). A juvenile early hominin skeleton from Dikika, Ethiopia. *Nature 443,* 296–301.

Zilhão, J. (2000). Fate of the Neandertals. *Archaeology 53* (4), 30.

Zimmer, C. (2009, September 21). The secrets inside your dog's mind. *Time.com.* www.time.com/time/magazine/article/0,9171,1921614-1,00.html (retrieved July 16, 2012)

Bibliography

Adams, R. M. (2001). Scale and complexity in archaic states. *Latin American Antiquity 11*, 188.

Adler, S. (1959). Darwin's illness. *Nature*, 1102–1103.

Allen, J. S., & Cheer, S. M. (1996). The non-thrifty genotype. *Current Anthropology 37*, 831–842.

Alper, J. S., et al. (Eds.). (2002). *The double-edged helix: Social implications of genetics in a diverse society*. Baltimore: Johns Hopkins University Press.

Alvard, M. S., & Kuznar, L. (2001). Deferred harvest: The transition from hunting to animal husbandry. *American Anthropologist 103* (2), 295–311.

Amábile-Cuevas, C. F., & Chicurel, M. E. (1993). Horizontal gene transfer. *American Scientist 81*, 338.

Ambrose, S. H. (2001). Paleolithic technology and human evolution. *Science 291*, 1748–1753.

American Anthropological Association. (1998). Statement on "race." www.aaanet.org/stmts/racepp.htm (retrieved August 1, 2012)

American Anthropological Association. (2007). Executive board statement on the Human Terrain System Project. www.aaanet.org/about/policies/statements/human-terrain-system-statement.cfm (retrieved November 15, 2012)

Andrews, L. B., & Nelkin, D. (1996). The Bell Curve: A statement. *Science 271*, 13.

Appadurai, A. (1996). *Modernity at large: Cultural dimensions of globalization*. Minneapolis: University of Minnesota Press.

Appenzeller, T. (1998). Art: Evolution or revolution? *Science 282*, 1451–1454.

Arnold, F., Kishor, S., & Roy, T. K. (2002). Sex-selective abortions in India. *Population and Development Review 28* (4), 759–785.

Ashmore, W. (Ed.). (1981). *Lowland Maya settlement patterns*. Albuquerque: University of New Mexico Press.

Aureli, F., & de Waal, F. B. M. (2000). *Natural conflict resolution*. Berkeley: University of California Press.

Ayalon, D. (1999) *Eunuchs, caliphs, and sultans: A study in power relationships*. Jerusalem: Mangess Press.

Babiker, M. A., et al. (1996). Unnecessary deprivation of common food items in glucose-6-phosphate dehydrogenase deficiency. *Annals of Saudi Arabia 16* (4), 462–463.

Bailey, R. C., & Aunger, R. (1989). Net hunters vs. archers: Variations in women's subsistence strategies in the Ituri forest. *Human Ecology 17*, 273–297.

Baker, P. (Ed.). (1978). *The biology of high altitude peoples*. London: Cambridge University Press.

Balikci, A. (1970). *The Netsilik Eskimo*. Garden City, NY: Natural History Press.

Balter, M. (1998). Why settle down? The mystery of communities. *Science 282*, 1442–1444.

Balter, M. (1999). A long season puts Çatalhöyük in context. *Science 286*, 890–891.

Balter, M. (2001). Did plaster hold Neolithic society together? *Science 294*, 2278–2281.

Balter, M. (2001). In search of the first Europeans. *Science 291*, 1724.

Barham, L. S. (1998). Possible early pigment use in South-Central Africa. *Current Anthropology 39*, 703–710.

Barkai, R., & Liran, R. (2008). Midsummer sunset at Neolithic Jericho. *Time and Mind: The Journal of Archaeology, Consciousness, and Culture 1* (3), 273–284.

Barnard, A. (1995). Monboddo's *Orang Outang* and the definition of man. In R. Corbey & B. Theunissen (Eds.), *Ape, man, apeman: Changing views since 1600* (pp. 71–85). Leiden: Department of Prehistory, Leiden University.

Barr, R. G. (1997, October). The crying game. *Natural History*, 47.

Barrett, L., et al. (2004). Habitual cave use and thermoregulation in chacma baboons (*Papio hamadryas ursinus*). *Journal of Human Evolution 46* (2), 215–222.

Bar-Yosef, O. (1986). The walls of Jericho: An alternative interpretation. *Current Anthropology 27*, 160.

Bar-Yosef, O., Vandermeesch, B., Arensburg, B., Belfer-Cohen, A., Goldberg, P., Laville, H., Meignen, L., Rak, Y., Speth, J. D., Tchernov, E., Tillier, A-M., & Weiner, S. (1992). The excavations in Kebara Cave, Mt. Carmel. *Current Anthropology 33*, 497–550.

Bates, D. G. (2001). *Human adaptive strategies: Ecology, culture, and politics* (2nd ed.). Boston: Allen & Bacon.

Bednarik, R. G. (1995). Concept-mediated marking in the Lower Paleolithic. *Current Anthropology 36*, 606.

Behrensmeyer, A. K., Todd, N. E., Potts, R., & McBrinn, G. E. (1997). Late Pliocene faunal turnover in the Turkana basin, Kenya, and Ethiopia. *Science 278*, 1589–1594.

Bekoff, M., et al. (Eds.). (2002). *The cognitive animal: Empirical and theoretical perspectives on animal cognition*. Cambridge, MA: MIT Press.

Bennett, R. L., et al. (2002, April). Genetic counseling and screening of consanguineous couples and their offspring: Recommendations of the National Society of Genetic Counselors. *Journal of Genetic Counseling 11* (2), 97–119.

Berdan, F. F. (1982). *The Aztecs of Central Mexico*. New York: Holt, Rinehart & Winston.

Bermúdez de Castro, J. M., Arsuaga, J. L., Cabonell, E., Rosas, A., Martinez, I., & Mosquera, M. (1997). A hominid from the lower Pleistocene of Atapuerca, Spain: Possible ancestor to Neandertals and modern humans. *Science 276*, 1392–1395.

Bernal, I. (1969). *The Olmec world*. Berkeley: University of California Press.

Bernard, H. R. (2006). *Research methods in anthropology: Qualitative and quantitative approaches* (4th ed.). Walnut Creek, CA: AltaMira Press.

Bernstein, R. E., et al. (1984). Darwin's illness: Chagas' disease resurgens. *Journal of the Royal Society of Medicine 77*, 608–609.

Berra, T. M. (1990). *Evolution and the myth of creationism*. Stanford, CA: Stanford University Press.

Binford, L. R. (1972). *An archaeological perspective*. New York: Seminar Press.

Binford, L. R., & Chuan, K. H. (1985). Taphonomy at a distance: Zhoukoudian, the cave home of Beijing man? *Current Anthropology 26*, 413–442.

Birdsell, J. H. (1977). The recalibration of a paradigm for the first peopling of Greater Australia. In J. Allen, J. Golson, & R. Jones (Eds.), *Sunda and Sahul: Prehistoric studies in Southeast Asia, Melanesia, and Australia* (pp. 113–167). New York: Academic Press.

Blackless, M., et al. (2000). How sexually dimorphic are we? Review and synthesis. *American Journal of Human Biology 12*, 151–166.

Blakey, M. (2003, October 29). Personal communication. *African Burial Ground Project*. Department of Anthropology, College of William & Mary.

Blakey, M. (2010, May). African Burial Ground Project: Paradigm for cooperation? *Museum International 62* (1–2), 61–68.

Blom, A., et al. (2004). Behavioral responses of gorillas to habituation in the Dzanga-Ndoki National Park, Central African Republic. *International Journal of Primatology 25*, 179–196.

Blumer, M. A., & Byrne, R. (1991). The ecological genetics and domestication and the origins of agriculture. *Current Anthropology 32*, 30.

Boas, F. (1909, May 28). Race problems in America. *Science 29* (752), 839–849.

Boas, F. (1966). *Race, language and culture.* New York: Free Press.

Bodley, J. H. (2007). *Anthropology and contemporary human problems* (5th ed.). Lanham, MD: AltaMira Press.

Bodley, J. H. (2008). *Victims of progress* (5th ed.). Lanham, MD: AltaMira Press.

Bogucki, P. (1999). *The origins of human society.* Oxford, UK: Blackwell Press.

Bongaarts, J. (1998). Demographic consequences of declining fertility. *Science 182*, 419.

Bonvillain, N. (2007). *Language, culture, and communication: The meaning of messages* (5th ed.). Upper Saddle River, NJ: Prentice-Hall.

Bordes, F. (1972). *A tale of two caves.* New York: Harper & Row.

Bornstein, M. H. (1975). The influence of visual perception on culture. *American Anthropologist 77* (4), 774–798.

Brace, C. L. (1981). Tales of the phylogenetic woods: The evolution and significance of phylogenetic trees. *American Journal of Physical Anthropology 56*, 411–429.

Brace, C. L. (1997). Cro-Magnons "R" us? *Anthropology Newsletter 38* (8), 1.

Brace, C. L. (2000). *Evolution in an anthropological view.* Walnut Creek, CA: AltaMira Press.

Brace, C. L., Nelson, H., & Korn, N. (1979). *Atlas of human evolution* (2nd ed.). New York: Holt, Rinehart & Winston.

Bradford, P. V., & Blume, H. (1992). *Ota Benga: The Pygmy in the zoo.* New York: St. Martin's Press.

Braidwood, R. J. (1960). The agricultural revolution. *Scientific American 203*, 130–141.

Braidwood, R. J. (1975). *Prehistoric men* (8th ed.). Glenview, IL: Scott, Foresman.

Brain, C. K. (1968). Who killed the Swartkrans ape-men? *South African Museums Association Bulletin 9*, 127–139.

Brain, C. K. (1969). The contribution of Namib Desert Hottentots to an understanding of australopithecine bone accumulations. *Scientific Papers of the Namib Desert Research Station*, 13.

Branda, R. F., & Eatoil, J. W. (1978). Skin color and photolysis: An evolutionary hypothesis. *Science 201*, 625–626.

Brettell, C. B., & Sargent, C. F. (Eds.). (2000). *Gender in cross-cultural perspective* (3rd ed.). Upper Saddle River, NJ: Prentice-Hall.

Brody, H. (1997). *Maps and dreams.* Long Grove, IL: Waveland Press.

Broecker, W. S. (1992, April). Global warming on trial. *Natural History*, 14.

Brothwell, D. R., & Higgs, E. (Eds.). (1969). *Science in archaeology* (rev. ed.). London: Thames & Hudson.

Brown, B., Walker, A., Ward, C. V., & Leakey, R. E. (1993). New *Australopithecus boisei* calvaria from East Lake Turkana, Kenya. *American Journal of Physical Anthropology 91*, 137–159.

Brown, P., et al. (2004). A new small-bodied hominin from the Late Pleistocene of Flores, Indonesia. *Nature 431*, 1055–1061.

Brunet, M., et al. (2002). A new hominid from the Upper Miocene of Chad, Central Africa. *Nature 418*, 145–151.

Burling, R. (1993). Primate calls, human language, and nonverbal communication. *Current Anthropology 34*, 25–53.

Butynski, T. M. (2001). Africa's great apes. In B. Beck et al. (Eds.), *Great apes and humans: The ethics of co-existence* (pp. 3–56). Washington, DC: Smithsonian Institution Press.

Byers, D. S. (Ed.). (1967). *The prehistory of the Tehuacan Valley: Environment and subsistence* (vol. 1). Austin: University of Texas Press.

Cachel, S. (1997). Dietary shifts and the European Upper Paleolithic transition. *Current Anthropology 38*, 590.

Callaway, E. (2007, December 3). Chimp beats students at computer game. *Nature.* doi:10.1038/news.2007.317

Capps, R., McCabe, K., & Fix, M. (2012). *Diverse streams: Black African migration to the United States.* Washington, DC: Migration Policy Institute. www.migrationpolicy.org/pubs/CBI-AfricanMigration.pdf (retrieved September 30, 2012)

Carbonell, E., et al. (2008). The first hominin of Europe. *Nature 452* (7186), 465–469.

Cardarelli, F. (2003). *Encyclopedia of scientific units, weights, and measures. Their SI equivalences and origins.* London: Springer.

Carneiro, R. L. (1970). A theory of the origin of the state. *Science 169*, 733–738.

Carneiro, R. L. (2003). *Evolutionism in cultural anthropology: A critical history.* Boulder, CO: Westview Press.

Caroulis, J. (1996). Food for thought. *Pennsylvania Gazette 95* (3), 16.

Carroll, J. B. (Ed.). (1956). *Language, thought and reality: Selected writings of Benjamin Lee Whorf.* Cambridge, MA: MIT Press.

Carroll, S. B. (2005). *Endless forms most beautiful: The new science of evo devo.* New York: Norton.

Cartmill, E. A., & Byrne, R. W. (2010) Semantics of orangutan gesture: Determining structure and meaning through form and use. *Animal Cognition.* doi: 10.1007/s10071-010-0328-7

Cartmill, M. (1998). The gift of gab. *Discover 19* (11), 64.

Cashdan, E. (1989). Hunters and gatherers: Economic behavior in bands. In S. Plattner (Ed.), *Economic anthropology* (pp. 21–48). Stanford, CA: Stanford University Press.

Cashdan, E. (2008). Waist-to-hip ratio across cultures: Trade-offs between androgen- and estrogen-dependent traits. *Current Anthropology 49* (6).

Cavalieri, P., & Singer, P. (1994). *The Great Ape Project: Equality beyond humanity.* New York: St. Martin's Press.

Cavalli-Sforza, L. L. (1977). *Elements of human genetics.* Menlo Park, CA: W. A. Benjamin.

Centers for Disease Control and Prevention. (2009). Differences in prevalence of obesity among black, white, and Hispanic adults—United States, 2006–2008. *Morbidity and Mortality Weekly Report 58* (27), 740–744.

Chagnon, N. A. (1988). Life histories, blood revenge, and warfare in a tribal population. *Science 239*, 935–992.

Chagnon, N. A., & Irons, W. (Eds.). (1979). *Evolutionary biology and human social behavior.* North Scituate, MA: Duxbury Press.

Chan, J. W. C., & Vernon, P. E. (1988). Individual differences among the peoples of China. In J. W. Berry (Ed.), *Human abilities in cultural context* (pp. 340–357). Cambridge, UK: Cambridge University Press.

Chang, K. C. (Ed.). (1968). *Settlement archaeology.* Palo Alto, CA: National Press.

Cheney, D. L., & Seyfarth, R. M. (2007). *Baboon metaphysics: The evolution of a social mind.* Chicago: University of Chicago Press.

Chicurel, M. (2001). Can organisms speed their own evolution? *Science 292*, 1824–1827.

Childe, V. G. (1951). *Man makes himself.* New York: New American Library. (orig. 1936)

Childe, V. G. (1954). *What happened in history.* Baltimore: Penguin Books.

Ciochon, R. L., & Fleagle, J. G. (Eds.). (1987). *Primate evolution and human origins.* Hawthorne, NY: Aldine.

Ciochon, R. L., & Fleagle, J. G. (1993). *The human evolution source book.* Englewood Cliffs, NJ: Prentice-Hall.

Clark, E. E. (1966). *Indian legends of the Pacific Northwest.* Berkeley: University of California Press.

Clark, G. (1967). *The Stone Age hunters.* New York: McGraw-Hill.

Clark, G. (1972). *Starr Carr: A case study in bioarchaeology.* Reading, MA: Addison-Wesley.

Clark, G. A. (1997). Neandertal genetics. *Science 277*, 1024.

Clark, G. A. (2002). Neandertal archaeology: Implications for our origins. *American Anthropologist 104* (1), 50–67.

Clark, J. G. D. (1962). *Prehistoric Europe: The economic basis.* Stanford, CA: Stanford University Press.

Clark, W. E. L. (1960). *The antecedents of man.* Chicago: Quadrangle Books.

Clark, W. E. L. (1966). *History of the primates* (5th ed.). Chicago: University of Chicago Press.

Clark, W. E. L. (1967). *Man-apes or ape-men? The story of discoveries in Africa.* New York: Holt, Rinehart & Winston.

Clarke, R. J. (1998). First ever discovery of a well preserved skull and associated skeleton of *Australopithecus. South African Journal of Science 94*, 460–464.

Clarke, R. J., & Tobias, P. V. (1995). Sterkfontein member 2 foot bones of the oldest South African hominid. *Science 269*, 521–524.

Coe, S. D. (1994). *America's first cuisines.* Austin: University of Texas Press.

Coe, S. D., & Coe, M. D. (1996). *The true history of chocolate.* New York: Thames & Hudson.

Coe, W. R. (1967). *Tikal: A handbook of the ancient Maya ruins.* Philadelphia: University of Pennsylvania Museum.

Coe, W. R., & Haviland, W. A. (1982). *Introduction to the archaeology of Tikal.* Philadelphia: University Museum.

Cohen, J. (1997). Is an old virus up to new tricks? *Science 277*, 312–313.

Cohen, J. (2009). Out of Mexico? Scientists ponder swine flu's origin. *Science 324* (5928), 700–702.

Cohen, M. N. (1977). *The food crisis in prehistory.* New Haven, CT: Yale University Press.

Cohen, M. N. (1995). Anthropology and race: The *Bell Curve* curve phenomenon. *General Anthropology 2* (1), 1–4.

Cohen, M. N. (1998). *Culture of intolerance: Chauvinism, class, and racism in the United States.* New Haven, CT: Yale University Press.

Cohen, M. N., & Armelagos, G. J. (1984). *Paleopathology at the origins of agriculture.* Orlando: Academic Press.

Cohen, M. N., & Armelagos, G. J. (1984). Paleopathology at the origins of agriculture: Editors' summation. In *Paleopathology at the origins of agriculture.* Orlando: Academic Press.

Colborn, T., Dumanoski, D., & Myers, J. P. (1996). Hormonal sabotage. *Natural History 3*, 45–46.

Colborn, T., Dumanoski, D., & Myers, J. P. (1997). *Our stolen future.* New York: Plume/Penguin Books.

Collins, B. (2005). *The trouble with poetry.* New York: Random House.

Conard, N. J. (2009). A female figurine from the basal Aurignacian deposits of Hohle Fels Cave in southwest Germany. *Nature 459* (7244), 248.

Conklin, H. C. (1955). Hanunóo color categories. *Southwestern Journal of Anthropology 11*, 339–344.

Conner, M. (1996). The archaeology of contemporary mass graves. *SAA Bulletin 14* (4), 6, 31.

Conroy, G. C. (1997). *Reconstructing human origins: A modern synthesis.* New York: Norton.

Coon, C. S. (1962). *The origins of races.* New York: Knopf.

Coon, C. S., Garn, S. N., & Birdsell, J. (1950). *Races: A study of the problems of race formation in man.* Springfield, IL: Thomas.

Cooper, A., Poinar, H. N., Pääbo, S., Radovci, C. J., Debénath, A., Caparros, M., Barroso-Ruiz, C., Bertranpetit, J., Nielsen-March, C., Hedges, R. E. M., & Sykes, B. (1997). Neanderthal genetics. *Science 277*, 1021–1024.

Copeland, S. R., et al. (2011, June 2). Strontium isotope evidence for landscape use by early hominins. *Nature 474*, 76–78. doi: 10.1038/nature10149

Coppa, A., et al. (2006). Early Neolithic tradition of dentistry. *Nature 440*, 755–756.

Coppens, Y., Howell, F. C., Isaac, G. L., & Leakey, R. E. F. (Eds.). (1976). *Earliest man and environments in the Lake Rudolf Basin: Stratigraphy, paleoecology, and evolution.* Chicago: University of Chicago Press.

Corbey, R. (1995). Introduction: Missing links, or the ape's place in nature. In R. Corbey & B. Theunissen (Eds.), *Ape,*

man, apeman: Changing views since 1600 (p. 1). Leiden: Department of Prehistory, Leiden University.

Cornwell, T. (1995, November 10). Skeleton staff. *Times Higher Education,* 20.

Corruccini, R. S. (1992). Metrical reconsideration of the Skhul IV and IX and Border Cave I crania in the context of modern human origins. *American Journal of Physical Anthropology 87*, 433–445.

Cottrell, L. (1963). *The lost pharaohs.* New York: Grosset & Dunlap.

Cowgill, G. L. (1997). State and society at Teotihuacan, Mexico. *Annual Review of Anthropology 26*, 129–161.

Crystal, D. (2002). *Language death.* Cambridge, UK: Cambridge University Press.

Culbert, T. P. (Ed.). (1973). *The Classic Maya collapse.* Albuquerque: University of New Mexico Press.

Culotta, E. (1995). New hominid crowds the field. *Science 269*, 918.

Culotta, E., & Koshland, D. E., Jr. (1994). DNA repair works its way to the top. *Science 266*, 1926.

D'Adesky, A.-C. (2004). *Moving mountains: the race to treat global AIDS.* New York: Verso.

Dalton, R. (2009). Fossil primate challenges Ida's place: Controversial German specimen is related to lemurs, not humans, analysis of an Egyptian find suggests. *Nature 461*, 1040.

Daniel, G. (1970). *The first civilizations: The archaeology of their origins.* New York: Apollo Editions.

Daniel, G. (1975). *A hundred and fifty years of archaeology* (2nd ed.). London: Duckworth.

Darwin, C. (1859). *On the origin of species.* New York: Atheneum.

Darwin, C. (1871). *The descent of man and selection in relation to sex.* New York: Random House (Modern Library).

Darwin, C. (1887). *Autobiography.* Reprinted in *The life and letters of Charles Darwin* (1902). F. Darwin (Ed.), London: John Murray.

Davenport, W. (1959). Linear descent and descent groups. *American Anthropologist 61*, 557–573.

Deetz, J. (1967). *Invitation to archaeology.* New York: Doubleday.

Deetz, J. (1977). *In small things forgotten: The archaeology of early American life.* Garden City, NY: Doubleday/Anchor.

de la Torre, S., & Snowden, C. T. (2009). Dialects in pygmy marmosets? Population variation in call structure. *American Journal of Primatology 71* (5), 333–342

del Carmen Rodríguez Martínez, M., et al. (2006). Oldest writing in the New World. *Science 313* (5793), 1610–1614.

del Castillo, B. D. (1963). *The conquest of New Spain* (translation and introduction by J. M. Cohen). New York: Penguin Books.

d'Errico, F., Zilhão, J., Julien, M., Baffier, D., & Pelegrin, J. (1998). Neandertal acculturation in Western Europe? *Current Anthropology 39*, 521.

DeSilva, J. M. (2009). Functional morphology of the ankle and the likelihood of climbing in early hominins. *Proceedings of the National Academy of Sciences USA 106*, 6567–6572.

Desowitz, R. S. (1987). *New Guinea tapeworm and Jewish grandmothers.* New York: Norton.

Dettwyler, K. A. (1994). *Dancing skeletons: Life and death in West Africa.* Prospect Heights, IL: Waveland Press.

Dettwyler, K. A. (1997, October). When to wean. *Natural History,* 49.

DeVore, I. (Ed.). (1965). *Primate behavior: Field studies of monkeys and apes.* New York: Holt, Rinehart & Winston.

de Waal, F. B. M. (1996). *Good natured: The origins of right and wrong in humans and other animals.* Cambridge, MA: Harvard University Press.

de Waal, F. B. M. (2000). Primates—A natural heritage of conflict resolution. *Science 28*, 586–590.

de Waal, F. B. M. (2001). *The ape and the sushi master.* New York: Basic Books.

de Waal, F. B. M. (2001). Sing the song of evolution. *Natural History 110* (8), 77.

de Waal, F. B. M. (2003). *My family album: Thirty years of primate photography.* Berkeley: University of California Press.

de Waal, F. B. M., & Johanowicz, D. L. (1993). Modification of reconciliation behavior through social experience: An experiment with two macaque species. *Child Development 64*, 897–908.

de Waal, F. B. M., Kano, T., & Parish, A. R. (1998). Comments. *Current Anthropology 39*, 408, 413.

de Waal, F. B. M., & Lanting, F. (1998). *Bonobo: The forgotten ape.* Berkeley: University of California Press.

Diamond, J. (1994). How Africa became black. *Discover 15* (2), 72–81.

Diamond, J. (1994). Race without color. *Discover 15* (11), 83–89.

Diamond, J. (1996). Empire of uniformity. *Discover 17* (3), 83–84.

Diamond, J. (1997). *Guns, germs, and steel.* New York: Norton.

Diamond, J. (1998). Ants, crops, and history. *Science 281*, 1974–1975.

Diamond, J. (2005). *Collapse: How societies choose to fail or succeed.* New York: Viking/Penguin Books.

Dixon, J. E., Cann, J. R., & Renfrew, C. (1968). Obsidian and the origins of trade. *Scientific American 218*, 38–46.

Dobzhansky, T. (1962). *Mankind evolving.* New Haven, CT: Yale University Press.

Dorit, R. (1997). Molecular evolution and scientific inquiry, misperceived. *American Scientist 85*, 475.

Draper, P. (1975). !Kung women: Contrasts in sexual egalitarianism in foraging and sedentary contexts. In R. Reiter (Ed.), *Toward an anthropology of women* (pp. 77–109). New York: Monthly Review Press.

Dubos, R. (1968). *So human an animal.* New York: Scribner.

Durant, J. C. (2000, April 23). Everybody into the gene pool. *New York Times Book Review,* 11.

Duranti, A. (2001). Linguistic anthropology: History, ideas, and issues. In A. Duranti (Ed.), *Linguistic anthropology: A reader* (pp. 1–38). Oxford: Blackwell Press.

Eaton, S. B., Konner, M., & Shostak, M. (1988). Stone-agers in the fast lane: Chronic degenerative diseases in evolutionary perspective. *American Journal of Medicine 84* (4), 739–749.

Edey, M. A., & Johannson, D. (1989). *Blueprints: Solving the mystery of evolution.* Boston: Little, Brown.

Edwards, J. (Ed.). (1999). *Technologies of procreation: Kinship in the age of assisted conception.* New York: Routledge.

Edwards, S. W. (1978). Nonutilitarian activities on the Lower Paleolithic: A look at the two kinds of evidence. *Current Anthropology 19* (1), 135–137.

Ehrlich, P. R., & Ehrlich, A. H. (2008). *The dominant animal: Human evolution and the environment.* Washington, DC: Island Press.

Eiseley, L. (1958). *Darwin's century: Evolution and the men who discovered it.* New York: Doubleday.

Elkin, A. P. (1964). *The Australian Aborigines.* Garden City, NY: Doubleday/Anchor.

Ellison, P. T. (2003). *On fertile ground: A natural history of human reproduction.* Cambridge, MA: Harvard University Press.

Enard, W., et al. (2002). Molecular evolution of FOXP2, a gene involved in speech and language. *Nature 418,* 869–872.

Erickson, C. L. (2001). Pre-Columbian fish farming in the Amazon. *Expedition 43* (3), 7–8.

Evans, W. (1968). *Communication in the animal world.* New York: Crowell.

Fagan, B. (2001). *The seventy great mysteries of the ancient world.* New York: Thames & Hudson.

Fagan, B. M. (1995). *People of the earth* (8th ed.). New York: HarperCollins.

Fagan, B. M. (1995). The quest for the past. In L. L. Hasten (Ed.), *Annual editions 95/96: Archaeology* (p. 10). Guilford, CT: Dushkin.

Fagan, B. M. (1999). *Archaeology: A brief introduction* (7th ed.). New York: Longman.

Fagan, B. M. (2000). *Ancient lives: An introduction to archaeology.* Englewood Cliffs, NJ: Prentice-Hall.

Fagan, B. M., Beck, C., & Silberman, N. A. (1998). *The Oxford companion to archaeology.* New York: Oxford University Press.

Falk, D. (1975). Comparative anatomy of the larynx in man and the chimpanzee: Implications for language in Neanderthal. *American Journal of Physical Anthropology 43* (1), 123–132.

Falk, D. (1989). Ape-like endocast of "Ape Man Taung." *American Journal of Physical Anthropology 80,* 335–339.

Falk, D. (1993). A good brain is hard to cool. *Natural History 102* (8), 65.

Falk, D. (1993). Hominid paleoneurology. In R. L. Ciochon & J. G. Fleagle (Eds.), *The human evolution source book.* Englewood Cliffs, NJ: Prentice-Hall.

Falk, D. (2004). *Braindance: New discoveries about human origins and brain evolution* (revised and updated). Gainesville: University Press of Florida.

Falk, D., et al. (2005). The brain of LB1, *Homo floresiensis. Science 308,* 242–245.

Farmer, P. (1992). *AIDS and accusation: Haiti and the geography of blame.* Berkeley: University of California Press.

Farmer, P. (1996). On suffering and structural violence: A view from below. *Daedalus 125* (1), 261–283.

Farmer, P. (2001). *Infections and inequalities: The modern plagues.* Berkeley: University of California Press.

Farmer, P. (2003). *Pathologies of power: Health, human rights, and the new war on the poor.* Berkeley: University of California Press.

Farmer, P. (2004, June). An anthropology of structural violence. *Current Anthropology 45,* 3.

Fausto-Sterling, A. (1993, March/April). The five sexes: Why male and female are not enough. *The Sciences 33* (2), 20–24.

Fausto-Sterling, A. (2000, July/August). The five sexes revisited. *The Sciences 40* (4), 19–24.

Fausto-Sterling, A., et al. (2000). How sexually dimorphic are we? Review and synthesis. *American Journal of Human Biology 12,* 151–166.

Feder, K. L. (2008). *Frauds, myths, and mysteries: Science and pseudoscience in archaeology* (6th ed.). New York: McGraw-Hill.

Fedigan, L. M. (1986). The changing role of women in models of human evolution. *Annual Review of Anthropology 15,* 25–56.

Fedigan, L. M. (1992). *Primate paradigms: Sex roles and social bonds.* Chicago: University of Chicago Press.

Fernandez-Carriba, S., & Loeches, A. (2001). Fruit smearing by captive chimpanzees: A newly observed food-processing behavior. *Current Anthropology 42,* 143–147.

Ferrie, H. (1997). An interview with C. Loring Brace. *Current Anthropology 38,* 851–869.

Finkler, K. (2000). *Experiencing the new genetics: Family and kinship on the medical frontier.* Philadelphia: University of Pennsylvania Press.

Flannery, K. V. (1973). The origins of agriculture. In B. J. Siegel, A. R. Beals, & S. A. Tyler (Eds.), *Annual review of anthropology* (vol. 2, pp. 271–310). Palo Alto, CA: Annual Reviews.

Flannery, K. V. (Ed.). (1976). *The Mesoamerican village.* New York: Seminar Press.

Fleagle, J. (1998). *Primate adaptation and evolution.* New York: Academic Press.

Food and Agriculture Organization of the United Nations. (2009, June 19). 1.02 billion people hungry: One sixth of humanity undernourished—more than ever before. www.fao.org/news/story/en/item/20568/icode/ (retrieved October 3, 2012)

Forbes, J. D. (1964). *The Indian in America's past.* Englewood Cliffs, NJ: Prentice-Hall.

Ford, A. The BRASS/El Pilar Program. www.marc.ucsb.edu/elpilar/ (retrieved November 15, 2012)

Fossey, D. (1983). *Gorillas in the mist.* Burlington, MA: Houghton Mifflin.

Fouts, R. S., & Waters, G. (2001). Chimpanzee sign language and Darwinian continuity: Evidence for a neurology continuity of language. *Neurological Research 23,* 787–794.

Fowke, K. R., Nagelkerke, N. J., Kimani, J., Simonsen, J. N., Anzala, A. O., Bwayo, J. J., MacDonald, K. S.,

Ngugi, E. N., & Plummer, F. A. (1996). Resistance to HIV-1 infection among persistently seronegative prostitutes in Nairobi, Kenya. *Lancet 348* (9038), 1347–1351.

Frake, C. (1961). The diagnosis of disease among the Subanun of Mindinao. *American Anthropologist 63,* 113–132.

Frake, C. O. (1992). Lessons of the Mayan sky. In A. F. Aveni (Ed.), *The sky in Mayan literature* (pp. 274–291). New York: Oxford University Press.

Frankfort, H. (1968). *The birth of civilization in the Near East.* New York: Barnes & Noble.

Franzen, J. L., et al. (2009). Complete primate skeleton from the middle Eocene of Messel in Germany: Morphology and paleobiology. *PLoS One 4* (5), e5723.

Frayer, D. W. (1981). Body size, weapon use, and natural selection in the European Upper Paleolithic and Mesolithic. *American Anthropologist 83,* 57–73.

Freeman, L. G. (1992). *Ambrona and Torralba: New evidence and interpretation.* Paper presented at the 91st Annual Meeting, American Anthropological Association.

Frisch, R. (2002). *Female fertility and the body fat connection,* Chicago: University of Chicago Press.

Frye, D. P. (2000). Conflict management in cross-cultural perspective. In F. Aureli & F. B. M. de Waal, *Natural conflict resolution* (pp. 334–351). Berkeley: University of California Press.

Galdikas, B. (1995). *Reflections on Eden: My years with the orangutans of Borneo.* New York: Little, Brown.

Gamble, C. (1986). *The Paleolithic settlement of Europe.* Cambridge, UK: Cambridge University Press.

Garn, S. M. (1970). *Human races* (3rd ed.). Springfield, IL: Thomas.

Gebo, D. L., Dagosto, D., Beard, K. C., & Tao, Q. (2001). Middle Eocene primate tarsals from China: Implications for haplorhine evolution. *American Journal of Physical Anthropology 116,* 83–107.

"Gene study suggests Polynesians came from Taiwan." (2005, July 4). Reuters. www.freerepublic.com/focus/f-news/1436791/posts (retrieved November 15, 2012)

Gero, J. M., & Conkey, M. W. (Eds.). (1991). *Engendered archaeology: Women and prehistory.* New York: Wiley-Blackwell.

Gettleman, J. (2011, July 9). South Sudan, the newest nation, is full of hope and problems. *New York Times.* www.post-gazette.com/pg/11190/1159402-82-0.stm (retrieved August 22, 2011)

Gibbons, A. (1993). Where are new diseases born? *Science 261,* 680–681.

Gibbons, A. (1997). Ideas on human origins evolve at anthropology gathering. *Science 276,* 535–536.

Gibbons, A. (1998). Ancient island tools suggest *Homo erectus* was a seafarer. *Science 279,* 1635.

Gibbons, A. (2001). The riddle of coexistence. *Science 291,* 1726.

Gibbons, A. (2001). Studying humans—and their cousins and parasites. *Science 292,* 627.

Gierstorfer, C. (2007). Peaceful primates, violent acts. *Nature 447,* 7.

Ginsburg, F. D., Abu-Lughod, L., & Larkin, B. (Eds.). (2009). *Media worlds: Anthropology on new terrain.* Berkeley: University of California Press.

Goldsmith, M. L. (2005). Habituating primates for field study: Ethical considerations for great apes. In T. Turner (Ed.), *Biological anthropology and ethics: From repatriation to genetic identity* (pp.49–64). New York: SUNY Press.

Goldsmith, M. L., Glick, J., & Ngabirano, E. (2006). Gorillas living on the edge: Literally and figuratively. In N. E. Newton-Fisher, et al. (Eds.), *Primates of western Uganda* (pp. 405–422). New York: Springer.

Goodall, J. (1986). *The chimpanzees of Gombe: Patterns of behavior.* Cambridge, MA: Belknap Press.

Goodall, J. (1990). *Through a window: My thirty years with the chimpanzees of Gombe.* Boston: Houghton Mifflin.

Goodall, J. (2000). *Reason for hope: A spiritual journey.* New York: Warner Books.

Goodman, A., & Armelagos, G. J. (1985). Death and disease at Dr. Dickson's mounds. *Natural History 94* (9), 12–18.

Goodman, M., et al. (1994). Molecular evidence on primate phylogeny from DNA sequences. *American Journal of Physical Anthropology 94,* 7.

Gould, S. J. (1983). *Hen's teeth and horses' toes.* New York: Norton.

Gould, S. J. (1989). *Wonderful life.* New York: Norton.

Gould, S. J. (1991). *Bully for brontosaurus.* New York: Norton.

Gould, S. J. (1991). *The flamingo's smile: Reflections in natural history.* New York: Norton.

Gould, S. J. (1994). The geometer of race. *Discover 15* (11), 65–69.

Gould, S. J. (1996). *Full house: The spread of excellence from Plato to Darwin.* New York: Harmony Books.

Gould, S. J. (1996). *The mismeasure of man* (2nd ed.). New York: Norton.

Gould, S. J. (1997). *Questioning the millennium.* New York: Crown.

Gould, S. J. (2000). The narthex of San Marco and the pangenetic paradigm. *Natural History 109* (6), 29.

Gould, S. J. (2000). What does the dreaded "E" word mean anyway? *Natural History 109* (1), 34–36.

Graves, J. L. (2001). *The emperor's new clothes: Biological theories of race at the millennium.* New Brunswick, NJ: Rutgers University Press.

Green, R. E., et al. (2010, May 7). A draft sequence of the Neandertal genome. *Science 328* (5979), 710–722.

Griffin, D., & Fitzpatrick, D. (2009, September 1). Donor says he got thousands for his kidney. *CNNWorld.com.* http://articles.cnn.com/2009-09-01/world/blackmarket.organs_1_kidney-transplants-kidney-donor-kidney-specialist?_s=PM:WORLD (retrieved June 10, 2012)

Grine, F. E. (1993). Australopithecine taxonomy and phylogeny: Historical background and recent interpretation. In R. L. Ciochon & J. G. Fleagle (Eds.), *The human evolution source book.* Englewood Cliffs, NJ: Prentice-Hall.

Grün, R., & Thorne, A. (1997). Dating the Ngandong humans. *Science 276,* 1575.

Guillette, E. A., et al. (1998, June). An anthropological approach to the evaluation of preschool children exposed to pesticides in Mexico. *Environmental Health Perspectives 106,* 347.

Gutin, J. A. (1995). Do Kenya tools root birth of modern thought in Africa? *Science 270,* 1118–1119.

Hager, L. (1989). *The evolution of sex differences in the hominid bony pelvis.* PhD dissertation. University of California, Berkeley.

Haglund, W. D., Conner, M., & Scott, D. D. (2001). The archaeology of contemporary mass graves. *Historical Archaeology 35* (1), 57–69.

Hahn, R. A. (1992). The state of federal health statistics on racial and ethnic groups. *Journal of the American Medical Association 267* (2), 268–271.

Hale, C. (2004). *Himmler's crusade: The true story of the 1938 Nazi expedition into Tibet.* New York: Bantam.

Halverson, J. (1980). Review of the book *Altamira revisited and other essays on early art. American Antiquity 54,* 883.

Hamblin, D. J., & the Editors of Time-Life. (1973). *The first cities.* New York: Time-Life.

Hamburg, D. A., & McGown, E. R. (Eds.). (1979). *The great apes.* Menlo Park, CA: Cummings.

Handwerk, B. (2005, March 8). King Tut not murdered violently, CT scans show. *National Geographic News,* 2.

Harcourt-Smith, W. E. H., & Aiello, L. C. (2004). Fossils, feet and the evolution of human bipedal locomotion. *Journal of Anatomy 204,* 403–416.

Hare, B., Brown, M., Williamson, C., & Tomasello, M. (2002). The domestication of social cognition in dogs. *Science 298* (5598). 1634–1636.

Harlow, H. F. (1962). Social deprivation in monkeys. *Scientific American 206,* 1–10.

Harpending, H., & Cochran, G. (2002). In our genes. *Proceedings of the National Academy of Sciences USA 99* (1), 10–12.

Harpending, J. H., & Harpending, H. C. (1995). Ancient differences in population can mimic a recent African origin of modern humans. *Current Anthropology 36,* 667–674.

Harrison, G. G. (1975). Primary adult lactase deficiency: A problem in anthropological genetics. *American Anthropologist 77,* 815–819.

Hart, D. (2006, April 21). Humans as prey. *Chronicle of Higher Education.*

Hart, D., & Sussman, R. W. (2005). *Man the hunted: Primates, predators, and human evolution.* Boulder, CO: Westview Press.

Hartwig, W. C. (2002). *The primate fossil record.* New York: Cambridge University Press.

Hartwig, W. C., & Doneski, K. (1998). Evolution of the hominid hand and toolmaking behavior. *American Journal of Physical Anthropology 106,* 401–402.

Hasnain, M. (2005, October 27). Cultural approach to HIV/AIDS harm reduction in Muslim countries. *Harm Reduction Journal 2,* 23.

Haviland, W. (1967). Stature at Tikal, Guatemala: Implications for ancient Maya, demography, and social organization. *American Antiquity 32,* 316–325.

Haviland, W. (1970). Tikal, Guatemala and Mesoamerican urbanism. *World Archaeology 2,* 186–198.

Haviland, W. A. (1972). A new look at Classic Maya social organization at Tikal. *Ceramica de Cultura Maya 8,* 1–16.

Haviland, W. A. (1975). The ancient Maya and the evolution of urban society. *University of Northern Colorado Museum of Anthropology,* Miscellaneous Series, 37.

Haviland, W. A. (1997). The rise and fall of sexual inequality: Death and gender at Tikal, Guatemala. *Ancient Mesoamerica 8,* 1–12.

Haviland, W. A. (2002). Settlement, society and demography at Tikal. In J. Sabloff (Ed.), *Tikal.* Santa Fe: School of American Research.

Haviland, W. A. (2003). *Tikal, Guatemala: A Maya way to urbanism.* Paper prepared for Third INAH/Penn State Conference on Mesoamerican Urbanism.

Haviland, W. A., & Moholy-Nagy, H. (1992). Distinguishing the high and mighty from the hoi polloi at Tikal, Guatemala. In A. F. Chase & D. Z. Chase (Eds.), *Mesoamerican elites: An archaeological assessment.* Norman: Oklahoma University Press.

Haviland, W. A., et al. (1985). *Excavations in small residential groups of Tikal: Groups 4F-1 and 4F-2.* Philadelphia: University Museum.

Hawkes, K., O'Connell, J. F., & Blurton Jones, N. G. (1997). Hadza women's time allocation, offspring, provisioning, and the evolution of long postmenopausal life spans. *Current Anthropology 38,* 551–577.

Hawks, J. (2009). Ankles of the Australopithecines. *John Hawks Weblog.* http://johnhawks.net/weblog/reviews/early_hominids/anatomy/desilva-2009-chimpanzee-climbing-talus.html (retrieved July 5, 2012).

Heita, K. (1999). Imanishi's world view. *Journal of Japanese Trade and Industry 18* (2), 15.

Helm, J. (1962). The ecological approach in anthropology. *American Journal of Sociology 67,* 630–649.

Helman, C. B. (2007). *Culture, health, and illness: An introduction for health professionals* (5th ed.). New York: Trans-Atlantic Publications.

Henry, D. O., et al. (2004). Human behavioral organization in the Middle Paleolithic: Were Neandertals different? *American Anthropologist 107* (1), 17–31.

Henshilwood, C. S., d'Errico, F., van Niekerk, K. L., Coquinot, Y., Jacobs, Z., Lauritzen, S.-E., Menu, M., & Garcia-Moreno. R. (2011). A 100,000-year-old ochre-processing workshop at Blombos Cave, South Africa. *Science 334* (6053), 219. doi:10.1126/science.1211535

Hewes, G. W. (1973). Primate communication and the gestural origin of language. *Current Anthropology 14,* 5–24

Higham, T., et al. (2012). Testing models for the beginnings of the Aurignacian and the advent of figurative art and music: The radiocarbon chronology of Geißenklösterle. *Journal of Human Evolution 62* (6), 664–676.

Himmelfarb, E. J. (2000, January/ February). First alphabet found in Egypt. Newsbrief. *Archaeology 53* (1).

Hobaiter, C., & Byrne, R. W. (2011, July). The gestural repertoire of the wild chimpanzee. *Animal Cognition 14* (4).

Holden, C. (1999). Ancient child burial uncovered in Portugal. *Science 283,* 169.

Hole, F. (1966). Investigating the origins of Mesopotamian civilization. *Science 153,* 605–611.

Hole, F., & Heizer, R. F. (1969). *An introduction to prehistoric archeology.* New York: Holt, Rinehart & Winston.

Holloway, R. L. (1980). The O. H. 7 (Olduvai Gorge, Tanzania) hominid partial brain endocast revisited. *American Journal of Physical Anthropology 53,* 267–274.

Holloway, R. L. (1981). The Indonesian *Homo erectus* brain endocast revisited. *American Journal of Physical Anthropology 55,* 503–521.

Holloway, R. L. (1981). Volumetric and asymmetry determinations on recent hominid endocasts: Spy I and II, Djebel Jhroud 1, and the Salb *Homo erectus* specimens, with some notes on Neanderthal brain size. *American Journal of Physical Anthropology 55,* 385–393.

Holloway, R. L., & de LaCoste-Lareymondie, M. C. (1982). Brain endocast asymmetry in pongids and hominids: Some preliminary findings on the paleontology of cerebral dominance. *American Journal of Physical Anthropology 58,* 101–110.

Hopkin, M. (2007, February 22). Chimps make spears to catch dinner. *Nature.* doi:10.1038/news070219–11

Houle, A. (1999). The origin of platyrrhines: An evaluation of the Antarctic scenario and the floating island model. *American Journal of Physical Anthropology 109,* 554–556.

Howell, F. C. (1970). *Early man.* New York: Time-Life.

Hrdy, S. B. (1999). Body fat and birth control. *Natural History 108* (8), 88.

Hymes, D. (1964). *Language in culture and society: A reader in linguistics and anthropology.* New York: Harper & Row.

Hymes, D. (Ed.). (1972). *Reinventing anthropology.* New York: Pantheon.

Hymes, D. (1974). *Foundations in sociolinguistics: An ethnographic approach.* Philadelphia: University of Pennsylvania Press.

Inda, J. X., & Rosaldo, R. (Eds). (2001). *The anthropology of globalization: A reader.* Malden, MA, and Oxford, UK: Blackwell Press.

Ingmanson, E. J. (1998). Comment. *Current Anthropology 39,* 409.

Inkeles, A., & Levinson, D. J. (1954). National character: The study of modal personality and socio-cultural systems. In G. Lindzey (Ed.), *Handbook of social psychology.* Reading, MA: Addison-Wesley.

Inoue, S., & Matsuzawa, T. (2007). Working memory of numerals in chimpanzees. *Current Biology 17,* 23, 1004–1005.

"Italy-German verbal war hots up." (2003, July 9). Reuters. *Deccan Herald.* http://archive.deccanherald.com/ deccanherald/july09/f4.asp (retrieved July 31, 2012)

Jacoby, R., & Glauberman, N. (Eds.). (1995). *The Bell Curve debate.* New York: Random House.

Jane Goodall Institute. www.janegoodall .org/janes-story (retrieved June 15, 2012)

Jennings, F. (1976). *The invasion of America.* New York: Norton.

Jennings, J. D. (1974). *Prehistory of North America* (2nd ed.). New York: McGraw-Hill.

Johanson, D., & Shreeve, J. (1989). *Lucy's child: The discovery of a human ancestor.* New York: Avon.

Johanson, D. C., & Edey, M. (1981). *Lucy, the beginnings of humankind.* New York: Simon & Schuster.

Johanson, D. C., Edgar, B., & Brill, D. (1996). *From Lucy to language.* New York: Simon & Schuster.

Johanson, D. C., & White, T. D. (1979). A systematic assessment of early African hominids. *Science 203,* 321–330.

Johanson, D. C., & Wong, K. (2009). *Lucy's legacy: The quest for human origins.* New York: Harmony.

John, V. (1971). Whose is the failure? In C. L. Brace, G. R. Gamble, & J. T. Bond (Eds.), *Race and intelligence.* Washington, DC: American Anthropological Association.

Jolly, A. (1985). *The evolution of primate behavior* (2nd ed.). New York: Macmillan.

Jolly, A. (1991). Thinking like a vervet. *Science 251,* 574.

Jolly, C. J. (1970). The seed eaters: A new model of hominid differentiation based on a baboon analogy. *Man 5,* 5–26.

Jolly, C. J., & Plog, F. (1986). *Physical anthropology and archaeology* (4th ed.). New York: Knopf.

Jones, S. (2005). Transhumance re-examined. *Journal of the Royal Anthropological Institute 11* (4), 841–842.

Jones, S., Martin, R., & Pilbeam, D. (1992). *Cambridge encyclopedia of human evolution.* New York: Cambridge University Press.

Joukowsky, M. A. (1980). *A complete field manual of archeology: Tools and techniques of fieldwork for archaeologists.* Englewood Cliffs, NJ: Prentice-Hall.

Joyce, C. (1991). *Witnesses from the grave: The stories bones tell.* Boston: Little, Brown.

Kaiser, J. (1994). A new theory of insect wing origins takes off. *Science 266,* 363.

Kaiser, J. (2011, May 4). 10 billion plus: Why world population projections were too low. *Science Insider.* http://news.sci encemag.org/scienceinsider/2011/05/10-billion-plus-why-world-population.html (retrieved October 1, 2012)

Kaplan, D. (2000). The darker side of the original affluent society. *Journal of Anthropological Research 53* (3), 301–324.

Kaplan, M. (2007, May 31). Upright orangutans point way to walking. *Nature.* doi:10.1038/news070528–8

Kaplan, M. (2008, August 5). Almost half of primate species face extinction. *Nature.* doi:10.1038/news.2008.1013 (retrieved June 23, 2012)

Karavanić, I., & Smith, F. H. (2000). More on the Neanderthal problem: The Vindija case. *Current Anthropology 41,* 839.

Kaw, E. (1993). Medicalization of racial features: Asian American women and cosmetic surgery. *Medical Anthropology Quarterly 7* (1), 74–89.

Kay, R. F., Fleagle, J. G., & Simons, E. L. (1981). A revision of the Oligocene apes of the Fayum Province, Egypt. *American Journal of Physical Anthropology 55,* 293–322.

Kay, R. F., Ross, C., & Williams, B. A. (1997). Anthropoid origins. *Science 275,* 797–804.

Kedia, S., & Van Willigen, J. (2005). *Applied anthropology: Domains of application.* New York: Praeger.

Keen, B. (1971). *The Aztec image in western thought.* New Brunswick, NJ: Rutgers University Press.

Kelly, R. L., & Thomas, D. H. (2012). *Archaeology* (6th ed.). Belmont, CA. Wadsworth.

Kenyon, K. (1957). *Digging up Jericho.* London: Ben.

Kibii, J. M., et al. (2011, September 9). A partial pelvis of *Australopithecus sebida. Science 333* (6048), 1407–1411.

King, J. (2010, July 28). Reducing the crack and powder cocaine sentencing disparity should also reduce racial disparities in sentences and prisons. *NACDL news release.* www.nacdl.org/ newsreleases.aspx?id=19533 (retrieved August 2, 2012)

Kirkpatrick, R. C. (2000). The evolution of human homosexual behavior. *Current Anthropology 41,* 384.

Kitchen, A., Miyamoto, M. M., & Mulligan, C. J. (2008). A three-stage colonization model for the peopling of the Americas. *PLoS One 3* (2), e1596. doi:10.1371/journal.pone.0001596

Kleinman, A. (1976). Concepts and a model for the comparison of medical systems as cultural systems. *Social Science and Medicine 12* (2B), 85–95.

Knauft, B. (1991). Violence and sociality in human evolution. *Current Anthropology 32,* 391–409.

Knight, C., Studdert-Kennedy, M., & Hurford, J. (Eds.). (2000). *The evolutionary emergence of language: Social function and the origins of linguistic form.* Cambridge, UK: Cambridge University Press.

Komai, T., & Fukuoka, G. (1934, October). Post-natal growth disparity in monozygotic twins. *Journal of Heredity 25,* 423–430.

Konner, M., & Worthman, C. (1980). Nursing frequency, gonadal function, and birth spacing among !Kung hunter-gatherers. *Science 207,* 788–791.

Koufos, G. (1993). Mandible of *Ouranopithecus macedoniensis* (hominidae: primates) from a new late Miocene locality in Macedonia (Greece). *American Journal of Physical Anthropology 91,* 225–234.

Krader, L. (1968). *Formation of the state.* Englewood Cliffs, NJ: Prentice-Hall.

Krajick, K. (1998). Greenfarming by the Incas? *Science 281,* 323.

Kramer, P. A. (1998). The costs of human locomotion: Maternal investment in child transport. *American Journal of Physical Anthropology 107,* 71–85.

Kroeber, A. L. (1939). Cultural and natural areas of native North America. In *American archaeology and ethnology* (vol. 38). Berkeley: University of California Press.

Kuhn, T. (1968). *The structure of scientific revolutions.* Chicago: University of Chicago Press.

Kummer, H. (1971). *Primate societies: Group techniques of ecological adaptation.* Chicago: Aldine.

Kunzig, R. (1999). A tale of two obsessed archaeologists, one ancient city and nagging doubts about whether science can ever hope to reveal the past. *Discover 20* (5), 84–92.

Lai, C. S. L., et al. (2001). A forkhead-domain gene is mutated in severe speech and language disorder. *Nature 413*, 519–523.

Lampl, M., Velhuis, J. D., & Johnson, M. L. (1992). Saltation and stasis: A model of human growth. *Science 258* (5083), 801–803.

Lancaster, J. B. (1975). *Primate behavior and the emergence of human culture.* New York: Holt, Rinehart & Winston.

Landau, M. (1991). *Narratives of human evolution.* New Haven, CT, & London: Yale University Press.

Lang, I. A., et al. (2008). Association of urinary bisphenol A concentration with medical disorders and laboratory abnormalities in adults. *Journal of the American Medical Association 300* (11), 1303–1310.

Lanning, E. P. (1967). *Peru before the Incas.* Englewood Cliffs, NJ: Prentice-Hall.

Larsen, C. S., Matter, R. M., & Gebo, D. L. (1998). *Human origins: The fossil record.* Long Grove, IL: Waveland Press.

Larsen, J. (2006, July 28). Setting the record straight: More than 52,000 Europeans died from heat in summer 2003. *Earth Policy Institute.* www .earth-policy.org/plan_b_updates/2006/update56 (retrieved October 3, 2012)

Lawler, A. (2001). Writing gets a rewrite. *Science 292*, 2419.

Leacock, E. (1981). *Myths of male dominance: Collected articles on women cross culturally.* New York: Monthly Review Press.

Leakey, L. S. B. (1965). *Olduvai Gorge, 1951–1961* (vol. 1). London: Cambridge University Press.

Leakey, L. S. B. (1967). Development of aggression as a factor in early man and prehuman evolution. In C. Clements & D. Lundsley (Eds.), *Aggression and defense.* Los Angeles: University of California Press.

Leakey, L. S. B., Tobias, P. B., & Napier, J. R. (1964). A new species of the genus *Homo* from Olduvai Gorge. *Nature 202*, 7–9.

Leakey, M. D. (1971). *Olduvai Gorge: Excavations in Beds I and II. 1960–1963.* London & New York: Cambridge University Press.

Leakey, M. G., Spoor, F., Brown, F. H., Gathogo, P. N., Kiare, C., Leakey, L. N., & McDougal, I. (2001). New hominin genus from eastern Africa shows diverse middle Pliocene lineages. *Nature 410*, 433–440.

"Leave none to tell the story: Genocide in Rwanda." (2004). www. hrw.org/legacy/reports/1999/rwanda/ (retrieved August 28, 2012)

Leavitt, G. C. (1990). Sociobiological explanations of incest avoidance: A critical review of evidential claims. *American Anthropologist 92*, 982.

Leclerc-Madlala, S. (2002). Bodies and politics: Healing rituals in the democratic South Africa. In V. Faure (Ed.), *Les cahiers de 'l'IFAS,* no. 2. Johannesburg: The French Institute.

Lee, R. B. (1993). *The Dobe Ju/'hoansi.* Fort Worth: Harcourt Brace.

Lee, R. B., & Daly, R. H. (1999). *The Cambridge encyclopedia of hunters and gatherers.* New York: Cambridge University Press.

Lee, R. B., & DeVore, I. (Eds.). (1968). *Man the hunter.* Chicago: Aldine.

Leeds, A., & Vayda, A. P. (Eds.). (1965). *Man, culture and animals: The role of animals in human ecological adjustments.* Washington, DC: American Association for the Advancement of Science.

Lees, R. (1953). The basis of glottochronology. *Language 29*, 113–127.

Leigh, S. R., & Park, P. B. (1998). Evolution of human growth prolongation. *American Journal of Physical Anthropology 107*, 331–350.

LeMay, M. (1975). The language capability of Neanderthal man. *American Journal of Physical Anthropology 43* (1), 9–14.

Leroi-Gourhan, A. (1968). The evolution of Paleolithic art. *Scientific American 218*, 58ff.

Lestel, D. (1998). How chimpanzees have domesticated humans. *Anthropology Today 12* (3).

Leth, P. M. (2007). The use of CT scanning in forensic autopsy. *Forensic Science, Medicine, and Pathology 3* (1), 65–69.

Levine, N. E., & Silk, J. B. (1997). Why polyandry fails. *Current Anthropology 38*, 375–398.

Lewellen, T. C. (2002). *The anthropology of globalization: Cultural anthropology enters the 21st century.* Westport, CT: Greenwood Publishing Group/Bergin & Garvey.

Lewin, R. (1983). Is the orangutan a living fossil? *Science 222*, 1223.

Lewin, R. (1985). Tooth enamel tells a complex story. *Science 228*, 707.

Lewin, R. (1986). New fossil upsets human family. *Science 233*, 720–721.

Lewin, R. (1987). Debate over emergence of human tooth pattern. *Science 235*, 749.

Lewin, R. (1987). The earliest "humans" were more like apes. *Science 236*, 1062–1063.

Lewin, R. (1987). Four legs bad, two legs good. *Science 235*, 969.

Lewin, R. (1987). Why is ape tool use so confusing? *Science 236*, 776–777.

Lewin, R. (1988). Molecular clocks turn a quarter century. *Science 235*, 969–971.

Lewin, R. (1993). Paleolithic paint job. *Discover 14* (7), 64–70.

Lewis-Williams, J. D. (1990). *Discovering southern African rock art.* Cape Town & Johannesburg: David Philip.

Lewis-Williams, J. D., & Dowson, T. A. (1988). Signs of all times: Entoptic phenomena in Upper Paleolithic art. *Current Anthropology 29*, 201–245.

Lewis-Williams, J. D., & Dowson, T. A. (1993). On vision and power in the Neolithic: Evidence from the decorated monuments. *Current Anthropology 34*, 55–65.

Lewis-Williams, J. D., Dowson, T. A., & Deacon, J. (1993). Rock art and changing perceptions of Southern Africa's past: Ezeljagdspoort reviewed. *Antiquity 67*, 273–291.

Lewontin, R. C. (1972). The apportionment of human diversity. In T. Dobzhansky et al. (Eds.), *Evolutionary biology* (pp. 381–398). New York: Plenum Press.

Lewontin, R. C., Rose, S., & Kamin, L. J. (1984). *Not in our genes.* New York: Pantheon.

Li, X., Harbottle, G., Zhang, J., & Wang, C. (2003). The earliest writing? Sign use in the seventh millennium BC at Jiahu, Henan Province, China. *Antiquity 77*, 31–44.

Lieberman, P. (2006). *Toward an evolutionary biology of language.* Cambridge, MA: Belknap Press.

Lindenbaum, S. (1978). *Kuru sorcery: Disease and danger in the New Guinea highlands.* New York: McGraw-Hill.

Livingstone, F. B. (1973). The distribution of abnormal hemoglobin genes and their significance for human evolution. In C. Loring Brace & J. Metress (Eds.), *Man in evolutionary perspective.* New York: Wiley.

Living Tongues. www.livingtongues.org (retrieved June 4, 2012)

Lock, M. (2001). *Twice dead: Organ transplants and the reinvention of death.* Berkeley: University of California Press.

Lorenzo, C., Carretero, J. M., Arsuaga, J. L., Gracia, A., & Martinez, I. (1998). Intrapopulational body size variation and cranial capacity variation in middle Pleistocene humans: The Sima de los Huesos sample (Sierra de Atapuerca, Spain). *American Journal of Physical Anthropology 106*, 19–33.

Loubser, J. H. N. (2003). *Archaeology: The comic.* Lanham, MD: AltaMira Press.

Lovejoy, C. O. (1981). Origin of man. *Science 211* (4480), 341–350.

Lucy, J. A. (1997). Linguistic relativity. *Annual Review of Anthropology 26*, 291–312.

MacCormack, C. P. (1977). Biological events and cultural control. *Signs 3*, 93–100.

MacLarnon, A. M., & Hewitt, G. P. (1999). The evolution of human speech: The role of enhanced breathing control. *American Journal of Physical Anthropology 109*, 341–363.

MacNeish, R. S. (1992). *The origins of agriculture and settled life.* Norman: University of Oklahoma Press.

Maggioncalda, A. N., & Sapolsky, R. M. (2002). Disturbing behaviors of the orangutan. *Scientific American 286* (6), 60–65.

Mair, L. (1957). *An introduction to social anthropology.* London: Oxford University Press.

Mann, A., Lampl, M., & Monge, J. (1990). Patterns of ontogeny in human evolution: Evidence from dental development. *Yearbook of Physical Anthropology 33*, 111–150.

Mann, C. C. (2002). The real dirt on rainforest fertility. *Science 297*, 920–923.

Mann, C. C. (2005). *1491: New revelations of the Americas before Columbus.* New York: Knopf.

Marcus, J., & Flannery, K. V. (1996). *Zapotec civilization: How urban society evolved in Mexico's Oaxaca Valley.* New York: Thames & Hudson.

Marks, J. (1995). *Human biodiversity: Genes, race, and history.* Hawthorne, NY: Aldine.

Marks, J. (2000, April 8). A feckless quest for the basketball gene. *New York Times.*

Marks, J. (2000, May 12). 98% alike (what our similarity to apes tells us about our understanding of genetics). *Chronicle of Higher Education,* B7.

Marks, J. (2002). *What it means to be 98 percent chimpanzee: Apes, people, and their genes.* Berkeley: University of California Press.

Marks, J. (2008). Caveat emptor: Genealogy for sale. *Newsletter of the ESRC Genomics Network 7,* 22–23.

Marks, J. (2008). Race: Past, present, and future. In B. Koenig, S. Lee, & S. Richardson (Eds.), *Revisiting race in a genomic age* (pp. 21–38). New Brunswick, NJ: Rutgers University Press.

Marks, J. (2009). *Why I am not a scientist: Anthropology and modern knowledge.* Berkeley: University of California Press.

Marshack, A. (1972). *The roots of civilization: A study in prehistoric cognition: The origins of art, symbol and notation.* New York: McGraw-Hill.

Marshack, A. (1976). Some implications of the Paleolithic symbolic evidence for the origin of language. *Current Anthropology 17* (2), 274–282.

Marshack, A. (1989). Evolution of the human capacity: The symbolic evidence. *Yearbook of physical anthropology* (vol. 32, pp. 1–34). New York: Alan R. Liss.

Marshall, E. (2001). Preclovis sites fight for acceptance. *Science 291,* 1732.

Martin, E. (1994). *Flexible bodies: Tracking immunity in American culture from the days of polio to the age of AIDS.* Boston: Beacon Press.

Martin, E. (1999). Flexible survivors. *Anthropology News 40* (6), 5–7.

Martin, E. (2009). *Bipolar expeditions: Mania and depression in American culture.* Princeton, NJ: Princeton University Press.

Martorell, R. (1988). Body size, adaptation, and function. *GDP,* 335–347.

Mascia-Lees, F. E., & Black, N. J. (2000). *Gender and anthropology.* Prospect Heights, IL: Waveland Press.

Mason, J. A. (1957). *The ancient civilizations of Peru.* Baltimore: Penguin Books.

Mathieu, C. (2003). *A history and anthropological study of the ancient kingdoms of the Sino-Tibetan borderland—Naxi and Mosuo.* New York: Mellen.

Matson, F. R. (Ed.). (1965). *Ceramics and man.* New York: Viking Fund Publications in Anthropology, no. 41.

Max Planck Institute of Evolutionary Anthropology. (2012). Denisova genome. Public data set: http://aws .amazon.com/datasets/2357 (retrieved July 19, 2012)

Mayr, E., & Diamond, J. (2002). *What evolution is.* New York: Basic Books.

McCorriston, J., & Hole, F. (1991). The ecology of seasonal stress and the origins of agriculture in the Near East. *American Anthropologist 93,* 46–69.

McDermott, L. (1996). Self-representation in Upper Paleolithic female figurines. *Current Anthropology 37,* 227–276.

McElroy, A., & Townsend, P. K. (2003). *Medical anthropology in ecological perspective.* Boulder, CO: Westview Press.

McGrew, W. C. (2000). Dental care in chimps. *Science 288,* 1747.

McHenry, H. (1975). Fossils and the mosaic nature of human evolution. *Science 190,* 425–431.

McHenry, H. M. (1992). Body size and proportions in early hominids. *American Journal of Physical Anthropology 87,* 407–431.

McHenry, H. M., & Jones, A. L. (2006). Hallucial convergence in early hominids. *Journal of Human Evolution 50,* 534–539.

McKenna, J. (1999). Co-sleeping and SIDS. In W. Trevathan, E. O. Smith, & J. J. McKenna (Eds.), *Evolutionary medicine.* London: Oxford University Press.

McKenna, J. J. (2002, September– October). Breastfeeding and bedsharing. *Mothering,* 28–37.

McKenna, J. J., Ball, H., & Gettler, L. T. (2007). Mother–infant cosleeping, breastfeeding and SIDS: What biological anthropology has discovered about normal infant sleep and pediatric sleep medicine. *Yearbook of Physical Anthropology 50,* 133–161.

McKenna, J. J., & McDade, T. (2005, June). Why babies should never sleep alone: A review of the co-sleeping controversy in relation to SIDS, bedsharing, and breastfeeding. *Pediatric Respiratory Reviews 6* (2), 134–152.

McNeil, W. (1992). *Plagues and people.* New York: Anchor.

Melaart, J. (1967). *Catal Hüyük: A Neolithic town in Anatolia.* London: Thames & Hudson.

Mellars, P. (1989). Major issues in the emergence of modern humans. *Current Anthropology 30,* 356–357.

Mellars, P. (2009). Archaeology: Origins of the female image. *Nature 459,* 176–177.

Merin, Y. (2002). *Equality for same-sex couples: The legal recognition of gay partnerships in Europe and the United States.* Chicago: University of Chicago Press.

Merrell, D. J. (1962). *Evolution and genetics: The modern theory of genetics.* New York: Holt, Rinehart & Winston.

Merzenich, H., Zeeb, H., & Blettner, M. (2010). Decreasing sperm quality: A global problem? *BMC Public Health.* doi: 10.1186/1471-2458-10-24 (retrieved September 11, 2011)

Michaels, J. W. (1973). *Dating methods in archaeology.* New York: Seminar Press.

Miles, H. (1983). Two-way communication with apes and the evolution of language. In E. de Grollier (Ed.), *Glossogenetics: The origin and evolution of language* (pp. 201–210). Paris: Harwood Academic Publishers.

Miles, H. (1986). How can I tell a lie? Apes, language and the problem of deception. In R. Mitchell & N. Thompson (Eds.), *Deception: Perspectives on human and nonhuman deceit* (pp. 145–266). Albany: SUNY Press.

Miles, H. (1990). The cognitive foundations for reference in a signing orangutan. In S. Parker & K. Gibson (Eds.), *"Language" and intelligence in monkeys and apes: Comparative developmental perspectives* (pp. 511–539). Cambridge, UK: Cambridge University Press.

Miles, H. (1993). Language and the orangutan: The "old person" of the forest. In

P. Cavalieri & P. Singer (Eds.), *The great ape project* (pp. 45–50). New York: St. Martin's Press.

Miles, H. (1994). ME CHANTEK: The development of self-awareness in a signing orangutan. In S. Parker, R. Mitchell, & M. Boccia (Eds.), *Self-awareness in monkeys and apes: Developmental Perspectives* (pp. 254–272). Cambridge, UK: Cambridge University Press.

Miles, H. (1999). Symbolic communication with and by great apes. In S. Parker, R. Mitchell, & H. Miles (Eds.), *The mentality of gorillas and orangutans: Comparative perspectives* (pp. 197–210). Cambridge, UK: Cambridge University Press.

Miles, H. (2003). Personhood. In J. Goodall et al. (Eds.). *The Great Ape Project Census: Recognition for the uncounted* (introduction by P. Singer, pp. 239–244). Portland, OR: Great Ape Project Books.

Miles, H., & Roberts, W. (1998). Methodologies, not method for primate theory of mind. *Behavioral and Brain Sciences 21* (1), 126.

Millon, R. (1973). *Urbanization of Teotihuacán, Mexico: The Teotihuacán map* (vol. 1, part 1). Austin: University of Texas Press.

Mintz, S. (1996). A taste of history. In W. A. Haviland & R. J. Gordon (Eds.), *Talking about people* (2nd ed., pp. 81–82). Mountain View, CA: Mayfield.

Minugh-Purvis, N. (1992). The inhabitants of Ice Age Europe. *Expedition 34* (3), 33–34.

Mitchell, R., & Miles, H. (1993). Apes have mimetic culture. *Behavioral and Brain Sciences 16* (4), 768.

Molnar, S. (1992). *Human variation: Races, types and ethnic groups* (3rd ed.). Englewood Cliffs, NJ: Prentice-Hall.

Montagu, A. (1964). *The concept of race.* London: Macmillan.

Montagu, A. (1975). *Race and IQ.* New York: Oxford University Press.

Montagu, A. (1998). *Man's most dangerous myth: The fallacy of race* (6th ed.). Lanham, MD: Rowman & Littlefield.

Morgan, L. H. (1877). *Ancient society.* New York: World Publishing.

Mydens, S. (2001, August 12). He's not hairy, he's my brother. *New York Times.* www.nytimes.com/2001/08/12/ weekinreview/ideas-trends-he-s-not-hairy-he-s-my-brother.html (retrieved June 25, 2012)

Nabhan, G. P. (2004). *Why some like it hot: Food, genes, and cultural diversity.* Washington, DC: Island Press.

Nader, L. (Ed.). (1996). *Naked science: Anthropological inquiry into boundaries, power, and knowledge.* New York: Routledge.

Neer, R. M. (1975). The evolutionary significance of vitamin D, skin pigment, and ultraviolet light. *American Journal of Physical Anthropology 43,* 409–416.

Nichols, J. (2008). Language spread rates as indicators of glacial-age peopling of the Americas. *Current Anthropology 49* (6), 1109–1117.

Nunney, L. (1998). Are we selfish because we are nice, or are we nice because we are selfish? *Science 281,* 1619.

Oakley, K. P. (1964). *Man the tool-maker.* Chicago: University of Chicago Press.

O'Carroll, E. (2008, June 27). Spain to grant some human rights to apes. *Christian Science Monitor.*

Otte, M. (2000). On the suggested bone flute from Slovenia. *Current Anthropology 41,* 271.

Parés, J. M., et al. (2000). On the age of hominid fossils at the Sima de los Huesos, Sierra de Atapuerca, Spain: Paleomagnetic evidence. *American Journal of Physical Anthropology 111,* 451–461.

Parish, A. (1998). Comment. *Current Anthropology 39,* 414.

Parnell, R. (1999). Gorilla exposé. *Natural History 108* (8), 43.

Patterson, F., & Linden, E. (1981). *The education of Koko.* New York: Holt, Rinehart & Winston.

Patterson, F., Miles, H., & Savage-Rumbaugh, E. (2003). *Maui Ape Preserve (MAP): The Ape Consortium for Global Research, Education and Conservation.* Woodside, CA: The Gorilla Foundation-koko.org

Patterson, F. G. P., & Gordon, W. (2002). Twenty-seven years of Project Koko and Michael. In B. Galdikas et al. (Eds.), *All apes great and small: Chimpanzees, bonobos, and gorillas* (vol. 1, pp. 165–176). New York: Kluwer Academic.

Patterson, T. C. (1981). *Archeology: The evolution of ancient societies.* Englewood Cliffs, NJ: Prentice-Hall.

Pelto, G. H., Goodman, A. H., & Dufour, D. L. (Eds.). (2000). *Nutritional anthropology: Biocultural perspectives on food and nutrition.* Mountain View, CA: Mayfield.

Pennisi, E. (1999). Genetic study shakes up out of Africa theory. *Science 283,* 1828.

Peters, C. R. (1979). Toward an ecological model of African Plio-Pleistocene hominid adaptations. *American Anthropologist 81* (2), 261–278.

Petersen, J. B., Neuves, E., & Heckenberger, M. J. (2001). Gift from the past: *Terra preta* and prehistoric American occupation in Amazonia. In C. McEwan & C. Barreo (Eds.), *Unknown Amazon* (pp. 86–105). London: British Museum Press.

Peterson, F. L. (1962). *Ancient Mexico: An introduction to the pre-Hispanic cultures.* New York: Capricorn Books.

Pickering, R., et al. (2011). *Australopithecus sediba* at 1.977 ma and implications for the origins of the genus *Homo. Science 333* (6048), 1421–1423.

Piggott, S. (1965). *Ancient Europe.* Chicago: Aldine.

Pike, A. W. G., et al. (2012). U-series dating of Paleolithic art in 11 caves in Spain. *Science 336,* 1409–1413.

Pilbeam, D. (1987). Rethinking human origins. In *Primate evolution and human origins.* Hawthorne, NY: Aldine.

Pilbeam, D., & Gould, S. J. (1974). Size and scaling in human evolution. *Science 186,* 892–901.

Pimentel, D. (1991). Response. *Science 252,* 358.

Pinker, S. (1994). *The language instinct: How the mind creates language.* New York: William Morrow.

Piperno, D. R., & Fritz, G. J. (1994). On the emergence of agriculture in the new world. *Current Anthropology 35,* 637–643.

Pohl, M. E. D., Pope, K. O., & von Nagy, C. (2002). Olmec origins of Mesoamerican writing. *Science 298,* 1984–1987.

Pollan, M. (2001). *The botany of desire: A plant's-eye view of the world.* New York: Random House.

Pollan, M. (2008). *In defense of food: An eater's manifesto.* New York: Penguin Books.

Pope, G. G. (1989). Bamboo and human evolution. *Natural History 10,* 56.

Pope, G. G. (1992). Craniofacial evidence for the origin of modern humans in China. *Yearbook of Physical Anthropology 35,* 291.

Power, M. G. (1995). Gombe revisted: Are chimpanzees violent and hierarchical in the "free" state? *General Anthropology 2* (1), 5–9.

Premack, A. J., & Premack, D. (1972). Teaching language to an ape. *Scientific American 277* (4), 92–99.

"President Obama descends from the first African enslaved for life in America." (2012, July). *Ancestry .com.* www.ancestry.com/obama (retrieved August 10, 2012)

Pringle, H. (1997). Ice Age communities may be earliest known net hunters. *Science 277,* 1203–1204.

Pringle, H. (1998). The slow birth of agriculture. *Science 282,* 1446–1449.

Profet, M. (1991). The function of allergy: Immunological defense against toxins. *Quarterly Review of Biology 66* (1), 23–62.

Profet, M. (1995). *Protecting your baby to be.* New York: Addison-Wesley.

Pruetz, J. D., & Bertolani, P. (2007, March 6). Savanna chimpanzees, *Pan troglodytes verus,* hunt with tools. *Current Biology 17,* 412–417.

Puleston, D. E. (1983). *The settlement survey of Tikal.* Philadelphia: University Museum.

Rapp, R. (1999). *Testing women, testing the fetus: The social impact of amniocentesis in America (The Anthropology of Everyday Life).* New York: Routledge.

Rasmussen, M., et al. (2011). An aboriginal Australian genome reveals separate human dispersals into Asia, *Science 334* (6052), 94–98. doi: 10.1126/science.1211177

Rathje, W., & Murphy, C. (2001). *Rubbish!: The archaeology of garbage.* Tucson: University of Arizona Press.

Rathje, W. L. (1974). The garbage project: A new way of looking at the problems of archaeology. *Archaeology 27,* 236–241.

Rathje, W. L. (1993). Rubbish! In W. A. Haviland & R. J. Gordon (Eds.), *Talking about people: Readings in contemporary cultural anthropology.* Mountain View, CA: Mayfield.

Read, C. E. (1973). *The role of faunal analysis in reconstructing human behavior: A Mousterian example.* Paper presented at the meetings of the California Academy of Sciences, Long Beach.

Read-Martin, C. E., & Read, D. W. (1975). Australopithecine scavenging and human evolution: An approach from faunal analysis. *Current Anthropology 16* (3), 359–368.

Recer, P. (1998, February 16). Apes shown to communicate in the wild. *Burlington Free Press,* 12A.

Redman, C. L. (1978). *The rise of civilization: From early farmers to urban society in the ancient Near East.* San Francisco: Freeman.

Reich, D., et al. (2010, December 23). Genetic history of an archaic hominin group from Denisova Cave in Siberia. *Nature 468,* 1053–1060.

Reich, D., et al. (2012). Reconstructing Native American population history. *Nature.* doi: 10.1038/nature11258

Reid, J. J., Schiffer, M. B., & Rathje, W. L. (1975). Behavioral archaeology: Four strategies. *American Anthropologist 77,* 864–869.

Relethford, J. H. (2001). Absence of regional affinities of Neandertal DNA with living humans does not reject multiregional evolution. *American Journal of Physical Anthropology 115,* 95–98.

Relethford, J. H., & Harpending, H. C. (1994). Craniometric variation, genetic theory, and modern human origins. *American Journal of Physical Anthropology 95,* 249–270.

Renfrew, C. (1973). *Before civilization: The radiocarbon revolution and prehistoric Europe.* London: Jonathan Cape.

Reynolds, V. (1994). Primates in the field, primates in the lab. *Anthropology Today 10* (2), 4.

Rice, D. S., & Prudence, M. (1984). Lessons from the Maya. *Latin American Research Review 19* (3), 7–34.

Rice, P. (2000). Paleoanthropology 2000—part 1. *General Anthropology 7* (1), 11.

Richmond, B. G., Fleagle, J. K., & Swisher III, C. C. (1998). First hominid elbow from the Miocene of Ethiopia and the evolution of the Catarrhine elbow. *American Journal of Physical Anthropology 105,* 257–277.

Richter, C. A., et al. (2007). In vivo effects of bisphenol A in laboratory rodent studies. *Reproductive Toxicology 24* (2), 199–224.

Ridley, M. (1999). *Genome: The autobiography of a species in 23 chapters.* New York: HarperCollins.

Rightmire, G. P. (1990). *The evolution of* Homo erectus: *Comparative anatomical studies of an extinct human species.* Cambridge, UK: Cambridge University Press.

Rightmire, G. P. (1998). Evidence from facial morphology for similarity of Asian and African representatives of *Homo erectus. American Journal of Physical Anthropology 106,* 61–85.

Rindos, D. (1984). *The origins of agriculture: An evolutionary perspective.* Orlando: Academic Press.

Rogers, J. (1994). Levels of the genealogical hierarchy and the problem of hominoid phylogeny. *American Journal of Physical Anthropology 94,* 81–88.

Romer, A. S. (1945). *Vertebrate paleontology.* Chicago: University of Chicago Press.

Roosevelt, A. C. (1984). Population, health, and the evolution of subsistence: Conclusions from the conference. In M. N. Cohen & G. J. Armelagos (Eds.), *Paleopathology at the origins of agriculture* (pp. 572–574). Orlando: Academic Press.

Rosas, A., & Bermúdez de Castro, J. M. (1998). On the taxonomic affinities of the Dmanisi mandible (Georgia). *American Journal of Physical Anthropology 107*, 145–162.

Rose, S. (2009). Darwin 200: Should scientists study race and IQ? NO: Science and society do not benefit. *Nature 457*, 786–788.

Rowe, M., & Mittermeier, R. A. (1996). *The pictorial guide to the living primates.* East Hampton, NY: Pogonias.

Rowe, T. (1988). New issues for phylogenetics. *Science 239*, 1183–1184.

Rupert, J. L., & Hochachka, P. W. (2001). The evidence for hereditary factors contributing to high altitude adaptation in Andean natives: A review. *High Altitude Medicine & Biology 2* (2), 235–256.

Russon, A., & Miles, H. (1995, November). Cultured orangutans: Culture beyond humans. In H. Miles (Chair), *Do apes have culture?* Annual meeting of the American Anthropological Association, Washington, DC.

Ruvolo, M. (1994). Molecular evolutionary processes and conflicting gene trees: The hominoid case. *American Journal of Physical Anthropology 94*, 89–113.

Rymer, R. (1994). *Genie: A scientific tragedy.* New York: HarperCollins.

Sabloff, J. A. (1989). *The cities of ancient Mexico.* New York: Thames & Hudson.

Sabloff, J. A. (1997). *The cities of ancient Mexico* (rev. ed.). New York: Thames & Hudson.

Sabloff, J. A., & Lambert-Karlovsky, C. C. (1973). *Ancient civilization and trade.* Albuquerque: University of New Mexico Press.

Sabloff, J. A., & Lambert-Karlovsky, C. C. (Eds.). (1974). *The rise and fall of civilizations, modern archaeological approaches to ancient cultures.* Menlo Park, CA: Cummings.

Sachs, E., Rosenfeld, B., Lhewa, D., Rasmussen, A., & Keller, A. (2008). Entering exile: Trauma, mental health, and coping among Tibetan refugees arriving in Dharamsala, India. *Journal of Traumatic Stress 21* (2), 199–208.

Sacks, O. (1998). *Island of the colorblind.* New York: Knopf.

Sahlins, M. (1972). *Stone Age economics.* Chicago: Aldine.

Sanday, P. R. (1975). On the causes of IQ differences between groups and implications for social policy. In M. F. A. Montagu (Ed.), *Race and IQ* (pp. 232–238). New York: Oxford University Press.

Sanday, P. R. (1981). *Female power and male dominance: On the origins of sexual inequality.* Cambridge, UK: Cambridge University Press.

Sapir, E. (1921). *Language.* New York: Harcourt.

Sapolsky, R. (2002). *A primate's memoir: Love, death, and baboons in East Africa.* New York: Vintage.

Savage-Rumbaugh, S., & Lewin, R. (1994). *Kanzi: The ape at the brink of the human mind.* New York: Wiley.

Sawert, H. (2002, October 11–12). TB and poverty in the context of global TB control. World Health Organization. Satellite Symposium on TB & Poverty. www.stoptb.org/assets/documents/ resources/publications/acsm/ H.RightsReport2001.pdf

Scarr-Salapatek, S. (1971). Unknowns in the IQ equation. *Science 174*, 1223–1228.

Schaller, G. B. (1971). *The year of the gorilla.* New York: Ballantine.

Schepartz, L. A. (1993). Language and human origins. *Yearbook of Physical Anthropology 36*, 91–126.

Scheper-Hughes, N. (2003, May 10). Keeping an eye on the global traffic in human organs. *Lancet 361* (9369), 1645–1648.

Schwartz, J. H. (1984). Hominoid evolution: A review and a reassessment. *Current Anthropology 25* (5), 655–672.

Scully, T. (2008). Online anthropology draws protest from aboriginal group. *Nature 453*, 1155. doi:10.1038/4531155a

Seiffert, E. R., et al. (2009). Convergent evolution of anthropoid-like adaptations in Eocene adapiform primates. *Nature 461*, 1118–1121.

Sellen, D. W., & Mace, R. (1997). Fertility and mode of subsistence: A phylogenetic analysis. *Current Anthropology 38*, 886.

Semenov, S. A. (1964). *Prehistoric technology.* New York: Barnes & Noble.

Senut, B., et al. (2001). First hominid from the Miocene (Lukeino formation, Kenya). *C. R. Academy of Science, Paris 332*, 137–144.

Seyfarth, R. M., Cheney, D. L., & Marler, P. (1980). Vervet monkey alarm calls: Semantic communication in a free-ranging primate. *Animal Behavior 28* (4), 1070–1094.

Seyfarth, R. M., et al. (1980). Monkey responses to three different alarm calls: Evidence for predator classification and semantic communication. *Science 210*, 801–803.

Sharer, R. J., & Ashmore, W. (2007). *Archaeology: Discovering our past* (4th ed.). New York: McGraw-Hill.

Sharpe, K., & Van Gelder, L. (2006). Evidence of cave marking by Paleolithic children. *Antiquity 80* (310), 937–947.

Sheets, P. D. (1993). Dawn of a new Stone Age in eye surgery. In R. J. Sharer & W. Ashmore. *Archaeology: Discovering our past* (2nd ed.). Palo Alto, CA: Mayfield.

Shipman, P. (1993). *Life history of a fossil: An introduction to taphonomy and paleoecology.* Cambridge, MA: Harvard University Press.

Shostak, M. (2000). *Nisa: The life and words of a !Kung woman.* Cambridge, MA: Harvard University Press.

Shreeve, J. (1994). Terms of estrangement. *Discover 15* (11), 60.

Shreeve, J. (1995). *The Neandertal enigma: Solving the mystery of modern human origins.* New York: William Morrow.

Shuey, A. M. (1966). *The testing of Negro intelligence.* New York: Social Science Press.

Sillen, A., & Brain, C. K. (1990). Old flame. *Natural History 4*, 10.

Silverstein, J. (2012). Bonds beyond blood: DNA testing and refugee family resettlement. *Anthropology News 53* (4), 11.

Simons, E. L. (1972). *Primate evolution.* New York: Macmillan.

Simons, E. L. (1989). Human origins. *Science 245*, 1349.

Simons, E. L., et al. (2009, July 22). Outrage at high price paid for a fossil. Correspondence. *Nature 460*, 456.

Simpson, G. G. (1949). *The meaning of evolution.* New Haven, CT: Yale University Press.

Simpson, S. W., et al. (2008). A female *Homo erectus* pelvis from Gona, Ethiopia. *Science 322* (5904), 1089–1092.

Skelton, R. R., McHenry, H. M., & Drawhorn, G. M. (1986). Phylogenetic analysis of early hominids. *Current Anthropology 27*, 21–43.

Sluka, J. A. (2007). Fieldwork relations and rapport: Introduction. In A. C. G. M. Robben & J. A. Sluka (Eds.), *Ethnographic fieldwork: An anthropological reader.* Malden, MA: Blackwell Press.

Small, M. F. (1997). Making connections. *American Scientist 85*, 503.

Small, M. F. (2008, August 15). Why red is such a potent color. *Live Science.* www.livescience.com/5043-red-potent-color.html (retrieved June 20, 2012)

Small, M. F. (2009, May 15). Why "Ida" inspires navel-gazing at our ancestry. *Live Science.* www.livescience.come/history/090520-hn-ida.html

Smedley, A. (2007). *Race in North America: Origin and evolution of a worldview.* Boulder, CO: Westview Press.

Smith, B. D. (1977). Archaeological inference and inductive confirmation. *American Anthropologist 79* (3), 598–617.

Smith, B. H. (1994). Patterns of dental development in *Homo, Australopithecus, Pan,* and gorilla. *American Journal of Physical Anthropology 94*, 307–325.

Smith, P. E. L. (1976). *Food production and its consequences* (2nd ed.). Menlo Park, CA: Cummings.

Smuts, B. (1987). What are friends for? *Natural History 96* (2), 36–44.

Snowden, C. T. (1990). Language capabilities of nonhuman animals. *Yearbook of Physical Anthropology 33*, 215–243.

Songok, E. M., Luo, M., Liang, B., Mclaren, P., Kaefer, N., Apidi, W., Boucher, G., Kimani, J., Wachihi, C., Sekaly, R., Fowke, K., Ball, B. T., & Plummer, F. A. (2012). Microarray analysis of HIV resistant female sex workers reveal a gene expression signature pattern reminiscent of a lowered immune activation state. *PLoS One 7* (1), e30048.

Spradley, J. P. (1979). *The ethnographic interview.* New York: Holt, Rinehart & Winston.

Spradley, J. P. (1980). *Participant observation.* New York: Holt, Rinehart & Winston.

Springen, K. (2008, September 15). What it means to be a woman: How women around the world cope with infertility. *Newsweek.com.* www.thedailybeast.com/newsweek/2008/09/14/what-it-means-to-be-a-woman.html (retrieved June 12, 2012)

Stahl, A. B. (1984). Hominid dietary selection before fire. *Current Anthropology 25*, 151–168.

Stanford, C. B. (1998). The social behavior of chimpanzees and bonobos: Empirical evidence and shifting assumptions. *Current Anthropology 39*, 399–420.

Stanford, C. B. (2001). *Chimpanzee and red colobus: The ecology of predator and prey.* Cambridge, MA: Harvard University Press.

Stanley, S. M. (1979). *Macroevolution.* San Francisco: Freeman.

Stedman, H. H., et al. (2004). Myosin gene mutation correlates with anatomical changes in the human lineage. *Nature 428,* 415–418.

Steward, J. H. (1972). *Theory of culture change: The methodology of multilinear evolution.* Urbana: University of Illinois Press.

Stiles, D. (1979). Early Acheulean and developed Oldowan. *Current Anthropology 20* (1), 126–129.

Stiles, D. (1992). The hunter-gatherer "revisionist" debate. *Anthropology Today 8* (2), 13–17.

Stocking, G. W., Jr. (1968). *Race, culture and evolution: Essays in the history of anthropology.* New York: Free Press.

Stone, R. (1995). If the mercury soars, so may health hazards. *Science 267,* 958.

Strier, K. (1993, March). Menu for a monkey. *Natural History,* 42.

Stringer, C. B., & McKie, R. (1996). *African exodus: The origins of modern humanity.* London: Jonathan Cape.

Strum, S., & Mitchell, W. (1987). Baboon models and muddles. In W. Kinsey (Ed.), *The evolution of human behavior: Primate models.* Albany: SUNY Press.

Stuart-MacAdam, P., & Dettwyler, K. A. (Eds.). (1995). *Breastfeeding: Biocultural perspectives.* New York: Aldine.

Suwa, G., Kono, R. T., Katoh, S., Asfaw, B., & Beyene, Y. (2007, August 23). A new species of great ape from the late Miocene epoch in Ethiopia. *Nature 448,* 921–924. doi:10.1038/nature06113

Swadesh, M. (1959). Linguistics as an instrument of prehistory. *Southwestern Journal of Anthropology 15,* 20–35.

Swaminathan, M. S. (2000). Science in response to basic human needs. *Science 287,* 425.

Swisher III, C. C., Curtis, G. H., Jacob, T., Getty, A. G., & Widiasmoro, A. S. (1994). Age of the earliest known hominids in Java, Indonesia. *Science 263,* 1118–1121.

Tamm, E., et al. (2007). Beringian standstill and spread of Native American frontiers. *PLoS One 2* (9), e829. doi: 10.1371/journal/pone.0000829

Tannen, D. (1990). *You just don't understand: Women and men in conversation.* New York: Morrow.

Tapper, M. (1999). *In the blood: Sickle-cell anemia and the politics of race.* Philadelphia: University of Pennsylvania Press.

Tattersall, I., & Schwartz, J. H. (1999). Hominids and hybrids: The place of Neanderthals in human evolution. *Proceedings of the National Academy of Sciences 96* (13), 7117–7119.

Templeton, A. R. (1994). Eve: Hypothesis compatibility versus hypothesis testing. *American Anthropologist 96* (1), 141–147.

Templeton, A. R. (1995). The "Eve" hypothesis: A genetic critique and reanalysis. *American Anthropologist 95* (1), 51–72.

Templeton, A. R. (1996). Gene lineages and human evolution. *Science 272,* 1363–1364.

Thompson, K. (2012, July 30). Obama's purported link to early American slave is latest twist in family tree. *Washington Post.* www.washingtonpost.com/politics/purported-obama-link-to-first-american-slave-is-latest-twist-in-presidents-family-tree/2012/07/30/gJQAYuG1KX_story.html?hpid=z4 (retrieved August 10, 2012)

Thomson, K. S. (1997). Natural selection and evolution's smoking gun. *American Scientist 85,* 516.

Thorne, A. G., & Wolpoff, M. D. H. (1981). Regional continuity in Australasian Pleistocene hominid evolution. *American Journal of Physical Anthropology 55,* 337–349.

Thornhill, N. Quoted in Haviland, W. A., & Gordon, R. J. (Eds.). (1993). *Talking about people* (p. 127). Mountain View, CA: Mayfield.

Thorpe, S. K. S., Holder, R. L., & Crompton, R. H. (2007). Origin of human bipedalism as an adaptation for locomotion on flexible branches. *Science 316,* 1328–1331.

Tobias, P. V., & von Königswald, G. H. R. (1964). A comparison between the Olduvai hominines and those of Java and some implications for hominid phylogeny. *Nature 204,* 515–518.

Toth, N., et al. (1993). Pan the toolmaker: Investigations in the stone tool-making and tool-using capabilities of a bonobo (*Pan paniscus*). *Journal of Archaeological Science 20* (1), 81–91.

Tracy, J. L., & Matsumoto, D. (2008). The spontaneous expression of pride and shame: Evidence for biologically innate nonverbal displays. *Proceedings of the National Academy of Sciences 105* (33), 11655–11660.

Trevathan, W., Smith, E. O., & McKenna, J. J. (Eds.). (1999). *Evolutionary medicine.* London: Oxford University Press.

Trifonov, V., Khiabanian, H., Greenbaum, B., & Rabadan, R. (2009). The origin of the recent swine influenza A (H1N1) virus infecting humans. *Eurosurveillance 14* (17). www.eurosurveillance.org/ViewArticle.aspx?ArticleId=19193 (retrieved July 16, 2012)

Trinkaus, E. (1986). The Neanderthals and modern human origins. *Annual Review of Anthropology 15,* 197.

Trinkaus, E., & Shipman, P. (1992). *The Neandertals: Changing the image of mankind.* New York: Knopf.

Trouillot, M. R. (1996). Culture, color, and politics in Haiti. In S. Gregory & R. Sanjek (Eds.), *Race.* New Brunswick, NJ: Rutgers University Press.

Turnbull, C. M. (1983). *The human cycle.* New York: Simon & Schuster.

Ucko, P. J., & Rosenfeld, A. (1967). *Paleolithic cave art.* New York: McGraw-Hill.

Ucko, P. J., Tringham, R., & Dimbleby, G. W. (Eds.). (1972). *Man, settlement, and urbanism.* London: Duckworth.

UNAIDS. (2009). *2009 AIDS epidemic update.* www.unaids.org/en/dataanalysis/epidemiology/2009aidsepidemicupdate/ (retrieved June 28, 2012)

United Nations, Universal Declaration of Human Rights. www.un.org/en/documents/udhr/index.shtml (retrieved October 1, 2012)

Van Willigen, J. (2002). *Applied anthropology: An introduction.* Westport, CT: Bergin & Garvey.

Vidya, R. (2002). Karnataka's unabating kidney trade. *Frontline.* www.frontlineonnet.com/fl1907/19070610.htm (retrieved June 10, 2012)

Vincent, J. (1979). On the special division of labor, population, and the origins of agriculture. *Current Anthropology 20* (2), 422–425.

Walrath, D. (2006). Gender, genes, and the evolution of human birth. In P. L. Geller & M. K. Stockett (Eds.), *Feminist anthropology: Past, present, and future.* Philadelphia: University of Pennsylvania Press.

Washburn, S. L., & Moore, R. (1980). *Ape into human: A study of human evolution* (2nd ed.). Boston: Little, Brown.

Washington, H. (2006) *Medical apartheid: The dark history of medical experimentation on black Americans from colonial times to the present,* New York: Anchor.

Weatherford, J. (1988). *Indian givers: How the Indians of the Americas transformed the world.* New York: Ballantine.

Weaver, M. P. (1972). *The Aztecs, Maya and their predecessors.* New York: Seminar Press.

Weiner, J. S. (1955). *The Piltdown forgery.* Oxford, UK: Oxford University Press.

Weiss, M. L., & Mann, A. E. (1990). *Human biology and behavior* (5th ed.). Boston: Little, Brown.

Wells, S. (2002). *The journey of man: A genetic odyssey.* Princeton, NJ: Princeton University Press.

Wernick, R., & the Editors of Time-Life. (1973). *The monument builders.* New York: Time-Life.

Wheeler, P. (1993). Human ancestors walked tall, stayed cool. *Natural History 102* (8), 65–66.

White, L. (1959). *The evolution of culture: The development of civilization to the fall of Rome.* New York: McGraw-Hill.

White, R. (1992). The earliest images: Ice Age "art" in Europe. *Expedition 34* (3), 37–51.

White, T., Asfaw, B., Degusta, D., Gilbert, H., Richards, G., Suwa, G., & Howell, F. C. (2003). Pleistocene *Homo sapiens* from the Middle Awash, Ethiopia. *Nature 423,* 742–747.

White, T. D. (1979). Evolutionary implications of Pliocene hominid footprints. *Science 208,* 175–176.

White, T. D. (2003). Early hominids—diversity or distortion? *Science 299,* 1994–1997.

White, T. D., & Toth, N. (2000). Cutmarks on a Plio-Pleistocene hominid from Sterkfontein, South Africa. *American Journal of Physical Anthropology 111,* 579–584.

White, T. D., et al. (2009, October). *Ardipithecus ramidus* and the paleobiology of early hominoids. *Science 326* (5949), 64, 75–86.

Whiting, J. W. M., Sodergem, J. A., & Stigler, S. M. (1982). Winter temperature as a constraint to the migration of preindustrial peoples. *American Anthropologist 84,* 289.

Whorf, B. (1946). The Hopi language, Toreva dialect. In *Linguistic structures of Native America*. New York: Viking Fund.

Whyte, A. L. H. (2005). Human evolution in Polynesia. *Human Biology 77* (2), 157–177.

"Why the stories are told," Aunty Beryl Carmichael. *Aboriginal culture: Dreamtime stories*. www.rmwebed.com.au/HSIE/y10/abc/dreamtime/dreamtime.htm (retrieved November 15, 2012)

Wiley, A. S. (2004). *An ecology of high-altitude infancy: A biocultural perspective*. Cambridge, UK: Cambridge University Press.

Willey, G. R. (1966). *An introduction to American archaeology: North America* (vol. 1). Englewood Cliffs, NJ: Prentice-Hall.

Willey, G. R. (1971). *An introduction to American archaeology: South America* (vol. 2). Englewood Cliffs, NJ: Prentice-Hall.

Wills, C. (1994). The skin we're in. *Discover 15* (11), 79.

Wilson, A. K., & Sarich, V. M. (1969). A molecular time scale for human evolution. *Proceedings of the National Academy of Sciences 63*, 1089–1093.

Wolpoff, M. (1996). *Australopithecus: A new look at an old ancestor. General Anthropology 3* (1), 2.

Wolpoff, M., & Caspari, R. (1997). *Race and human evolution*. New York: Simon & Schuster.

Wolpoff, M. H. (1977). Review of earliest man in the Lake Rudolf Basin. *American Anthropologist 79*, 708–711.

Wolpoff, M. H. (1982). *Ramapithecus* and hominid origins. *Current Anthropology 23*, 501–522.

Wolpoff, M. H. (1993). Evolution in *Homo erectus*: The question of stasis. In R. L. Ciochon & J. G. Fleagle (Eds.), *The human evolution source book*. Englewood Cliffs, NJ: Prentice-Hall.

Wolpoff, M. H. (1993). Multiregional evolution: The fossil alternative to Eden. In R. L. Ciochon & J. G. Fleagle (Eds.), *The human evolution source book*. Englewood Cliffs, NJ: Prentice-Hall.

Wolpoff, M. H., Wu, X. Z., & Thorne, A. G. (1984). Modern *Homo sapiens* origins: A general theory of hominid evolution involving fossil evidence from east Asia. In F. H. Smith & F. Spencer (Eds.), *The origins of modern humans* (pp. 411–483). New York: Alan R. Liss.

Wood, B., & Aiello, L. C. (1998). Taxonomic and functional implications of mandibular scaling in early hominines. *American Journal of Physical Anthropology 105*, 523–538.

Wood, B., Wood, C., & Konigsberg, L. (1994). *Paranthropus boisei*: An example of evolutionary stasis? *American Journal of Physical Anthropology 95*, 117–136.

Woodford, M. H., Butynski, T. M., & Karesh W. (2002). Habituating the great apes: The disease risks. *Oryx 36*, 153–160.

Woodward, V. (1992). *Human heredity and society*. St. Paul, MN: West.

World Health Organization, Preamble to the Constitution. (1948). www.who.int/about/definition/en/print.html (retrieved November 15, 2012)

Wrangham, R., & Peterson, D. (1996). *Demonic males*. Boston: Houghton Mifflin.

Wu, X., & Poirier, F. E. (1995). *Human evolution in China*. New York: Oxford University Press.

Yates, D. (2011). *Archaeological practice and political change: Transitions and transformations in the use of the past in nationalist, neoliberal and indigenous Bolivia*. PhD dissertation, Department of Archaeology, Cambridge, UK: University of Cambridge.

Young, A. (1981). The creation of medical knowledge: Some problems in interpretation. *Social Science and Medicine 17*, 1205–1211.

Zeder, M. A., & Hesse, B. (2000). The initial domestication of goats (*Capra hircus*) in the Zagros Mountains 10,000 years ago. *Science 287*, 2254–2257.

Zeresenay, A., et al. (2006). A juvenile early hominin skeleton from Dikika, Ethiopia. *Nature 443*, 296–301.

Zilhão, J. (2000). Fate of the Neandertals. *Archaeology 53* (4), 30.

Zimmer, C. (1999). New date for the dawn of dream time. *Science 284*, 1243.

Zimmer, C. (2005). *Smithsonian intimate guide to human origins*. New York: HarperCollins.

Zimmer, C. (2009, September 21). The secrets inside your dog's mind. *Time.com*. www.time.com/time/magazine/article/0,9171,1921614-1,00.html (retrieved July 16, 2012)

Zohary, D., & Hopf, M. (1993). *Domestication of plants in the Old World* (2nd ed.). Oxford, UK: Clarendon Press.

Index

abduction, 138
Abell, Paul, 140
absolute dating, 121
acclimatization, 305, *305*
Acheulean tool tradition, 179, *179*
action archaeology, *256*,
　256–258, *258*
action theory, 269–270
adaptation (biological), 12–13, 44–45
　to climate, 306–308, *307*, *308*
　of Darwin's finches, 49, *49*
　defined, 43
　physical variation and, 47
　See also physiological adaptation
adaptation (developmental), 14, *301*,
　301–302, *302*
adaptation (genetic), 300, 301
adaptive radiation, 57
adduction, 138
adenine, 32, *32*
Aegyptopithecus, *136*
affiliative actions, 91
Afghanistan, *217*, 217–218, *250*, 251
Africa, 142, 178, *210*
　archaic *Homo sapiens*, 187–188, *188*
　Australopithecus, 141, 142, *144*, *145*,
　　145–146, *146*, *149*, 149–155, *150*,
　　152, *153*, *154*
　Bantu culture, *251*, 262
　Fertile Crescent, 229–232, *230*, *231*
　fingerprint patterns, *279*
　Homo erectus, 176, *176*
　Homo ergaster, 173, *174*
　Homo habilis, 159, 159–161, *160*, 188
　limestone Cave sites, 150
　Nile Valley, *251*
　Olduvai Gorge specimens, 140, *140*,
　　159, *159*, *173*
　refugee family unification and DNA
　　testing, *36*, 36–37
　Timbuktu, 102, *102*
　See also Homo sapiens
African Burial Ground Project, New York
　City, 14–15, *15*, 278
African Wildlife Foundation, 76, *76*
agriculture
　agricultural innovation,
　　258–259
　defined, 245
　intensive, *243*, 243–245, *244*, 245
　Maya forest, *256*, 256–258, *258*
alleles
　defined, 32
　genes and, *32*, 32–34, *33*, *34*
　genotype and, *38*
　of human blood groups, 288, *288*
　sickle-cell allele and malaria,
　　45–47, *46*
　Tay-Sachs allele, *33*, 270
Allen's rule, 306, *306*
alpaca, 235, 271

altitude, 304, 306, *306*
　acclimatization, 305, *305*
　atmospheric pressure, *305*
　Machu Picchu, 265, *265*
altruism, 94
Alzheimer's disease, *33*, 301
amaranth, *235*
Ambrose, Stanley, 192
American Sign Language, *28*
Americas, *210*
　Neolithic revolution, 242
　See also North America;
　　South America
amino acids, 235–236
amniocentesis, 35
amylin, *33*
anagenesis, 48
analogies, 27
analogous wings, 27–28, *28*
anatomical modernity, 197–198
ancestral characteristics, 59
Anderson, David, 9
Angkor Wat, Cambodia, 248, *248*
animal domestication, 228, *231*,
　231–232
Animal Welfare Act, 98, *98*
ankles, *Australopithecus*, *147*,
　147–148
anorexia nervosa, 303
anthropocentrism, 53
anthropoids, 27, *27*, *132*
　defined, 60
　relationships among Old World
　　anthropoids, *136*
　skulls, *133*
Anthropologists of Note
　Berhane Asfaw, 201, *201*
　Franz Boas, 12–13, *13*, 277, *302*
　Peter Ellison, 304, *304*
　Jane Goodall, *12*, 39, 85, *85*, 98,
　　98, 140
　Kinji Imanishi, *85*, 85–87
　Fatimah Jackson, 278, *278*
　Louis S. B. Leakey, 53, 85, 140, *140*,
　　159, *159*
　Mary Nicol Leakey, 140, *140*, 151
　Claude Lévi-Strauss, 309
　Matilda Coxe Stevenson, 13, *13*
　Xinzhi Wu, 201, *201*
anthropology, 3
　applied, 6
　cities of past and future, 272, *272*
　forensic, 14–15, *15*
　four fields of, *5*, 5–6
　linguistic, 8
　lumpers and splitters debate, *160*,
　　160–161
　medical, 6, 308–310, *309*
　molecular, 11
　physical, 11
　See also paleoanthropology

Anthropology Applied, boxed features
　African Burial Ground Project,
　　New York City, 14–15, *15*
　Amazonia fish farming, 260–261,
　　261, *262*
　Congo Heartland Project, *76*, 76–77
　stone tools for modern surgeons,
　　190, *190*
apes, 71–73, *72*, *73*, *74*
　humans compared with, 12
　See also primate(s); primate behavior
applied anthropology, 6
　See also Anthropology Applied; forensic
　　anthropology
arboreal, 58
arboreal hypothesis, 133
archaeology, 9
　bio-, 10, *10*
　experimental, 166
　historical, 10
　as science of discovery, 128
　zoo-, 11
Archaic cultures, 226
archaic *Homo sapiens*, 183, *183*
　cultural innovations, 184, *185*, 190
　defined, 184
　Denisovans, 188
　in Java, Africa, and China,
　　187–188, *188*
　Levalloisian technique of, 184, *184*
　Middle Paleolithic culture, 188–193,
　　189, *190*, *191*, *192*
　See also Neandertal
Ardipithecus, *136*, 140–142, *141*, *152*
Ardipithecus kadabba, *144*
Ardipithecus ramidus, *144*, *154*
Armelagos, George, 221
arrested development (primate), 88–90,
　89, *90*
Arsuaga, Juan Luis, *106*
art
　bronze sculpture, 259, *259*
　Chauvet Cave, 212, *212*
　entoptic phenomena, 211, *211*
　Hohle Fels Cave Venus, 209, *209*
　Neolithic, 239, *240*, 240–241, *241*
　Peche Merle Cave, 212–213, *213*
　red ochre, 210, *210*, 216
　on spear-thrower, *208*
artifact, 104
Aryan race, *284*
Asfaw, Berhane, 201, *201*
Ashkenazi Jews, 270
Asia, 181, 229–232, *230*, *231*
　fingerprint patterns, *279*
　primate behavior, 88–90, *90*
asparagus, 224
Atapuerca site, *173*
atlatls, 207, 208, *208*
atmospheric pressure, *305*
Atsalis, Sylvia, 78

Aurignacian tradition, 204
Australia, *210*
  entoptic phenomena in cave art,
    211, *211*
  fingerprint patterns, *279*
  Sahul and Sunda land masses, *216*,
    216–219, *217*
Australian Aborigines, 288, *288*
Australopithecus, 136, *142*, 142–143
  ankles of, *147*, 147–148
  central Africa specimens, 149
  defined, 142
  east Africa specimens, *144*, *145*,
    145–146, *146*, 149, *149*
  Homo and, *152*, 152–154, *153*,
    154, 161
  in human origins scenarios, *154*
  robust australopithecines, *144*, *151*,
    151–152, *152*
  south Africa specimens, *144*, *150*,
    150–151
Australopithecus aethiopicus, *144*, *152*
  in human origins scenarios, *154*
Australopithecus afarensis, *144*, 144–145,
    149, *152*
  in human origins scenarios, *154*
  modern human, chimp skeletons
    comparison to, *146*
Australopithecus africanus, *144*, *152*
  foot, 150, *150*
  in human origins scenarios, *154*
Australopithecus anamensis, *144*,
    149, *152*
Australopithecus bahrelghazali, *144*, 149
Australopithecus boisei, *144*, *152*
  in human origins scenarios, *154*
Australopithecus garhi, *144*, *152*,
    153, *153*
  in human origins scenarios, *154*
Australopithecus robustus, *144*, *151*,
    151–152, *152*
  in human origins scenarios, *154*
Australopithecus sediba, *144*, *152*, 153,
    155, *155*
  in human origins scenarios, *154*
Avian influenza, 271
avocado, *235*
Aztec culture, 207, *236*
  earth mother goddess, 157, *157*
  Teotihuacan, Mexico, 250–252, *251*,
    252, 253

baboons, 71
  conservation strategies for, 76–77
  Old World anthropoid relations of, *136*
Bacon's Rebellion, 277
Bambanani Women's Group, 298, *298*
bamboo construction, *180*
Bangladesh, 320, *320*
Bantu culture, 251, *262*
barley, *234*, 235–236
Basque culture, 288, *288*
beaks, 52, *52*
beans, *234*, *235*
bees, 235, 257
Beger, Bruno, *284*
The Bell Curve (Herrnstein and
    Murray), 286
Berger, Lee, 155, *177*
Bergmann's rule, 306, *306*
Bering Strait land bridge, *219*, 219–220
Bilzingsleben site, *173*
binocular vision, 64
bioarchaeology, 10, *10*
biocultural approach, 12
Biocultural Connections, boxed features
  childbirth and evolution, 157, *157*
  chimpanzees in biomed research, 98, *98*

dogs, *232*, 232–233
epicanthic eye fold, *289*, 289–290
  Kennewick Man, 120, *120*,
    219, 220
  organ transplantation, 6
  pesticides, 322
  red color, 65, *65*
  swine-borne disease in Americas, 271
bipedalism, 130, *130*
  anatomy of, *137*, 137–140, *138*,
    139, *140*
  climate and vegetation zone impact
    on, 154–155, *155*
  defined, 135
  fully erect bipedals, 155–159,
    157, *158*
  heat stress control and, 156–158, *158*
  Orrorin tugenensis, *137*
  Taung Child, 142
  Toumai skull, *137*
Birdsell, Joseph, 216
bisphenol-A (BPA), 321
Black, Davidson, 177–178
blade technique, 206
Blakey, Michael, 15
Blombos Cave, *209*
blood type, 32, *33*, 38–39
  clines, *291*
  as example of polymorphism,
    287–288, *288*
Blumenbach, Johann, 276, *276*
Boas, Franz, 12–13, *13*, 277, *302*
Boaz, Noel T., 170
body maps, 298, *298*
Boesch, Christophe, 171
Bolivia, 260–261, *261*, *262*
bonobos, 73, *74*
  conservation strategies for, 76, *76*
  female dominance among, 86
  Imanishi's studies of, 85, *85*–87
  Kanzi, 167
  Old World anthropoid relations
    of, *136*
  relationship to other primates, *61*
  sexual behavior, 80, *80*
bow and arrow, 209
Bowen, Paul, *177*
Bowen, Richard M., *177*
Boxgrove site, *173*
Bozza, Diana, *301*
Brace, C. Loring, 186
brachiation, 67
brain
  cranium size, *174*
  Homo diet and, 172, *172*
  Homo sapiens, 27, *203*, *205*
  Neandertal, *186*, 186–187, *187*
  personhood, brain death, and organ
    transplantation, 6
  primate, 66
  temperature control, 156–158, *158*
  Wernicke's area, *182*
  See also intelligence; skulls
breastfed babies, 4–5, 57, *57*
Brill, David, *155*
Brinkmeier, Dan, 261, *261*, *262*
Britain, 277, 288, *288*
  Piltdown specimens, *143*, 143–144
Bronze Age, 259, *259*
bubonic plague, 271
burial
  African Burial Ground Project,
    New York City, 14–15, *15*, 278
  City of the Dead, Cairo, *272*
  in forensic anthropology, 14–15, *15*
  grave goods, 266
  at Kebara, 191, *191*
  at Shanidar, *186*, 191

  at Sima de los Huesos, 106, *183*,
    183–184
  See also rituals
burin, 179, 188, 207
Bwindi Impenetrable National Park, *55*,
    55–56, *56*

cacao, *234*
Caddoan-speaking civilization, Texas-
    Arkansas, 271
capitalism, 224
Carmichael, Aunty Beryl, *217*, 217–218
Caspari, Rachel, 198
cassava, 278
caste system, 282, *283*
Çatalhöyük, Turkey, 250–251, *251*
catarrhines, 61
cattle, *245*
cell division, 34–39, *38*
Census Bureau, US, 282–287, *287*
Central African Republic, *217*, 217–218
Central America, *253*, 253–256, *254*, *256*
  See also Maya culture
Ceprano site, *173*
Cercopithecus, *136*
Chad, *142*, *144*
Châtelperronian tradition, *204*
Chauvet Cave, 212, *212*
chicken, 239, *239*
chicle, 257
chiefdom, 27
Childe, V. Gordon, 229
Chile, *217*, 217–218, 219, 288
chili pepper, 235, 236, *236*
chimpanzees, 73
  Australopithecines and human jaws
    vs., 149
  breastfeeding among, 57, *57*
  climbing capacity of, 147–148
  Goodall's studies of, *12*
  human DNA compared to, 39–40
  hypoglossal canal, *182*
  leopard consumption of, 171
  life cycle, *92*
  modern human and *A. afarensis*
    compared to, *146*
  Nellie, 130, *130*
  Old World anthropoid relations of, *136*
  relationship to other primates, *61*
  Save the Chimps, 98, *98*
  toolmaking, 85, *85*
China, *217*–218, 288, *288*
  Neolithic cities, *177*, 177–178, *178*,
    187–188, *188*, 250, *251*
  Zhoukoudian Cave, 170, *173*, *177*,
    177–178, *178*, 179
Chippewa culture, 288, *288*
chocolate, *234*
chordates, 27, *27*
Chororapithexus abyssinicus, 135, *136*
Christianity
  creation story, 25
  scriptural interpretation for fossils,
    28–29
chromatid, 32
chromosomes, 31, 32–33, *33*
chronometric dating, 121
Ciochon, Russell L., 170
cities
  agricultural innovation and, 258–259
  ancient past and future, 272, *272*
  Cahokia, southern Illinois, US, 269
  central government, 262, 262–266,
    263, *264*, 265
  disease and, 270
  diversification of labor, 259–262,
    261, *262*
  emergence of, 249–25

Great Zimbabwe, *251, 262*
Kabul, Afghanistan, *250*
Machu Picchu, 265, *265*
Mohenjo-Daro, 251
Nile Valley, *251*
policing ancient, *267*
social stratification, 266, *266*
Teotihuacan, 250–252, *251, 252, 253*
Tikal, *253*, 253–256, *254, 256*
Ur, *267*
vitamin D deficiencies, *292*
civilization
defining, 250–253
disease and colonialism, 270–271
earliest currently known, *251*
ecological theories for, *267*,
267–269, *269*
clade, 60
cladogenesis, 48, *48*
clans, 280–281
Clark, Desmond, 201
class, 27, *27*
classification, 26, *26–28, 27*
See also taxonomy
climate
in Allen's rule, 306, *306*
in Bergmann's rule, 306, *306*
continental drift and, 126
diet and vegetation zones,
154–155, *155*
ecological niches and, 57, 66
fire use favored by, 179–181
food production *vs.* foraging, 229–232,
230, 231
mammal diversification and, 58
Neandertal adaptation to, *186*,
186–187, *187, 188*
physiological adaptation to cold,
306–307, *307*
physiological adaptation to heat,
307–308, *308*
clines, 47, 287–293, *288, 289, 291,
292, 293*
clothing, Upper Paleolithic, 215
Coca-Cola bottling plant, *323*
cocaine, 285
codes of ethics, 19–21
co-dominant allele, *38*
codon, 32–33
coffee, *234*
cognitive capacity, 220
Cohen, Mark Nathan, 221
Collins, Billy, 232, 233
colobus, *136*
colonialism, 270–271
colorblindness, 32–33, *33*, 42–43, *43*,
65, *65*
coltan, 2, *2*, 75, *75*
communication
American Sign Language, *28*
Homo erectus, *182*, 182–183
humans as prey and development of,
170–171, *171*
language areas of brain, *182*
Neandertal, 193
pointing with human hand, *232*,
232–233
primate capacity for, *161*, 193
community, 83
Congo Heartland Project, *76*, 76–77
Conkey, Margaret, 214–215
conservation strategies, 74–78, *75, 76, 78*
continental drift, 126
contraceptive use, 311, *311*
convergent evolution, 59
cooking, by *H. erectus*, 179–181
Coosa city-states, Georgia, 271
coprolites, 114

core-fringe-legume pattern (CFLP), 236
corn. See maize
corporations, 224
co-sleeping, 4, *5*
cosmetic surgery, 288–290, *289*
cotton, *234*, 235, *235*, 241
Coulston, Frederick, 98, *98*
Crabtree, Don, 190
Croatia, 191
Cro-Magnon, 197–198, *198*
See also Upper Paleolithic
cultural anthropology, 6
applied, 8
See also ethnography; ethnology
cultural resource management, 11
culture
ape, 12, 85
defined, 7
primate, 99
See also specific culture
culture-bound, 4
culture shock, 16, 17
Cuvier, George, 29
cystic fibrosis, *33*
cytoplasm, 33–34, *34*
cytosine, 32, *32*

Dani culture, *234*
Dart, Raymond, 142, 171
Darwin, Charles, 28–30, *29*, 49, *49*,
143, 151
Darwinian gradualism, 49
dating methods, 121–125, *122, 123, 125*
datum point, 111
Dawson, Charles, 143, *143*
demographics, 69
dendrochronology, 124
Denisovans, 188
dental formula, 62
See also teeth, chewing apparatus and
derived features, 59
DES (diethylstilbestrol), 321
The Descent of Man (Darwin), 143
descriptive linguistics, 8
DeSilva, Jeremy, 147
developmental adaptation, 14, *301*,
301–302, *302*
development trajectories, *302*
DeVore, Irven, 190, *190*
de Waal, Frans, 49, 86
diabetes, *33*
diastema, 149
diffusion, 239
Mesoamerican plant domestication,
228, 232
dinosaurs, *132*
disease, *33*
bone, *292*
brought to Americas, 271
civilization, cities, and, 270
colonialism and, 270–271
defined, 310
DES and cancer, 321
from domesticated animals, *245*
evolutionary medicine insights into,
315, 315–316
immune system *vs.*, *315*
infectious, *243*, 243–245, *244, 245*, 271
political ecology of, 317
poverty and infection, 270
prion diseases, *317*, 317–318
science, illness, and, 310–312, *311*
social stratification and, 270
diurnal, 58
Dmanisi site, *173*
DNA (deoxyribonucleic acid), 24, 31,
33–34, *34*
human compared to chimpanzee, 39–40

refugee family unification and DNA
testing, 36, *36*–37
structure of, 32
Doctors Without Borders, 298, *298*
doctrine, 16
dogs, *232*, 232–233, 235, *245*, 271
domestication
animal, 228
defined, 227
diseases from animals, *245*
early centers of, 232–236, *234,
235, 236*
plant, 227–228, *228, 232*
See also specific animal; specific plant
dominance hierarchies, 84
dominant, 37
Donis, Ruben, 239, *239*
Dryopithecus, 135, *136*
ducks, 235, *245*, 271
Dupain, Jeff, 76, *76*
Durkheim, Émile, 39

Eaton, Boyd, 221
ecofact, 104
ecological niche, 57, 66
egalitarian societies, 242
Egypt, *217*, 217–218, 250, *251*, 272
Eldredge, Niles, 49
Ellison, Peter, 304, *304*
El Pilar, Central America, *256*,
257–258, *258*
Emancipation Proclamation (United
States), 277
empirical science, 16
endangered language, *9*
endangered species, 52, *52*
endemic, 310
endocast, 117
endoplasmic reticulum, 33–34, *34*
entoptic phenomena, 211, *211*
environment
deprivation, 286–287
diet and, in human origins debates,
154–155, *155*
habitat disturbance/destruction, 224
health disparities and, *320*, 320–321
primate arrested development *vs.*
social, 88–90, *89, 90*
See also physiological adaptation
environmental toxins, *42*, 320, *320*
pesticides, 321–322, *322*
enzymes, 32
Eocene epoch, *132*
epicanthic eye fold, *289*, 289–290
epigenetics, 286
Erickson, Clark, 261, *261, 262*
Eskimo culture, 288, *288*
Ethiopia, 311, *311*
Australopithecus specimens, 141, 142,
144, 152, 152–154, *153, 154*
World Heritage sites, *217*, 217–218
ethnic cosmetic surgery, 288–290, *289*
ethnobotany, 11
ethnocentrism
Boas's concerns about, 12–13, *13*, 277, *302*
defined, 4
European, 197–198
ethnography, 7
ethnology, 7
eukaryotic cell, 33–34, *34*
Europe/Europeans, 143–144, *210*
blood type B, *291*
colonialist, and spread of infectious
diseases, 270–271
ethnocentrism in, 197–198
fingerprint patterns, *279*
organ trafficking, 20, *20*
organ transplantation, 6

evolution
  Darwin's theory of, 28–30, *29*, 49, *49*, 143, 151
  defined, 41
  Hardy-Weinberg principle, 40–41
  primate behavior as model for human, 81–83, *82*
  race and human, 294–295, *295*
evolutionary medicine, 221
  defined, 314
  on infectious disease, *315*, 315–316
  symptoms as defense mechanisms, 314–315
experimental archaeology, 166

factory farming, 239, *239*
Falk, Dean, 156
Faraday, Deborah, *301*
farming
  agricultural innovation, 258–259
  Amazonia fish farming, 260–261, *261*, *262*
  factory farming, 239, *239*
  hydraulic theory, 267
  intensive, *243*, 243–245, *244*, *245*
  at Mesa Verde, 269, *269*
  roots of, 225–227
  See also horticulture
fava beans, *293*, 293–294, *294*
Fay, Michael, 171
Fenn, Elizabeth, 271
Fertile Crescent, 229–232, *230*, *231*
fertility (human), 35–36
  diet and, *303*
  reproductive physiology *vs.* social stimuli, *304*, *304*
  reproductive success, 43–44, 321
field methods
  concepts and methods for most distant past, *125*, 125–128, *126*, *127*
  dating methods, 121–125, *122*, *123*, *125*
  recovering cultural and biological remains, 104–109, *105*, *106*, *107*, *108*
  searching for artifacts and fossils, 109–115, *110*, *112*, *113*, *114*, *115*
  sorting evidence, 115–120, *116*, *117*, *118*, *119*, *120*
fieldwork, 7, 16–17, *18*
figurative art, 210
fingerprint patterns, *279*
fire, *H. erectus* use of, 179–181
fishing, 260–261, *261*, *262*
flax, 241
Flood, Robert, *26*
flotation, 111
fluorine dating, 121, 144
food
  gracile and robust australopithecine, *151*, 151–152
  H. erectus cooking, 179–181
  Homo, 172, *172*
  in human origins debates, 154–155, *155*
  Neolithic, *243*, 243–245, *244*, *245*
  population size and, 236–237, *237*
  production *vs.* foraging, 229–232, *230*, *231*
  slow release, 292
  spread of agriculture, 239, 240
  women's nutrition and fertility, *303*, 303–304
food foraging, food production *vs.*, 229–232, *230*, *231*
foramen magnum, 66, *137*
Ford, Anabel, 257–258, *258*
Fore culture, 317

forensic anthropology, 14–15, *15*
forest gardeners, *256*, 256–258, *258*
fossils
  Bible interpretation of, 28–29
  defined, 104
  field methods for finding, 109–115, *110*, *112*, *113*, *114*, *115*
  first *Homo*, 152
  fossilization process, 104–105
  global distribution of living and fossil primates, *54*
founder effects, 42–43
fovea centralis, 64
France, 197, *198*, 212, *212*
fruit fly, *48*
Fukuoka, Masanubu, 257

G-6-PD deficiency, *293*, 293–294, *294*
Galapagos Islands, *29*, 29–30, 49, *49*
Galdikas, Biruté M. F., 88
Galloway, Patricia, 271
gardening, *256*, 256–258, *258*
gelada estrus, *87*
gender bias, 169
gender identity, 167
genealogy, for sale, 280–281
gene flow, 43
gene pool, 40, 41, 42
genera, *26*, 26–28, *27*
genes, 285–286, *286*
  alleles and, *32*, 32–34, *33*, *34*
  defined, 31
  homeobox, *48*
  human karyotype, 32–33, *33*
  regulatory, *48*
  transmission of, 31–32
  See also DNA
genetic adaptations, 301
  defined, 300
genetically modified organisms (GMOs), 232
genetic code, 12, 34
genetic drift, 42–43
genetics, Mendel's laws of heredity, 30–31
genetic testing, prenatal, 35, *35*
genocide, 14, 282, *284*
genome, *32*, *33*, *33*, 278
genotype, 37, *38*, 292
genus (genera), *26*, 26–28, *27*
geographic information systems (GIS), 9
Georgia (country), *217*, 217–218
Germany, 209, *209*, 282–284, *284*
gibbons, 61, *136*
gigantism, *33*
Glasse, Robert, 317
globalization, 21, 318
Globalscapes, boxed features
  Iraqi ancient artifacts in New York City, 268, *268*
  organ trafficking, 20, *20*
  primate conservation strategies, 75, 75–76, *76*
  radio programs and medical clinics, 311, *311*
  swine flu, 238, *238*
  World Heritage sites, *217*, 217–218
goats, 234
gods and goddesses
  Aztec culture, 157, *157*
  large-scale sculptures, 259, *259*
golden lion tamarin, 78
Goldsmith, Michelle L., 55, 55–56
Gombe Chimpanzee Reserve, Tanzania, 85, *85*
Goodall, Jane, 12, 39, 85, *85*, 98, *98*, 140
gorillas, 52, *52*
  conservation strategies, 75, 75–76, *76*
  dentition, 62

  ecotourism, 55, 55–56, *56*
  Homo habilis hand and, 159, *159*
  lowland, 55, 78
  mountain, 55–56, 74, 76–77, 78
  Old World anthropoid relations of, *136*
  relationship to other primates, 61
  sexual dimorphism, 72–73, *73*
Gould, Stephen Jay, 16, 49
gourds, 234, 235, *235*
government, central, *262*, 262–266, *263*, *264*, 265
gracile australopithecus, *144*, 150, *150*, *151*
grade, 60
Grand Dolina site, 178
Grant, Madison, 282
grave goods, 266
  See also burial
Gray, Peter, 304, *304*
Great Chain of Being, *26*
Great Rift Valley, 144
Great Ziggurat, Ur, 267
Great Zimbabwe city, *251*, 262
Greece, 259, *259*
grid system, 111
grooming (primate), *86*, 86–87
Grotte de Chauvet, 212, *212*
ground-penetrating radar (GPR), 9
guanine, 32, *32*
Guatemalan Foundation for Forensic Anthropology, *15*
Gugar Goge (Tell It to Me Straight), 311, *311*
Guillette, Elizabeth, 322
guinea pig, 271

habitat destruction, 224
habituation, 55, 55–56, *56*
hafting, 184, *185*, 190
hand-axe, Acheulean, 179, *179*
hands
  Australopithecus sediba, 155, *155*
  bipedals' weapon function of, 155
  dog and human communication via, *232*, 232–233
  environmental toxins and missing, *42*
  in Neandertal cave art, 196, *196*
  prehensile, 67
  wings compared to, 27–28, *28*
haplorhines, 60
Hardenberg, Firmon, 190
Hardy, Godfrey H., 40–41
Hardy-Weinberg principle, 40–41
Hare, Brian, 232
Harris lines, *243*
Hawks, John, 146
Hayek, Salma, *293*
healing, *189*, 191
  Doctors Without Borders, 298, *298*
  evolutionary principles applied to, 221
  HIV/AIDS intervention, 17–19, *18*, 34, 298, *298*
  medical pluralism, 318
  medical systems, 309, *309*
  obsidian scalpels, 190, *190*
  red ochre, 210, *210*, 216
health disparities
  environmental impact on, 320, 320–321
  globalization and structural violence, 318
  population size and, 318–319, *319*
  poverty and, 319–320
  poverty *vs.* health, *319*
Hemings, Sally, *279*
hemoglobin, *33*, 38, *38*, 39
hemp, 234
heredity, 30–31, 286
  See also genes

Herrnstein, Richard, 286
heterozygous, 37
Hexian site, *173*
hierarchy
  18th/19th century European, 275–278, *276, 277*
  in primate behavior, 84–86, *85, 86*
higher primates, 60
Hinduism, 25
historical archaeology, 10
historical linguistics, 8–9
Hitler, Adolf, 282
HIV/AIDS, 17–19, *18,* 34, 298, *298*
Hlwele, Nondomiso, 298, *298*
Hohle Fels Cave, Germany, 209, *209*
holistic perspective, 3
homeobox genes, *48*
homeotherm, 57
home range, 84, *84*
Hominids, 27, *27,* 61, *136*
Hominins, 61
  climbing capacity of, 147–148
  Pliocene diversity of, *144,* 144–154, *145, 146, 147, 148, 149, 150, 151, 152, 153*
hominoid, 61
Homo (genus)
  Australopithecus and, *152,* 152–154, *153, 154,* 161
  brain size and diet, 172, *172*
  defined, 165
  discovery of first stone toolmaker, *166,* 166–167
  first fossil record of, *152*
  as hunters or gatherers, 168–172, *169, 171*
  Lake Turkana specimens, *159,* 159–160, *160*
  Old World anthropoid relations of, *136*
  sex, gender, and early, 167–168, *169*
Homo antecessor, 174, 183, 184
Homo erectus, 105, 172
  in Africa, 176, *176*
  in China, 170, *173,* 177, 177–178, *178,* 179
  cranial capacity range, *174*
  culture of, *178,* 178–182, *179, 181*
  entering Eurasia, 176
  evidence of complex thought, 181–182
  fossils of, *173,* 173–174, *188*
  Homo habilis relationship with, 175–176
  in Indonesia, 176–177
  language, *182,* 182–183
  linguistic abilities, *182,* 182–183
  physical characteristics, *174,* 174–175, *175*
  as prey and development of communication, 170–171, *171*
  skull, 174–175, *175, 188*
  in western Europe, 178
Homo ergaster, 173, 174
Homo florensis, 181
Homo habilis, 159, 160, 160–161
  defined, 159
  skull comparison, *188*
Homo heidelbergensis, 174
homologies, 27–28
Homo sapiens, 12
  chimpanzee DNA compared to, 39–40
  classification of, *26,* 26–28, *27*
  cultural milestones in evolution of, *205*
  future, 321–323, *323*
  Neandertal relationship to, 186, *204*
  See also archaic *Homo sapiens*

Homo sapiens idaltu, 200, *200*
homosexual behavior (primate), 80, *80,* 88
homozygous, 36, 39
Honduras, 217, 217–218
horticulture, 227
  See also agriculture; gardening
housing
  mammoth bone, 215, *215*
  Mesa Verde, southwest US, 269, *269*
  Neolithic, 239–241, *240, 241*
  reindeer-skin tent, *5*
Hudson, Charles, 271
human body modification
  cosmetic surgery, 288–290, *289*
  environmental toxins causing, *42*
Human Genome Project, 33, *33,* 278
human origins debate, *198*
  Aboriginal views, *216,* 216–219, *217*
  in Americas, *219,* 219–220
  anatomical evidence, *202,* 202–204, *203*
  apes and, 134–137, *135, 136, 137,* 140
  coexistence and cultural continuity, 204–206, *205*
  cultural evidence, 204, *204*
  environment, diet, and, 154–155, *155*
  expansion and colonization, 215
  first fossil record of *Homo, 152*
  genetic evidence, 202
  multiregional hypothesis, 199–200
  possible scenarios, *154*
  problematic definition of modern human, 197–198, *199*
  race and human evolution, 206
  recent African origins hypothesis, 34, *200, 200*
  Sahul and Sunda, *216,* 216–219, *217*
  Upper Paleolithic technology, 206–208, *207, 208*
human variation
  blood-groups, 287–288, *288*
  culture and biological diversity, 290, *291,* 292–293
  facial features and shape, 288–290, *289*
  See also modern human; skin color
hunting
  atlatls, 207, 208, *208*
  bow and arrow, 209
  cliff-fall strategy of, 189–190, 220
  fluted spear points, 220
  Homo, 168–172, *169, 171*
  Mousterian tool tradition and Neandertal, *189,* 189–191, *204*
  net, 208–209
  obsidian blades, 190, *190*
  primate, 97, *97,* 99
hunting response, 306–307, *307*
Huntington's disease, *33*
Hutus, Rwanda, 284
Huxley, Thomas Henry, 30
hydraulic theory, 267
hypoglossal canal, 182, *182*
hypoplasias, *243,* 243–245, *244, 245*
hypothesis, 16
hypoxia, 304–305

Ice Man (Ötsi), *105*
Imanishi, Kinji, *85,* 85–87
immune system, *315*
Inca civilization, 265, *265,* 266, *266,* 271
Indonesia, 181
  World Heritage sites, *217,* 217–218
  See also Homo erectus
Indus civilization, *251*
influenza, 245
inheritance of acquired characteristics theory, 29

innovation, 227
intelligence, 285, *291*
  cranial capacity range, *174*
  genetic components and expression of, 286–287
  Homo diet and, 172, *172*
  of *Homo sapiens,* 27, *203,* 205
  Neandertal, *186,* 186–187, *187*
  primate, 66
  See also chimpanzees; language; orangutans
intelligent design (ID), 25
intensive agriculture, *243,* 243–245, *244, 245*
Iran
  World Heritage sites, *217,* 217–218
  Zagros Mountains, 231–232
Iraq
  ancient artifacts stolen from, 268, *268*
  first Neolithic cities, 250, *251*
  Shanidar Cave, *186,* 191
  World Heritage sites, *217,* 217–218
  Zagros Mountains, 231–232
Ireland, 277
irrigation. *See* farming
ischial callosities, 83
isolating mechanisms, 48
isotherm, 57
Israel, 191

Jackson, Fatimah, 278, *278*
Japan, 6, 288, *288*
Java, 173, 187–188, *188*
Jefferson, Thomas, *279*
Jericho, Tower of, *240*
Jerusalem, *217,* 217–218
Jhala, Jayasinhji, *4*
Jianshi site, *173*
joint attention, 233
Judaism, 25, 270, *284*

Kanzi (bonobo), *167*
karyotype, 32, 33, *33*
Kebara site, 191, *191*
Kemps, Willy, *207*
Kennewick Man, 120, *120,* 219, 220
Kenya, 142, *144,* 279
  Lake Turkana, *159,* 159–160, *160*
Kenyanthropus platyops, 144, 149, *152,* 154
kingdom, *27*
knuckle walking, 141
Konner, Melvin, 221
Konso Gardula site, *173*
Koobi Fora site, *173*
Koro language, *9*
k-selected, 58
kuru, 317
Kwakiutl culture, 13

labor, diversification in cities, 259–262, *261, 262*
lactase/lactose, 292
Lake Turkana, Kenya, *159,* 159–160, *160*
Lamarck, Jean-Baptiste, 29
Landau, Misia, 165
land ownership, concept of, 229
  See also water/land resources
language
  American Sign Language, *28*
  areas of brain involved in, *182*
  endangered, *9*
  gene, 193
  Homo erectus, 182, 182–183
  Neandertal, 193
  primate capacity for, 193
  Wernicke's area of brain, *182*
Lantian site, *173*
law of competitive exclusion, 152

law of independent assortment, 31
law of segregation, 31
Leakey, Louis, 53, 85, 140, *140*, 159, *159*
Leakey, Mary Nicol, 140, *140*, 151
Leakey, Richard, 140, 159
learning, 92–96, *93*, *94*, *95*
legumes, 235–236
lemurs, *59*, 61, 68, *68*, *92*
lentils, 235–236
Levalloisian technique, 184, *184*
Lévi-Strauss, Claude, 309
life cycles, *92*
limestone cave sites, Africa, 150
Lin, Jeremy, *274*
Lindenbaum, Shirley, 317
linguistic anthropology, 8
linguistics, descriptive, 8
Linnaeus, Carolus, *26*, *26*–28, *27*
Linnean suborders, 60
Living Tongues Institute for Endangered
    Languages, *9*
llama, *234*, 235, 271
Lock, Margaret, 6
Lomako Conservation Science Center,
    DRC, *76*, 76–77
long bone growth, *302*
Longgupo site, *173*
Lorblanchet, Michel, 212–213, *213*
lorises, *61*, 68, *68*
lost wax casting method, 259, *259*
Lower Paleolithic, 166
lowland gorillas, 55, 78
Lucy (fossil specimen), *144*, 145
lumpers and splitters debate, 160–161
Lyell, Charles, 29, 30

macaques, 71, 85, 86, *92*, *136*
Machu Picchu, Andes, 265, *265*
macroevolution, speciation and, 47–49,
    48, *49*
mad cow disease, 317
maize, 228, *228*, *234*, 235, *235*
    GMO corn, *232*
    Maya forest, *256*, 256–258, *258*
Makiritares, 288, *288*
malaria, *293*
    cassava treatment of, 278
    sickle-cell allele and, 45–47, *46*
Malawi, 142
male dominance display, *88*
Mali, *311*, 312–314
malnutrition, *243*, 243–245, *244*, *245*,
    319, 319–320
    vitamin D deficiency, *292*
Malthus, Thomas, 30
mammals, 12, *132*
    classification of, *26*, *26*–28, *27*
    defined, 26
    jaw and teeth, *58*
    reptiles compared to, *57*, 57–58, *58*
*Man's Most Dangerous Myth: The Fallacy of
    Race* (Montagu), 277
Mapuche culture, 288, *288*
Marks, Jonathan, *39*
marrow, 169
Marshack, Alexander, 192
mass graves, 15
mass media, 311, *311*
material culture, 104
Mauer site, *173*
Maya culture, *253*, 253–256, *254*, *256*,
    257–258, *258*, 288, *288*
McDermott, LeRoy, 214–215
measles, 245, 271
medical anthropology, 6, 308–310, *309*
medical pluralism, 318
medical system, 309, *309*
Mediterranean Sea, 142

Mehdiganj, India, *323*
meiosis, 35–36
melanin, 290
Melka Kunturé site, *173*
Mellars, Paul, 214–215
menarche, 302, *303*
Mendel, Gregor, 30
menopause, 303
Mesa Verde, southwest US, 269, *269*
Mesoamerica, 250–252, *251*, *252*, *253*
    pottery and weaving, 242
Mesolithic, 225, 227, *243*, 243–245,
    244, *245*
    defined, 226
Mesopotamia, *251*, *264*
    See also Iraq
messenger RNA (mRNA), 33–34, *34*
metabolic rate, 307, *307*
Mexico, 250–252, *251*, *252*, *253*, 311,
    311, 322
microlith, 226
middens, 110
Middle Paleolithic
    archaic *Homo sapiens*, 188–193, *189*,
        190, *191*, *192*
    Mousterian tool tradition, *189*, 189–
        191, *204*
    Neandertal, 188–193, *189*, *190*, *191*,
        192
milk, 292–294, *293*, *294*
millet, *234*
million years ago (mya), 12
Mintz, Sidney, 236
Miocene epoch, *132*
    apes and human origins, 134–137, *135*,
        136, *137*, 140
    climate change, diet, and vegetation
        zones, 154–155, *155*
    fully erect bipedals, 155–159, *157*, *158*
    timeline of hominins, *152*
mitochondria, 33–34, *34*
mitochondrial DNA (mtDNA), 34,
    200, *200*
    genealogy for sale, 280–281
mitosis, 35
modern human
    A. afarensis, chimp skeletons compari-
        son to, *146*
    Aurignacian tradition, 204, *204*
    biological diversity of, 287–293, *288*,
        289, *291*, *292*, *293*
    classification of, 27, *27*
    cultural milestones in evolution
        of, *205*
    Homo habilis hand and, 159, *159*
    hypoglossal canal, *182*
    life cycle, *92*
    problematic definition of,
        197–198, *199*
    relationship to other primates, *61*
modernity, anatomical, 197–198
Mohenjo-Daro, Pakistan, 251
Mojokerto site, *173*
molecular anthropology, 11
molecular clock, 126
monkeys
    colobus, *136*
    on evolutionary timeline, *132*
    gelada estrus, *87*
    golden lion tamarin, *78*
    lemurs, *59*, 61, 68, *68*, *92*
    lorises, *61*, 68, *68*
    macaques, 71, 85, 86, *92*, *136*
    Old World, *61*, 70–71, *71*
    relationship to other primates, *61*
monogamy, 91
Montagu, Ashley, 277
Monti, Laurie, 292

mountain gorillas, 55–56, 74, 76–77, 78
mouse, life cycle, *92*
Mousterian tool tradition, *189*,
    189–191, *204*
multiregional hypothesis, 199–200
mumps, 271
Mundorff, Amy Zelson, 15
Murray, Charles, 286
musical art
    Neandertal flute, 192, *192*
    Upper Paleolithic, *209*, 209–215, *211*,
        212, *213*
Muslim creation story, 25
mutation, 42, *42*
    defined, 41
    malaria and sickle-cell anemia, 45–47, *46*
    preventing powerful jaw muscle, 181
myths, 25

Nabhan, Gary, 292
Nariokotome site, *173*, 176, *176*
natal group, 83
Native American Graves Protection and
    Repatriation Act (NAGPRA), 11
    Kennewick Man debate, 120, *120*,
        219, 220
Native Americans, 288, *288*
    Caddoan-speaking civilization, Texas-
        Arkansas, 271
    Cahokia city, southern Illinois, 269
    infectious diseases from Europeans,
        270–271
    See also specific culture; specific language
Natufian culture, *226*, 229–230, *230*, 240
    defined, 226
natural selection, 30
Navajo culture, 288, *288*
Neandertal
    Châtelperronian tradition, *204*
    defined, 185
    Homo sapiens relationship to, 186
    language, 193
    Middle Paleolithic, 188–193, *189*, *190*,
        191, *192*
    Mousterian tool tradition, *189*,
        189–191, *204*
    skull shape, brain size, culture, *186*,
        186–187, *187*, 188
    symbolisms and culture, *191*,
        191–192, *192*
Nellie (chimpanzee), 130, *130*
Nenet culture, *5*
Neolithic, 225
    culture, 239–240, *240*
    modern concept of progress applied
        to, 245
    social structure, 241–242, *242*
    toolmaking, pottery, housing, clothing,
        239, 240, 240–241, *241*
    tooth decay, intensive agriculture, and
        stress, *243*, 243–245, *244*, *245*
Neolithic revolution, 225
    in Americas, 242
    animal domestication, 228, *231*,
        231–232
    human biology impacted by, *243*,
        243–245, *244*, *245*
    plant domestication, 227–228,
        228, 232
    spread of food production, 237, 239
net hunting, 208–209
New World monkeys, *61*, 69, 69–70,
    70, 134
Nez Perce culture, 25
niche, ecological, 57, 66
Nichols, Johanna, 219
Niger, *217*, 217–218, 288, *288*
Nigeria, 311, *311*

Nile Valley, north Africa, *251*
Nilotes, 288, *288*
nocturnal, 57
North America
    Bering Strait land bridge, *219*, 219–220
    Kennewick Man, 120, *120*, 219, 220
    Mesa Verde, 269, *269*
    organ transplantation, 6
notochord, 27, *27*

Oakley, Kenneth, 144
oasis theory, 229
Obama, Barack, 279
obesity, *319*, 319–320
obsidian blades, 190, *190*
ochre, 210, *210*, 216
Oldowan tool tradition, 166, *167*
Olduvai Gorge, 140, *140*, 159, *159*, 173
Old World anthropoids, *136*
Old World monkeys, *61*, 70–71, *71*,
    87, *132*
Oligocene epoch, *132*, 133–134, *136*
Omo site, *173*
One Straw Revolution (Fukuoka), 257
On Man's Place in Nature (Huxley), 30
On the Origin of Species (Darwin), 30, 151
opposable toe, 67, 130, *130*
orangutans
    Goodall's early studies, 85, *85*
    Old World anthropoid relations of, *136*
    rape among, 88–90, *90*
    relationship to other primates, *61*
    spear fishing, *73*
order, 27, *27*
organ donation, 6
Original Studies, boxed features
    action archaeology, *256*, 256–258, *258*
    Australopithecus ankles, *147*, 147–148
    genealogy for sale, 280–281
    history of mortality and physiological
        stress, *243*, 243–244, *244*
    Mali: science, medicine, and culture,
        311, 312–314
Orrorin tugenensis, *136*, 136–137, *137*, *152*
Ota Benga, 277, *277*
Otte, Marcel, 192, *192*
ovulation, 88

Pääbo, Svante, 193
paint fabrication, *210*
painting toolkits, 192
Pakistan, 243, *243*, 250, 251, *251*
    World Heritage sites, *217*, 217–218
paleoanthropology
    dating methods, 121–125, *122*, *123*, *125*
    defined, 12
    field methods, *125*, 125–128, *126*, *127*
    recovering cultural and biological
        remains, 104–109, *105*, *106*,
        107, *108*
    searching for artifacts and fossils,
        109–115, *110*, *112*, *113*, *114*, *115*
    sorting evidence, 115–120, *116*, *117*,
        118, *119*, *120*
Paleocene epoch, *132*
Paleolithic. *See* Lower Paleolithic; Middle
    Paleolithic; Upper Paleolithic
palynology, 123
pantheon, 259, *259*
Papua, New Guinea (PNG), 317
    Dani culture, *234*
participant observation, 7, *7*, 16
pastoralism, 227
peanuts, *234*, 235
Peche Merle Cave, 212–213, *213*
Pei, W. C., 177
Peking Man, *177*, 177–178, *178*, 201
Pemons, 288, *288*

percussion method, toolmaking, 166
personhood, as cultural concept, 6
Perttula, Timothy K., 271
pertussis (whooping cough), *245*, 271
Peru, 223, 224, 250–251, *251*
    World Heritage sites, *217*, 217–218
pesticides, 321–322, *322*
phenotype, 38, *38*, 39
Philippines, *217*, 217–218
phosphates, 32, *32*
phylum, 27, *27*
physical anthropology, 11
physiological adaptation
    to cold, 306–307, *307*
    defined, 304
    to heat, 307–308, *308*
    to high altitude, 304–306, *305*, *306*
    human-made (unnatural) stressors
        requiring, 308
pigs, *234*, 245
    factory farming, 239, *239*
    swine-borne disease in Americas, 271
Piltdown specimens, Sussex, *143*, 143–144
Pizarro, Francisco, 271
plant domestication, 227–228, *228*, 232
platyrrhines, 61
Pleistocene epoch, *152*, 210
Pliocene epoch, *132*
    climate change, diet, and vegetation
        zones, 154–155, *155*
    hominin diversity during, *144*,
        144–154, *145*, *146*, *147*, *148*, *149*,
        150, *151*, *152*, *153*
    timeline of hominins, *152*
Poirier, Frank, 201
Pokotylo, David, 190
pollination, 257
pollution, *320*, 320–321
    pesticides, 321–322, *322*
polygenetic inheritance, 38, *38*, 39
polymerase chain reaction (PCR), 117
polymorphism, 287–288, *288*
polytypic, 288
population
    defined, 40, 41
    food production and size of,
        236–237, *237*
    health disparities and size of,
        318–319, *319*
    US Census Bureau and concept of race,
        282–284
    variation, *203*
    world, *319*
Population Media Center (PMC),
    311, 311
population variation, *203*
potassium-argon dating, 124
potatoes, 224, *234*, 235
pottery, 232, 239, *241*
    Mesoamerica, 242
    Neolithic, *240*, 240–241
    Yuchanyan Cave, 227, *227*
poverty, *243*, 243–245, *244*, *245*, 319,
    319–320
    environmental deprivation *vs.* expres-
        sion of intelligence, 286–287
    infectious disease thriving in, 270
preadapted, 57
prehensile, 67
prehistory, 103
Presbytis, *136*
pressure flaking, 207, *207*
primary innovation, 227
primate(s)
    apes and human origins, 134–137, *135*,
        136, *137*, 140
    brain, 66
    classification of, *26*, 26–28, *27*

conservation strategies, 74–78, *75*, *76*, *78*
    culture, 99
    defined, 26
    dentition, *62*, 62–64, *63*
    as endangered species, 52, *52*
    on evolutionary timeline, *132*
    global distribution of living and
        fossil, *54*
    language capacities, 193
    life cycle, *92*
    Linnean suborders of, 60
    origins, *131*, 131–133, *132*, *133*
    relationships among, *61*
    sensory organs, *64*, 64–66, *65*
    skeleton, 66–67, *67*
    taxonomy, 58–62, *59*, *60*, *61*
primate behavior
    arrested development *vs.* social envi-
        ronment, 88–90, *89*, *90*
    communication and learning, 92–96,
        93, *94*, *95*
    grooming, *86*, 86–87
    home range, 84, *84*
    hunting, *97*, *97*, 99
    individual interaction and bonding,
        87, *87*
    as model for human evolution,
        81–83, *82*
    rape, 88–90, *90*
    reconciliation, 86, 87
    reproduction and care of young,
        91–92, *92*
    sexual behavior, 80, *80*, *87*, 87–91,
        88, *90*
    social hierarchy, 84–86, *85*, *86*
    social organization, *83*, 83–84
    tool usage, 96, 96–97, *167*
primatology, 12
    anthropocentrism in, 53
    gorilla ecotourism, *55*, 55–56, *56*
    methods and ethics in, 54–55
Principles of Geology (Lyell), 30
prion, *317*, 317–318
Proboscis monkey, 70–71, *71*
Proconsul, 134–135, *135*, *136*
prosimians, 60, *62*, 64, 66, *68*, *132*, *133*
Prusiner, Stanley, 317
Pueblo cultures, 269, *269*
Punch, John, 279
punctuated equilibria, 48, *49*
Punnett Squares, *38*
Punta Lobos site, Huarmey River Valley, *9*

Quechua culture, 266

race
    as cultural category, *282*, 282–287, *283*,
        284, *287*
    as human classification, 275–281, *279*,
        280, *281*
    human evolution and, 294–295, *295*
    as taxonomic category, 274, 278,
        278–281, *279*
"Racial Problems in America" (Boas), 277
racism, 274, 284, 286, 287, *287*
    Blumenbach's classification of humans,
        276, *276*
    defined, 285
radiocarbon dating, 123
radio drama, medical clinic and, 311, *311*
rainforests, 260–261, *261*, *262*
Ramenofsky, Anne, 271
rape, 88–90, *90*
Recent African Origins hypothesis, 34,
    200, *200*
recessive, 38, *38*
reconciliation, 86, 87
red ochre, 210, *210*, 216

refugees, family unification via DNA testing, *36*, 36–37
regulatory gene, 48
relative dating, 121
religion, secularization from, 301
reproductive success, 43–44, 321
reptiles, mammals compared to, *57*, 57–58, *58*
residence
    Mesa Verde, southwest US, 269, *269*
    Neolithic, 239–241, *240*, *241*
    reindeer-skin tent, *5*
    Upper Paleolithic mammoth bone, 215, *215*
retrovirus, 34
rhinoplasty, 288–290, *289*
ribosomes, 33
rice, *234*
Ridley, Matt, 32
rifting, 144, *145*
rituals
    burial, *106*, *186*, 191, *191*
    at Jericho, *240*
    ochre, 210, *210*, 216
RNA (ribonucleic acid), 33
Roosevelt, A. C., *243*, 243–245, *244*
Rosenbaum, Levy Izhak, 20, *20*
r-selected, 58
Russia/Russians, 288, *288*
Rwanda, 14, *74*, *75*, 75–76, *76*, 284

Saami reindeer herders, Siberia, *7*, 288, *288*
Sabido, Miguel, 311, *311*
sagittal crest, 151
Sahelanthropus tchadensis, 135, *136*, *137*, *152*
Sahlins, Marshall, 229
Sahul land mass, 216, 216–219, *217*
Salé site, *173*
Sambungmachan site, *173*
Sangiran site, *173*
sapote, *235*
Savage-Rumbaugh, Sue, 193
savannah, 144, *145*, 156–158, *158*
Save the Chimps, 98, *98*
Sawert, Holger, 270
scapula, 67
Scheper-Hughes, Nancy, 20, *20*
schizophrenia, *33*
Schuster, Gerd, 73
secondary innovation, 227
secularization, 301
sedentary living patterns
    Neolithic revolution and, *243*, 243–245, *244*, *245*
    obesity, *319*, 319–320
Senegal, 130, *130*, 217, 217–218
sensory organs, 64, 64–66, *65*
Serbia, *217*, 217–218
seriation, 121
serotonin receptor, 33
sexual behavior
    early *Homo*, 167–168, *169*
    primate, 80, *80*, 87, 87–91, *88*, *90*
sexual dimorphism
    in *A. afarensis*, 145–146, *146*
    in canine teeth, *63*, 63–64, *134*, *146*
    defined, 64, 82
    gorillas, 72–73, *73*
    in lumpers and splitters debate, *160*, 160–161
    in monogamous species, 91
sexual reproduction, 35–36
shaman, 309
Shanidar Cave, *186*, 191
Shea, John, 190
sheep, *234*
Sheets, Payson D., 190

Shostak, Marjorie, 221
Shreeve, James, *186*, 281
siamangs, *61*, *136*
Siberia, *210*, *219*, 219–220, 309, *309*
    Nenet culture, *5*
    Saami reindeer herders, *7*, 288, *288*
sickle-cell anemia, 45–47, *46*
Sidi Abderrahman site, *173*
Sifford, Charles, 285
silkworm, *234*
Sima del Elefante, Spain, 178
Sima de los Huesos, Spain, *106*, *183*, 183–184
Sivapithecus, 136
six degrees of separation, 2, *2*, 21, *21*
skin, adaptive response of, 307–308, *308*
skin color, 275, *276*, 278
    conflagration of biological into cultural categories, 282–287, *283*, *284*, *287*
    global distribution of pigmentation, *291*
    key factors in adaptation of, 290
    melanin, 290
skulls
    anthropoid, *133*
    Blumenbach's classification of, 276, *276*
    comparison of, *188*
    Cro-Magnon, 197–198, *198*
    foramen magnum and bipedalism, *137*
    Homo erectus, 174–175, *175*, *188*
    Homo habilis, *188*
    Kenyanthropus platyops, *144*, *149*, *152*, *154*
    Lucy, 144, *145*
    Neandertal, *186*, 186–187, *187*, *188*
    Piltdown hoax, *143*, 143–144
    prosimian, *133*
    remnants of genocide, *284*
    Taung Child, 142
    Toumai, *137*
    Trinil site, *173*
slavery, 14–15, 271, 278, 279, *279*, 285–287, *286*, *287*
smallpox, 245, 265, 271
Smedley, Audrey, 277
Smits, Willie, *73*
Snow, Clyde C., 14
social hierarchy (primate), 84–86, *85*, *86*
social organization, *83*, 83–84
soil enrichment methods, ancient, 235
soil marks, 110
Solomon, Jane, 298, *298*
Solomon Islanders, 288, *288*
sorghum, *234*
Soto, Hernando de, 271
South America, 219, *265*, 265–266, *266*, 271
Spain, 178, *265*, 270–271, 282, *283*
spear-throwers, 207, 208, *208*
speciation
    macroevolution and, 47–49, *48*, *49*
    punctuated equilibria pattern of, 48, *49*
species, 30, 151
    classification of, *26*, 26–28, *27*
    defined, 26
    endangered, 52, *52*
    natural selection and diversity of, 30
squash, 235, *235*
stabilizing selection, *43*, 44
Stammler, Florian, *7*
starchy grains, 235
starvation, *319*, 319–320
state
    action theory on, 269–270
    ecological theories for emergence of, *267*, 267–269, *269*
stereoscopic vision, 64
Stevenson, Matilda Coxe, 13, *13*
stratified, defined, 111

stratified societies
    disease and, 270
    grave goods evidencing, 266, *266*
stratigraphy, 121
strepsirhines, 60
stress
    bipedal heat stress control, 156–158, *158*
    history of mortality and physiological, *243*, 243–244, *244*
    human-made (unnatural) stressors, 308
structural violence, 285–287, *287*
Strumm, Shirley, 76
subfamily, 27, *27*
suborder, 27, *27*
subphylum, 27, *27*
sudden infant death syndrome (SIDS), 4–5, *5*
sugarcane, 32, *32*, 234
Sumatra, Indonesia, *216*, 216–219, *217*
Sunda land mass, *216*, 216–219, *217*
sunflowers, 235
superfamily, 27, *27*
suspensory hanging apparatus, 67
Swartkrans site, *173*
swine flu, 238, *238*
symbolism (Neandertal), *191*, 191–192, *192*

tamarin, *78*
taphonomy, 104
taro, *234*
tarsiers, *61*, 69, *69*
Taung Child, 142
taxonomy, 26–28, *27*, 58–62, *59*, *60*, *60*, *61*
Tay-Sachs, *33*, 270
technology
    Upper Paleolithic, 206–208, *207*, *208*
    See also toolmaking
teeth, chewing apparatus and
    chimp, *Australopithecines*, and human jaws, *149*
    gracile and robust australopithecine, *151*, 151–152
    mammals' compared to reptiles', *57*, 57–58, *58*
    in Mesolithic and Neolithic, *243*, 243–245, *244*, *245*
    mutation preventing powerful jaw muscle growth, 181
    primate, 62, 62–64, *63*
    prosimian, *62*
    sexual dimorphism in canine, *146*
Teilhard de Chardin, Pierre, 177
Teotihuacan, Mexico, 250–252, *251*, *252*, *253*
Ternifine site, *173*
tertiary scavenger, 169
Thailand, 180, 288, *288*
theory, 16
Thinkers of the Jungle (Schuster, Smits, and Ullal), 73
Thomas Quarries site, *173*
Thorne, Alan, 201
Thornton, Russell, 271
thrifty genotype, 292
thymine, 32, *32*
Tibet, 284
Tikal, Central America, 253, 253–256, *254*, *256*
Timbuktu, Mali, 102, *102*
toe, opposable big, 67, 130, *130*
tomatoes, 235
toolmaking
    Acheulean tool tradition, 179, *179*
    Aurignacian tradition, 204
    blade technique, 206
    burins, 179, *188*, 207

chimp, 85, *85*
earliest known stone toolmaker, *166*, 166–167
hafting, 184, *185*, 190
Levalloisian technique, 184, *184*
Mousterian tool tradition, *189*, 189–191, *204*
Neolithic, 239–241, *240*, *241*
obsidian blades, 190, *190*
Oldowan tool tradition, 166, *167*
percussion method, 166
pressure flaking, 207, *207*
tool use, 164, *164*
atlatls, 207, 208, *208*
bamboo construction, *180*
Olduvai Gorge specimens, 159, *159*
orangutan spear fishing, *73*
painting toolkits, 192
primate, *96*, 96–97, *167*
stone tools for modern surgeons, 190, *190*
Toumai skull, *137*
Tower of Jericho, *240*
Toyne, J. Marla, *9*
transcription, 33
transfer RNA (tRNA), 33–34, *34*
translation, 33
Trinil site, *173*
Trouillot, Michel-Rolph, 282
Tsukahara, Takahiro, 171
tuberculosis (TB), 245
Ashkenazi Jews and Tay-Sachs allele, *33*, 270
turkey, *234*, 235, 271
Tuskegee Syphilis Study, 299, *300*
Tutsis, Rwanda, 284
Twa Pygmy, Congo, 277, *277*
twins, *286*
Tzunux, Diego Lux, *15*

Uganda
primate conservation strategies, *75*, 75–76, *76*
World Heritage sites, *217*, 217–218
Ullal, Jay, *73*
UNESCO World Heritage sites, *217*, 217–218
uniformitarianism, 29

United States (US)
African Burial Ground Project, New York City, 14–15, *15*, 278
Cahokia, southern Illinois, 269
concept of race, 282–287, *287*
Mesa Verde, southwest, 269, *269*
organ trafficking, 20, *20*
race and racism, 286
slavery, 277, *277*
World Heritage sites, *217*, 217–218
Upper Paleolithic, 197–198, *198*
in Americas, *219*, 219–220
art and music, *209*, 209–215, *211*, *212*, *213*
cultural innovations of, *210*
dwellings, clothing, and long-distance trade, 215
expansion and colonization, 215
female representational art, *209*, 214–215
major trends, 220–222
mammoth bone dwellings, *215*
medical prescriptions from, 221
in Sahul and Sunda, *216*, 216–219, *217*
technology, 206–208, *207*, *208*
Ur, Mesopotamia, *267*
urban centers. *See* cities

Valle, Mellisa Lund, *9*
vegeculture, 232, *234*
Verano, John, *9*
Verner, Samuel, 277, *277*
vertebrates, 66
vervet monkeys, 71
vetebrates, 27, *27*
violence
forensic documentation of, 15, *15*
orangutan rape, 88–90, *90*
See also warfare
vision, primate, *64*, 64–66, *65*
visual predation hypothesis, 133
vitamin D deficiency, *292*

Wallace, Alfred Russel, 30
warfare, 248, *248*
waste disposal, 11
water/land resources, 321–323, *323*
habitat disturbance/destruction, 224

hydraulic theory, 267
land ownership concept, 229
Peru, 224
weaving, Mesoamerican, 242
Weidenreich, Franz, 177–178, *178*, 201
Weinberg, Wilhelm, 40–41
Wernicke's area, *182*
whale hunting, *307*
wheat, *234*, 235–236
Wheeler, Peter, 156–158
whooping cough, *245*, 271
wings, 27–28, *28*
Wolpoff, Milford, *187*, 198, 201
women, 80, 302
Bambanani Women's Group, 298, *298*
nutrition and fertility, *303*, 303–304
in Paleolithic art, *209*, 214–215
phenotype, 32–33, *33*
See also gender
women's rights, 311, *311*
Woods, Tiger, 285
World Health Organization (WHO), 239, *239*
World Heritage sites, *217*, 217–218
The World of Living Things (Imanishi), 85, *85*
World War II, *284*
writing systems, 255, *255*, *264*, 264–265
written history, 103
Wu, Xinzhi, 201, *201*

Xavantes, 288, *288*

yams, *234*
Yaqui culture, 322
Yemen, World Heritage sites, *217*, 217–218
Yuanmou site, China, *173*
Yuchanyan Cave, 227, *227*

Zagros Mountains, Iraq and Iran, 231–232
Zelson, Amy, 14
Zhoukoudian Cave, 170, *173*, *177*, 177–178, *178*, 179
Zimbabwe, 251, 262
zooarchaeology, 11
Zulu culture, 17–19, *18*
Zuni culture, 13, *13*